Communications
in Computer and Information Science

1776

Rationale

The CCIS series is devoted to the publication of proceedings of computer science conferences. Its aim is to efficiently disseminate original research results in informatics in printed and electronic form. While the focus is on publication of peer-reviewed full papers presenting mature work, inclusion of reviewed short papers reporting on work in progress is welcome, too. Besides globally relevant meetings with internationally representative program committees guaranteeing a strict peer-reviewing and paper selection process, conferences run by societies or of high regional or national relevance are also considered for publication.

Topics

The topical scope of CCIS spans the entire spectrum of informatics ranging from foundational topics in the theory of computing to information and communications science and technology and a broad variety of interdisciplinary application fields.

Information for Volume Editors and Authors

Publication in CCIS is free of charge. No royalties are paid, however, we offer registered conference participants temporary free access to the online version of the conference proceedings on SpringerLink (http://link.springer.com) by means of an http referrer from the conference website and/or a number of complimentary printed copies, as specified in the official acceptance email of the event.

CCIS proceedings can be published in time for distribution at conferences or as post-proceedings, and delivered in the form of printed books and/or electronically as USBs and/or e-content licenses for accessing proceedings at SpringerLink. Furthermore, CCIS proceedings are included in the CCIS electronic book series hosted in the SpringerLink digital library at http://link.springer.com/bookseries/7899. Conferences publishing in CCIS are allowed to use Online Conference Service (OCS) for managing the whole proceedings lifecycle (from submission and reviewing to preparing for publication) free of charge.

Publication process

The language of publication is exclusively English. Authors publishing in CCIS have to sign the Springer CCIS copyright transfer form, however, they are free to use their material published in CCIS for substantially changed, more elaborate subsequent publications elsewhere. For the preparation of the camera-ready papers/files, authors have to strictly adhere to the Springer CCIS Authors' Instructions and are strongly encouraged to use the CCIS LaTeX style files or templates.

Abstracting/Indexing

CCIS is abstracted/indexed in DBLP, Google Scholar, EI-Compendex, Mathematical Reviews, SCImago, Scopus. CCIS volumes are also submitted for the inclusion in ISI Proceedings.

How to start

To start the evaluation of your proposal for inclusion in the CCIS series, please send an e-mail to ccis@springer.com.

Deep Gupta · Kishor Bhurchandi ·
Subrahmanyam Murala ·
Balasubramanian Raman · Sanjeev Kumar
Editors

Computer Vision and Image Processing

7th International Conference, CVIP 2022
Nagpur, India, November 4–6, 2022
Revised Selected Papers, Part I

 Springer

Editors
Deep Gupta
Visvesvaraya National Institute
of Technology Nagpur
Nagpur, India

Kishor Bhurchandi
Visvesvaraya National Institute
of Technology Nagpur
Nagpur, India

Subrahmanyam Murala
Indian Institute of Technology Ropar
Rupnagar, India

Balasubramanian Raman
Indian Institute of Technology Roorkee
Roorkee, India

Sanjeev Kumar
Indian Institute of Technology Roorkee
Roorkee, India

ISSN 1865-0929   ISSN 1865-0937 (electronic)
Communications in Computer and Information Science
ISBN 978-3-031-31406-3   ISBN 978-3-031-31407-0 (eBook)
https://doi.org/10.1007/978-3-031-31407-0

This Springer imprint is published by the registered company Springer Nature Switzerland AG
The registered company address is: Gewerbestrasse 11, 6330 Cham, Switzerland

Preface

The 7th International Conference on Computer Vision and Image Processing (CVIP 2022) was organized by Visvesvaraya National Institute of Technology Nagpur, Maharashtra, INDIA. CVIP is a premier conference focused on image/video processing and computer vision. Previous editions of CVIP were held at IIT Ropar (2021), IIIT Allahabad (CVIP 2020), MNIT Jaipur (CVIP 2019), IIIT Jabalpur (CVIP 2018), and IIT Roorkee (CVIP 2017 and CVIP 2016). The conference witnessed extraordinary success with publications in multiple domains of computer vision and image processing.

The Team composed of Kishor Bhurchandi (VNIT Nagpur), Pritee Khanna (IIIT DMJ), Prashant Patil (Deakin University, Australia), Gaurav Bhatnagar (IIT Jodhpur), Satish Kumar Singh (IIIT Allahabad) and Shiv Ram Dubey (IIIT Allahabad) organized CVIP 2022 and coordinated the event so efficiently. Moreover, the publicity for the submissions of research articles at CVIP' 2022 by Herkeerat Kaur (IIT Jammu), Nidhi Goel (IGDTUW, Delhi), Sneha Singh (CWRU, USA) and R. B. Keskar (VNIT Nagpur) made CVIP 2022 altogether a great success, with an overwhelming submission of 307 research papers. Also, the efficient teamwork by volunteers of VNIT Nagpur helped to overcome the different challenges during the event.

CVIP 2022 received 307 regular paper submissions that went through a rigorous review process by approx. 300 reviewers from various renowned national and international institutes and universities. The technical program chairs, Vishal R. Satpute (VNIT Nagpur), Santosh Kumar Vipparthi (IIT Ropar), Deepak Mishra (IIST Trivandrum), Ananda S. Chowdhury (Jadavpur University), Debashis Sen (IIT Kharagpur), Rama Krishna Sai Gorthi (IIT Tirupati), Saugta Sinha (VNIT Nagpur), Puneet Goyal (IIT Ropar), Emanuela Marasco (George Mason University, USA), Shital S. Chiddarwar (VNIT Nagpur) and Snigdha Bhagat (Blackrock Gurugram), coordinated the overall review process which resulted in the acceptance of 121 research articles. Out of them, 113 papers were scheduled for oral presentation in 22 technical sessions around the research areas of Medical Image Analysis, Image/Video Processing for Autonomous Vehicles, Activity Detection/Recognition, Human-Computer Interaction, Segmentation and Shape Representation, Motion and Tracking, Image/Video Scene Understanding, Image/Video Retrieval, Remote Sensing, Hyperspectral Image Processing, Face, Iris, Emotion, Sign Language and Gesture Recognition, etc.

Keynote Talks: CVIP 2022 was scheduled with four keynote talk sessions for each day. CVIP 2022 commenced with a keynote talk on "Digital pathology for detection of cancer from breast FNAC and oral histopathology images" by Ajoy Kumar Ray (IIT Kharagpur) followed by keynote talks by Petia Ivanova Radeva (University of Barcelona, Spain), Fabio Dell'Acqua (University of Pavia, Italy) and Ayellet Tal (Technion, Israel). On the second day, Daniel P. Lopresti (Lehigh University, USA) presented his talk on "Research reproducibility research: Opportunities and challenges". The keynote talks by Bharat Biswal (New Jersey Institute of Technology, USA), Ramesh Jain (University of California, Irvine, USA), and Prabir Kumar Biswas (Indian Institute of Technology, Kharagpur) also gave an informative discussion on image processing and computer vision. The last day of the conference began with an informative keynote talk on "Advances in adversarial robustness and domain adaptation of deep models" by R. Venkatesh Babu, (Indian Institute of Science, Bangalore), and the keynote talks by Jayanta Mukhopadhyay (Indian Institute of Technology, Kharagpur), Vikram M. Gadre (Indian Institute of Technology, Bombay), and Sumantra Dutta Ray (Indian Institute of Technology, Delhi) enlightened the audience with an informative discussion on image processing.

Awards: CVIP 2022 presented high-quality research works with innovative ideas. All the session chairs were invited to vote for five different categories of awards. Five different awards were announced: IAPR Best Paper Award, IAPR Best Student Paper, CVIP 2022 Best Paper Award, CVIP 2022 Best Student Paper Award, Sir M. Visvesvaraya Best Student Paper Award.

Also, CVIP 2022 awarded to Santanu Chaudhury, IIT Jodhpur a CVIP Lifetime Achievement Award for his remarkable research in the field of Image Processing and Computer Vision. The awards were announced in the valedictory ceremony by Conference Chair, Deep Gupta (VNIT Nagpur).

The next edition of CVIP will be organized by IIT Jammu, India.

November 2022

Deep Gupta
Kishor Bhurchandi
Balasubramanian Raman
Sanjeev Kumar
Subrahmanyam Murala

Organization

Patron

Bidyut Baran Chaudhuri   ISI Kolkata, India

General Chairs

Pramod M. Padole (Director)	VNIT Nagpur, India
Petia Radeva	University of Barcelona, Spain
Tom Gedeon	Curtin University, Australia

General Co-chairs

Balasubramanian Raman	IIT Roorkee, India
Avinash Keskar	VNIT Nagpur, India

Conference Chairs

Deep Gupta	VNIT Nagpur, India
Subrahmanyam Murala	IIT Ropar, India
Partha Pratim Roy	IIT Roorkee, India
Sanjeev Kumar	IIT Roorkee, India

Conference Convenors

Kishor Bhurchandi	VNIT Nagpur, India
Pritee Khanna	IIITDM Jabalpur, India
Gaurav Bhatnagar	IIT Jodhpur, India
Satish Kumar Singh	IIIT Allahabad, India
Shiv Ram Dubey	IIIT Allahabad, India

Technical Program Chairs

Vishal R. Satpute	VNIT Nagpur, India
Santosh Kumar Vipparthi	IIT Ropar, India
Deepak Mishra	IIST Trivandrum, India
Ananda S. Chowdhury	Jadavpur University, India
Debashis Sen	IIT Kharagpur, India
Rama Krishna Sai Gorthi	IIT Tirupati, India
Snigdha Bhagat	Blackrock Gurugram, India
Saugata Sinha	VNIT Nagpur, India
Abhinav Dhall	IIT Ropar, India
Puneet Goyal	IIT Ropar, India
Emanuela Marasco	George Mason University, USA
Shital S. Chiddarwar	VNIT Nagpur, India

Website Chairs

Ankit Bhurane	VNIT Nagpur, India
Poonam Sharma	VNIT Nagpur, India

Publicity Chairs

Harkeerat Kaur	IIT Jammu, India
Sneha Singh	CWRU, USA
Nidhi Goel	IGDTUW, India
R. B. Keskar	VNIT Nagpur, India
M. H. Kolekar	IIT Patna, India

Publication Chairs

Poonam Sharma	VNIT Nagpur, India
Prashant W. Patil	Deakin University, Australia
Sachin Chaudhary	PEC, India

Local Organizing Committee

Ashwin Kothari	VNIT Nagpur, India
Vipin Kamble	VNIT Nagpur, India
Joydeep Sen Gupta	VNIT Nagpur, India
Pradnya Ghare	VNIT Nagpur, India
K. Surender	VNIT Nagpur, India
Neeraj Rao	VNIT Nagpur, India
Prabhat Sharma	VNIT Nagpur, India
Punitkumar Bhavsar	VNIT Nagpur, India
Anamika Singh	VNIT Nagpur, India
Praveen Pawar	VNIT Nagpur, India
Amit Agrawal	VNIT Nagpur, India
Himanshu Padole	VNIT Nagpur, India
Arvind Kumar	VNIT Nagpur, India
Vivek Raghuwanshi	VNIT Nagpur, India

International Advisory Committee

Daniel P. Lopresti	Lehigh University, USA
Sebastiano Battiat	Università di Catania, Italy
Bharat Biswal	NJIT, USA
Jonathan Wu	University of Windsor, Canada
Pallavi Tiwari	CWRU Cleveland, USA
Gaurav Sharma	University of Rochester, USA
Nalini K. Ratha	State University of New York at Buffalo, USA
Satish Viswanath	CWRU Cleveland, USA
Paula Brito	University of Porto, Portugal
Ankit Chaudhary	University of Missouri, USA
Henry Leung	University of Calgary, Canada
Rangaraj M. Rangayyan	University of Calgary, Canada
Anup Basu	University of Alberta, Canada
Kiran Raja	NTNU, Norway
B. S. Manjunath	University of California, Santa Barbara, USA
Mohan S. Kankanhalli	NUS, Singapore
Sule Yildirim Yayilgan	NTNU, Norway
Emanuela Marasco	George Mason University, USA
Ali Reza Alaei	Southern Cross University, Australia
Thinagaran Perumal	Universiti Putra Malaysia, Malaysia
Xiaoyi Jiang	University of Münster, Germany
Sudeep Sarkar	University of South Florida, USA

Vishal M. Patel   Johns Hopkins University, USA
Richard Hartley   Australian National University, Australia
Luc Van Gool   ETH Zurich, Switzerland
Junsong Yuan   State University of New York at Buffalo, USA
Petra Perner   FutureLab Artificial Intelligence, Germany
Rajkumar Buyya   University of Melbourne, Australia
Elisa Barney Smith   Boise State University, USA

National Advisory Committee

Ajoy Kumar Ray   IIT Kharagpur, India
Uday B. Desai   IIT Hyderabad, India
Venkatesh Babu   IISc Bangalore, India
Vikram M. Gadre   IIT Bombay, India
Prabir Kumar Biswas   IIT Kharagpur, India
S. N. Singh   IIT Kanpur, India
A. G. Ramakrishnan   IISc Bangalore, India
Phaneendra K. Yalavarthy   IISc Bangalore, India
Prasanna Chaporkar   IIT Bombay, India
Ram Bilas Pachori   IIT Indore, India
Sibi Raj B. Pillai   IIT Bombay, India
Jayanta Mukhopadhyay   IIT Kharagpur, India
R. S. Anand   IIT Roorkee, India
Sanjay Kumar Singh   IIT BHU, India
Umapada Pal   ISI Kolkata, India
Abhay S. Gandhi   VNIT Nagpur, India
Aparajita Ojha   IIITDM Jabalpur, India
Sushmita Mitra   ISI Kolkata, India
Kishor Kulat   VNIT Nagpur, India

CVIP Reviewers

Alireza Alaei   Southern Cross University, Australia
A. Prabhakar Rao   VNIT Nagpur, India
Amitesh Singh Rajput   Birla Institute of Technology and Science, Pilani
Ananda S. Chowdhury   Jadavpur University, India
Anil Balaji Gonde   SGGS Nanded, India
Anish Kumar Vishwakarma   VNIT Nagpur, India
Anjali Gautam   IIIT Allahabad, India
Ankit Ashokrao Bhurane   VNIT Nagpur, India

Ankush Jamthikar	VNIT Nagpur, India
Anoop Jacob Thomas	IIIT Tiruchirappalli, India
Ansuman Mahapatra	NIT Puducherry, India
Anuj Sharma	Panjab University, Chandigarh, India
Aparajita Ojha	IIITDM, Jabalpur, India
Arif Ahmed Sekh	XIM University, Bhubaneswar, India
Arijit De	Jadavpur University, India
Arindam Sikdar	University of Bristol, UK
Arun Kumar Sivapuram	Indian Institute of Technology, Tirupati, India
Ashish Mishra	Jaypee Institute of Information Technology, India
Ashish Phophalia	IIIT Vadodara, India
Ashutosh C. Kulkarni	Indian Institute of Technology, Ropar, India
Aswathy M. A.	MIT Pune, India
Avishek Ghosh	University of California, San Diego, USA
Ayan Seal	IIIT Jabalpur, India
Ayatullah Faruk Mollah	Aliah University
B. N. Chatterji	IIT, Kharagpur, India
B. Surendiran	NIT Puducherry, India
Bindu Verma	Delhi Technological University, India
Binsu C. Kovoor	Cochin University of Science and Technology, India
Bishshoy Das	Indian Institute of Technology Delhi, India
Bunil K. Balabantaray	NIT Meghalaya, India
Chandra V. Sekhar	Indian Institute of Information Technology, Sri City
Chhavi Dhiman	Delhi Technological University, India
Chirag Paunwala	Sarvajanik College of Engineering and Technology, Surat, India
Chithra A. V.	Indian Institute of Space Science and Technology, India
Daniel Lopresti	Lehigh University, USA
Debanjan Sadhya	ABV-IIITM Gwalior, India
Deep Gupta	VNIT Nagpur, India
Deepak Ranjan Nayak	NIT Jaipur, India
Deepak Gupta	NIT Arunachal Pradesh, India
Deepak Mishra	IIST Trivendrum, India
Durga Prasad Bavirisetti	NTNU, Norway
Dushyant Kumar Singh	MNNIT Allahabad, India
Elisa Barney Smith	Boise State University, USA
Emanuela Marasco	George Mason University, USA
Fabio Dell'Acqua	University of Pavia, Italy
Gaurav Bhatnagar	IIT Jodhpur, India

Gaurav Gupta	Wenzhou-Kean University, China
Gautam Bhattacharya	UIT, BU, India
Gopa Bhaumik	NIT Sikkim, India
Gorthi Rama Krishna Sai Subrahmanyam	IIT Tirupati, India
Guoqiang Zhong	Ocean University of China, China
Gurinder Singh	IIT Ropar, India
Hadia Showkat Kawoosa	IIT Ropar, India
Harkeerat Kaur	IIT Jammu, India
Himanshu Agarwal	Information Technology Noida, India
Himanshu P. Padole	VNIT Nagpur, India
Indra Deep Mastan	LNMIT Jaipur, India
Irshad Ahmad Ansari	IIITDM Jabalpur, India
Jagadeesh Kakarla	IIITDM, India
Jagannath Sethi	Jadavpur University, India
Jagat Sesh Challa	BITS Pilani, India
Jagdeep Kaur	NIT Jalandhar, India
Jasdeep Singh	IIT Ropar, India
Jayashree Vivekanand Khanapuri	K. J. Somaiya Institute of Engineering & Information Technology, India
Jaydeb Bhaumik	Jadavpur University, India
Jayendra Kumar	NIT Jamshedpur, India
Jeevan J.	Exafluence Inc., USA
Jignesh S. Bhatt	IIIT Vadodara, India
Jitendra A. Maddarkar	NDS Infoserv
Joohi Chauhan	Indian Institute of Technology Ropar, India
Juan E. Tapia	Hochschule Darmstadt, Germany
Junsong Yuan	State University of New York at Buffalo, USA
K. M. Bhurchandi	VNIT Nagpur, India
Kalidas Yeturu	Indian Institute of Technology Tirupati, India
Kapil Rana	IIT Ropar, India
Karthick Seshadri	National Institute of Technology, Andhra Pradesh, India
Kaushik Roy	West Bengal State University, India
Kaustuv Nag	IIIT Guwahati, India
Kiran Raja	NTNU
Kishor K. Bhoyar	YCCE Nagpur, India
Krishan Kumar	NIT Kurukshetra, India
Krishna P. Miyapuram	Indian Institute of Technology, Gandhinagar, India
Krishna Pratap Singh	IIIT Allahabad, India
Krishna Siva Prasad Mudigonda	VIT-AP University, India
Kuldeep Biradar	SGGSIET

Kuldeep Singh	MNIT Jaipur, India
Kushall Pal Singh	MNIT Jaipur, India
Lalatendu Behera	NIT Jalandhar, India
Madhurima Bandyopadhyay	Continental Automotive Components (India) Pvt. Ltd., India
Maheshkumar H. Kolekar	IIT Patna, India
Malaya Kumar Nath	NIT Puducherry, India
Mandhatya Singh	IIT Ropar, India
Manesh B. Kokare	SGGSIE&T Nanded, India
Manisha Das	VNIT Nagpur, India
Manisha Sawant	VNIT Nagpur, India
Mayur R. Parae	IIIT, Nagpur, India
Milind Mushrif	YCCE, Nagpur, India
Mohamed Akram Ulla Shariff	Samsung R&D Institute India-Bangalore, India
Mohammad Farukh Hashmi	National Institute of Technology Warangal, India
Mohammed Javed	IIIT Allahabad, India
Mohan Kankanhalli	National University of Singapore, Singapore
Monu Verma	MNIT Jaipur, India
Mrinal Kanti Bhowmik	Tripura University, India
Muhammad Suhaib Kanroo	IIT Ropar, India
Naga Srinivasarao Batta Kota	NIT Warangal, India
Nagashettappa Biradar	Bheemanna Khandre Institute of Technology, Bhalki, India
Nancy Mehta	Indian Institute of Technology Ropar, India
Narendra D. Londhe	National Institute of Technology Raipur, India
Naveen Cheggoju	IIIT Una, India
Neetu Sood	Dr BR Ambedkar National Institute of Technology, Jalandhar, India
Neha Nawandar	VNIT Nagpur, India
Nidhi Goel	IGDTUW, India
Nidhi Lal	VNIT Nagpur, India
Nikhil Dhengre	VNIT Nagpur, India
Nikita S. Rathi	Accenture, India
Nirmala Murali	IIST, India
Nishant Jain	Jaypee University of Information Technology, India
N. V. Subba Reddy	Manipal University, India
Palak H.	Delhi Technological University, India
Pallavi K. Parlewar	RCOEM, India
Pankaj Pratap Singh	Central Institute of Technology (CIT) Kokrajhar, India
Paresh Kamble	VNIT Nagpur, India

Partha Pratim Sarangi	Seemanta Engineering College, India
Partha Pakray	NIT Silchar, India
Parul Sahare	IIIT, Nagpur, India
Parveen Kumar	National Institute of Technology Uttarakhand, India
Petia Radeva	University of Barcelona, Spain
Piyush Kumar	National Institute of Technology Patna, India
Poonam Sharma	VNIT Nagpur, India
Praful Hambarde	Indian Institute of Technology Ropar, India
Prafulla Saxena	MNIT Jaipur, India
Pranav Kumar Singh	Central Institute of Technology Kokrajhar, India
Prashant Patil	IIT Ropar, India
Pratistha Mathur	Manipal University Jaipur, India
Pratyusha Rakshit	Jadavpur University, India
Preeti Rai	GGITS, India
Prem S. Yadav	MNIT Jaipur, India
Prerana Mukherjee	Jawaharlal Nehru University, India
Pritee Khanna	IIITDM Jabalpur, India
Pritpal Singh	National Taipei University of Technology, Taiwan, India
Puneet Goyal	IIT Ropar, India
Puneet Gupta	IIT Indore, India
Punitkumar Bhavsar	VNIT Nagpur, India
Raghunath S. Holambe	RJIT, India
Rameswar Panda	MIT-IBM Watson AI Lab, USA
Ratnapal K. Mane	VNIT Nagpur, India
Richa R. Khandelwal	RCOEM, India
Rohini Suhas Ochawar	RCOEM, India
Rubell Marion Lincy George	Indian Institute of Information Technology Kottayam, India
Rubin Bose S.	Madras Institute of Technology, India
Rukhmini Bandyopadhyay	University of Texas MD Anderson Cancer Centre, India
Rusha Patra	IIIT Guwahati, India
S. N. Tazi	RTU, India
Sahana M. Prabhu	RBEI, India
Sahu Abhimanyu	Seemanta Engineering College, India
P. S. SaiKrishna	Indian Institute of Technology Tirupati, India
Sanjay Talbar	SGGSIET, India
Sanjeev Kumar	IIT Roorkee, India
Sanjit N.	IIIT Una, India
Sanjit Maitra	Indian Statistical Institute, India

Sanjiv Vedu Bonde	SGGSIET, Nanded, India
Sanjoy Pratihar	IIIT Kalyani, India
Sanjoy K. Saha	Jadavpur University, India
Santosh Singh Rathore	ABV-IIITM Gwalio, India
Sathiesh Kumar V.	Madras Institute of Technology, India
Satya Prakash Sahu	NIT Raipur, India
Satya Narayan	Government Engineering College Ajmer, India
Satyasai Jagannath Nanda	Malaviya National Institute of Technology Jaipur, India
Satyendra Singh Yadav	NIT, Meghalaya, India
Saugata Sinha	VNIT Nagpur, India
Sevakram Tanaji Kumbhare	Jadavpur University, Kolkata, India
Shanmuganathan Raman	Indian Institute of Technology Gandhinagar, India
Shashi Shekhar Jha	IIT Ropar, India
Shashi Poddar	CSIR- Central Scientific Instruments Organisation, India
Shelly Sachdeva	NIT Delhi, India
Shipla Metkar	COEP Technological University, Pune, India
Shital Chiddarwar	VNIT Nagpur, India
Shitala Prasad	Institute for Infocomm Research, India
Shiv Ram Dubey	Indian Institute of Information Technology, Allahabad, India
Shivakumara Palaiahnakote	University of Malaya, Malaysia
Shruti Jain	Jaypee University of Information Technology, Solan, India
Shruti S. Phutke	Indian Institute of Technology Ropar, India
Sivaiah Bellamkonda	Indian Institute of Information Technology Kottayam, India
Smita Agrawal	TIET, Patiala, India
Snehasis Mukherjee	Shiv Nadar University, India
Snigdha Bhagat	Indian Institute of Technology Delhi, India
Somenath Das	Indian Institute of Science Bangalore, India
Soumen Bag	IIT Dhanbad, India
Soumyadip Sengupta	University of North Carolina at Chapel Hill, USA
Sree Rama Vamsidhar S.	Indian Institute of Technology Tirupati, India
Srimanta Mandal	DA-IICT, Gandhinagar, India
Subrahmanyam Murala	IIT Ropar, India
Sudeep Sarkar	University of South Florida, Tampa, USA
Suman Kumar Maji	IIT Patna, India
Sumantra Dutta Roy	Indian Institute of Technology Delhi, India
Suresh C. Raikwar	Thapar Institute of Engineering and Technology, India

Sushanta Kumar Sahu	Jadavpur University, India
Suvidha Tripathi	LENS Corp., India
Swarup Roy	Sikkim University, India
Syed Taqi Ali	VNIT Nagpur, India
T. Veerakumar	NIT Goa, India
Tannistha Pal	NIT Agartala, India
Tapabrata Chakraborty	University of Oxford
Tapas Si	Bankura Unnayani Institute of Engineering, India
Tasneem Ahmed	Integral University, India
Uday V. Kulkarni	SGGSIET, India
Umarani Jayaraman	IIITDM Kancheepuram, India
Umesh Chandra Pati	National Institute of Technology, Rourkela, India
Vibha Vyas	COEP Technological University, India
Vibhor Kant	IIT BHU, India
Vidya More	COEP Technological University, India
Vijay N. Gangapure	Government Polytechnic, Kolhapur, India
Vijaya Thool	SGGSIET, Nanded, India
Vincenzo Piuri	Università degli Studi di Milano, Italy
Vinti Agarwal	BITS Pilani, India
Vipin Milind Kamble	VNIT, Nagpur, India
Vipin P. Yadav	MIT Academy of Engineering, India
Vishal Ramesh Satpute	VNIT Nagpur, India
Vishnu Srinivasa Murthy Yarlagadda	Vellore Institute of Technology, India
Vishwas Rathi	Indian Institute of Technology Ropar, India
Vivek Tiwari	IIIT Naya Raipur, India
Watanabe Osamu	Takushoku University, Japan
Xiaoyi Jiang	University of Münster, Germany
Yadunath Pathak	VNIT Nagpur, India
Yogesh Sariya	NIT Agartala, India
Yogita	NIT Meghalaya, India

Contents – Part I

Contents – Part II

Anomaly Detection in ATM Vestibules Using Three-Stream Deep Learning Approach

Mehant Kammakomati$^{(\boxtimes)}$ ⓘ, Suryadevara Deepak Chowdary, Srikanth Naik Varthya, and Karthick Seshadri ⓘ

National Institute of Technology, Andhra Pradesh, Tadepalligudem, India
{411843,411877,411878}@student.nitandhra.ac.in,
karthick.seshadri@nitandhra.ac.in

Abstract. Anomalies are abnormal events that deviate from typical behavioral patterns. Video anomaly detection is the problem of identifying anomalies in video feeds. ATM vestibules are one of the critical places where such anomalies must be detected. The problem lies around how we represent a video and further perform analysis on it to predict an anomaly. Another problem is the unavailability of data for this task specific to the ATM vestibule. To tackle these, this paper uses a three-stream deep learning architecture and contributes two novel datasets: box annotated image and temporal annotated video dataset. The three streams correspond to contextual, spatial and motion information. It is first-of-its-kind attempt to leverage box annotated image dataset for finetuning object detection models to detect ATM class and temporal annotated video dataset to train the model for video anomaly detection in ATM vestibule. The presented work achieves a recall score of 0.93, and false positive rate of 0.13.

Keywords: ATM security · Anomaly detection · Deep Learning · Computer vision · ATM dataset

1 Introduction

With advancements in computer vision and deep learning, there is a surge in the cognification of devices to impart intelligence while tackling tasks. This reduces the need for human interventions in such tasks and promotes a better living. Cameras are such devices that assist computer vision algorithms and support deep learning systems to solve real-world challenges, which can include chest radiography diagnosis [1], counting objects [2], pedestrian tracking [3], and anomaly detection [4]. In many use-cases, this is done to ensure people's wellbeing. Video surveillance is one such challenge where researchers are proposing various approaches to solve real-world problems such as anomalous event detection. Some anomalous events of typical interest [7] are abuse, arrest, arson, assault, burglary, explosion, fighting, road accident, robbery, shooting, shoplifting, stealing, and vandalism.

D. Gupta et al. (Eds.): CVIP 2022, CCIS 1776, pp. 1–12, 2023.
https://doi.org/10.1007/978-3-031-31407-0_1

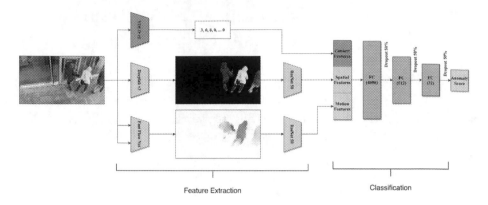

Fig. 1. Diagram of the three-stream deep learning architecture.

Video surveillance cameras are everywhere and their usage is increasing at a faster rate. One core task in video surveillance is identifying abnormal activities. They are being used not only in public places such as banks, shopping malls, parks, etc., but in private places such as gated communities, individual houses, and private spaces as well. However, effective surveillance requires human monitors who can flag and counter anomalies by observing the cameras' live streams. This process comes with certain challenges. Firstly, abnormal events can happen at lightning speeds, sometimes tracking them would be infeasible. Next, they are unpredictable and a human monitor naturally cannot be attentive at all times. Further, manual anomaly detection involves significant wastage of human resources. Finally, humans are not always trustworthy to report anomalous events at all times. The solution to intelligent computer vision model is, only if it is trained on the right set of data mitigating false positive and negative rates.

Generalized algorithms can be devised to detect most anomalous events. Rather than using them as they are for a particular use-case, those algorithms can be further finetuned using use-case specific data to specialize them for performing well for a particular real-world setting. This approach can deliver better results if the model is meant only for that use case and at the same time leverages generalization capabilities to detect multiple anomalous events. ATM (Automated Teller Machine) vestibules are one of those use-cases that require a high degree of security. ATM is prone to several anomalous events such as fighting, robbery, explosion and assault. Hence, generalized anomaly detection models that are fine-tuned with ATM-specific data can perform well in detection.

We use a modified deep learning architecture (as shown in Fig. 1) for real-time video anomaly detection in ATM vestibules that was originally introduced by Petrocchi et al. [5]. The modification involves the usage of the semantic segmentation technique in the spatial feature extraction process where the video image frame is broken into segments. The task-specific segments are kept as is, and the rest of their pixels are set to 0. The image feature extractor extracts features from this modified video image frame where the focus is on extracting features from task-specific segments. Also, the modified architecture leverages a deep learning approach to generate optical flow frames for the given two consecutive video image frames. The downstream classification task takes up a modified architecture with 3 layers. Finally, we curate two datasets. First is the image dataset which consists of 1491 images. These images come with bounding box annotations for ATM and person classes. The dataset is suitable for finetuning a pre-trained object detection model to perform well in an ATM setting. We name this dataset ATM-Image (ATM-I). Second is the video dataset which consists of 65 videos that come with temporal annotations for anomalous and normal classes. The dataset is useful to train and test real-world video anomaly models. We name this dataset ATM Anomaly-Video (ATMA-V). In summary, this paper provides the following contributions:

- We use a modified three-stream deep learning architecture where the three streams correspond to contextual, spatial, and motion features. The modification involves the usage of the semantic segmentation technique in the spatial feature extraction process where the video image frame is broken into segments relevant to the ATM anomaly use case.
- We curated two datasets. First is the image dataset consisting of 1491 images to finetune object detection models to detect ATM class. Second is the video dataset consisting of 65 real-world videos to detect ATM video anomalies.

The next section includes an overview of the seminal related research works addressing the problem of anomaly detection in ATM vestibules; the third section describes in detail the curated datasets; the fourth section mentions the proposed methodology; the fifth section includes implementation details and results of the work and the final section provides a conclusion and possible future amendments to the proposed method.

2   Related Work

Anomalous events in ATM vestibules are a problem that has been daunting for ages. One of the ways to track down such events is through video footage. This section outlines various seminal research attempts that address this challenging problem.

Angadi et al. [6] have prepared a smallscale video dataset that includes various anomalous events that happen in ATM vestibules. The video data is synthetically prepared in one location whereas the actual real-world events might differ significantly in terms of location, environment, and people. The dataset does not include hard anomalies such as assault, explosion, fighting, and robbery.

Viji et al. [22] have proposed a Machine Learning algorithm. The work uses K-means clustering algorithm and Support Vector Machine (SVM) to detect anomalous activities in ATM surveillance videos. Histogram of Oriented Gradients (HOG) technique is used to extract features from the video stream that is further mapped using K-means. SVM algorithm is used for the classification task to identify normal and abnormal activities.

Parab et al. [23] have proposed a deep learning approach where feature extraction from the video frames is done with the help of Long-Short Term Memory (LSTM) and Convolutional Neural Network (CNN) where temporal features are extracted. The extracted features are used in the downstream classification task for an anomaly in the ATM vestibule. The approach is trained and tested on a non-ATM-specific dataset.

Tripathi et al. [24] have proposed a new framework for detecting abnormal events at ATM installations. The work uses HOG for feature generation from video image frames. Further, random forest technique is used for the downstream classification task.

Nar et al. [25] have proposed a model where anomalous behavior is identified based on a person's posture. The work uses a logistic regression algorithm for the classification task. Postures can't completely tell if the person is part of an anomalous event. In rural areas, people tend to involve in such postures simply which are not intentionally meant to do something abnormal in the ATM vestibule. This approach might increase the false positive rate.

Fig. 2. Examples of different box-annotated images taken from ATM-I dataset.

3   Dataset

This section describes in detail the data collection approach, bounding box-annotated image dataset, and temporal annotated video dataset that has been prepared for ATM vestibule use case as part of the research work. The ATM-I dataset is available at: https://doi.org/10.34740/kaggle/ds/2080545, and the ATMA-V dataset is available at https://doi.org/10.34740/kaggle/dsv/3455016.

3.1   Previous Datasets

We searched extensively for the existing video anomaly detection datasets specialized for ATM use cases. The dataset [6] that was prepared by Angadi et al. [6]

consists of 11 surveillance videos, where different human actions are covered such as money withdrawal, wearing a cap/helmet, and carrying a suspicious object. All the videos present in the dataset are synthetically prepared and are recorded in exactly one location. Those videos do not cover some of the important anomalous events such as fighting, robbery, and explosion. Moreover, they only cover soft anomalies and miss out on hard anomalies which are primary interests for researchers. Datasets like UCF-Crime developed by Sultani et al. [7] comprise long untrimmed surveillance videos which cover most of the real-world anomalies that can be used for training the classification model. To finetune the model for the ATM anomaly use case, we construct a bounding box annotated image and temporal annotated video dataset.

3.2 Data Collection

To ensure diversification in terms of location and people, the data for both image and video formats have been collected manually from the internet. Mostly, multimedia sharing platforms such as YouTube, Kaotic, Dailymail, Itemfix, leakedreality, GettyImages, and Shutterstock are leveraged as sources. Collection from internet sources is done with the help of multiple text-based search queries that are slightly varied in terms of vocabulary and language such as "atm robbery", "atm theft", "atm chori", and "atm Diebstahl". Genuine ATM-based data on the internet is meager, so this approach of search and collection has mitigated the challenge to some extent. To prepare a high-quality dataset, certain conditions are imposed during the collection process such as: avoiding shaky, overly labeled videos/images, and videos that are compiled.

3.3 ATM-I Dataset

MS COCO [13] is an image dataset that has 80 classes which include persons, vehicles, animals, furniture, and other common real-world objects. However, the dataset does not include the ATM class. Due to this reason, the image dataset has been created where each image is a bounding box annotated for the ATM and person class. To ensure good quality annotation following measures are taken: tight bounding boxes, completeness, and consistency across images. The dataset comprises 1491 images that cover different angles in which an ATM box can be viewed in ATM vestibules. Images are collected and annotated ensuring they are equally distributed among the classes. In Fig. 2, some of the bounding box annotated images are shown. One of the main reasons for the image dataset is, to train the object detection model to extract contextual information from the video image frames that include ATM objects, which is usually the primary focus of the attacker in most anomalous events. Moreover, this dataset can be used to finetune a pre-trained object detection model to specialize detection tasks in an ATM vestibule setting. Images in the dataset are augmented with blur (up to 2.25px) and noise (up to 6% of pixels) effects. Augmentation is done to expand the dataset and increase model performance.

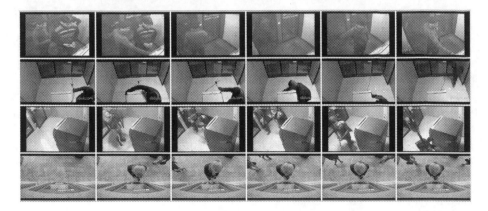

Fig. 3. Examples of different temporal annotated videos taken from ATMA-V dataset.

Table 1. A comparison of video datasets specific to anomalies in ATM.

	# of Videos	Dataset Length
Angadi et al. [6]	11	11 min
Ours	**65**	**43 min**

3.4   ATMA-V Dataset

The video dataset comprises 65 videos that consist of both anomalous and normal video segments. The dataset is free from skewness to one class where segments are equally distributed between anomalous and normal classes. In Fig. 3, some of the anomalous and normal video segments are shown. These videos are temporally annotated by human annotators for anomalous and normal segments. Annotations are cross-validated by a different person who was not part of the annotators' group, this is done to minimize human error to a certain extent. Annotation data for videos is represented as a set of frame ranges that contain anomalous segments and those frames that are not included within the range are considered normal video segments. The dataset is compared with a previous effort from Angadi et al. [6] and is shown in Table 1.

4   Proposed Methodology

The following section describes the proposed method that includes the process involved in feature extraction and video representation, classification model, and calculating anomaly score.

4.1   Contextual Feature Extraction

Contextual information is represented as a vector of object counts. In order to extract the contextual information, we utilize an existing pre-trained object detection model. Object detection problem is widely researched [8] and has implementations. The model is further trained on the ATM-I dataset so as to include ATM and person class along with the other classes that are part of the pre-train dataset. Each video image frame is given as input to the object detection model. Then, the number of instances of each object is extracted from the object detector output. Using this information the final vector for each frame is constructed of size total number of classes. The index of the vector represents a specific class and the value represents the number of instances of that class. This vector can be defined as an object count vector.

4.2   Motion Feature Extraction

The motion of the objects in the scene is captured from the temporal structure of the video by finding the difference between two adjacent video image frames. This can be achieved with the help of optical flow estimation [9] between two video image frames. Optical flow estimation captures the apparent motion of each pixel on the image plane. There is a significant research effort [10] to solve the optical flow estimation problem. One of the existing deep learning approaches is used to draw optical flow image frames. FastFlowNet [14] is leveraged that is partial fully connected structure with dilated convolution that obtains a good balance among accuracy, speed and number of parameters compared with sequential connected and dense connected structures. Two adjacent video image frames are given to the optical flow estimator and the obtained output can be defined as an optical flow frame. To extract features from the optical flow frame, an image feature extractor can be used [11]. The output from the image feature extractor is the motion information.

4.3   Spatial Feature Extraction

Spatial feature extraction follows a two-step process. First, semantic segmentation is performed on the video image frame. Semantic segmentation helps in identifying relevant objects and their boundaries in the image space, giving out a semantic mask as output. With the help of the mask, the pixels that are covered by the mask are kept unaltered in the original image frame and the rest of the pixel values are changed to zero. This way, unrelated parts from the image are removed and the resulting image can be defined as a spatial image frame. Second, this image is given as input to an existing image feature extractor. The extracted features are from spatial information.

4.4   Classification Model

Contextual, motion, and spatial features are concatenated to form the input layer. The model has three hidden layers each having 4096, 512, and 32 neurons respectively and the output layer has 1 neuron. The output layer gives the probability of anomaly.

4.5   Anomaly Score Function

The anomaly score is high in an anomalous segment and low in a normal segment of the video. Typically, an anomalous event is continuous until the normal event begins. All the frames belonging to the anomalous segment should give out high probability values. It is possible that the model can give out false positives or false negatives which contribute to noise. This noise should not affect the anomaly score of the overall video segment. To ensure this, we propose the usage of rolling mean which helps in smoothening the overall anomaly score graph over a video producing a much more confident qualitative result. We plot the sum of absolute differences between noisy and smoothened values for different window sizes. The point that looks forms the knee in the curve or where the slope varies largely is considered the optimal window size.

5   Experiment and Results

5.1   Implementation Details

The state-of-the-art object detection model, YOLO [12] (version 5) is used to detect objects in the video image frame. YOLO model, the version that was pre-trained on MS COCO is further trained on the ATM-I dataset. Contextual features of a video image frame are represented as a vector of fixed size (81 classes), where the indices represent the class id and the value represents the count of the instances of the class detected in the video image frame.

Pltflow tool kit is used as it would give quick access to several pre-trained models for optical flow estimation. FastFlowNet (FFN) [14] method is leveraged to obtain optical flow image frames quickly with a decent error rate as compared to other techniques [10]. FFN was pre-trained on sintel [15], an optical flow dataset that has most of the real-world objects. Deeplabv3 [16] from Google is used to perform semantic image segmentation tasks. The model is pre-trained on the Pascal VOC dataset [17].

To extract image features from the optical flow frame and spatial image frame, RESNET-50v2 [18], a convolutional neural network, is used that was pre-trained on the Imagenet dataset. The outputs from RESNET-50v2 undergo global average pooling. These three features are then concatenated to form the input layer to a 4-layer fully connected neural network. The first layer has 4096 neurons followed by 512 neurons followed by 32 neurons and 1 neuron layer. Dropout regularization [19] with a dropout rate of 0.5 is used between the fully connected layers. Activation functions ReLU [20] are used for the hidden layers and softmax for the last layer. Adam [21] optimizer is used with a learning rate of 0.001. Categorical cross-entropy is used as the loss function. Input video images preprocessed to have the dimensions 112X112 and pixels are normalized between 0 to 1 range.

5.2 Datasets

ATM-I: The ATM-I dataset consists of 1491 box-annotated images. It is divided into a training set, and validation set consisting of 1342, and 149 images, respectively.

ATMA-V: The ATMA-V dataset consists of 65 real-world videos. It is divided into a training set, and test set containing 52, and 13 videos, respectively.

Table 2. Ablation study results.

Architecture	#params	Recall	Precision	Accuracy	F1	ROC AUC	FPR
(4096,2)	**40.7M**	0.46	0.62	0.80	0.53	0.75	**0.08**
(4096,4096,2)	42.8M	0.87	0.67	0.87	0.76	0.91	0.13
(4096,512,32,2)	42.8M	**0.94**	**0.69**	**0.88**	**0.79**	**0.92**	0.13

Table 3. Quantitative analysis of proposed method and previous works.

Method	Recall	Precision	Accuracy	F1	ROC AUC	FPR
Tripathi et al. [24]	0.26	0.38	0.55	0.31	0.32	0.63
Viji et al. [22]	0.39	0.47	0.68	0.43	0.42	0.56
Parab et al. [23]	0.82	0.68	0.79	0.74	0.8	0.21
Ours	**0.94**	**0.69**	**0.88**	**0.79**	**0.92**	**0.13**

5.3 Ablation Study

An ablation study is performed to assess the effect of different components in the deep neural architecture on the performance of the model. Table 2 demonstrates how layer and neuron count affects the performance of the classification model. It could be observed that increasing the layer count would not always improve the model performance. Secondly, layers with decreasing neuron count in the direction of input to output improved the model performance for the classification task.

5.4 Quantitative Comparison with Previous Works

Comparison results of the proposed method with previous works are shown in Table 3. From the table, we observe that the proposed work outperforms (0.94 Recall and 0.13 False Positive Rate) other methods on the ATMA-V dataset. Among the performance metrics, the recall and false positive rate are crucial here as we want the model to correctly identify most of the anomalous events that are in the testing set.

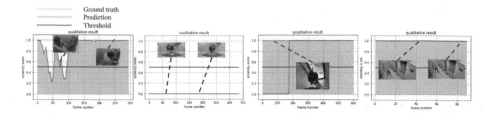

Fig. 4. Qualitative results.

5.5   Qualitative Results

The Fig. 4 shows qualitative results of the model on some videos taken from the testing set. Results demonstrate that the proposed model effectively identifies normal and anomalous video segments.

6   Conclusion and Future Work

We have curated two datasets specific to ATMs: ATM-I and ATMA-V. ATM-I dataset can be used for finetuning object detection models for ATM use cases. ATMA-V dataset can be used for ATM video anomaly detection and benchmarking. We have presented a modified three-stream deep learning architecture where the three streams correspond to contextual, spatial and motion information. We provided qualitative and quantitative results on video anomaly detection task in ATM vestibules that achieved a recall score of 0.93, and false positive rate of 0.13.

In the present work, there is a scope for improvement in resource utilization and time taken for the feature extraction process. There could be better models or other approaches to improve this process. Along with the contextual, motion, and spatial features, we can consider audio features that might improve anomaly score prediction. Moreover, we can consider other end-to-end deep learning architectures that might improve the downstream classification task.

References

1. Kim, E., Kim, S., Seo, M., Yoon, S.: XProtoNet: diagnosis in chest radiography with global and local explanations. In: 2021 IEEE/CVF Conference on Computer Vision and Pattern Recognition (CVPR) (2021). https://doi.org/10.1109/cvpr46437.2021.01546
2. Ranjan, V., Sharma, U., Nguyen, T., Hoai, M.: Learning to count everything. In: 2021 IEEE/CVF Conference on Computer Vision and Pattern Recognition (CVPR) (2021). https://doi.org/10.1109/cvpr46437.2021.00340
3. Stadler, D., Beyerer, J.: Improving multiple pedestrian tracking by track management and occlusion handling. In: 2021 IEEE/CVF Conference on Computer Vision and Pattern Recognition (CVPR) (2021). https://doi.org/10.1109/cvpr46437.2021.01081

4. Pang, G., Shen, C., Cao, L., Hengel, A.V.: Deep learning for anomaly detection. ACM Comput. Surv. **54**, 1–38 (2022). https://doi.org/10.1145/3439950

5. Petrocchi, S., Giorgi, G., Cimino, M.G.: A real-time deep learning approach for real-world video anomaly detection. In: The 16th International Conference on Availability, Reliability and Security (2021). https://doi.org/10.1145/3465481.3470099

6. Angadi, S., Nandyal, S.: Database creation for normal and suspicious behaviour identification in ATM video surveillance. SSRN Electron. J. (2021). https://doi.org/10.2139/ssrn.3835113

7. Sultani, W., Chen, C., Shah, M.: Real-world anomaly detection in surveillance videos. In: 2018 IEEE/CVF Conference on Computer Vision and Pattern Recognition (2018). https://doi.org/10.1109/cvpr.2018.00678

8. Zaidi, S.S., Ansari, M.S., Aslam, A., et al.: A survey of modern deep learning based object detection models. Digit. Signal Process. **126**, 103514 (2022). https://doi.org/10.1016/j.dsp.2022.103514

9. Gibson, J., Marques, O.: Optical flow fundamentals. Opt. Flow Trajectory Estimation Methods 1–7 (2016). https://doi.org/10.1007/978-3-319-44941-8_1

10. Hur, J., Roth, S.: Optical flow estimation in the deep learning age. Model. Hum. Motion 119–140(2020). https://doi.org/10.1007/978-3-030-46732-6_7

11. Salau, A.O., Jain, S.: Feature extraction: a survey of the types, techniques, applications. In: 2019 International Conference on Signal Processing and Communication (ICSC) (2019). https://doi.org/10.1109/icsc45622.2019.8938371

12. Redmon, J., Divvala, S., Girshick, R., Farhadi, A.: You only look once: unified, real-time object detection. In: 2016 IEEE Conference on Computer Vision and Pattern Recognition (CVPR) (2016). https://doi.org/10.1109/cvpr.2016.91

13. Lin, T.-Y., et al.: Microsoft COCO: common objects in context. In: Fleet, D., Pajdla, T., Schiele, B., Tuytelaars, T. (eds.) ECCV 2014. LNCS, vol. 8693, pp. 740–755. Springer, Cham (2014). https://doi.org/10.1007/978-3-319-10602-1_48

14. Kong, L., Shen, C., Yang, J.: FastFlowNet: a lightweight network for fast optical flow estimation. In: 2021 IEEE International Conference on Robotics and Automation (ICRA) (2021). https://doi.org/10.1109/icra48506.2021.9560800

15. Butler, D.J., Wulff, J., Stanley, G.B., Black, M.J.: A naturalistic open source movie for optical flow evaluation. In: Fitzgibbon, A., Lazebnik, S., Perona, P., Sato, Y., Schmid, C. (eds.) ECCV 2012. LNCS, vol. 7577, pp. 611–625. Springer, Heidelberg (2012). https://doi.org/10.1007/978-3-642-33783-3_44

16. Liang-Chieh, C., Papandreou, G., Schroff, F., Hartwig, A.: Rethinking Atrous Convolution for Semantic Image Segmentation (2017). https://doi.org/10.48550/arXiv.1706.05587

17. Everingham, M., Van Gool, L., Williams, C.K., et al.: The pascal visual object classes (VOC) challenge. Int. J. Comput. Vision **88**, 303–338 (2009). https://doi.org/10.1007/s11263-009-0275-4

18. He, K., Zhang, X., Ren, S., Sun, J.: Deep residual learning for image recognition. In: 2016 IEEE Conference on Computer Vision and Pattern Recognition (CVPR) (2016). https://doi.org/10.1109/cvpr.2016.90

19. Srivastava, N., Hinton, G., Krizhevsky, A., et al.: Dropout: A Simple Way to Prevent Neural Networks from Overfitting (2014)

20. Agarap, A.F.: Deep Learning using Rectified Linear Units (ReLU) (2018)

21. Kingma, D., Ba, J.: Adam: A Method for Stochastic Optimization (2017)

22. Viji, S., Kannan, R., Jayalashmi, N.Y.: Intelligent anomaly detection model for ATM booth surveillance using machine learning algorithm: intelligent ATM survillance model. In: 2021 International Conference on Computing, Communication, and Intelligent Systems (ICCCIS) (2021). https://doi.org/10.1109/icccis51004.2021.9397103
23. Parab, A., Nikam, A., Mogaveera, P., Save, A.: A new approach to detect anomalous behaviour in ATMs. In: 2020 6th International Conference on Advanced Computing and Communication Systems (ICACCS) (2020). https://doi.org/10.1109/icaccs48705.2020.9074417
24. Tripathi, V., Mittal, A., Gangodkar, D., Kanth, V.: Real time security framework for detecting abnormal events at ATM installations. J. Real-Time Image Proc. **16**(2), 535–545 (2016). https://doi.org/10.1007/s11554-016-0573-3
25. Nar, R., Singal, A., Kumar, P.: Abnormal activity detection for bank ATM Surveillance. In: 2016 International Conference on Advances in Computing, Communications and Informatics (ICACCI) (2016). https://doi.org/10.1109/icacci.2016.7732351
26. Hackeling, G.: Mastering machine learning with scikit-learn. Packt, Birmingham, West Midlands (2017)

MIS-Net: A Deep Residual Network Based on Memorised Pooling Indices for Medical Image Segmentation

Emerson Nithiyaraj E.$^{(\boxtimes)}$ (iD) and Arivazhagan Selvaraj (iD)

Department of Electronics and Communication Engineering, Mepco Schlenk Engineering College, Sivakasi 626005, Tamil Nadu, India
ej.jeshua@gmail.com, sarivu@mepcoeng.ac.in

Abstract. Deep learning has recently become vitally important in the field of medical image segmentation. Segmentation architectures include more network layers than classification architectures and require roughly twice as many network parameters. This large number of network layers may result in vanishing gradient or redundant computation, increased computational complexity and more memory consumption. Therefore, it is essential to develop an efficient deep model for segmenting medical images. In this work, a novel deep model named MIS-Net is proposed for medical image segmentation. The proposed MIS-Net model is a 69-layer encoder/decoder convolutional model that employs the concept of memorised pooling indices and residual learning. The proposed model is examined for three medical segmentation challenges, namely liver segmentation from the LITS and 3DIRCADb datasets, lung and COVID-19 infection segmentations from the COVID-19 CT dataset. The experiment results for the segmentation of the liver, lung, and COVID-19 infection acquire average dice scores of 0.989, 0.992, and 0.934, respectively. The MIS-Net model surpasses the other deep segmentation models with 0.34M (million) network parameters. The proposed model is a parameter efficient model that reduces the computational complexity and memory utilisation of the model.

Keywords: Medical image segmentation · Deep learning · Convolutional Neural Network

1 Introduction

The boom of deep learning has augmented several image-processing applications including classification, segmentation, recognition, and detection. Traditional machine learning methods in the past relied on manually extracted features to categorise every pixel in the image. With the evolution of deep learning, deep models have automated the process of learning from the data instead of extracting manual features [1]. Several Deep Convolutional Neural Networks (DCNN) such as AlexNet [2], GoogleNet [3], ResNet [4], U-Net [5], SegNet [6] and VGG [7] have been proposed for various image processing

© The Author(s), under exclusive license to Springer Nature Switzerland AG 2023
D. Gupta et al. (Eds.): CVIP 2022, CCIS 1776, pp. 13–28, 2023.
https://doi.org/10.1007/978-3-031-31407-0_2

applications. Semantic segmentation is an active research area in which DCNN accomplishes the task of classifying each pixel in the image according to a specified set of classes [8]. Semantic segmentation in medical images is an alluring and arduous approach where automated segmentation of medical images can help doctors in diagnostic tests. Medical imaging modalities include X-rays, ultrasound, Computer Tomography (CT), and Magnetic Resonance Imaging (MRI). Researchers are working on a number of Computer-Aided Diagnostic (CAD) solutions to minimize the workload of doctors in this area. The aim of the CAD tool is to achieve a faster and more precise diagnosis so that a large number of individuals can be treated more effectively at the same time. Additionally, automatic processing of medical images using CAD tools reduces human error and improves the diagnosis time and quality. Deep models have shown that they are accurate and superior for segmentation tasks, and many deep learning-based CAD solutions have been proposed for medical image segmentation tasks [9, 10].

In this work, a novel deep model named MIS-Net is proposed for medical image segmentation. The proposed MIS-Net model is 69-layer encoder/decoder convolutional model that utilises the concept of memorised pooling indices and residual learning with skip connections. The proposed model is examined for three clinical segmentation problems, namely liver segmentation from the 3DIRCADb dataset, lung and COVID-19 infection segmentations from the COVID-19 CT dataset.

2 Related Works

The Fully Convolutional Network (FCN) is a prominent deep network that provides exceptional performance among all the deep models. Long et al. [11] developed a basic model for semantic segmentation using FCN. FCN-8s is a network that, during the upsample stage, integrates the final prediction layer with the lower layers using finer strides. U-Net is a standard and most popular deep model for segmentation of medical images. U-Net is a deep convolutional network comprised of two networks: a contraction network, or encoder, and an expansion network, or decoder. The stack of convolution and max-pooling layers that make up the contraction path are used to derive features from images. The size of the image decreases along the expansion path as the depth of the network increases. The expansion path is a stack of transposed convolutions that generates the accurate localization by using up-sampling. Skip connections are used to combine the feature maps from the encoder at the same level with the output of the transposed convolution layers at the decoder. Meanwhile, different versions of U-Net models were proposed for medical image segmentation. Weng et al. [12] proposed NAS-UNet for medical image segmentation that is validated on Promise12, Chaos and ultrasound nerve datasets. Zhou et al. [13] designed U-Net++ for medical image segmentation in which the skip connections are revised in a way to close the semantic gap between the feature maps of the encoder and decoder sub-networks. Alom et al. [14] proposed Recurrent Residual Convolutional Neural Network based U-Net named R2UNet which utilises the power of recurrent and residual networks. This proposed model is validated on three different datasets for lung lesion segmentation, retinal blood vessel segmentation and skin cancer segmentation. Zhang et al. [15] developed a DENSE-Inception UNet that integrates the Inception-Res module and densely connected convolutional model into the U-Net architecture. This model is tested on datasets such as retinal blood vessel segmentation, lung segmentation and brain tumour segmentation. Badrinarayanan et al. proposed a semantic segmentation framework named SegNet for road scenes and indoor scenes segmentation tasks. The convolutional layers of VGG16 and the encoder network of SegNet are identical. The decoder network first up-samples the input feature maps using the previously memorised max-pooling indices from the related encoder feature maps. Dense feature maps are created by convolving the obtained sparse feature maps with the decoder filter bank. Some versions of SegNet [16, 17] are also proposed for biomedical segmentation tasks. The SegNet model consumes less memory since the memorised pooling indices are only transferred from the encoder to the decoder. The U-Net model consumes a large amount of memory as the entire feature maps are transferred from contraction path to expansion path.

As the literature review reveals, various deep models based on U-Net and SegNet are proposed for medical image segmentation. Deep models usually suffer from the vanishing gradient problem, which prevents the model from updating its weights. This may completely stop the model from further training and result in poor performance. In comparison to classification tasks, segmentation architectures demand a vast number of network parameters since they have a large number of network layers. A model with fewer network parameters directly reduces the memory usage and computational complexity. Therefore, it is imperative to create efficient deep segmentation models that can guarantee greater performance with fewer network parameters. As a result, the objective of this work is to propose a deep network for segmenting medical images that is free of vanishing gradients and outperforms the state-of-the-art models in terms of fewer network parameters.

3 Proposed MIS-Net Model

The architecture of the proposed MIS-Net model is presented in Fig. 1. The proposed MIS-Net is a symmetrical structured model that contains two networks known as the encoder and decoder. The proposed model has an encoder/decoder network up to a depth of four. The group of convolutional, batch normalization, and ReLU layers are stacked twice in each encoder and decoder depth. The first two depths have 32 convolution filters each, while the latter two depths have 64 convolution filters each. The convolutional layer is a core component of any CNN model, where the filter bank in it is responsible for extracting meaningful representations or features from the input image. Batch normalization [18] neglects the internal covariance shift problem by normalizing incoming feature maps over a mini-batch. The concept of residual learning from the deep residual networks is employed in the proposed model [19]. As the name suggests, skip connections skip between layers of a network so that the output of one layer is supplied as input to certain other layers while being skipped from the layer after it. The input feature map prior to the first convolutional layer and the feature map following the second ReLU layer are added using additive skip connections in each encoder depth.

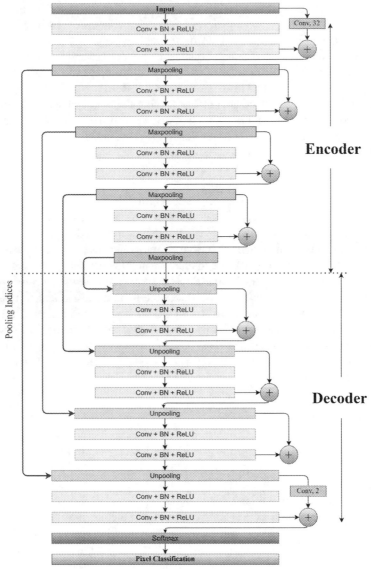

Conv - 2D Convolutional Layer; **BN** - Batch Normalization; **ReLU** - Rectified Linear Unit
(Conv, n) - 'n' denotes the number of kernels in the convolutional layer

Fig. 1. The proposed MIS-Net model for medical image segmentation

As evident in Fig. 1, the max-pooling layers of each encoder depth are fed with these accumulated feature maps instead of the direct feature maps from the previous layer. The encoder network ensures improved and more robust feature representation through feature accumulation using skip connections. The pooling operation is accountable for dimensionality reduction and translation invariance over minute spatial alterations in the input feature map. The locations of the maximum feature value in each pooling window are stored at each encoder feature map, which was influenced by the semantic segmentation model SegNet. In the decoder network, the incoming feature maps are first up-sampled using the unpooling operation. The memorised max-pooling locations from the encoder networks are shared with each of the corresponding decoder networks. The resulting sparse feature maps are convolved with the decoder filter bank to obtain dense feature maps. In the same way, the up-sampled feature map and the feature map after the second ReLU layer are added using skip connections at each decoder depth in the decoder network. The feature accumulation via additive skip connections guarantees superior image reconstruction in the decoder network. The softmax and pixel classification layers are used at the end of the decoder to generate class probabilities and pixel labels from the input image.

The difference between the proposed MIS-Net and U-Net models is that the U-Net model does not reuse pooling indices but instead transfers the entire feature map to the corresponding decoders at the cost of more memory. The proposed MIS-Net model has different layer and filter size configurations than the SegNet model, which reduces the amount of network parameters and lowers memory use. The main advantage of the proposed MIS-Net model is the use of additive skip connections, and the summation blocks are seen on the right side of Fig. 1. The summation blocks perform element-wise addition, which adds the incoming feature maps of the same size. These additive skip connections solve the vanishing gradient problem encountered during back propagation. The gradients are preserved by the skip connections when the earlier layers of the deep network are approached. Additionally, the skip connection enables lateral layers in deeper networks to gain knowledge from the features of the preceding layers.

3.1 Training or Network Parameters

Back propagation is the process of adjusting the parameters such as weights based on the loss function between the output and target (actual) values [20]. The training or network parameters are the parameters that are modified or updated by the back propagation algorithm during training of the network [21]. The amount of training parameters in a CNN model determines the network complexity. The quantity of training parameters in a convolutional layer is determined based on the filter size (m × n), number of the filters in the prior layer 'p' and current layer 'k'. The calculation for the amount of training parameters in a convolutional layer is given in Eq. (1).

$$N_{conv} = ((m \times n \times p) + 1) \times k \tag{1}$$

4 Experimental Setup

4.1 Dataset Summary

The liver segmentation is experimented on the 'LITS - Liver Lesion Segmentation Challenge' dataset and the 3DIRCADb (3D Image Reconstruction for Comparison of Algorithm Database) datasets [22, 23]. LITS training data contains 130 3D CT images and 3DIRCADb dataset contains 20 3D CT images. The corresponding binary masks for every CT slice are provided in both the datasets. The original image size of (512 × 512) is used in this work. The lung segmentation and the COVID-19 infection segmentation are experimented on the COVID-19 CT scan dataset provided by Kaggle [24]. This dataset has 20 CT images with the expert segmentations of lung and Covid-19 infection regions. Some sample images of liver, lung and COVID-19 infection along with ground truths are depicted in Fig. 2.

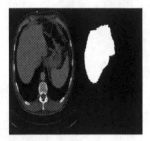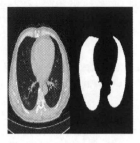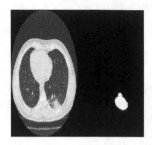

Fig. 2. Liver CT image in the left, lung CT image in the middle and COVID-19 infection CT image in the right with its corresponding ground truths.

4.2 Performance Analysis Metrics

The MIS-Net model is statistically evaluated based on five performance metrics, i.e., Sensitivity (SE), Specificity (SP), Mean Accuracy (ACC), Dice coefficient (DSC) and Jaccard index (JC) [25, 26]. The metrics are defined in the Eqs. (2) to (6). The values of variables such as true positive (TP), false positive (FP), true negative (TN), and false negative (FN) are obtained from the confusion matrix.

$$\text{Sensitivity (SE)} = \frac{TP}{TP + FN} \tag{2}$$

$$\text{Specificity (SP)} = \frac{TN}{TN + FP} \tag{3}$$

$$\text{Mean Accuracy (ACC)} = \frac{TP + TN}{TP + TN + FP + FN} \tag{4}$$

$$\text{Dice coefficient (DSC)} = \frac{2TP}{2TP + FP + FN} \tag{5}$$

$$\text{Jaccard Index (JI)} = \frac{TP}{TP + FP + FN} \tag{6}$$

4.3 Hyperparameter Settings

In the training process, mini-batch stochastic gradient descent with momentum (MB-SGDM) optimizer is used [27]. Optimizers are algorithms that adjust the characteristics of a neural network, such as weights and learning rate, in order to minimise losses. While implementing the MIS-Net model with many other optimization algorithms, MB-SGDM optimizer brought the best results. For network training, concept of adaptive learning rate is employed. The initial learning rate is predetermined for a given number of epochs, and the learning rate is multiplied by the learning rate drop factor for every predetermined number of epochs. The network is trained for 20 epochs, with the initial learning rate set at 0.1 and the learning rate drop factor set at 0.001 every 10 epochs. Epochs 1 through 10 have a learning rate of 0.1, whereas epochs 11 through 20 have a learning rate of 10^{-4}. The initial bias is set to zero and the initial weights of the model are assigned using Gaussian distribution with a mean value zero and standard of 0.01. To prevent the overfitting issues, the training and validation images are randomly shuffled before every epoch [28]. The ReLU function is used as the activation function and the binary cross entropy loss function is used.

5   Experimental Results and Discussion

The effectiveness of the proposed MIS-Net model is tested on three clinical segmentation problems. These include liver segmentation from the LITS and 3DIRCADb datasets, lung segmentation and COVID-19 infection segmentation from the COVID-19 CT dataset. The identical segmentation problem is also carried out using standard deep models such as U-Net, SegNet, FCN-8s, and ResU-Net to validate the MIS-Net model for better comparability. The implementation of U-Net, SegNet, FCN-8s and ResU-Net used the same datasets and same hyper-parameter settings (epochs, weights initialization, loss function, learning rate and optimization algorithm) as MIS-Net. The experiments are carried out using Matlab 2021a on a PC with an Intel Xeon CPU running at 2.1 GHz and a 16 GB RAM GPU from NVIDIA.

5.1   Liver Segmentation Using the LITS and 3DIRCADb Datasets

For this study, 540 slices from the 20 CT images of 3DIRCADb dataset and 3445 slices from the 130 CT images of LITS dataset are used. These 3985 slices exhibit a broader range and complexity in terms of the size and structure of the liver. The Hounsfield unit (HU) of each CT slice is windowed between [100, 400] [29]. The HU windowing process eliminates the unwanted regions from the CT image and raises the contrast. To each windowed CT slice is applied a Gaussian filter with a sigma value of 0.2 to effectively reduce granular noise [30]. The dataset has a split ratio of 80% for training, 10% for validation, and 10% for testing. The original image size of (512×512) is used in this work. The validation accuracy of the MIS-Net model for liver segmentation is 99.68%. The pictorial results of the proposed MIS-Net model for liver segmentation are shown in Fig. 3. The first and second columns display the actual CT slices together with the results using the LITS dataset. The third and fourth columns display the actual CT slices with the ground truth and the results using the 3DIRCADb dataset. As shown in Fig. 3, the MIS-Net model has the ability to segment the liver region accurately irrespective of the shape and size of the liver region.

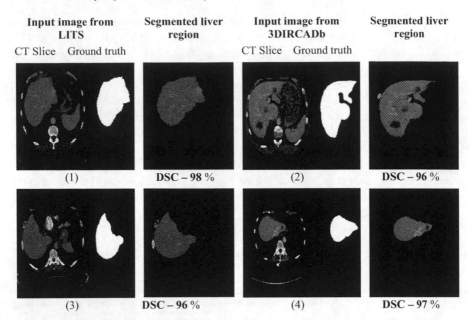

Input image from LITS	Segmented liver region	Input image from 3DIRCADb	Segmented liver region

Fig. 3. Pictorial results of the MIS-Net model for liver segmentation using LITS and 3DIRCADb datasets.

Table 1 summarises the confusion matrix for liver segmentation using the test set images. As evident in Table 1, the obtained classification accuracies of the proposed model for liver pixels (TP) and background pixels (TN) are 98.2% and 99.8%, respectively. 0.2% of background pixels and 1.8% of liver pixels are misclassified as liver pixels (FN) and background pixels (FP), respectively.

Table 1. Normalized confusion matrix for 398 liver slices

Actual class		
Predicted class	Liver	Background
Liver	0.982	0.002
Background	0.018	0.998

Table 2 summarises the segmentation performance of MIS-Net for liver segmentation and also presents a comparison with the other traditional networks. As seen in Table 2, the proposed model is 99.7% precise in predicting the liver pixels out of all the positive predictions (TP, FP). A specificity value of 98.2% shows the model's ability to predict the non-liver pixels out of all actual negatives (TN, FP). The average Dice score and Jaccard index of MIS-Net are 98.9% and 98% respectively. The proposed MIS-Net model has resulted in a Dice score that is 6.4% higher than the second-best segmentation performance. The MIS-Net model produced better results for liver segmentation while

Table 2. Experimental results of MIS-Net model for liver segmentation and comparison against other networks

Model	SE	SP	ACC	DSC	JI
FCN – 8s	0.862	0.978	0.897	0.890	0.801
U-Net	0.867	0.971	0.912	0.908	0.831
SegNet	0.851	0.962	0.901	0.894	0.808
Res-UNet	0.864	0.971	0.930	0.925	0.860
MIS-Net	**0.997**	**0.982**	**0.990**	**0.989**	**0.980**

experimenting with two different datasets. The quantitative investigation has shown that the proposed MIS-Net model outperformed all other conventional deep networks under all evaluation metrics.

5.2   Lung Segmentation Using the COVID-19 CT Dataset

The 20 CT images of the COVID-19 CT dataset have a total of 3250 2D slices in it. Among the 3250 slices, 2314 slices have the lung region. These slices are subjected to data augmentation techniques such as horizontal flipping and rotation of angles +45 and –45°. A total of 9256 images combining the original and augmented images are used to evaluate the proposed model for lung segmentation. The dataset has a split ratio of 80% for training, 10% for validation, and 10% for testing. The MIS-Net model attained a validation accuracy of 99.63% for lung segmentation. The segmentation results of the MIS-Net model for lung segmentation are shown in Fig. 4. The first and third columns display the CT slices with the ground truths, while the second and fourth columns display the lung segmentation results of the corresponding CT slices.

Table 3 summarises the confusion matrix for lung segmentation using the test set images. As shown in Table 3, the obtained classification accuracies of the proposed model for lung pixels (TP) and background pixels (TN) are 98.8% and 99.8%, respectively. 1.2% of lung pixels and 0.2% of background pixels are misclassified as background pixels (FN) and lung pixels (FP), respectively. Table 4 provides results of MIS-Net for lung segmentation and comparison with other networks in terms of quantitative analysis. From Table 4, the proposed model is 99.7% precise in predicting the lung pixels out of all the positive predictions (TP, FP). A specificity value of 99.8% shows the model's ability to predict the non-lung pixels out of all actual negatives (TN, FP).

Further, the Table 4 shows that the MIS-Net results in better performance under each evaluation score. The average dice score and average Jaccard index obtained using the proposed method are 99.2% and 98.4%, respectively. In terms of SE, SP, ACC, DSC and JC, the results from the MIS-Net model are 5.5%, 3.04%, 1.8%, 2.1% and 4.1% higher than the second segmentation performance. As a result, the outcomes demonstrate that the proposed MIS-Net model performs effectively for lung segmentation.

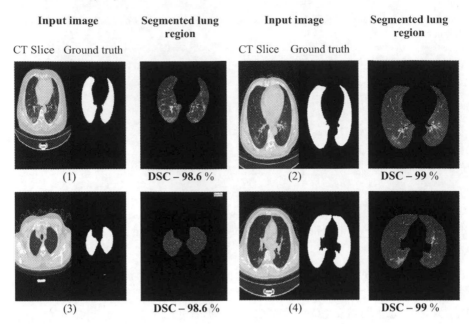

Fig.4. Pictorial results of the MIS-Net model for lung segmentation using COVID-19 CT dataset.

Table 3. Normalized confusion matrix for 926 slices of COVID19 CT dataset

Actual class		
Predicted class	Lung	Background
Lung	0.988	0.012
Background	0.002	0.998

Table 4. Experimental results of MIS-Net model for lung segmentation and comparison against other networks

Model	SE	SP	ACC	DSC	JI
FCN – 8s	0.932	0.982	0.941	0.938	0.883
U-Net	0.939	0.984	0.969	0.962	0.926
SegNet	0.936	0.979	0.970	0.966	0.934
Res-UNet	0.942	0.985	0.975	0.971	0.943
MIS-Net	**0.997**	**0.988**	**0.993**	**0.992**	**0.984**

5.3 Covid-19 Infection Segmentation Using the COVID-19 CT Dataset

Among the 20 CT images of the COVID-19 CT dataset, only 1630 slices contain the COVID-19 infection region. These 1630 slices are also subjected to data augmentation techniques such as horizontal flipping and rotation of angles +45 and −45°. A total of 6520 images are used to experiment the MIS-Net model for the COVID-19 infection segmentation. The dataset has a split ratio of 80% for training, 10% for validation, and 10% for testing. The MIS-Net model obtained a validation accuracy of 99.24% for COVID-19 segmentation. The COVID-19 infection segmentation results of the proposed MIS-Net model are shown in Fig. 5. The first and third columns display the actual CT slices with the ground truths, while the second and fourth columns show the COVID-19 infection segmentation results of the corresponding slices.

Table 5 summarises the confusion matrix for COVID-19 infection segmentation using the test set images. The proposed model has resulted in an average classification accuracy of 99.7% for background pixels (TN) and 87.9% for COVID-19 infection pixels (TP). 0.3% of background pixels and 12.1% of COVID-19 pixels are incorrectly labelled or misclassified.

Input image	COVID-19 infection region	Input image	COVID-19 infection region
CT Slice Ground truth		CT Slice Ground truth	

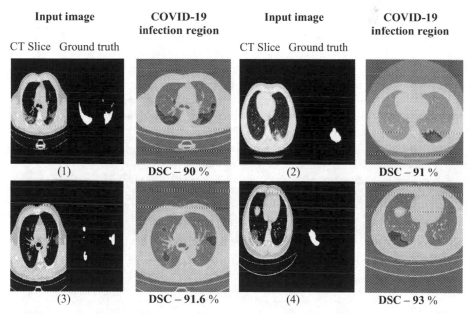

(1)	DSC – 90 %	(2)	DSC – 91 %
(3)	DSC – 91.6 %	(4)	DSC – 93 %

Fig. 5. Pictorial results of the MIS-Net model for COVID-19 infection segmentation using COVID-19 CT dataset.

Table 6 summarises the statistical analysis of MIS-Net and its comparison to other networks for COVID-19 infection segmentation. As seen in Table 6, the proposed model is 90.1% precise in predicting the non-COVID-19 pixels out of all actual negatives (TN, FP). A sensitivity value of 99.6% shows the model's ability to predict the COVID-19 pixels out of all the positive predictions (TP, FP). The MIS-Net model has produced

Table 5. Normalized confusion matrix for 652 slices of COVID19 CT dataset

Actual class		
Predicted class	COVID19	Background
COVID19	0.879	0.121
Background	0.003	0.997

Table 6. Experimental results of MIS-Net model for COVID-19 infection segmentation and comparison against other networks

Model	SE	SP	ACC	DSC	JI
FCN – 8s	0.754	0.647	0.699	0.698	0.536
U-Net	0.774	0.612	0.734	0.733	0.578
SegNet	0.872	0.766	0.802	0.749	0.598
Res-UNet	0.891	0.795	0.826	0.824	0.700
MIS-Net	**0.996**	**0.901**	**0.938**	**0.934**	**0.876**

an average Dice score of 0.934 and the average Jaccard index, SE, SP and ACC are 0.876, 0.996, 0.901 and 0.938. For COVID-19 infection segmentation, the Dice score of the MIS-Net model is 11.7% higher than the second segmentation performance. These results verify the feasibility and robustness of the proposed MIS-Net model for COVID-19 infection segmentation.

The training parameters of MIS-Net are computed including both the encoder and decoder networks. The number of training parameters for FCN-8s, U-Net, SegNet, and ResUNet is identified from the literature. Table 7 presents the comparison of the number of training parameters between the proposed MIS-Net model and other networks.

Table 7. Comparison of training parameters between MIS-Net and other models

Model Name	Number of parameters (million)	Parameters computation
FCN-8s [11]	134.5M	Encoder and decoder
U-Net [5]	31M	Encoder and decoder
SegNet [6]	14.7M	Encoder only
ResUNet [14]	31M	Encoder and decoder
MIS-Net	**0.34M**	Encoder and decoder

From Table 7, it is observed that the number of training parameters for the proposed MIS-Net model is 0.34M, which is very much less compared to FCN-8s, U-Net, SegNet and ResUNet models. The primary benefit of the MIS-Net model is the number of training parameters, which lowers the computational complexity and memory usage of the model. For all three segmentation tasks, the gap between training and testing accuracies is extremely small, ensuring that the model is not overfitted to the training data. The additive skip connections in MIS-Net promise robust feature representations, and the results are better than the other models for all three clinical segmentation problems. The optimal MIS-Net model is proposed after conducting vast experimentation with different hyperparameter settings. The evaluation of the proposed model for different model settings is depicted in Fig. 6.

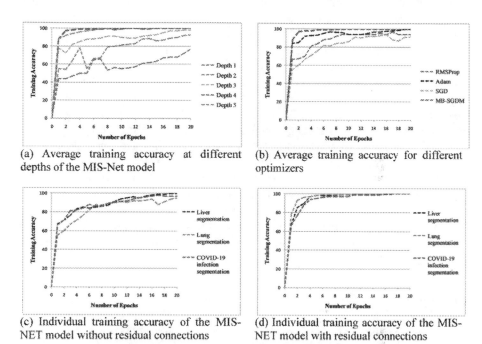

(a) Average training accuracy at different depths of the MIS-Net model

(b) Average training accuracy for different optimizers

(c) Individual training accuracy of the MIS-NET model without residual connections

(d) Individual training accuracy of the MIS-NET model with residual connections

Fig. 6. Results of the MIS-Net model for different hyper-parameter settings

The average training accuracy of the three segmentation problems for different depths of the encoder/decoder network in the MIS-Net model is shown in Fig. 6(a). The MIS-Net model at depth 4 converges faster and achieves a minimal number of network parameters than at depth 5. The average training accuracy for different optimizers is illustrated in Fig. 6(b). The MB-SGDM optimizer resulted in optimal training performance than the other optimizers. The momentum term in the MB-SGDM optimizer aggregates the gradients during weights update instead of using single gradient. This accounts for faster and smoother convergence, as evident in Fig. 6(b). Figure 6(c) depicts the individual training accuracy of the three segmentation problems with no residual connections. Figure 6(d) depicts the individual training accuracy with residual connections. The MIS-Net model with residual connections performs better than the model with no residual connections. The residual connections account for preventing the vanishing gradient and overfitting problems. Thus, the proposed MIS-Net model is efficient using the concepts of memorised pooling indices and residual learning for medical image segmentation tasks.

6   Conclusion

In this work, an effective deep network named MIS-Net is proposed for the segmentation of medical images. The proposed approach addresses both the vanishing gradient problem and the huge number of network parameters in a deep segmentation model. This is achieved by utilising the concepts of memorised pooling indices and residual learning. The proposed MIS-Net model has produced great results on three different clinical datasets. The MIS-Net model resulted in a dice score of 0.989, 0.992 and 0.934 for liver segmentation, lung segmentation and COVID-19 infection segmentation. For better evaluation, the same task is performed with the standard U-Net, SegNet, FCN-8s and ResU-Net models and their results are compared with those. The dice scores of the MIS-Net model are 6.4%, 2.1% and 11.7% higher than the second segmentation performance for the liver, lung, and COVID-19 segmentations. According to the experimental findings, the proposed MIS-Net model performs better than the existing typical deep segmentation models. The proposed MIS-Net is a parameter-efficient model that outperforms the comparable models by having 0.34 million network parameters. Therefore, this work demonstrates the effectiveness of residual learning and memorised pooling indices in a DCNN for medical image segmentation task. The outcome of the experiments demonstrates that the proposed MIS-Net is an accurate and effective model for segmenting medical images. In the future, the MIS-Net model could be applied to other imaging modalities.

References

1. Castiglioni, I., Rundo, L., Codari, M., et al.: AI applications to medical images: from machine learning to deep learning. Physica Med. **83**, 9–24 (2021). https://doi.org/10.1016/j.ejmp.2021.02.006
2. Krizhevsky, A., Sutskever, I., Hinton, G.E.: ImageNet classification with deep convolutional neural networks. Commun ACM **60**, 84–90 (2017). https://doi.org/10.1145/3065386
3. Szegedy, C., Liu, W., Jia, Y., et al.: Going Deeper with Convolutions. arXiv:14094842 [cs] (2014)
4. He K, Zhang X, Ren S, Sun J.: Deep Residual Learning for Image Recognition. arXiv:151203385 [cs] (2015)
5. Ronneberger O, Fischer P, Brox T (2015) U-Net: Convolutional Networks for Biomedical Image Segmentation. arXiv:150504597 [cs]
6. Badrinarayanan V, Kendall A, Cipolla R (2016) SegNet: A Deep Convolutional Encoder-Decoder Architecture for Image Segmentation. arXiv:151100561 [cs]
7. Simonyan K, Zisserman A (2015) Very Deep Convolutional Networks for Large-Scale Image Recognition. arXiv:14091556 [cs]
8. Minaee, S., Boykov, Y.Y., Porikli, F., et al.: Image Segmentation using deep learning: a survey. IEEE Trans. Pattern Anal. Mach. Intell. **44**, 3523–3542 (2021). https://doi.org/10.1109/TPAMI.2021.3059968

9. Hesamian, M.H., Jia, W., He, X., Kennedy, P.: Deep learning techniques for medical image segmentation: achievements and challenges. J. Digit. Imaging **32**(4), 582–596 (2019). https://doi.org/10.1007/s10278-019-00227-x

10. Nithiyaraj, E.E., Arivazhagan, S.: Survey on Recent works in computed tomography based computer - aided diagnosis of liver using deep learning techniques. Int. J. Innov. Sci. Res. Techol. **5**:173–181 (2020). https://doi.org/10.38124/IJISRT20JUL058

11. Long, J., Shelhamer, E., Darrell, T.: Fully convolutional networks for semantic segmentation. In: 2015 IEEE Conference on Computer Vision and Pattern Recognition (CVPR). Recurrent Residual Convolutional Neural Network based on U-Net (R2U-Net) for Medical Image Segmentation (2015)

12. Weng, Y., Zhou, T., Li, Y., Qiu, X.: NAS-Unet: neural architecture search for medical image segmentation. IEEE Access **7**, 44247–44257 (2019). https://doi.org/10.1109/ACCESS.2019.2908991

13. Zhou, Z., Rahman Siddiquee, M.M., Tajbakhsh, N., Liang, J.: UNet++: a nested U-Net architecture for medical image segmentation. In: Stoyanov, D., et al. (eds.) DLMIA/ML-CDS -2018. LNCS, vol. 11045, pp. 3–11. Springer, Cham (2018). https://doi.org/10.1007/978-3-030-00889-5_1

14. Alom, Z., Taha, T.M., Asari, V.K.: Recurrent residual convolutional neural network based on U-Net (R2U-Net) for medical image segmentation, 12p (2018)

15. Zhang, Z., Wu, C., Coleman, S., Kerr, D.: DENSE-INception U-net for medical image segmentation. Comput. Methods Programs Biomed. **192**, 105395 (2020). https://doi.org/10.1016/j.cmpb.2020.105395

16. Almotairi, S., Kareem, G., Aouf, M., et al.: Liver tumor segmentation in CT scans using modified SegNet. Sensors (Basel) **20**, 1516 (2020). https://doi.org/10.3390/s20051516

17. Budak, Ü., Guo, Y., Tanyildizi, E., Şengür, A.: Cascaded deep convolutional encoder-decoder neural networks for efficient liver tumor segmentation. Med. Hypotheses **134**, 109431 (2020). https://doi.org/10.1016/j.mehy.2019.109431

18. Ioffe, S., Szegedy, C.: batch normalization: accelerating deep network training by reducing internal covariate shift. arXiv:150203167 [cs] (2015)

19. Hemalakshmi, G.R., Santhi, D., Mani, V.R.S.. et al.: Deep residual network based on image priors for SingleImage super resolution in FFA Images. Comput. Model. Eng. Sci. **125,** 125–143 (2020). https://doi.org/10.32604/cmes.2020.011331

20. Gupta, T.: Deep learning: back propagation. In: Medium. https://towardsdatascience.com/back-propagation-414ec0043d7. Accessed 29 Apr 2021

21. Vasudev, R.: Understanding and calculating the number of parameters in convolution neural networks (CNNs). In: Medium (2021). https://towardsdatascience.com/understanding-and-calculating-the-number-of-parameters-in-convolution-neural-networks-cnns-fc88790d530d. Accessed 29 Apr 2021

22. LITS – Liver Tumor Segmentation Challenge (LITS17). In: Academic Torrents. https://academictorrents.com/details/27772adef6f563a1ecc0ae19a528b956e6c803ce. Accessed 17 Jun 2021

23. 3DircadbIIRCAD France. https://www.ircad.fr/research/3dircadb/. Accessed 17 Jun 2021

24. COVID-19 CT scans. https://kaggle.com/andrewmvd/covid19-ct-scans. Accessed 25 Nov 2021

25. Wang, Z., Wang, E., Zhu, Y.: Image segmentation evaluation: a survey of methods. Artif. Intell. Rev. **53**(8), 5637–5674 (2020). https://doi.org/10.1007/s10462-020-09830-9

26. Sathananthavathi, V., Indumathi, G.:. Encoder Enhanced Atrous (EEA) UNet architecture for retinal blood vessel segmentation. Cogn. Syst. Res. **67,** 84–95 (2021). https://doi.org/10.1016/j.cogsys.2021.01.003

27. Mahmood, H.: Gradient descent. In: Medium (2019). https://towardsdatascience.com/gradient-descent-3a7db7520711. Accessed 29 Apr 2021

28. Salman, S., Liu, X.: Overfitting mechanism and avoidance in deep neural networks. arXiv:190106566 [cs, stat] (2019)
29. Hounsfield Scale - an overview|ScienceDirect Topics. https://www.sciencedirect.com/topics/medicine-and-dentistry/hounsfield-scale. Accessed 29 Apr 2021
30. Mayasari, R., Heryana, N.: Reduce noise in computed tomography image using adaptive Gaussian filter. Int. J. Comput. Tech. **6,** 4 (2019)

HD-VAE-GAN: Hiding Data with Variational Autoencoder Generative Adversarial Networks

Rohit Gandikota[1]([✉])[ID] and Deepak Mishra[2][ID]

[1] Northeastern University, Boston, MA, USA
gandikota.ro@northeastern.edu
[2] Department of Space, Indian Institute of Space Science and Technology,
Thiruvananthapuram, Kerala, India
deepak.mishra@iist.ac.in
https://rohitgandikota.github.io/

Abstract. This manuscript proposes an end-to-end trainable model, VAE-GAN, engineered to hide messages (image) inside a container (image). The model consists of an embedder network (to hide a message inside the container) and an extractor network(to extract the hidden message from the encoded image). In the proposed method, we employ the generative power of a variational autoencoder with adversarial training to embed images. At the extractor, a vanilla convolutional network with adversarial training has provided the best results with clean extracted images. To analyse the noise sensitivity of the model, the encoded image is subjected to multiple attacks, and it is established that the proposed method is inherently robust towards attacks like Gaussian blurring, rotation, noise, and cropping. However, the model can be trained on any possible attacks to reduce noise sensitivity further. In this manuscript, we explore the application of hiding images inside images, but the method can be extended to hide various combinations of data hiding.

Keywords: steganography · generative adversarial networks · neural network · variational autoencoder

1 Introduction

Based on applications and requirements, numerous categories of data hiding techniques can be identified. Generally speaking, hiding can be split into two categories based on the amount of information needed to discover it: i) A blind approach [14,22] that extracts the embedded data from an encoded or embedded image without the aid of the original container signal. Techniques of blind concealment are less resistant to attacks [15]. (ii) Non-blind methods can decode an encoded message using both the original container signal and the secret keys, which are both present at the transmission end. These strategies are more resistant to different attacks than blind strategies. Since a more reliable model is required, blind data hiding-the topic of this work-is more difficult.

D. Gupta et al. (Eds.): CVIP 2022, CCIS 1776, pp. 29–43, 2023.
https://doi.org/10.1007/978-3-031-31407-0_3

There are two popular theories regarding how to conceal information in images. The first is steganography, where the objective is to achieve secret communication between a sender and a receiver, while a potential adversary is unable to determine whether the image contains any message. The purpose of digital watermarking, the second idea, is to encrypt data while overcoming or withstanding any challenging circumstances. Even if an attacker distorts the image, the recipient can still decipher the message. Data ownership and copyright identification are frequently done through the use of watermarking. This research explores the effectiveness of steganography for watermarking and proposes a method for its use. Additionally, the method is invisible to the naked eye, and the network is naturally resistant to the majority of attacks.

This paper proposes a generic deep learning approach named Hiding Data with VAE-GAN (HD-VAE-GAN) for data concealing. The proposed method is a blind technique using Variational Autoencoding compared to the existing methods using various CNN architectures [15,18,20,23]. Unlike the existing GAN based methods that use adversarial training for embedding alone [5,14,16], our proposed method has adversarial training for both embedder and extractor. We have introduced the variational factor in the embedding procedure that significantly improved the extraction robustness. Due to the sampling in VAE, the encoded images fall onto a wider distribution, and varying samples improves the extraction robustness as these sampled encoded images are used for extractor training. Experiments show that HD-VAE-GAN outperforms state-of-the-art methods in terms of robustness.

The main contributions of this work are

- Proposing, to our best knowledge, the first generic end-to-end trainable model with Adversarial VAE encoder for data hiding.
- Introducing variational inference in data hiding to improve the method's robustness by modelling a wider distribution of the encoded image. This variational sampling improves the extraction robustness as the sampled encoded images are used for extractor training.

The rest of this paper is organised as follows: First, in Sect. 2, we discuss the previous work related to the field of data hiding. Then, in Sect. 3, we formulate the problem and introduce all the networks used in this method. We discuss the training procedure designed for our method. Later, we provide the experimental details in Sect. 4 and the performance results of our method in Sect. 5. Finally, we conclude in Sect. 6 that variational encoding does improve the inherent robustness of the network towards transmission attacks while not majorly compromising on the encoding efficiency.

2   Related Work

Mun *et al.* [22] introduced a custom training of CNN to embed and extract watermarks. While Kandi *et al.* [15] uses two differently initialized auto-encoders for embedding. Their method requires information about the original cover and only embed binary watermarks. Shumeet *et al.* [4] uses Deep Neural Networks for steganography by implementing three different networks: Prep Network, Hiding Network, and a Reveal Network. Some techniques use domain transforms to embed watermarks [6–8,13], and others using spatial domain watermarking [25] in order to calculate LSB in the cover image and replace it with the secret information.

Recently, Zhu *et al.* [14] and [5] have introduced the adversarial component in watermarking using an encoder-decoder model to embed and extract respectively. For the first time, Le.*et al.* [19] have used GANs in watermarking. However, unlike our work, they have used it to generate a texture image and then embed it using a different concealing network making their watermark visually invisible. Kevin *et al.* [16] have compared res and dense connections in the generator that mitigate the vanishing gradient problem in GAN with a basic CNN as the generator. Gandikota *et al.* [9] have attempted hiding audio in images using GAN with speech specific objective functions. This work was specific to audio hiding due to speech signals' one-dimensional non-stationary characteristics.

GAN is a prevalent idea present in the machine learning community. While it is mainly used to generate images [1,21] and [11], Wu *et al.* [26] have used them to remove mesh noise from the images which are further used for face identification. They have perceived the generative property of GAN as domain transform from which we have taken the inspiration.

3 Proposed Method

In this section, we formulate the problem statement and describe all the networks in detail. We also discuss the training procedure and possible transmission attacks that may affect the extraction process.

3.1 Problem Formulation

Data hiding is the practice of concealing a message image MSG into a cover image CI. The resultant encoded image EI may look similar to the CI. It is also essential to extract the message image MSG_{ex} from the encoded image.

In this paper, we suggest an innovative approach to the two goals listed above. To embed messages, a modified VAE-GAN network is presented, and to extract the embedded messages, a separate extractor network with adversarial training is suggested. The variational inference makes our method efficient compared to [5,14,16], that uses adversarial networks alone.

HD-VAE-GAN consists of four neural networks; an embedder Emb, an embedding discriminator D_{emb}, an extractor Ex, and an extraction discriminator D_{ex}. Emb is a variational autoencoder network with skip connections from the encoder Emb_{enc} to a decoder Emb_{dec} that is in the same dimensions. Emb is designed to generate an encoded image EI that has a distribution close to the cover image CI by taking the cover image CI and message image MSG as inputs. Embedding Discriminator D_{emb} is designed to distinguish the encoded

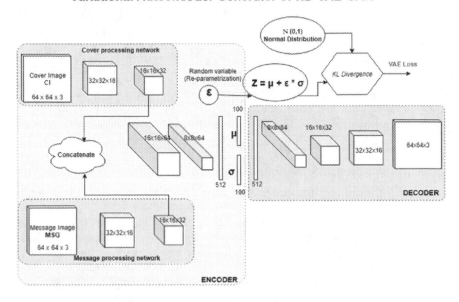

Fig. 1. The architecture of embedder of HD-VAE-GAN. A variational autoencoder with concatenation leaks from the encoder to the decoder is used as an embedder. The reparameterisation trick is used with the help of a variable ϵ, making the rest of the network deterministic. The KL divergence with the sampled z and normal distribution will force the μ and σ to follow the mean and variance of a normal distribution, respectively.

image generated by Emb from the corresponding cover image CI. The encoder Emb_{enc} of the VAE Emb as shown in Fig. 1, is used to transform the domain from a combination of cover and message to normal distribution. This variational inference that brings the domain to normal distribution makes the task easy for the decoder to generate the encoded image. The process of embedding through a concatenation of message and cover is shown in Fig. 1. At the receiver end, the extractor Ex decodes the hidden message from the encoded image. The Extraction Discriminator D_{ex} is designed to distinguish the extracted message MSG_{ex} from the original hidden message MSG

It is significant to remember that GANs are unstable during the training [2] and may result in image distortions. For the training of HD-VAE-GAN, we provide a special multi-objective training method that has fixed the mode-collapse problem in GAN training. The binary cross-entropy and L1 loss are combined in the GANs to increase the output's crispness at higher frequencies. In order to make the generator train quicker and assist the neural network approach the nash equilibrium, a deep convolution loss (feature loss from a pre-trained network) is included.

3.2   VAE Embedder Network

A detailed representation of the embedder is depicted in Fig. 1. The embedding is done by concatenating features in the encoder of the Emb. As proposed in the standard VAE [17], we implement the encoder as shown in Eq. 1, transforming the domain from cover and message images to a normal distribution with a dimensional size of dim.

$$Emb_{enc}(CI, \ MSG) \implies \mu, \ \sigma \in \mathbb{N}_{dim}(0, 1) \tag{1}$$

The decoder samples from the distribution $\mathbb{N}_{dim}(0, 1)$ and constructs an encoded image that is similar to cover image as shown in Eq. 2. The VAE can be seen as the embedder as it takes cover image and message images, process them to produce encoded image as shown in Eq. 3.

$$Emb_{dec}(\mu, \ \sigma) \implies EI \tag{2}$$

$$Emb(CI, \ MSG) \implies Emb_{dec}(Emb_{enc}(CI, \ MSG)) \implies EI \tag{3}$$

To elaborate, the embedder takes two inputs of the same size $cW \times cH \times cC$, and the encoder outputs two arrays μ and σ, representing the mean and variance of a distribution. A sampled point from these distribution parameters of the encoder will, in turn, be input to the decoder, which upsamples it back to the array, EI of size $cW \times cH \times cC$. Leaking identical layer activations from the encoder and concatenating them at the decoder has significantly improved the embedder training.

The variational sampling at the decoder of the VAE helps in varying samples of encoded images from the same message-cover image pairs. Since these encoded images are used as training samples for the extractor, the robustness of the network is increased. In other words, the VAE sampling acts like an inherent noisy channel that helps to improve the extractor training. However, this approach produces less accurate encoded images than the traditional techniques, and hence this method is preferred to be applied in steganography purposes where embedding efficiency is not of a higher priority.

3.3   Extractor Network

The extractor Ex, as the name suggests, is assigned the task of extracting the hidden message MSG in the encoded image EI. This can be done by simply devising an autoencoder with EI of size $cW \times cH \times cC$ as input and training it to extract the MSG of size $cW \times cH \times cC$ as output as shown in Eq. 4. We propose adversarial training to the extractor and formal training with pixel loss to help improve the extraction efficiency. The discriminator used in this case ensures that the extractor extracts only the correct hidden message from the corresponding encoded image and trains the extractor to distinguish between the cover and encoded images. The extractor was trained in an adversarial manner using the same discriminator used for the embedder's training. This adversarial training ensures that the extractor can differentiate between the cover and the encoded image.

$$\textbf{EXTRACTOR}(EI) \implies MSG \tag{4}$$

3.4 Discriminator Networks

The output of the embedder network must be indistinguishable from that of the original container image. We adopt adversarial training as the generative models produce hyper realistic images. We therefore deploy a discriminator network with leaky relu activations to add adversarial training to the embedder network. To illustrate clearly, as shown in Fig. 2, the discriminator takes an image of size $cW \times cH \times cC$ discriminates it as fake or real by outputting a single number(0 or 1).

Similarly, a discriminator is used for the adversarial training of the extractor. The extractor's adversarial generation capacity will help estimate the cover image distribution sampled by the VAE embedder. The discriminator improved the extraction efficiency compared to a vanilla CNN.

3.5 Training

Training of HD-VAE-GAN can be disintegrated into a two-stage process as shown in Algorithm 1. The embedder is taught in the first stage to insert the message inside a cover image and produce an encoded image that resembles the cover as depicted in Fig. 2. A cover image CI and a message image MSG are inputs for the embedder with parameters θ, and it produces an embedded image EI as the output. The use of adversarial loss, $Entropy_{emb}$ in Eq. 6 and variational inference, $VLoss$ in Eq. 5 , alone to build the encoded image was insufficient because the higher frequencies are not recorded. To overcome this blurry effect, we introduced an L1 loss between the encoded image and the cover image, referred to as $L1_{emb}$ that is represented in Eq. 7.

HD-VAE-GAN

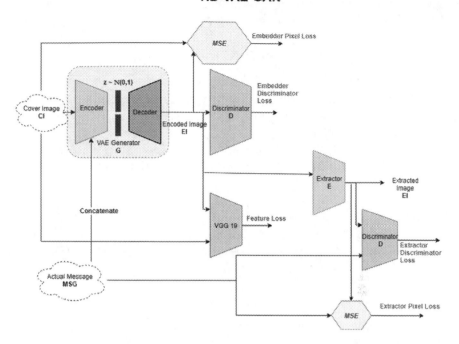

Fig. 2. Architecture of HD-VAE-GAN. It consists of one generator and one discriminator. A pre-trained VGG19 [24] is used to compute feature loss. The message is embedded in the generator through the concatenation process. An adversarial extractor extracts the embedded message from the encoded image.

$$V_{Loss} = KL((\mu + \epsilon * \sigma), \mathbb{N}(0,1)) \qquad (5)$$

Where μ and σ are outputs of Encoder(CI, MSG) shown in Fig. 1

$$Entropy_{emb} = log D_{emb}(CI) + log(1 - D_{emb}(EI)) \qquad (6)$$

$$L1_{emb} = \sum_{i=1}^{cH} \sum_{j=1}^{cW} \sum_{k=1}^{cC} |EI_{i,j,k} - CI_{i,j,k}| \qquad (7)$$

Where $EI = Emb_\theta(CI)$ and D_{emb} is Discriminator

The images showed some color distortion despite the fact that the sharpness had improved. We included a feature loss, as indicated in Eq. 8 to produce accurate images and speed up generator training. Deep features are generated from the final pooling layer of a pre-trained VGG19 [24] network (*chi*). The features of the created image WMI were compared to the features of the original cover image CI, and the results were represented as the loss function $FLoss$, which is shown in Eq. 8. The feature loss has assisted in reconstructing the encoded images' finer features. This made the message visually unidentifiable by maintaining identical texture and color information to the cover image.

$$F_{Loss} = \frac{1}{wH \times wW} \sum_{i=1}^{wH} \sum_{j=1}^{wW} (\chi(EI)_{i,j} - \chi(CI)_{i,j})^2 \tag{8}$$

We train the extractor with parameters λ in the second stage to decode the hidden message MSG given the EI from the first stage as input. The L1 loss between the original message and the encoder output, $L1ex$ in Eq. 9, and the cross-entropy loss from the GAN framework, $Entropyex$, for extractor output, as shown in Eq. 10, are designed as extractor loss functions.

$$L1_{ex} = \sum_{i=1}^{cH} \sum_{j=1}^{cW} \sum_{k=1}^{cC} |MSG_{i,j,k}^{extracted} - MSG_{i,j,k}^{actual}| \tag{9}$$

$$Entropy_{ex} = log\mathbf{D}(MSG^{actual}) + log(1 - \mathbf{D}(MSG^{extracted}) \tag{10}$$

$$Where \ MSG^{extracted} = Ex_\lambda(EI)$$

Algorithm 1. Two stage implicit training procedure for HD-VAE-GAN

- Train the embedder with parameters θ such that:

$$\min_\theta \ \beta_1 L1_{emb} + \beta_2 V_{Loss} + \beta_3 F_{Loss} + \beta_4 Entropy_{emb}$$

- Train the extractor with parameters λ such that:

$$\min_\lambda \ \beta_5 L1_{ex} + \beta_6 Entropy_{ex}$$

The total loss (HD-VAE-Loss) used for training the model is a weighted sum of the above-mentioned losses as shown in Eq. 11. The coefficients, $\beta_1, \beta_2, \beta_3, \beta_4, \beta_5, \beta_6$ were chosen in such a way that all the losses are scaled to have similar contribution in the total loss. Although, a slightly higher contribution for the F_{Loss} is given since experimentally, it has been proven to generate more appealing images. The typical values for $(\beta_1, \beta_2, \beta_3, \beta_4, \beta_5, \beta_6)$ were (0.1, 0.5, 0.1, 0.8, 0.1, 0.8).

$$HD - VAE - Loss = \min_{Ex} \min_{Emb} \max_{D_{emb}} \max_{D_{ex}} \beta_1 L1_{emb} + \beta_2 V_{Loss} + \beta_3 F_{Loss}$$

$$+\beta_4 Entropy_{emb} + \beta_5 L1_{ex} + \beta_6 Entropy_{ex} \tag{11}$$

3.6   Transmission Attacks

On encoded images, a few common attacks such as Gaussian blurring, rotation, cropping, and various noises were simulated to assess the network's robustness to intermediate transmission attacks. The model is found to be inherently resistant to the majority of attacks, but its performance falls short, as shown in Table 2. To reduce the model's sensitivity to harmful external attacks, we continue to train the model to extract the hidden message even when the encoded image is doctored or distorted. This can be accomplished by feeding the attacked encoded images into the model and training the extractor to extract messages, as described in Algorithm 1. As shown in Table 2, training over attack simulations improved the model's performance in terms of Peak Signal to Noise Ratio (PSNR) between the encoded image and cover image. This metric indicates the degree to which hidden messages are visible (similarity between encoded and cover images).

4   Experiment

4.1   Dataset Details

To train and evaluate our model, we used the DIV2K dataset [3]. The dataset contains 900 images, and the average PSNR and SSIM on the test set are reported in Table 1. The training data set contains 900 images, 800 of which are train sets and 100 of which are test images.

4.2   Implementation Details

For the embedder, convolution with stride two was used instead of max pooling to avoid the losses due to the pooling layer. This has shown an improvement in the embedder's loss. Also the input dimensions were chosen as $64 \times 64 \times 3$. The VAE encoder's output is designed with two arrays of sizes 100 each. The discriminators used are pix-2-pix patch GAN [12]. To avoid overfitting and accelerate the training process, batch Normalisation is used after every convolution layer followed by activation layers. Using L1 regularisation for clipping the weights has significantly improved training. We had 14 million parameters in the embedder and around 45k parameters in the discriminator. The training time of HD-VAE-GAN with a training set of 800 images for 50000 epochs was around one week with a GTX 1080Ti GPU and Intel's Xeon Gold 6128 processor from DevCloud through Intel's AI student ambassador program for intense processing. The entire project is open-sourced on GitHub [10].

4.3   Results

For training and testing of HD-VAE-GAN, random pairs of images from the dataset are used as cover and message images. By comparing the results in table 1, our models provide competing results compared to the existing work like *SteganoGAN* [16] and *DeepStego* [4]. Two models that were proposed by [16], *SteganoGAN Res* with Res connections in generator and *SteganoGAN basic* with vanilla CNN as the generator was used in the comparison.

Table 1. Comparison of embedding and extraction capacity without any attacks on DIV2K dataset

Method	SSIM	PSNR-CI	PSNR-EX
HD-VAE-GAN	0.9059	27.89	27.34
SteganoGAN Res	0.9000	38.25	-
SteganoGAN Basic	0.6700	24.62	-

HD-VAE-GAN achieved exciting results compared to the SteganoGAN Res model, even though our method does not contain Res layers. *PSNR-CI* refers to the similarity between the encoded image and the cover image, whereas *PSNR-EX* refers to the extraction efficiency. SSIM refers to the Structure Similarity Index Measure between the cover and encoded images.

The model is robust to various attacks, but the visual results were unsatisfactory. Hence we can improve that by training the models on different attacks and thus making it more robust. The comparison of extraction accuracy before and after training on attacks is shown in Table 2. The PSNR has improved by 20dB and the extracted images improved visually. HD-VAE-GAN performs very well in terms of extraction efficiency compared to existing models. Since VAE is known for variational inference, it could be the reason for the lower PSNR than SteganoGAN. The variational inference makes the encoded image space smoother, generating blurry images. It can be handled by reducing the dimensions of latent space or by giving less weight for V_{Loss}. Nevertheless, this smooth latent space helps with the robustness of the extractor network. Attacked encoded images fall apart in the actual data dimensional space but are closely spaced in the latent space due to the variational inference, helping the extractor easily extract the corresponding hidden messages.

Table 2. Extraction efficiency (PSNR-EX (in dB)) of extracted messages from attacked encoded image before and after training on attacks

Simulated Attack	Before Training	After Training
Gaussian Blur	20.77	40.41
Rotation 90	9.57	35.57
Rotation 10	6.68	37.51
Cropping 10%	12.13	36.08
Speckle	21.07	29.74
S&P Noise	16.15	39.83
Gaussian noise	15.90	26.86
Blur + Crop †	-	28.56
Gaussian + Rot90†	-	24.74
Gaussian + Rot10†	-	26.23
Crop +Rot 90†	-	19.31
Crop +Rot 10†	-	21.42

A few combinations of the attacks used in training were used to test on the network. Even though the network did not see the combined attacks during training, the generalised model extracted the messages efficiently. The (†) marked rows of Table 2 provide the evidence that the networks distinguishes between attacks and take appropriate measures to minimise the reconstruction loss.

5   Analysis

5.1   Feeding an Empty Container Image to the Extractor

The unanswered question by [14, 16], and [4] is the output of the extractor when a non-encoded, empty container image is fed as an input. During the training of the extractor network, the embedding discriminator is used for transfer learning of the extractor discriminator. This plays the role of distinguishing between encoded and cover images. Cover images are negative samples, and encoded images are positive samples during the embedding training, by using the same parameters at extraction forces the extractor to output garbage values when the non-encoded image is fed as input. Here, the discriminator helps train the extractor rather than playing a min-max game. As a result extractor of HD-VAE-GAN was not showing any signs of the message when a non-encoded image was fed, as shown in Fig. 3.

Fig. 3. Extractor output when a non-encoded image is fed as input to the extractor of HD-VAE-GAN. No patterns of the message were observed.

5.2   Pixel Level Distortion Due to Embedding

We have compared the histograms of the cover image and the encoded image. HD-VAE-GAN has been shown to distort the cover image's pixels after embedding, as shown in Fig. 4. This poor embedding efficiency of HD-VAE-GAN is due to the blurry output of VAE. It suggests that the method to be used in scenarios where embedding quality is not of a higher priority.

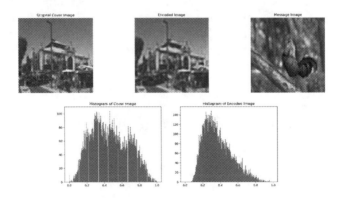

Fig. 4. Even though both the images look the same, there is a distinguishable change in the histogram after HD-VAE-GAN does the embedding

5.3   What if an Attacker Gets Access to the Cover Image

There is a chance that the attacker can get access to the original cover image and use it to eliminate or extract the message in the encoded image. To check for the robustness of our method in such cases, we have subtracted the cover image from the encoded image, as shown in Fig. 5. There is no information about the message in the different images of HD-VAE-GAN that is magnified ten times. Therefore, the network does not embed the message in the pixel space and is robust to this attack.

Fig. 5. The difference between the cover image and encoded image by **HD-VAE-GAN** shows that the message is not embedded directly in the pixel space, but rather done in the deep feature space. It clarifies that an adversary with access to the original cover image can not decode the image without the extractor network.

6 Conclusion

This paper proposes a robust end-to-end trainable VAE-GAN (HD-VAE-GAN) to conceal message images capable of extracting the hidden message from a distorted encoded image. We introduced adversarial training in both embedder and extractor while introducing variational inference into the embedder. Though the proposed HD-VAE-GAN is attempted on images, it is a general framework and can be applied directly to other data hiding frameworks, such as audio, video, and 3D model frameworks. Adversarial learning proves to be efficient for this kind of application.

References

1. Brock, A., Simonyan, K.: Large scale GAN training for high fidelity natural image synthesis. arXiv preprint arXiv:1809.11096 (2018)
2. Radford, A., Chintala, S.: Unsupervised representation learning with deep convolutional generative adversarial networks. In: International Conference on Learning Representations (2016)
3. Agustsson, E., Timofte, R.: Ntire 2017 challenge on single image super-resolution: dataset and study. In: 2017 IEEE Conference on Computer Vision and Pattern Recognition Workshops (CVPRW), pp. 1122–1131 (2017)
4. Baluja, S.: Hiding images in plain sight: Deep steganography. In: Guyon, I., Luxburg, U.V., Bengio, S., Wallach, H., Fergus, R., Vishwanathan, S., Garnett, R. (eds.) Advances in Neural Information Processing Systems, vol. 30, pp. 2069–2079. Curran Associates, Inc. (2017)
5. Chang, C.C.: Adversarial learning for invertible steganography. IEEE Access **8**, 198425–198435 (2020)
6. Chen, B.J., Coatrieux, G.: Full 4-d quaternion discrete Fourier transform based watermarking for color images. Digital Signal Process **28**(1), 106–119 (2014)
7. Das, C., Panigrahi, S.: A novel blind robust image watermarking in DCT domain using inter-block coefficient correlation. Int. J. Electron. Commun. **68**(3), 244–253 (2014)
8. Feng, L.P., Zheng, L.B.: A DWT-DCT based blind watermarking algorithm for copyright protection. In: Proceedings of IEEE ICCIST. **7**, 455–458 (2010). https://doi.org/10.1109/ICCSIT.2010.5565101
9. Gandikota, R., Mishra, D.: Hiding audio in images: a deep learning approach. In: Deka, B., Maji, P., Mitra, S., Bhattacharyya, D.K., Bora, P.K., Pal, S.K. (eds.) Pattern Recognition and Machine Intelligence, pp. 389–399. Springer International Publishing, Cham (2019). https://doi.org/10.1007/978-3-030-34872-4_43
10. GitRepo: Hd-vae-gan (2019). https://github.com/RohitGandikota/Hiding-Images-using-VAE-Generative-Adversarial-Networks. Accessed 11 Sep 2019
11. Goodfellow, I.J., Pouget-Abadie, J., Bengio, Y.: Generative adversarial nets. Adv. Neural Inf. Process. Syst. **27**, 2672–2680 (2013)
12. Isola, P., Zhu, J.Y., Zhou, T., Efros, A.A.: Image-to-image translation with conditional adversarial networks. In: CVPR (2017)
13. Ouyang, J., Coatrieux, G., Chen, B., Shu, H.: Color image watermarking based on quaternion Fourier transform and improved uniform log-polar mapping. Comput. Elect. Eng. **46**, 419–432 (2015)
14. Zhu, J., Kaplan, R., Jhonson, J., Li, F.-F.: Hidden: hiding data with deep networks. In: The European Conference on Computer Vision (ECCV), pp. 657–672. Springer, Cham (2018). https://www.springerprofessional.de/hidden-hiding-data-with-deep-networks/16180210
15. Kandi, H., Mishra, D., Gorthi, S.: Exploring the learning capabilities of convolutional neural networks for robust image watermarking. Comput. Secur. **65**, 2506–2510 (2017). https://doi.org/10.1016/j.cose.2016.11.016
16. Zhang, K.A., Cuesta-Infante, A., Xu, L.: SteganoGAN: High capacity image steganography with GANs. arXiv preprint arXiv:1901.03892, January 2019
17. Kingma, D.P., Welling, M.: Auto-encoding variational Bayes. In: 2nd International Conference on Learning Representations (ICLR) (2013)
18. Lee, J.E., Seo, Y.H., Kim, D.W.: Convolutional neural network-based digital image watermarking adaptive to the resolution of image and watermark. Appl. Sci. **10**(19), 6854 (2020)

19. Li, C., Jiang, Y., Cheslyar, M.: Embedding image through generated intermediate medium using deep convolutional generative adversarial network. Comput. Mater. Continua. **56**(2), 313–324 (2018)

20. Liu, Y., Guo, M., Zhang, J., Zhu, Y., Xie, X.: A novel two-stage separable deep learning framework for practical blind watermarking. In: Proceedings of the 27th ACM International Conference on Multimedia, pp. 1509–1517 (2019)

21. Lu, Y., Tai, Y.W., Tang, C.K.: Attribute-guided face generation using conditional cycleGAN. In: Proceedings of the European Conference on Computer Vision (ECCV), pp. 282–297. Springer, Cham (2018). https://www.springerprofessional. de/en/attribute-guided-face-generation-using-conditional-cyclegan/16177286

22. Mun, S.M., Nam, S.M., Jang, H.U., Kim, D., Lee, H.K.: A robust blind watermarking using convolutional neural network. arXiv preprint arXiv:1704.03248 (2017)

23. Sharma, K., Aggarwal, A., Singhania, T., Gupta, D., Khanna, A.: Hiding data in images using cryptography and deep neural network. arXiv preprint arXiv:1912.10413 (2019)

24. Simonyan, K., Zisserman, A.: Very deep convolutional networks for large-scale image recognition. In: International Conference on Learning Representations, pp. 1–14 (2015)

25. Sun, Q.T., Niu, Y.G., Wang, Q., Sheng, G.: A blind color image watermarking based on dc component in the spatial domain. Optik. **124**(23), 6255–6260 (2013). https://doi.org/10.1016/j.ijleo.2013.05.013

26. Wu, J., Shi, H., Zhang, S., Lei, Z., Yang, Y., Li, S.Z.: De-mark GAN: removing dense watermark with generative adversarial network. In: International Conference on Biometrics (ICB), pp. 69–74, February 2018. https://doi.org/10.1109/ICB2018. 2018.00021

Share-GAN: A Novel Shared Task Training in Generative Adversarial Networks for Data Hiding

Rohit Gandikota[1]([⊠]) and Deepak Mishra[2]

[1] Northeastern University, Boston, MA, USA
gandikota.ro@northeastern.edu
[2] Department of Space, Indian Institute of Space Science and Technology,
Thiruvananthapuram, Kerala, India
deepak.mishra@iist.ac.in
https://rohitgandikota.github.io/

Abstract. This manuscript proposes a novel training process for a pre-existing architecture of GANs to enable task-sharing or multi-tasking of sub-modules. We explore the application of data hiding to analyse the model's performance. Share-GAN consists of an embedder network (to encode secret messages into a cover), a U-Net autoencoder (that consists of encoder and decoder). The embedder's encoder network is custom trained to act as an extractor network (to extract the hidden message from the encoded image). The multi-tasking of the embedder's encoder is, to our knowledge, never explored prior to this work. The encoded image is subjected to multiple attacks to analyse the noise sensitivity of the model. The proposed method shows inherent robustness towards attacks like Gaussian blurring, rotation, noise, and cropping. However, the model can be trained on any possible attacks to reduce noise sensitivity further. In this manuscript, we considered images as both messages and containers. However, the method can be extended to any combination of multi-media data.

Keywords: messaging · generative adversarial networks · neural network · deep learning

1 Introduction

Existing data concealment methods can be divided into several categories based on their applications and requirements. Hide can be broadly classified into two types based on the level of information required to detect it: (i) Blind method [13, 21] that detects embedded information from encoded/embedded image without using an original container signal. Blind concealment techniques are less resistant to attacks [15]. (ii) Non-blind methods detect the encoded message using all available information at the transmission end, namely the original container signal and the secret keys. These techniques are more resistant to different types of attacks than blind techniques. Blind data hiding, which is the focus of this work, is more difficult because a more robust model is required.

© The Author(s), under exclusive license to Springer Nature Switzerland AG 2023
D. Gupta et al. (Eds.): CVIP 2022, CCIS 1776, pp. 44–57, 2023.
https://doi.org/10.1007/978-3-031-31407-0_4

There are two common ideas for concealing information in images. The first is steganography, which aims to achieve secret communication between a sender and a receiver while an adversary cannot tell if the image contains any message. The second concept is digital messaging, in which the goal is to encode data while overcoming or withstanding any adverse conditions. Even if an adversary distorts the image, the receiver can still deduce the message. Messaging is commonly used to determine who owns the copyright to data. In this paper, we present a method for using steganography and investigate its efficacy for message encryption. Furthermore, the technique is visually indistinguishable, and the network is inherently resistant to the majority of attacks.

This paper proposes a novel training procedure in GANs named Share-GAN and explores its applications in data hiding. The proposed method is a blind technique that uses a single network to embed and extract a secret message. Compared to the existing methods using various CNN architectures [15,17,19,22], the proposed method uses similar architectures, but a novel training process. Unlike the existing GAN based methods that use adversarial training for embedding alone [5,13,16], our proposed method has adversarial training for both embedder and extractor. The introduced task-sharing drastically reduced the computational burden while keeping the model's performance on par.

The rest of this paper is organized as follows: First, in Sect. 2, we discuss the previous work related to the field of data hiding. Then, in Sect. 3, we formulate the problem and introduce all the networks used in this method. We discuss the training procedure designed for our method. Later, we provide the experimental details in Sect. 4 and the performance results of our method in Sect. 5. Finally, we conclude in Sect. 6 that task-sharing does help in reducing trainable parameters while not compromising on the performance of GAN.

2 Related Work

Mun et al. [21] introduced a custom training of CNN to embed and extract messages. While Kandi et al. [15] uses two differently initialized auto-encoders for embedding. Their method requires information about the original cover and only embed binary messages. Shumeet et al. [4] uses Deep Neural Networks for steganography by implementing three different networks: Prep Network, Hiding Network, and a Reveal Network. Some techniques use domain transforms to embed messages [6,7,9,12], and others using spatial domain messaging [24] in order to calculate LSB in the cover image and replace it with the secret information.

Recently, Zhu et al. [5,13] have introduced the adversarial component in messaging using an encoder-decoder model to embed and extract respectively. For the first time, Le.et al. [18] have used GANs in messaging. However, unlike our work, they have used it to generate a texture image and then embed it using a different concealing network making their message visually invisible. Kevin et al. [16] have compared res and dense connections in the generator that mitigate the vanishing gradient problem in GAN with a basic CNN as the generator.

Gandikota *et al.* [10] have attempted hiding audio in images using GAN with speech specific objective functions. This work was specific to audio hiding due to speech signals' one-dimensional non-stationary characteristics.

GAN is a prevalent idea present in the machine learning community. While it is mainly used to generate images [1,11,20], Wu *et al.* [25] have used them to remove mesh noise from the images which are further used for face identification. They have perceived the generative property of GAN as domain transform from which we have taken the inspiration.

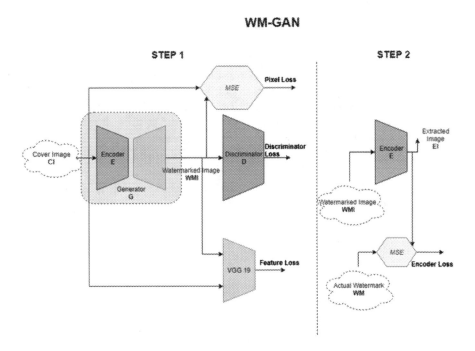

Fig. 1. The architecture of Share-GAN. It consists of one generator and one discriminator. A pre-trained VGG19 [23] is used to compute feature loss. This figure represents the two-stage training process explained in Algorithm 1. The encoder is trained separately in stage 2, and L1 loss is computed against the original secret message, acting like an extractor.

3   Proposed Method

3.1   Problem Formulation

Data hiding is the practice of concealing a message image MSG into a cover image CI. The resultant encoded image EI may look similar to the CI. It is also essential to extract the message image MSG_{ex} from the encoded image.

In this paper, instead of training two different networks for the tasks mentioned above, we train a single network that can embed and extract the desired message. Making the proposed method efficient compared to [5,13], and [16], who have used two different networks. Unlike our method that uses GANs, Shumeet *et al.* [4] have used a deep vanilla CNN approach with three different networks for steganography purposes.

Share-GAN consists of three nets: an embedder Emb, embedding discriminator D_{emb}, and extracting discriminator D_{ex}. **Emb** is a convolution U-Net auto-encoder with skip connections from the hidden layers of the encoder to hidden layers of the decoder that are of similar dimensions. Its target is to generate an encoded image by injecting a message into a cover image while not distorting the cover image. The embedding discriminator D_{emb} is designed to distinguish the encoded image generated by Emb from the corresponding cover image. The encoder of the Embedder $E_{encoder}$ which is a sub-model of Emb is used to extract the message from the encoded image. As the encoder of the generator can extract the message, any cover image that is passed through Emb is "embedded" because the generator has information about the message.

It is important to note that GANs are unstable during the training state [2], which can result in distortions in the output images. We propose a custom multi-objective training procedure for Share-GAN training that overcomes the mode-collapse limitation in GAN training.

3.2   Generator Network

Inspired from the work of Wu *et al.* [25], we devised the generator **G** as a domain transformer. As shown in Eq. 1. The encoder **E** transforms the domain from encoded image to message and hence can be perceived as an extractor.

$$\mathbf{ENCODER}(encoded\,Image) \implies message \tag{1}$$

We comprehend the generator as the embedder as it has information about the message and processes the cover image to produce encoded image as shown in Eq. 2.

$$\mathbf{GENERATOR}(Cover\,Image) \implies encoded\,Image \tag{2}$$

To exemplify, the encoder of the generator takes input of size $cW \times cH \times cC$ and outputs a downsampled array of size $wW \times wH \times wC$. This output of the encoder will in-turn be input to the decoder which upsamples it back to array of size $cW \times cH \times cC$. Leaking identical layer activations from encoder and concatenating them at decoder has shown a significant improvement in the embedder training.

3.3   Discriminator Network

The output of the embedder network must be indistinguishable from that of the original container image. We adopt adversarial training as the generative models produce hyper realistic images. We therefore deploy a discriminator network with leaky relu activations to add adversarial training to the embedder network. To illustrate clearly, as shown in Fig. 1, the discriminator accepts an image (either a cover image or an encoded picture) of size $cW \times cH \times cC$ as input and outputs a number (o or 1) to differentiate between the two. This ensures the message's obscurity and, to some extent, that a deep learning steganalysis tool cannot detect the message's presence.

3.4   Training GAN for Message Embedding

As illustrated in Algorithm, Share-GAN training is split into a two-stage implicit process. 1. First, we teach the generator how to incorporate the message. The generator with parameter θ gets a cover image CI as input and is taught to generate an image that is comparable to the cover image and is designated encoded image WMI, as shown in Fig. 1. In the ablation investigation, we discovered that employing adversarial loss, $DLoss$ in Eq. 3, alone caused dilution near the resulting image's edge. To mitigate the damage, we apply a typical L2 loss comparing the encoded and cover images, denoted as $GLoss$ in Eq. 4.

$$D_{Loss} = log\mathbf{D}(CI) + log(1 - \mathbf{D}(WMI)) \tag{3}$$

$$G_{Loss} = \frac{1}{cH \times cW} \sum_{i=1}^{cH} \sum_{j=1}^{cW} (WMI_{i,j} - CI_{i,j})^2 \tag{4}$$

Where $WMI = Generator_{\theta}(CI)$ *and* $\mathbf{D}$ *is Discriminator*

We discovered that the images were still not crisp enough and had significant color distortion. To achieve clearer and more colorful photos, we used a deep feature loss, as shown in Eq. 5. As features, we used the activation outputs of the χ final convolution layers of a pre-trained VGG19 [23] network. We used a conventional L2 loss function F_{Loss} to compare the characteristics of the generated image WMI to the features of the actual cover image CI, as stated in Eq. 5. Deep feature loss has aided in the restoration of finer features in encoded images. This also helps to keep the texture and color information consistent with the cover image, making the message visually indistinguishable.

$$F_{Loss} = \frac{1}{wH \times wW} \sum_{i=1}^{wH} \sum_{j=1}^{wW} (\chi(WMI)_{i,j} - \chi(CI)_{i,j})^2 \tag{5}$$

The second stage of training involves merely training the generator's encoder with parameters λ to output the message WM when given the current loop's WMI as input. This step guarantees that the encoder behaves similarly to an extractor. The encoder pixel loss between the original message and the encoder output, E_{Loss}, is tailored for the second stage of Share-GAN training, as stated in Eq. 6.

$$E_{Loss} = \frac{1}{wH \times wW} \sum_{i=1}^{wH} \sum_{j=1}^{wW} (WM_{i,j}^{extracted} - WM_{i,j}^{actual})^2 \tag{6}$$

Where $WM^{extracted} = Extractor_{\lambda}(WMI)$

Algorithm 1. Two stage implicit training procedure for the proposed model of Share-GAN
- Train the generator with parameters θ such that:

$$\min_{\theta} \quad \beta_1 G_{Loss} + \beta_2 F_{Loss} + \beta_3 D_{Loss}$$

- Train the extractor with parameters λ such that:

$$\min_{\lambda} \quad \beta_4 E_{Loss}$$

As demonstrated in Eq. 7, the total loss used for training the model is a weighted sum of the losses mentioned above. The coefficients, $\beta_1, \beta_2, \beta_3, \beta_4$ were chosen in such a way that all losses are scaled to contribute equally to the total loss Although a little bigger contribution for the F_{Loss} is offered because it has been shown experimentally to yield more appealing photos.

$$Loss = \min_{G} \; \max_{D} \; \beta_1 G_{Loss} + \beta_2 F_{Loss} + \beta_3 D_{Loss} + \beta_4 E_{Loss} \qquad (7)$$

It is important to note that since the proposed method is designed for messaging rather than steganography, we de-emphasize the requirement of embedding multiple messages by a single network. Hence, our model is message specific. To be precise, Share-GAN can be trained to encode only a single message into any desired cover image.

3.5 Training on Attack Simulations

The successful implementation of the messaging procedure also involves efficient extraction of the embedded message even under various attacks that the encoded image goes through. Some of the common attacks performed on the encoded image to remove the hidden message are blurring, cropping, rotation, noise addition, etc. The mentioned attacks were simulated using methods mentioned in [14] and applied on the encoded images. These attacked encoded images are then fed to extractor for recovery of the actually embedded message. It is observed that the proposed network is very efficient in the recovery of the message from the attacked encoded images. After the initial training, we continue to train the encoder of **G** to extract message even when the encoded image is doctored or distorted. This can be done by inputting the attacked encoded images and train the encoder to extract messages which are attacked in a similar fashion, using the same procedure as elucidated in stage 2 of Algorithm.1.

3.6 Implementation Details

We avoid the usage of maxpool layers and instead use the convolution filters with stride 2 to avoid the information loss. For an input of size $128 \times 128 \times 3$, the encoder generates an output of size $2 \times 2 \times 1024$ which is reshaped to $64 \times 64 \times 1$

for a valid message dimension. The discriminator used was a typical CNN with an output layer of 1 dimension. To avoid overfitting, batch Normalization is used after every convolution layer. By using L2 regularization for clipping the weights, a significant improvement in training was observed. Usage of fully connected layers was avoided to regulate the number of parameters. We had a total of 60 million parameters in the generator and around 45k parameters in discriminator. Training time of Share-GAN for 5000 epochs was around 15 min with GTX 1080Ti graphics processor.

4   Experiment

4.1   Dataset Details

In order to have a fair comparison, we have used the DIV2K dataset [3] to train and test our model. The dataset comprises of 900 pictures, and we provide the average PSNR, and SSIM on the test set in Table 1. The training data set contains 900 photos, 800 of which are train images and the remaining 100 are test images. To compare with [4], we used cover pictures from the ImageNet dataset [8] for testing. As illustrated in the table. According to 1, the use of a limited training dataset on Share-GAN is sufficient to produce engaging results when compared to works that employed the entire training dataset [16].

4.2   Metrics Used

In order to compare our results with other state of the art methods, following metrics are used. The metrics used to check the invisibility of message and quality of extraction are MSE and $PSNR$ as shown in Eq. 8 and Eq. 9.

$$MSE(\alpha, \beta) = \frac{1}{H \times W} \sum_{i=1}^{H} \sum_{j=1}^{W} (\alpha_{i,j} - \beta_{i,j})^2 \tag{8}$$

$$PSNR(\alpha, \beta) = 10 \times log(\frac{1}{MSE(\alpha, \beta)}) \ (in \ dB) \tag{9}$$

For binary messages, the Normalised Correlation metric NC in Eq. 10 is used.

$$NC(\alpha, \beta) = \frac{1}{H \times W} \sum_{i=1}^{H} \sum_{j=1}^{W} \delta(\alpha_{i,j}, \beta_{i,j}) \tag{10}$$

$$\delta(a, b) = \begin{cases} 0 \ if \ a \neq b \\ 1 \ if \ a = b \end{cases}$$

Bit Error Rate (BER), as shown in Eq. 11., was also used. Assuming that in the case of grayscale image, each pixel has a capacity of 8 bits and in case of binary message, each pixel is of size 1 bit.

$$BER = 100 \times \frac{Number \ of \ Bits \ in \ error}{Number \ of \ Bits \ Tansmitted} \ \% \tag{11}$$

4.3   Grayscale Messaging

The work is extended for grayscale messages and partial training dataset was used to train Share-GAN to evaluate the requirement of training data for the model to be well generalised. By comparing the results in Table. 1, our model provides competing results compared to the existing work like *SteganoGAN* [16] and *DeepStego* [4]. Two models that were proposed by [16], *SteganoGAN Res* with Res connections in generator and *SteganoGAN basic* with vanilla CNN as generator were used in the comparison.

Table 1. Comparison of invisibility of message and extraction efficiency without any attacks on DIV2K dataset in terms of PSNR.

Method	SSIM	PSNR-CI (in dB)	PSNR-WM (in dB)
Share-GAN (N = 50)	0.9875	36.02	23.04
Share-GAN (N = 100)	0.9899	37.02	23.28
Share-GAN (N = 200)	0.9930	38.12	24.01
SteganoGAN Res (N = 800)	0.9000	38.25	–
SteganoGAN Basic (N = 800)	0.6700	24.62	–
DeepStego †	–	35.29	37.79
Share-GAN (N = 50) †	0.9801	36.05	25.78

*N – Number of samples used in training

Share-GAN achieved better results compared to SteganoGAN Res model. It is important to note that the proposed model does not contain Res layers and uses partial training dataset. The rows marked (†) are the results tested on 1000 random images from ImageNet dataset as cover images. *PSNR-CI* refers to the similarity between encoded image and the cover image, whereas, *PSNR WM* refers to the extraction efficiency. SSIM refers to the Structure Similarity Index Measure between cover and encoded images.

The model is robust to various attacks, but the visual results were not satisfactory. Hence, we improve that by retraining the model on different attacks and thus making it more robust. The comparison of extraction accuracy before and after training on attacks is shown in Table 2. Clearly, the PSNR has improved on average by 20dB and the extracted messages improved visually.

A few combinations of the attacks used in training were used to test on the network. Even though the combined attacks were not seen by the network during training, the model generalized well and extracted the messages efficiently.

Table 2. PSNR of extracted messages from attacked encoded image before training on attacks and after training on attacks

Attack	Before training (in dB)	After training (in dB)
Gaussian Blur	16.55	36.96
Rotation 90°	7.48	32.49
Rotation 10°	7.62	31.14
Cropping 10%	8.34	32.03
Speckle	4.57	18.28
Salt and Pepper Noise	9.88	33.30
Gaussian noise	7.01	20.84
Gaussian Blur + Crop *	–	21.70
Gaussian + Rotation 90° †	–	19.42
Gaussian + Rotation 10° †	–	20.66
Crop +Rotation 90° †	–	10.82
Crop +Rotation 10° †	–	12.31

The † marked rows of Table 2 provide the evidence that the network distinguishes between attacks and takes appropriate measures to minimize the reconstruction loss.

Table 3. Comparison of Robustness of extracted messages from attacked encoded images in terms of NC and BER(%).

Attack	Our	[21]	[6]	[7]	[9]	[15]	Our (BER)
Blur ($\sigma = 0.1$)	**1.0**	0.95	0.84	0.81	0.80	0.76	0.00
Rotation 90	**1.0**	**1.0**	-4e-3	-7e-3	−0.02	–	0.00
Rotation 10	**1.0**	0.98	–	–	–	0.3	0.00
Crop (10%)	**1.0**	0.99	0.81	0.78	0.57	0.96	0.00
Salt and Pepper Noise	**1.0**	0.88	0.90	0.82	0.88	**1.0**	0.00
Speckle Noise	**0.97**	–	–	–	–	0.47	2.08
Gaussian Noise	**0.84**	–	**0.84**	0.73	0.83	0.53	16.32
Crop (10%) + Rotation 90†	**0.76**	–	–	–	–	–	24.08
Blur ($\sigma = 0.1$) + Rotation 90†	**0.98**	–	–	–	–	–	2.08

4.4   Binary Messaging

To compare our results with a few of the recent methods that can embed only binary messages, Binarization of the messages were done with Scipy's [14] default

Otsu thresholding function. The details have been shown in Table 3 and the metrics used were Normalised Correlation(NC) and Bit Error Rate (BER). The proposed method is able to achieve a perfect extraction. As can be in seen Table 3, our network is more robust and effective than the works in comparison. We simulated attacks for different ranges in various categories and plotted the normalized correlation metrics in Fig. 2. From the figure, it is evident that the network is inherently robust to the attacks under consideration. Visual results for the binary extracted messages from different attacked encoded images are shown in Fig. 3.

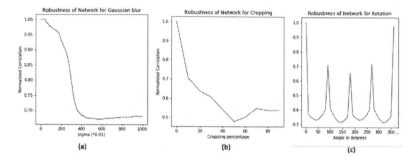

Fig. 2. Robustness of the models before training on attacks. The normalised correlation decreases with increase in (a)blur and (b)crop, but for (c)rotation the repeatablity is due to the 90°C symmetry in the outdoor nature images.

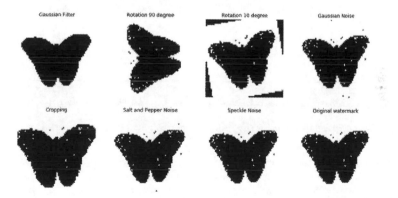

Fig. 3. Extracted message samples from attacked encoded image. As desired, the extractor is able to identify various distortions and take appropriate actions.

5   Analysis

5.1   Feeding a Non-encoded Image to the Extractor

The unanswered question by [13, 16], and [4] is, what the output of an extractor would be if a non-encoded image is fed as an input. To answer that, we have trained the extractor by feeding encoded images as positive samples and the cover images as negative samples. For cover images, the extractor is trained to output an image with all the pixel values as black. However, when tested, the extractor was giving some patterns of the message when the cover image is fed as shown in Fig. 4. The reason behind this behavior could be that the extractor is partially using some visual features of the encoded image to extract the message and given the cover image looks similar to the encoded image, there are some visual patterns of the message in the output.

Fig. 4. Extractor output when a non-encoded image is fed as input. Partial visual patterns of message can be observed.

5.2   What if an Attacker Gets Access to the Cover Image

There is a chance that the attacker can get access to the original cover image and use it to eliminate the message in the encoded image. To check for robustness of our method in such cases, we have subtracted the cover image from the encoded image and visualized the results as shown in Fig. 5. Clearly, there is no information about the message in the difference image that is magnified by 10 times. Therefore, Share-GAN does not plainly embed the message into the pixels and is robust to this attack.

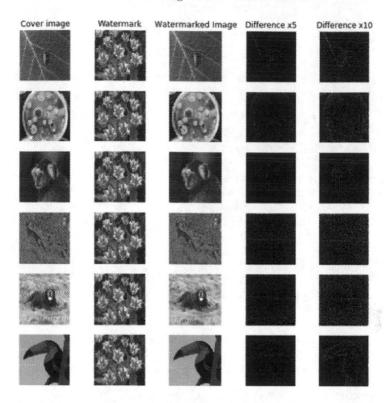

Fig. 5. The difference between the cover image and encoded image shows that the message's information is not embedded directly into the pixels of the cover image. This ensures that even if an attacker get's access to the original cover image, the message can not be removed.

6   Conclusion

In this paper, we propose a robust end-to-end trainable GAN (Share-GAN) to embed messages that are also capable of extracting the message from a distorted encoded image. We introduced adversarial training in both embedder and extractor while, reducing the model parameters compared to state-of-the-art methods. Though the proposed is attempted on images, it is a general framework and can be applied to other messaging frameworks directly, such as audio, video and 3D model frameworks. Adversarial learning proves to be efficient for this kind of applications.

References

1. A. Brock, J.D., Simonyan, K.: large scale GAN training for high fidelity natural image synthesis. arXiv preprint arXiv:1809.11096 (2018)

2. Radford, A., Metz, L., Chintala, S.: Unsupervised representation learning with deep convolutional generative adversarial networks. In: International Conference on Learning Representations (2016)
3. Agustsson, E., Timofte, R.: Ntire 2017 challenge on single image super-resolution: dataset and study. In: 2017 IEEE Conference on Computer Vision and Pattern Recognition Workshops (CVPRW), pp. 1122–1131 (2017)
4. Baluja, S.: hiding images in plain sight: deep steganography. In: Guyon, I., et al. (eds.) Advances in Neural Information Processing Systems 30, pp. 2069–2079. Curran Associates, Inc. (2017). http://papers.nips.cc/paper/6802-hiding-images-in-plain-sight-deep-steganography.pdf
5. Chang, C.C.: Adversarial learning for invertible steganography. IEEE Access **8**, 198425–198435 (2020)
6. Chen, B., et al.: Full 4-d quaternion discrete fourier transform based watermarking for color images. Digital Signal Proc. **28**(1), 106–119 (2014). https://doi.org/10.1016/j.dsp.2014.02.010
7. Das, C., et al.: A novel blind robust image watermarking in DCT domain using inter-block coefficient correlation. Int. J. Electron. Commun. **68**(3), 244–253 (2014)
8. Deng, J., Dong, W., Socher, R., Li, L.J., Li, K., Fei-Fei, L.: Imagenet: a large-scale hierarchical image database. In: Conference on Computer Vision and Pattern Recognition (2009)
9. Feng, L.P., Zheng, L.B., Cao, P.: A dwt-dct based blind watermarking algorithm for copyright protection. In: Proceedings of IEEE ICCIST, vol. 7, pp. 455–458 (2010). https://doi.org/10.1109/ICCSIT.2010.5565101
10. Gandikota, R., Mishra, D.: Hiding audio in images: a deep learning approach. In: Deka, B., Maji, P., Mitra, S., Bhattacharyya, D.K., Bora, P.K., Pal, S.K. (eds.) PReMI 2019. LNCS, vol. 11942, pp. 389–399. Springer, Cham (2019). https://doi.org/10.1007/978-3-030-34872-4_43
11. Ian, J.G., et al.: Generative adversarial nets. Adv. Neural Inf. Process. Syst. **27**, 2672–2680 (2013)
12. Ouyang, J., et al.: Color image watermarking based on quaternion fourier transform and improved uniform log-polar mapping. Comput. Electr. Eng. **46**, 419–432 (2015)
13. Zhu, J., et al.: Hidden: Hiding data with deep networks. In: The European Conference on Computer Vision (ECCV), pp. 657–672 (2018)
14. Jones, E., Oliphant, T., Peterson, P., et al.: SciPy: open source scientific tools for Python (2001). http://www.scipy.org/
15. Kandi, H., et al.: Exploring the learning capabilities of convolutional neural networks for robust image watermarking. Comput. Secur. **65**, 2506–2510 (2017). https://doi.org/10.1016/j.cose.2016.11.016
16. Zhang, K.A., et al.: Steganogan: high capacity image steganography with GANs. arXiv preprint arXiv:1901.03892 (January 2019)
17. Lee, J.E., Seo, Y.H., Kim, D.W.: Convolutional neural network-based digital image watermarking adaptive to the resolution of image and watermark. Appl. Sci. **10**(19), 6854 (2020)
18. Li, C., et al.: Embedding image through generated intermediate medium using deep convolutional generative adversarial network. Comput. Mater. Continua **56**(2), 313–324 (2018)
19. Liu, Y., Guo, M., Zhang, J., Zhu, Y., Xie, X.: A novel two-stage separable deep learning framework for practical blind watermarking. In: Proceedings of the 27th ACM International Conference on Multimedia, pp. 1509–1517 (2019)

20. Lu, Y., Tai, Y.W., Tang, C.K.: Attribute-guided face generation using conditional cyclegan. In: Proceedings of the European Conference on Computer Vision (ECCV), pp. 282–297 (2018)
21. Mun, S.M., et al.: A robust blind watermarking using convolutional neural network. arXiv preprint arXiv:1704.03248 (2017)
22. Sharma, K., Aggarwal, A., Singhania, T., Gupta, D., Khanna, A.: Hiding data in images using cryptography and deep neural network. arXiv preprint arXiv:1912.10413 (2019)
23. Simonyan, K., Z.A.: Very deep convolutional networks for large-scale image recognition. In: International Conference on Learning Representations, pp. 1–14 (2015)
24. Sun, Q.T., et al.: A blind color image watermarking based on dc component in the spatial domain. Optik **124**(23), 6255–6260 (2013). https://doi.org/10.1016/j.ijleo.2013.05.013
25. Wu, J., Shi, H., Zhang, S., Lei, Z., Yang, Y., Li, S.Z.: De-mark GAN: removing dense watermark with generative adversarial network. International Conference on Biometrics (ICB), pp. 69–74, February 2018. https://doi.org/10.1109/ICB2018.2018.00021

Hiding Video in Images: Harnessing Adversarial Learning on Deep 3D-Spatio-Temporal Convolutional Neural Networks

Rohit Gandikota[1]([✉])[ID], Deepak Mishra[2][ID], and Nik Bear Brown[1]

[1] Northeastern University, Boston, MA, USA
gandikota.ro@northeastern.edu
[2] Indian Institute of Space Science and Technology, Department of Space,
Valiamala, Kerala, India

Abstract. This work proposes end-to-end trainable models of Generative Adversarial Networks (GAN) for hiding video data inside images. Hiding video inside images is a relatively new topic and has never been attempted earlier to our best knowledge. We propose two adversarial models that hide video data inside images: a base model with Recurrent Neural Networks and a novel model with 3D-spatiotemporal Convolutional Neural Networks. Both the models have two distinct networks: (1) An embedder to extract features from the time variate video data and inject them into the deep latent representations of the image. (2) An extractor that reverse-engineers the embedder function to extract the hidden data inside the encoded image. A multi-discriminator GAN framework with multi-objective training for multimedia hiding is one of the novel contributions of this work.

Keywords: video hiding · steganography · generative adversarial networks · 3D-spatio-temporal convolutions · recurrent neural networks

1 Introduction

Audio and video are two primary essential means of communication in the modern era, with a unique capacity to communicate information compared to images and text. Applications like strategical and secret communications require immunity towards eavesdropping by an adversary node. Our work focuses on understanding the requirements for such scenarios and formulating novel solutions using generative models [10] considering the temporal variability of video data. Videos can convey both temporal and spatial information simultaneously that either images or audio can not convey. With the primary objective of the work being video hiding inside images, the method can also be looked at from a video compression point of view. Transmitting a video signal takes up a lot of transmission channel bandwidth, and these methods essentially transmit a video injected image instead of the whole video, making them efficient and lighter video transmission techniques. Hiding video inside images is a novel proposal, and to our best knowledge, our methods are the first to attempt the same.

Earlier techniques in data hiding involved domain transforms to embed message [2,3,6,11], and others using spatial domain [18]. Recently with advent of deep learning, data hiding using neural networks were introduced [12,13,16]. Zhu et al. [12] has introduced the adversarial component in data hiding using an encoder-decoder model to embed and extract respectively. Most of the works [12,13,16] and, [14] deal with hiding image signals while not address the temporal dimension.

This paper first discusses the possibilities and limitations of embedding non-stationary audio signals and spatio-temporal video signals (usually perceived as images that progress in temporal dimension) inside images using the existing deep learning methods. Then we deal with video hiding by discussing the advantages of the temporal dynamic behaviour of deep learning models like Recurrent Neural Networks (RNN) on achieving "video hiding inside images". We also discuss the advantages of the adversarial training of RNN in this application by comparing it with 3D convolution modules to study the influence of the internal temporal state (memory) of RNN.

We propose two models to hide video in the image: **Vid-in-Img-RAN**, a recurrent model with stacks of Convolutional LSTMs to hide video into images and **Vid-in-Img-3DGAN**, a GAN framework with 3D Spatio-temporal convolutions with dual discriminator. Both methods are based on multi-objective training and are end-to-end trainable. **Vid-in-Img-RAN** consists of an embedder network (designed with a Recurrent Neural Network (RNN) video processing network and hiding network), a discriminator (to distinguish between the cover and encoded image), and finally, an extractor (a one to many RNN to restore the hidden video). **Vid-in-Img-3D-GAN**, a more refined model consists of an embedder (with message processing and hiding network with 3D Spatio-temporal convolution layers), an extractor with dual discriminators (with motion loss to add temporal dependencies between the extracted video frames). The main contributions of this work are

- Introducing the first generic end-to-end trainable GAN models, **Vid-In-Img-RAN**, **Vid-In-Img-3DGAN**, that can hide temporal multimedia data inside images.
- Multi-discriminator GAN framework with multi-objective training for hiding video inside images.
- Designing a dual discriminator GAN, one in a video level and the other in a frame level, ensures both temporal and spatial level efficiency.

The rest of this paper is organized as follows: First, in Sect. 2, we discuss the previous work related to video processing and data hiding. Then, in Sect. 3, we formulate the problem, introduce the model architectures and, discuss the training procedure designed for our method. Later, we provide the preliminary experimental results and analysis in Sect. 4. Finally, we conclude our work in Sect. 5 with a note on the models' exciting initial results and future implementations to improve the models.

2   Related Work

Gandikota et al. [7] addressed the problem of audio hiding inside images. They proposed a model, VoI-GAN, explicitly engineered to consider the non-stationary audio signals and embed them inside images. Using a custom-designed objective function, their model injects a spectrogram of the audio message inside images. Their custom-objective functions inspire our method, and we propose objective functions to address the complex requirements of video data. Qiyang et al. [9] have proposed a new method to automatically generate a video sequence from a single image and a user-provided motion stroke. The critical component in their proposed architecture is a recursive predictor that generates features of a new frame given the features of the previous frame. Using an autoencoding constraint and adversarial training, they later train a generator to map the features into temporally coherent image sequences. Yijun et al. [15] formulate the multi-frame prediction task as a multiple time-step flow (multi-flow) prediction phase followed by a flow-to-frame synthesis phase. The multi-flow prediction is modelled in a variational probabilistic manner with spatial-temporal relationships learned through 3D convolutions. [5] proposes a user-controllable approach to generate video clips of various lengths from a single face image. To that end, they design a neural network architecture that can incorporate the user input into its skip connections and propose several improvements to the adversarial training method for the neural network.

Yingwei et al. [17] present a novel Temporal GANs conditioning on Captions, namely TGANs-C, in which the input to the generator network is a concatenation of a latent noise vector and caption embedding, and then is transformed into a frame sequence with 3D Spatio-temporal convolutions. Our work draws inspiration from [17] when it comes to the extraction process since we need to extract a video from a single image. Carl et al. [19] propose a generative adversarial network for video with a Spatio-temporal convolutional architecture that untangles the scene's foreground from the background. All these methods deal with video generation from images or random noise and hence are equivalent to the extraction process of our method. The embedding in our work is done by concatenating latent data of the video into the cover image.

3   Proposed Method

In this section, we first formulate the problem of hiding video in images and later discuss the proposed methods "Vid-in-Img-RAN" that uses recurrent neural networks and "-in-Img-3D-GAN" that uses 3D spatiotemporal convolutions to hide video in images. We discuss the architectures and training procedures for the proposed methods in detail.

3.1   Problem Formulation

Hiding video in an image is to embed a message video ($VMSG$) into a cover image (CI) and then later be able to extract the video from the encoded image

Skeltal Workflow of Vid-in-Img Models

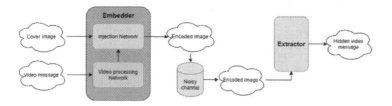

Fig. 1. The figure represents the standard workflow of the Vid-in-Img models in block representation. The embedder has a video processing/message processing network and an injection network. The extractor takes the received encoded image and extracts the hidden video message

(EI). So there is a need for two processes to accomplish this task: embedding and extracting.

In this work, we propose two different methods for hiding video inside images, and these methods have two distinct networks as basic building blocks, an embedder Emb, and an extractor Ex as shown in Fig. 1. The objective of Emb is to encode the video inside a cover image without distorting the image. Extractor Ex is used at the receiver end to recover the hidden video inside the encoded image that is generated by Emb.

We propose a multi discriminator GAN framework with multi-objective training to stabilize the training. Video has much spatial redundancy in the temporal dimension, and we exploit this property to propose efficient and unique techniques. Detailed explanations about the Emb and Ex networks are given below.

3.2 Embedder Network

The embedder has two building blocks based on the functionality: a video processing network and an injection network. The video processing network extracts information from video and generates the deep latent representations of the video that is feasible to infuse with the latent representations of the cover image. The injection network processes the cover image and concatenates the output of the video processing network with the cover image's latent space. The training of the embedder is done with adversarial and deep feature losses as objective functions. To elaborate, the embedder takes cover image of size $cW \times cH \times cC$ and message video of size $mT \times mW \times mH \times mC$ as inputs. The video processing network converts the video into latent dimensions of size $lW \times lH \times lC$. These latent representations are concatenated with the cover image information and processed by the hiding network of the embedder.

Both the methods (Vid-in-Img-RAN and Vid-in-Img-3D-GAN) have similar injection networks but are unique in the architecture of the message processing networks. The message processing network in Vid-in-Img-RAN consists of a many-to-one LSTM recurrent network to extract the latent representations of the secret video message processed and outputted with the exact dimensions as the cover image's latent representations. This whole embedding process is represented in Fig. 2.

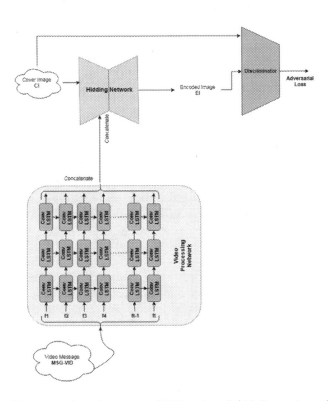

Fig. 2. Embedder network architecture of Vid-in-Img-RAN. It consists of a video processing network and a hiding network. The video processing network converts the 4D video data into a 3D latent representation. The hiding network hides this latent data inside the cover image by concatenation.

The message processing network in Vid-in-Img-3D-GAN consists of a 3D convolution autoencoder network to process the 4D video and output 3D latent representations of the secret video message that are later injected inside the cover image by the injection network. This whole embedding process is represented in Fig. 3.

3.3   Extractor Network

The extraction network is designed to process the encoded image to extract the hidden video message. It is achieved in the Vid-in-Img-RAN by designing a one-to-many recurrent neural network that takes the encoded image as input and

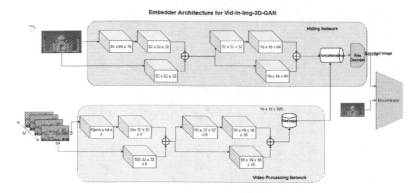

Fig. 3. Embedder network architecture of Vid-in-Img-3D-GAN. It consists of a video processing network and a hiding network. The video processing network with 3D convolutions converts the 4D video data into a 3D latent representation. The hiding network hides this latent data inside the cover image by concatenation. Both the networks have residual connections and U-net shape for a boost in training.

outputs the hidden video in the image, as shown in Fig. 4. The extractor network Ex, at each time step, takes evidence from the temporal information provided by the previous time-step recurrent cell and the encoded image and outputs the next frame.

The extractor network in the Vid-in-Img-3D-GAN is shown in Fig. 5, has been designed using a 3D convolutional neural network that takes the encoded image as input and outputs the hidden video in the image. The extractor network Ex is a feed-forward neural network with 3D Spatio-temporal convolutions. To maintain the motion flow of the video, we introduce a motion loss, as shown in Fig. 5.

3.4 Embedder Discriminator Network

Since the embedder aims to embed the video message inside the image with minimal distortion of the cover image, the encoded image should look similar to the cover image. Introducing adversarial training will provide the embedder with the power of imagination [10]. A discriminator network is designed for the embedder with stacked convolutional layers with batch normalization and the activation function to evaluate whether each output of embedder is authentic or fake through the lower level and semantic features. To illustrate clearly, as shown in Fig. 2 and Fig. 3, the discriminator takes an image of size $cW \times cH \times cC$ as an input and outputs a number (either 0 or 1) to discriminate between the cover image and encoded image.

Extractor Network of Vid-in-Img-RAN

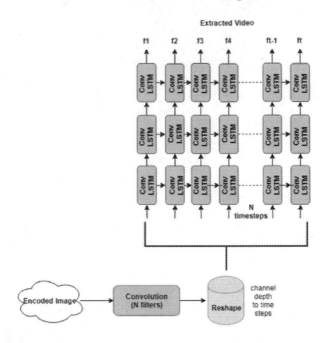

Fig. 4. Extractor network architecture of Vid-in-Img-RAN. It consists of a recurrent network that is a one-to-many variant. The extractor produces a video from just the encoded image as input.

3.5   Video Discriminator Networks

We introduce adversarial training into the extractor of Vid-in-Img-3D-GAN using a dual discriminator setting. It is introduced to compensate for the missing temporal components in the 3D convolution network architecture. The first discriminator, video level discriminator **D1**, is used to differentiate between a real video and the extracted video. We use a 3D convolutional network with res layers and skip connections. It is done to maintain the temporal and spatial features of the video and simultaneously introduce adversarial training. As shown in Fig. 5, **D1** takes video of size $vT \times vW \times vH \times vC$ as an input and outputs a single number to discriminate between real video and the extracted video.

To maintain the frame-level efficiency, a frame-level discriminator **D2** with time distributed convolutions. This helped in a more accurate video extraction, ensuring better frame efficiency. As shown in Fig. 5, **D2** takes video of size $vT \times vW \times vH \times vC$ as an input and outputs and array of size $vT \times 1$ to discriminate between real video frames and the extracted video frames.

Extractor Network of Vid-in-Img-3D-GAN

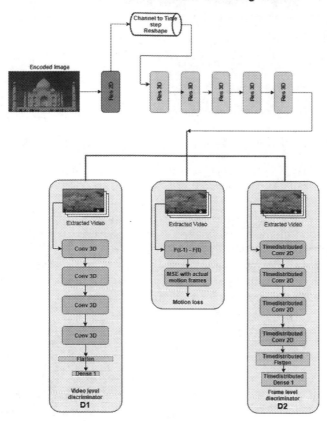

Fig. 5. Extractor network architecture of Vid-in-Img-3D-GAN. It consists of a 3D-spatiotemporal convolutional network. A video level discriminator is used to distinguish between the real video and the extracted video. To ensure frame-level efficiency, we introduce a frame-level discriminator. Also, to maintain the flow motion of the extracted video, we introduce a motion loss. The motion is computed by simply taking the difference between the consecutive frames.

3.6 Training Procedure for Vid-in-Img-RAN

Training of Vid-in-Img-RAN can be disintegrated into a two-stage process as shown in the Algorithm 1. The first stage trains the embedder to inject a video message inside a cover image and output the encoded image similar to the cover image. As shown in Fig. 2, the embedder with parameters θ receives a cover image CI of size $cH \ x \ cW \ x \ cC$ and the secret video message $VMSG$ of size $mT \ x \ mH \ x \ mW \ x \ mC$ as inputs and outputs a similar image EI with same dimension as CI. Using the cross-entropy loss $Entropy_{Emb}^{RAN}$ in adversarial training using D_{emb}^{RAN} with parameters δ, in Eq. 1, alone to generate the encoded image was not sufficient as the embedder produced blurry encoded images with missing higher frequency features. To overcome this blurring, we introduced a pixel level L1 loss between the encoded image and the cover image, referred to as $L1_{Emb}^{RAN}$ that is represented in Eq. 2.

$$Entropy_{emb}^{RAN} = log(D_{emb}^{RAN}(CI)) + log(1 - D_{emb}^{RAN}(EI)) \tag{1}$$

$$L1_{Emb}^{RAN} = \sum_{i=1}^{cH}\sum_{j=1}^{cW}\sum_{k=1}^{cC} |EI_{i,j,k} - CI_{i,j,k}| \tag{2}$$

$$Where\ EI = Embedder_\theta(CI)\ and\ D_{emb}^{RAN}\ is\ Discriminator$$

A deep feature loss has been used to eliminate the colour distortions in the reconstructed image and is named feature loss, as shown in Eq. 3. A pre-trained VGG 19 network without the FCC layers with untrainable parameters is used to extract the deep features of images. These features of the EI are compared with the features of the cover image CI, both with sizes $fH\ X\ fW\ X\ fC$ and represented it as loss function F_{Loss}. This new deep learning-based loss function has helped in restoring the minute details like band-to-band misregistration, colour distortions and finally produce a sharper, similar encode image as CI making the video message visually indistinguishable.

$$F_{Loss} = \sum_{i=1}^{fH}\sum_{j=1}^{fW}\sum_{k=1}^{fC}(\chi(EI)_{i,j,k} - \chi(CI)_{i,j,k})^2 \tag{3}$$

The second stage of training is to train the extractor, with parameters λ, to extract the video message $VMSG^{ex}$ given the current loop's EI as input. As shown in Eq. 4, the extractor pixel-level L1 loss between the original message and the output of the extractor, $L1_{ex}^{RAN}$, is designed for the second stage of Vid-in-Img-RAN's training.

$$L1_{ex}^{RAN} = \sum_{i=1}^{mH}\sum_{j=1}^{mW}\sum_{k=1}^{mC}\sum_{l=1}^{mT} |VMSG_{l,i,j,k}^{ex} - VMSG_{l,i,j,k}| \tag{4}$$

$$Where\ VMSG^{extracted} = Extractor_\lambda(EI)$$

Algorithm 1. Two stages implicit training procedure for the proposed model of Vid-in-Img-RAN

- Train the embedder with parameters θ such that:

$$\min_\theta \max_\delta\ \beta_1 L1_{Emb}^{RAN} + \beta_2 F_{Loss} + \beta_3 Entropy_{emb}^{RAN}$$

- Train the extractor with parameters λ such that:

$$\min_\lambda\ \beta_4 L1_{ex}^{RAN}$$

The total loss used for training the model is a weighted sum of the losses mentioned above. The coefficients, $\beta_1, \beta_2, \beta_3, \beta_4$ were chosen so that all the losses are scaled to have an equal contribution in the total loss. Although a slightly higher contribution for the F_{Loss} is given since experimentally, it showed more appealing encoded images.

$$Loss = \min_{Emb} \max_{D_{emb}^{RAN}} \min_{Ex} beta_1 L1_{Emb}^{RAN} + \beta_2 F_{Loss} + \beta_3 Entropy_{emb}^{RAN}$$

$$\beta_4 L1_{ex}^{RAN}$$

3.7 Training Procedure for Vid-in-Img-3D-GAN

Training of Vid-in-Img-3D-GAN can also be disintegrated into a two-stage process as shown in the Algorithm 2. The first stage of training the embedder is similar to the method mentioned earlier in the Algorithm 1 and uses exact functions as the RAN version.

The difference is in the second stage of training viz. is to train the extractor, with parameters λ, to output the video message $VMSG$ given the current loop's EI as input. Similar to Eq. 4, the extractor pixel-level L1 loss between the original message and the output of the extractor, $L1_{ex}^{3D}$ is designed. To ensure the temporal flow motion of the extracted video, we also introduce a motion loss (m_{Loss}). To calculate the motion flow $\vec{m}$, we opt for a conventional way of taking the difference between consecutive frames.

$$\vec{m} = frame_t - frame_{t-1}$$

The MSE between the motion flow of extracted video and the real motion flow is taken as motion loss m_{Loss}. This is shown in Eq. 5.

$$m_{Loss} = \frac{1}{vT \times vH \times vW} \sum_{i=1}^{vH} \sum_{j=1}^{vW} \sum_{k=1}^{vT} (\overrightarrow{m_{Ex}}_{i,j,k} - \overrightarrow{m_{act}}_{i,j,k})^2 \qquad (5)$$

We propose a video level discriminator that distinguishes between the original embedded video and the extracted video. The extractor tries to minimize the proposed $Entropy_{ex}^{video}$ in Eq. 6, while the **D1** with parameters δ_1 tries to maximize it. We also propose a frame-level discriminator that distinguishes whether each frame is real or not. It helps in a more frame-level realistic video. The extractor tries to minimize the proposed $Entropy_{ex}^{frame}$ in Eq. 7, while the **D2** with parameters δ_2 tries to maximize it.

$$Entropy_{ex}^{video} = log\mathbf{D1}(VMSG) + log(1 - \mathbf{D1}(VMSG^{Ex})) \qquad (6)$$

$$Entropy_{ex}^{frame} = \sum_{t=1}^{T} (log\mathbf{D2}(VMSG_t) + log(1 - \mathbf{D2}(VMSG_t^{Ex}))) \qquad (7)$$

Where T is total number of frames in the video

The total loss used for training the model is a weighted sum of the losses mentioned above, as shown in Eq. 8. The coefficients, $\beta_1, \beta_2, \beta_3, \beta_4, \beta_5, \beta_6, \beta_7$ were chosen in such a way that all the losses are scaled to have similar contribution in the total loss. Although a slightly higher contribution to the discriminator losses is given since it has generated more appealing images experimentally.

$$Loss = \min_{Emb} \max_{D_{emb}^{3D}} \min_{Ex} \max_{D1} \max_{D2} \beta_1 L1_{emb}^{3D} + \beta_2 F_{Loss} + \beta_3 Entropy_{emb}^{3D}$$

$$+\beta_4 L1_{ex}^{3D} + \beta_5 m_{Loss} + \beta_6 Entropy_{ex}^{video} + \beta_7 Entropy_{ex}^{frame} \qquad (8)$$

Algorithm 2. Two stage-implicit training procedure for the proposed model of Vid-in-Img-3D-GAN

- Train the embedder with parameters θ such that:

$$\min_{\theta} \max_{\delta} \beta_1 L1_{emb}^{3D} + \beta_2 F_{Loss} +$$

$$\beta_3 Entropy_{emb}^{3D}$$

- Train the extractor with parameters λ such that:

$$\min_{\lambda} \max_{\delta_1} \max_{\delta_2} \beta_4 L1_{ex}^{3D} + \beta_5 m_{Loss} + \beta_6 Entropy_{ex}^{video} + \beta_7 Entropy_{ex}^{frame}$$

---

4   Experiment

For the experiment, we have used the Nvidia GTX 1080Ti and Tesla V100 graphics processors in the Virtual Reality Lab of IIST. We have used the Discovery cluster of Northeastern University for intense processing. All the codes are open-sourced on GitHub [8].

4.1   Dataset Details

DIV2K dataset, a diverse 2K resolution image collection of about 900 indoor and outdoor scenes [1] is used for cover images. Imagenet [4], an extensive visual database designed for use in visual object recognition software research, is also used for evaluation. For the video dataset, we have used the Object Tracking Benchmark [20]. We have trained both models to embed 50 frames per image.

4.2   Results

Since, to our best knowledge, the proposed problem statement is novel and lacks prior work, we compare our two methods with each other in terms of embedding efficiency (in *PSNR* and *SSIM*) and extraction efficiency (*PSNR*). PSNR-CI refers to the pixel level closeness between the encoded and cover image. PSNR-EX refers to the pixel level similarity between the extracted and actual video frames. As shown in Table 1, it is clear that the Vid-in-Img-RAN under-performs compared to Vid-in-Img-3D-GAN. The ablation study provides conclusive proof for the choice of objective functions. Adding L1 loss did improve embedding SSIM drastically and restored higher frequencies in the encoded image. F-Loss improved the colour distortions, and the combination of all the three led to a holistic performance by the model.

The first and last frames of Vid-in-Img-RAN are shown in Fig. 6 and of Vid-in-Img-3D-GAN in Fig. 7. The observed blurry initial frames are due to the lack of past information in the initial time stamps of the RNN. However, 3D-GAN performs very well with the motion loss included, as the computation is very compact and the video, frame-level discriminators worked very effectively. Visually, the video generated by 3D-GAN is better perceptible than the RNN-GAN.

Table 1. Comparison of embedding and extraction efficiency of Vid-in-Img models with ablation study

Vid-in-Img Model	SSIM	PSNR-CI	PSNR-EX
RAN	0.77	38.41	20.05
3D-GAN (Entropy)	0.75	35.28	34.66
3D-GAN (Entropy+L1)	0.91	50.17	36.41
3D-GAN (Entropy+L1+F-Loss)	0.98	55.45	36.84

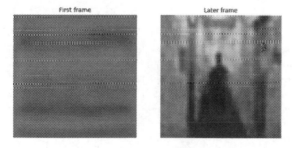

Fig. 6. Sample frames of the extracted video by Vid-in-Img-RAN. The first frame of the extracted video is shown on the right and the last frame on the left. The last frame is visually better. A good last frame extraction is due to the high past information from RNN cells.

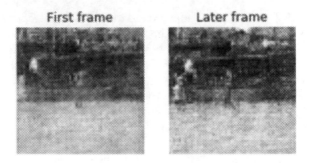

Fig. 7. Sample frames of the extracted video by Vid-in-Img-3D-GAN. The first frame of the extracted video is shown in the right and the last frame is shown in the left.

5   Conclusion

This work proposes a novel research direction of hiding video inside images and proposes two deep generative models with LSTMs and 3D-CNNs. The proposed usage of both the video-level and frame-level discriminators with motion loss ensures Spatio-temporal efficiency in the extracted video. In the future, we would like to improve the proposed models in a more theoretical way by considering the limit on the number of frames that can be embedded, improving the loss functions and, adding un-tried regularizers. We would also like to explore the choices of bi-directional LSTM to avoid information bias across the extracted frames. Adopting deep learning methods may open new directions and pave for exciting applications and research fields in data hiding.

References

1. Agustsson, E., Timofte, R.: NTIRE 2017 challenge on single image super-resolution: dataset and study. In: 2017 IEEE Conference on Computer Vision and Pattern Recognition Workshops (CVPRW), pp. 1122–1131 (2017)
2. Chen B.J., et al.: FULL 4-D quaternion discrete Fourier transform based watermarking for color images. Digit. Signal Process. **28**(1), 106–119 (2014), https://doi.org/10.1016/j.dsp.2014.02.010
3. Das C, Panigrahi S, Sharma,V.K., Mahapatra, K.K.: A novel blind robust image watermarking in dct domain using inter-block coefficient correlation. Int. J. Electron. Commun. **68**(3), 244–253 (2014)
4. Deng, J., Dong, W., Socher, R., Li, L.J., Li, K., Fei-Fei, L.: ImageNet: a large-scale hierarchical image database. In: Conference on Computer Vision and Pattern Recognition (2009)
5. Fan, L., bing Huang, W., Gan, C., Huang, J., Gong, B.: Controllable image-to-video translation: A case study on facial expression generation. CoRR abs/1808.02992 (2019)
6. Feng, L.P., Zheng, L.B., C.P.: A DWT-DCT based blind watermarking algorithm for copyright protection. Proc. IEEE ICCIST **7**, 455–458 (2010). https://doi.org/10.1109/ICCSIT.2010.5565101

7. Gandikota, R., Mishra, D.: Hiding audio in images: a deep learning approach. In: Deka, B., Maji, P., Mitra, S., Bhattacharyya, D.K., Bora, P.K., Pal, S.K. (eds.) PReMI 2019. LNCS, vol. 11942, pp. 389–399. Springer, Cham (2019). https://doi.org/10.1007/978-3-030-34872-4_43

8. GitRepo: Video-hiding-GAN (2019). https://github.com/RohitGandikota/Hiding-Video-in-Images-using-Deep-Generative-Adversarial-Networks

9. Hu, Q., Waelchli, A., Portenier, T., Zwicker, M., Favaro, P.: Video synthesis from a single image and motion stroke. CoRR abs/1812.01874 (2018)

10. Ian, J., et al.: Generative adversarial nets. Adv. Neural Inf. Process. Syst. **27**, 2672–2680 (2013)

11. J. Ouyang, G. Coatrieux, B.C.H.S.: Color image watermarking based on quaternion fourier transform and improved uniform log-polar mapping. Comput. Electr. Eng. **46**, 419–432 (2015)

12. Zhu, J., Kaplan, R., Johnson, J., Fei-Fei, L.: HiDDeN: Hiding Data With Deep Networks. In: Ferrari, V., Hebert, M., Sminchisescu, C., Weiss, Y. (eds.) ECCV 2018. LNCS, vol. 11219, pp. 682–697. Springer, Cham (2018). https://doi.org/10.1007/978-3-030-01267-0_40

13. Kandi, H., Mishra, D., Sai Gorthi, S.R.K.: Exploring the learning capabilities of convolutional neural networks for robust image watermarking. Comput. Secur. **65**, 2506–2510 (2017). https://doi.org/10.1016/j.cose.2016.11.016

14. Zhang, K.A., Cuesta-Infante, A., Xu, L., Veeramachaneni, K.: SteganoGAN: high capacity image steganography with GANs. arXiv preprint arXiv:1901.03892 (January 2019)

15. Li, Y., Fang, C., Yang, J., Wang, Z., Lu, X., Yang, M.-H.: Flow-Grounded spatial-temporal video prediction from still images. In: Ferrari, V., Hebert, M., Sminchisescu, C., Weiss, Y. (eds.) ECCV 2018. LNCS, vol. 11213, pp. 609–625. Springer, Cham (2018). https://doi.org/10.1007/978-3-030-01240-3_37

16. Mun, S.M., et al.: A robust blind watermarking using convolutional neural network. arXiv preprint arXiv:1704.03248 (2017)

17. Pan, Y., Qiu, Z., Yao, T., Li, H., Mei, T.: To create what you tell: generating videos from captions. In: Proceedings of the 25th ACM International Conference on Multimedia, pp. 1789–1798. MM 2017 (2017), http://doi.acm.org/10.1145/3123266.3127905

18. Sun, Q.T., Niu, Y.G., Wang, Q., Sheng, G.: A blind color image watermarking based on dc component in the spatial domain. Optik **124**(23), 6255–6260 (2013). https://doi.org/10.1016/j.ijleo.2013.05.013,https://doi.org/10.1016/j.ijleo.2013.05.013

19. Vondrick, C., Pirsiavash, H., Torralba, A.: Generating videos with scene dynamics. In: Proceedings of the 30th International Conference on Neural Information Processing Systems, pp. 613–621. NIPS2016, Curran Associates Inc., USA (2016), http://dl.acm.org/citation.cfm?id=3157096.3157165

20. Wu, Y., Lim, J., Yang, M.: object tracking benchmark. IEEE Trans. Pattern Anal. Mach. Intell. **37**(9), 1834–1848 (2015). https://doi.org/10.1109/TPAMI.2014.2388226

An Explainable Transfer Learning Based Approach for Detecting Face Mask

T. Anjali[(✉)] and V. Masilamani

Department of Computer Science and Engineering, Indian Institute of Information and Technology Design and Manufacturing, Kancheepuram, Chennai 600127, India
{coe20d001,masila}@iiitdm.ac.in

Abstract. COVID-19 has made a serious impact throughout the world. Wearing a face mask properly in public is considered an effective strategy to prevent infection. To contribute to community health, this work intends to develop an accurate real-time system for detecting non-mask faces in public. The proposed system can be used by law enforcement authorities to monitor and enforce the proper use of masks. A novel transfer learning-based method to detect face masks efficiently is proposed in this paper. Inspired by EfficientNetV2, a transfer learning model has been proposed to use for detecting whether a person is wearing a mask or not. To our knowledge, the EfficientNetV2 has not been used for detecting face masks. The model building is done based on two standard face mask datasets. The images in the first dataset consist of multiple people wearing masks, not wearing masks, and wearing the mask incorrectly. The second dataset consists of masked faces and faces without masks. To validate the generalization capability of the proposed model, the trained model is tested on two new standard datasets. In addition to that, the testing is done on a dataset created by ourselves. The proposed model performs well even on images with distortions such as blurred and noisy images. The model predicts whether the person in the input image is wearing a mask or not and also the correctness of mask-wearing with significantly better accuracy than the existing methods. The explainability of the proposed model is explained using a class activation map.

Keywords: EfficientNetV2 · Transfer Learning · Deep Learning · Masked Face Images

1 Introduction

COVID-19 has been reported towards the end of 2019 and it has become a public health concern all over the world. The pandemic is having an impact on society and the economy everywhere [1]. Centers for Disease Control and Prevention (CDC) has reported that the coronavirus is transferred mostly by respiratory droplets created when people cough, talk, sneeze, or breath [2]. This epidemic has resulted in several shutdowns in various industries. The studies suggested that [3] there are mainly two ways to prevent the disease. The first one is to

© The Author(s), under exclusive license to Springer Nature Switzerland AG 2023
D. Gupta et al. (Eds.): CVIP 2022, CCIS 1776, pp. 72–86, 2023.
https://doi.org/10.1007/978-3-031-31407-0_6

avoid physical contact with the infected people as much as possible via physical distancing and the second method is to use a face mask when you are in public.

As suggested by Bassi et al. in [4], it is always better to take routine temperature screening. Wearing face masks properly when you are outdoor is very important to reduce the spread of infection. Some people are still finding it difficult to wear a mask properly or are hesitant to use a mask. As a consequence, identifying the presence of face masks automatically has emerged as an important computer vision problem [5].

In the past years, the progress in computer vision and deep learning has been widely made in face recognition [6], facial expression recognition [7], illness diagnostics [8], object detection, [9] etc. The existing face mask detection algorithms are mainly binary classification problems. Ie, checking whether the mask is there or not. A MobileNet and Single Shot MultiBox Detector based model, called BlazeFace is proposed by Bazarevsky et al., which is for fast detection of faces and is suitable for mobile phone like devices [10]. ResNet50 based Transfer learning [11] along with You Only Look Once Version 2 (YOLOv2) is proposed by Loey et al. [12]. Wu et al. considered a three-class face mask detection problem using Im-Res2Net-101 and YOLOv2 [13].

In the literature, it has been observed that the current methods are mainly discussed face mask detection as just an object detection problem. The author [13] motivated that detecting if one is wearing a mask or not is not only the way to approach the problem. But we also should have to think of whether the worn mask is correct. This implies localization of the mask on the face has importance, which can identify if the mask is worn in the right manner.

Transfer learning is reusing the previously learned knowledge to solve a new problem. Transfer learning is common in deep learning because it can re-train the model with a minimum amount of data [14]. It's essential in the field of computer vision as most real-world situations don't provide millions of labelled data for complex models to be trained. Literature suggests that even though these new tasks may contain classes that are completely different from those of the original task, the learned features can be useful for a variety of computer vision problems [15]. Edges are detected in the first layer, shapes in the intermediate layer, and task-specific properties in the final layers by neural networks [16]. The initial and middle layers are employed in transfer learning, and the subsequent layers only require re-training for the new task. Transfer learning has several advantages, the most prominent of which are shorter training time, and better neural network performance (in most cases), even when there is a lack of a huge amount of labelled data [17].

This paper proposes an explainable transfer learning-based method to detect face masks from images of people. According to our knowledge, EfficientNets are not used for detecting face masks. EfficientNets [18] are a family of Convolutional Neural networks built by Google ranging from B0 to B7. It is reported that they have the state-of-the-art results on the ImageNet dataset. We conducted Various studies on the latest neural network architectures and EfficientNetV2, version 2 of the EfficientNet, has been recognized to operate well. A novel transfer learning using EfficientNetV2 inspired model is used for detecting the correctness mask worn is proposed in the paper. On the chosen datasets, the method proposed in our paper outperformed existing models.

The rest of the paper is written as follows: Related work is written in Sect. 2. In Sect. 3, the proposed method is explained, and in Sect. 4, the results and discussions are presented, followed by the conclusion.

2   Related Works

Transfer learning is a machine learning technique in which a model trained for one task is used as the base for another task's model [19]. Transfer learning is commonly used with predictive modelling issues that employ picture data as input. A deep learning model pre-trained on ImageNet 1000 class photograph categorization competition is commonly used for transfer learning [20]. Due to the COVID-19 pandemic, some of the approaches in deep learning are introduced to detect the infected patients and also used to see if someone is taking the necessary precautions to avoid catching COVID-19.

Dey et al. proposed a model based on MobileNet for detecting face masks trained and tested on two different datasets [21]. The first dataset, known as IDS1, has a 3835 collection of images from two categories: 1916 of them are images with masks and 99 are faces without masks. The second dataset, IDS2 consists of 1376 images of which 690 are with masks and 686 are without masks. IDS1 contains images collected from the Kaggle and Bing Search API and images for IDS2 are gathered from Simulated Masked Face Dataset (SMFD). The accuracy achieved for IDS1 is 93% and almost 100% achieved for IDS2. The advantage is that their model has the advantage of being able to be implemented on low-power embedded computing systems.

In [22], Chowdari et al. proposed a InceptionV3 based face mask detection model. The model is trained and tested on SMFD. To overcome the issue of availability of less images, they applied an image augmentation technique. This helped the authors to improve the result. The model produced a training accuracy of 99.9% accuracy and 100% testing accuracy.

Teboulbi et al. in [23] proposed a system for detecting face masks and measuring social distancing. They have created their dataset consisting of 3835 images. It is a well balanced dataset containing images of two classes, 1919 images of faces with masks and 1916 images of faces without masks. They have conducted experiments on VGG-19, VGG-16, DenseNet, Inception V3, MobileNet, MobileNet V2 and ResNet-50. The accuracy for DenseNet is 91% and Inception V3 is 88%. For the lightweight models such as MobileNet and MobileNet V2, the accuracy was reported as 98% and 95% respectively. The highest accuracy of 99% is given by ResNet-50, VGG-16, and VGG-19. In [12], Loey et al. proposed a medical face mask detection approach with YOLOv2 and ResNet-50. The experiment is conducted on two datasets from Kaggle. They have combined both datasets and finally had 1415 images after removing redundant and bad-quality images. The proposed method has an accuracy of 81% [12]. In [24], Ieamsaard et al. proposed an effective face mask detection technique using YOLOv5. It is a region-based one-stage object detection network. They reported an accuracy of 96.5% for the dataset collected from Kaggle. Nagrath et al. in [25] proposed a face mask detection system using a single-shot multi-box detector and MobileNetV2. This model is light weighted and can be implemented in the NVIDIA Jetson Nano like embedded devices and Raspberry pi. The dataset is created by collecting images from various open-source datasets, which include Kaggle, PyImageSearch, etc. They have 5512 images of people with masks and without masks images in their dataset. The paper reported an accuracy of 92.64% for their dataset.

Samuel Adi Sanjaya et al. suggested a MobileNet V2-based model for the classification of masked and unmasked images [26]. They have created a dataset with 1916 masked images and 1930 unmasked images collected from various online resources. The accuracy obtained for their model is 96.8%. They have tested their model in the images obtained from 25 cities in Indonesia and analyzed the percentage of people wearing a mask. The cities with the highest and lowest percentage of people not wearing a mask is reported in their paper.

In the paper [27], Sethi et al. proposed a transfer learning-based face mask detection model. They have come up with AlexNet, MobileNet, and ResNet50 based models to train the dataset MAsked Face Analysis (MAFA) and reported an accuracy of 98.2% for ResNet50. This paper also proposes a method to recognize identities wearing masks. Identity predictions are reported in terms of precision and recall and it is 98.86%, and 98.22% respectively.

Wu et al. in [13] proposed a model, Face Mask Detection-You Only Look Once (FMD-YOLO) for efficient face mask detection for the prevention of coronavirus. The paper contributes a Res2Net101 based model for the classification of images into with mask, without a mask, and mask worn incorrectly. The proposed model uses YOLOv3 for mask detection. The model is trained on two datasets named MD2 and MD3, where MD stands for Mask detection Dataset. cAP50 (category Average Precision for IoU = 0.5) is considered the evaluation metric of the proposed model and it is reported as 0.86 and 0.91 for without mask and with mask classes respectively for the dataset MD2. cAP50 for MD3 is 0.89, 0.93, and 0.82 for without mask, with mask and mask, wore incorrectly classes respectively.

3 Proposed Model

3.1 Dataset and Preprocessing

In this paper, two standard datasets containing face mask images have been selected for verifying the efficiency of the model, which are available at the Kaggle online platform, https://www.kaggle.com/andrewmvd/face-mask-detection and GitHub repository of Chandrika Deb, https://github.com/chandrikadeb7/Face-Mask-Detection/. For convenience, they are denoted as Masked Dataset-1 (DS1) and Masked Dataset-2 (DS2). DS1 contains three classes of the mask, without a mask and mask worn incorrectly. There are a total of 853 labelled face images available in DS1 and each image may have multiple persons with or without wearing the mask. Some of the persons in the images are not facing the camera.

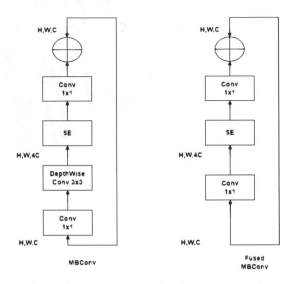

Fig. 1. MBConv block and Fused-MBConv block of EfficientNetv2

The bounding boxes for the masked region are annotated in pascal visual object classes format. Only the region enclosed by the bounding box is used as input, and the labels associated with it are used as output. Then we have a total number of individual persons wearing masks is 3232, not wearing masks is 717 and wearing masks incorrectly is 123.

There are 2166 images of people wearing masks and 1930 images of people without wearing a mask are available in the dataset called DS2. Each image has only one person in the frame. The dataset consists various types of images such as .jpeg, .png etc. As a part of preprocessing, all the images are converted to a uniform format. Initially, all the images are of different sizes and orientations. Then they have been resized it to $224 \times 224 \times 3$ for the convenient working of the proposed model. In both datasets, 70% of the total images are divided for training and 10% for validation and 20% for testing the model.

3.2   Classifier

EfficientNets are a family of CNNs that uniformly scales all dimensions using a compound coefficient [18]. A new version of EfficientNets called EfficientNetV2 [28] is progressed recently. It is a smaller and faster model for object recognition tasks. Some of the MBConv blocks of EfficientNets are replaced by Fused MBConv in EfficientNetV2 [29].

Instead of a depthwise convolution, they have used a Fused MBConv block which has a convolution with a 3×3 filter as shown in the Fig. 1. As far as we know, no one has used EfficientNetV2 for detecting face masks. The novelty of

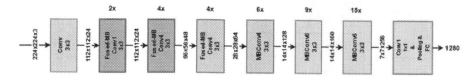

Fig. 2. Architecture of EfficientNetV2-s

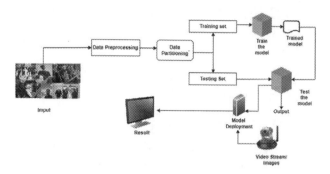

Fig. 3. The flowchart of proposed model

this work is that we are getting good results in a lighter model and it can easily be embedded in devices like mobile phones.

We have used an EfficientNetV2-s inspired transfer learning model for our experiments. This model has 22M parameters and gives a Top-1 accuracy of 83.9% on ImageNet datasets. The architecture of EfficientNetV2-s is as shown in the Fig. 2.

4 Result and Discussion

4.1 Experiment Setup

The EfficientNetV2-s have been initialized with pre-trained weights and set necessary parameters. Timm [30] PyTorch library is used for the implementation of the model. The general flowchart of the proposed system is as shown in Fig. 3. Both the datasets are trained for a different number of epochs for identifying the optimum number. EfficientNetV2-s have been trained on DS1 for 300 epochs and 200 epochs for DS2. The model trained on DS1 is called model1 and the model used for training DS2 is called as model2. The batch size used here is 16 with a learning rate of 0.01. The Cross entropy loss is used as the loss function along with Adabound [31] optimizer.

4.2 Model Comparison

The performance of the model has been measured in terms of Accuracy, Precision, F1 score and Recall. Macro averaging is used for classification models with two or more target classes. Macro averaged recall (MAR), Macro averaged precision (MAP) and Macro averaged F1 Score (MAF-1) can be calculated using the Eqs. (1–3) respectively.

$$MAP = \frac{\sum_{i=1}^{n} Precision_i}{(Total\, No\, of\, classes)} \tag{1}$$

$$MAR = \frac{\sum_{i=1}^{n} Recall_i}{(Total\, No\, of\, classes)} \tag{2}$$

$$MAF - 1 = \frac{(2 * MAP * MAR)}{(MAP + MAR)} \tag{3}$$

To compare existing models, various deep learning models that have been used for face mask recognition in the literature are implemented. All the models have been trained on 70% of the datasets, 10% for validation and the remaining images are used for testing. The same experiment setup is used for all the comparison models.

Face mask detection on models suggested by [11,18,28,32,33], are tested on the datasets and compared the results with the proposed model. The comparison of the proposed model with the precision, recall, accuracy and F1 score obtained for ResNet 50, ResNet 101, VGG19, Inception V3, EfficientNet B0-B4 is explained in Table 1. This experiment helped to choose EfficientNetV2 as the best model to detect the presence of a mask on a face. As we can see in the Table 1, the proposed model gives the highest result on both datasets, DS1 and DS2.

Table 1. Proposed method compared with existing models

Model	Accuracy		MAP		MAR		MAF-1	
	DS1	DS2	DS1	DS2	DS1	DS2	DS1	DS2
ResNet-18 [11]	0.92	0.89	0.92	0.88	0.92	0.89	0.92	0.89
ResNet-50 [11]	0.91	0.9	0.92	0.91	0.91	0.9	0.91	0.9
ResNet-101 [11]	0.9	0.91	0.93	0.91	0.89	0.9	0.89	0.9
VGG-19 [32]	0.82	0.84	0.83	0.84	0.82	0.84	0.82	0.84
Inception_V3 [34]	0.84	0.85	0.86	0.84	0.84	0.84	0.84	0.84
EfficientNet_B0 [18]	0.93	0.94	0.94	0.93	0.95	0.94	0.94	0.94
EfficientNet_B1 [18]	0.94	**0.97**	0.94	0.96	0.94	**0.96**	0.94	**0.96**
EfficientNet_B2 [18]	0.96	0.94	0.95	0.94	0.94	0.94	0.95	0.94
EfficientNet_B3 [18]	0.94	0.94	0.93	0.95	0.93	0.95	0.93	0.95
EfficientNet_B4 [18]	0.94	0.96	0.93	0.95	0.93	0.96	0.93	0.95
EfficientNet_lite0 [33]	0.95	0.96	0.96	0.95	0.95	0.95	0.95	0.95
Proposed Model	**0.97**	0.96	**0.98**	**0.97**	**0.97**	**0.96**	**0.97**	**0.96**

The detailed class-wise results of the EfficientNetV2-s inspired models, model 1 and 2 can be seen in Fig. 4. In the first model, For the class of images with people wearing masks, the precision, recall and F1 score are 0.99. The same for images without masks is 0.94, 0.99 and 0.96 respectively. For the third class, where the people wore their masks inappropriately has 0.91, 0.76 and 0.83 precision, recall and F1 Score respectively. In the second model, For the class of images with people wearing masks, the precision, recall and F1 score are 0.95, 0.98 and 0.96 respectively. The same for images without masks is 0.97, 0.94 and 0.96 respectively.

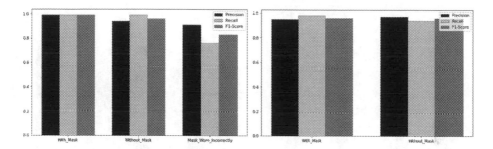

Fig. 4. Representation of class-wise results of proposed model-1 and model-2 respectively

The DS1 consists of three categories of images such as with a mask, without a mask and mask worn incorrectly. The model trained using DS1 is tested on two other datasets called DS3 and DS4. The standard dataset Moxa3K is used as DS3 [35]. This dataset has 3000 images containing multiple persons and the masks are labelled in Pascal VOC format. Similarly, a model trained on DS2 is tested on DS4 as well as on DS5. DS4 is a standard dataset containing 2135 images with masked and 1930 images of faces without mask. The model-2 is tested on DS5, the dataset created by ourselves by collecting 50 masked and unmasked images of 10 identities and applied scaling, rotation and shearing to create 5000 images. To test the performance of model-1, an extra class consists of 500 images of 10 individuals not worn their masks correctly is added. The results of the testing is shown in the Fig. 6. The ROC curve is plotted for the models tested on DS1 and DS2 and is shown in Fig. 5 From the ROC curve of model-1, it is clear that the model is able to predict class0 (With mask), class1 (without mask), class2 (mask wore incorrectly) with almost accurately.

The dataset is imbalanced, and we have fewer images for the third class, resulting in lower accuracy for the class, the mask wore incorrectly. Class0 indicates with mask and class1 represents without mask class for model-2. It gives similar results for both the classes as it has the same number of images in the classes.

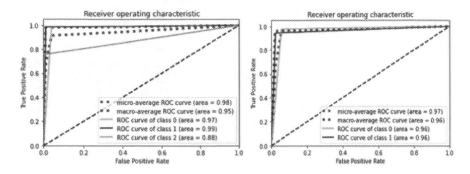

Fig. 5. ROC curve of Model-1 and Model-2 respectively

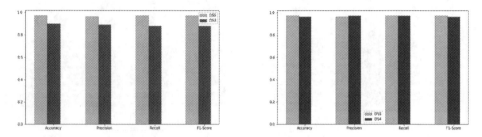

Fig. 6. Testing model-1 and model-2 with other datasets

The Fig. 7 gives the confusion matrix obtained by the models for the datasets DS1 and DS2 respectively. Model-1 predicted 1196 images correctly out of 1222 images with 97.95% accuracy. Out of 808 images, 766 images are correctly classified in the case of Model-2. Model-2 gives an accuracy of 96.04%.

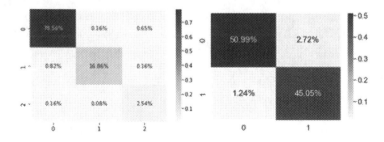

Fig. 7. Confusion matrix of Model-1 and Model-2 respectively

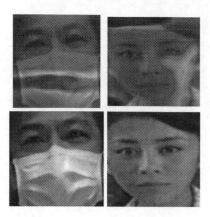

Fig. 8. Left Top: Class activation map image with mask, Left bottom: Image with mask. Right Top: class activation map image without mask, Right Bottom: Image without mask (Color figure online)

4.3 Explainability of the Model

The Class Activation Map (CAM) of the model is given by the Fig. 8. To obtain CAM, the output of the last convolutional layer was used. The CAM is produced by running GradCAM on it. We observed that such output on the with mask and without mask images is well distinguished. The emphasized region in red represents the presence of mask in the first image. This indicates the explainability of the proposed model. During model inference, the masked region is exposed to make the decision.

4.4 Performance of Model on Distortions

The correctness of the trained models is checked on different image conditions. 1000 images are selected from DS4 in which 500 masked images and 500 unmasked images were there. Salt and pepper noise, Speckle noise and White Gaussian noise are added in different amounts and observed the changes happening in the model performance. Similarly blurring using different kernel sizes is also done to monitor the variation in performance. Random noise function from Scikit library is used for adding noise [36]. Salt and pepper noise is added in a different amounts between 0.1–1.0 and the performance is evaluated. The salt and pepper noise is tried to remove using a median filter and significant improvement in the performance is observed. The results are observed as shown in the Fig. 10. The mean and variance of random distribution is adjusted to add different amount of speckle and white Gaussian noise. The Table 2 shows the result of adding noise to the image. From the experiment, it is observed that a median kernel of size 5×5 helps to improve the performance of a noisy image to a greater extent. The corresponding results are also reported in Table 2.

Similarly, blurring of images using different kernel sizes have also done to monitor the variation in performance. The corresponding results are shown

Table 2. The performance of proposed model under different distorted conditions

Type of Noise	Mean	Variance	Noisy image Results				Denoised with median filter, size = 5 × 5			
			Accuracy	MAP	MAR	MAF-1	Accuracy	MAP	MAR	MAF-1
Speckle Noise	0	0.01	0.87	0.87	0.87	0.87	0.89	0.89	0.89	0.89
		0.05	0.86	0.86	0.86	0.86	0.87	0.87	0.87	0.87
		0.1	0.86	0.86	0.86	0.86	0.87	0.88	0.87	0.87
		0.5	0.82	0.83	0.82	0.82	0.85	0.85	0.85	0.85
		1	0.74	0.79	0.74	0.74	0.75	0.77	0.74	0.74
	0.5	0.01	0.83	0.84	0.84	0.84	0.84	0.84	0.84	0.84
		0.05	0.84	0.84	0.84	0.84	0.85	0.85	0.85	0.85
		0.1	0.83	0.84	0.84	0.84	0.86	0.86	0.85	0.85
		0.5	0.8	0.8	0.8	0.8	0.83	0.83	0.83	0.83
		1	0.78	0.79	0.79	0.79	0.81	0.82	0.81	0.81
White Gaussian Noise	0	0.01	0.87	0.87	0.87	0.87	0.9	0.91	0.9	0.9
		0.05	0.86	0.86	0.86	0.86	0.89	0.9	0.89	0.89
		0.1	0.85	0.85	0.85	0.85	0.86	0.85	0.85	0.85
		0.5	0.81	0.82	0.81	0.81	0.81	0.82	0.82	0.82
		1	0.78	0.79	0.79	0.78	0.79	0.79	0.78	0.78
	0.5	0.01	0.68	0.76	0.68	0.66	0.71	0.71	0.71	0.71
		0.05	0.67	0.76	0.67	0.65	0.68	0.68	0.68	0.68
		0.1	0.7	0.76	0.7	0.69	0.72	0.78	0.72	0.72
		0.5	0.67	0.72	0.67	0.66	0.69	0.73	0.69	0.8
		1	0.58	0.73	0.59	0.55	0.61	0.74	62	0.55

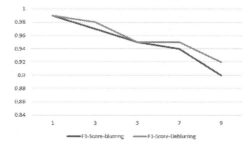

Fig. 9. Analysing the F1-Score in the in the blurred and deblurred images in different kernel sizes

in the Fig. 9. The performance of the model is diminishing as the kernel size increases. Images have to be deblurred and denoised for the better performance of the model in real-time. Noise removal can be done after deblurring is performed. This will help us to remove the noise added to the image during the process of deblurring. This will improve the accuracy of the model to a greater extent. The good quality image is an important factor to get good classification results. The performance of the model is improved when the image quality is good [37,38].

4.5   Real-Time Implementation of the Model

The trained model is implemented to detect the masks from the faces in real time as well. The model trained for three category classification is used for

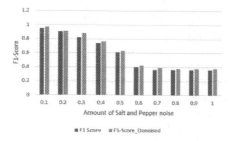

Fig. 10. Analysing the F1-Score of the model when salt and pepper noise is present and when the noise has been removed

detecting face masks from the video streams captured using the camera. The Multi-task Cascaded Convolutional Networks (MTCNN) framework [39] is used for detecting the face from the input. The algorithm is able to detect faces even when there is low light. Five facial landmarks such as right eye, left eye, left mouth corner, right mouth corner and nose are identified using the facial landmark feature of MTCNN [40]. The region of interest is restricted to the lower part of the face by focusing on the features of nose, left and right corners of mouth. The trained model used to detect the mask from the selected area. The model is able to detect around 98% of the subjects from the captured video and detecting the mask accurately. The predictions of the real-time system is shown in the Fig. 11. The bounding boxes are drawn around the faces in three different colours. Green is used to indicate the faces with masks, red is for faces without mask and yellow is denoting the images with incorrectly worn masks. The mask worn incorrectly class is identified with a confidence of 0.97 and the with mask and without mask classes are predicted with a confidence score of 1.

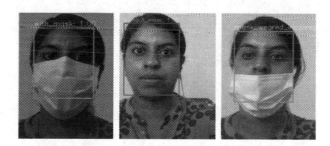

Fig. 11. Real-time implementation of the model (Color figure online)

5 Conclusion

A novel transfer learning-based model is proposed for detecting face masks. The proposed model uses an EfficientNetV2 inspired model for transfer learning for the first time. The model is trained on two standard dataset after doing some necessary pre-processing. The first dataset consists of three different categories of images. The model is trained on one more standard dataset with two categories of images i.e. images of people wearing the mask and not wearing the mask. The results have shown that transfer learning on EfficientNetV2 has outperformed the prior approaches. The proposed model produced an accuracy of 97.95% for the three-class model and 96.6% accuracy is reported for the binary class model. The EfficientNetV2 based model is compared with existing models based on other transfer learning techniques. Images containing different types of noise and other distortions such as blurring are tested to check the performance of the model. Inspite of being light, the model outperforms the existing methods on standard datasets. In addition, the model can detect people wearing masks in real-time. The model can be deployed in hand held devices such as mobile phones. This enhances the applicability of the model for practical purposes. For instance, CCTV cameras connected to micro controllers can be fed into the microcontroller and the number of people not wearing mask can be identified. The explainability of the proposed model was illustrated using the class activation map.

References

1. Rahmani, A.M., Mirmahaleh, S.Y.H.: Coronavirus disease (COVID-19) prevention and treatment methods and effective parameters: a systematic literature review. Sustain. Urban Areas **64**, 102568 (2021)
2. Wang, Z., Wang, P., Louis, P.C., Wheless, L.E., Huo, Y.: WearMask: fast in-browser face mask detection with serverless edge computing for COVID-19. arXiv preprint arXiv:2101.00784 (2021)
3. Howard, J., et al.: An evidence review of face masks against COVID-19. Proc. Natl. Acad. Sci. **118**(4), e2014564118 (2021)
4. Bassi, A., Henry, B.M., Pighi, L., Leone, L., Lippi, G.: Evaluation of indoor hospital acclimatization of body temperature before COVID-19 fever screening. J. Hosp. Infect. **112**, 127–128 (2021)
5. Fan, X., Jiang, M.: RetinaFaceMask: a single stage face mask detector for assisting control of the COVID-19 pandemic. In: 2021 IEEE International Conference on Systems, Man, and Cybernetics (SMC), pp. 832–837. IEEE (2021)
6. Parmar, D.N., Mehta, B.B.: Face recognition methods & applications. arXiv preprint arXiv:1403.0485 (2014)
7. Jain, D.K., Zhang, Z., Huang, K.: Multi angle optimal pattern-based deep learning for automatic facial expression recognition. Pattern Recogn. Lett. **139**, 157–165 (2020)
8. Esteva, A., et al.: Deep learning-enabled medical computer vision. NPJ Digit. Med. **4**(1), 1–9 (2021)
9. Zhao, Z.-Q., Zheng, P., Xu, S.-T., Wu, X.: Object detection with deep learning: a review. IEEE Trans. Neural Netw. Learn. Syst. **30**(11), 3212–3232 (2019)
10. Bazarevsky, V., Kartynnik, Y., Vakunov, A., Raveendran, K., Grundmann, M.: BlazeFace: sub-millisecond neural face detection on mobile GPUs. arXiv preprint arXiv:1907.05047 (2019)
11. He, K., Zhang, X., Ren, S., Sun, J.: Deep residual learning for image recognition. In: Proceedings of the IEEE Conference on Computer Vision and Pattern Recognition, pp. 770–778 (2016)

12. Loey, M., Manogaran, G., Taha, M.H.N., Khalifa, N.E.M.: Fighting against COVID-19: a novel deep learning model based on YOLO-v2 with ResNet-50 for medical face mask detection. Sustain. Urban Areas **65**, 102600 (2021)
13. Wu, P., Li, H., Zeng, N., Li, F.: FMD-Yolo: an efficient face mask detection method for COVID-19 prevention and control in public. Image Vis. Comput. **117**, 104341 (2022)
14. Olivas, E.S., Guerrero, J.D.M., Martinez-Sober, M., Magdalena-Benedito, J.R., Serrano, L., et al.: Handbook of Research on Machine Learning Applications and Trends: Algorithms, Methods, and Techniques: Algorithms, Methods, and Techniques. IGI Global (2009)
15. Jason, B.: A gentle introduction to transfer learning for deep learning (2022). https://machinelearningmastery.com/transfer-learning-for-deep-learning/
16. Pan, S.J., Yang, Q.: A survey on transfer learning. IEEE Trans. Knowl. Data Eng. **22**(10), 1345–1359 (2009)
17. Zhuang, F., et al.: A comprehensive survey on transfer learning. Proc. IEEE **109**(1), 43–76 (2020)
18. Tan, M., Le, Q.: EfficientNet: rethinking model scaling for convolutional neural networks. In: International Conference on Machine Learning, PMLR, pp. 6105–6114 (2019)
19. AnalyticsVidhya, Understanding transfer learning for deep learning. https://www.analyticsvidhya.com/blog/2021/10/understanding-transfer-learning-for-deep-learning/
20. Deng, J., Dong, W., Socher, R., Li, L.-J., Li, K., Fei-Fei, L.: ImageNet: a large-scale hierarchical image database. In: 2009 IEEE Conference on Computer Vision and Pattern Recognition, pp. 248–255. IEEE (2009)
21. Dey, S.K., Howlader, A., Deb, C.: MobileNet mask: a multi-phase face mask detection model to prevent person-to-person transmission of SARS-CoV-2. In: Kaiser, M.S., Bandyopadhyay, A., Mahmud, M., Ray, K. (eds.) Proceedings of International Conference on Trends in Computational and Cognitive Engineering. AISC, vol. 1309, pp. 603–613. Springer, Singapore (2021). https://doi.org/10.1007/978-981-33-4673-4_49
22. Jignesh Chowdary, G., Punn, N.S., Sonbhadra, S.K., Agarwal, S.: Face mask detection using transfer learning of InceptionV3. In: Bellatreche, L., Goyal, V., Fujita, H., Mondal, A., Reddy, P.K. (eds.) BDA 2020. LNCS, vol. 12581, pp. 81–90. Springer, Cham (2020). https://doi.org/10.1007/978-3-030-66665-1_6
23. Teboulbi, S., Messaoud, S., Hajjaji, M.A., Mtibaa, A.: Real-time implementation of AI-based face mask detection and social distancing measuring system for COVID-19 prevention. Sci. Program. **2021**, 1–20 (2021)
24. Ieamsaard, J., Charoensook, S.N., Yammen, S.: Deep learning-based face mask detection using YOLOv5. In: 2021 9th International Electrical Engineering Congress (iEECON), pp. 428–431. IEEE (2021)
25. Nagrath, P., Jain, R., Madan, A., Arora, R., Kataria, P., Hemanth, J.: SSDMNV2: a real time DNN-based face mask detection system using single shot multibox detector and MobileNetV2. Sustain. Urban Areas **66**, 102692 (2021)
26. Sanjaya, S.A., Rakhmawan, S.A.: Face mask detection using MobileNetV2 in the era of COVID-19 pandemic. In: 2020 International Conference on Data Analytics for Business and Industry: Way Towards a Sustainable Economy (ICDABI), pp. 1–5. IEEE (2020)
27. Sethi, S., Kathuria, M., Kaushik, T.: Face mask detection using deep learning: an approach to reduce risk of coronavirus spread. J. Biomed. Inform. **120**, 103848 (2021)

28. Tan, M., Le, Q.: EfficientNetV2: smaller models and faster training. In: International Conference on Machine Learning, PMLR, pp. 10096–10106 (2021)
29. Gupta, S., Tan, M.: EfficientNet-EdgeTPU: creating accelerator-optimized neural networks with AutoML. Google AI Blog **2**, 1 (2019)
30. Wightman, R.: Pytorch image models. https://github.com/rwightman/pytorch-image-models
31. Luo, L., Xiong, Y., Liu, Y., Sun, X.: Adaptive gradient methods with dynamic bound of learning rate. arXiv preprint arXiv:1902.09843 (2019)
32. Simonyan, K., Zisserman, A.: Very deep convolutional networks for large-scale image recognition. arXiv preprint arXiv:1409.1556 (2014)
33. Ab Wahab, M.N., Nazir, A., Ren, A.T.Z., Noor, M.H.M., Akbar, M.F., Mohamed, A.S.A.: EfficientNet-lite and hybrid CNN-KNN implementation for facial expression recognition on raspberry Pi. IEEE Access **9**, 134065–134080 (2021)
34. Szegedy, C., Vanhoucke, V., Ioffe, S., Shlens, J., Wojna, Z.: Rethinking the inception architecture for computer vision. In: Proceedings of the IEEE Conference on Computer Vision and Pattern Recognition, pp. 2818–2826 (2016)
35. Machine Learning Mastery: MOXA: a deep learning based unmanned approach for real-time monitoring of people wearing medical masks. https://shitty-bots-inc.github.io/MOXA/index.html
36. SciKit-image, Scikit-random noise. https://scikit-image.org/docs/stable/api/skimage.util.htmlrandom-noise
37. Kiruthika, S., Masilamani, V.: Image quality assessment based fake face detection. Multimed. Tools Appl. **82**, 8691–8708 (2023). https://doi.org/10.1007/s11042-021-11493-9
38. Kiruthika, S., Masilamani, V.: Goal oriented image quality assessment. IET Image Process. **16**(4), 1054–1066 (2022)
39. Zhang, K., Zhang, Z., Li, Z., Qiao, Y.: Joint face detection and alignment using multitask cascaded convolutional networks. IEEE Sig. Process. Lett. **23**(10), 1499–1503 (2016)
40. Ma, M., Wang, J.: Multi-view face detection and landmark localization based on MTCNN. In: 2018 Chinese Automation Congress (CAC), pp. 4200–4205. IEEE (2018)

Left Ventricle Segmentation of 2D Echocardiography Using Deep Learning

Swati Upadhyay⬭, A. Shamla Beevi⁽⬭⁾⬭, and Saidalavi Kalady⬭

National Institute of Technology Calicut Kozhikode, Kattangal, Kerala, India
shamlabeevia@gmail.com

Abstract. To identify the heart-related issues the very first step used by clinicians in diagnosis is to correctly identify the clinical indices which are possible by accurate Left Ventricle (LV) segmentation. Our work is related to building a deep learning model that automatically segments the cardiac left ventricle in an echocardiographic image into epicardium, endocardium, and left atrium. We propose the Vgg16 U-Net architecture for LV segmentation in this paper. On the CAMUS dataset, the Vgg16 Unet model is new, and it has demonstrated promising results for endocardium segmentation. The dice metric values achieved for endocardium, epicardium, and left atrium are **0.9412±0.0289**, **0.8786±0.0420**, and **0.9020±0.0908** respectively.

Keywords: Echocardiography · Segmentation U-Net · CNN (Convolutional Neural Network) · CVD (Cardiac Vascular Diseases) · Deep Learning

1 Introduction

Cardiac disease is a major reason for demise, according to the World Health Organization, it is estimated to claim about 17.9 million lives every year [1]. Doctors frequently recommend echocardiography to patients who have heart problems. Echocardiography is ultrasound imaging which is a non-invasive method to get live heart images. There are other methods like MRI and CT scan available for getting live heart images but those methods emit harmful radiation and are very expensive, whereas echocardiography is very cost-effective and thus more preferred by clinicians. The LV Segmentation in the echocardiographic image allows us to calculate the indices like systolic volumes and diastolic volumes, ejection fraction (EF), myocardium mass, and left atrium (LA), these cardiac parameters are very essential for disease diagnosis.

The automatic echocardiographic segmentation of the ultrasound image is a very complicated and challenging task to do because there are a lot of flecks and some other artifacts in the images, therefore manual or semi-automatic annotation is more preferred by clinicians. But these approaches have various disadvantages like it needs to be carried out only by an experienced clinician also there is always some inter-observer and intra-observer variability in the annotations, it

D. Gupta et al. (Eds.): CVIP 2022, CCIS 1776, pp. 87–98, 2023.
https://doi.org/10.1007/978-3-031-31407-0_7

is a very time-consuming process as well the whole process needs to be repeated for every patient. Therefore there is a need for a fully automatic method that can segment the cardiac images precisely and saves time. Many researchers have tried to resolve this issue and come up with methods to automatically delineate the left ventricle. However, some of them used non-deep learning methods to segment LV and some were based on deep learning used, in-house dataset, and only a few methods used publicly available CAMUS dataset.

There have been many methods for left ventricle segmentation however [5] [6], they did not involve deep learning because a large dataset is a type of prerequisite for it however in 2015, Olaf Ronneberger [2] introduced an approach that uses the data augmentation concept to very efficiently use the dataset. They built a fully convolutional neural network (FCNN) architecture called the U-Net. The U-Net model gave very good results for different medical image segmentation. This started a revolution in biomedical imaging and several new models were suggested for segmenting images. Leclerc et al. [3] introduced two U-Net models U-Net1 and U-Net2 which were slightly non-identical to the original U-Net model. These models were trained and tested on the CAMUS dataset and gave a dice value of 0.928 for the endocardium and 0.888 left atrium. It was however found out that the original U-Net surpasses the U-Net1 and U-Net2 architectures on an in-house dataset in which out of 1098 available frames, 992 frames were annotated [4] but they did not do the segmentation for the left atrium and epicardium and only segmented the endocardium with a dice value of 0.92 from original U-Net.

Daimary [8] introduced the three hybrid CNN models for the segmentation of the brain tumor in the MRI. The Seg-UNet is a hybrid architecture that combines SegNet5 with U-Net. This model has a downsampling property from the SegNet5 and upsampling property of U-Net which is the concatenation of features map size from many levels. Another architecture was U-SegNet, which was similar to Seg-UNet architecture with the only variation in the number of convolution blocks or depth, Seg-UNet has five convolution blocks whereas only three blocks are used in the U-SegNet. Another model was Res-SegNet which was a fusion of SegNet5 and ResNet18. This model has downsampling and upsampling properties similar to the SegNet5 and in it Resnet18 prompted the inclusion of inputs from many levels. These hybrid methods showed better performance in comparison to the original CNN methods for brain MRI images, but there was no model for echocardiographic image segmentation. K. Simonyan [10] introduced an architecture for image recognition and classification purpose.

Jie Hu [11] introduced Squeeze and Excitation Networks (SENets) which are a type of convolutional neural network that increases channel inter-dependencies at a very negligible computational expense. SENets were used in the ImageNet competition and won the competition by increasing the preceding year's result by 25%. In 2014 in an ImageNet Visual Recognition Challenge Vgg16 stood first but since it has high depth, it is computationally quite expensive. In 2015 C C. Szegedy [10] introduced inception v3 architecture. They tested their result on the 2012, ImageNet Large Scale Visual Recognition Competition and achieved a result of 17.2% and 3.58% top-1 and top-5 error values respectively. Vasily Zyuzin [7] did the echocardiographic segmentation by building a hybrid model of ResNet and U-Net having ResNet-34 in the downsampling part of the U-Net and achieved a dice coefficient value of 0.935 for endocardium and 0.904 for the left atrium. From the given literature survey we can conclude that variations of U-Net models are more effective in giving accurate segmentation of the left ventricle. Table 1 shows the dice value of endocardium achieved by the various models on the CAMUS dataset.

The remaining sections of the paper are organised as follows: Sect. 2 gives a brief of the key contribution of the paper, Sect. 3 discuss about methodology that we have used, Sect. 4 presents details about the dataset used, evaluation matrices, results obtained during experimentation and performance analysis and Sect. 5 concludes the paper.

Table 1. Dice coefficient of existing methodologies for endocardium

	Method Used	Dice Coefficient
Leclerc, Sarah, et al. [12]	Refining U-Net	0.921±0.054
Zyuzin, Vasily, et al. [7]	U-Net ResNet34	0.935±0.008
Yang, Yingyu, et al. [13]	Shape Constraints in Deep learning model	0.931±0.041

2   Contribution

In echocardiography, we performed multi-class segmentation of the left ventricle. We applied the transfer learning approach by using imagenet weights to build a Vgg16 U-Net architecture, which we then compared to the U-Net, Res U-Net, and Res-34 U-Net models on the CAMUS dataset. The Dice Coefficient and IoU metrics were used to evaluate the models, and the Friedman test was used to justify their significance level. For Vgg16 U-Net network we achieved higher dice coefficient values for endocardium and epicardium than the other 3 three networks.

3   Methodology

We have experimented with different deep learning models for LV segmentation like U-Net, Res UNet, Res34 UNet and Vgg16 UNet architectures.

3.1   U-Net

U-Net [2] is a convolutional neural network having U-shaped architecture. It uses long skip connections to transfer important features from the encoder to the decoder. We built a U-Net model having four downsampling layers and four

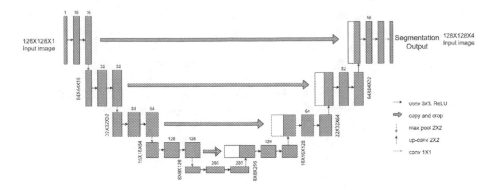

Fig. 1. General Architecture of U-Net [2]

up sampling layers with 1 layer acting as a bridge. We resized all the images to a 128×128 size.

Figure 1 shows the U-Net model used.

3.2   Res U-Net

A Convolutional Neural Network can be made better for image-related tasks by adding more layers. However, it is possible that it will lose accuracy as a result of this. In order to extract critical properties from complicated images, deep learning practitioners often add a number of layers. But when we add more levels to the network, the performance degrades. It's mostly there due to the vanishing gradient issue.

The residual network [14] is used to overcome this problem. The residual network has residual units or blocks that have identity links or skip connections. Figure 2 represents the Residual Block. Adding these residual blocks instead of the regular convolutional blocks in the U-Net model gives the Res U-Net architecture.

3.3   Res34 U-Net

A ResNet is formed by repeating the residual units. A ResNet-34 will have 34 such layers. Figure 3 represents the Residual network-34 unit. We have used the ResNet-34 architecture as the backbone of the U-Net. Figure 1 gives the complete description of the U-Net architecture that we have used as our base model. In the U-Net architecture, in the encoder or in the down-sampling part instead of using convolutional layers we used residual blocks. The encoder is ResNet-34 while the decoder or the up-sampling has a deconvolutional layer followed by a regular convolutional layer.

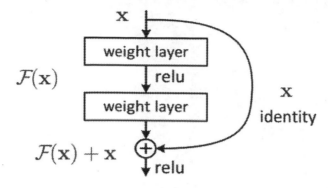

Fig. 2. Residual Block Unit [14]

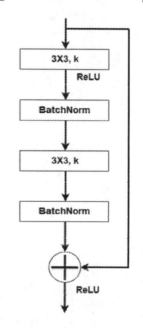

Fig. 3. ResNet-34 Block [7]

3.4 Vgg16 U-Net

We have used the Vgg16 U-Net architecture using transfer learning approach. The transfer learning approach involves using pre-trained models on large datasets at the neural network's beginning. Because that model has been trained on a large amount of data, it can discover some features and we take advantage of those qualities by modifying specific aspects of the trained model to suit our needs. We used the Vgg16 [10] layers with pre-trained weights on the ImageNet dataset as the encoder in the U-Net model. We used the 13 convolutional layers in the encoder. Figure 5 shows the Vgg16 U-Net model. We did not include the

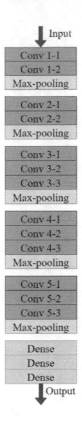

Fig. 4. Vgg16 Architecture [10]

3 dense layers as shown in Fig. 4 of the Vgg16 architecture, instead used the deconvolutional layers of the U-Net model. We used a stride 2 max pooling layer for downsampling and a transposed convolution with a kernel size of 2×2 for upsampling, and we trained the model for 23,748,676 trainable parameters at a 1e-3 learning rate. We used two loss functions Dice Loss (1) and Categorical Focal Loss [15] (2). In Eq. (1) DC refers to dice coefficient and it is defined in Eq. (4).

$$Dice\ Loss = (1 - DC) \tag{1}$$

$$Categorical\ Focal\ Loss = -(1 - P)^{\gamma} \log(P),\ where\ \gamma = 2 \tag{2}$$

In Eq. (2) P refers to the probability of the ground truth and γ is the focusing parameter having a value greater than equal to 0, we experimented that the best value for γ is 2.

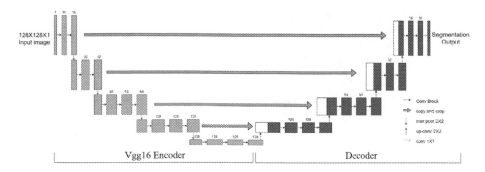

Fig. 5. Vgg16 U-Net Architecture

4   Experimental Results

We trained four models U-Net model, Res-UNet, Vgg-16 U-Net, and Res-34 U-Net model. We used the same training, testing, and validation set and also used the same set of other hyperparameters during the training of all the models. Table 2 gives the complete description of the hyper-parameters used in each model.

4.1   Dataset

The only publicly available echocardiographic images dataset is the CAMUS dataset [9]. It includes end-systolic volume and end-diastolic volume images from echocardiography apical two-chamber (AP2C) and apical four-chamber (AP4C). Images from 500 patients ranging in age from 20 to 90 years old are examined by the same machine out of which 450 patient images are manually annotated by an expert. There were 1800 fully annotated images in total. These images were divided into three sets: training, testing, and validation. The first 10% of the images were used for testing, the next 10% for validation, and the remaining images were used for training.

4.2   Network Training

The model is built using Keras and Tensorflow python libraries which have inbuilt modules to support the CNN models, also the system has a RAM of 8 GB, Intel(R) UHD Graphics 620 and NVIDIA GeForce MX130 GPU, Intel(R) Core(TM) i5-8250U CPU and 64-bit operating system, x64-based processor.

4.3   Evaluation Metrics

For measuring the performance and to see how well the model works for segmentation, the following metrics are considered:-

Table 2. Model Characteristics

	U-Net	ResU-Net	Vgg16 U-Net	Res-34 U-Net
Total parameters used:	1,946,756	2,037,492	23,752,708	24,456,589
Trainable parameters:	1,943,812	2,033,076	23,748,676	24,439,239
Non-trainable parameters:	2,944	4,416	4,032	17,350
Lowest Resolution:	(16, 16)	(16, 16)	(16, 16)	(16, 16)
Batch Size:	16	16	8	8
Optimizer:	Adam	Adam	Adam	Adam
Learning rate:	0.001	0.001	0.0001	0.0001
Activation function:	ReLU and softmax (for output layer)	ReLU and softmax (for output layer)	ReLU and softmax (for output layer)	ReLU and softmax (for output layer)
Stride:	(2,2)	(2,2)	(2,2)	(2,2)
No. of epochs:	250	250	250	250
Kernel initializer:	he normal	he normal	he normal	he normal
Loss function:	Categorical Crossentropy	Weighted Categorical Crossentropy	Dice Loss and Categorical Focal Loss	Dice Loss and Categorical Focal Loss
Normalization scheme:	Batch Normalization	Batch Normalization	Batch Normalization	Batch Normalization

Intersection Over Union (IoU or Jaccard Index):– It is a metric for evaluation that is calculated image by image between the predicted segmentation (Ps) by the model and the actual segmentation by the experts (As). IoU can be mathematically expressed as in the Eq. (3).

$$IoU = \frac{|Ps \cap As|}{|Ps \cup As|} \tag{3}$$

If the IoU value is 1 means that the ground truth and the predicted image are the same. A lower IoU value denotes poor prediction results.

Dice Coefficient (DC):– It measures the overlapping regions of the predicted segment (P) and the ground truth (GT). The mathematical equation for DC is expressed in the Eq. (4).

$$DC = \frac{2|P \cap GT|}{|P| + |GT|} \tag{4}$$

The range of value is between 0 (zero overlap) and 1 (complete overlap).

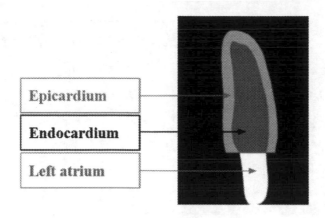

Fig. 6. Training mask

Table 3. Mean IoU and Mean Dice values of U-Net, Res U-Net, Res-34 U-Net and Vgg16 U-Net models for endocardium, epicardium and left atrium

Model	Dice Coefficient			IoU Values		
	Endocardium	Epicardium	Left Atrium	Endocardium	Epicardium	Left Atrium
U-Net	0.9195	0.8373	0.8692	0.8551	0.7244	0.7831
	±0.0539	±0.0585	±0.1155	±0.0819	±0.0826	±0.1416
Res U-Net	0.9166	0.8381	0.8773	0.8493	0.7258	0.7926
	±0.0450	±0.0589	±0.1000	±0.0727	±0.0833	±0.1255
Res34 U-Net	0.9388	0.8760	**0.9047**	0.8864	0.7818	**0.8550**
	±0.0315	±0.0418	**±0.0930**	±0.0536	±0.0637	**±0.1129**
Vgg16 U-Net	**0.9412**	**0.8786**	0.9020	**0.8904**	**0.7861**	0.8306
	±0.0289	**±0.0420**	±0.0908	**±0.0498**	**±0.0647**	±0.1118

Table 4. Performance evaluation of dice value in endocardium

	Dice Coefficient
Leclerc, Sarah, et al. [12]	0.921±0.054
Zyuzin, Vasily, et al. [7]	0.935±0.008
Yang, Yingyu, et al. [13]	0.931±0.041
U-Net	0.9195±0.0539
Res U-Net	0.9166±0.0450
Res34 U-Net	0.9388±0.0315
Vgg16 U-Net	**0.9412±0.0289**

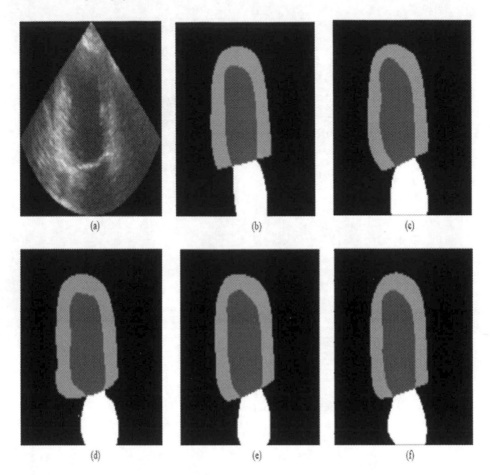

Fig. 7. Segmentation output of each model (a)Echocardiography image, (b)Ground truth, (c)Predicted image by U-Net model, (d)Predicted image by Res U-Net model, (e)Predicted image by Vgg16 U-Net model, (f)Predicted image by Res34 U-Net model.

4.4   Segmentation Results

We have experimented with four deep learning models. Figure 6 shows the three classes in which we segment the left ventricle i.e. the epicardium, the endocardium, and the left atrium. The epicardium is the outermost layer of the heart while the endocardium is the innermost layer. The left atrium receives blood from the lungs and then supplies it to the left ventricle of the heart for pumping oxygenated blood to other parts of the body. Table 3 shows the result of our Model. Res34 U-Net has given better values for the Left atrium than the U-Net, Res U-Net, and Vgg16 U-Net models. For the endocardium and epicardium segmentation, the Vgg16 U-Net model has shown the highest dice and IoU values. Figure 7 shows the segmented output of each model. To evaluate the segmentation performance achieved by Vgg16 U-Net, we compare this proposed method with existing methods [7] [12] [13] based on dice coefficient.

The statistical significance of the results of the proposed methods in left ventricle segmentation was analyzed using the Friedman test for each metric to assess their influence. The results showed that the Vgg16 U-Net produced statistically different (p-value = 0.05) scores for the majority of metrics at the endocardium, epicardium, and left atrium. Table 4 shows the performance of the existing literature and our models for dice coefficient values in the endocardium. It can be seen that Vgg16 U-Net outperforms all the other methods.

5   Conclusion

Four different architectures were used to segment the left ventricle into the endo-cardium, epicardium, and left atrium. We have presented the results by comparing U-Net, Res U-Net, Res34 U-Net, and Vgg16 U-Net architectures. Out of all these methods, Vgg16 U-Net model gave the best results.

In further studies, we can include attention modules that perform feature fine-tuning at the spatial and channel levels to enhance the local features and suppress the irrelevant features.

Acknowledgment. We would like to acknowledge Sudhish N. George for his comments on the earlier versions of the manuscript.

References

1. American Heart Association. "Heart Disease and Stroke Statistics Update Fact Sheet At-a-Glance; 2021." (2021)
2. Ronneberger, O., Fischer, P., Brox, T.: U-Net: convolutional networks for biomedical image segmentation. In: Navab, N., Hornegger, J., Wells, W.M., Frangi, A.F. (eds.) MICCAI 2015. LNCS, vol. 9351, pp. 234–241. Springer, Cham (2015). https://doi.org/10.1007/978-3-319-24574-4_28
3. Leclerc, S., et al.: Deep learning for segmentation using an open large-scale dataset in 2D echocardiography. IEEE Trans. Med. Imag. 38(9), 2198–2210 (2019)
4. Azarmehr, N., et al.: Automated segmentation of left ventricle in 2D echocardiography using deep learning. arXiv preprint: arXiv:2003.07628 (2020)
5. Lacerda, S.G., et al.: Left ventricle segmentation in echocardiography using a radial-search-based image processing algorithm. In: 2008 30th Annual International Conference of the IEEE Engineering in Medicine and Biology Society. IEEE (2008)
6. Bernard, O., et al.: Standardized evaluation system for left ventricular segmentation algorithms in 3D echocardiography. IEEE Trans. Med. Imag. 35(4), 967–977 (2015)
7. Zyuzin, V., et al.: Segmentation of 2D echocardiography images using residual blocks in U-net architectures. In: 2020 Ural Symposium on Biomedical Engineering, Radioelectronics and Information Technology (USBEREIT). IEEE (2020)
8. Daimary, D., et al.: Brain tumor segmentation from MRI images using hybrid convolutional neural networks. Procedia Comput. Sci. 167, 2419–2428 (2020)

9. Leclerc, S., et al.: Deep learning segmentation in 2D echocardiography using the CAMUS dataset: automatic assessment of the anatomical shape validity. arXiv preprint: arXiv:1908.02994 (2019)
10. Simonyan, K., Andrew Z.: Very deep convolutional networks for large-scale image recognition. arXiv preprint: arXiv:1409.1556 (2014)
11. Hu, J., et al.: Squeeze-and-excitation networks. In: Proceedings of the IEEE Conference on Computer Vision and Pattern Recognition, vol. 4 (2018)
12. Leclerc, S., et al.: RU-Net: a refining segmentation network for 2D echocardiography. In: 2019 IEEE International Ultrasonics Symposium (IUS). IEEE (2019)
13. Yang, Y., Sermesant, M.: Shape constraints in deep learning for robust 2D echocardiography analysis. In: Ennis, D.B., Perotti, L.E., Wang, V.Y. (eds.) FIMH 2021. LNCS, vol. 12738, pp. 22–34. Springer, Cham (2021). https://doi.org/10.1007/978-3-030-78710-3_3
14. He, K., et al.: Deep residual learning for image recognition. In: Proceedings of the IEEE Conference on Computer Vision and Pattern Recognition (2016)
15. Lin, T.-Y., et al.: Focal loss for dense object detection. In: Proceedings of the IEEE International Conference on Computer Vision (2017)

Multi Modal 2-D Canvas Based Gallery Content Retrieval

Pragya Paramita Sahu[✉][ID], Vikrant Singh[ID], and Viswanath Veera[ID]

Samsung Research Institute, Bangalore, India
pragya.sahu@samsung.com

Abstract. Clicking pictures using mobile cameras is an ubiquitous part of daily human lives. However, finding the same photo, after a couple of weeks, is a herculean task. Conventional gallery search is based on a 1D query input, limited to keywords, without any smart understanding of the user's needs. The user is needed to scroll through hundreds of images to find the one. In this work, we propose a multi-modal canvas based content retrieval system. Our system allows the users to write/draw on a 2-D canvas, instead of a single line. We use the relative position of the keywords to better understand the user's needs and retrieve the photo he needs faster. Complex ideas of perception, nearness and object relations are more easily explained through a 2-D input, rather than complex sentences. We integrate a handwriting recognition system with a clustering based sketch recognition engine, to allow users a truly multi-modal system to interact with their devices. Our system also allows users to specify the finer features of the objects, thus providing increased ease of retrieval. We show that using the proposed system, users are able to find the required image faster with a 33% reduction in human effort. Proposed system allows users to creatively search for images rather than monotonously scrolling through hundreds of images.

Keywords: Multimodal interaction · Positional search · Handwritten stroke recognition

1 Introduction

Past years have seen massive headway in the development of mobile cameras. State-of-art cameras, coupled with extensive phone and cloud storage, translates to users being able to click as they wish. Every moment can be easily documented. However, revisiting the same photos is an arduous process. Looking for a photo taken a while back involves scrolling through hundreds of similar images. Current gallery search methodologies are limited to a text query input. Expressing relational information in the search query is a difficult task. Conventional systems are limited by the growth of robust Natural Language Understanding (NLU) engines. Additionally, extensive usage of the system is limited to users ability to form grammatically correct phrases and sentences.

Recent years have also seen work on the development of Sketch Based Image Retrieval (SBIR) systems. These match a hand-drawn sketch with the closest image in the gallery. Realizing the ease of conveying finer details, fine-grained SBIR saw significant progress in recent works [1,2]. However, all such works depend on: 1. Users looking for an extremely specific type of object and 2. Users are competent in sketching to accurately represent finer details. Most retrieval results are ranked temporally, without any further intelligence in understanding human intentions.

In this work, we bring together text, handwriting and sketch modes of input, to build a system that understands user needs without any additional effort. Our system looks at the query from a 2-D canvas based input, rather than a traditional 1-D input. As the adage goes, "A picture is worth a thousand words". A rough painting can better express user needs. Complex ideas of inter object relations and relative object nearness and perception, are easier to explain with a rough sketch rather than complex sentences. However, not every person is adept at sketching complex objects. With these two important aspects in mind, we propose a 2-D multi-modal canvas based input methodology that allows users to express themselves clearer and for our systems to understand better. User can choose to write, type or sketch the keyword on a 2-D canvas, inherently providing an idea of its approximate position in the required image. They can also choose to input a finer feature descriptor, further refining the search criteria. Proposed system develops a smarter understanding of user needs through the required keywords and their inherent relationships (using a novel scoring system), retrieving the required image faster and with higher accuracy.

2 Related Work

2.1 Text Based Image Retrieval

Most gallery applications today are limited to a text input based image retrieval. Conventional systems match the input tag to object information in the metadata, and retrieve the results, sorted temporally. Some advanced applications allow users to input basic adjectives (eg. colour) to further describe the object. Retrieval problems however have been tackled from different aspects. The works of Zheng et al. [3] and Savvas et al. [4] look at using image features for increased accuracy in image retrieval applications. A significant amount of work has also been seen in the domain of face recognition and retrieval from huge gallery datasets [5,6]. However, the scope of text based image retrieval is limited by the huge constraining factors of language and NLU.

2.2 Sketch Based Image Retrieval

Work has also grown in the domain of sketch based image retrieval. SBIR systems can broadly be classified into Category-level SBIR and Fine-grained SBIR. Category level SBIR classifies the drawn sketch into a pre-defined class category and retrieves images matching that category through traditional [7] or zero-shot [8] methodologies. Fine-grained SBIR is a more recent addition to the community. Recently, Pang et.al [2] looked at a cross-category SBIR. Progressive systems for zero-shot SBIR systems have also been explored by in [9] and [10].

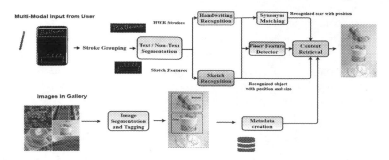

Fig. 1. System Flowchart for Multi-Modal Content Retrieval *(Detailed description of modules defined in Section 3)*

2.3 Handwriting Recognition

The domain of Handwriting Recognition (HWR) has also seen growth in the past years [11]. Handwriting recognition, or any stroke recognition technique, can be broadly categorized into online (temporal coordinate based) and offline (pixel based, 2-D) recognition. Alex Graves' work in [13] developed a Bidirectional Long Short Term Memory (Bi-LSTM) network in conjugation with a Connectionist Temporal Classification (CTC) cost function, to accurately recognize sequential data without the need of pre-segmentation. More recently, Carbune et.al [15] looked at an attention based methodology using Bezier curves.

3   Proposed Approach

In most gallery applications, every photo is stored with the information of the objects in it and its bounding box (the bounding box is returned as a output from **Image Segmentation and Object Recognition** algorithms, even if it is not stored separately). This is stored as **Image Metadata**. Conventional retrieval systems use the object names as a tag for the image, but make no use of this positional information.We propose using this additional information to make image retrieval faster and more efficient. Users can use the canvas to inherently input the relative position and size of the object (depending on the position/size of the written/sketched keyword), without any additional effort in creating complex textual input query. As our content retrieval system is based on tag matching, the implemented sketch recognition module follows a C-SBIR (categorical sketch based image retrieval) approach.

In Fig. 1, we present a detailed flowchart of the various modules and engines that build up our system, along with a sample scenario. A search query which may be a combination of handwritten text and a rough sketch is given as an input to our retrieval engine. After stroke grouping, a text/non-text segmentation engine separates the multi-modal input into separate stroke patterns. The text strokes are passed to a HWR engine and the image strokes are given as input to the sketch recognition engine. The recognized text as well as the recognized objects alongside the relevant finer features (including shape, size and position information) extracted from the canvas input are passed to the retrieval engine where our ranking algorithm outputs the best possible matched results to the given query. In addition to the proposed novel pipeline, we also propose a new scoring system for ranking retrieved images in Sect. 3.5. This multi-headed scoring system in addition to the multi-modal input pipeline forms the pillars behind our proposed system.

3.1   Sketch Segmentation and Classification

A canvas input, especially ones created to better describe object relations, will contain multiple objects. Object stroke segmentation thus becomes the first step to support multi-modal, multi-object input. Sun et.al looked at a proximity based sketch segmentation in [19]. However, a purely distance based proximity measure returned erroneous results in the cases where new strokes are drawn farther away from the existing incomplete object. To solve this problem, we incorporated temporal distance as an additional proximity measure. The strokes which are drawn just after one another are considered temporally close and vice versa. This hybrid proximity measure, using both spatial and temporal distance, increased sketch segmentation accuracy by 18% (from 72% to 84.9%).

The grouped strokes are then classified as text or non-text input. The classification module consists of a RNN-GRU (Recurrent Neural Network - Gate Recurrent Unit) feed forward network, trained on the IAMonDb data-set [20]. We follow the approach shown in Khomenko et.al's work in [12] for this paper. Text strokes are sent as input to the HWR module while all non-text strokes are grouped and sent as input to the Sketch Recognition (SR) module.

3.2   Handwritten Text Recognition and Synonym Matching

A 2 layer Bi-LSTM (100 units) based online HWR engine with a CTC cost function was built, to recognize handwritten English text. The output layer has 113 units (112 unique characters, numbers and special characters and one 'blank' label). This network was trained on labeled data of 1.5 million words from 100 writers, with a learning rate of 0.0001 and momentum of 0.9. All parameters were used directly as quoted from the work of Alex Graves in [13]. As we expect text inputs to be no more than 3–4 words (finer feature adjective + category name), we used a 3-gram language model. While the number of objects segmented in the gallery application is a constant (used gallery application supported 500 categories of object detection), we did not want the user to be limited to using just the exact keywords. Thus, a general HWR engine was built [14]. For every word that the user writes, its closest matching keyword was found using a FastText [16] based word similarity calculator. The closest synonym matching the supported category and its corresponding position was sent to the content retrieval module.

3.3   Sketch Recognition

In this work, we deploy an offline model for the classification task utilizing a CNN based deep learning pipeline. Our model implements a categorical SR, supporting 345 distinct categories (as present in QuickDraw data-set). For the purposes of SR, we choose to use a offline model rather than an online model. This is because, unlike handwritten words, sketches have no sequence of drawing. Using an online model biased the recognition to the sequence of strokes, and any free-hand sketch drawn in a way different from the data-set saw inaccurate results. The offline model, however, sees the complete 2-D image and performed better on these rough free-hand sketches. Our classification model is a modified RESNET (residual network) based architecture. We prune the vanilla RESNET model layers to optimize for size and latency without significant drop in the accuracy levels. Our architecture is described in detail in Fig. 2.

Model Pruning. A mobile compatible model needs to be memory efficient without loss of accuracy. To prune the network, we first remove the last layer of a trained RESNET-34 model. Next we add a $1{\times}1$ convolution layer between the input and output of this layer (Fig. 3), initialized with linear weights obtained by minimizing L2-loss between input and output of this layer obtained from the base RESNET model for a subset of training images. This replacement of layers allows for models to retain information while reducing the number of weights.

Let $X_{7\times7\times512}$ be the input to the layer. We average across first two dimensions to obtain a 1-D vector X'_{512}. Similarly we get, Y'_{512}.

$$X'_{512} = \sum_{i,j} X_{i,j,512} \tag{1}$$

Let $X'_{1000\times512}$ be such a vector for a set of 1000 images and $Y'_{1000\times512}$ be the output. Then we minimize,

$$||Y' - W_{1\times1\times512}X'||_2 \tag{2}$$

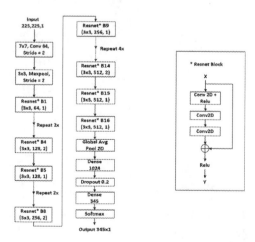

Fig. 2. Sketch Recognition Model Architecture

Fig. 3. Layer Pruning

where, $W_{1\times1\times512}$ represents the initial weights for the $1 \times 1 \times 512$ convolution layer. The network is then fine-tuned on the whole training set.

To further handle the loss of accuracy, we noted that often users don't provide important finer details (e.g necessary details that would distinguish a pen from a marker). We theorized that instead of limiting the search result to a specific category, providing results belonging to objects of similar categories can give more flexibility to the user. On the basis of class similarity, we divided the 345 sketch classes into 152 'super classes'. For example, truck, car and ambulance are clustered together as a single class, 'vehicles'. This broader categorization helped in retrieving the closest images intended by the user.

3.4   Finer Feature Classifier

Our system allows the user to specify additional finer features of the drawn/written object. For the purposes of this work, we define a finer feature as an adjective descriptor of the object, which helps the refinement of the result list. This can be of the form shown in Fig. 4. Currently, our system only supports text based descriptor. After text recognition, we separate out the words meant to specify the finer features, and use it as an additional input for our content retrieval engine. Currently our system supports words describing the colour, luminance, perspective and texture of the object. As of now we were limited to the features that our gallery object segmenter could easily classify.

Fig. 4. Possible ways of denoting finer feature in input

3.5   Positional Content Retrieval

The content retrieval (CR) engine receives the category name and its bounding box coordinates from the HWR and SR modules. The confidence matching score for each image is calculated by a combined spatial and localization score for the given sketch. The individual scores are detailed below.

Spatial Confidence. Spatial score is calculated to provide a measure of the inter object relations. For every object in the canvas and the photo, the number and type of categories present in each side is store in a hashmap for every direction (left, right, top and bottom). We define a score parameter S_{ik} as:

$$S_{ik} = \sum min(MapI[ImageObject_i], MapS[CanvasObject_k]) \qquad (3)$$

where i is the index for image and k is the index for canvas. $MapI$ and $MapS$ denote the hashmap data structure for all 4 directions in which key is the object class and value is it's frequency, when i^{th} image object ($ImageObject_i$) is the same as k^{th} canvas object ($CanvasObject_k$).

We also define a parameter of $CanvasMatch_k$, which denotes the summation of $MapS$ for k^{th} canvas object in all 4 directions.

$$CanvasMatch_k = \sum_{d \in (l,r,t,b)} MapS_d[(CanvasObject_k)] \qquad (4)$$

where $MapS_d$ represents the hashmap in d direction.

Finally, the spatial score is calculated as the maximum of the ratio of score parameter S_{ik} to $CanvasMatch_k$.

$$conf_{spatial} = max_{\forall i,k}(S_{ik}/CanvasMatch_k) \qquad (5)$$

Locational Confidence. Locational score calculated the closeness of the objects in the canvas and photo. The Euclidean distance $d_{i,k}$ between the bounding box centres of the matched classes in the i_{th} image and k_{th} canvas is calculated as:

$$\|d_{i,k}\| = d(Image_i, Canvas_k) \qquad (6)$$

The locational confidence score is defined as inverse of the minimum distance score for each matched object in the image.

$$conf_{loc} = \sum_{i,k} 1/(min(d_{i,k})) \qquad (7)$$

We take the inverse score because the closer the input position is to the image object position, the better is our match.

Final Confidence. The final confidence score for each image was calculated as a weighted average of the spatial and locational confidence scores.

$$conf_{Final} = (1 - \alpha) * conf_{spatial} + (\alpha) * conf_{loc} \qquad (8)$$

where α was empirically 0.1. To include finer feature support, the descriptor was added as additional input, and marked as N/A if not provided. The final image list is sorted in decreasing order of the $conf_{Final}$ and output to the user.

4 Experiments and Results

4.1 Training Data-Sets

The English HWR model was trained on a dataset of 1.5 million words, obtained from 100 writers. This model gave a character recognition accuracy of $\approx 96\%$ and word recognition accuracy of $\approx 84\%$ when tested on a dataset of $\approx 16k$ samples. The SR model was trained and tested on the QuickDraw dataset [17] consisting of rough, free-hand sketches from 345 discrete categories. We chose the QuickDraw dataset because users were time constrained during data collection process (all samples were drawn within 20 secs). This translates to the sketch samples being rough and sparse. For the widespread adaptability of our solution, it is important that the SR module is robust enough to handle extremely rough sketches. Our training and evaluation sets consist of 70000 images and 1000 images of each class. Cross-entropy loss function and Adam optimizer with a batch size of 64 was used. Our model metrics are documented in Table 1.

Table 1. Performance for single sketch recognition

Model	Top-1 Acc (345 classes)	Top-3 Acc (345 classes)	Model Size (MB)	Latency (ms)
Base RESNET	80.93%	92.77%	93 MB	285 ms
Pruned RESNET	79.15%	91.74%	10 MB	50 ms

4.2 Testing Environment

For the purposes of system experimentation, we collected test data from 200 different users on a Samsung Note-9 device. The test participants were spread equally across both genders, and their age demographics is mentioned in Table 2. Participants were explained the purpose and application usage before starting. The built application took a 2-D input, and retrieved the images from the gallery, most matching the input. The interface showed images retrieved by conventional approach as well as the proposed positional approach. As the results were stored after every step, we did not need the user's to specifically mark when the required image was retrieved. The input could be refined after every retrieval. Participants could choose to add/remove/move the objects on the screen. The gallery for the purposes of this experimentation, contained 5000 different images, obtained from Open Images Dataset [18]. The recognized objects and their bounding box information (available in the dataset) was stored in the application database. The test data was primarily collected in 2 phases, enumerated below:

Phase 1 - Uniform Testing. Set-A of the test data was aimed at measuring how accurately our model is able to retrieve the required image. The participants were shown an image and asked to provide a 2-D canvas input to retrieve that image. The canvas input could be multi-modal, and the participants could choose to either draw or write. To measure model robustness, participants were asked to start with one category, and keep on adding categories till they were able to retrieve the required photo in both modes. They could also "move" the object strokes on the screen, to change the relative distance and positions more easily. **Set-B** of the test data was aimed to measure the differences between sketch, text and multi-modal based input. Thus, for every test case, the user was required to input three test samples, a. using only sketches b. using only handwritten text and c. using a combination of both, as they deemed fit. **Set-C** of the test data was collected with the aim of testing the finer feature descriptor support in the system. The participants were asked to provide a descriptor for the categories, to better refine the results. This descriptor could be colour, texture or luminance.

Table 2. Age demographics of test subjects

Age Group	16–33	34–45	46–70
Percentage of respondents	68%	24%	8%

Phase 2 - Personal Testing. The accuracy and efficacy of any gallery retrieval solution, is dependent on the number and type of images present in the gallery. Thus, for the first phase of data collection, we ensured that a fixed gallery was used, to provide a comprehensive analysis of the results. However, for the proposed system, an analysis of the accuracy of input and corresponding retrieval is also important. Thus, we asked a subset of 50 participants, to install the developed application on their phones and provide gallery access permissions. Participants could then use the solution to retrieve images from their gallery, by providing input from memory. This provided an accurate measure of the real-life usage of our solution. As before, participants could edit the input, adding, removing or moving categories, till the required image was retrieved satisfactorily.

4.3   Experiments

Our solution proposes to use the inherently provided position and size information, from a 2-D canvas based input from the user, as an additional input for gallery content retrieval. As we focus our work on the complete system, in the following experiments we compared our work to a similar content retrieval solution that uses only keyword tags for searching, and sorts all returned images by its temporal information. From henceforth, we will refer to such a solution as **Conventional Gallery Search** and our proposed solution as **Multi-Modal Gallery Search**. Multi-Modal Search can be used in addendum to any state of the art content retrieval algorithm, increasing its efficiency by similar numbers. Below, we discuss various experiments that we conducted to prove model efficacy, robustness and accuracy.

Experiment 1: System Accuracy Comparisons. The first and foremost metric to measure any system efficacy is its accuracy. The aim of our system is to ensure that users can find the required image faster, without the need of any additional scrolling. On an average, most phones support a maximum of around 10–12 images at once (dependent on user selected size and phone size). Thus, we provide a measure of the average number of times the required image appeared in Top-3, Top-5 and Top-10 results in both the systems (Conventional Search and Multi-Modal Search) in Fig. 5. Our results show, that using the additional measure of position and size, we see nearly **20% improvement in Top-5** and 23% improvement in Top-10 results. This additional information, provided by the user inherently when inputting through a 2-D canvas, allows us to refine the results and ensure that the system ranks images with higher accuracy. We believe that such a scored ranking of images is a more cohesive measure than simple temporal ranking of the results. The system is able to intelligently get a better understanding of user needs. The accuracy measures here are highly dependent on the available gallery images. Thus, these numbers will vary with the choice of test data and type of images in the gallery. This can be specifically seen in Table 3, where we tabulate the retrieval accuracies in Top-10 results for 10 random users collected during the personal testing phase (Sect. 4.2). With a difference in gallery, we can see a significant variation in retrieval results. User 2 and User 5 see the most significant gain. Their image galleries had a lot of photos, and an equally large number of similar looking images. Simple category tag returned a huge amount of images and adding the position and size information allowed for better retrieval. User 3 and 8 see minimal improvement by using the proposed system. This can be explained by the fact that their

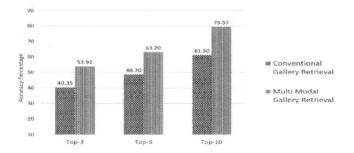

Fig. 5. Top-N accuracy with conventional and proposed gallery search methods

Table 3. Top-10 retrieval accuracies for 10 users in personal testing phase

	User-1	User-2	User-3	User-4	User-5	User-6	User-7	User-8	User-9	User-10
Conventional Gallery Search	68%	57%	85%	64%	52%	62%	73%	91%	81%	79%
Multi-Modal Gallery Search	75%	82%	89%	78%	69%	77%	82%	93%	92%	94%

galleries had limited photos, and a simple keyword tag retrieved the required image, as it was only one of a few of that kind. This is further strengthened by the fact that for User 8, even without using positional information, he was able to retrieve the required image in 91% of the test scenarios. Hence, the average accuracy numbers, calculated over a fixed and decent sized gallery, provide a more reliable measure of the strength brought in by the addition of the proposed features.

Experiment 2: System Efficacy: Spatial Versus Size Variance. Using a sketch based input, one can specify not only the position, but also the relative size of the object more accurately. Complex descriptions, like nearness and perspective, can be very easily specified through simple size variations in the sketches. This same feature, however, is lost when the user chooses to use a handwritten text based input. While the relative positions can still be accurately specified, text is 1-dimensional in nature, with its length dependent on the text length and constant height. To provide a measure of the affect of this loss in size, we compare the Top-N accuracies (average number of times required image appears) when using an only text based input VS an only sketch based input (using the data collected in Sect. 4.2) in Fig. 6. As predicted, we see a slight drop in the retrieval accuracies when moving to a purely text based input. The size variations are often an invaluable metric in a lot of scenarios. Thus, a multi-modal system becomes more crucial. Users can choose to draw/sketch elements that they believe need a higher measure of size specified, and stick to text input for others. We believe that a multi-modal system, like the one proposed here, will provide users the flexibility of choice, thus increasing convenience.

Additionally, as our sketch recognition module is trained on the Quick Draw data set, which collected samples drawn within 20 s, for the purposes of our system the user does not need to draw a perfect rendition of the required object category. A rough sketch, with the bare minimum features, can be recognized accurately and efficiently by the system.

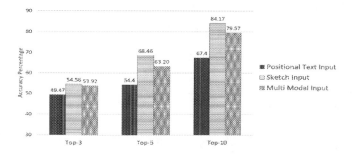

Fig. 6. Top-N accuracy with variation in input mode

Experiment 3: System Convenience. While we see a improvement in the efficiency of obtaining results, it is also important that this improvement is not at the cost of user effort. For mass acceptance, any solution should be convenient and easy to use, and show a significant reduction in user effort. To provide a measure of the same, we estimate two major features: 1. Effort in providing keyword tags and 2. Time spent in inputting the keyword tags. For the purposes of this experiments, we have used the data collected during the personal phase of testing (4.2), to get a more accurate representation of the human effort involved. To provide a measure of the reduction in human effort, we estimate the difference in the average number of keyword input needed before the participant obtained the required result in Top-5 results (Table 5). We choose Top-5 as the main metric of comparison, because that is the minimum number of images returned by any gallery search application. However, for the sake of completion, we also provide the metrics for Top-3 and Top-10 results. As can be seen in the results, we see an ≈ 34% reduction in the average number of keywords that the user needed to input to obtain the required image in Top-5 results. While the number of keywords to be specified is significantly lower, the solution still looses its potency if the effort and time spent in sketching/writing an object is significantly higher than the time it would have taken to scroll through the gallery list. To provide a measure of this, we provide a comprehensive timing analysis in Table 4. In scenario-1, user types/writes the keywords in search bar and scrolls through the retrieved results to select the intended one. In scenario-2, user writes/draws the same keywords in 2-D input canvas and scrolls (if needed) to select the intended result. We further divided the total time taken into two parts, time elapsed in providing input (input time) and time elapsed in retrieval (processing and searching time). The processing time includes segmentation, recognition an retrieval times. While the average input time is comparatively lower in a text input, the average searching time is significantly higher making the process much slower. This gives the proposed approach a huge advantage. As the intended result is generally present in the Top-10 candidates, users do not have to scroll a

Table 4. Time Comparison

Solution	Input Time (s)	Retrieval Time (s)		Total Time (s)
		Processing Time	Searching Time	
Conventional Gallery Search	7.9	0.05	12.6	20.55
Multi Modal Gallery Search	9.2	0.21	6.4	15.81

Table 5. Average Number of Keywords to Retrieve Image in Top-N Candidates

Approach	Top-3	Top-5	Top-10
Conventional Gallery Search	4.12	3.95	3.17
Multi Modal Gallery Search	3.03	2.61	2.14

lot to find their target image. The total searching time sees a significant reduction with the proposed approach (Scenario-2). Thus, our system is able to provide a two-fold benefit to the user. Not only is the number of average keywords needed as an input significantly lower, the positional result ensures that substantial searching time is saved as well.

Experiment 4: System Robustness. One of the bigger bottlenecks of a positional retrieval system is its dependence on the memory of the user. Hazy recollections would lead to inaccurate inputs. Any system, to prove its efficacy, needs to be robust enough to handle such variations in the size and position without a significant fall in accuracies. To provide a measure of this, we provide results from scenarios with a significant distance and size shift between the drawn input and the expected image in Table 6. These cases are a subset of the scenarios collected in Phase-2 of user testing (Sect. 4.2). Our results demonstrate that even with a 60% variation in shift or size, proposed model is able to retrieve the required image. This robustness is a due to the usage of a spatial score in addition to the localization score (Sect. 3.5). The spatial score focuses on the relative positions of the objects, allowing the model to handle human errors of size and position shifts.

Experiment 5: System Precision. Finally, to truly understand the importance of the proposed system, we evaluated two metrics. We define system precision as the average number of cases in which the proposed solution was able to retrieve the result, when the conventional solution was unable to retrieve the required image in the Top-50 results. Searching through 50 images involves a significant amount of scrolling, and we hypothesized that users would refine the search query rather than scroll any further. We see that in nearly 10% (1993 out of 20,000) of the test scenarios, our proposed solution was able to retrieve the required image which conventional systems could not. We also look at the other extreme, i.e. the cases in which the conventional solution performed better than the proposed solution. Temporal ranking in conventional solutions focus on recent photos whereas proposed solution can be overwhelmed by similar photos. This was seen in nearly 2% (527 out of 20,000) cases. However, in such scenarios, the user can provide an additional approximate time information (last week, May etc.) as additional input. We aim at including this feature in future.

Table 6. Variation in Average Top-N accuracy, with percentage size and location shift of keyword

	0–30%	31–60%	> 60%
Top-5	63.20%	62.59%	57.72%
Top-10	79.57%	78.18%	75.51%

Experiment 6: Support for Finer Feature Descriptors. As described in Sect. 3.4, user can choose to provide an additional 'finer feature' descriptor, in addition to the keyword, to further elaborate and refine the result space. This can be an adjective (currently we support colour, texture, luminance and perspective), written beside or inside the corresponding object. Addition of this feature ensured that the required image is retrieved even more accurately. Using this, our system was able to retrieve the required image in the Top-10 result list ≈ 38% more frequently, than without using this feature.

4.4   User Survey

Before starting the testing process, we asked them a few questions regarding the current image retrieval solutions. We also asked them about their comfort with 'sketching' as a method of explaining ideas. The result of this survey is shown in Fig. 7. On an average people found the existing solutions only 40% convenient. 78% participants stated that they regularly used sketches to demonstrate ideas more effectively. We also gave users certain scenarios, and asked them whether they would prefer to sketch the scene or provide a text input. For scenes with finer features, 92% participants preferred to sketch. These numbers, while validating the need of a better content retrieval solution, also prompted us to look at a multi-modal system. At the end of testing, participants were asked to submit another feedback form about their experience and rate the ease and efficiency of solution on a scale of 10. The results (mean and standard deviation) of the interview have been shown in Fig. 8.

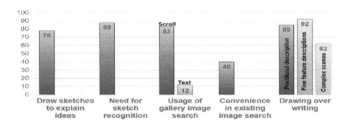

Fig. 7. User Survey : Need for Solution

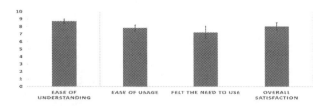

Fig. 8. User Feedback of built solution

5   Conclusion and Future Work

In this work, we propose a end-to-end multi-modal system for a 2-D canvas based input system for easy and efficient gallery image retrieval. Our system allows users to input through a 2-D canvas, rather than a traditional 1-D input. This translates to users being able to provide information of size, shape and location saliently, without any additional effort from their end. Users can provide inherent understanding of perspective and nearness to the system, without the need to form complex sentences that current NLP solutions would be unable to support. Users can choose to type, speak or input through a handwritten text. Our novel, positional content retrieval system returns the required photo faster and with higher accuracy, thus eliminating the need for scrolling. Our results show that users are 22% more likely to get the required image in the Top-5 results, with a $1/3^{rd}$ reduction in human effort. Allowing for easy finer feature description further improves the ease of retrieval. Our proposed system can be built as an addition on any state-of-art content retrieval engines to significantly improve performance. Our hypothesis is validated by the conducted user survey, wherein $\approx 75\%$ participants felt that the solution was need-of-the-hour. In the future, we want to include a scene classification module to our system as well, to further understand the user needs and overcome the errors in sketch recognition. We also want to extend the feature support to include temporal information, thus allowing users more smart control in the way they interact with their devices.

References

1. Song, J., Yu, Q., Song, Y.Z., Xiang, T., Hospedales, T.M.: Deep spatial-semantic attention for fine-grained sketch-based image retrieval. In: IEEE International Conference on Computer Vision (2017)
2. Pang, K., et al.: Generalising fine-grained sketch-based image retrieval. In: Proceedings of the IEEE Conference on Computer Vision and Pattern Recognition, pp. 677–686 (2019)
3. Zheng, L., Wang, S., Liu, Z., Tian, Q.: Packing and padding: coupled multi-index for accurate image retrieval. In: Proceedings of the IEEE Conference on Computer Vision and Pattern Recognition, pp. 1939–1946 (2014)
4. Chatzichristofis, S.A., Boutalis, Y.S.: Fcth: fuzzy color and texture histogram-a low level feature for accurate image retrieval. In: 2008 Ninth International Workshop on Image Analysis for Multimedia Interactive Services, pp. 191–196 (2008)
5. Parcalabescu, L., Frank, A.: Exploring phrase grounding without training: contextualisation and extension to text-based image retrieval. In: Proceedings of the IEEE/CVF Conference on Computer Vision and Pattern Recognition Workshops, pp. 962–963 (2020)
6. Krishnan, A., Rajesh, S., Shylaja, S.S.: Text-based image retrieval using captioning. In: 2021 Fourth International Conference on Electrical, Computer and Communication Technologies (ICECCT), pp. 1–5 (2021)
7. Collomosse, J., Bui, T., Jin, H.: Livesketch: query perturbations for guided sketch-based visual search. In: Proceedings of the IEEE Conference on Computer Vision and Pattern Recognition, pp. 2879–2887 (2019)

8. Dey, S., Riba, P., Dutta, A., Llados, J., Song, Y.Z.: Doodle to search: practical zero-shot sketch-based image retrieval. In: Proceedings of the IEEE Conference on Computer Vision and Pattern Recognition (2019)
9. Deng, C., Xu, X., Wang, H., Yang, M., Tao, D.: Progressive cross-modal semantic network for zero-shot sketch-based image retrieval. IEEE Trans. Image Process. **29**, 8892–8902 (2020)
10. Xu, X., Yang, M., Yang, Y., Wang, H.: Progressive domain-independent feature decomposition network for zero-shot sketch-based image retrieval (2020)
11. Bahlmann, C., Burkhardt, H.: The writer independent online handwriting recognition system frog on hand and cluster generative statistical dynamic time warping. IEEE Trans. Pattern Anal. Mach. Intell. **26**, 299–310 (2004)
12. Khomenko, V., Volkoviy, A., Degtyarenko, I., Radyvonenko, O.: Handwriting text/non-text classification on mobile device. In: Fourth International Conference on Artificial Intelligence and Pattern Recognition (AIPR), pp. 42–49 (2017)
13. Graves, A., Liwicki, M.: A novel connectionist system for unconstrained handwriting recognition. IEEE Trans. Pattern Anal. Mach. Intell. **31**, 855–868 (2008)
14. Sahu, P.P., et al.: Personalized hand writing recognition using continued LSTM training. In: 2017 14th IAPR International Conference on Document Analysis and Recognition (ICDAR), vol. 1. IEEE (2017)
15. Carbune, V., et al.: Fast multi-language LSTM-based online handwriting recognition. Int. J. Doc. Anal. Recogn. (IJDAR) **23**, 1–14 (2020)
16. Bojanowski, P., Grave, E., Joulin, A., Mikolov, T.: Enriching word vectors with subword information. Trans. Assoc. Comput. Linguist. **5**, 135–146 (2017)
17. Ha, D., Eck, D.: A neural representation of sketch drawings. arXiv preprint arXiv:1704.03477 (2017)
18. Kuznetsova, A., et al.: The open images dataset v4: Unified image classification, object detection, and visual relationship detection at scale. arXiv preprint arXiv:1811.00982 (2018)
19. Sun, Z., Wang, C., Zhang, L., Zhang, L.: Free hand-drawn sketch segmentation. In: Fitzgibbon, A., Lazebnik, S., Perona, P., Sato, Y., Schmid, C. (eds.) ECCV 2012. LNCS, vol. 7572, pp. 626–639. Springer, Heidelberg (2012). https://doi.org/10.1007/978-3-642-33718-5_45
20. Liwicki, M., Bunke, H.: IAM-OnDB-an on-line English sentence database acquired from handwritten text on a whiteboard. In: International Conference on Document Analysis and Recognition, pp. 956–961 (2005)

A Segmentation Based Robust Fractional Variational Model for Motion Estimation

Pushpendra Kumar, Muzammil Khan$^{(\boxtimes)}$ (ID), and Nitish Kumar Mahala

Department of Mathematics, Bioinformatics and Computer Applications,
Maulana Azad National Institute of Technology, Bhopal 462003, India
{pkumarfma,mk.193104002}@manit.ac.in

Abstract. In this paper, we introduce a nonlinear robust fractional order variational framework for motion estimation from image sequences (video). Particularly, the presented model provides a generalization of integer order derivative based variational functionals and offers an enhanced robustness against outliers while preserving the discontinuity in the dense flow field. The motion is estimated in the form of optical flow. For this purpose, a level set segmentation based fractional order variational functional composed of a non-quadratic Charbonnier norm and a regularization term is propounded. The non-quadratic Charbonnier norm introduces a noise robust character in the model. The fractional order derivative demonstrates non-locality that makes it competent to deal with discontinuous information about edges and texture. The level set segmentation is carried on the flow field instead of images, which is a union of disjoint and independently moving regions such that each motion region contains objects of equal flow velocity. The resulting fractional order partial differential equations are numerically discretized using Grünwald–Letnikov fractional derivative. The nonlinear formulation is transformed into a linear system which is solved with the help of an efficient numerical technique. The results are evaluated by conducting experiments over a variety of datasets. The accuracy and efficiency of the propounded model is also depicted against recently published works.

Keywords: Charbonnier norm · Fractional derivative · Level set segmentation · Optical flow · Variational methods

1 Introduction

Digital video cameras can work in a broad range of electromagnetic spectrum [16]. Therefore, nowadays, these are used in various fields such as medical field, undersea navigations, security surveillances, transportation sites, space explorations, etc. to record the object activities in the form of image sequences. These image sequences lay out the motion information of the scene. This motion information is a fundamental requirement for various applications such as fire detection, medical image registration, cloud motion prediction, etc. [13, 19, 21]. For these such applications, there arises the need of accurate motion estimation. This motion is generally extracted from image sequences in the form of optical flow. Optical flow is a two dimensional vector field $\boldsymbol{u} = (u, v)^T$, which corresponds to the displacement of the respective pixel between

© The Author(s), under exclusive license to Springer Nature Switzerland AG 2023
D. Gupta et al. (Eds.): CVIP 2022, CCIS 1776, pp. 115–128, 2023.
https://doi.org/10.1007/978-3-031-31407-0_9

the reference and the target image frame [34]. Therefore, optical flow estimation is placed in the category of correspondence problems. There exists a number of methods in the literature which lend themselves to optical flow estimation. However, differential variational methods have come up as the most successful approaches in this direction. This is a result of their straightforward problem formulation, simulation, and accuracy in the estimated results [5,10,38]. These methods use pixel intensity values from all the pixels in the image and minimize the corresponding energy functional. A number of variational methods have been proposed in the literature starting from the pioneering works by Horn & Schunk [18] and Lucas & Kanade [29]. The differential models are developed under two fundamental assumptions (1) brightness constancy assumption (BCA) and (2) smoothness assumption. BCA assumes that the pixel intensity value is constant as it moves between image frames, whereas smoothness assumption tells that in a window neighboring pixels have the same flow vectors. Therefore, an accurate estimation of motion becomes a hard task due to the presence of several factors such as noise, motion blur, large displacements, illumination change, and other outliers [17,37,42,46]. In literature, various models have been presented to address these problems. In order to deal with the problem of illumination change in a scene, Zimmer et al. [46] proposed a robust data term by using HSV color space representation and a constraint normalization scheme. Brox et al. [6] attempted to solve the problem of large motion by combining a descriptor matching algorithm and an energy minimization method. Some of the models such as [5,7,40,41] used convex robust data terms such as Lorentzian, Tukey, Leclerc, and Charbonnier to increase the robustness against outliers and dealt with the problem of large motion. Dong et al. [12] applied a deep learning-based optical flow estimation framework, which provided significantly accurate results. Since deep learning-based optical flow estimation techniques require large volumes of data to train a model properly, whereas the variational methods for optical flow estimation require a very few amount of data to set the model parameter values and still provide satisfactory results for test data [22].

The models presented in [34,39,47] deal with the over-smoothing problem by introducing oriented smoothness constraints that restrict the displacement vector field variations and prevent over-segmentation. The work presented in [3,27,44,45] regularized their models in the estimation by employing a total variational (TV) smoothing term and L_1-norm. Lu et al. [28] introduced an edge preserving optical flow estimation model for nonuniform fluid flow by combining a non-local quadratic data term with a segmentation model. These segmentation models are generally based on active contours. In the applications of image processing, active contours are extensively implemented by using level set segmentation methods due to their high accuracy in boundary detection. In level set segmentation methods, the active contours are presented by the level sets and the evolution of these level sets is executed in accordance with a set of partial differential equations [11]. This segmentation process helps in detecting the topological changes taking place on the boundaries.

All these techniques bound to their dependency upon integer order differentiation. The accuracy of the existing models can be improved by using fractional derivatives. These derivatives are capable to deal with discontinuous functions whereas the integer order derivatives can not [33,35]. Also, the fractional order derivatives possess a non-local character whereas the integer order derivatives do not [22]. Moreover, fractional order derivatives are capable to provide an optimal value for fractional order α which corresponds to a stable solution [25]. A number of fractional derivatives are available in the literature. Some well-known of them are as follows: Marchaud fractional derivative, Grünwald–Letnikov fractional derivative, Riemann-Liouville fractional derivative and Caputo fractional derivative [8, 14, 31, 32].

2   Contribution

This work introduces a nonlinear robust fractional order variational model based on a level set segmentation framework for motion estimation. The presented model is formulated by using a noise robust Charbonnier norm and discontinuity preserving Marchaud fractional derivative. The work is unique in four-folds: (i) It can be reduced to the existing variational models which are based on integer order differentiation. (ii) The presented model employed a level set segmentation framework on the flow field instead of images, which helps in detecting the topological changes taking place on the boundaries. (iii) The non-quadratic Charbonnier norm imparts the ability to increase the robustness of the model in the presence of outliers. (iv) The Marchaud fractional derivative helps in preserving the discontinuities in the flow field such as moving boundaries and edges, and furnishes a flow field which is dense. In order to numerically implement the proposed model, the fractional order partial differential equations are discretized with help of Grünwald-Letnikov fractional derivative. The resulting system of equations is a nonlinear system. An outer fixed point iteration scheme is utilized in transforming this nonlinear system into a linear system of equations, and further solved by using an efficient numerical scheme. The experiments are performed over a variety of datasets. A comparison of the estimated results with ground truth (GT) flow fields and the recently republished works is presented both in qualitative and quantitative forms. The accurate and robust performance of the model is also exhibited in the presence of noise.

The remaining part of the paper is constituted by the forthcoming sections: Sect. 3 immerses itself into the proposed model formulation and its numerical solution implementation. Section 4 demonstrates the experiments along with result discussion. Finally, the conclusion along with future work remarks are described in Sect. 5.

3   Mathematical Formulation of the Proposed Model

3.1   Level Set Segmentation Framework Based Fractional Order Variational Model

We propose an accuracy and robustness enhanced variational model incorporated by the level-set segmentation, Charbonnier norm and Marchaud fractional derivative for estimating optical flow from image sequences as

$$\mathcal{F} = \lambda \mathcal{F}_{dp} + \mathcal{F}_{sc} \tag{1}$$

where, the first and the second terms are the Charbonnier norm based segmented data penalty and smoothness terms, respectively. The mathematical formulations of these are given in the next sections.

3.2   Charbonnier Norm Based Segmented Data Penalty Term

The data penalty term based on Charbonnier norm in optical flow estimation is defined as

$$\mathcal{F}_{dp} = \int_{\mathcal{R}} \psi \left[(\mathcal{I}_t + \nabla \mathcal{I}^T \boldsymbol{w})^2 \right] d\boldsymbol{X} \tag{2}$$

where, $\psi(z^2) = \sqrt{\kappa^2 + z^2}$ represents the Charbonnier norm, z is a variable and $\kappa \in \mathbb{R}^+$ which is chosen in accordance with the model of Bruhn et al. [7].

Let π_0 and π_0^C be the two different regions of an image. Thus, the segmented data penalty term based on Charbonnier norm is given as

$$\mathcal{F}_{dp} = \int_{\pi_0} \sqrt{\kappa^2 + (\mathcal{I}_t + \nabla \mathcal{I}^T \boldsymbol{w})^2} d\boldsymbol{X} + \int_{\pi_0^C} \sqrt{\kappa^2 + (\mathcal{I}_t + \nabla \mathcal{I}^T \boldsymbol{w})^2} d\boldsymbol{X} \tag{3}$$

where, π_0 is a segmented component by $\mathcal{L}_\cup = \mathcal{L}_u \cup \mathcal{L}_v$ and π_0^C is a complement of π_0. Here, $\mathcal{L}_u$ and $\mathcal{L}_v$ denote the level sets or level curves corresponding to the optical flow components u and v, respectively. The level set function corresponding to the level set $\mathcal{L}_u$ is defined as

$$\Lambda(x, y) = \begin{cases} \eta(x, y) > 0 \text{ on } \omega_u \\ \eta(x, y) = 0 \text{ on } \partial \omega_u \\ \eta(x, y) < 0 \text{ on } \omega_u^C \end{cases}$$

where, $\eta(x, y)$ denotes the value of the function and ω_u is the region enclosed by $\mathcal{L}_u$. Similarly, we can consider the level set function corresponding to the $\mathcal{L}_v$. We further simplify the above expression (3) with the help of Heaviside's function $\mathcal{H}$ as

$$\mathcal{F}_{dp} = \int_{\mathcal{R}} \left[\mathcal{H}(\Lambda_\cup) \sqrt{\kappa^2 + (\mathcal{I}_t + \boldsymbol{w}^T \nabla \mathcal{I})^2} + (1 - \mathcal{H}(\Lambda_\cup)) \sqrt{\kappa^2 + (\mathcal{I}_t + \boldsymbol{w}^T \nabla \mathcal{I})^2} \right] d\boldsymbol{X} \tag{4}$$

on simplifying (4), we have

$$\mathcal{F}_{dp} = \int_{\mathcal{R}} \sqrt{\kappa^2 + (\mathcal{I}_t + \boldsymbol{w}^T \nabla \mathcal{I})^2} d\boldsymbol{X} \tag{5}$$

This expression is called the Charbonnier norm based segmented data penalty term.

3.3   Segmented Smoothness Constraint

The level set segmentation based smoothness term is defined as [43]

$$\mathcal{F}_{sc} = \int_{\mathcal{R}} \left[\| \mathcal{D}^\alpha \boldsymbol{w}^T \mathcal{H}_w^{d \frac{1}{2}} \|_F + \| \mathcal{D}^\alpha \boldsymbol{w}^T (I - \mathcal{H}_w^d)^{\frac{1}{2}} \|_F + \vartheta \| \nabla \mathcal{H}_w^T \|_{\mathrm{Col2}} \right] d\boldsymbol{X} \tag{6}$$

where $\boldsymbol{w} = (u, v)^T$ and $\mathcal{D}^\alpha = (\mathcal{D}_x^\alpha, \mathcal{D}_y^\alpha)^T$ denotes the Marchaud fractional order derivative of order $\alpha \in (0, 1)$, $\mathcal{H}_w = (\mathcal{H}(\Lambda_u), \mathcal{H}(\Lambda_v))^T$, I is an identity matrix and $\|.\|_{\mathrm{Col2}}$ represents the sum of L_2-norm of columns in a matrix. This expression segments and locally smoothes the segmented regions on both the flow components u and v. On solving (6), we get

$$\mathcal{F}_{sc} = \int_{\mathcal{R}} \| \mathcal{D}^\alpha \boldsymbol{w}^T \|_F + \vartheta \| \nabla \Lambda_w \delta_w^d \|_{\mathrm{Col2}} d\boldsymbol{X} \tag{7}$$

where, $\Lambda_w = (\Lambda_u, \Lambda_v)^T$ and $\delta_w = (\delta(\Lambda_u), \delta(\Lambda_v))^T$. Here, δ denotes dirac delta function. The expression (7) helps in segmenting the flow field both in horizontal and vertical directions. Thus, the proposed model (1) can be expressed as

$$\mathcal{F} = \int_{\mathcal{R}} \left[\lambda \sqrt{\kappa^2 + (\mathcal{I}_t + \boldsymbol{w}^T \nabla \mathcal{I})^2} + \|\mathcal{D}^\alpha \boldsymbol{w}^T\|_F + \vartheta \|\nabla \Lambda_w \delta_w^d\|_{\mathrm{Col2}} \right] d\boldsymbol{X} \qquad (8)$$

The variational functional as given by (8) is written down as the following system of functionals for determining the optical flow [9]

$$\mathcal{F}(\hat{\boldsymbol{w}}) = \int_{\mathcal{R}} \left[\lambda \sqrt{\kappa^2 + (\mathcal{I}_t + \hat{\boldsymbol{w}}^T \nabla \mathcal{I})^2} + \frac{1}{2\Phi} \|\boldsymbol{w} - \hat{\boldsymbol{w}}\|_2^2 \right] d\boldsymbol{X} \qquad (9)$$

$$\mathcal{F}(\boldsymbol{w}, \Lambda_w) = \int_{\mathcal{R}} \left[\frac{1}{2\Phi} \|\boldsymbol{w} - \hat{\boldsymbol{w}}\|_2^2 + \|\mathcal{D}^\alpha \boldsymbol{w}^T\|_F + \vartheta \|\nabla \Lambda_w \delta_w^d\|_{\mathrm{Col2}} \right] d\boldsymbol{X} \qquad (10)$$

where Φ is a small parameter such that $\hat{\boldsymbol{w}} = (\hat{u}, \hat{v})$ is a close approximation of $\boldsymbol{w} = (u, v)$. The variational functional (9) is to be minimized according to the calculus of variation in variable $\hat{\boldsymbol{w}}$. Hence, we get the following Euler-Lagrange equations

$$\left(\frac{\lambda}{\mathcal{T}} \nabla \mathcal{I} \nabla \mathcal{I}^T + \frac{1}{\Phi} I \right) \hat{\boldsymbol{w}} = \frac{1}{\Phi} \boldsymbol{w} - \frac{\lambda}{\mathcal{T}} \mathcal{I}_t \nabla \mathcal{I} \qquad (11)$$

where $\mathcal{T} = \sqrt{\kappa^2 + (\mathcal{I}_t + \hat{\boldsymbol{w}}^T \nabla \mathcal{I})^2}$. The expression given in (10) is solved according to Chan et al. [43]. For this, we write $\boldsymbol{w} = \boldsymbol{w}^+ \odot \mathcal{H}_w + \boldsymbol{w}^- \odot (1 - \mathcal{H}_w)$. Here, $\odot$ denotes Hadamard product and $\boldsymbol{w}^+$ and $\boldsymbol{w}^-$ are the segmented flow fields inside and outside $\mathcal{L}_w$ while $\boldsymbol{w}^+ = \boldsymbol{w}^-$ on $\mathcal{L}_w$. Thus, the expression (10) can be written as

$$\mathcal{F}(\boldsymbol{w}^+, \boldsymbol{w}^-, \Lambda_w) - \int_{\mathcal{R}} \left[\frac{1}{2\Phi} \|\mathcal{H}_w^{d\frac{1}{2}} (\boldsymbol{w}^+ - \hat{\boldsymbol{w}})\|^2 + \frac{1}{2\Phi} \|(1 - \mathcal{H}_w^d)^{\frac{1}{2}} (\boldsymbol{w}^- - \hat{\boldsymbol{w}})\|^2 \right.$$
$$\left. + \|\mathcal{D}^\alpha \boldsymbol{w}^{+T} \mathcal{H}_w^{d\frac{1}{2}}\|_F + \|\mathcal{D}^\alpha \boldsymbol{w}^{-T} (I - \mathcal{H}_w^d)^{\frac{1}{2}}\|_F + \vartheta \|\nabla \Lambda_w \delta_w^d\|_{\mathrm{Col2}} \right] d\boldsymbol{X} \qquad (12)$$

In order to minimize the above variational functional (12) according to the calculus of variation [30], the following Euler-Lagrange equations are obtained

$$u^+ - \hat{u} = -2\Phi \{ (\mathcal{D}_-^\alpha \mathcal{D}_+^\alpha)^T e \} u^+ \text{ on } \{(x, y) | \Lambda_u(x, y, t) > 0\} \qquad (13)$$

$$u^- - \hat{u} = -2\Phi \{ (\mathcal{D}_-^\alpha \mathcal{D}_+^\alpha)^T e \} u^- \text{ on } \{(x, y) | \Lambda_u(x, y, t) < 0\} \qquad (14)$$

$$\frac{\partial}{\partial t} \Lambda_w(x, y, t) = -\delta_w^d \left[\frac{1}{2\Phi} (\boldsymbol{w}^+ - \hat{\boldsymbol{w}})^d (\boldsymbol{w}^+ - \hat{\boldsymbol{w}}) - \frac{1}{2\Phi} (\boldsymbol{w}^- - \hat{\boldsymbol{w}})^d (\boldsymbol{w}^- - \hat{\boldsymbol{w}}) \right.$$
$$+ diag \{ (\mathcal{D}^\alpha \boldsymbol{w}^+)^T (\mathcal{D}^\alpha \boldsymbol{w}^+) \} - diag \{ (\mathcal{D}^\alpha \boldsymbol{w}^-)^T (\mathcal{D}^\alpha \boldsymbol{w}^-) \}$$
$$\left. - \vartheta \left\{ \nabla^T \left\{ (\nabla \Lambda_w^T) \left(diag(diag((\nabla \Lambda_w^T)^T (\nabla \Lambda_w^T)))^{-\frac{1}{2}} \right) \right\} \right\}^T \right] \qquad (15)$$

where, ∂t denotes the time step in which the level set functions evolve. Similarly, we get a system of equations for v. These equations allow to compute $\boldsymbol{w}^+$ and $\boldsymbol{w}^-$ over the auxiliary flow field $\hat{\boldsymbol{w}}$.

On discretizing the Eqs. (13), (14) and (15) as per the concepts of [32] and [43], we obtain a discretized system of equations for optical flow $w = (u, v)$ estimation in terms of iteration equations as

$$\left(\frac{\lambda}{\mathcal{T}^n}\nabla\mathcal{I}\nabla\mathcal{I}^T + \frac{1}{\Phi}I\right)\hat{w}^n_{i,j} = \frac{1}{\Phi}w^n_{i,j} - \frac{\lambda}{\mathcal{T}^n}\mathcal{I}_t\nabla\mathcal{I} \tag{16}$$

$$w^{+,n+1}_{i,j} = \mathfrak{R}^{-1}\left[\hat{w}^n_{i,j} + 2\Phi\sum_{(\bar{i},\bar{j})\in p(i,j)}\omega^{(\alpha)}_{p_{i,j}}w^{+,n}_{\bar{i},\bar{j}}\right] \tag{17}$$

$$w^{-,n+1}_{i,j} = \mathfrak{R}^{-1}\left[\hat{w}^n_{i,j} + 2\Phi\sum_{(\bar{i},\bar{j})\in p(i,j)}\omega^{(\alpha)}_{p_{i,j}}w^{-,n}_{\bar{i},\bar{j}}\right] \tag{18}$$

$$\begin{aligned}
\Lambda^{n+1}_{w,i,j} = (\mathcal{C}^w)^{-d}&\Big[\Lambda^n_{w,i,j} + (\tau^w)^d\Big\{(\mathcal{C}^w_1)^d\Lambda^n_{w,i+1,j} + (\mathcal{C}^w_2)^d\Lambda^n_{w,i-1,j} + (\mathcal{C}^w_3)^d\Lambda^n_{w,i,j+1}\\
&+ (\mathcal{C}^w_4)^d\Lambda^n_{w,i,j-1}\Big\} + (\vartheta^{-1}\tau^w)^d\Big\{\frac{-1}{2\Phi}(w^{+,n}_{i,j} - \hat{w}_{i,j})^d(w^{+,n}_{i,j} - \hat{w}_{i,j})\\
&+ \frac{1}{2\Phi}(w^{-,n}_{i,j} - \hat{w}_{i,j})^d(w^{-,n}_{i,j} - \hat{w}_{i,j}) - diag\Big((\sum_{k=0}^{W}\omega^{(\alpha)}_k E_x^{-k}w^{+,T})^T\\
&(\sum_{k=0}^{W}\omega^{(\alpha)}_k E_x^{-k}w^{+,T})\Big) + diag\Big((\sum_{k=0}^{W}\omega^{(\alpha)}_k E_x^{-k}w^{-,T})^T(\sum_{k=0}^{W}\omega^{(\alpha)}_k\\
&E_x^{-k}w^{-,T})\Big)\Big\}\Big]
\end{aligned} \tag{19}$$

where, $\mathcal{T}^n = \sqrt{\kappa^2 + (\mathcal{I}_t + \hat{w}^{T,n}_{i,j}\nabla\mathcal{I})^2}$, $\mathfrak{R} = 1 + 2\Phi\sum_{(\bar{i},\bar{j})\in p(i,j)}\omega^{(\alpha)}_{p_{i,j}}$, $\mathcal{C}^{\mathcal{W}} = \sum_{\pi=1}^{4}\mathcal{C}^{\mathcal{W}}_\pi$ for $\mathcal{W} = u$ or v, $\mathcal{C}^w = (\mathcal{C}^u, \mathcal{C}^v)^T$ and $\mathcal{C}^w_l = (\mathcal{C}^u_l, \mathcal{C}^v_l)^T$ for $l = 1, 2, 3, 4$, $\tau^w = (\tau^u, \tau^v)^T$ with $\tau^{\mathcal{W}} = \frac{\Delta t}{h^2}\delta_\epsilon(\Lambda^n_{\mathcal{W},i,j})\vartheta$ for $\mathcal{W} = u$ or v. This system of Eqs. (16)–(19) is nonlinear. Therefore, it is transformed into a linear system by making use of an outer fixed point iteration technique and finally solved to get the optical flow field.

4   Experiments, Results and Discussions

4.1   Datasets

Datasets from different spectrums have been taken in order to analyzed the performance of the presented model. These datasets are as follows:

- **Synthetic dataset:** Venus, Grove, GroveSun [1,2].
- **Underwater dataset:** Tortoise [26].
- **Thermal dataset:** Home [23].
- **Real dataset:** Heart [4].

Figure 1 gives an illustration of the reference frames from the datasets used. The works given in [1,2,4,23,26] provide a detailed information regarding these datasets.

Fig. 1. Reference image frames corresponding to all the datasets.

4.2 Performance Measure

The assessment and comparisons of performance of the presented algorithm with other existing models are carried on in terms of the following error measures which are defined as follows:

- **Average angular error ($\mathcal{AAE}$):**

$$\mathcal{AAE} = \frac{1}{MN} \sum \arccos \left(\frac{u_C u_E + v_C v_E + 1}{\sqrt{u_C^2 + v_C^2 + 1} \sqrt{u_E^2 + v_E^2 + 1}} \right)$$

where, M and N represent the horizontal and vertical dimensions of the image frames, respectively. Here, (u_C, v_C) denotes GT optical flow and (u_E, v_E) represents estimated optical flow [4].

- **Average endpoint error ($\mathcal{AEE}$):**

$$\mathcal{AEE} = \frac{1}{MN} \sum \left| \sqrt{u_E^2 - u_C^2} + \sqrt{v_E^2 - v_C^2} \right| \tag{20}$$

This measure gives the mean value of the euclidean distances between the head of the flow vectors of (u_C, v_C) and (u_E, v_E). This error measure is highly benefitting when $\mathcal{AAE}$ is zero, since it prevents the false predictions of accuracy [36]. The drawback of this measure is that it penalizes large flows strongly.

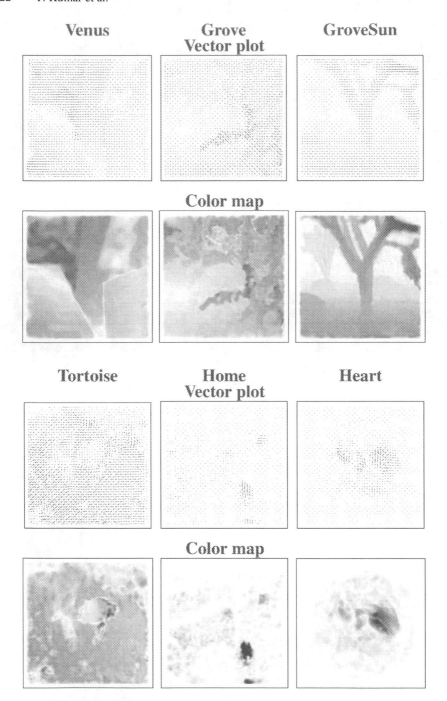

Fig. 2. Optical flow estimation results as vector plots and color maps.

– **Average Error normal to the gradient** $(\mathcal{AENG})$:

$$(\mathcal{AENG})((u_E, v_E)(u_C, v_C)) = \frac{1}{MN}\|((u_E - u_C),(v_E - v_C))(-\partial_y\mathcal{I}, \partial_x\mathcal{I})^T\| \quad (21)$$

This error is aimed at measuring the flow perpendicular to an edge at (x,y). Smaller values of $\mathcal{AENG}$ provide more effectiveness in compensating against aperture problem. The complete details regarding aperture problem are available in [15].

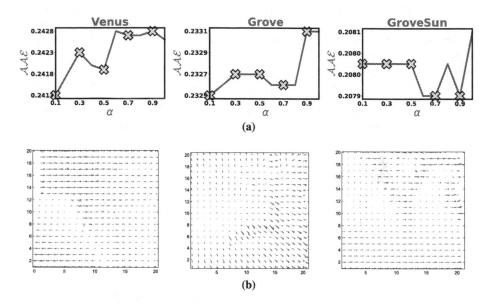

Fig. 3. (a) Changes in value of $\mathcal{AAE}$ as α varies. (b) Overlapping of the vector plots obtained from estimated optical flow (red) and GT flow (blue). (Color figure online)

4.3   Experimental Discussions

MATLAB R2014b is the platform on which all the experimental results have been evaluated. The results have been comprehensively assessed and analyzed, and their comparison with other existing models is also established. In all the experiments, we consider $\vartheta = 10^3$, $\Phi = 10^{-5}$, $\mathcal{N}_{warp} = 5$, $\mathcal{N}_{pyr} = 5$ and $\mathcal{N}_{it} = 10^2$, $\lambda = 500$, and the values of α is chosen corresponding to the optimal solutions as shown in Fig. 3(a). A 5×5 sized window is convolved with image frames and the fractional order derivatives are calculated. Quantitative and qualitative both the forms of the output results have been estimated for all the datasets, and also depicted for the datasets deteriorated by Gaussian noise. Color maps and vector plots are used to represent the results in qualitative form. Different motion directions in optical flow field are denoted by different colors. A manifestation of the accuracy of the proposed model is also implemented by overlapping the estimated vector plot with the corresponding GT vector plot. The quantitative results are illustrated with the help of $\mathcal{AAE}$, $\mathcal{AEE}$ and $\mathcal{AENG}$.

First experiment discusses the estimated qualitative results for all the datasets as shown in Fig. 2. These results in terms of vector plots and color maps depict the fact that the estimated flow field is 100% dense and each segmented region is sufficiently smooth inside each region and preserve the discontinuous information at motion boundaries. In Grove dataset, the minuscule motion details such as tree branches are well-preserved in color map. The vector plot for GroveSun clearly demonstrates the translational motion. The thermal, medical and underwater image sequences are considered based upon their applications in real life such as surveillance, medical diagnosis and robot navigation etc. These datasets suffer from many degradation factors such as noise, low contrast, turbidity, etc. In medical image sequence, a pumping heart shows a divergent motion. The obtained results given in Fig. 2 verify the applicability of the proposed model.

Second experiment demonstrates the relationships between α and AAE corresponding to different datasets through $2D$ plots as described in Fig. 3(a). Here, $\alpha \in (0, 1)$ as per the result stability. The optimal value of α is chosen depending upon the minimum value of AAE corresponding to all the datasets with GT flow. These observations infer a fair validation for the choice of an optimal value of α in the presented model. An overlapping between the estimated and GT vector plots is also provided to visualize the precision in the estimated results. These comparisons clearly exhibit the congruency between the estimated and the ground truth results. Hence,

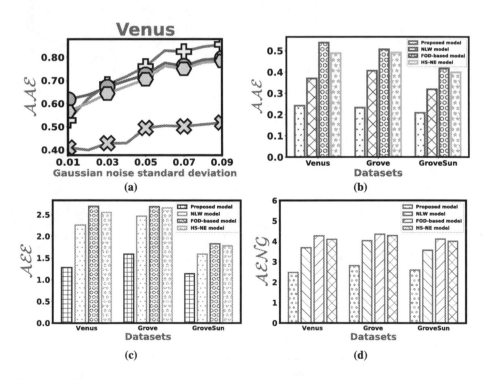

Fig. 4. (a) Effect of Gaussian noise: comparison of the robustness of the proposed model v/s NLW model [20] v/s FOD-based model [10] v/s HS-NE model [24]. (b), (c) and (d) Comparison of results estimated in terms of $\mathcal{AAE}$, $\mathcal{AEE}$ and $\mathcal{AENG}$ from the Proposed model v/s NLW model [20] v/s FOD-based model [10] v/s HS-NE model [24], respectively. (Color figure online)

it is observed that under different conditions the proposed model is capable to generate a decent optical flow field.

Third experiment analyses the robust character of the presented model against Gaussian noise in terms of AAE. In order to carry on this experiment, the image sequences are deteriorated with Gaussian noise of zero mean and different standard deviations. The robustness of the proposed model is depicted through comparisons with some recent techniques such as HS-NE model [24], FOD-based model [10] and NLW model [20] in Fig. 4(a).

Fourth experiment provides a detailed result comparison between the propounded model and the techniques [10,20,24] in Fig. 4(b). It is seen that the presented model produces comparatively better results. Figure 5(a) illustrates the strength of the level set segmentation framework in the proposed model in comparison to the techniques presented in [10,20,24] for Venus image sequence. The estimated results from different techniques for a particular region are denoted by yellow, green and gray color boxes. It is worth mentioning that the proposed model furnishes a very good result with respect to GT flow, whereas the models [10,20,24] either over-smooth the edges or provide false flow. The Fig. 5(b) illustrates an upper gray line pixel row of optical flow inside the gray box region. It is obvious that the presented model demonstrates the superiority of the segmentation technique.

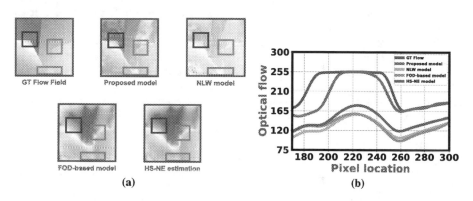

(a)   (b)

Fig. 5. (a) Segmented color map comparison of the proposed model v/s GT flow [2] v/s NLW model [20] v/s FOD-based model [10] v/s HS NE model [24], (b) Optical flow representation along a row of region (gray box) in the estimated results. (Color figure online)

5   Conclusions and Future Work

This work presented a nonlinear fractional order variational model for motion estimation through optical flow. The model is formulated with a level set segmentation framework that incorporates Charbonneir norm and Marchaud fractional order derivative. The level set segmentation process takes place on the flow field instead of images. It can be seen that for different values of fractional order α and κ, the proposed model can be scaled down to integer order variational models. The estimated flow fields are dense, smooth inside each of the segmented region and follow the discontinuous information at motion boundaries. The choice of the optimal fractional order corresponds to the minimum value of AAE. The robustness of the model is shown under the effect of Gaussian noise and compared with the existing techniques. The overlapped vector plot results with the GT flow field depict the accuracy of the proposed model. In future works, this model can be further modified for the applications of image denoising.

Acknowledgements. The authors Pushpendra Kumar and Nitish Kumar Mahala acknowledge the support of NBHM, Mumbai for grant no. 02011/24/2021 NBHM (R.P)/ R&D- II/8669 and the author Muzammil Khan expresses gratitude to MHRD, New Delhi, Government of India.

References

1. http://visual.cs.ucl.ac.uk/pubs/flowconfidence/supp/index.html (2011)
2. Baker, S., Scharstein, D., Lewis, J., Roth, S., Black, M.J., Szeliski, R.: A database and evaluation methodology for optical flow. Int. J. Comput. Vis. **92**(1), 1–31 (2011). https://doi.org/10.1007/s11263-010-0390-2
3. Ballester, C., Garrido, L., Lazcano, V., Caselles, V.: A TV-L1 optical flow method with occlusion detection. In: Pinz, A., Pock, T., Bischof, H., Leberl, F. (eds.) DAGM/OAGM 2012. LNCS, vol. 7476, pp. 31–40. Springer, Heidelberg (2012). https://doi.org/10.1007/978-3-642-32717-9_4
4. Barron, J.L., Fleet, D.J., Beauchemin, S.S.: Performance of optical flow techniques. Int. J. Comput. Vis. **12**(1), 43–77 (1994)
5. Black, M.J., Anandan, P.: The robust estimation of multiple motions: parametric and piecewise-smooth flow fields. Comput. Vis. Image Underst. **63**(1), 75–104 (1996)
6. Brox, T., Bregler, C., Malik, J.: Large displacement optical flow. In: Conference on Computer Vision and Pattern Recognition, pp. 41–48 (2009)
7. Bruhn, A., Weickert, J., Schnörr, C.: Lucas/Kanade meets Horn/Schunck: combining local and global optic flow methods. Int. J. Comput. Vis. **61**(3), 211–231 (2005). https://doi.org/10.1023/B:VISI.0000045324.43199.43
8. Caputo, M.: Linear models of dissipation whose Q is almost frequency independent-2. Geophys. J. Int. **13**(5), 529–539 (1967)
9. Chambolle, A.: An algorithm for total variation minimization and applications. J. Math. Imaging Vis. **20**(1–2), 89–97 (2004). https://doi.org/10.1023/B:JMIV.0000011325.36760.1e
10. Chen, D., Sheng, H., Chen, Y., Xue, D.: Fractional-order variational optical flow model for motion estimation. Philos. Trans. Roy. Soc. A Math. Phys. Eng. Sci. **371**(1990), 20120148 (2013)
11. Cremers, D., Rousson, M., Deriche, R.: A review of statistical approaches to level set segmentation: integrating color, texture, motion and shape. Int. J. Comput. Vis. **72**(2), 195–215 (2007). https://doi.org/10.1007/s11263-006-8711-1
12. Dong, C.Z., Celik, O., Catbas, F.N., OŠBrien, E.J., Taylor, S.: Structural displacement monitoring using deep learning-based full field optical flow methods. Struct. Infrastruct. Eng. **16**(1), 51–71 (2020)
13. Fang, N., Zhan, Z.: High-resolution optical flow and frame-recurrent network for video super-resolution and deblurring. Neurocomputing **489**, 128–138 (2022)
14. Ferrari, F.: Weyl and Marchaud derivatives: a forgotten history. Mathematics **6**(1), 6 (2018)
15. Galvin, B., McCane, B., Novins, K., Mason, D., Mills, S., et al.: Recovering motion fields: an evaluation of eight optical flow algorithms. In: BMVC, vol. 98, pp. 195–204 (1998)
16. Gonzalez, R.C., Woods, R.E.: Digital Image Processing, 4th edn (2018)
17. Guan, L., et al.: Study on displacement estimation in low illumination environment through polarized contrast-enhanced optical flow method for polarization navigation applications. Optik **210**, 164513 (2020)
18. Horn, B.K., Schunck, B.G.: Determining optical flow. Artif. Intell. **17**(1–3), 185–203 (1981)

19. Huang, H., et al.: Cloud motion estimation for short term solar irradiation prediction. In: International Conference on Smart Grid Communications, pp. 696–701 (2013)
20. Huang, Z., Pan, A.: Non-local weighted regularization for optical flow estimation. Optik **208**, 164069 (2020)
21. Jeon, M., Choi, H.S., Lee, J., Kang, M.: Multi-scale prediction for fire detection using convolutional neural network. Fire Technol. **57**(5), 2533–2551 (2021). https://doi.org/10.1007/s10694-021-01132-y
22. Khan, M., Kumar, P.: A nonlinear modeling of fractional order based variational model in optical flow estimation. Optik **261**, 169136 (2022)
23. Kumar, P., Khan, M., Gupta, S.: Development of an IR video surveillance system based on fractional order TV-model. In: 2021 International Conference on Control, Automation, Power and Signal Processing (CAPS), pp. 1–7. IEEE (2021)
24. Kumar, P., Kumar, S.: A modified variational functional for estimating dense and discontinuity preserving optical flow in various spectrum. AEU-Int. J. Electron. Commun. **70**(3), 289–300 (2016)
25. Kumar, P., Kumar, S., Balasubramanian, R.: A fractional order total variation model for the estimation of optical flow. In: Fifth National Conference on Computer Vision, Pattern Recognition, Image Processing and Graphics, pp. 1–4 (2015)
26. Kumar, P., Kumar, S., Balasubramanian, R.: A vision based motion estimation in underwater images. In: International Conference on Advances in Computing, Communications and Informatics, pp. 1179–1184 (2015)
27. Kumar, P., Raman, B.: Motion estimation from image sequences: a fractional order total variation model. In: Raman, B., Kumar, S., Roy, P.P., Sen, D. (eds.) Proceedings of International Conference on Computer Vision and Image Processing. AISC, vol. 460, pp. 297–307. Springer, Singapore (2017). https://doi.org/10.1007/978-981-10-2107-7_27
28. Lu, J., Yang, H., Zhang, Q., Yin, Z.: A field-segmentation-based variational optical flow method for PIV measurements of nonuniform flows. Exp. Fluids **60**(9), 1–17 (2019). https://doi.org/10.1007/s00348-019-2787-1
29. Lucas, B.D., Kanade, T.: An iterative image registration technique with an application to stereo vision. In: 7th International Joint Conference on Artificial Intelligence, pp. 674–679 (1981)
30. Gelfand, I.M., Fomin, S.V.: Calculus of Variations. Dover Publications (2012)
31. Marchaud, A.: Sur les dérivées et sur les différences des fonctions de variables réelles. J. de Mathématiques Pures et Appliquées **6**, 337–426 (1927)
32. Miller, K.S.: Derivatives of noninteger order. Math. Mag. **68**(3), 183–192 (1995)
33. Miller, K.S., Ross, B.: An Introduction to the Fractional Calculus and Fractional Differential Equations. Wiley (1993)
34. Nagel, H.H., Enkelmann, W.: An investigation of smoothness constraints for the estimation of displacement vector fields from image sequences. IEEE Trans. Pattern Anal. Mach. Intell. **5**, 565–593 (1986)
35. Oldham, K., Spanier, J.: The Fractional Calculus Theory and Applications of Differentiation and Integration to Arbitrary Order. Elsevier (1974)
36. Otte, M., Nagel, H.-H.: Optical flow estimation: advances and comparisons. In: Eklundh, J.-O. (ed.) ECCV 1994. LNCS, vol. 800, pp. 49–60. Springer, Heidelberg (1994). https://doi.org/10.1007/3-540-57956-7_5
37. Rao, S., Wang, H., Kashif, R., Rao, F.: Robust optical flow estimation to enhance behavioral research on ants. Digit. Sig. Process. **120**, 103284 (2022)
38. Rinsurongkawong, S., Ekpanyapong, M., Dailey, M.N.: Fire detection for early fire alarm based on optical flow video processing. In: 9th International Conference on Electrical Engineering/Electronics, Computer, Telecommunications and Information Technology, pp. 1–4 (2012)

39. Schnorr, C.: Segmentation of visual motion by minimizing convex non-quadratic functionals. In: 12th International Conference on Pattern Recognition, vol. 1, pp. 661–663 (1994)
40. Senst, T., Eiselein, V., Sikora, T.: Robust local optical flow for feature tracking. IEEE Trans. Circ. Syst. Video Technol. **22**(9), 1377–1387 (2012)
41. Sun, D., Roth, S., Black, M.J.: Secrets of optical flow estimation and their principles. In: Computer Society Conference on Computer Vision and Pattern Recognition, pp. 2432–2439 (2010)
42. Tu, Z., Poppe, R., Veltkamp, R.: Estimating accurate optical flow in the presence of motion blur. J. Electron. Imaging **24**(5), 053018 (2015)
43. Vese, L.A., Chan, T.F.: A multiphase level set framework for image segmentation using the Mumford and Shah model. Int. J. Comput. Vis. **50**(3), 271–293 (2002). https://doi.org/10.1023/A:1020874308076
44. Werlberger, M., Trobin, W., Pock, T., Wedel, A., Cremers, D., Bischof, H.: Anisotropic Huber-L1 optical flow. In: BMVC, vol. 1, p. 3 (2009)
45. Zach, C., Pock, T., Bischof, H.: A duality based approach for realtime TV-L^1 optical flow. In: Hamprecht, F.A., Schnörr, C., Jähne, B. (eds.) DAGM 2007. LNCS, vol. 4713, pp. 214–223. Springer, Heidelberg (2007). https://doi.org/10.1007/978-3-540-74936-3_22
46. Zimmer, H., Bruhn, A., Weickert, J.: Optic flow in harmony. Int. J. Comput. Vis. **93**(3), 368–388 (2011). https://doi.org/10.1007/s11263-011-0422-6
47. Zimmer, H., et al.: Complementary optic flow. In: Cremers, D., Boykov, Y., Blake, A., Schmidt, F.R. (eds.) EMMCVPR 2009. LNCS, vol. 5681, pp. 207–220. Springer, Heidelberg (2009). https://doi.org/10.1007/978-3-642-03641-5_16

FlashGAN: Generating Ambient Images from Flash Photographs

Abdul Wasi[1] , Iktaj Singh Bhinder[1], O. Jeba Shiney[1] ,
Mahesh Krishnananda Prabhu[2], and L. Ramesh Kumar[2(✉)]

[1] Chandigarh University, Mohali, India
[2] Samsung Research Institute, Bangalore, India
{mahesh.kp,ram.kumar}@samsung.com

Abstract. Mobile Cameras capture images deftly in scenarios with ample light and can meticulously highlight even the finest detail from the visible spectrum. However, they perform poorly in low-light setups owing to their sensor size, and so, a flash gets triggered to capture the image better. Photographs taken using a flashlight have artefacts like atypical skin tone, sharp shadow, non-uniform illumination, and specular highlights. This work proposes a conditional generative adversarial network (cGAN) to generate ambient images with uniform illumination from the flash photographs and mitigate other artefacts introduced by the triggered flash. The proposed architecture's generator has a VGG-16 inspired encoder at its core, pipelined with a decoder. A discriminator is employed to classify patches from each image as real or generated and penalize the network accordingly. Experimental results demonstrate that the proposed architecture significantly outperforms the current state-of-the-art, performing even better on facial images with homogenous backgrounds.

Keywords: Conditional Generative Adversarial Network (cGAN) ·
Generator · VGG-16 · Encoder · Decoder · Discriminator

1 Introduction

Since the advent of cameras on mobile phones, there has been an increasing shift in capturing images using them. Attributable to the limited size of their sensors, the resolution and quality of the images captured using mobile cameras are relatively low when compared to professional DSLR cameras. Despite this, these cameras are able to capture the finest details of the objects in evenly-distributed lighting conditions. However, due to hardware constraints, the camera lens and aperture are relatively small and using them to capture images in low-light conditions results in poor quality. As a result, these cameras employ a flashlight to compensate for the low-light conditions. Such photographs, captured using a flash have a number of anomalies induced in them. These include an even and

© The Author(s), under exclusive license to Springer Nature Switzerland AG 2023
D. Gupta et al. (Eds.): CVIP 2022, CCIS 1776, pp. 129–140, 2023.
https://doi.org/10.1007/978-3-031-31407-0_10

unnatural skin tone, shadows that are more sharp than normal, areas overexposed to a flashlight, and specular highlights resulting in a degenerated image [1]. Consequently, reconstructing such images into ambient ones poses a challenge. Prior work done to address this problem involved training a convolutional neural network (CNN) to generate uniformly illuminated portraits from flash images [2]. However, these models have been trained in studio environment with a homogeneous background. As a result, they fail to perform on random day-to-day images captured with flash in uncontrolled environments. Also, even though they perform well under control setups, they fail to successfully reconstruct certain features like the hue of the face and also, have a low peak signal-to-noise ratio.

The dataset used in this research consists of pairs of flash and no-flash images of human faces and an array of other objects captured in an indoor setup with diverse backgrounds, generally 0.5–1.0 s apart, with the source of illumination being indoor lights [3]. The absence of natural light source helps in proper flash exposure of the input images. This work seeks to investigate the prospect of taking the images captured with a flash and using a conditional generative adversarial network (cGAN) to convert them into ambient images that seem to be captured using a uniformly distributed lighting condition. The generator takes a flash image as an input and reconstructs the output image without the flash artifacts. The discriminator takes pairs of the input and target image as inputs and tries to infer if it is the ground truth or a generated image, minimizing the loss function accordingly. Finally, it learns an optimal function to map an input flash image to the desired output image. The output image is then subtracted from the unfiltered flash image to get the uniformly illuminated ambient image.

2 Related Work

This section provides a concise overview of the literature relevant to our problem. Ronneberger *et al.* [4] demonstrate how an encoder-decoder based architecture, trained on a few input images helps generate a corresponding segmented image in the output. The encoder here converts the input images to a lower-dimensional latent space representation from which the decoder generates an output. Isola *et al.* [5] propose a cGAN inspired generic solution to problems where the output image is generated from a paired input image. The authors employ a U-Net and a Markovian discriminator to generate the output images while trying to minimize the GAN loss and the mean absolute error between the target and generated image. Liu *et al.* [6] use coupled GANs based framework for image-to-image translation. Their model is essentially an unsupervised one and performs well on animal and facial image translation, among others. Pertinent to mention is that most of these methods use pairs of aligned images for training purposes. Zhu *et al.* [7] attempted to solve the problem by presenting an architecture that tries to learn a mapping from a source image to the target without depending on paired examples. This method gives good results in photo enhancement, style transfer, etc. Capece *et al.* [2] propose an encoder-decoder based CNN, to be

Fig. 1. Samples of flash and ambient images from the dataset. For pairs of images with faces, the foreground is extracted using MODNet [8].

used for translating pictures captured using flash into portraits with uniform illumination. It uses a dataset of human faces captured in a studio, with and without flash. The encoder part of this model uses the weights of a pre-trained VGG-16 which helps in extracting low-dimensional features from the image. The decoder is symmetric to the encoder and it up-samples the features to generate the output image. In order to minimize the Spatial Information loss, the model further uses skip connections between encoder and decoder layers. Although this architecture mitigates the anomalies introduced by a flash, it fails to regenerate the actual skin tone of the subject. Chávez *et al.* [1] use a conditional GAN to generate uniformly illuminated images from flash ones. Although they are able to generate somewhat uniform skin texture in the output and reduce the effect of flash, their model gives a less score on the structural similarity index measure. This indicates that even though the model removes the abnormalities that come from flash and generate a realistic skin tone, the output image has features that are divergent from normal. Inspired by the above-mentioned work, we propose a conditional GAN which fixes the shortcomings and generates the output with higher accuracy.

3 Methodology

3.1 Dataset

The dataset used in this research is acquired from the Flash and Ambient Illuminations Dataset (FAID) [3]. It consists of 2775 pairs of properly aligned images of People, Shelves, Plants, Toys, Rooms, and Objects captured with and without using a flash, usually 0.5 to 1 s apart (Fig. 1). The images are captured in an artificially illuminated indoor set up so as to give them a proper flash exposure. The images in the FAID dataset are resized to 256 * 256 pixels and split into two sets: the one with facial images and the other with the rest. The dataset of facial images is further reduced to 275 images, removing images with

less light exposure and misaligned flash-no-flash pairs. What follows is the foreground extraction on such images using MODNet [8]. Afterward, the dataset is
augmented to generate a total of 1100 images, 935 of which are used to train
the network and the remaining 165 to test it. The rationale behind removing the
background from images of people is to be able to compare the accuracy with
the previous work that used a uniform studio-like background with such images.
The dataset with the rest of the pictures is used as such, with 300 of its 2000
images used for testing the model and the rest to train it.

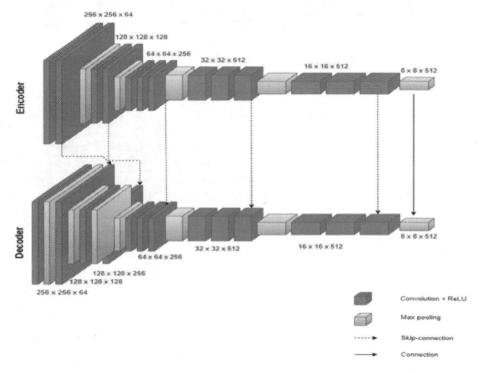

Fig. 2. The encoder-decoder architecture of the generator. The encoder takes a
$256 \times 256 \times 3$ flash filtered image $Bil(I_f)$ as an input, the target being $Bil(I_f)$ - $Bil(I_a)$
normalized in the range $[0, 1]$. It gives I_o as output which is then denormalized in $[-1, 1]$.

3.2 Conditional GAN

A Conditional GAN [9] aids the creation of particular kind of images. It consists
of a Generator and a Discriminator, both of which are fully convolution networks.
In addition to a latent vector, a class label concatenated to it is provided as an
input to the generator. This class label or data from other modalities directs
the generator in terms of the image it is expected to generate. In image-to-
image translation, the encoder-decoder architecture of the generator allows it to

extract high-level features from an input image and construct the output close to the expected one. Afterward, the discriminator takes pairs of input and target images as inputs and tries to determine whether the target image is real or not while trying to minimize the discriminator loss. Here, fake corresponds to the image generated by the generator. The purpose served by a cGAN can be put as follows:

$$\eta_{cGAN}(\theta_G, \theta_D) = T_{a,b}[\log \theta_D(a, b)] + T_{a,c}[\log(1 - \theta_D(a, \theta_G(a, c)))] \tag{1}$$

Here, the generator θ_G works towards minimizing the objective function while the discriminator θ_D tries to maximize it i.e.

$$\theta_G^{res} = \arg \min_{\theta_G} \max_{\theta_D} \eta_{cGAN}(\theta_G, \theta_D) \tag{2}$$

3.3   Training

Problem Encoding. The proposed network may be used to tackle the problem in a variety of ways, the most basic of which is a model that takes a flash image I_f as an input and tries to generate its uniformly illuminated ambient equivalent I_a. The discriminator can then try to distinguish it from the expected output and learn to improvise the same. However, such a setup exhibits a decreased efficiency while learning to decouple details that have a sharp contrast from the surrounding features. The resultant image has visible artifacts and is faintly blurred. In this research, a bilateral filter [10] is used to address this problem. It is essentially a non-linear filter that smoothens an image, doing so without altering the pixel composition of the sharp image edges. Mathematically, the bilateral filter $F_{Bil}[.]$ is defined as:

$$F_{Bil}[Im]_x = \frac{1}{W_x} \sum_{y \epsilon S} K_{\upsilon_s}(||x - y||) K_{\sigma_r}(|Im_x - Im_y|) Im_y \tag{3}$$

where the weighted pixel sum is ensured by W_x given as:

$$W_x = \sum_{y \epsilon S} G_{\sigma_s}(||x - y||) G_{\sigma_r}(|Im_x - Im_y|) \tag{4}$$

For an Image Im, the values of σ_s and σ_r signify the amount of filtering and G_{σ_s} and G_{σ_r} are Gaussian weightings for spatial and range intensity respectively and Im_θ signifies the intensity at pixel θ.

The result is an image whose high-frequency features are replaced with the spatially weighted average of the intensity of its surrounding pixels. The input to the network used in this work is a bilateral flash image $Bil(I_f)$, the target being the difference between the bilateral flash image $Bil(I_f)$ and the filtered no-flash image $Bil(I_a)$, normalized in the range [0, 1] (Fig. 2).

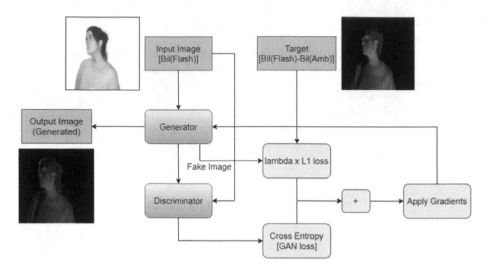

Fig. 3. Training of a generator. Here, the generator output I_o are the generated (fake) images and the L1 loss tries to minimize the difference between I_o and the target $Bil(I_f)$ - $Bil(I_a)$. The discriminator gets as input pairs of the expected and generated images ($Bil(I_f)$ - $Bil(I_a)$ and I_o), both labelled as real and uses the sigmoid cross entropy to distinguish between the two. The gradient tries to minimize both the errors as shown in Eq. (7).

Generator. The generator [9] in this work is essentially an encoder-decoder [11], with its encoder a VGG-16 network [12] and the decoder constructed accordingly. A VGG-16 is composed of 16 layers, the first 13 being the convolution layers that learn features from the input image while periodically downsampling it so that each pixel represents a larger input image context. The rest of the layers are fully connected and primarily, have a role in image classification. Here, the VGG-16 is pre-trained on the ImageNet dataset. We retain the 13 convolution layers of this network, whose weights have been updated in a way that they can classify images with high accuracy. It is called transfer learning. The activation function used is ReLU with the kernels of size 3×3 being used to pool features and a stride value of 1.

After a further convolution operation, a decoder almost symmetric to the encoder is developed. The input to the decoder is essentially this output from the last convolution operation. Here, the aim is to reconstruct the output I_o similar to $Bil(I_f)$ - $Bil(I_a)$. So, the data is upsampled in a way so that at each step, it is symmetric to the corresponding encoding layer. Also, batch normalization is performed so that the output at each layer is a valid input to the next. To make the gradient non-zero, the activation tensor thus obtained goes through LeakyReLU [13], a non-saturating nonlinear activation function. Lastly, skip connections are introduced to address the degradation and vanishing gradient problems as the proposed network has many layers. Pertinent to mention is that the Generator was trained on pairs of images to map its performance without a discriminator, the output of which has been mentioned in the results section (Fig. 3).

Loss Function. This work uses the Adam Optimizer, which is an extension of the stochastic gradient descent to minimise the loss function. Another major objective is to minimize the difference between the low contrast frequencies of $Bil(I_f)$ and $Bil(I_a)$ which we expect to retrieve later. This objective function can be put as:

$$O(p,t) = \frac{4}{3N} \sum_o ((t_o - I_o) + E|I_o - t_o|)^2 \tag{5}$$

where

$$t_o = Bil(I_f) - Bil(I_a) \tag{6}$$

and I_o is the predicted output. This output is then denormalized in the range $[-1, 1]$ and later subtracted from I_f to get the reconstructed ambient image.

While trying to minimize the model loss, using both the mean absolute error $L1$ and the Conditional GAN loss in the ratio of 100:1 gives reasonably good results. Therefore, the combined loss function is given by:

$$\theta_{FlashGAN} = \arg \min_{\theta_G} \max_{\theta_D} \eta_{cGAN}(\theta_G, \theta_D) + \lambda \eta_{L1}(\theta_G) \tag{7}$$

where $\lambda = 100$ and $\eta_{L1}(\theta_G)$ is the L1 loss given as:

$$\eta_{L1}(\theta_G) = T_{a,b,c}[||b - \theta_G(a,b)||_1] \tag{8}$$

Discriminator. A discriminator [14] tries to distinguish an image developed by the generator from the ground truth expected in the output. In this paper, a PatchGAN [15] has been used as a discriminator. As opposed to classifying an entire image, a PatchGAN discriminator convolves on an image and attempts to determine whether each NxN patch in a picture is real or not. In the output, it averages all such responses. Each activation in the output layer is a projection of an area from the input image described by the receptive field [16] R_f. A 70×70 PatchGAN is employed that convolves over each 70×70 patch of the input image of size $256 \times 256 \times 3$. This PatchGAN produces sharp outputs, both spatially and in color. All the ReLUs used are leaky with a slope of 0.2. The given discriminators architecture is:

$$C64 - C128 - C256 - C512$$

where the receptive field increases from four in the output convolution layer to seventy in the first one (C64). This receptive field maps an area from the input image to a final activation.

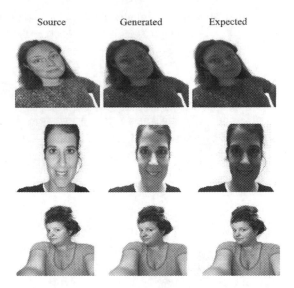

Fig. 4. Results on Segmented facial image dataset

Fig. 5. Results on the generic dataset

4   Results

FlashGAN was trained on pairs of images of resolution 256×256 on an Nvidia GeForce GTX 1050 Ti GPU for about 17 h. At this point, the value of Structural Similarity Index (SSIM) [17] was high indicating that the generated image is highly similar to the ground truth.

Figures 4, 5 and 6 show the output generated from the test images after the training was stopped. The generated images here are the FlashGAN outputs denormalized in the range $[-1, 1]$ and then subtracted from I_f. SSIM and Peak signal-to-noise ratio (PSNR) [18] are the metrics used to evaluate the efficiency of our model. SSIM measures the similarity between the ground truth I_a and the generated image denormalized and subtracted from the flash image $I_f - I_o$.

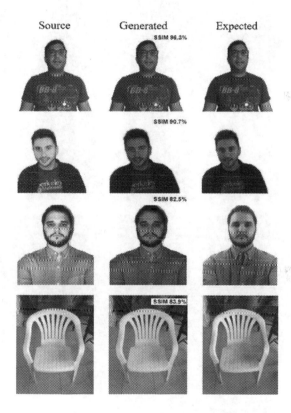

Fig. 6. Generated images along with their SSIM.

Both the segmented and the generic dataset were evaluated individually using the given metrics. The model performed equally well on images with multiple faces. The average SSIM and PSNR value on a sample of 70 images from the test set of facial images is 0.951 and 29.37 dB respectively. On a similar sample for the generic images, these values are 0.926 and 23.18 dB. A high value of PSNR signifies a better-reconstructed output. The results also indicate the proposed model is significantly better than the state-of-the-art as shown in Table 1. In this table, the SSIM and PSNR for FlashGAN is an average on a mixed sample of facial and generic images. Also, when the generator (encoder-decoder) was trained on the same sample, the SSIM and PSNR values obtained were 0.894 and 21.89 dB indicating that pairing it with a discriminator to make an adversarial network significantly improves the overall performance (Fig. 7).

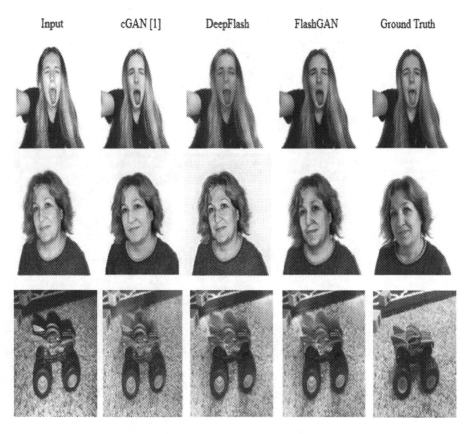

Fig. 7. A comparison between Guided cGAN, DeepFlash and the proposed network (FlashGAN).

Table 1. Mean SSIM and PSNR of DeepFlash [2], guided cGAN by J Chávez [1] and FlashGAN (proposed network).

Method	SSIM	PSNR
DeepFlash	0.8878	20.58 dB
Guided cGAN	0.684	15.67 dB
FlashGAN	0.937	25.14 dB

5 Conclusion and Future Scope

The results achieved by the proposed architecture suggest that conditional GANs outperform the other methods of image-to-image translation. In this work, it was pivotal in reconstructing the overexposed areas, generating the exact skin tone, and removing artifacts from the flash images with high efficiency.

Despite this, the models' accuracy dropped when it was trained without applying a bilateral filter on the input and target images. Filtering the images before they are passed through FlashGAN results in increased complexity. The attempt to reconstruct portrait images with heterogeneous background resulted in a decreased accuracy too. Also, an attempt to generate the ambient image as an output of the decoder (as opposed to I_o, the actual output) resulted in a decreased accuracy. In some cases, a low SSIM score was attributed to misaligned images. Models to address these problems can be part of future work. The model must be further optimized to remove or reconstruct the background without the shadow artifacts generated because of the flash light.

References

1. Chávez, J., Mora, R., Cayllahua-Cahuina, E.: Ambient lighting generation for flash images with guided conditional adversarial networks. arXiv preprint arXiv:1912.08813 (2019)
2. Capece, N., Banterle, F., Cignoni, P., Ganovelli, F., Scopigno, R., Erra, U.: Deep-Flash: turning a flash selfie into a studio portrait. Sig. Process. Image Commun. **77**, 28–39 (2019)
3. Aksoy, Y., et al.: A dataset of flash and ambient illumination pairs from the crowd. In: Ferrari, V., Hebert, M., Sminchisescu, C., Weiss, Y. (eds.) ECCV 2018. LNCS, vol. 11213, pp. 644–660. Springer, Cham (2018). https://doi.org/10.1007/978-3-030-01240-3_39
4. Ronneberger, O., Fischer, P., Brox, T.: U-Net: convolutional networks for biomedical image segmentation. In: Navab, N., Hornegger, J., Wells, W.M., Frangi, A.F. (eds.) MICCAI 2015. LNCS, vol. 9351, pp. 234–241. Springer, Cham (2015). https://doi.org/10.1007/978-3-319-24574-4_28
5. Isola, P., Zhu, J.Y., Zhou, T., Efros, A.A.: Image-to-image translation with conditional adversarial networks. In: Proceedings of the IEEE Conference on Computer Vision and Pattern Recognition, pp. 1125–1134 (2017)
6. Liu, M.Y., Breuel, T., Kautz, J.: Unsupervised image-to-image translation networks. In: Advances in Neural Information Processing Systems, vol. 30 (2017)

7. Zhu, J.Y., Park, T., Isola, P., Efros, A.A.: Unpaired image-to-image translation using cycle-consistent adversarial networks. In: Proceedings of the IEEE International Conference on Computer Vision, pp. 2223–2232 (2017)
8. Ke, Z., Sun, J., Li, K., Yan, Q., Lau, R.W.: MODNet: real-time trimap-free portrait matting via objective decomposition. In: AAAI (2022)
9. Mirza, M., Osindero, S.: Conditional generative adversarial nets. arXiv preprint arXiv:1411.1784 (2014)
10. Elad, M.: On the origin of the bilateral filter and ways to improve it. IEEE Trans. Image Process. **11**(10), 1141–1151 (2002)
11. Zhou, S., Nie, D., Adeli, E., Yin, J., Lian, J., Shen, D.: High-resolution encoder-decoder networks for low-contrast medical image segmentation. IEEE Trans. Image Process. **29**, 461–475 (2019)
12. Simonyan, K., Zisserman, A.: Very deep convolutional networks for large-scale image recognition. arXiv preprint arXiv:1409.1556 (2014)
13. Xu, B., Wang, N., Chen, T., Li, M.: Empirical evaluation of rectified activations in convolutional network. arXiv preprint arXiv:1505.00853 (2015)
14. Goodfellow, I., et al.: Generative adversarial nets. In: Advances in Neural Information Processing Systems, vol. 27 (2014)
15. Li, C., Wand, M.: Precomputed real-time texture synthesis with Markovian generative adversarial networks. In: Leibe, B., Matas, J., Sebe, N., Welling, M. (eds.) ECCV 2016. LNCS, vol. 9907, pp. 702–716. Springer, Cham (2016). https://doi.org/10.1007/978-3-319-46487-9_43
16. Luo, W., Li, Y., Urtasun, R., Zemel, R.: Understanding the effective receptive field in deep convolutional neural networks. In: Advances in Neural Information Processing Systems, vol. 29 (2016)
17. Wang, Z., Bovik, A.C., Sheikh, H.R., Simoncelli, E.P.: Image quality assessment: from error visibility to structural similarity. IEEE Trans. Image Process. **13**(4), 600–612 (2004)
18. Hore, A., Ziou, D.: Image quality metrics: PSNR vs. SSIM. In: 2010 20th International Conference on Pattern Recognition, pp. 2366–2369. IEEE, August 2010

CT Image Synthesis from MR Image Using Edge-Aware Generative Adversarial Network

Jiffy Joseph[1]([envelope]) [ORCID], Rita Prasanth[1], Sebin Abraham Maret[1], P. N. Pournami[1], P. B. Jayaraj[1], and Niyas Puzhakkal[2]

[1] Department of Computer Science and Engineering, National Institute of Technology Calicut, Calicut, Kerala, India
{jiffy_p190037cs,pournamipn,jayarajpb}@nitc.ac.in
[2] Department of Medical Physics, MVR Cancer Centre and Research Institute, Calicut, Kerala, India
niyas.puzhakkal@mvrccri.co

Abstract. Magnetic Resonance Imaging (MRI) and Computed Tomography (CT) are two widely used medical imaging techniques in radiology to form pictures of the anatomy and the human body's physiological processes. Radiotherapy planning requires the use of CT as well as MR images. The high radiation exposure of CT and the cost of acquiring multiple modalities motivate a reliable MRI-to-CT synthesis. The MRI-to-CT synthesiser introduced in this paper implements a deep learning model called Edge-aware Generative Adversarial Network (EaGAN). This model includes edge information into the traditional Generative Adversarial Network (GAN) using the Sobel operator to compute edge maps along two directions. Doing this allows us to focus on the structure of the image and the boundary lines present in the image. Three variants of the EaGAN model are trained and tested. A model called discriminator-induced EaGAN (dEaGAN) that adversarially learns the edge information in the images is proven to generate the best results. It possesses a Mean Absolute Error (MAE) of 67.13HU, a Peak Signal to Noise Ratio (PSNR) of 30.340 dB, and a Structural Similarity Index (SSIM) of 0.969. The proposed model outperforms the state-of-the-art models and generates CT images closer to the ground truth CTs. The synthesised CTs are beneficial in medical diagnostic and treatment purposes to a greater extent.

Keywords: Computed tomography · Generative adversarial network · Image synthesis · Magnetic resonance imaging

1 Introduction

MRI is a tool for imaging human body anatomy; it uses magnetic fields and radio waves to record detailed images of internal structures and soft tissues. On the other hand, a CT scan uses X-rays and is preferred while imaging bones and

© The Author(s), under exclusive license to Springer Nature Switzerland AG 2023
D. Gupta et al. (Eds.): CVIP 2022, CCIS 1776, pp. 141–153, 2023.
https://doi.org/10.1007/978-3-031-31407-0_11

blood vessels and detecting calcification. However, CT scans are more harmful than MRI because of the ionizing X-Rays.

Often CT scans are required in addition to MRI to form an accurate medical diagnosis of the patient. For example, MRI scans do not differentiate a void of air from bone structures, whereas CT distinguishes bones as bright areas and air as dark areas. CT scans are also required to design precise treatment planning for cancer patients. Studies suggest that there is a 1 in 300 chance of getting cancer due to CT scans. The longer-lasting effects of CT scans on patients become a primary concern when diagnosing cancer patients and pregnant patients. An MRI scan is the safer alternative.

CT images are widely used in various medical practices, such as detecting infarction, tumours, and calcification and are also a crucial part of cancer treatment planning. However, the use of CT should be limited due to the risk of radiation exposure. Hence, synthesizing CT images from other modalities, specifically MRI, is crucial. Eventually, the synthesis also helps in MRI-only radiotherapy.

The remainder of the paper is structured as follows; Sect. 2 gives a concise view of the related works, Sect. 3 describes the proposed methodology, Sect. 4 gives the results obtained from the proposed model and comparison with other state-of-the-art methods, and finally, Sect. 5 composed of the summary and future scopes.

2   Related Works

Medical image synthesis has been a well-researched area in the recent past. Many techniques have been developed, including those using atlas maps and random forests. Lee et al. [13] used multi-atlas and multi-channel registration to synthesise CT images from MR images of abnormal tissue regions in the brain, such as tumours. The atlas contains co-registered MR and CT images. A structural similarity measure is used to synthesise CT images from the registered atlas of CT images. Synthesis is further refined by using another multi-channel deformable registration. The remaining erroneous areas are detected using the sum of square differences and are refined using a patch-based synthesis approach with a similarity weighted average.

The performance of atlas-based models is highly dependent on registration accuracy. Techniques based on random forests have also been explored in image synthesis. Huynh et al. [10] used a structured random forest model for CT synthesis from corresponding MRI images of the brain and prostate region. The spatial information is captured by explicitly using a rigid body registration to register the CT images instead of deformable registration, where the spatial information may be lost or corrupted. The feature set of the random forest consists of spatial coordinates of the patch being used, pairwise voxel difference, Haar-like feature, and a Discrete Cosine Transform. This set of features aims to accommodate information about an image at multiple levels. The features mentioned above are applied at multiple resolutions of the original MR image to obtain a final set of features fed into the model. The proposed structured random forest consists of an ensemble model with a median of medians and a mean of median to combine the output from multiple decision trees. An Auto Context Model (ACM) is used to refine the generated images further.

More recent advances in image synthesis have focused on deep learning models, specifically Convolutional Neural Networks (CNNs) and GANs. Bahrami et al. [2] and Chen et al. [5] used the UNet-based CNNs for CT synthesis from pelvic MRI scans by minimising the Mean Absolute Error between the synthetic and ground truth CTs. Specifically, the model used by the former was VGG16 without a fully connected layer paired with a residual network. Both Islam et al. [11] and Florkow et al. [6] used 3D-UNet for MRI-to-CT synthesis. The former efficiently used the model in brain image synthesis, and the latter used it in hip morphology.

A conditional GAN (cGAN) is used by Ziljlstra et al. [21] for synthesising CT images from MRI scans of the lower arm for orthopaedic applications such as segmentation, planning of orthopaedic surgery, and 3D printing. The use of MRI in orthopaedic applications is limited as bones appear as single voids on conventional MRI sequences. The sensitivity of CT to bone density makes it ideal in such applications. The model gives a good result on segmentation only when there is high quality paired dataset. Ang et al. [1] used a composite loss function that incorporates a spatially-correlative map-based loss, L1-loss, and adversarial loss for accurate electron density generated from the MRI voxel values using cGAN. An anorectal MRI-to-CT synthesiser proposed by Bird et al. [4] used cGAN that incorporated a domain-specific loss called focal loss. They obtained a minimal dosimetric difference by employing this loss function. Olberg et al. [15] used a DenseNet-based cGAN to synthesise the CT images from the MRI scans of the abdominal region. The model was enabled by creating a clinically unavailable training set with matching representations of intestinal gas that helps in accurate dosimetry.

Nie et al. [14] used a cGAN to synthesise CT images from the brain and pelvic MRI scans and generate 7T MRI from 3T MRI scans. The author used a Fully Convolutional Neural Network (FCN) as the generator with an additional image-gradient-difference-based loss function to obtain sharper CT images. A long-term residual unit used benefits the convergence of training deep networks. The method proposed in this paper uses a patch-based learning technique; hence, they employ ACM to refine generated images and maintain global context information. The model is trained over a paired set of MR-CT images. The model proposed by Jiangtao et al. [12] is a kind of cGAN called contrastive unpaired translation network (CUT). They introduced the structural similarity and contrast losses to the objective function of the generator. They proved that the model outperforms other state-of-the-art models in the brain MRI-to-CT synthesis task.

CycleGAN is a GAN variant specialising in synthesising images using unpaired training datasets by maintaining cycle consistency. Hiasa et al. [9] used cycleGAN to synthesise CT from MR images of muscles around the thigh, pelvis and femur bones. They used landmark-based registration to align the MR and CT images. The generators of the cycleGAN were CNNs with nine residual blocks. PatchGAN, which applies FCN on every patch, was used as the discriminator. In addition to the cycle consistency loss, this paper also includes an explicit gradient consistency loss function. This loss is a normalised crosscorrelation in both the horizontal and vertical directions of the synthesised and source images. Wolterink et al. [18] also used cycleGAN to create brain CT images from MR images. This cycleGAN differs from those mentioned above in the generator and discriminator architectures. The generators and discriminators are 2D FCNs with nine residual blocks. In addition, the discriminator network classifies the image by first classifying smaller patches of the image and then later combining the results of all the patches. The training of this cycleGAN also differs by having a forward and backward cycle for each epoch, thereby maintaining training stability. Yang et al. [19] used cycleGAN with an additional loss to maintain structural consistency utilising the feature extraction using modality independent neighbourhood descriptor(MIND). They also incorporated a self-attention module to keep the spatial dependencies in the generated CTs. The application of the model to the brain and abdomen produced reasonable synthesis accuracy. CycleGAN is also used for MRI-only treatment planning via CT synthesis in the case of spinal code injuries [3].

This paper employs a deep learning technique to synthesize CT images from MRI images. Specifically, a derivation of the Generative Adversarial Network [7] is used for the synthesis. The proposed model is an Edge-aware GAN (EaGAN) [20] that uses a 2D spatial gradient measurement called Sobel operator to measure and penalize for the error in edge formation in a synthetic image. The Sobel operator loss function ensures sharper edges in the synthetic images.

3   Methodology

The proposed network, detailed below, consists of a generator network based on UNet and a CNN-based discriminator network. The network is trained using paired brain MRI-CT images.

3.1   Data Acquisition and Preprocessing

The dataset consists of the paired MRI-CT scans of 13 patients. Both scans were in DICOM format, with the CT scans in axial view and MRI scans in sagittal view. The preprocessing stages followed are given in Fig. 1. The images in DICOM format are converted into NIfTI format using the software tool Plastimatch. Next, the MR scans in sagittal view are converted into axial view using 3D-Slicer software. The CT images are then masked to remove the artefacts like scanner, bed etc., as shown in Fig. 2. Then, MR scans are registered to the CT scans using rigid registration technique in ImageJ software, specifically, Mattes mutual information algorithm. These images are then converted into patches of size 128 × 128, with each MR patch paired with the corresponding CT patch. Data augmentation techniques are also used to increase the size of the training dataset. Three types of flip augmentations are used; flip with respect to the Y-axis, flip with respect to the X-axis, and flip with respect to the Y-axis, followed by a flip with respect to the X-axis. The MRI and CT values are scaled to a range of $(-1, 1)$ before being given as input to the model.

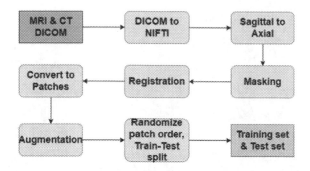

Fig. 1. Preprocessing stages

Fig. 2. Masking procedure; unmasked CT (left), mask to be applied (middle), and masked CT (right)

3.2   EaGAN for MRI-to-CT Synthesis

Generator Networks. The workflow of the proposed EaGAN is represented in Fig. 3. The EaGAN consists of a generator network and an adversarial network that trains separately on the paired MRI-CT data. The source image (MRI) is given as the input to the generator. The generator network trains to generate the target image (CT) and fool the discriminator. The discriminator network trains to distinguish between the synthetic and actual CT images. With time the generator learns to create foolproof images which the discriminator cannot determine. The generator of the EaGAN is a standard UNet architecture illustrated in Fig. 4 [16], which is popularly used for medical image synthesis, particularly in cases where the source modality is different from the target modality. The base model is designed for 2D MR input patches; the output will be the corresponding 2D CT patches. The UNet architecture is built using five convolution blocks and five up-convolution blocks. After each block, the first four convolution blocks have a max-pooling layer with a kernel size 2×2. The block architecture of the UNet is shown in Fig. 5.

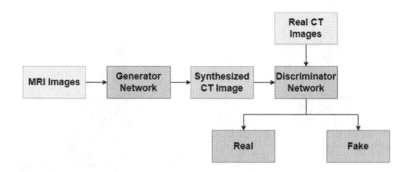

Fig. 3. Workflow of EaGAN

The convolution block consists of two convolution layers followed by batch normalization and a ReLU activation function for each layer. The layer uses a kernel of size 3×3, a stride of 1 and padding of 1. The convolution block takes the number of input and output channels while initializing the network. This block is used in the UNet to increase the number of channels while maintaining the height and width.

The up-convolution block consists of a transpose convolution layer and two convolution layers. Each layer is followed by batch normalization and ReLU activation function. The transpose convolution layer uses a kernel of size 2×2 with a stride of 2, and the convolution layer uses a kernel of size 3×3 with a stride of 1 and padding 1. The transpose convolution layer of the block is used here to halve the number of channels.

The generator loss function L_G defined in Eq. 1 has 3 parts; an L2 loss function L_{L2}, an adversarial loss function L_{adv} (Eq. 2), and an edge detector loss L_{edge} (Eq. 4).

$$L_G = \lambda_{L2}L_{L2} + \lambda_{adv}L_{adv} + \lambda_{edge}L_{edge} \qquad (1)$$

$$L_{adv}(X) = log(1 - D(X, G(X))) \qquad (2)$$

The model also includes a Sobel edge detector S from [20] which uses two Sobel kernels, F_i and F_j since the base model is 2D, for x and y directions. The two kernels are convolved on the image I, and edge maps from both kernels are merged to obtain a final edge map. The computation of the final edge map is given in Eq. 3. The edge map is computed for both synthesised and ground truth

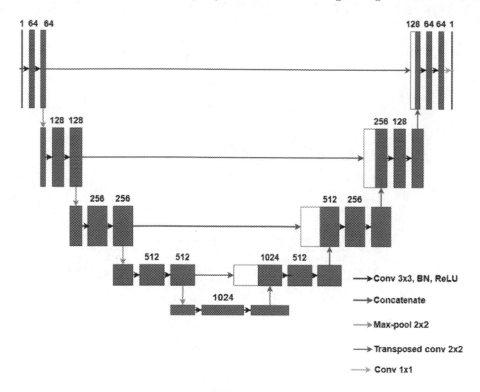

Fig. 4. UNet architecture

patches, and the L1-loss is calculated by comparing the two maps. This loss is added to the loss function of the generator.

$$S(I) = \sqrt{(F_i * I)^2 + (F_j * I)^2} \tag{3}$$

$$L_{edge}(X,Y) = \| S(Y) - S(G(X)) \| \tag{4}$$

The output patch obtained from the generator network is then given to the discriminator network.

Discriminator Network. The discriminator network of the base model is a CNN with three layers of convolution. Each layer is followed by batch normalisation, ReLU activation, and max-pooling. Three fully connected layers follow the final layer of convolution. The first two layers use ReLU activation, and the final layer uses a sigmoid function that outputs the probability of the input being an original CT patch. The convolution layers use kernels of sizes 9, 5, and 5 for each layer with stride 1 and padding 0. The fully connected layers use 512, 64, and 1 as the number of output nodes for the respective layer. The architecture

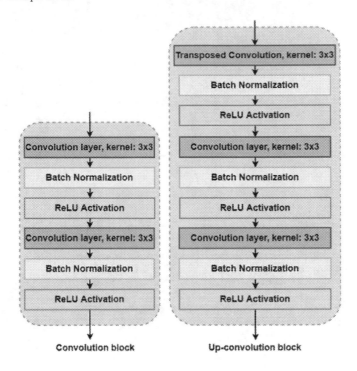

Fig. 5. Block architecture for UNet

of CNN is shown in Fig. 6. The loss function for the discriminator L_D is Binary Cross-Entropy (BCE) loss (Eq. 5).

$$L_D(X, Y) = -log(D(X, Y)) - log(1 - D(X, G(X))) \qquad (5)$$

Two more models are also developed with slight changes in the generator network and discriminator loss function as described below.

Res-UNet Generator. The first model uses a UNet architecture with its standard blocks. In the second model, the competitor for the traditional convolution blocks of the UNet is residual blocks adapted from [8]. Residual blocks have been shown to be superior in many applications. The architecture remains the same except for the generator, where residual convolution blocks are used instead of standard convolution blocks. These differ by having a skip connection from the block's input to the output. The Res-UNet architecture also has its up-convolution blocks, which are used in place of the standard up-convolution blocks of the base model. The rest of the architecture, including the discriminator and the edge detector, remains the same.

Modified Discriminator. In the third model, the discriminator is modified to accept the Sobel edge maps [20]. It allows the GAN to learn the edge information

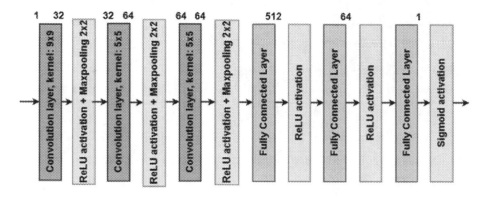

Fig. 6. CNN architecture of discriminator

of the CT adversarially. Such a model is called dEaGAN. The discriminator function now becomes:

$$L_D(X, Y) = -log(D(X, Y, S(Y))) - log(1 - D(X, G(X), S(G(X)))) \quad (6)$$

3.3 Training

Pytorch implementation of the UNet and the discriminator network are used and trained on NVIDIA Tesla V100 32 GB GPU. Models are run for 50 epochs with a batch size of 10 patches, and it takes around 3 h to train a dataset of approximately 2400 batches. The models are trained with Adam Optimizer with a generator learning rate of 10^{-3} and 10^{-4} for the discriminator. The training set consists of patches from 11 patients, while the test set contained patches of 2 patients. The training set contains approximately 25000 patches in total, including augmented patches. The lambda values are tuned manually for each model by observing the model performance for each set of lambdas. The models worked best at lambda values of $\lambda_{L2} = 6$, $\lambda_{Adv} = 0.02$, and $\lambda_{Edge} = 8$.

A model with a modified discriminator to accept Sobel edge maps was also trained using a similar technique. The EaGAN with Res-UNet is made, where the UNet block is replaced with a Res-UNet block and trained in a similar manner as given above.

In addition to the edge-aware networks, models which resemble the state-of-the-art models like Res-UNet [2] and CGAN with Res-UNet [17] were also trained and tested with optimal parameter settings.

4   Results

We used SSIM, PSNR, and MAE values calculated on the corresponding test sets to compare the models. The metrics are computed and averaged over reconstructed slices rather than patches. The reconstructed 512×512 slice is cropped to 384 × 384 slice centred on the initial 512 × 512 slice. The values given in the table below are computed over these 384 × 384 sized slices of predicted and real CT. Results obtained from all the models are furnished in Table 1 and sample image slices and patches are given in Fig. 7 and Fig. 8.

Table 1. Comparison of MAE, PSNR, SSIM values of the models

Model	MAE (HU)	PSNR (dB)	SSIM
dEaGAN (Proposed)	**67.13**	30.340	**0.969**
Normal EaGAN	74.39	**30.556**	0.950
EaGAN with Res-UNet	76.20	30.437	0.969
CGAN with Res-UNet [17]	79.64	29.98	0.928
Res-UNet [2]	79.81	29.90	0.930

The normal EaGAN performs well during testing having good PSNR, SSIM, and MAE values as well as having good quality visually with well-defined edges and structures (Fig. 7(c)). Most of the slices above the nasal cavity region perform well in testing with PSNR and SSIM values ranging from 29–33 and 0.97–0.98, respectively. The slices in the nasal cavity region do not perform on par with the rest. It is primarily due to the much noisier MRI in the nasal cavity region, having less defined structures and higher pixelation of structures. The slices in these regions have PSNR and SSIM values ranging from 26–28 and 0.90–0.94, respectively.

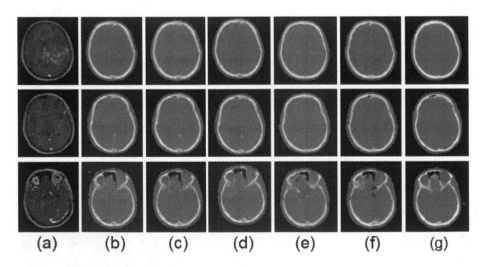

(a)   (b)   (c)   (d)   (e)   (f)   (g)

Fig. 7. Predicted CT for each model. (a) MRI, (b) CT from CGAN with Res-UNet, (c) CT from normal EaGAN, (d) CT from Res-UNet, (e) CT from Res-UNet EaGAN, (f) CT from dEaGAN and (g) ground truth CT

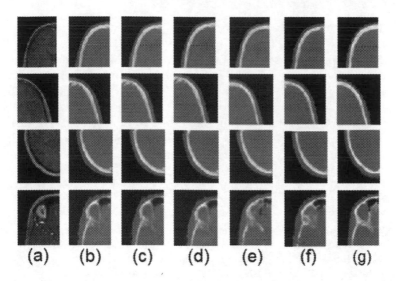

Fig. 8. CT patches from each model. (a) MRI, (b) CT from CGAN with Res-UNet, (c) CT from normal EaGAN, (d) CT from Res-UNet, (e) CT from Res-UNet EaGAN, (f) CT from dEaGAN and (g) ground truth CT

The dEaGAN mentioned in Table 1 is the EaGAN with the modified discriminator and generator. The SSIM and MAE values are better than the normal EaGAN but have slightly lower PSNR. Visually the results of dEaGAN have similar performance to the normal EaGAN except for the nasal region of the test subject, where dEaGAN has slightly blurry results (Fig. 7(f)).

The EaGAN with Res-UNet blocks (Fig. 7(e)) does similar in terms of PSNR, SSIM, and MAE metrics as compared to the normal EaGAN. The visual quality is also on par or better than the normal EaGAN in many regions, having better edges. But, we observed the Res-UNet model bringing more artefacts to some internal structures in the nasal cavity and the bones.

The CT image produced by a simple Res-UNet is given in Fig. 7(d); in this case, all three metrics show poor values compared to the proposed model. Similarly, the results from CGAN with Res-UNet are given in Fig. 7(b). The MAE is higher than normal EaGAN, and the PSNR and SSIM are comparatively lower. The visual quality is similar to the normal EaGAN.

As per our observation, the dEaGAN is a good all-rounder. Though the dEaGAN and the EaGAN with Res-UNet do slightly better than normal EaGAN in many aspects, they also have defects. The predicted images' quality heavily depends on the input MRI and CT; higher quality MRI and CT images (less noisy and higher resolution) can produce better predictions as the networks can learn the structures well. The accuracy of registration is also another essential factor in prediction quality.

5   Conclusion

Medical imaging techniques like MRI and CT play vital roles in disease diagnosis and treatment. The replacement of multimodal imaging with a single imaging modality is cost-effective, time-saving, and helps to avoid harmful radiations from the human body. An edge-aware cGAN is proposed above for synthesising a CT image from an MRI image. From the results obtained from three variants of the EaGAN, dEaGAN appears to perform the best. The model can be improved in the future by using more input data and incorporating ACM.

References

1. Ang, S.P., Phung, S.L., Field, M., Schira, M.M.: An improved deep learning framework for MR-to-CT image synthesis with a new hybrid objective function. In: 2022 IEEE 19th International Symposium on Biomedical Imaging (ISBI), pp. 1–5. IEEE (2022). https://doi.org/10.1109/ISBI52829.2022.9761546
2. Bahrami, A., Karimian, A., Fatemizadeh, E., Arabi, H., Zaidi, H.: A new deep convolutional neural network design with efficient learning capability: application to CT image synthesis from MRI. Med. Phys. **47**(10), 5158–5171 (2020). https://doi.org/10.1002/mp.14418
3. Bajger, M., et al.: Lumbar spine CT synthesis from MR images using CycleGAN-a preliminary study. In: 2021 Digital Image Computing: Techniques and Applications (DICTA), pp. 1–8. IEEE (2021). https://doi.org/10.1109/DICTA52665.2021.9647237
4. Bird, D., et al.: Multicentre, deep learning, synthetic-CT generation for ano-rectal MR-only radiotherapy treatment planning. Radiother. Oncol. **156**, 23–28 (2021). https://doi.org/10.1016/j.radonc.2020.11.027
5. Chen, S., Qin, A., Zhou, D., Yan, D.: U-Net-generated synthetic CT images for magnetic resonance imaging-only prostate intensity-modulated radiation therapy treatment planning. Med. Phys. **45**(12), 5659–5665 (2018)
6. Florkow, M.C., et al.: MRI-based synthetic CT shows equivalence to conventional CT for the morphological assessment of the hip joint. J. Orthop. Res.® **40**(4), 954–964 (2022). https://doi.org/10.1002/jor.25127
7. Goodfellow, I.J., et al.: Generative adversarial nets. In: Advances in Neural Information Processing Systems, vol. 3, pp. 2672–2680, January 2014. https://doi.org/10.3156/jsoft.29.5_177_2
8. He, K., Zhang, X., Ren, S., Sun, J.: Deep residual learning for image recognition. In: Proceedings of the IEEE Computer Society Conference on Computer Vision and Pattern Recognition, December 2016, pp. 770–778 (2016). https://doi.org/10.1109/CVPR.2016.90
9. Hiasa, Y., et al.: Cross-modality image synthesis from unpaired data using Cycle-GAN. In: Gooya, A., Goksel, O., Oguz, I., Burgos, N. (eds.) SASHIMI 2018. LNCS, vol. 11037, pp. 31–41. Springer, Cham (2018). https://doi.org/10.1007/978-3-030-00536-8_4
10. Huynh, T., et al.: Estimating CT image from MRI data using structured random forest and auto-context model. IEEE Trans. Med. Imaging **35**(1), 174–183 (2016). https://doi.org/10.1109/TMI.2015.2461533

11. Islam, K.T., Wijewickrema, S., O'Leary, S.: A deep learning framework for segmenting brain tumors using MRI and synthetically generated CT images. Sensors **22**(2), 523 (2022). https://doi.org/10.3390/s22020523

12. Jiangtao, W., Xinhong, W., Xiao, J., Bing, Y., Lei, Z., Yidong, Y.: MRI to CT synthesis using contrastive learning. In: 2021 IEEE International Conference on Medical Imaging Physics and Engineering (ICMIPE), pp. 1–5. IEEE (2021). https://doi.org/10.1109/ICMIPE53131.2021.9698888

13. Lee, J., Carass, A., Jog, A., Zhao, C., Prince, J.L.: Multi-atlas-based CT synthesis from conventional MRI with patch-based refinement for MRI-based radiotherapy planning. In: Medical Imaging 2017: Image Processing, vol. 10133, p. 101331I. International Society for Optics and Photonics (2017). https://doi.org/10.1117/12.2254571

14. Nie, D., et al.: Medical image synthesis with deep convolutional adversarial networks. IEEE Trans. Biomed. Eng. **65**(12), 2720–2730 (2018). https://doi.org/10.1109/TBME.2018.2814538

15. Olberg, S., et al.: Abdominal synthetic CT reconstruction with intensity projection prior for MRI-only adaptive radiotherapy. Phys. Med. Biol. **66**(20), 204001 (2021). https://doi.org/10.1088/1361-6560/ac279e

16. Ronneberger, O., Fischer, P., Brox, T.: U-Net: convolutional networks for biomedical image segmentation. In: Navab, N., Hornegger, J., Wells, W.M., Frangi, A.F. (eds.) MICCAI 2015. LNCS, vol. 9351, pp. 234–241. Springer, Cham (2015). https://doi.org/10.1007/978-3-319-24574-4_28

17. Tao, L., Fisher, J., Anaya, E., Li, X., Levin, C.S.: Pseudo CT image synthesis and bone segmentation from MR images using adversarial networks with residual blocks for MR-based attenuation correction of brain PET data. IEEE Trans. Radiat. Plasma Med. Sci. **5**(20), 193–201 (2021). https://doi.org/10.1109/trpms.2020.2989073

18. Wolterink, J.M., Dinkla, A.M., Savenije, M.H.F., Seevinck, P.R., van den Berg, C.A.T., Išgum, I.: Deep MR to CT synthesis using unpaired data. In: Tsaftaris, S.A., Gooya, A., Frangi, A.F., Prince, J.L. (eds.) SASHIMI 2017. LNCS, vol. 10557, pp. 14–23. Springer, Cham (2017). https://doi.org/10.1007/978-3-319-68127-6_2

19. Yang, H., et al.: Unsupervised MR-to-CT synthesis using structure-constrained CycleGAN. IEEE Trans. Med. Imaging **39**(12), 4249–4261 (2020). https://doi.org/10.1109/TMI.2020.3015379

20. Yu, B., Zhou, L., Wang, L., Shi, Y., Fripp, J., Bourgeat, P.: Ea-GANs: edge-aware generative adversarial networks for cross-modality MR image synthesis. IEEE Trans. Med. Imaging **38**(7), 1750–1762 (2019). https://doi.org/10.1109/TMI.2019.2895894

21. Zijlstra, F., et al.: CT synthesis from MR images for orthopedic applications in the lower arm using a conditional generative adversarial. arXiv, vol. 10949, p. 109491J. International Society for Optics and Photonics (2019). https://doi.org/10.1117/12.2512857

Modified Scaled-YOLOv4: Soccer Player and Ball Detection for Real Time Implementation

Banoth Thulasya Naik[1]([⊠]) [iD], Mohammad Farukh Hashmi[1] [iD],
and Avinash G. Keskar[2]

[1] Department of Electronics and Communication Engineering, National Institute of Technology, Warangal, India
thulasyramsingh@student.nitw.ac.in, mdfarukh@nitw.ac.in
[2] Department of Electronics and Communication Engineering, Visvesvaraya National Institute of Technology, Nagpur, India
agkeskar@ece.vnit.ac.in

Abstract. Detecting players and the football at the same time is a challenging task in soccer due to the zigzag movements of the players, high velocity of the football, and the passage of the football from one player to another, as well as significant interference between the football and players. Moreover, the diminished pixel resolution of players that are farther away and smaller in the frame in football matches, and the high velocity of the ball, will have a certain impact on the detection accuracy. The major difficulties in deploying player/ball detection networks to embedded devices are the high computation and memory requirements. To address the above mentioned challenges and difficulties, this paper proposes a lightweight network i.e. modified Scaled YOLOv4 for player, referee and ball detection in soccer. The proposed approach demonstrates 0. 938 precision and 0.923 recall in detecting the player/referee/ball and achieved 20.8 FPS with 46.9 ms of inference time on Jetson TX2 Board.

Keywords: Player and Ball Detection · Soccer · YOLOv4 · Jetson TX2

1 Introduction

Sport analysis is gaining popularity around the world and it motivates coaches to reorganize their players' positions or improve their performance by evaluating prior games. The objective of sport analysis can be classified into three categories: player/referee/ball detection, activity categorization, and movement classification. Soccer player, referee and ball detection is a challenging task because of many challenges, which include the complex occlusions to detect events [1, 2], automatic event annotation [3, 4], an unconstrained field environment, background, unpredictable movements to track multiple players [5], unstable camera motion, behavior analysis and extracting the highlights [6, 7], and video summarization [8]. In soccer, detecting the ball aids in the detection and categorization of a variety of ball-related events such as goals, ball possession

© The Author(s), under exclusive license to Springer Nature Switzerland AG 2023
D. Gupta et al. (Eds.): CVIP 2022, CCIS 1776, pp. 154–165, 2023.
https://doi.org/10.1007/978-3-031-31407-0_12

etc. Moreover, it is still an active challenge to detect the ball in soccer sports due to its size, velocity, and irregular motion. A result of a number of difficulties, including unexpected and sudden changes in player motions and similar appearance, players with extreme aspect ratios, and frequent occlusions, detection of players, and assistant referees, semantic scene interpretation in computer vision applications of sports is still progressive research.

2   Literature

In soccer video analysis, identifying the players and the soccer ball is essential. In order to analyze the ball location, Mazzeo et al. [9] experimented with several of feature extraction algorithms. Motion-based player detection using background elimination was presented in [10, 11], while global motion estimation based player action detection in dynamic background was proposed in [12]. These techniques have the drawback of being unable to identify players while they are examined by moving cameras. A comprehensive review of sports video analysis is presented in [13]. Introduced a blob-guided based particle swarm optimization (PSO) approach [14] for player recognition in soccer footage, a two-stage blob identification process was paired with an efficient search method based on PSO. Players under severe occlusion situations were not detected using this method. Yang et al. [15, 16] devised a Bayesian-based multi-dimensional model to generate a probabilistic and identifiable occupancy map for detecting and identifying the player's position. Kamble et al. [17] presented a deep learning-based ball identification and tracking (DLBT) method for soccer videos. This approach detects and classifies background, players, and ball in soccer sport with 87.45% of accuracy.

People outside the playfield and players on the playfield have the same appearance. Earlier methods used a court mask to avoid people detected beyond the playfield, but this approach cannot identify an official (referee) who closely monitors a game to ensure that the rules are obeyed and that any disputes arising from the game are addressed. Therefore, by detecting as the background and eliminating people outside the playfield, the proposed technique efficiently identifies the players, ball, and referee in the playfield.

3   Proposed Methodology

The advantage of Scaled YOLOv4 [18] is the utilization of effective feature layer, as it is analogous to splitting the input frame into grids, with each grid responsible for object identification in the region corresponding to that grid. This grid is then utilized to handle object detection when the center of an object falls within this zone. So, to detect the players, soccer ball, referee, and to eliminate people outside the playfield by detecting as the background without using a court mask, Scaled YOLOv4 network is considered and modified as shown in Fig. 1. As a result, the design is composed of three main components: the backbone, the neck, and the head, which are used for feature extraction, feature fusion, and object identification and classification. The backbone network is a convolution neural network that uses multiple convolutions and pooling to extract feature maps of various sizes from the input image. The neck network integrates the feature maps of different levels with these feature maps of different sizes to gain additional contextual information and decrease information loss. Feature pyramid networks (FPN) and path aggregation networks (PAN) [19] were employed in the fusion process. The FPN structure is used to communicate significant semantic properties from top feature maps to bottom feature maps. Simultaneously, significant localization features are transported from lower to higher feature maps through the PAN framework. The combination of both structures improves the feature fusion performance of the neck subnet. It can be observed that there are two feature fusion layers, each of which generates two scales of new feature maps, $256 \times 256 \times 255$, and $128 \times 128 \times 255$, where 255 denotes the number of channels. The smaller the feature maps are, the larger the portions of the frame that each grid cell in the feature maps refers to. This suggests that the $128 \times 128 \times 255$ feature maps are suitable for detecting large objects, whereas the $256 \times 256 \times 255$ feature maps are suitable for detecting tiny object as 128×128 refers the number of grid cells in a frame which can detects the large objects, where as 256×256 refers the number grid cells in the same frame to detect the tiny objects. The head section in the network conducts object detection and classification using these updated feature maps. YOLO model detect the objects based on the anchor boxes and grid cells.

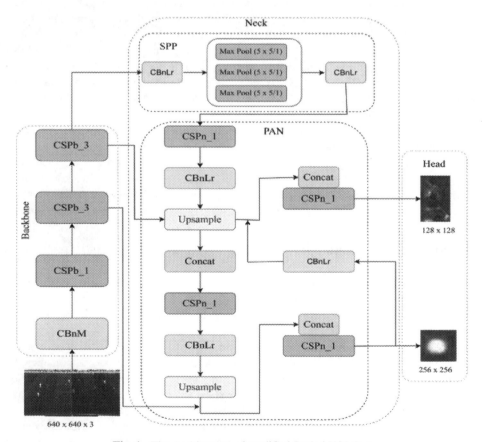

Fig. 1. The Architecture of modified Scaled YOLOv4

The CBnM (convolution + batch normalization + Mish activation) module in the backbone chunks and concatenates images with the purpose of extracting more features while downsampling. Convolution, normalization, and the Leaky relu activation function are all part of the CBnLr module, and in modified Scaled YOLOv4, two types of cross-stage partial networks (CSP) [20] were used. One is utilized in the backbone network as CSPb, while the other is used in the neck as CSPn. The CSP network aims to enhance inference time thereby maintaining precision with significantly reducing the model size by connecting the network's front and back layers via a cross-layer interconnection. The structure of the two types of CSP networks differs quite considerably. The CSP network in the neck employs CBnLr modules to replace the residual units that are present in the backbone's CSP network. Furthermore, spatial pyramid pooling (SPP) performs maximum pooling with various kernel sizes such as 5×5, 9×9, and 13×13 and fuses the features by concatenating them. Whereas, the Concat module in the network performs the concatenation operations on the tensors. By applying dimensionality reduction (downsampling) techniques to represent image features at a higher level of abstraction, the input feature map is primarily compressed.

Objectness Loss: The coordinate loss term trains the network to predict a better box, while the objectness loss term instructs it to predict a precise IOU (As a result, the IoU tries to reach 1.0).

Generalized IoU is defined as [21]

$$\text{GIoU Loss: IoU} - \frac{\left| \frac{C}{A \cap B} \right|}{|C|} \tag{1}$$

where C is the tiny convex hull that encloses A and B and A is the predicted bounding box, B is the ground truth bounding box as shown in Fig. 2.

The architecture contains 232 convolution layers with with total parameters of 7254609, and a batch normalization (Bn) layer and a mish activation layer connect each convolution layer. Additionally, leaky-ReLU is used in place of all activation functions throughout the architecture, which involves less computation and the size of weight file is 43.7 MB. Whereas, Scaled YOLOv4 contains a total of 334 layers.

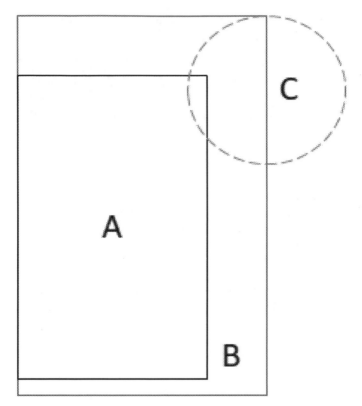

Fig. 2. Representation of GIoU loss using bounding boxes.

4   Dataset and Experimentation

Since a dedicated dataset was not available, the ISSIA dataset [22] by adding classes for the player, soccer ball, referee, and playfield background. The desired dataset was prepared by considering around 7500 frames in which contains soccer ball from six videos of ISSIA databases as shown in Fig. 3.

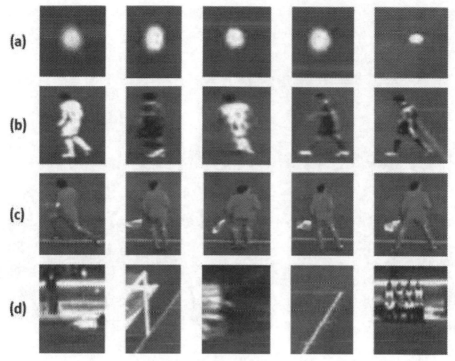

Fig. 3. Examples from the updated ISSIA dataset include a) soccer ball, b) player, c) referee, and d) background.

Google Colab was used to train the detection and classification model, which has 27.3 GB of RAM and a Tesla P100-PCIE-16GB GPU, and finally, the testing phase was performed both on the Google Colab and Jetson TX2 evaluation board. The experimental setup and real-time player/referee/ball detection on the Jetson TX2 evaluation board was shown in Fig. 4.

Fig. 4. Testing Setup on Jetson TX2 Board

5   Real-Time Implementation and Results

In this section, the performance of the proposed algorithm for soccer player, referee, and ball detection is demonstrated using the ISSIA dataset.

The training and validation results of detection and classification of players, referee, soccer ball, and background were measured in terms of precision of 0.938 and recall of 0.923 with 34.48 FPS which were shown in Table 1 and graphical representation of performance measures and loss functions were shown in Fig. 5 and Fig. 6. Fig. 7 depicts the suggested detection algorithm, which recognizes four classes (player, soccer ball, referee, and background). In this section, the performance of the proposed algorithm for soccer player, referee, and ball detection is demonstrated using the ISSIA dataset.

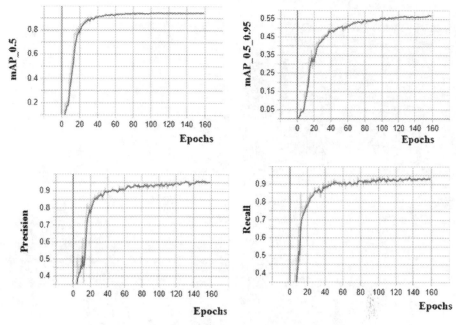

Fig. 5. Graphical representation of performance metrics

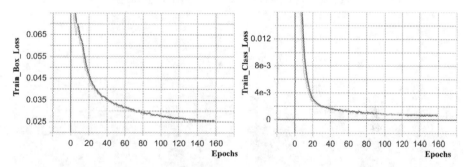

Fig. 6. Graphical representation of bounding box and class loss

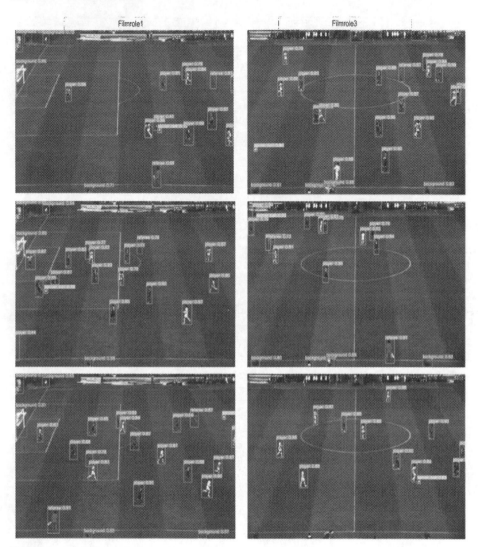

Fig. 7. Detection and classification results of player, referee, soccer ball, and background from two filmroles of ISSIA dataset.

Table 1. Training and validation measures of proposed methodology

Class	Precision	Recall	mAP@0.5	mAP@.5:.95
Background	0.924	0.865	0.879	0.443
Player	0.944	0.95	0.972	0.67
Referee	0.954	0.965	0.971	0.668
Ball	0.931	0.913	0.952	0.49
Average	**0.938**	**0.923**	**0.943**	**0.56**

5.1 Real-Time Testing Results on Jetson TX2

Proposed detection and classification algorithm was implemented on Jetson TX2 board. One of the most important components of deploying a deep neural network in a commercial environment is the architecture latency. The most of real-world applications requires fast inference time, which can be from a few milliseconds to one second. Therefore, the methodology was tested on two filmroles (filmrole1 and filmrole 3) of ISSIA dataset as shown in Fig. 8. And achieved 20.8 FPS on the frame resolution of 640 × 640 with 46.9 ms of inference time which is encircled in yellow colour as shown in Fig. 9.

Fig. 8. Player, referee, soccer ball, and background detection and classification results on Jetson TX2 Board.

Fig. 9. Total inference time taken to detect players, soccer ball, and referee using proposed methodology on Jetson TX2 Board.

6 Conclusion and Future Scope

This paper has presented a lightweight network for real-time implementation of player, soccer ball, referee, and background detection in soccer sport. The algorithm detected the peoples outside the playfield as background, which improved the performance of detecting the players, soccer ball, and referees on the playfield. The proposed approach demonstrates 97.8% precision and 98.1% recall in detecting the player/referee/ball and achieved 20.8 FPS with 46.9 ms of inference time on Jetson TX2 Board. The limitation of the proposed algorithm is that the tiny white spots (such as players shoes, far view of the flag etc.) detects as soccer ball.

In future work, in addition to addressing the above limitations, the proposed methodology is deployed in other low-edge devices such as PYNQ board, Jetson Nano etc., while other methods are considered to optimize the proposed method to enhance scalability.

References

1. D'Orazio, T., et al.: An investigation into the feasibility of real-time soccer offside detection from a multiple camera system. IEEE Trans. Circ. Syst. Video Technol. **19**(12), 1804–1818 (2009)
2. Tavassolipour, M., Karimian, M., Kasaei, S.: Event detection and summarization in soccer videos using Bayesian network and copula. IEEE Trans. Circ. Syst. Video Technol. **24**(2), 291–304 (2013)
3. Tjondronegoro, D.W., Chen, Y.P.P.: Knowledge-discounted event detection in sports video. IEEE Trans. Syst. Man Cybern.-Part A Syst. Hum. **40**(5), 1009–1024 (2010)

4. Xu, C., Wang, J., Hanqing, L., Zhang, Y.: A novel framework for semantic annotation and personalized retrieval of sports video. IEEE Trans. Multimedia **10**(3), 421–436 (2008)
5. Baysal, S., Duygulu, P.: Sentioscope: a soccer player tracking system using model field particles. IEEE Trans. Circ. Syst. Video Technol. **26**(7), 1350–1362 (2015)
6. Zhu, G., Huang, Q., Changsheng, X., Xing, L., Gao, W., Yao, H.: Human behavior analysis for highlight ranking in broadcast racket sports video. IEEE Trans. Multimedia **9**(6), 1167–1182 (2007)
7. Kolekar, M.H., Sengupta, S.: Bayesian network-based customized highlight generation for broadcast soccer videos. IEEE Trans. Broadcast. **61**(2), 195–209 (2015)
8. Chen, F., Delannay, D., De Vleeschouwer, C.: An autonomous framework to produce and distribute personalized team-sport video summaries: a basketball case study. IEEE Trans. Multimedia **13**(6), 1381–1394 (2011)
9. Mazzeo, P.L., Leo, M., Spagnolo, P., Nitti, M.: Soccer ball detection by comparing different feature extraction methodologies. Adv. Artif. Intell. **2012**, 1–12 (2012)
10. Martín, R., Martínez, J.M.: A semi-supervised system for players detection and tracking in multi-camera soccer videos. Multimedia Tools Appl. **73**(3), 1617–1642 (2013)
11. Laborda, M.A.M., Moreno, E.F.T., del Rincón, J.M., Jaraba, J.E.H.: Real-time GPU color-based segmentation of football players. J. RealTime Image Process. **7**(4), 267–279 (2012)
12. Li, H., Tang, J., Si, W., Zhang, Y., Lin, S.: Automatic detection and analysis of player action in moving background sports video sequences. IEEE Trans. Circ. Syst. Video Technol. **20**(3), 351–364 (2009)
13. Naik, B.T., Hashmi, M.F., Bokde, N.D.: A comprehensive review of computer vision in sports: open issues, future trends and research directions. Appl. Sci. **12**(9), 4429 (2022). https://doi.org/10.3390/app12094429M
14. Manafifard, M., Ebadi, H., Moghaddam, H.A.: Appearance-based multiple hypothesis tracking: application to soccer broadcast videos analysis. Sig. Process. Image Commun. **55**, 157–170 (2017)
15. Yang, Y., Zhang, R., Wu, W., Peng, Y., Xu, M.: Multi-camera sports players 3D localization with identification reasoning. In: Proceedings of the 25th International Conference on Pattern Recognition (ICPR), pp. 4497–4504 (2021)
16. Yang, Y., Xu, M., Wu, W., Zhang, R., Peng, Y.: 3D multiview basketball players detection and localization based on probabilistic occupancy. In: Proceedings Digital Image Computing, Techniques and Applications (DICTA), pp. 1–8 (2018)
17. Kamble, P.R., Keskar, A.G., Bhurchandi, K.M.: A deep learning ball tracking system in soccer videos. Opto-Electron. Rev. **27**(1), 58–69 (2019)
18. Wang, C.Y., Bochkovskiy, A., Liao, H.Y.M.: Scaled-yolov4: scaling cross stage partial network. In: Proceedings of the IEEE/CVF Conference on Computer Vision and Pattern Recognition, pp. 13029–13038 (2021)
19. Liu, S., Qi, L., Qin, H., Shi, J., Jia, J.: Path aggregation network for instance segmentation. In: Proceedings of the IEEE/CVF Conference Computer Vision Pattern Recognition, pp. 8759–8768 (2018)
20. Wang, C.Y., Liao, H.Y.M., Wu, Y.H., Chen, P.Y., Hsieh, J.W., Yeh, I.H.: CSPNet: a new backbone that can enhance learning capability of CNN. In: Proceedings of the IEEE/CVF Conference Computer Vision Pattern Recognition Workshops (CVPRW), pp. 390–391 (2020)
21. Rezatofighi, H., Tsoi, N., Gwak, J., Sadeghian, A., Reid, I., Savarese, S.: Generalized intersection over union: a metric and a loss for bounding box regression. In: Proceedings of the IEEE/CVF Conference on Computer Vision and Pattern Recognition, pp. 658–666 (2019)
22. D'Orazio, T., Leo, M., Mosca, N., Spagnolo, P., Mazzeo, P.L: A semi-automatic system for ground truth generation of soccer video sequences. In: Proceedings 6th IEEE International Conference on Advanced Video and Signal Based Surveillance, pp. 559–564 (2009)

CandidNet: A Novel Framework for Candid Moments Detection

Gaurav Ramola$^{(\boxtimes)}$, Nikhar Maheshwari, and Sudha Velusamy

Samsung R&D Institute, Bengaluru, India
gauravramola007@gmail.com

Abstract. Candid photography is a relatively recent trend among both professional and amateur photographers. However, capturing decisive candid moments with a natural head pose, body pose, eye gaze, facial expressions, human-object interactions, and background understanding is not a trivial task. It requires the timing and intuition of a professional photographer to capture fleeting moments. We propose a novel and real-time framework for detecting a candid moment in this work. The method includes a two-stream network, namely, Attribute Network and Visual Embedder Network. The former network stream collaboratively learns high-level semantic features from the candid feature pool and the latter network stream focuses on learning visual image features. Lastly, we have extended our solution, by fine-tuning CandidNet, to output candid scores for frames in the range 0 to 4 (0: non-candid; 4: extreme candid). The scoring mechanism allows us to compare images based on their candidness. A detailed ablation study conducted on the proposed framework with various configurations proves the efficacy of the method with a classification accuracy of 92% on CELEBA-HQ [16] and 94% on CANDID-SCORE [13]. With a high processing speed, the proposed solution is suitable for real-time applications like candid moment indication to the user in-camera preview. First-in-the-market, the solutionis being deployed on the Samsung Galaxy S22 flagship phone as part of the Single Take Photo application.

Keywords: Candid Moment · Feature Disentanglement · Local Features · Global Features

1 Introduction

With the increased ease of access to smartphones, digital photography today has advanced from being an art practiced by professional photographers to the everyday activity of many amateur photographers using regular smartphone cameras. This has led to a considerable volume of digital multimedia content being captured and shared on various social networking platforms like Instagram, Facebook, and Twitter. Users' demand for a simple point-and-shoot solution that can capture visually stunning photographs has created immense research and commercial opportunity in the field of computational photography. Compute power

Fig. 1. Illustration of Traditional Vs Candid frame selection from a scenes [2]

and advanced camera hardware available to the general population through smartphones are now being leveraged to elevate an amateur photographer to the levels of a seasoned photographer.

While there are various kinds of shots like Selfie, Groupie, etc., that trend and gain popularity from time to time on popular media platforms, 'Candid' photographs are among the most perennial, with over 10 million photos being tagged on Instagram every week. The defining aspect of a photograph that is termed 'Candid' is that it has been captured without creating a posed appearance, which makes it look natural. Natural human characteristics like expressions, gaze, head pose, body pose, and interactions are the highlighting features of candidness.

The popularity of candid pictures has been attributed to observers feeling more connected with the subject present in the photograph. The absence of pose makes the subject seem more genuine or real [3]. However, the fact that a candid image needs to capture natural and fleeting moments poses the greatest challenge for any photographer. Professional Photographers with years of experience have honed their skills and the art of timing such moments. However, the same cannot be expected from amateur photographers and everyday smartphone users. This created a space to engineer an automated solution for smartphone photographers to enable them to capture good quality candid photographs of interesting moments in a single click. With growing interest in smartphone photography, there have been many automated applications like 'Smile shot' to aid the users to capture traditional smiling moments with ease. The proposed solution here is one such an advanced application that automatically understands different factors of candidness and help the users to get perfect candid moments. To our knowledge, very minimal research work exists to this end. We discuss some of these works in the next section. Upon analyzing a large set of images tagged with hashtags like #candid on Instagram like photo-sharing platforms, we determined the primary characteristics of photographs that defines the candidness of an image. We clubbed the factors, namely, eye-gaze, head pose, body pose, and expressions, into our attribute list, and call this candid feature pool. The attributes in candid feature pool are the ones that metrically differ the most between traditionally captured photos and candid captures. Figure 1) highlights the differences between a set of photos selected based on traditional photo selection parameters versus candid parameters, on a set of frames captured during a single photo session for relative comparisons.

We propose a novel framework with two streams, one for learning the candid feature pool and the other for learning the semantics of candid pictures through scene understanding. Our accuracy results, presented in a later section, prove the efficacy of the proposed image candidness prediction technique. Being a real-time solution makes it highly suitable for deployment on smartphone devices

We summarize our contributions as follows:

1. A novel framework design for the problem of image candidness prediction.
2. Low-latency, high accuracy network architecture design that utilizes both, high-level image semantics as well as low-level visual features.
3. Customization of the candid solution to suit various smartphone applications on camera preview and gallery.

2   Related Work

Prior work in image aesthetics mostly deals with identifying a good image by scoring them based on parameters like exposure, composition, clarity, and other semantic variables like smile intensity and blink. This kind of aesthetic analysis has evolved drastically in recent times, and this section briefly tracks the various advances in research and commercialization in this field. Automated aesthetic analysis of photographic images in [8] analyses the frames with respect to capture parameters like sharpness, depth, clarity, tone, and colorfulness. Many of the initial commercial applications like Adobe Moments [3] made use of such an analysis. The work presented in [10] made use of expressions, specifically smile, as a parameter to score a sequence of shots of a group of people. This kind of aesthetic evaluation of shots became more sophisticated and started taking into account several other expressions, as well as artifacts in the images like blink and red-eye. Samsung's Best Photo [7] and Google's Top Shot [6] are two of the most popular aesthetic engines deploying such an approach to score and select frames. There has been growing interest in context-aware photography, and candid photography is related to this approach as context plays a very important role in determining a shot's candidness. Candid portrait selection from video [13] describes a method where the authors have made use of temporal context by taking into account frames before and after the frame being evaluated i.e., blanket frames. This research suggests that candidness is associated with suddenness, and thus, taking into account blanket frames makes it easier to zero down on exact candid moment. However, this approach is computationally expensive as for a desired high-quality output, the entire video needs to be captured and processed in high definition and hence, is less viable for commercial purposes. The other way to take temporal context into account is by taking burst shot captures as is done in various successful commercial products like ProCamera [1], where the creators have made a compromise between complete temporal context, quality of frames captured, and commercial feasibility. The other approach towards a better scene understanding is using spatial context where an aesthetic and semantic analysis of frame background and foreground is used to determine attributes like the attractiveness of a frame. Google Clips [5] is one such product that uses this approach to capture the important moments from a sequence of shots.

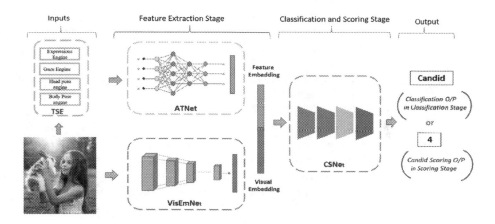

Fig. 2. An Overall Illustration of CandidNet.

3   Model Architecture

We propose a Deep Learning architecture, CandidNet, comprising two streams: a) Attribute Network (ATNet) that explicitly learns high-level candidness characteristics directly from the candid-feature pool. b) Visual Embedding Network (VisEmNet), which learns low-level visual image features from the input image. To predict an image's candidness score, we concatenate the feature maps from these two streams and feed them to the final Candidness Scoring Network (CSNet). A pictorial flow diagram of the proposed CandidNet is shown in Fig. 2. We performed a detailed analysis of 2000 images tagged as Candid from Instagram, Twitter, and Tumblr to manually analyze the objective visual characteristics responsible for an image's candidness. We noticed that eye gaze, head pose, body pose, and expressions were the factors that contribute most to an image's candidness. Hence we added these features to our attribute list, candid feature pool.

Task Specific Engines (TSEs). The attribute values for the candid feature pool are extracted from images using the basic human attribute engines already present in the Samsung camera pipeline. These human attribute engines are referred to as Task-Specific Engines (TSEs). We have used TSEs as they are already well-optimized for their relevant tasks. Furthermore, training a new network to predict all of these would have required a large database, annotated with all these attributes. Using TSEs to extract information for the candid feature pool enabled us to make CandidNet a computationally light model, increasing its portability to real-time applications.

Attribute Network (ATNet). The outputs from the TSEs are concatenated to form a candid feature pool, which is subsequently fed as input to the ATNet. The role of ATNet, a 3-layer fully connected network, is to capture the local context of the image by mapping the candid feature pool to a 256-dimensional feature vector, Attribute Embedding, which carries meaningful semantic and structural information beneficial for the task of candid moment detection.

Visual Embedder Network (VisEmNet). The candid feature pool is very limited to human subjects and does not take into account human-object interactions and foreground-background understanding. From our analysis, we found out that these global features also played a major role in determining the candidness of the shot. VisEmNet is a convolutional neural network (CNN) that is trained to extract the visual image features capturing the global context of the scene. The output of this network is a 256-dimensional vector, Visual Embedding, which represents the global context that will aid the network in making candidness predictions for an image. Due to the superior performance of MobileNet techniques, MobileNetV2 [19] is used as a backbone network for implementing VisEmNet.

Candidness Scoring Network (CSNet). CSNet takes in a 512-dimensional input vector composed by concatenating Attribute Embedding (256d) and Visual Embedding (256d). Since CSNet works on previously learned features, we have kept it to be a shallow network with 4 fully-connected layers, each followed by Batch Norm [15] and ReLU activations, except for the last layer. As highlighted in Fig. 3, CSNet is trained with different objectives during the Classification Stage and Scoring Stage. In the Classification stage, CSNet classifies the input image as Candid/Non-Candid, whereas in Scoring Stage, CSNet is fine-tuned to output a candid score (0–4). A higher candid score indicates a stronger presence of candidness in the scene.

4 Feature Extraction Stage

In the feature extraction stage, ATNet and VisEmNet are trained to learn a rich and meaningful representation of the image, as shown in Fig. 3, which serves as the optimal initialization for the downstream task of candid image classification. We have experimented with various learning methods, including supervised

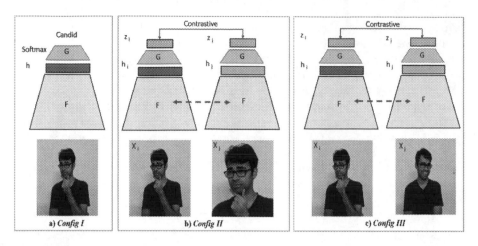

Fig. 3. Different learning method employed in Feature extraction stage to generate meaningful representations.

learning, contrastive learning [14] and self-supervised learning [11,12,18,20] to learn these discriminative features. These methods were combined and experimented with in various configurations, as described below:

Config I: The network is trained in a supervised fashion making use of annotated labels. A linear layer is applied to both ATNet and VisEmNet separately. It is used to map the output embedding (Attribute Embedding/Visual Embedding) to a binary classification output: Candid/Non-Candid. ATNet and VisEmNet are independently trained in a supervised fashion with a cross-entropy loss for the gradient flow. There is no large-scale open-source dataset available that has annotated Candid/Non-Candid labels. This limits the effectiveness of the fully supervised training in Config I for learning network parameters.

Config II: Here, we combine the benefits of Self Supervised and Contrastive learning. We used a simple framework for contrastive learning of visual representations, SimCLR [9], to train both networks (ATNet and VisEmNet) as this framework does not require any specialized architectures or a memory bank. We use the normalized temperature-scaled cross-entropy loss (NT-Xent) defined by SimCLR [9] to train ATNet and VisEmNet. The network tries to generate representations for the input image such that it is closer in representation space to positive samples compared to the negative samples via NT-Xent loss. In the latent/representation space, positives for contrastive learning are generated as data augmentations of a given sample (random crop with face present, resize with random flip, color distortions, and Gaussian blur), and negatives are randomly sampled from the mini-batch. However, this can result in false negatives, which may not be mapped correctly, resulting in a worse representation.

Config III: In this configuration, provided labels are used to select the positives and negatives for contrastive learning. The network is trained using supervised contrastive loss defined in [18]. Supervised Contrastive learning uses many positives per anchor in addition to many negatives as opposed to the convention in self-supervised contrastive learning, which only uses a single positive. By using many positives and negatives, we can better model intra-class and inter-class variability. This translates to representations that provide improved generalization since they better capture the representation for a particular class.

All configurations are shown in Fig. 3. In Config I, after training, we remove the linear layers, and the learned embeddings (h) serve as an input to Classification Stage. Note in Config II and III that the loss operates on top of an extra projection of the representation via G (.), z, rather than on the representation h directly. But only the representation h is used for the downstream task of predicting the candidness of the scene.

5   Classification Stage

While annotating a large dataset, it is easier to assign a classification label (Candid/Non-Candid) to a given image than to assign a score, which is indicative of the candidness of the scene. Therefore, after the feature extraction stage, we introduce a classification stage where CSNet is trained for binary classification tasks (Candid/Non-Candid). By concatenating the features from these two streams, we can capture both the global (from VisEmNet) and local (from ATNet) context of the scene. The concatenated features are given as input to CSNet, which uses a cross-entropy loss to classify the input image. The significance of the introduction of the Classification Stage before the Scoring Stage is described in detail in Sect. 8.3 (Fig. 4).

6   Scoring Stage

After training the network on a larger dataset in the Classification stage, the CandidNet can differentiate between Candid and Non-Candid Images. We make use of this understanding to fine-tune the CandidNet network to output a candid score. The candid score is useful in scenarios where we need to compare multiple images based on their candidness, like selecting top candid moments from a continuous sequence of shots. In such cases, we can sort the images based on the candid score and select the top-most candid moments captured during the session. In the absence of a large dataset of images with candid score ground truth annotation, we took CandidNet (pre-trained for binary classification) and fine-tuned it for the scoring task where it just needs to focus on intra-class variations (levels of candidness). We modeled the candidness scoring problem as a classification problem where the goal was to map images to one of the 5 classes (0: Non-Candid; [1–4]: Candid) where each mapped label represents the corresponding candid score. We fine-tuned the weights of CandidNet by training it end-to-end on the CANDID-SCORE dataset using cross-entropy loss.

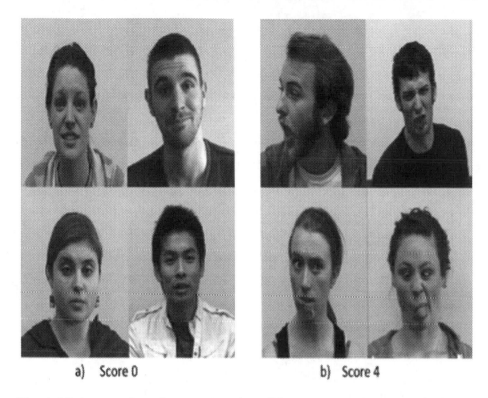

a) Score 0   b) Score 4

Fig. 4. Minimum and maximum averaged candid scores assigned to images by human annotators

7   Experimentatal Setup

7.1   Datasets

CELEBA-HQ: CELEBA-HQ is a large-scale face attributes dataset with 30,000 high resolution ($1024 \times 1024 \times 3$) celebrity images. For this research, we resized these images to a smaller resolution ($114 \times 114 \times 3$). We randomly selected 12,000 images from this dataset and conducted an internal user study with five volunteers to annotate images as candid or non-candid. The volunteers were asked to apply their understanding of candidness while assigning a label to an image. Out of 12000, we used 10000 images for training, 1200 images for validation, and 800 images for testing.

CANDID-Score: We selected 2000 images from work by Fiss et al. [4] and assigned them a score between 0 and 4 based on the candidness of the scene. Images in the dataset include people talking, spontaneous laughter, the six basic emotions associated with canonical facial expressions, transitions between

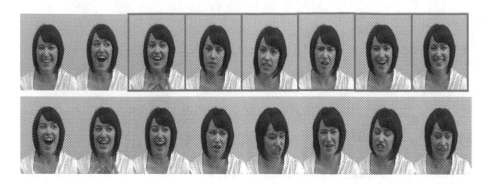

Fig. 5. Top: Eight highest-scoring peak frames in the score predicted by Fis et al. [4] for frames from Video 6; Bottom: Eight highest-scoring peak frames in the score predicted using our proposed CandidNet for frames from Video 6 in video Dataset by Fis et al. Note the automatic score in Fis et al. [4] predicts some non-candid images as candid (Images highlighted in red) (Color figure online)

expressions, and funny faces. We conducted a user study with 10 volunteers. The volunteers were given random images in sets of 5 and were asked to score the images from 0 to 4 based on their inherent understanding of candidness. A volunteer can assign the same score to multiple images in a set. The scores are then averaged and assigned as a label to the image. Figure 5 shows the minimum and maximum ranking assigned to different images. For training purposes, we resized these images to a smaller resolution ($114 \times 114 \times 3$). We used 1200 images for training, 600 images for validation, and 200 images for testing.

Fig. 6. Images from CELEBA-HQ dataset classified as Non-Candid by CandidNet

Fig. 7. Images from CELEBA-HQ dataset classified as Candid by CandidNet

7.2 Training Details

Our model was trained using Pytorch [17]. Due to the major role played by eye gaze in determining the candidness of a scene, we used MobileNetV2 [19] pre-trained on MPII Face Gaze dataset [21] as VisEmNet backbone. ATNet and CSNet were initialized using Xavier initialization [22]. In the Feature Extraction stage, ATNet and VisEmNet are trained on the CELEBA-HQ dataset in different configurations (Config I, II, and III, described in Sect. 3.2) for 5000 epochs. The minibatch size for all configurations was set to 256 to rule out variations introduced by differing batch sizes. Adam optimization was used with an initial learning rate of 0.0001, with a rate decay of 0.001. Data augmentation in the form of random crop, brightness, gamma, and the color shift was performed randomly on the fly. During random crop, we make sure that the cropped image contains the face. In the Classification stage, we freeze the ATNet and VisEmNet weights and train CSNet on CELEBA-HQ for 2000 epochs with a batch size of 64. In the Scoring stage, we fine-tune the network on the CANDID-SCORE dataset by training CandidNet end-to-end for 1000 epochs with a batch size of 32. We evaluate the performance of CandidNet by measuring the precision and recall on the CELEBA-HQ dataset and CANDID-SCORE dataset.

Table 1. Quantitative Comparison of the accuracy different Modules on datasets.

Modules Used	CELEBA-HQ	CANDID-Score
ATNet + Linear Layer	79%	81%
VisEMNet + Linear Layer	81%	84%
CandidNet	**86%**	**89%**

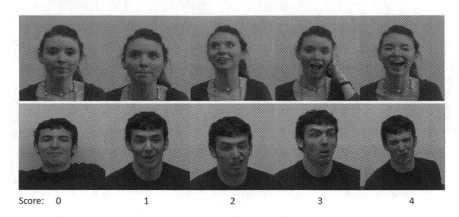

Score: 0   1   2   3   4

Fig. 8. Scores assigned to various images from CANDID-Score dataset by CandidNet

8   Ablation Studies

We performed three ablation studies to evaluate the impact of each module in CandidNet, compare different learning stages in the feature extraction stage, and effect of the introduction of the Classification Stage before the Scoring Stage.

8.1   CandidNet Modules

We trained CandidNet on the CELEBA-HQ dataset to classify an image as Candid/Non-Candid and later fine-tuned it on the CANDID-SCORE dataset to assign a candid score to an image.

ATNet: A linear layer is added to ATNET to utilize the attribute embedding in assigning a candidness label to the input image. We observed that ATNet is not able to capture candid moments when a person is exhibiting extreme emotions like laughing with eyes closed. We conclude that this happened because ATNet is trained on the input image's candid feature pool and not on the input image directly, it is limited by the accuracy of the TSEs as detailed in Sect. 3 (Table 2).

Table 2. Quantitative Comparison of different learning techniques used in feature extraction stage.

Configurations	CELEBA-HQ	CANDID-Score
CandidNet + Config I	86%	89%
VisEMNet + Linear Layer	88%	91%
CandidNet	**92%**	**94%**

VisEmNet: We trained a linear classifier on the visual embedding to detect the candidness of an image. We observed that the network could not make correct predictions in unaligned poses like when the eye gaze was not aligned with the head pose and when a person turned back to look at the camera. This indicated that VisEmNet is not able to assign importance to eye gaze, head pose, and body pose properly in these cases.

CSNet: As ATNet and VisEmNet were trained on different inputs, they deduce candidness by learning different discriminative features for the same image. For a complete understanding of the candidness present in the scene, we fused the attribute embedding and visual embedding from both networks and analyzed them. By concatenating the features from these two streams, we were able to make use of both the global (from VisEmNet) and local (from ATNet) context of the scene, as detailed in Sect. 3. Similar experiments were repeated in the Scoring Stage on the CANDID-SCORE dataset, as detailed in Sect. 6. The results of these studies are highlighted in Table 1. The study clearly showed a drastic improvement in candid moment prediction when we combined two streams of information from ATNet and VisEmNet: the Attribute embedding and Visual embedding, respectively.

Table 3. Quantitative effect different learning Stages on Candid Score Assignment.

Stages	Accuracy
Scoring Stage	86%
Scoring + Classification stage	**94%**

8.2 Feature Extraction Stage

In the feature extraction stage, we trained both ATNet and VisEmNet on the configurations described in Sect. 3 to enforce them to embed information in different contexts (local and global) for a discriminative learned representation. The performance of these configurations is tabulated in Table 3. We observed that the performance of networks in Config I is limited by the amount of labeled Candid data. Although Config II suffers from false negatives as discussed in Sect. 4, Config II was still able to outperform Config I. This demonstrates the effectiveness of a contrastive form of learning to understand the generic representations of images on an unlabeled dataset. The networks benefit the most when trained in Config III, making use of both, provided labels and contrastive learning to separate the features in the representation stage.

8.3 Classification Stage Before Scoring Stage

In the Classification Stage, we were able to learn discriminative features for inter-class (Candid/Non-Candid) variability. The Scoring Stage was built on top of this understanding to focus more on modeling the intra-class variability of the candid class, to predict a measure of candidness. Table 3 shows the improvement in candid score assignment when the Classification Stage is introduced before the Scoring Stage.

9   Results and Discussion

Figure 5 shows the comparison of CandidNet with the automatic score method described in Fis et al. [4]. They first computed a series of features designed to capture the candid moment present in the scene and then trained their model using supervised learning. As highlighted in the top row in a red bounding box in Fig. 5, the automatic score wrongly classifies some images as candid, whereas CandidNet was able to successfully assign a high candid score to more expressive subjects present in the CANDID-SCORE dataset. Figure 6 and Fig. 7 show the example results from CELEBA-HQ dataset. Table 1 and Table 3 highlights the CandidNet model's accuracy in predicting the candid moment. Figure 8 indicates the candid score assigned to different images by the scoring stage depending on the level of candidness present in the scene. CandidNet assigns a higher score to extreme emotions in non-frontal cases, while lower scores are assigned to images in frontal cases. The qualitative, as well as quantitative results presented thus far on both the CELEBA-HQ and CANDID-SCORE datasets, demonstrate the efficacy of CandidNet in detecting the top candid moments in a sequence of shots.

10   Conclusion

In this paper, we have proposed a novel deep learning-based solution Candid-Net that automates candid moment detection, which is a fairly straightforward task for humans. The main novelty of our work is the introduction of two parallel streams to generate image embeddings during the Feature Extraction Stage, ATNet and VisEmNet, and defining a small set of very specific semantic attributes that contribute the most to determining the candidness of a subject, candid feature pool. While ATNet focuses solely on the higher-level semantic features, VisEmNet learns the lower-level features in an image that are not quantifiable or categorical, but which we found to be equally important in determining an image's candidness. Our method of parallel streams forced the network to simultaneously learn local as well as global/spatial context features through ATNet and VisEmNet, respectively. Finally, the representations generated in Feature Extraction Stage were fused and fed to CSNet to perform candid moment classification. We observed that this fusion of features from two streams resulted in a significant improvement in classification accuracy compared to classification based on individual streams, as shown in Table 1. To make the solution work in real-time, and suitable for smartphone devices, we took steps to make each module individually cost-efficient, like using a candid feature pool reduced the number of features to be learned, which translated into a small-sized ATNet, whereas, for VisEmNet, we made use of a MobileNetV2 backbone which is aimed at cost-effective deployment on mobile devices. We have kept CSNet as a shallow (4-layered) network as it had to work on learned representations from ATNet and VisEmNet and not on high-dimensional data. In the last stage, to build a candidness scoring engine, we used an already trained binary classifier and performed fine-tuning on the same, by training on the CANDID-SCORE dataset, to output a candid score for images in the range 0–4, both inclusive. This kind of approach helped us in training a scorer in the absence of a large dataset of manually scored images as the network had already learned inter-class differences and just needed to focus on intra-class separation. This kind of scoring mechanism will find use in applications where multiple images need to be compared to pick the top candid moments among them. CandidNet has the potential to offer several commercialization opportunities in Samsung flagship devices, with a few example applications listed below: a. Top candid moments for a Single Take Photo session can be selected and stitched as a collage and presented as a 'candid collage', b. Auto-candid mode in the native camera app that notifies the user, in real time, when a candid moment is detected. c. Post processing feature in gallery that can sample through high resolution frames of 4K/8K video and find good quality candid moments.

References

1. Prakoso, C.: The Best iPhone Camera App for Candid and Street Photography. https://moblivious.com/reviews/the-best-iphone-camera-app-for-candid-and-street-photography/
2. Image is from internet
3. So Long, Selfies: Why Candid Photos Make a Better Impression (2017). https://knowledge.wharton.upenn.edu/article/power-candid-photos/
4. Candid Moments (2018). https://helpx.adobe.com/in/premiere-elements/using/candid-moments.html
5. Google Clips (2018). https://ai.googleblog.com/2018/05/automatic-photography-with-google-clips/
6. Top Shot on Pixel 3 (2018). https://ai.googleblog.com/2018/12/top-shot-on-pixel-3
7. Capture More of What You Love with New Features on Galaxy S10 and Galaxy Note10 (2020). https://news.samsung.com/global/capture-more-of-what-you-love-with-new-features-on-galaxy-s10-and-galaxy-note10
8. Aydın, T.O., Smolic, A., Gross, M.: Automated aesthetic analysis of photographic images. IEEE Trans. Visual Comput. Graphics **21**(1), 31–42 (2014)
9. Chen, T., Kornblith, S., Norouzi, M., Hinton, G.: A simple framework for contrastive learning of visual representations. In: International Conference on Machine Learning, pp. 1597–1607. PMLR (2020)
10. Dhall, A., Goecke, R., Gedeon, T.: Automatic group happiness intensity analysis. IEEE Trans. Affect. Comput. **6**(1), 13–26 (2015)
11. Doersch, C., Gupta, A., Efros, A.A.: Unsupervised visual representation learning by context prediction. In: Proceedings of the IEEE International Conference on Computer Vision, pp. 1422–1430 (2015)

12. Doersch, C., Zisserman, A.: Multi-task self-supervised visual learning. In: Proceedings of the IEEE International Conference on Computer Vision, pp. 2051–2060 (2017)
13. Fiss, J., Agarwala, A., Curless, B.: Candid portrait selection from video. In: Proceedings of the 2011 SIGGRAPH Asia Conference, pp. 1–8 (2011)
14. Hadsell, R., Chopra, S., LeCun, Y.: Dimensionality reduction by learning an invariant mapping. In: 2006 IEEE Computer Society Conference on Computer Vision and Pattern Recognition (CVPR 2006), vol. 2, pp. 1735–1742. IEEE (2006)
15. Ioffe, S., Szegedy, C.: Batch normalization: accelerating deep network training by reducing internal covariate shift. In: International Conference on Machine Learning, pp. 448–456. PMLR (2015)
16. Karras, T., Aila, T., Laine, S., Lehtinen, J.: Progressive growing of GANs for improved quality, stability, and variation. arXiv preprint arXiv:1710.10196 (2017)
17. Ketkar, N., Moolayil, J.: Introduction to PyTorch. In: Ketkar, N., Moolayil, J. (eds.) Deep Learning with Python, pp. 27–91. Apress, Berkeley (2021). https://doi.org/10.1007/978-1-4842-5364-9_2
18. Noroozi, M., Favaro, P.: Unsupervised learning of visual representations by solving jigsaw puzzles. In: Leibe, B., Matas, J., Sebe, N., Welling, M. (eds.) ECCV 2016. LNCS, vol. 9910, pp. 69–84. Springer, Cham (2016). https://doi.org/10.1007/978-3-319-46466-4_5
19. Sandler, M., Howard, A., Zhu, M., Zhmoginov, A., Chen, L.C.: Mobilenetv 2: inverted residuals and linear bottlenecks. In: Proceedings of the IEEE Conference on Computer Vision and Pattern Recognition, pp. 4510–4520 (2018)
20. Zhang, R., Isola, P., Efros, A.A.: Colorful image colorization. In: Leibe, B., Matas, J., Sebe, N., Welling, M. (eds.) ECCV 2016. LNCS, vol. 9907, pp. 649–666. Springer, Cham (2016). https://doi.org/10.1007/978-3-319-46487-9_40
21. Zhang, X., Sugano, Y., Fritz, M., Bulling, A.: It's written all over your face: full-face appearance-based gaze estimation. In: Proceedings of the IEEE Conference on Computer Vision and Pattern Recognition Workshops, pp. 51–60 (2017)

Cost Efficient Defect Detection in Bangle Industry Using Transfer Learning

Anuranjan Dubey[1] and Abhinandan Dubey[2]($\boxtimes$)

[1] Jaypee Institute of Information Technology, A 10 Block A, Industrial Area,
Sector 62, Noida 201309, Uttar Pradesh, India
anuranjandubey@outlook.com
[2] Stony Brook University, 100 Nicolls Road, Stony Brook, NY 11794, USA
adubey@cs.stonybrook.edu

Abstract. Bangle industry in India has been notoriously at the epicenter of child-labour. Even though the government has passed several laws in the last few decades to end child-labour, this problem is barely at bay, and thousands of young children still work in dingy bangle making factories and hazardous units where they are exposed to toxic fumes over long periods of time only to shape bangles, sort them and identify defects. In this study, we dived deeper into this problem to identify at which stages deep learning and artificial intelligence can be used, present a dataset and perform an evaluation. Since one of the most crucial aspects of bangle manufacturing process is to make sure bangles come out round and without defects, we present a system which uses a unique image processing technique and transfer learning to identify these defects. We have also compiled a dataset which consists of human-labeled images collected from one of the bangle factories, which act as a seed to train the network which can detect common defects. We present an extensive evaluation of performance of various machine learning algorithms on our dataset using traditional features, and features extracted from popular neural networks. We also discuss how our method can be extended to identify defects in size. Furthermore, we briefly discuss how this can be implemented and used in the bangle industry without any significant costs.

Keywords: dataset · neural networks · image processing

1 Introduction

The United Nations Convention on Children Rights states that a child is entitled to fundamental rights of survival, development and protection at birth [1]. However, in India, there are several towns which have long disregarded these fundamental rights, and instead see children as cheap labour. Often, underage children from poor families and neighborhoods are made to work in factories for hours. The northern town of Firozabad is notoriously known for such factories [3], and is lined up with bangle factories where poor and underage children

D. Gupta et al. (Eds.): CVIP 2022, CCIS 1776, pp. 181–194, 2023.
https://doi.org/10.1007/978-3-031-31407-0_14

are dragged into arduous tasks. These children are deprived of their fundamental rights, just because of abject poverty in the families and communities they belong to. Several studies have shown how these factories continue to deprive these children aged as little as 5–14 years, of their childhood [23]. Even though the country has enacted several laws aimed at this very issue of child labour, this problem is still at the epicenter of the bangle industry. Various acts have been specifically passed by the government to target child labour in factories such as The Factories Act of 1948, The Mines Act of 1952, The Child Labour (Prohibition and Regulation) Act of 1986, The Juvenile Justice (Care and Protection) of Children Act of 2000, which have all failed to an extent in rooting out the issue [23].

More than two decades have passed since these acts were passed, yet these factories continue to employ and exploit young children in hazardous units. In this study, we surveyed these factories, and found out exactly why these bangle factories are still dependent on child labour. Talking to experts, it became clear to us that bangle-making was a multi-stage process. Much of the work is done by large machines which molten glass and shape them into a circle, however, these machines are anything but state-of-the-art. Humans are employed to make sure the bangles come out nicely shaped, and most factory owners hire underage children for this step because they see them as cheap labour.

While most of the bangle making process is now run using machines, and most of the industrial equipment required is usually set up by industry owners, one critical piece of equipment is left out and instead requires humans. This is one of the last steps in bangle making process, which requires verification and testing. There are essentially two kinds of test performed - (i) diameter test to check if the bangle has a perfect round shape, (ii) defect test to check if the material in the bangle has any bubbles or deformities. If any of these tests fail, the bangle is considered defective, the glass is melted, and goes through the process of bangle making again. Currently, this process is carried out in part using infrared thermography to identify defects, and then humans to check the shape and diameter of the bangles using molds. The equipment required for infrared thermography is often expensive and owners of these factories often avoid buying this equipment, relying solely on child labour to inspect the bangles.

Despite being such a big social issue, there has been no prior research done which can identify "mechanisms" to prevent child labour. Most research done on this tries to identify how lawmakers can enforce these laws. While laws which prohibit and criminalize child labour are absolutely essential, we believe artificial intelligence can be applied to this problem in a cost efficient way, which incentivizes industry owners to use artificial intelligence instead of child labour.

There are no published works on this, partly also because of absence of public datasets on bangles. In this paper, we present (i) a human-labeled dataset of 1080 bangle images in varying radius and colors. (ii) a process which uses neural networks and machine learning to identify defective bangles with an accuracy of 92%.

To collect images of bangles, we contacted a factory owner, and collected images of bangles, of varying sizes and colors. From a machine learning perspective, this is quite a challenging problem because i) defects can be of varying degree and depth, ii) illumination and perspective can pose challenges in identification of defects. Finally, no datasets are publicly available which can help cover any of these problems. Thus, any solution developed for this problem needs to be versatile enough to capture these aspects.

To solve these challenges, we have devised a multi-step process, which start with pre-processing of images, generating embeddings for these images, and finally training a model to classify bangle as either non-defective or defective. Our experiments on test data show an accuracy of 92%. In addition, we provide a comparison of this method with various image features, and also show a cost-benefit which can incentivise this for bangle-making factory owners, thus eliminating child labour.

1.1 Problem Scope

As mentioned earlier in this section, defects in bangles are primarily of three kinds - size, shape and deformities such as bubbles. We have limited the scope of our problem to defects of only two kinds; (i) defects in shape (broken bangles or bangles with gaps) or (ii) defect in material (such as bubbles or deformities). Our methods do not check for differences in size of the bangle, however, we briefly show how this capability can be easily added to our proposed method. We intentionally left this to make sure our method generalizes well in bangles of all sizes.

1.2 Contributions

To summarize, our contributions are following:

- Our research helps curb child labour in unprivileged and low-economy communities, which has drawn little attention. To best of our knowledge, this is one-of-a-kind and a novel approach in terms of using AI to solve this social issue. The youth of children is at risk, and our method could be a great solution towards providing a cheap alternative to factory owners, thus eliminating child labour.
- We propose a human-labeled data-set of 1080 bangle images, which opens the door for this problem to be investigated in even greater detail by the industry experts and further advance the proposed methods.
- We investigate various traditional feature based approaches, transfer learning and machine learning algorithms to classify bangle images, and propose a cost-efficient method which shows an accuracy of 92% on test data.

2 Related Work

To best of our knowledge, this is the first research done to solve this problem of defect detection in bangles using artificial intelligence. The primary reason for this has been (i) Most of the bangle manufacturing occurs in low-income countries which do not have enough capital to use advanced techniques, and thus industry draws little attention towards this issue, and (ii) Existing methods employ use of either manual inspection by humans, or use infrared thermography to identify subtle defects like bubbles. Most of the existing literature, thus, can be grouped broadly into two categories.

The first category of papers are around physical techniques of defect detection. Most of the research in this group focuses on using infrared thermography to identify defects in glass materials. [18] However, an important thing to note here is that even with infrared thermography, a human has to look for broken bangles, the reason is that infrared thermography focuses on identifying defects in the material, and not on uniqueness of the shape and size of bangles.

The second category of papers are around defect detection using image processing, machine learning and deep learning. This could also be grouped into whether the study is based on finding defects using methods in computer vision like image thresholding [19], contour methods, edge detection [25] and image segmentation [11]. The research specifically focuses on specific materials, such as PCBs [2], which is significantly different from our problem, both in the problem statement, and the kind of material.

Literature focusing on defect detection using machine learning and deep learning is present, but not quite applicable. There are some studies done for detecting defects in glass surfaces [14] using image processing and machine learning but these focus exclusively on material defects, and thus cannot be used for classifying broken bangles. Some of the literature [24], focus on the problem of surface defect detection on flat surfaces and images, and use convolutional neural networks for segmenting images [5], and identifying defects. These methods do not make sense in our case, because (i) These methods use flat-surface material defects which do not involve identifying defects as "deformities" in form of shapes and (ii) The emphasis is usually on segmentation to identify defects, which is an overkill and not a requirement in the case of defect detection in bangles. Some of the literature is related to this problem, such as [17] which involves defect classification of bearings based on autoencoder neural networks. Although the shape is an aspect of defects in such problems, the inherent difference in materials and kind of defects make these methods inapplicable at least directly. There's some research [4] which involves infrared thermography and neural networks combined to identify defects in glasses. While their research is really good at identifying defects such as bubbles, it cannot be applied to classify a broken bangle from a complete one (Fig. 1).

3   Dataset

We collected a set of 1080 bangle images under average lighting condition. Each image is 3000×3000 pixels, and has three channels (RGB). These images were compiled from a base set of images, where each image was rotated by clockwise by $90°$ to yield four images, which gives us more images to train with. No specific apparatus or setup was put in place to ensure proper illumination or hide

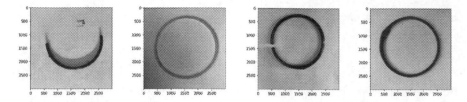

Fig. 1. Types of broken and defective bangles. The first from the left is labeled "broken", the second is "defective" since it has a minor gap and varying thickness, the third and fourth are also defective, as the third one has a small gap, and both have "bubbles" or blobs of glass of varying thickness.

shadows. These images were also labeled, at the time when the pictures were taken, by humans who work as sorters in the last stage of bangle manufacturing process. These people have years of expertise and can identify defects like broken bangles, bubbles or thickness variation at a glimpse. We cross-validated these labels across different humans to make sure these labels were indeed correct. The labels classify images into three classes (i) "good" which implies a bangle is fit to be shipped and has no visible defects, (ii) "defect" which implies a bangle might have a gap, a bubble or thickness variation and finally (iii) "broken" which implies a bangle is broken, which in most cases is either just an arc or a huge gap in the circular shape of bangle. Since a bangle coming out as broken, could also be considered defective, we also show results of our method, if only two classes are used.

4   Methods

In this section, we will show the methods we used to analyse these images, and various approaches we tried to classify them. This also includes the methods we tried to pre-process these images such as image thresholding, dilation etc., to be used along with "traditional" methods such as SIFT [16].

4.1   Traditional Methods

To form a baseline, we used individual features mentioned below, and some combinations of these to train various machine learning models. The individual methods are briefly described below and results are shown in Table 1.

Hough Transform. One of the first things to try was to use hough transform to detect perfect "circles" in the images [8], and a perfect circle would classify as a "good" label. However, this method cannot distinguish between "defect" images and "good" images even when complex image pre-processing methods are used.

The reason is that any image transformations cannot capture the versatility and different nature of defects.

Contour Features. Contour features like finding out whether a contour is convex and closed were also good candidates for classifying them. We tried classifying images based on contour area, arc lengths and whether or not the contour was closed, however this also yields poor results at identifying defective bangles.

SIFT-Based Correlation and Features. We tried formulating this problem as a correlation or rule-based classification problem without using any models, and just using statistics, such as average, minimum and maximum values, of top-K matches on SIFT feature descriptors to "match" an image and assign it a class. This method takes a very long time to complete, and fails to achieve results anywhere close to the proposed method. Another approach we tried using SIFT was to use Bag of Visual Words (BoVW) [15]. We extracted the SIFT keypoints and descriptors and used them construct vocabularies which represent each image as a histogram of features which are in the image. This bag of visual words is then used to compute the nearest neighbors. Finally, a machine learning algorithm is used to train a model to classify using the visual vocabulary representation as an input. While the results are better than other traditional features, they are still far from the results obtained using transfer learning.

Image Moments. Image moments are highly efficient features for shape detection. We extracted Hu moments [13] from the images and trained a machine learning model to classify the images just based on their Hu moments. However the accuracy scores for these models are nowhere close to the one with the proposed method below.

4.2   Proposed Method

Our proposed method involves a three stage process (i) pre-processing the images by a unique technique described below, and resizing them to 224 × 224 pixels (ii) using ResNet50 model [10] to get embeddings of each image as a vector and finally (iii) using the feature vectors obtained as training inputs to train a multi-class classifier. We further compare performance of different machine learning and neural network based classifiers in the analysis section.

4.3   Pre-processing

Our pre-processing involves removing shadows from the pictures of the bangle images. We use basic morphological operations to achieve this. Starting with an input image $\mathcal{I}$, with RGB channels c, the image is dilated and subtracted with the original to remove any background noise like shadows. This step also helps to amplify the bangle edges. Dilation step involves convolving an the bangle image with a 15×15 square kernel. We perform dilation for each channel in the image.

$$\mathcal{D}(u_c, v_c) = \max_{(u'_c, v'_c): \texttt{element}(u',v') \neq 0} \mathcal{I}(u_c + u', v_c + v') \tag{1}$$

After dilation we use a non-linear filtering technique, which involves replacing pixel values with a median of all the pixels under the kernel area. This is done to remove any grainy noise from the image, while avoiding edge blurring.

$$\mathcal{D}'(u_c, v_c) \leftarrow median\{\mathcal{D}(u_c + i, v_c + j) | (i, j) \in R\} \tag{2}$$

As shown in Fig. 3, we then take the difference of the original image $\mathcal{I}$ with the dilated, median blurred image $\mathcal{D}'$, i.e.; $\mathcal{S} = |\mathcal{I} - \mathcal{D}'|$, to remove shadows. Our peculiar method for image pre-processing allows our model to learn features in absence of any shadows. Figure 2 shows a nice example where our pre-processing method helps clear out the unwanted data in the image. Finally, we perform min-max normalization on the obtained image, which is resized to 224×224 to be fed to our feature extraction engine.

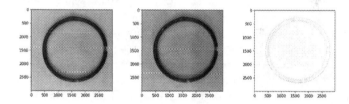

Fig. 2. How our image pre-processing method can progressively remove any shadows which can negatively impact the model. The image is taken from a pi camera. The important observation here is in the original image has a small gap where the shadow almost "completes" the bangle. As shown in the third image from the left, this noise is completely eliminated.

4.4   Feature Extraction

We use transfer learning on pre-trained ResNet50 model, which is a Convolutional Neural Network (CNN) that is 50 layers deep. Convolutional neural networks have been long established as one of the most expressive ways to extract image features. A CNN is comprised of several convolutional layers which are connected to spatially connected neurons. A max-pooling layer follows the convolutional layer to keep the computational complexity in check. This also avoids feature maps getting too large by only selecting the maximum feature response in a neighborhood. These convolutional and pooling layers are often in pairs, and are followed by some fully-connected layers. These layers are great at learning the non-linear nature of local features which are the output of previous layers. At the end, a CNN has a layer which distributes the probability into various

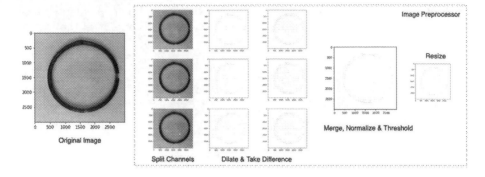

Fig. 3. Pre-processing images using the proposed method.

classes. This layer normalizes the output classes and uses functions such as soft-max function to do so. CNNs can be trained from scratch by initializing weights at random, and optimization is performed using back-propagation algorithm. However, models such as VGG and ResNet are deep models which may require lots of training data, processing power and time. This is where **transfer learning** fills the gap. Transfer learning uses pre-trained weights from a model trained on a huge image dataset such as ImageNet [20], which allows the model to learn subtle features of the real world. VGG-19 (a variant of VGG model) is a deep convolutional network which contains five convolutional blocks, and was considered state-of-the-art CNN until more deep neural networks started to give slightly better results with reduced model size, such as ResNet [10]. For feature extraction, we use the pretrained ResNet50 model [22] with ImageNet weights. Training this CNN with random weights can take a really long time because of the amount of layers, besides by training on ImageNet dataset [7] the model has learned a good representation of low-level features such as lighting, edges, and shapes which are crucial for bangle defect classification. For extracting features from this pretrained model, we strip the softmax (last) layer of ResNet50 network so we get a 1×2048 feature vector for each image (Fig. 4).

4.5   Classification

The extracted features from various neural networks are fed to a machine learning algorithm to classify the image as "broken", "defective" or "good". The reason we classify some as defective is that some bangles might have small infractions, or bubbles, or a blob of material which makes the bangle not broken, yet unusable. We will also perform experiments (as shown in later sections) by using only two class labels ("defective" and "non-defective"), which gives a really high accuracy.

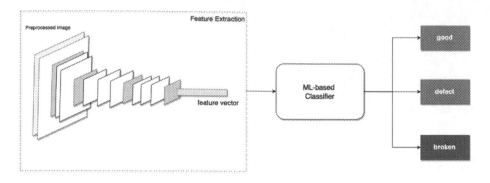

Fig. 4. Training process using the proposed method.

5   Experiments and Results

Since the goal in bangle detection is to reduce the chances of a defective or broken bangle be assigned a "good" category, we use accuracy to measure the performance of the model. Precision is also an important metric to us as we need to reduce false positives, i.e.; bangles which were assigned a "good" label while they were either "broken" or "defective". All our metrics are calculated by a train-test split of 75–25 and by performing a 4-fold cross-validation. Our results show an accuracy of 91% using SVM with the features obtained from the pre-trained ResNet50 model. We have also obtained results from VGG-16, VGG-19 [21] and Xception [6]. Results have been summarised in Table 2.

Table 1. Performance of various machine learning algorithms with traditional features

Technique	Hough Transform				Contour Features			
	Accuracy	Precision	Recall	F1-Score	Accuracy	Precision	Recall	F1-Score
SVM	0.45	0.20	0.45	0.28	0.45	0.20	0.45	0.28
Decision Tree	0.45	0.20	0.45	0.28	0.43	0.37	0.43	0.33
Perceptron	0.29	0.09	0.29	0.13	0.41	0.27	0.41	0.31
SGD	0.29	0.09	0.29	0.13	0.30	0.32	0.31	0.21
KNN	0.29	0.09	0.29	0.13	0.28	0.25	0.28	0.17
Random Forest	0.45	0.20	0.45	0.28	0.45	0.30	0.55	0.39
Technique	Image Moments				SIFT Features			
	Accuracy	Precision	Recall	F1-Score	Accuracy	Precision	Recall	F1-Score
SVM	0.45	0.20	0.45	0.28	0.75	0.56	0.75	0.64
Decision Tree	0.45	0.20	0.45	0.28	0.42	0.83	0.42	0.39
Perceptron	0.29	0.09	0.29	0.13	0.42	0.83	0.42	0.39
SGD	0.29	0.09	0.29	0.13	0.75	0.78	0.75	0.76
KNN	0.29	0.09	0.29	0.13	0.55	0.30	0.55	0.39
Random Forest	0.45	0.20	0.45	0.28	0.55	0.30	0.55	0.39

Table 2. Comparison of various machine learning methods with features extracted from various neural networks through transfer learning.

Technique	VGG16				VGG19			
	Accuracy	Precision	Recall	F1-Score	Accuracy	Precision	Recall	F1-Score
SVM	0.88	0.88	0.88	0.88	0.86	0.86	0.86	0.86
Decision Tree	0.72	0.72	0.72	0.72	0.75	0.74	0.75	0.74
Perceptron	0.85	0.85	0.85	0.85	0.84	0.85	0.84	0.84
SGD	0.82	0.82	0.82	0.82	0.83	0.84	0.83	0.82
KNN	0.75	0.78	0.75	0.76	0.73	0.77	0.73	0.74
Random Forest	0.81	0.83	0.81	0.79	0.81	0.83	0.81	0.79
Technique	ResNet50				Xception			
	Accuracy	Precision	Recall	F1-Score	Accuracy	Precision	Recall	F1-Score
SVM	0.91	0.92	0.91	0.91	0.60	0.58	0.60	0.58
Decision Tree	0.79	0.78	0.79	0.78	0.47	0.46	0.47	0.46
Perceptron	0.88	0.90	0.88	0.88	0.60	0.58	0.60	0.56
SGD	0.77	0.82	0.77	0.72	0.56	0.57	0.56	0.56
KNN	0.75	0.78	0.75	0.75	0.47	0.41	0.47	0.43
Random Forest	0.77	0.81	0.77	0.74	0.53	0.41	0.53	0.44
XGBoost	0.87	0.87	0.87	0.86	0.60	0.62	0.60	0.56

5.1 Binary Classification

Since most of the times, the task would be to identify and sort bangles as "defective" or "non-defective", we considered this as a binary classification problem, and clubbed the "defect" and "broken" classes as "defective" while the rest being "non-defective". We used our proposed method to achieve an accuracy score of 0.92.

5.2 Combining Traditional Features

One of the subtle features about images is that often using several techniques can result in a nice mix of signals which encapsulate local as well global features of an image. To test this, we tried combining some traditional features such as SIFT Features and Hu Moments obtained from preprocessed images and added them to the feature vector obtained from the neural networks. However, this resulted in more bangles being classified incorrectly and results did not improve, this could be because traditional features alone as features perform worse on this training task (Fig. 5).

5.3 Variations in Pre-processing Techniques

As mentioned before in the paper, we tried using transfer learning just on plain bangle images but it was only able to achieve an accuracy score of 0.86. We tried dilating the images with different kernel sizes, trying various techniques

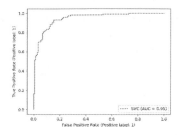

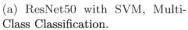

(a) ResNet50 with SVM, Multi-Class Classification.

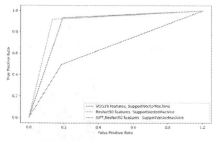

(b) Binary Classification.

Fig. 5. ROC Curves of major experiment

like erosion. However, increasing the kernel size for dilation has worse effects as it also dilates and "fills" the gaps in the bangle thus making it hard to find defects. On the contrary, making the kernel smaller does not dilate the image enough to really remove the shadows (Table 3).

Table 3. Results from experiments performed. First two experiments make use of Hu moments. "BIN" indicates the bangles were only classified as defective or non-defective. "ORG" indicates only original images were used, without any image pre-processing techniques applied

Technique	Accuracy	Precision	Recall	F1-Score
Hu+VGG19+SVM	0.77	0.81	0.77	0.74
Hu+SVM (BIN)	0.75	0.56	0.75	0.64
SIFT+ResNet50+SVM (BIN)	0.75	0.56	0.75	0.64
VGG19+SVM (BIN)	**0.91**	**0.92**	**0.91**	**0.91**
ResNet50+SVM (BIN)	**0.92**	**0.92**	**0.92**	**0.92**
VGG19+SVM (ORG)	0.83	0.83	0.83	0.82
ResNet50+SVM (ORG)	0.86	0.87	0.86	0.86

5.4   Extending to Detect Size Defects

Our method is agnostic to size and thickness of the bangles. However, it might be important in certain cases to ensure the size of the bangle is accurate. This can be done using Circular Hough Transform (CHT). As evident in Table 1, while Hough Features themselves are not a sufficient indicator of a defect, the transform can be used to find the radius of the bangle. If given a min and a max radius, CHT can be used efficiently to detect the radius of a circle in the image. However, without this constraint, this might be inefficient, since it has a three dimensional parameter space (equation of a circle), which requires lots of memory and computation. An extensive comparison of this technique is discussed in [12].

The work also discusses Fast Hough Transform (FHT), and some space-saving approaches introduced by Gerig and Klein [9] which can be combined with our transfer learning approach as an additional layer to catch defects in size (Fig. 6).

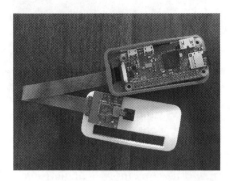

Fig. 6. Hardware setup using a raspberry pi and a pi camera.

6   Conclusion

In this paper, we show how transfer learning can be used to classify defects in bangle industry which provides a cost-efficient method that can be used in factories with minimal human intervention. The experimental results that we have obtained and the dataset which we have collected can serve as a mechanism to curb the issue of child labour in bangle industry. The proposed method can accurately classify images as good, broken or defective, in bangles of varying sizes, colors, and in different lighting conditions. As for the future, this work can be extended to also check for the radius or size of bangles by adding superior image transformation methods and having mechanisms to train models to discard bangles with incorrect size. We are also interested in using hand-crafted traditional features which can be good indicators of presence of defects. It would also be interesting to see how our transfer learning can work with other state-of-the-art CNNs. We are also interested in exploring how our method adapts to manufacturing of other parts and products. Our main focus for this study was to show how existing tools and techniques in artificial intelligence can be easily applied to solve ethical issues in poor communities. This work can also serve as a stage to draw attention to the issue of child labour, thus helping address the issue by more preventative actions.

7   Ethical Impact

Bangle Industry is a big industry in India. It still runs partially on child labour. This approach enables the factory owners to get rid of this wretched practice by providing them a cheaper alternative to the unfair practice of child labour.

There's a considerable cost benefit in using this method. Our method only needs a raspberry pi with a camera to work with, and can provide same results as a human sorter used with an infrared thermography camera. The average starting cost of a thermography equipment is USD 900, compared to a raspberry pi 4, with a pi camera (USD 160 for 4 GB version) and a breadboard, for GPIO (USD 20), which comes at most USD 200. This method allows the factory owners to see a cost benefit and can be easily used without the need of either.

References

1. Convention on the rights of the child. UN General Assembly, United Nations, Treaty Series, vol. 1577 (1989)
2. Baygin, M., Karakose, M., Sarimaden, A., Akin, E.: Machine vision based defect detection approach using image processing. In: 2017 International Artificial Intelligence and Data Processing Symposium (IDAP), pp. 1–5 (2017). https://doi.org/10.1109/IDAP.2017.8090292
3. Burra, N.: Glass factories of Firozabad: II: plight of child workers. Econ. Polit. Wkly **21**(47), 2033–2036 (1986). http://www.jstor.org/stable/4376352
4. Campa, A., Hsieh, S.J., Wang, H.J.: Non-visible defect detection in glass using infrared thermography and artificial neural networks. In: Stockton, G.R., Colbert, F.P. (eds.) Thermosense: Thermal Infrared Applications XXXV, vol. 8705, pp. 197–208. International Society for Optics and Photonics, SPIE (2013). https://doi.org/10.1117/12.2015650
5. Chen, J., Li, Y., Zhao, J.: X-ray of tire defects detection via modified faster R-CNN. In: 2019 2nd International Conference on Safety Produce Informatization (IICSPI), pp. 257–260 (2019). https://doi.org/10.1109/IICSPI48186.2019.9095873
6. Chollet, F.: Xception: deep learning with depthwise separable convolutions (2016). https://doi.org/10.48550/ARXIV.1610.02357. https://arxiv.org/abs/1610.02357
7. Deng, J., Dong, W., Socher, R., Li, L.J., Li, K., Fei-Fei, L.: Imagenet: a large-scale hierarchical image database. In: 2009 IEEE Conference on Computer Vision and Pattern Recognition, pp. 248–255. IEEE (2009)
8. Duda, R.O., Hart, P.E.: Use of the hough transformation to detect lines and curves in pictures. In: Graphics and Image Processing, Association for Computing Machinery, vol. 15, pp. 11–14 (1972)
9. Gerig, G., Klein, F.: Fast contour identification through efficient hough transform and simplified interpretation strategy. In: IJCPR, Paris, vol. 8, no. 1, pp. 498–500 (1986). https://doi.org/10.5244/C.3.29
10. He, K., Zhang, X., Ren, S., Sun, J.: Deep residual learning for image recognition (2015). https://doi.org/10.48550/ARXIV.1512.03385. https://arxiv.org/abs/1512.03385
11. He, Z., Sun, L.: Surface defect detection method for glass substrate using improved Otsu segmentation. Appl. Opt. **54**(33), 9823–9830 (2015). https://doi.org/10.1364/AO.54.009823. http://ao.osa.org/abstract.cfm?URI=ao-54-33-9823
12. Yuen, H.K., Princen, J., Illingworth, J., Kittler, J.: A comparative study of hough transform methods for circle finding. Image Vis. Comput. **8**(1), 71–76 (1989). https://doi.org/10.5244/C.3.29
13. Hu, M.K.: Visual pattern recognition by moment invariants. IRE Trans. Inf. Theory **8**(2), 179–187 (1962). https://doi.org/10.1109/TIT.1962.1057692

14. Jiang, J.B., Xiao, X., Feng, G., Lu, Z., Yang, Y.: Detection and classification of glass defects based on machine vision (2019)
15. Karim, A., Sameer, R.: Image classification using bag of visual words (BOVW), pp. 76–82 (2018). https://doi.org/10.22401/ANJS.21.4.11
16. Lowe, D.: Object recognition from local scale-invariant features. In: Proceedings of the Seventh IEEE International Conference on Computer Vision, vol. 2, pp. 1150–1157 (1999). https://doi.org/10.1109/ICCV.1999.790410
17. Lu, M., Mou, Y.: Bearing defect classification algorithm based on autoencoder neural network. Adv. Civil Eng. **2020**(6680315) (2020). https://doi.org/10.1155/2020/6680315
18. Meola, C., Carlomagno, G.M.: Infrared thermography to evaluate impact damage in glass/epoxy with manufacturing defects. Int. J. Impact Eng. **67**, 1–11 (2014). https://doi.org/10.1016/j.ijimpeng.2013.12.010
19. Ng, H.F.: Automatic thresholding for defect detection. Pattern Recognit. Lett. **27**(14), 1644–1649 (2006). https://doi.org/10.1016/j.patrec.2006.03.009. https://www.sciencedirect.com/science/article/pii/S016786550600119X
20. Russakovsky, O., et al.: Imagenet large scale visual recognition challenge (2015)
21. Simonyan, K., Zisserman, A.: Very deep convolutional networks for large-scale image recognition (2014). https://doi.org/10.48550/ARXIV.1409.1556. https://arxiv.org/abs/1409.1556
22. Simonyan, K., Zisserman, A.: Very deep convolutional networks for large-scale image recognition (2015)
23. Syed, M.I.: Child Labour and the new legislation; A study of home based bangle industries of Firozabad, U.P. Ph.D. thesis, Aligarh Muslim University, Aligarh, UP, India (2011)
24. Xiao, L., Wu, B., Hu, Y.: Surface defect detection using image pyramid. IEEE Sens. J. **20**(13), 7181–7188 (2020). https://doi.org/10.1109/JSEN.2020.2977366
25. Zhao, J., Kong, Q., Zhao, X., Liu, J., Liu, Y.: A method for detection and classification of glass defects in low resolution images. In: 2011 Sixth International Conference on Image and Graphics, pp. 642–647 (2011)

Single Image Dehazing Using Multipath Networks Based on Chain of U-Nets

S. Deivalakshmi$^{(\boxtimes)}$ and J. Sudaroli Sandana

Department of Electronics and Communication Engineering, National Institute of Technology,
Tiruchirappalli, India
deiva@nitt.edu, sandhana3000@gmail.com

Abstract. Single-image haze removal is a necessary pre-processing step for several computer vision applications and may be a challenging task. The images captured outdoors are seriously degraded in color and contrast due to extreme weather conditions like fog, haze, snow and rain. This poor visual quality can inhibit the performance, which is intended to operate on clear conditions like object detection. In recent years, single-image dehazing, which recovers clean images from haze-affected images, has gained popularity. This paper proposes a unique and efficient multipath supported U-Net called Ladder-Net to directly restore a hazy free image from a hazy image. Utilizing only a single set of encoder and decoder branches within the U-Net structure, the proposed Ladder-Net has numerous encoder and decoder branches and dense skip connections between each pair of adjoining encoder and decoder branches at every level. The encoder and decoder are designed to acquire the contextual information in the input images and to evaluate the role of each input to the resulting hazy-free images, respectively, without relying on the atmospheric scattering model. The proposed model is trained and tested using RESIDE benchmark dataset. Experiments conducted on hazy images and a synthetic dataset obtained naturally show that the proposed method proves effective in achieving superior performance over previous methods. The experimental results convey that the proposed architecture achieves exceptional performance over the prevailing methods concerning the qualitative and the quantitative performance, PSNR and SSIM.

Keywords: Single image haze removal · U-Net · multipath networks · Ladder-Net

1 Introduction

Images captured under extreme weather conditions such as mist, fog, snow and dust lack visual pleasantness [1] and deteriorate in terms of contrast and color. Haze dramatically adds noise to the images captured by the cameras and causes a major problem in terrestrial photography because it is difficult to capture distant objects, as the penetration of light in a dense atmosphere is necessary. It is very difficult to detect haze as there is a difference in the concentration of haze from one place to another. Haze is a phenomenon that depends on depth. The light reflected by the hazy particles causes the visual effect of

D. Gupta et al. (Eds.): CVIP 2022, CCIS 1776, pp. 195–208, 2023.
https://doi.org/10.1007/978-3-031-31407-0_15

a decrease in contrast to the image captured. This degraded image pleasantness poses serious challenges to the best computer vision algorithms, which are intended to operate on clear images for tracking [2], segmentation [3] and object detection [4, 5]. Hazy weather also causes degradation in the images captured by various systems such as aerial photography systems [6], image classification [7], target recognition systems and satellite remote sensing systems [8] which depend on optical imaging instruments. Therefore, in the present scenario, haze removal and improving the visual perceptional quality of the images are drawing the attention of the researchers. Image dehazing is the task of reconstructing a crystal-clear image from a hazy image or multiple hazy images. The previous techniques which are proposed for image processing used a wide range of visual information to obtain the statistical and deterministic properties of hazy images, including histogram-based [9, 10], saturation based and contrast-based algorithms for image dehazing are suggested to obtain the hazy free clean image from a single image by the early researchers. Later, researchers tried to achieve similar performance by using multiple images. In [11], image dehazing based on the polarization method is used. In polarization-based haze removal techniques, multiple images must be taken with different degrees of polarization.

In [12], numerous images of the same scene are captured under distinct weather conditions. These are called multiple constraint-based dehazing methods. Many dehazing algorithms are proposed for restoring clear images through additional prior knowledge or multiple hazy images [13]. But in practice, multiple hazy images captured from the same scene or depth-related information are not always available. This difficulty can be avoided if single image dehazing techniques were introduced. In recent years, single image haze removal based on a physical model achieved significant progress. It was carried out by making assumptions that the contrast of the clear image is more than in the image captured under the haze. But restoring a clean image from a single hazy image is more difficult.

Recently, algorithms proposed based on convolutional neural networks (CNN) are giving better solutions for several high-level vision applications, including dehazing. CNN has shown tremendous popularity due to its capability to produce state-of-the-art performance. DehazeNet [14], proposed for haze removal using a single image, uses bilateral ReLU as a nonlinear activation function. DehazeNet algorithm maps functions between the haze image and its medium transmissions. This model assumes that the global constant atmospheric light should be learned along with the medium transmission parameters. In AMEF - Artificial Multiple Exposure Fusion [16], haze is removed using two steps. First, gamma correction operations are used to sequentially under-expose the hazy image artificially. In the second step, the set of artificially under-exposed images are merged through a multi-scale Laplacian blending scheme to yield a haze-free image. In All-in-One Dehazing Network (AOD-Net) [15], a haze removal algorithm has been proposed using convolutional neural networks (CNN). AOD-Net is based on an improvised version of the atmospheric scattering model in which a hazy free image is produced via a lightweight CNN instead of separately estimating atmospheric light and transmission matrix.

In this work, Ladder-Net, a chain of numbers of U-Nets that aims at achieving image dehazing effectively, is proposed. As presented in Fig. 2, multipath networks based on

U-Net consists of U-Nets of different depths in which decoders of the same resolution are densely connected via the skip recursive paths. The proposed architecture enables the following benefits. First, Ladder-Net is not inclined to choose network depth as it embeds U-Nets of various depths in its design. Secondly, it is not blinded by restrictive skip connections, which are unnecessary where only the same scale feature maps from the encoder and the decoder branches can be fused. To observe the efficiency of this proposed multipath network based on U-Net, its performance should be compared to the state-of-the-art methods with the RESIDE benchmark dataset [18] and also with images captured from some real world.

The most significant contributions of the proposed work are as follows:

- A unique multipath network based on the chain of U-Nets is proposed for effective dehazing in an end-to-end manner without relying on the concept of the atmospheric scattering model.
- The proposed Ladder-Net is the interconnection of U-Nets of variable depths and skip connections between each pair of adjoining encoder and decoder branches at every level.
- The concept of densely connected convolutions is used to refrain the network from learning redundant features and enhance the flow of information through the network.
- Two U-nets are used, as more encoder and decoder branches tend to increase the number of parameters and training difficulty.

The remaining portion of this paper is summed up in the following manner. Section 2 provides the work associated with haze removal. In Sect. 3, the proposed architecture for image dehazing is discussed. Sections 4 and 5 discuss experimental results and ablation studies. Section 6 presents the concluding remarks of the proposed work.

2 Related Work

Even though Image dehazing literature is available in a wide variety, haze removal is still an open topic to investigate. In contemporary research, there are three types of images dehazing techniques: image enhancement, image fusion and restoration, developed based on physical modeling. Methods based on the image enhancement technique do not consider the specific reason for the degradation of images. No fog is eliminated from the haze-affected image to return to the original clean image. Because of this, these image dehazing approaches are not adaptable to different images and scenes. Physical modeling-based image restoration approaches explore a fixed set of reasons behind the degradation of an image. In addition, this technique also creates a degraded model for images deteriorated due to fog. The physical modeling-based image restoration method follows the concept of the atmospheric scattering model. Atmospheric scattering can be categorized into two parts: The first is because of the light attenuation reflected from the object's surface to the camera; The second is because of air-light scattering of the camera. The theory of atmospheric scattering is proposed to explain how a hazy image formed in 1976 [17]. In [12], this theory is primarily used in computer vision applications and image recognition.

The formula for the atmospheric scattering model is as follows.

$$K(i) = I(i)t(i) + A(1 - t(i)) \tag{1}$$

where K is a degraded image because of haze, I is a clear hazy free image, and i is the position of a pixel within the image. Vector A used here is a three-dimensional constant that is in RGB space. A is the atmospherical light, and $t(i)$ is the medium for transmission that explains the quantity of light reaching the receiver. This parameter for medium transmission is inversely proportional to the depth and is formulated as follows.

$$t(i) = exp^{(-\beta d(i))} \tag{2}$$

t is a parameter related to transmission within the medium, and β is the atmospheric scattering coefficient. Here, the deterioration of atmospheric light and the transmission are combined and then it is defined by the $A(1 - t(i))$ term; air-light has been included to discuss the chance of scene color variation. The shift is because of various sources of illumination in addition to sunlight.

Methods based on Image fusion augment useful information from many different sources and achieve an image of high quality. These techniques do not require the physical model. But for information from multiple sources, the fusion strategy is very complicated. The fusion technique integrates necessary information from multiple sources into an image of highly noticeable quality. Fusion techniques extract relevant information from each channel to enhance the extent of utilizing the information of an image. In recent years, these approaches have also been utilized to remove the haze from the image. A single image haze removal algorithm that eliminates the visually degraded versions due to the haze has been described [16]. This algorithm does not depend on physical model inversion for haze formation, but it is considered a few basic ideas to get a clear image. An end-to-end training model called DehazeNet for estimating medium transmission parameters has been proposed in [14]. Input to this model is the deteriorated image due to the haze, producing a transmission matrix as its output. It aims at estimating the global atmospherical light by using some practical rules, and recovery of the hazy free image is achieved by using the concept of atmospheric scattering. AMEF - Artificial Multiple Exposure Fusion [16] used gamma correction operations to sequentially under-expose the hazy image artificially and a multi-scale Laplacian blending scheme to yield a haze-free image. In All-in-One Dehazing Network (AOD-Net) [15], a hazy free image is produced via a lightweight CNN instead of separately estimating atmospheric light and transmission matrix. The coarse scale net and fine scale net in Multi-Scale Convolutional Neural Networks (MSCNN) [27] enhance results locally by learning the mapping between hazy images and their related transmission maps.

To overcome the issues in physical modelling and fusion techniques, in this paper, a unique multipath network based on the chain of U-Nets is proposed for effective dehazing in an end-to-end manner without relying on the concept of the atmospheric scattering model. Multiple path networks designed based on the U-net architecture have a chain of numerous U-Nets. Rather than utilizing just one set of encoder branches and decoder branches in the U-Net structure, the proposed model uses multiple sets of encoder branches and decoder branches and has skip connections also between each adjoining encoder and decoder branches pair at every level. This enables the information flow and thereby improves the dehazing performance.

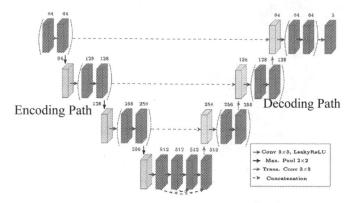

Fig. 1. Architecture of U-Net structure

3 Method

The architecture of the multipath networks is based on the chain of U-Nets architecture used for haze removal and is explained in this section. Then the superiority in performance by using the chain of multiple U-Nets and the benefit of using concatenation is presented. The basic idea of using the proposed model for single image dehazing is that hazy and hazy free images are directly mapped instead of learning from the air propagation (atmospheric scattering) model, comparing it to many previous CNN methods. As Ladder-Net is seen as a chain of multiple U-Nets, first, the U-Net architecture is discussed and then the basic U-Net architecture to the chain of two U-Nets, which forms a Ladder-Net, is extended. The basic U-Net architecture is shown in Fig. 1 and the Ladder-Net architecture is shown in Fig. 2. Training details and the model computational complexity are also explained in this section.

3.1 Motivation Behind the New Architecture

The architecture of the U-Network is as shown in Fig. 1. The proposed network takes advantage of the strength of densely connected convolutions by allowing it to learn different kinds of features. In U-net, the encoder branch extracts the desirable features from the sequential set of convolutional layers. The decoder branch then takes these feature maps extracted from the encoder as an input and rebuilds the required result by using these features. This encoder and decoder pairs in U-net improve the performance in several applications such as image segmentation and image recognition.

In the method, the single image haze removal is adopted by designing the encoding (contracting) path symmetric to the decoding (expansive) path, and it results in a U-shaped architecture (U-Net architecture). Specifically, in a U-Net, two layers of 3×3 convolution are applied repeatedly in the contracting path, in which each convolution layer is followed by the ReLU function and the max-pooling layer of size 2×2. Zero padding is used in the convolutional layers so that size won't get reduced. Usage of Pooling layers will help in reducing input size thereby speeding up the computations. It gives robustness to feature detection. The number of feature maps is doubled at each

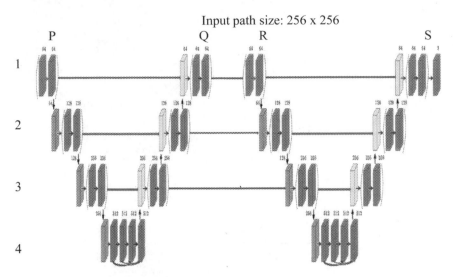

Fig. 2. Overall architecture of Multipath networks based on U-Net (Ladder-Net)

step of down sampling. A sequence of convolutional layers is used in the last step of the contracting path. Feature maps which are learned from all the previous convolutional layers and the current layer are concatenated and these are then forwarded so that they can be the input for the next convolution. On other hand, each step-in decoding path performs a transposed convolution over the previous layer output. The corresponding feature maps extracted in the encoding path are cropped and copied to the decoding path. Then these feature channels are concatenated with up-sampling function output. This helps the network in learning a diverse set of feature maps avoiding redundant features and eliminates the risk of gradients vanishing or exploding. It is found that the feature of a great way to combine feature and spatial information can benefit by studying the mathematical features of image dehazing. This type of integration can be provided by performing the up convolutions and the concatenations sequentially with the features of high resolution resulting from the contracting path.

3.2   Ladder-Net and U-Net

"Figure 2" shows the overall architecture of Multipath networks based on U-Net (Ladder-Net) with an input size of 256 × 256 pixels. Embedded input to the Ladder-Net is a haze degraded image.

U-net-based Multipath networks are viewed as a sequence of U-Nets. 1 and 2 Columns come under one U-Net whereas 3 and 4 Columns come under the second U-Net. There are skip connections at levels P-S between two U-Nets. By concatenating the features from encoder branches and decoder branches, the features are added from two branches from different U-Net. The proposed network allows numerous paths for the information flow and a few paths are listed as follows: (a) P1 → Q1 → R1 → S1, (b) P1 → Q1 → R2 → S2 → S1, (c) Q1 → Q2 → R2 → R3 → R4 → S3. In the proposed Ladder-Net, the skip connections also enable numerous paths for the information flow and the number of these paths exponentially increases with the increase in the number of encoder-decoder pairs. More encoder and decoder branches cause an increase in the number of parameters and because of this, training also becomes difficult so the proposed architecture is limited to only two U-nets.

3.3 Advantages of Using Dense Connections

Instead of just adding the features are concatenated. The input and the output images for dehazing using Encoding and Decoding structures are highly correlated. Because of this, carrying all the input pixel values till the end of the deeper network is unavoidable. This, however, increases the training burden and because of this, the network works inefficiently. These skip concatenations provide the solution to this problem through the introduction of shorter paths for carrying input values to the next layers of the deeper network. As components in longer paths make zero gradient vector and result in vanishing gradient problem in deeper networks. Therefore, skip connections forms shorter paths for the gradient backpropagation and reduces the vanishing gradient problem. However, reuse of preceding layer features is allowed by dense skip connections and the redundancy in re-learning of features is avoided.

3.4 Computational Complexity

Computational complexity plays a major role while designing any network. It is the key factor in deciding the deployment of the network in real-time. The total number of parameters that the network can optimize theoretically is defined as computational complexity. The below Eq. 3 provides computational complexity for any Fully connected Convolutional Neural network (FCN).

$$C = \sum_{l=1}^{D} n_{l-1} \times f^2 \times n_l \times S_l^2 \qquad (3)$$

where D is the network depth, l denotes the index of the layers used, S represents the size of the image from which the haze is to be removed and n_l denotes the total number of filters used in the l_{th} layer. n_0 represents the total number of channels in the input patch (3 color channels). The difference between practical computational complexity and theoretical computational complexity is based on the hardware implementation and the type of framework used.

3.5 Loss Function

Let's use $\{\ddot{\eta}_k \ \ddot{\Upsilon}_k\}$ to represent the number of samples to be trained. Similarly, let $\delta^p = \{x^p, y^p\}$ indicate the network parameters present in the individual layers. k stands for the kth training sample. Then the formula to minimize Mean Squared Error (MSE) ($N(\delta)$) can be as follows.

$$N(\delta) = \frac{1}{L} \sum_{k=1}^{L} \left\| F(\eta^k, \delta) - \gamma^k \right\|^2 + \pounds \|\delta\|^2 \qquad (4)$$

where δ is the network parameter vector, $F(\eta^k, \delta)$ is the network prediction for the kth sample out of L samples. Adam optimizer [21] is used with parameters μ_1, μ_2 being set to 0.9, 0.999 and ϵ being set to 10^{-8} respectively. Standard mini-batch gradient descent is used with each batch of size 64. The pth layer gradients are computed as.

$$g_{tl} = \Delta_{\delta p} N(\delta_p) \tag{5}$$

The formulas for momentum vectors are as given below.

$$\hat{m}_1 = \mu_1 \hat{m}_{t-1+}(1 - \mu_1)\, gt_1 .\, (vt) = \mu_2 v_{t-1+}(1 - \mu_2)\, gt_1^2 \tag{6}$$

The parameter can be finally updated as given below.

$$\delta_{p+1} = \delta_p - \frac{\eta}{\sqrt{\hat{v}_t} + \epsilon} \hat{m}_t \tag{7}$$

where $\hat{m}_t$ t and $\hat{v}_t$ prevents the formation of null vectors because mt and vt are initialized as zero and can be computed as follows.

$$\hat{m}_t = \frac{m_t}{1 - \mu_1^t}$$
$$\hat{v}_t = \frac{v_t}{1 - \mu_2^t} \tag{8}$$

4   Experiments

Experimental analysis for dehazing is explained in this section. The datasets used for training, performance comparison with the newest top dehazing approaches and network parameters are included in this section. Quantitative and qualitative analyses are also included.

4.1   Dataset Setup

The publicly available RESIDE benchmark dehaze dataset is used for training, validation, and testing because it has diverse and large-scale data sources and image contents. There is a total of synthetic hazy 313,950 outdoor images and 10,500 indoor images respectively in the RESIDE dataset from stereo and depth datasets as the extensive training and the testing pairs of hazy images. From the training pairs of RESIDE benchmark, 320 images from the dataset are used for training. From the 100 images 18960 training samples are cropped and each sample has a size of 37 × 37. 80 separate images are cropped to produce a validation set. The 91 separate images are considered for testing.

4.2 Training Details

The Chained U-Net is chosen with 4 levels (P-S) and a dropout rate of 0.25. In the first level (level P) the total number of channels is taken to be 64 and Adam optimizer with default parameters. The learning rate is reduced based on the plateau strategy and set to 0.01, 0.001 and 0.0001 on 0, 20 and 80 epochs respectively, and the total learning epochs are set as 120. The factor of regularization is fixed to $10 - 5$. During training, l_2 regularization is adopted, and the weight decay factor is set at a value of 5×10^{-5} to address over-and-under fitting. Gradient explosion will not occur because of employing a very low learning rate, so gradient clipping is not used. For training, a PC with the following specifications: Intel core I7 processor with 64 GB RAM and 2 GB NVIDIA GeForce 730 GPU and for the training followed by testing, MATLAB deep learning toolbox is used.

4.3 Metrics Used

For quantitative performance comparison, the metrics Pixel Signal to Noise ratio (PSNR) and Structural similarity (SSIM) index are used widely.

$$PSNR(I_G, I_D) = 10log_{10} \frac{I_{G_{max}}^2}{\frac{1}{N} \sum_{i=1}^{N} (I_{G_i} - I_D)^2} \tag{9}$$

$$SSIM(I_G, I_D) = \frac{\left(2\mu_{I_G}\mu_{I_D} + C_1\right)\left(2\sigma_{I_G I_D} + C_2\right)}{\left(\mu_{I_G}^2 + \mu_{I_D}^2 + C_1\right)\left(\sigma_{I_G}^2 + \sigma_{I_D}^2 + C_2\right)} \tag{10}$$

where I_G and I_D are the ground truth image and image dehazed respectively, μ I_G, μ_{I_D} represents the means of I_G and $\sigma_{I_G I_D}$, $\sigma_{I_G}^2$ represents the variance of ground truth I_G, $\sigma_{I_D}^2$ represents the variance of dehazed image I_D, $\sigma_{I_G I_D}$ is cross-covariance of ground truth haze-free image x and dehazed clean image I_D.

4.4 Compared Methods

To evaluate the performance efficiency of Multipath networks based on U-Net architecture, many top haze removal state of art methods has been chosen for comparing with our proposed network. These methods includes DehazeNet [14], DCP [22], CAP [23], AOD-Net [15], GFN [24], MSCNN [27], DCPDN [28], RYF-Net [25], PFF-Net [26] and AMEF [16].

4.5 Quantitative Metrics

The comparison of quantitative metrics for outdoor and indoor images is represented in Tables 1 and 2 respectively. The proposed method proves to be the top performer for both the metrics PSNR and SSIM when compared with different state-of-the-art dehazing methods. All the networks used the same RESIDE benchmark dataset for training. The improved performance in the proposed Ladder-Net is because it takes advantage of the strength of densely connected convolutions by allowing it to learn different kinds of features. In addition to this, the skip connections also enable multiple paths of the information flow and the number of these paths increases exponentially along with the increase in the number of encoder and decoder pairs.

Table 1. Comparison of the proposed model with existing dehazing algorithms for outdoor images.

Model	PSNR	SSIM
DCP [22]	19.13	0.8148
CAP [23]	19.05	0.8364
DehazeNet [14]	23.48	0.8915
MSCNN [27]	17.57	0.8102
AOD-Net [15]	20.29	0.8765
GFN [24]	21.55	0.8444
DCPDN [28]	22.49	0.8565
RYF-Net [25]	21.44	0.8716
PFF-Net [26]	21.12	0.8422
AMEF [16]	17.68	0.8349
Proposed	**26.88**	**0.9288**

Table 2. Comparison of the proposed model with existing dehazing algorithms for indoor images.

Model	PSNR	SSIM
DCP [22]	16.62	0.8179
CAP [23]	19.05	0.8364
DehazeNet [14]	21.14	0.8472
MSCNN [27]	19.06	0.8504
AOD-Net [15]	17.57	0.8102
GFN [24]	22.3	0.88
DCPDN [28]	19.13	0.8191
RYF-Net [25]	21.44	0.8716
PFF-Net [26]	24.7	0.8951
AMEF [16]	22.05	0.8472
Proposed	**24.69**	**0.9098**

4.6 Qualitative Comparison

The qualitative comparison of the dehazed images with other approaches is represented in "Fig. 3 and Fig. 4". The proposed method produces a better visual perceptual quality of the image when compared to dehazed images produced with different methods.

Ground truth   Hazy   DCP   AOD-Net   DehazeNet   Amef   **Proposed**

Fig. 3. Visual comparison of the proposed method with different methods qualitatively for outdoor images

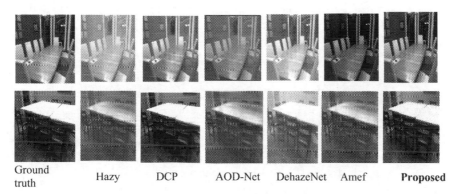

Ground truth   Hazy   DCP   AOD-Net   DehazeNet   Amef   **Proposed**

Fig. 4. Visual comparison of the method proposed with different methods qualitatively for Indoor images

5 Ablation Experiments

Before finalizing the Multipath networks based on U-Net (Ladder-Net) architecture, exhaustive ablation studies were done. First, the U-Net architecture is introduced to achieve single image dehazing without relying on the atmospheric scattering model. Experiments on the components of the basic U-Net architecture have been conducted. For this purpose, RESIDE benchmark set is used. From this, it is observed that skip connections increase the reconstruction accuracy. However, the number of paths for the flow of information is limited in U-Net. Then, it is hypothesized that a chain of U-Net architectures may be effective for the aggregation of local statistics and effective learning of features for haze removal. The number of paths increases exponentially along with the increase in the number of pairs of encoder and decoder branches and with the number of spatial levels. The PSNR and SSIM comparisons for these two variants in U-net models on RESIDE benchmark dataset are provided in Table 3 and Table 4 for outdoor and indoor images.

Table 3. Comparison of PSNR and SSIM between basic U-Net and the Ladder-Net architectures for outdoor images.

Structure	PSNR (dB)	SSIM
U-NET	25.05	0.9204
Proposed Ladder-Net	26.88	0.9288

Table 4. Comparison of PSNR and SSIM between basic U-Net and the Ladder-Net architectures for indoor images.

	PSNR (dB)	SSIM
U-NET	23.99	0.9080
Proposed Ladder-Net	24.69	0.9098

6 Conclusion

In this paper, the novelty of the deep learning based approach to the removal of haze using a single image has been proposed. The proposed method learns a mapping between haze and dehaze images end-to-end. By using a greater number of encoder-decoder pairs, better performance is achieved by the proposed model for PSNR and SSIM than that of the existing state-of-the-art dehazing methods for both outdoor images and indoor images. In the proposed Ladder-Net, the skip connections also enable multiple paths of the information flow and the number of these paths increases exponentially along with the increase in the number of encoder and decoder pairs. The proposed model achieved better PSNR and SSIM when compared to the existing algorithms.

References

1. Nayar, S.K., Narasimhan, S.G.: Vision in bad weather. In: Proceedings of IEEE Conference on Computer Vision, vol. 2, pp. 820–827, September 1999
2. Shehata, M.S., et al.: Video-based automatic incident detection for smart roads: the outdoor environmental challenges regarding false alarms. IEEE Trans. Intell. Transp. Syst. **9**(2), 349–360 (2008)

3. Sakaridis, C., Dai, D., Van Gool, L.: Semantic foggy scene understanding with synthetic data. Int. J. Comput. Vis. **126**(9), 973–992 (2018)
4. Liu, Y., et al.: Improved techniques for learning to dehaze and beyond: a collective study (2018). arXiv:1807.00202
5. Li, B., et al.: Benchmarking single-image dehazing and beyond. IEEE Trans. Image Process. **28**(1), 492–505 (2019)
6. Woodell, G., Jobson, D.J., Rahman, Z., Hines, G.: Advanced image processing of aerial imagery. In: Proceedings of SPIE 6246, Visual Information Processing XV, 62460E (12 May 2006)
7. Shao, L., Liu, L., Li, X.: feature learning for image classification via multiobjective genetic programming. IEEE Trans. Neural Netw. Learn. Syst. **25**(7), 1359–1371 (2014). https://doi.org/10.1109/TNNLS.2013.2293418
8. Liu, Q., Gao, X., He, L., Lu, W.: Haze removal for a single visible remote sensing image. Signal Process. **137,** 33–43 (2017). ISSN 0165-1684. https://doi.org/10.1016/j.sigpro.2017.01.036
9. Kim, T.K., Paik, J.K., Kang, B.S.: Contrast enhancement system using spatially adaptive histogram equalization with temporal filtering. IEEE Trans. Consum. Electr. **44**(1), 82–87(1998). https://doi.org/10.1109/30.663733
10. Stark, J.A.: Adaptive image contrast enhancement using generalizations of histogram equalization. IEEE Trans. Image Process. **9**(5), 889–896 (2000). https://doi.org/10.1109/83.841534
11. Schechner, Y., Narasimhan, S., Nayar, S.: Polarization-based vision through haze, Appl. Opt. **42**, 511–525 (2003)
12. Narasimhan, S.G., Nayar, S.K.: Contrast restoration of weather degraded images. IEEE Trans. Pattern Anal. Mach. Intell. **25**(6), 713–724 (2003). https://doi.org/10.1109/TPAMI.2003.1201821
13. Li, Y., You, S., Brown, M.S., Tan, R.T.: Haze visibility enhancement: a survey and quantitative benchmarking. Comput. Vis. Image Understand. **165**, 1–16 (2017)
14. Cai, B., Xu, X., Jia, K., Qing, C., Tao, D.: DehazeNet: an end-to-system for single image haze removal. IEEE Trans. Image Process. **25**(11), 5187–5198 (2016). https://doi.org/10.1109/TIP.2016.2598681
15. Li, B., Peng, X., Wang, Z., Xu, J., Feng, D.: AOD-net: all-in-one dehazing network. Proc. IEEE Int. Conf. Comput. Vis. **1**(4), 4770–4778 (2017)
16. Galdran, A.: Image dehazing by artificial multiple-exposure image fusion. Signal Process. **149,** 135–147 (2018). ISSN:0165-1684,https://doi.org/10.1016/j.sigpro.2018.03.008
17. Cantor, A.: Optics of the atmosphere–scattering by molecules and particles. IEEE J. Quant. Electr. **14**(9), 698–699 (1978). https://doi.org/10.1109/JQE.1978.1069864
18. Li, B., et al.: RESIDE: a benchmark for single image dehazing, arXiv preprint arXiv:1712.04143 (2017)
19. Gondara, L.: Medical image denoising using convolutional denoising autoencoders. In: IEEE 16th International Conference on Data Mining Workshops (ICDMW), pp. 241–246 (2016)
20. Mao, X., Shen, C., Yang, Y.-B.: Image restoration using very deep convolutional encoder-decoder networks with symmetric skip connections. Adv. Neural Inf. Process. Syst. 2810–2818 (2016)
21. Kingma, D.B., Jimmy, B.: Adam: a method for stochastic optimization. In: international Conference on Learning Representations (2014)
22. He, K., Sun, J., Tang, X.: Single image haze removal using dark channel prior. IEEE Trans. Pattern Anal. Mach. Intell. **33**(12), 2341–2353 (2011)
23. Zhu, Q., Mai, J., Shao, L.: A fast single image haze removal algorithm using color attenuation prior. IEEE Trans. Image Process. **24**(11), 3522–3533 (2015)

24. Ren, W., et al.: Gated fusion network for single image dehazing. In: Proceedings of the IEEE Computer Society Conference on Computer Vision and Pattern Recognition, pp. 3253–3261, June 2018
25. Dudhane, A., Murala, S.: RYF-Net: deep fusion network for single image haze removal. IEEE Trans. Image Process. **29**, 628–640 (2019)
26. Mei, K., Jiang, A., Li, J., Wang, M.: Progressive feature fusion network for realistic image dehazing. In: Proceedings Asian Conference on Computer Vision pp. 203–215 (2018)
27. Ren, W., Liu, S., Zhang, H., Pan, J., Cao, X., Yang, M.-H.: Single image dehazing via multi-scale convolutional neural networks. In: Leibe, B., Matas, J., Sebe, N., Welling, M. (eds.) ECCV 2016. LNCS, vol. 9906, pp. 154–169. Springer, Cham (2016). https://doi.org/10.1007/978-3-319-46475-6_10
28. Zhang, H., Patel, V.M.: Densely connected pyramid dehazing network. In: Proceedings of the IEEE Conference on Computer Vision and Pattern Recognition, pp. 3194–3203, June 2018

Leveraging Tri-Planar Views and Weighted Average Fusion Technique to Classify Lung Nodule Malignancy

Samiksha Gupta[1]($^{\boxtimes}$) (iD), Satish Kumar Singh[1] (iD), and Xiaoyi Jiang[2]($^{\boxtimes}$) (iD)

[1] Department of Information Technology, IIIT Allahabad, Allahabad, India
{mit2020105,sk.singh}@iiita.ac.in
[2] Faculty of Mathematics and Computer Science, University of Münster, Münster, Germany
xjiang@uni-muenster.de

Abstract. Lung cancer is among the world's worst malignancies. The textured features of a nodule are crucial indications of malignancy in the diagnosis of lung cancer. Effectively in A CAD system, extracting the nodule's features from CT (computed tomography) images is difficult due to a lack of huge annotated training datasets. In our work, we propose a weighted average fusion technique based on transferred models to improve the performance of lung nodule classification in the CAD system. Initially, the performance of learning architectures (such as InceptionV3, ResNet50, DenseNet121, VGG16, ResNet50V2 and ResNet152V2) was evaluated. It was found that transfer learning technique performed better than the traditional machine learning models. We leveraged the triplanar views and the GAP layer to improve the accuracy. The results are presented for the publicly available LIDC/IDRI dataset. After that, we built a weighted average fusion model upon the transferred models to derive the better accuracy from the highest-achieving model and achieved the best performance on an unbiased test set with an accuracy of $90.25 \pm 0.45\%$ and AUC of 0.97.

Keywords: Lung nodule malignanacy classification · computer tomography · convolutional neural network · transfer learning · triplanar view · weighted average model · fusion model

1 Introduction

Lung cancer is one of the most lethal cancers with a rising prevalence. It has a dreadful impact on people's life [22]. This condition can be effectively treated with radiotherapy and chemotherapy. Lung cancer patients, on the contrary, for a period of five years have a rate of survival of 16% [16]. Early diagnosis of pulmonary cancer detection is essential since it can enhance the survival chances [8].

Computer aided detection (CAD) has become an important system for radiologists to detect cancer of lungs as technology advances. It also aids in detection of lung nodules with accuracy and cut down on the amount of misdiagnoses and missed nodules [6]. A well-functioning pulmonary CAD system should be able to detect nodule candidates and reduce false positives. False positive reduction is a critical to reduce wrong diagnoses. The diversity of nodules makes it challenging for CAD systems to detect them. Lung nodules include several distinct characteristics, including margin information, size, shape, and patterns of calcification. Above mentioned characteristics are used to identify nodules [17]. In recent years, texture characteristics for image classification have gotten a lot of attention. [12], as well as for nodule classification in the medical diagnostics [10]. Meanwhile, deep learning techniques, particularly CNNs, have recently been applied to classify lung nodules with encouraging results [20,21].

Setio et al. [19] proposes to break down a three-dimensional pulmonary nodule into nine fixed view planes. Using a multi-view architecture, these are further processed to have patches of image are extracted on every plane trained using 2D CNN and then the outputs of all CNNs are combined using a strategy called late-fusion. Medical images are classified using a deep network. Zhu et al. utilises a completely automated three-dimensional deep CNN [4] for classification and identification of lung nodule. In the LUNGx challenge dataset, Wang et al. [1] achieved an accuracy and AUC score of 90.38% and 94.48%, respectively using a CNN model for pulmonary nodule classification.

From the set of pixels observed in medical imaging, CNNs eventually build higher-level features. However, CNN needs more training data to extract these features more efficiently, otherwise leading to epistemic uncertainty. To overcome this problem pre-trained model has been introduced. As a result, various attempts are done to use the transfer learning approaches for solving difficulty of small medical datasets [7,9]. For the classification of lung nodule, Zhao et al. [25] applied a transfer learning and fine-tuning technique. All four layers of the CNN architectures, which had previously been trained on natural images, were fine-tuned. Xie et al. [24] offered a deep model for malignancy classification. Using LIDC-IDRI dataset, they had achieved an 91.60% accuracy. [5] CNN's adaptation is impeded by the lack of a categorised medical database, additionally to worries about privacy with medical images. Where in previous findings they have used a complex or highly computationally expensive 3D CNN models and CNN models built from scratch require more data to be trained properly. Pre-trained models were utilised in some studies, although the AUC and accuracy were quite low.

In our work, we introduced and analysed six models of different types for malignant and benign nodule classification (using LIDC/IDRI dataset). ResNet50, InceptionV3, DenseNet121, VGG16, ResNet50V2 and ResNet152V2 are the six transfer learning models. On top of the convolution base of the transfer learning model, GAP layers have been added to substitute (via pooling operation) the fully connected layers in classical CNNs for binary classification. Moreover, a novel methodology is proposed by us that merges the two best-performing models, and weights are assigned to each model to get better accuracy. The following is a list of our study's contributions. (1) The proposed approach of transfer learning is able to acquire important features from the training data and accomplish seamless classification rather than building specific CNNs from zero. (2) The approach of transfer learning beat both the CNN model and the classic model of machine learning, while the weighted average fusion model merging Resnet-50 and Inception-V3 outperformed all other non fused models.

The later section of the work is structured in the following manner. Section 2 outlines the methodology and the architecture of our proposed lung nodule malignancy classification scheme, as well as lays the design of the proposed architecture. Section 3 contains the information about data, including a brief on database description and data preprocessing. The results and evaluation are discussed in Sect. 4 while the conclusion of the work carried out is described in Sect. 5.

2   Method and Workflow

Due to the limited training dataset, training a CNN model from the ground up is a highly extensive process. So, pre-training a network over a dataset of imagenet and performing the fine-tuning, for a small medical dataset is an effective method of achieving acceptable accuracy while cutting down on training time. Even though the classification of lung cancer in LIDC/IDRI images differs from object detection in the imagenet dataset though may share similar learned features. The core strategy of our study is briefly outlined in this part, followed by DCNN models. Following that, we present the weighted average fusion strategies.

2.1   Pre-trained Deep Convolutional Neural Network (DCNN) Architectures

ResNet: The ResNet model is made up of a series of comparable (or residual) blocks, each of which is comprised of convolutional layers. Through an identity mapping path, a block's output is linked to its own input. This method eliminates vanishing gradients and improves gradient backward flow, allowing for much more extensive network training. The three ResNet models employed in our research were ResNet50, ResNet50V2, and ResNet152V2. The model, trained on the dataset of ImageNet, has a top 1 accuracy rate of 78.0% and top 5 accuracy rate of 94.2%.

InceptionV3: InceptionV3 is reimagining of InceptionV1 and InceptionV2 initial structure. The ImageNet dataset was used to train the model, which can recognise the classes having top 5 error rate of 3.5% and a top 1 error rate of 17.3%. In general, InceptionV3 beats prior CNN models in terms of memory retention.

*DenseNet:*Feature propagation, feature reuse, and decreasing the amount of parameters has been improved by eliminating the problem of vanishing gradient which is provided by DenseNets. It has a top 5 accuracy rate of 92.3% and a top 1 accuracy rate of 75.3%.

Many deep CNN architectures have been pre-trained on the imagenet dataset for object classification, and are open to the public. As a result, have no need to train those DCNN from the ground up. In our analysis, we employed the Keras module, which offered the best performing pretrained model weights. Our research does include a two-stage process for training (1) using a model that had been pre-trained on a huge dataset in the target domain with common features for the majority of computer vision issues, and (2) freeze the few top layers on a LIDC/IDRI dataset in the target domain and then fine-tune it.

2.2   Importance of Global Average Pooling (GAP) Layer

To fastrack the training process and reduce the sensitivity of network initialization, the GAP is utilised to substitute completely connected layers in classical CNNs and ReLU layers. Convolution is performed in the lowest layers of traditional convolutional neural networks. Flatten layer vectorizes the feature maps from the final convolutional layer, which are then sent into a fully connected layer (Dense), followed by a sigmoid classifier. The fully connected layers, on the contrary, are vulnerable to overfitting, thus limiting the generalization of the overall network. Hinton et al. [15] propose Dropout is a regularizer that, during training, turns 50% of the activations to fully connected layers to zero at random. It has increased generalization ability and reduced overfitting to a great extent [11].

To overcome the vanishing gradient problem and promote generalizations, the rectified linear unit (ReLU) is utilised. It has been used as an activation function at the ending of the convolutional layer [2]. When employing back-propagation to train a neural network, the function is linear for values greater than zero, indicating that it possesses many of the desirable characteristics of a linear activation function (Fig. 1).

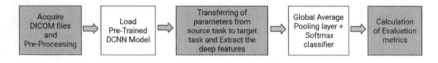

Fig. 1. The process for a nodule classification by using pre-trained CNN model.

2.3   Proposed Weighted Average Fusion Technique

Initially, we have classified the images using single pre-trained architectures, in which include-top set to False to prevent the pre-trained model from including the fully connected and final pooling layer. A global average pooling layer has been added, succeeded by a one dense layer with a kernel size of 64×64 and a dropout layer with just a value of 0.5. The GAP layer was firstly used by Min Lin and Yan in 2014 [14]. To substitute the typical fully connected layers in the CNN for improving generalization capability, they introduced the GAP layer. Basic strategy is to generate one feature map for all the categories in the final layer. We average each feature map, and the resultant vector is sent straight into the softmax layer.

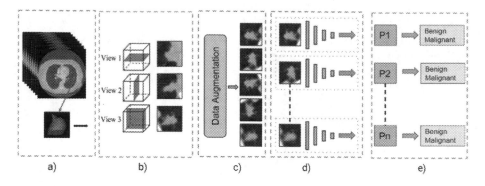

Fig. 2. The framework of proposed method. (a) Pulmonary candidate nodule extraction (b) Generating 2D images of a candidate nodule cube from three distinct angles (c) On all views, data augmentation (flip, rotation at different angles, blur) was applied. (d) Various pre-trained CNN models are employed to extract Feature, followed by GAP layer. (e) Binary classification performed using Softmax classifier.

Using the above methodology, we achieved a remarkable AUC, but the accuracy was not satisfactory, so to improve the accuracy we have proposed a weighted average fusion technique by fusing two models to get better results. Using this technique we improved the accuracy by around 1.5%.

A single algorithm might not have been able to produce the best prediction for a particular dataset. ML algorithms contain flaws, and developing a high-accuracy model is challenging. If we build and integrate several models, the model's overall accuracy may increase. Combining the outputs from each model may be done with two aims in mind: decreasing model error while retaining generalization.

To determine whether a lung nodule is malignant or benign, we propose a novel approach that merges the two best performing models, and based on the performance of each model, weights have been assigned to the model. The argmax of the accumulated probabilities for each class label is used to compute the prediction. A weighted fusion approach is an extension of model averaging in which each member's contribution to the final prediction has been given a weights based on their performance. The model weights are positive real numbers with a total of one, indicating the performance of each model. Figure 2 illustrates the suggested design.

Based on the above findings Table 3 shows that ResNet50, InceptionV3 and DenseNet121 are the top-performing models. We fused these models in different combinations, and found the fusion of ResNet50 and InceptionV3 outperform other combinations. ResNet is based on residual learning which incorporates skipping connections using which vanish gradient problems in the lower layer are avoided, whereas Three highly developed convolution modules constitute InceptionV3, which can both provide distinguishing features and lessen the number of parameters. It is frequently used in medical imaging to classify irregularities, in particular to determine the illness stage. Compared to the other transfer learning models like VGG, DenseNet family, Inception is more efficient, has a deeper network, and yet maintains its speed. It is also computationally less costly and employs additional Classifiers as regularizers (Fig. 3).

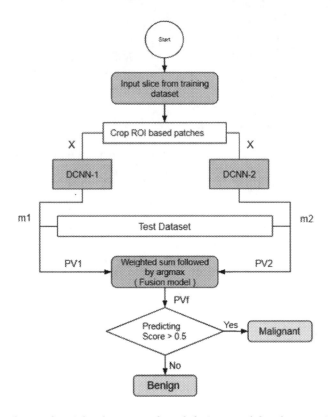

Fig. 3. Flow-chart of weighted average based fusion model: where × is the images patches, m1, m2 are the best saved model, PV1, PV2 are a predicting vectors and PVf is the final prediction value.

The weighted average fusion model has been based on the maximum likelihood of two classification results using ResNet50 and Inception-V3's output features. Consider the following dataset to train the model:

$$(X_1, Y_1), (X_2, Y_2), (X_3, Y_3)....(X_N, Y_N) \tag{1}$$

where Xi is the image patch's feature vector, Yi is the associated class's label, and N denotes the total number of image patches for training. For all the lung nodule image patches, feature maps have been obtained from ResNet50 and Inception-V3. We retrieved j feature maps for a nodule if a lung nodule has j slices. where PV1 and PV2 are the prediction vectors which are obtained from different models. After finding a vector from each model, We find a weighted average using tensordot across all the model, then apply argmax across the classes.

$$tdot = tensordot(\{PV_1, PV_2\}, W, axes = (0, 0)) \tag{2}$$

As shown in Eq. 2, the prediction vector is updated based on the greatest likelihood of the each feature map.

$$PV_f = argmax(tdot) \tag{3}$$

The final prediction vector is PVf. The labels were then assigned based on final prediction on vector's prediction score for each class, as shown in Eq. 3

$$Y_C = \begin{cases} Malignant, & \text{if } Score \geq 0.5 \\ Benign, & \text{otherwise.} \end{cases} \tag{4}$$

3   Dataset and Data Handling

First, the annotations from the LIDC/IDRI dataset are preprocessed, and images of nodules of pulmonary are extracted. Following that, pylidc library is applied to the above-mentioned dicom files to extract the annotated information, and relevant area and convert it into cross-sectional images, resulting in a new dataset (Fig. 4).

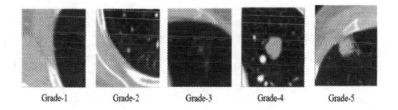

Grade-1   Grade-2   Grade-3   Grade-4   Grade-5

Fig. 4. 5 categories of nodules based on malignancy.

The publicly available LIDC-IDRI database comprises 244,527 thoracic CT scan data from 1,010 people. XML annotation files consist of each nodule's x and y-axis coordinates, as well as its boundary information, and additionally include semantic diagnostic features that were identified by four pulmonary radiologists with extensive experience. They assigned a score of 1 to 5 to each feature. To determine which annotation is assigned to the corresponding nodule, we used available XML files. The degree of malignancy for each lung nodule was graded by radiologists into 1 of 5 categories, as shown in Table 1.

Table 1. Severity of Cancer for each lung nodules.

Onset of cancer	Severity of Cancer
High unlikely for cancer	1
Moderate unlikely for cancer	2
Indeterminate likelihood	3
Moderate likely for cancer	4
High likely for cancer	5

3.1 Data Transformation and Patch Generation

The database of LIDC-IDRI contains a diverse group of scans obtained by utilizing various reconstruction and capture parameters. The DICOM format is used for all of the slices, where pixels have a depth of 16 bits and a size of 512×512. All the CT scans are firstly transformed to the Hounsfield (HU) scales, then to a range of values to normalise the pixels ($-1000, 500$ HU). Then the creation of patches of image is done in two steps. [5] Firstly, coordinates of centre (x, y, z) are obtained and sliced the number of benign and malignant nodules from the related XML file to extract a Region of Interest (ROI) around nodule. Then some pixels are taken around the central coordinates considering slice thickness to get the voxel coordinates of $48 \times 48 \times 48$ volume. For the LIDC-IDRI database, nodule sizes range from 3 mm to 30 mm, while thickness of slice ranges from 0.6 mm to 5 mm. Later, we used voxel coordinates obtained in the previous phase to extract triplanar view patches of size 32×32. During the extraction of each patch, we used identical central coordinates (x, y) for every slice. Three planar views (Axial, Sagittal, Coronal) are reconstructed based on the centroid of each connected component [13].

Moreover, on the other end, attempts to solve two-class problem by developing system that can distinguish among malignant and benign nodule images. As a result, non-malignant nodules were categorized as classes 1 and 2, class 3 nodules were ignored, and malignant nodules were characterized as classes 4 and 5. Finally, just 850 nodules remain from the original 7371 nodules, with 448 benign and 402 malignant nodules.

3.2 Image Augmentation

With a limited quantity of training data, augmentation of image is a wonderful approach to increase the deep networks' performance. To increase the deep CNN's testing accuracy, a large amount of sample data can be used to minimize the loss function and, as a result, improve the network's robustness. Image augmentation uses various methods of image processing, like translation, resizing, flips, rotation and construct training images artificially. Image processing operations like, random rotation (90, 180, 270), flips, translation, resize and blur are performed in proposed method. Six images have been generated for each view.

Figure 5 are augmented images of the Axial plane in (fig. a) and (fig. b). where the original image is on the top left, the blurred image is on the bottom right, and others are rotated images.

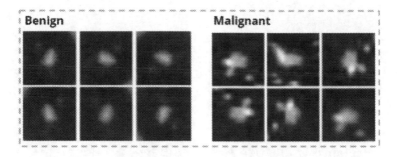

Fig. 5. Top left is original image, bottom right is blurred and other images are rotated and flipped a) Benign Nodule Augmentation b) Malignant Nodule Augmentation.

4   Results and Evaluation

In our work, the task of classifying lung nodule is carried out by using weighted average fusion model by selecting feature maps which are obtained from pretrained DCNNs. All experiments are carried out on a local machine with Intel(R) Core(TM) i5 processor, 16 GB RAM.

4.1   Evaluation Metrics

Evaluation metrics can be used to explain a model's performance. Evaluation metrics has ability to distinguish between model results

Accuracy: For evaluating the problems of classification one of the great option is accuracy that is balanced and isn't skewed, or the classes are balanced.

Precision: It explains what percentage of anticipated Positives are actually Positive. The percentage of your results that are relevant is referred to as precision.

Recall: It specifies the percentage of actual Positives that are appropriately classified. When we aim to acquire as many positives as possible, recall is a good option of evaluation metric.

Area under curve: The AUC ROC shows how well the positive and negative groups' probabilities are differentiated. Scaling has no effect on the AUC. It measures how effectively predictions are ordered rather than assessing absolute values.

F1-score: To construct a single score, F1-score will take into consideration the harmonic mean of a classifier's recall and precision. Basically it is used for comparing the outcomes which are obtained by two different classifiers (Table 2).

Table 2. Details of evaluation metrics.

Evaluation metrics	Mathematical Expression
Accuracy	$\frac{TP+TN}{TP+FP+FN+TN}$
Recall	$\frac{TP}{TP+FN}$
Precision	$\frac{TP}{TP+FP}$
F1-Score	$2 * \frac{Precision*recall}{Precision+recall}$

Where The true positive is TP, the true negative is TN, the false positive is FP, and the false negative is FN.

4.2 Performance Evaluation Based on Single Model

This section describes the experimental findings obtained by using Global averaging pooling on features extracted by InceptionV3, ResNet50, DenseNet121, VGG16, ResNet50V2, and ResNet152V2. The results are divided into two sections: first compares deep extractors using the evaluation metrics ACC, AUC, Precision, and Recall then seeks to find the best deep transfer learning model; the second compares the best results achieved with other ways described in the literature. The ROC curve (Area Under the Curve) is an evaluation metric for different threshold levels of classification methods. The AUC is a indicator of separability, while the ROC is a probabilistic curve. It demonstrates how well the model differentiates across classes. The AUC represents how effectively the model predicts first and second classes as first and second, respectively. The greater the AUC, the better the model predicts first and second classes as first and second, respectively. In general, the higher the AUC, the better the model discriminate between people having illness or not (Fig. 6).

The fundamental measure for evaluating the prediction ability of categorization systems has been predictive accuracy. The majority of classifiers also generate classification probability estimates, but they are entirely ignored in the accuracy measure. The area covered under the curve of ROC, or simply AUC, is a more appropriate metric than accuracy [26]. The significance of their findings implies that AUC should be used instead of accuracy when evaluating and comparing categorization systems.

All the above-mentioned researchers use the same dataset LIDC/IDRI. Authors have used a variety of methodologies in relation to pretrained models and their combinations. Table 3 shows the performance analysis of different deep transfer learning model. In terms of lung nodule malignancy classification our result demonstrated, ResNet-50, DenseNet121, and Inception-V3 are giving best performance compare to other specified models. The classification results were based on model's maximum computed likelihood score. Figure 5 shows a ROC

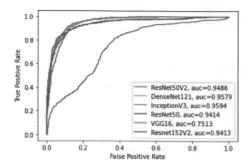

Fig. 6. ROC comparison of Six transfer learning model.

Table 3. Comparison of the performance among different Pre-trained models.

Model	ACC	Precision	Recall	AUC
ResNet50	88.09	84.5	85.66	94.14
InceptionV3	**89.05**	85.4	87.39	**95.94**
VGG16	68.56	57.5	85.14	75.53
ResNet152v2	87.92	82.81	87.82	94.13
DenseNet121	88.84	87.76	83.59	95.79
ResNet50V2	87.40	78.22	94.64	94.86

plot comparison of six pre-trained models. Among the other networks, InceptionV3 has the largest area under the ROC curve. Table 4 shows a comparison of our suggested model with state-of-the-art approaches.

As per score of 95.94%, it could be seen that the proposed approach outperforms in terms of AUC. respectively.

Table 4. Comparison between the Performance of the suggested approach with state-of-the-art methods on the LIDC-IDRI database.

Model	Year	AUC
local-global [3]	2018	95.62
Xie et al. [23]	2018	94.43
S. Akila at el. [24]	2020	94.9
Wang at el. [1]	2020	94.48
I. Ali at el. [5]	2021	94.46
P. Zahi at el. [18]	2020	95.59
Proposed GAP-DCNN model	2022	**95.94**
Proposed fusion model	2022	**97.00**

In local-global [3] for local feature extraction Residual Blocks are used with a kernel of size 3×3 and then to extract the global features Non-Local Blocks are used, achieving good results of $AUC = 95.62\%$. Xie et al. [23] used multi-view knowledge-based collaborative (MV-KBC) model in which 9 views of voxel have been considered and achieved an AUC of percentage 95.70 for pulmonary nodule classification. The suggested model has a rather high computational complexity during training due to the inclusion of 27 ResNet-50 models. training the model takes roughly 20 h. However, Akila et el. [24] for classification of patches of the 2D nodule, several DCNNs such as LSTM, RNN, and CNN were used. The AUCs of the LSTM and CNN models are 0.912 and 0.944. Recently, Wang at el. [1] The multi-scale method uses different sized filters to extract nodule features from local regions more effectively, for global regions nodule extraction the architecture of multi-path along with features being extracted from various ConvNet layers used and achieved an AUC of 0.948. P. Zahi at el. [18] multi-task CNN (MT-CNN) is employed and achieved an AUC of 95.59% in LIDC-IDRI. By leveraging fewer computationally intensive resources, the suggested technique surpasses the state-of-the-art AUC and attains the 0.97 AUC.

4.3   Results for Weighted Average Based Fusion Model

The weighted average fusion has been used on ResNet-50 and Inception-V3, two of the best lung nodule classification systems available. Between both DCNNs models, the maximum obtained likelihood score was used to classify the fusion results. Table 5 shows a comparison of all the fusion models based on different weights. The findings reveal that utilising weights [0.4,0.6], the suggested fusion technique effectively categorised each and every class with an overall accuracy of 90.70% for benign and 90.20% for malignant on ResNet-50 and Inception-V3 (Fig. 7).

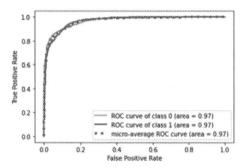

Fig. 7. ROC plot for malignant and benign class using fusion model.

Although using accuracy as a defining parameter for our model makes intuitive sense, it is usually good to include Precision and Recall as well. There may be additional instances when our precision or recall is great but our accuracy

Table 5. Performance comparison based on different weights of fusion model Resnet-50 + Inception-v3.

weights	ACC	Precision	Recall	AUC	F1-score
[0.7,0.3]	89.5	83.36	91.21	96.7	87.11
[0.6,0.4]	89.94	84.6	90.9	96.8	87.6
[0.5,0.5]	90.39	87.58	89.43	96.85	88.4
[0.45,0.55]	**90.67**	89.45	88.38	**96.87**	**88.9**
[0.4,0.6]	90.3	89.81	87.5	96.8	88.6
[0.3,0.7]	89.87	91.39	85.58	96.5	88.4

is poor. In an ideal scenario, We want to avoid any scenarios where the patient has lung cancer but our model says he doesn't, therefore we're aiming for a high recall. Other than that, in cases where the patient does not have lung cancer but our model predicts the contrary, we would like to avoid treating a patient who does not have cancer.

Although we try for high precision and recall value, we cannot achieve both at the same time. For example, if we alter the model to one that has a high recall of 91.21 using weights [0.7,0.3], we may be able to detect all of the patients who have lung cancer, but we may also treat a large number of patients who do not. Similarly, if we seek for high precision of 91.39 using weights [0.3,0.7] to prevent offering any unnecessary or incorrect therapy, we may end up with a large number of people with lung cancer who go untreated. We can just aim for a high F1 score, which indicates good Accuracy as well as balancing the precision and recall.

Based on the given observations, it's seen that with the increase in weights of ResNet-50 accuracy decreases and Recall increases, and with the increase in weights of inception-V3 accuracy decreases and precision increases. By transferring two CNN models (ResNet50 and InceptionV3) with weights [0.45, 0.5], the suggested technique performed well in lung cancer classification, as shown in Table 5. The transferred InceptionV3 model had the greatest accuracy of the six models. With score of 90.46 ± 0.4%, 88.4 ± 0.11%, 88.9 ± 011% and 96.8 ± 0.11%, the proposed methodology surpasses the accuracy, recall, F1-score, and AUC.

5   Conclusion

We attempted to show that a deep neural network trained on the imagenet achieves a high accuracy despite consuming minimal processing power. Our method was able to detect salient features that aided in the classification of pulmonary nodule malignancy. By fine-tuning suitable hyper-parameters, we compared the performance of several pre-trained models. Our studies found that the proposed model can generalize to unseen datasets, which is a great step toward robustness. Instead of employing several fully connected layers after feature extraction, which may lead to overfitting, we employed a global average pooling layer followed by a two FC layers for pulmonary nodule malignancy classification. To evaluate performance, features were collected from six state of the art transferable architectures. The global average pooling (GAP) layer helped to enhance classification accuracy.

Among the above-mentioned CNN models, transferred InceptionV3 was able to achieve exemplary results on the LIDC dataset touching an accuracy of 89.05% and AUC of 0.9594, which outperformed the traditional models learning from scratch. Transferring the InceptionV3 model from an imagenet dataset to the LIDC/IDRI dataset can be a good method to construct a DCNN model for the classification problem. Finally, we demonstrate that the suggested methodology of weighted average fusion performed better in comparision to the recent state-of-the-art techniques. The accuracy, AUC, and precision, the classification scores attained is $90.25 \pm 0.45\%$, $96.8 \pm 0.11\%$ and $89.4 \pm 0.11\%$.

References

1. Abdelrahman, S.A., Abdelwahab, M.M., Sayed, M.S.: Pulmonary nodule and malignancy classification employing triplanar views and convolutional neural network. In: 2019 IEEE 62nd International Midwest Symposium on Circuits and Systems (MWSCAS), pp. 594–597. IEEE (2019)
2. Agnes, S.A., Anitha, J.: Automatic 2D lung nodule patch classification using deep neural networks. In: 2020 Fourth International Conference on Inventive Systems and Control (ICISC), pp. 500–504. IEEE (2020)
3. Al-Shabi, M., Lan, B.L., Chan, W.Y., Ng, K.H., Tan, M.: Lung nodule classification using deep local-global networks. Int. J. Comput. Assist. Radiol. Surg. **14**(10), 1815–1819 (2019)
4. Ali, I., Muzammil, M., Haq, I.U., Khaliq, A.A., Abdullah, S.: Efficient lung nodule classification using transferable texture convolutional neural network. IEEE Access **8**, 175859–175870 (2020)
5. Ali, I., Muzammil, M., Haq, I.U., Khaliq, A.A., Abdullah, S.: Deep feature selection and decision level fusion for lungs nodule classification. IEEE Access **9**, 18962–18973 (2021)
6. Awai, K., et al.: Pulmonary nodules at chest CT: effect of computer-aided diagnosis on radiologists' detection performance. Radiology **230**(2), 347–352 (2004)
7. Banerjee, I., Crawley, A., Bhethanabotla, M., Daldrup-Link, H.E., Rubin, D.L.: Transfer learning on fused multiparametric MR images for classifying histopathological subtypes of rhabdomyosarcoma. Comput. Med. Imaging Graph. **65**, 167–175 (2018)
8. Knight, S.B., Crosbie, P.A., Balata, H., Chudziak, J., Hussell, T., Dive, C.: Progress and prospects in early detection in lung cancer. Open Biol. **7**(9), 170070 (2017)
9. Cheng, P.M., Malhi, H.S.: Transfer learning with convolutional neural networks for classification of abdominal ultrasound images. J. Digit. Imaging **30**(2), 234–243 (2017)
10. Han, F., et al.: Texture feature analysis for computer-aided diagnosis on pulmonary nodules. J. Digit. Imaging **28**(1), 99–115 (2015)

11. Hinton, G.E., Srivastava, N., Krizhevsky, A., Sutskever, I., Salakhutdinov, R.R.: Improving neural networks by preventing co-adaptation of feature detectors. arXiv preprint arXiv:1207.0580 (2012)
12. Jia, S., Deng, B., Zhu, J., Jia, X., Li, Q.: Local binary pattern-based hyperspectral image classification with superpixel guidance. IEEE Trans. Geosci. Remote Sens. **56**(2), 749–759 (2017)
13. Krizhevsky, A., Sutskever, I., Hinton, G.E.: Imagenet classification with deep convolutional neural networks. In: Advances in Neural Information Processing Systems, vol. 25 (2012)
14. Lin, M., Chen, Q., Yan, S.: Network in network. arXiv preprint arXiv:1312.4400 (2013)
15. Ling, C.X., Huang, J., Zhang, H.: AUC: a better measure than accuracy in comparing learning algorithms. In: Xiang, Y., Chaib-draa, B. (eds.) AI 2003. LNCS, vol. 2671, pp. 329–341. Springer, Heidelberg (2003). https://doi.org/10.1007/3-540-44886-1_25
16. Midthun, D.E.: Early diagnosis of lung cancer. F1000prime Reports, vol. 5 (2013)
17. Ost, D., Fein, A.M., Feinsilver, S.H.: The solitary pulmonary nodule. New Engl. J. Med. **348**(25), 2535–2542 (2003)
18. Pang, S., Yu, Z., Orgun, M.A.: A novel end-to-end classifier using domain transferred deep convolutional neural networks for biomedical images. Comput. Methods Programs Biomed. **140**, 283–293 (2017)
19. Setio, A.A.A., et al.: Pulmonary nodule detection in CT images: false positive reduction using multi-view convolutional networks. IEEE Trans. Med. Imaging **35**(5), 1160–1169 (2016)
20. Shen, W., Zhou, M., Yang, F., Yang, C., Tian, J.: Multi-scale convolutional neural networks for lung nodule classification. In: Ourselin, S., Alexander, D.C., Westin, C.-F., Cardoso, M.J. (eds.) IPMI 2015. LNCS, vol. 9123, pp. 588–599. Springer, Cham (2015). https://doi.org/10.1007/978-3-319-19992-4_46
21. Wei Shen, M., et al.: Multi-crop convolutional neural networks for lung nodule malignancy suspiciousness classification. Pattern Recogn. **61**, 663–673 (2017)
22. Torre, L.A., Bray, F., Siegel, R.L., Ferlay, J., Lortet-Tieulent, J., Jemal, A.: Global cancer statistics, 2012. CA: Cancer J. Clin. **65**(2), 87–108 (2015)
23. Wang, Y., Zhang, H., Chae, K.J., Choi, Y., Jin, G.Y., Ko, S.B.: Novel convolutional neural network architecture for improved pulmonary nodule classification on computed tomography. Multidimens. Syst. Signal Process. **31**(3), 1163–1183 (2020)
24. Xie, Y., et al.: Knowledge-based collaborative deep learning for benign-malignant lung nodule classification on chest ct. IEEE Trans. Med. Imaging **38**(4), 991–1004 (2018)
25. Zhao, X., et al.: Deep CNN models for pulmonary nodule classification: model modification, model integration, and transfer learning. J. Xray Sci. Technol. **27**(4), 615–629 (2019)
26. Zhu, W., Liu, C., Fan, W., Xie, X.: Deeplung: deep 3D dual path nets for automated pulmonary nodule detection and classification. In: 2018 IEEE Winter Conference on Applications of Computer Vision (WACV), pp. 673–681. IEEE (2018)

A Bayesian Approach to Gaussian-Impulse Noise Removal Using Hessian Norm Regularization

Suman Kumar Maji[✉] and Anirban Saha

Department of Computer Science and Engineering, Indian Institute of Technology Patna, Patna 801106, India
{smaji,anirban_2021cs13}@iitp.ac.in

Abstract. The problem of removing mixed noise from images is a challenging problem due to their ill-posed nature. In this paper, we propose a Bayesian technique for the removal of mixed Gaussian-Impulse noise from images. The proposed optimization problem is derived from the maximum a posteriori (MAP) estimates of the noise statistics and makes use of a total variation (TV) and a nuclear norm of the Hessian as its two regularization terms. While TV ensures smoothness to the solution, the use of Hessian takes into account detail preservation in the final optimized output. The proposed problem is then solved under the framework of primal-dual algorithms. Experimental evaluation shows that the proposed method can significantly improve the restoration quality of the images, compared to the existing techniques.

Keywords: Mixed noise removal · Gaussian-impulse noise · primal dual algorithms

1 Introduction

Random noise components are inevitably introduced to the original data during image acquisition and transmission. This results in unwanted contamination of desired data that is targeted for processing. Thus the acquired data needs to be pre-processed efficiently, removing the unwanted noisy components with minimal effect on the information depicted by the original data. This pre-processing step is known as denoising, and prior knowledge about the contaminating noise component plays a vital role during this step. Mixed Gaussian-Impulse noise is very common among image data. The most frequently encountered Gaussian noise is the Additive White Gaussian Noise (AWGN), which gets induced during the acquisition of the image with the impulse component, like Salt and Pepper Impulse Noise (SPIN) and Random Valued Impulse Noise (RVIN), largely corrupts the image during transmission.

D. Gupta et al. (Eds.): CVIP 2022, CCIS 1776, pp. 224–234, 2023.
https://doi.org/10.1007/978-3-031-31407-0_17

With the intent to restore an image, many denoising techniques have been recorded in the literature. Amongst these techniques, Deng et al. [11] have presented an adaptive Gaussian filtering algorithm that has resulted in promising denoised outcomes. Alongside, several noisy pixel detections and elimination methodologies were also researched upon [6]. In [23], the authors demonstrated a similar approach with a filter-based mixed noise elimination strategy. Whereas, the authors of [22] differentiated the impulse-distorted pixels and Gaussian-distorted pixels for processing separately with adaptive directional weighted mean filter and adaptive anisotropic diffusion model, respectively. Simultaneous processing of Gaussian and impulse components with a weighted encoding method has also been experimented [19]. Moreover, a promising proximal approach for denoising was even analyzed by [4]. Apart from this, a denoising method utilizing a non-divergence diffusion equation with an impulse noise indicator and a regularised Perona-Malik (RPM) diffusion operator as its components is proposed in [29]. Transform-domain enhanced sparse representation-based image denoising technique has also been explored in [9] involving three sequential steps, which include 3-D group transformation, shrinking of the transform spectrum, and inverse 3-D transformation. The work, presented in [24], demonstrated image denoising by learning a sparse signal-adapted basis set and exploiting the self similarities of natural images. Analyzing the performance of regularization-based approaches in denoising an image, methods like l1-l0 minimization technique [30], TV regularisation with l2 and l1 data fidelity [28], and weighted l2-l0 norms energy minimization model [21] were also explored. The performance of a two-phase denoising method implementing detectors and detail-holding regularisation was recorded by Zeng et al. [31]. The work [18] utilizes the advantage of adaptive weight setting and demonstrated a weighted low-rank model for noise elimination. Furthermore, the authors of [5] instigated the evolution of non-local means (NL-means) as an image denoising model. In addition to this, a patch-based denoising model was also surveyed in [10]. Alongside this, several CNN-based image restoration models, learning residual components, were being researched in recent times. One such model includes a convolutional-based denoiser prior model as proposed in [33]. Similarly, the work demonstrated in [35] proposes another dedicated denoising convolutional model architecture, capable of restoring the original image. Besides this, Islam et al. [16] presented a CNN-based denoising model that learns an end-to-end mapping from noisy to noise-free data adopting a computationally efficient transfer learning approach. In addition, the performance of a two-phase cascaded residual convolutional model for removing mixed noise has been recorded in [13]. Apart from this, the work [3] proposed an ensemble model, considering a loss function as derived in a Bayesian setting, enhancing the model performance. Parallelly, the authors of [1] also demonstrated a CNN-based denoising model inspired by the Bayesian maximum a posteriori (MAP) derivation of the Gaussian-impulse likelihood.

In this paper, we propose a Bayesian-based image denoising technique that is capable of dealing with mixed Gaussian-Impulse noise. The proposed method has been designed as a joint formulation for the MAP estimates of Gaussian and impulse noise statistics and consists of two data fidelity terms and two prior terms. For the prior terms, we make use of a TV norm and a nuclear norm of the Hessian respectively. The proposed problem is then minimized/solved under the framework of primal dual hybrid gradient descent algorithms [7,8]. This involves computation of the proximal operators associated to each cost term (data fidelity + prior) as well as some other parameters, which we have listed. Our method is focused on implementing Gaussian and impulse noise removal strategies applied jointly on the same degraded sample, although this can also be done by variable splitting [2,25,26]. Experimental results, both visual and quantitative, have shown the merit of the proposed technique in comparison with several existing methodologies in the literature.

The rest of the paper is organized as given. Section 2 introduces the noise formulation followed by Sect. 3, which derives the objective function that is to be optimized by the model. Section 4 describes the proposed method. Then the extensive experimental data is provided in Sect. 5 and finally concluded by Sect. 6.

2   Preliminaries

Assuming that the observed noisy image is of dimension $m \times n$, the image formation model can be given by:

$$f = u + g + s \tag{1}$$

where $u \in R^{m \times n}$ is the original clean image, $f \in R^{m \times n}$ is the noisy observation, $g \sim \mathcal{N}(0, \sigma_g^2)$ denotes the Gaussian noise with zero mean and variance σ_g^2 and $s \sim \mathcal{L}(0, \sigma_s)$ represents the sparse or impulse noise (approximated as Laplacian noise [27]) where 0 is the location parameter and σ_s the shape parameter. f is therefore represents an image corrupted by mixed Gaussian-impulse noise and our objective is to reconstruct an image $\hat{u}$, which is as close as possible to the original image u, from f.

3   Problem Formulation

In the Bayesian MAP framework, the problem of estimating u from f can be expressed as a posterior probability $p(u|f)$ as:

$$\hat{u} = \arg \max_u p(u|f) = \arg \max_x \frac{p(f|u) \times p(u)}{p(f)} \tag{2}$$

where $p(f|u)$ is the likelihood term and $p(u)$ the prior term. Maximizing the above equation is equivalent to minimizing its negative logarithm, which gives us:

$$\hat{u} = \arg \min_u - \log p(f|u) - \log p(u) + \log p(f) \tag{3}$$

Since f is known, $p(f)$ is a constant and hence the above estimation equation reduces to:

$$\hat{u} = \arg \min_{u} -\log p(f|u) - \log p(u) \tag{4}$$

If the underlying distribution is Gaussian, then the estimation problem of Eq. (4) takes the form:

$$\hat{u} = \arg \min_{u} -\log \frac{1}{\sqrt{2\pi\sigma_g^2}}\exp\left(-\frac{(f-u)^2}{2\sigma_g^2}\right) - \log(p(u) \tag{5}$$

and considering Gibbs model for $p(u) = e^{-\alpha R(u)}$; $\alpha > 0$ Eq. (5) is simplified to:

$$\hat{u} = \arg \min_{u} \frac{(f-u)^2}{2\sigma_g^2} + \alpha R(u) \tag{6}$$

and is equivalent to minimizing the functional:

$$\hat{u} = \arg \min_{u} \frac{\lambda_1}{2}\|f-u\|_2^2 + R(u) \tag{7}$$

Similarly, if the underlying distribution is Laplacian in nature [14], and a Gibbs prior $p(u) = e^{-\alpha Q(u)}$; $\alpha > 0$, the estimation problem in Eq. (4) can be written as:

$$\hat{u} = \arg \min_{u} -\log \frac{1}{2\sigma_s}\exp\left(-\frac{|f-u|}{\sigma_s}\right) - \log e^{-\alpha Q(u)} \tag{8}$$

and is equivalent to minimizing the functional:

$$\hat{u} = \arg \min_{u} \lambda_2\|f-u\|_1 + Q(u) \tag{9}$$

where λ_1 and λ_2 are positive regularization hyper-parameters.

4   Proposed Methodology

Our proposed method is therefore aimed at combining the Gaussian and laplacian MAP formulations, as expressed in Eq. (7) and (9) respectively, in order to formulate an optimization problem aimed at removing mixed Gaussian-impulse noise from images. The proposed formulation is expressed as:

$$\hat{u} = \arg \min_{u} \frac{\lambda_1}{2}\|f-u\|_2^2 + \lambda_2 \|f-u\|_1 + R(u) + Q(u) \tag{10}$$

We consider the nuclear norm $\|\cdot\|_*$ of the Hessian operator as $R(u)$ and the total variational (TV) norm $\|\cdot\|_1$ as $Q(u)$ for our prior terms. Since it is a

Table 1. Detail of the cost terms and associated functions and operators.

k	$\varphi_k(\cdot)$	$\mathrm{prox}_{\gamma\varphi_k}(\cdot)$	$\mathbf{T}_k$	$\mathbf{T}^*{}_k$
1	$\frac{\lambda_1}{2}\|f - \cdot\|_2^2$	$\frac{\cdot + \lambda_1 \gamma \mathbf{f}}{1 + \lambda_1 \gamma}$	$\mathbf{I}$	$\mathbf{z}$
2	$\lambda_2\|f - \cdot\|_1$	$\max(0, |\cdot| - \gamma)\,\mathrm{sgn}(\cdot)$	$\mathbf{I}$	$\mathbf{z}$
3	$\lambda_3\|\cdot\|_*^2$	$\mathbf{U}\mathrm{soft}_{\lambda_3\gamma}(\mathbf{S})\mathbf{V}^*$	$\begin{bmatrix}\mathbf{D}_{11}\\\mathbf{D}_{12}\\\mathbf{D}_{21}\\\mathbf{D}_{22}\end{bmatrix}$	$\begin{bmatrix}\mathbf{D}_{11}^*\\\mathbf{D}_{12}^*\\\mathbf{D}_{21}^*\\\mathbf{D}_{22}^*\end{bmatrix}^\top$
4	$\|\cdot\|_1$	$\begin{cases}1 - \dfrac{\gamma}{\|\cdot\|_1}\cdot & \text{if } \|\cdot\|_1 \geq \gamma\\[2mm]0 & \text{otherwise}\end{cases}$	$\begin{bmatrix}\mathbf{D}_1\\\mathbf{D}_2\end{bmatrix}$	$\begin{bmatrix}\mathbf{D}_1^*\\\mathbf{D}_2^*\end{bmatrix}^\top$

denoising problem, no penalty term is imposed on the TV prior in order to ensure smoothness. The resultant optimization problem will therefore be:

$$\hat{u} = \arg\min_u \frac{\lambda_1}{2}\|f - u\|_2^2 + \lambda_2\|f - u\|_1 + \lambda_3\left\|\begin{bmatrix}D_{11}\\D_{12}\\D_{21}\\D_{22}\end{bmatrix}u\right\|_* + \|Du\|_1 \tag{11}$$

where the Hessian operator is composed of the second order derivatives D_{11}, D_{12}, D_{21} and D_{22} stacked in a single operator, with an additional penalty imposed by the regularization hyper-parameter λ_3. D is the gradient operator with D_1 and D_2 being its directional derivative components.

We propose to minimize Eq. (11) using the multi-term version of primal dual hybrid gradient algorithm (PDHG) [8]. In order to do so, we need to formulate Eq. (11) in the form $\sum_k \phi_k(\mathbf{T}_k\mathbf{x})$ where $\mathbf{T}_k$ are operators, ϕ_k are functions and k denotes the number of terms in the cost function. We therefore need to define ϕ_k and $\mathbf{T}_k$ for all the four cost functions of Eq. (11). In addition for the purpose of minimization using PDHG we also need to define the proximity operator associated to every ϕ_k as well as the adjoint $\mathbf{T}_k^*$. The proximity operator is defined as:

$$\mathrm{prox}_{\gamma\phi_k}(\cdot) = \arg\min_u \phi_k(u) + \frac{1}{2\gamma}\|u - \cdot\|_2^2 \tag{12}$$

with $\gamma > 0$.

4.1 Proximal Operator Associated with Function $\phi_1(\mathbf{T}_1\mathbf{x})$

$\phi_1(\cdot)$ is the function associated with the term $\frac{\lambda_1}{2}\|f - \cdot\|^2$ with $\mathbf{T}_1 = \begin{bmatrix}0 & \mathbf{I}\end{bmatrix}$. The proximal operator for ϕ_1 will therefore be:

$$\mathrm{prox}_\gamma \phi_1(\mathbf{z}) = \arg\min_\mathbf{x} \varphi_1(\mathbf{x}) + \frac{1}{2\gamma}\|\mathbf{x} - \mathbf{z}\|^2 \tag{13a}$$

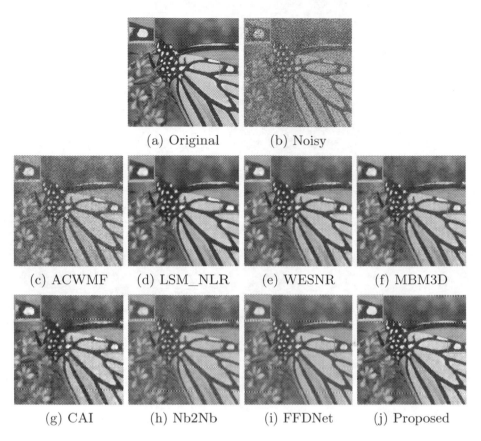

Fig. 1. Visual Comparison over simulated data (Monarch) with $\{o, p_{im}\} - \{25, 25\%\}$. The hyper-parameters for the proposed method: $\{\lambda_1, \lambda_2, \lambda_3\} = \{0.8, 0.5, 0.8\}$.

$$= \arg \min_{\mathbf{x}} \ \frac{\lambda_1}{2}\|f - \mathbf{x}\|_2^2 + \frac{1}{2\gamma}\|\mathbf{x} - \mathbf{z}\|_2^2 \tag{13b}$$

$$= \frac{\mathbf{z} + \lambda_1 \gamma f}{1 + \lambda_1 \gamma} \tag{13c}$$

Here $\mathbf{I}$ represents the identity operator and $\mathbf{z}$ its adjoint.

4.2 Proximal Operator Associated with Function $\phi_3(\mathbf{T}_3\mathbf{x})$

The proximity operator associated to the nuclear norm is defined as the soft thresholding of the eigen values: $\text{prox}_{\gamma\|\cdot\|_*} = \mathbf{U}\text{soft}_\gamma(\mathbf{S})\mathbf{V}^*$ where $\mathbf{U}\mathbf{S}\mathbf{V}^*$ is the singular value decomposition of the argument.

The rest of the operators can be calculated accordingly. A summary of the needed function and operators are presented in Table 1.

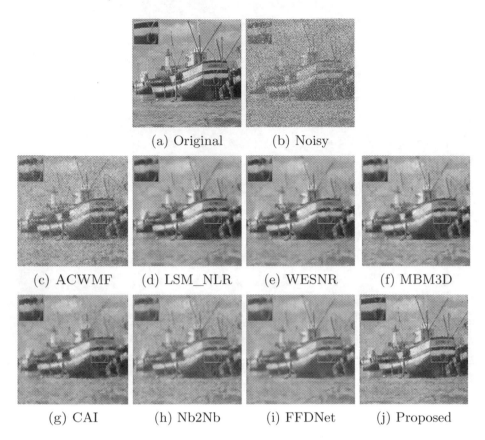

Fig. 2. Visual Comparison over simulated data (Boat) with $\{\sigma, p_{im}\} = \{25, 30\%\}$. The hyper-parameters for the proposed method: $\{\lambda_1, \lambda_2, \lambda_3\} = \{0.2, 0.5, 0.2\}$.

5   Experimental Results

In order to demonstrate the overall performance of the proposed model, experiments were carried on several standard image dataset namely Classic5 [12] and Set12 [32]. Mixed noise components ($AWGN + RVIN$), that is simulated to record the results, is a combination of additive white Gaussian noise with $\sigma \in \{25, 30\}$ and random valued impulse noise with probability $p_{im} \in \{25\%, 30\%\}$. Apart from recording the performance measure of the proposed model, it is compared with the output of other methods in the literature: ACWMF [20], LSM_NLR [14], WESNR [19], MBM3D [9], CAI [17], Nb2Nb [15], and FFDNet [34]. Both the visual and the qualitative performance have been compared to manifest the effectiveness of the proposed model.

To quantify the variation in denoised image quality provided by different methods, peak signal-to-noise ratio (PSNR) has been considered as one of the evaluation measure. Equation (14) provides the mathematical formulation to compute the PSNR in decibels (dB). Another evaluation measure include

Table 2. Evaluation Results (PSNR and SSIM) of Mixed Noise Removal (AWGN + RVIN)

Dataset	Noise_Label	Metric	Noisy	ACWMF	LSM_NLR	WESNR	MBM3D	CAI	Nb2Nb	FFDNet	Proposed
Classic_5	{25, 25%}	PSNR	14.646	20.217	23.047	22.616	23.042	21.690	20.866	21.255	**24.012**
		SSIM	0.211	0.454	0.662	0.654	0.656	0.597	0.581	0.632	**0.681**
	{25, 30%}	PSNR	14.172	19.432	23.441	22.710	22.922	21.817	19.980	20.277	**24.061**
		SSIM	0.182	0.438	0.657	0.643	0.638	0.585	0.562	0.611	**0.671**
	{30, 25%}	PSNR	14.682	18.773	22.565	21.872	22.413	20.201	19.300	19.525	**23.572**
		SSIM	0.205	0.413	0.629	0.622	0.618	0.555	0.540	0.588	**0.664**
	{30, 30%}	PSNR	14.195	18.903	21.505	21.345	21.426	20.408	19.499	19.741	**23.976**
		SSIM	0.181	0.400	0.618	0.606	0.599	0.547	0.527	0.581	**0.658**
Set_12	{25, 25%}	PSNR	14.471	19.564	22.889	22.413	22.802	21.545	19.941	20.346	**24.393**
		SSIM	0.207	0.463	**0.708**	0.698	0.691	0.630	0.601	0.661	0.707
	{25, 30%}	PSNR	13.898	19.488	22.358	22.157	22.455	21.385	19.999	20.410	**24.389**
		SSIM	0.185	0.446	0.694	0.682	0.671	0.619	0.589	0.654	**0.695**
	{30, 25%}	PSNR	14.253	18.882	21.661	21.274	21.860	20.383	19.327	19.641	**24.182**
		SSIM	0.201	0.425	0.674	0.663	0.656	0.591	0.566	0.632	**0.691**
	{30, 30%}	PSNR	14.006	18.609	21.720	21.321	21.975	20.237	19.108	19.396	**23.945**
		SSIM	0.184	0.409	0.665	0.648	0.637	0.581	0.550	0.617	**0.675**

structural similarity (SSIM) that can be expressed by Eq. (15). In both the equations, the original noise-free image is represented by u and the processed image is denoted by $\hat{u}$. And the functions $E[\bullet]$, $Var[\bullet]$, and $Cov[\bullet, \bullet]$ computes the spatial average, variance and co-variance of the input. Nevertheless, the parameter P denotes the total number of image patches taken consideration.

$$\text{PSNR} = 10 \log_{10} \frac{(u_{max})^2}{E[(u^i - \hat{u}^i)^2]} \tag{14}$$

$$\text{SSIM} = \frac{1}{P} \sum_{i=1}^{P} \left(\frac{2E[u^i]E[\hat{u}^i] + \alpha_1}{E[(u^i)^2] + E[(\hat{u}^i)^2] + \alpha_1} \times \frac{2Cov[u^i, \hat{u}^i] + \alpha_2}{Var[u^i] + Var[\hat{u}^i] + \alpha_2} \right) \tag{15}$$

The results of the evaluation matrices are recorded in Table 2. The table shows the qualitative comparison of different models over the simulated input with noise levels $\{(\sigma, p_{im})\} \in \{(25, 25\%), (30, 30\%), (25, 30\%), (30, 25\%)\}$. Comparing the results recorded in this table, it is obvious that the proposed model outperforms the other denoising techniques. Beside analysing the performance based on quality measures, visual aspects of the outputs provided by various models are also seen through. Some of these visuals has been represented by Fig. 1, and 2. Visual comparison over the standard "Monarch" data simulated with noise level $\{\sigma, p_{im}\} \in \{25, 25\%\}$ is shown in Fig. 1. Similarly, Fig. 2 represents the "Boat" data contaminated with noise levels $\{25, 30\%\}$. With detailed observation of the zoomed view, that are extracted and visualised in the figures, it is evident that the proposed model is capable to remove the noisy component more effectively as compared to other denoising models. The model also keeps the structural information intact preserving sharp edges and patterns depicted by the original data.

6 Conclusion

In this paper, we have proposed a Bayesian based image denoising technique for the removal of mixed Gaussian-Impulse noise from images. The proposed optimization problem has been derived from the MAP estimates of the Gaussian and impulse noise statistics and consists of two data fidelity terms and two prior terms. For the prior terms, we have considered the TV norm and the nuclear norm of the Hessian respectively. The proposed optimization problem is then minimized using primal dual hybrid gradient descent algorithms. Experimental results, both visual and quantitative, have shown the merit of the proposed technique in comparison with the state-of-the-art existing methodologies.

References

1. Aetesam, H., Maji, S.K.: Noise dependent training for deep parallel ensemble denoising in magnetic resonance images. Biomed. Signal Process. Control **66**, 102405 (2021). https://doi.org/10.1016/j.bspc.2020.102405. https://www.sciencedirect.com/science/article/pii/S1746809420305115
2. Aetesam, H., Maji, S.K., Boulanger, J.: A two-phase splitting approach for the removal of gaussian-impulse noise from hyperspectral images. In: Singh, S.K., Roy, P., Raman, B., Nagabhushan, P. (eds.) CVIP 2020. CCIS, vol. 1376, pp. 179–190. Springer, Singapore (2021). https://doi.org/10.1007/978-981-16-1086-8_16
3. Aetesam, H., Maji, S.K., Yahia, H.: Bayesian approach in a learning-based hyperspectral image denoising framework. IEEE Access **9**, 169335–169347 (2021). https://doi.org/10.1109/ACCESS.2021.3137656
4. Aetesam, H., Poonam, K., Maji, S.K.: Proximal approach to denoising hyperspectral images under mixed-noise model. IET Image Process. **14**(14), 3366–3372 (2020). https://doi.org/10.1049/iet-ipr.2019.1763. https://ietresearch.onlinelibrary.wiley.com/doi/abs/10.1049/iet-ipr.2019.1763
5. Buades, A., Coll, B., Morel, J.M.: A non-local algorithm for image denoising. In: 2005 IEEE Computer Society Conference on Computer Vision and Pattern Recognition (CVPR 2005), vol. 2, pp. 60–65 (2005). https://doi.org/10.1109/CVPR.2005.38
6. Cai, J.F., Chan, R., Nikolova, M.: Two-phase approach for deblurring images corrupted by impulse plus gaussian noise. Inverse Problems and Imaging 2 (05 2008). https://doi.org/10.3934/ipi.2008.2.187
7. Chambolle, A., Pock, T.: A first-order primal-dual algorithm for convex problems with applications to imaging. J. Math. Imaging Vis. **40**(1), 120–145 (2010). https://doi.org/10.1007/s10851-010-0251-1
8. Condat, L.: A primal-dual splitting method for convex optimization involving lipschitzian, proximable and linear composite terms. J. Optim. Theory Appl. **158**(2), 460–479 (2012). https://doi.org/10.1007/s10957-012-0245-9

9. Dabov, K., Foi, A., Katkovnik, V., Egiazarian, K.: Image denoising by sparse 3-D transform-domain collaborative filtering. IEEE Trans. Image Process. **16**(8), 2080–2095 (2007). https://doi.org/10.1109/TIP.2007.901238

10. Delon, J., Desolneux, A.: A patch-based approach for removing impulse or mixed gaussian-impulse noise. SIAM J. Imaging Sci. **6**, 1140–1174 (2013). https://doi.org/10.1137/120885000

11. Deng, G., Cahill, L.: An adaptive gaussian filter for noise reduction and edge detection. In: 1993 IEEE Conference Record Nuclear Science Symposium and Medical Imaging Conference, pp. 1615–1619 (1993). https://doi.org/10.1109/NSSMIC.1993.373563

12. Foi, A., Katkovnik, V., Egiazarian, K.: Pointwise shape-adaptive DCT for high-quality deblocking of compressed color images. In: 2006 14th European Signal Processing Conference, pp. 1–5 (2006)

13. Guan, J., Lai, R., Xiong, A., Liu, Z., Gu, L.: Fixed pattern noise reduction for infrared images based on cascade residual attention CNN. Neurocomputing **377**, 301–313 (2020). https://doi.org/10.1016/j.neucom.2019.10.054. https://www.sciencedirect.com/science/article/pii/S0925231219314341

14. Huang, T., Dong, W., Xie, X., Shi, G., Bai, X.: Mixed noise removal via laplacian scale mixture modeling and nonlocal low-rank approximation. IEEE Trans. Image Process. **26**(7), 3171–3186 (2017). https://doi.org/10.1109/TIP.2017.2676466

15. Huang, T., Li, S., Jia, X., Lu, H., Liu, J.: Neighbor2neighbor: self-supervised denoising from single noisy images. In: 2021 IEEE/CVF Conference on Computer Vision and Pattern Recognition (CVPR), pp. 14776–14785 (2021). https://doi.org/10.1109/CVPR46437.2021.01454

16. Islam, M.T., Mahbubur Rahman, S., Omair Ahmad, M., Swamy, M.: Mixed gaussian-impulse noise reduction from images using convolutional neural network. Signal Process. Image Commun. **68**, 26–41 (2018). https://doi.org/10.1016/j.image.2018.06.016. https://www.sciencedirect.com/science/article/pii/S0923596518300705

17. Cai, J.F., Chan, R.H., Nikolova, M.: Two-phase approach for deblurring images corrupted by impulse plus gaussian noise. Inverse Probl. Imaging **2**(2), 187–204 (2008)

18. Jiang, J., Yang, J., Cui, Y., Luo, L.: Mixed noise removal by weighted low rank model. Neurocomputing **151**, 817–826 (2015). https://doi.org/10.1016/j.neucom.2014.10.017

19. Jiang, J., Zhang, L., Yang, J.: Mixed noise removal by weighted encoding with sparse nonlocal regularization. IEEE Trans. Image Process. **23**, 2651–2662 (2014). https://doi.org/10.1109/TIP.2014.2317985

20. Ko, S.J., Lee, Y.: Center weighted median filters and their applications to image enhancement. IEEE Trans. Circ. Syst. **38**(9), 984–993 (1991). https://doi.org/10.1109/31.83870

21. Liu, J., Tai, X.C., Huang, H., Huan, Z.: A weighted dictionary learning model for denoising images corrupted by mixed noise. IEEE Trans. Image Process. **22**, 1108–1120 (2012). https://doi.org/10.1109/TIP.2012.2227766

22. Ma, H., Nie, Y.: Mixed noise removal algorithm combining adaptive directional weighted mean filter and improved adaptive anisotropic diffusion model. Math. Probl. Eng. **2018**, 1–19 (2018). https://doi.org/10.1155/2018/6492696

23. Madhura, J.J., Babu, D.R.R.: An effective hybrid filter for the removal of gaussian-impulsive noise in computed tomography images. In: 2017 International Conference on Advances in Computing, Communications and Informatics (ICACCI), pp. 1815–1820 (2017). https://doi.org/10.1109/ICACCI.2017.8126108

24. Mairal, J., Bach, F., Ponce, J., Sapiro, G., Zisserman, A.: Non-local sparse models for image restoration. In: 2009 IEEE 12th International Conference on Computer Vision, pp. 2272–2279 (2009). https://doi.org/10.1109/ICCV.2009.5459452

25. Maji, S.K., Boulanger, J.: A variational model for poisson gaussian joint denoising deconvolution. In: IEEE 18th International Symposium on Biomedical Imaging, pp. 1527–1530 (2021)

26. Maji, S.K., Dargemont, C., Salamero, J., Boulanger, J.: Joint denoising-deconvolution approach for fluorescence microscopy. In: IEEE 13th International Symposium on Biomedical Imaging, pp. 128–131 (2016)

27. Marks, R.J., Wise, G.L., Haldeman, D.G., Whited, J.L.: Detection in laplace noise. IEEE Trans. Aerosp. Electron. Syst. AES-**14**(6), 866–872 (1978). https://doi.org/10.1109/TAES.1978.308550

28. Rodríguez, P., Rojas, R., Wohlberg, B.: Mixed gaussian-impulse noise image restoration via total variation. In: 2012 IEEE International Conference on Acoustics, Speech and Signal Processing (ICASSP), pp. 1077–1080 (2012). https://doi.org/10.1109/ICASSP.2012.6288073

29. Shi, K., Zhang, D., Guo, Z., Sun, J., Wu, B.: A non-divergence diffusion equation for removing impulse noise and mixed gaussian impulse noise. Neurocomputing **173**, 659–670 (2015). https://doi.org/10.1016/j.neucom.2015.08.012

30. Xiao, Y., Zeng, T., Yu, J., Ng, M.: Restoration of images corrupted by mixed gaussian-impulse noise via l. Pattern Recognit. **44**, 1708–1720 (2011). https://doi.org/10.1016/j.patcog.2011.02.002

31. Zeng, X., Yang, L.: Mixed impulse and gaussian noise removal using detail-preserving regularization. Opt. Eng. **49**, 097002 (2010). https://doi.org/10.1117/1.3485756

32. Zhang, K., Zuo, W., Chen, Y., Meng, D., Zhang, L.: Beyond a gaussian denoiser: residual learning of deep CNN for image denoising. IEEE Trans. Image Process. **26**(7), 3142–3155 (2017). https://doi.org/10.1109/TIP.2017.2662206

33. Zhang, K., Zuo, W., Gu, S., Zhang, L.: Learning deep CNN denoiser prior for image restoration. In: Proceedings of the IEEE Conference on Computer Vision and Pattern Recognition (CVPR) (2017)

34. Zhang, K., Zuo, W., Zhang, L.: FFDNet: toward a fast and flexible solution for CNN-based image denoising. IEEE Trans. Image Process. **27**(9), 4608–4622 (2018). https://doi.org/10.1109/TIP.2018.2839891

35. Zuo, W., Zhang, K., Zhang, L.: Convolutional neural networks for image denoising and restoration. In: Bertalmío, M. (ed.) Denoising of Photographic Images and Video. ACVPR, pp. 93–123. Springer, Cham (2018). https://doi.org/10.1007/978-3-319-96029-6_4

DeepTemplates: Object Segmentation Using Shape Templates

Nikhar Maheshwari[1], Gaurav Ramola[1(✉)], Sudha Velusamy[1],
and Raviprasad Mohan Kini[2]

[1] Samsung R&D Institute India, Bengaluru, India
gauravramola007@gmail.com
[2] Thoughtworks, Bengaluru, India

Abstract. Object segmentation is a crucial component for many vision applications like object editing and augmented reality. Traditional pixelwise segmentation techniques result in irregularities around object boundaries. However, applications like lip makeup require smooth boundaries that resemble a typical lip *"template-shape"*. We propose an encoder-decoder architecture that is explicitly conditioned to utilize the underlying *template-shape* of an object for segmentation. The decoder was trained separately to generate a template-shaped segment obtained from landmark points of an object. The encoder is then trained to predict these landmarks using Euclidean loss. Finally, we jointly train the encoder and decoder by incorporating the decoder's segmentation loss to refine the landmarks, which conditions the network to produce template-shaped object segments. The performance of the proposed method was evaluated with **mIOU** and **f-score** measures on the HELEN data set for lip segmentation. We observed perceptually superior segments with smooth object boundaries when compared to state-of-the-art techniques.

Keywords: Object Segmentation · Template Generation · Face Parsing

1 Introduction

Object segmentation is amongst the most researched topics in the field of computer vision for its diverse range of applications including object recognition, scene understanding and face editing. Many real-world objects have a specific underlying shape template for their corresponding class. Typically, state-of-the-art object segmentation techniques aim to predict every pixel belonging to an object accurately. But the large variance in the appearance of captured objects due to illumination conditions, material type, and possible occlusions leads to unnatural irregularities at object boundaries, when segmented using conventional methods.

An example is shown in Fig. 1, where the *frisbee* and *lip* objects have specific template shapes (Fig. 1(c)). Applying conventional segmentation techniques

---

This work was done when all the authors were part of Samsung R&D Institute India.

D. Gupta et al. (Eds.): CVIP 2022, CCIS 1776, pp. 235–245, 2023.
https://doi.org/10.1007/978-3-031-31407-0_18

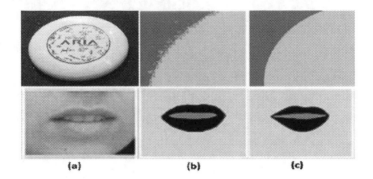

Fig. 1. (a) Input; (b) Traditional method [4]; (c) Proposed

for these images results in irregular shapes as demonstrated in Fig. 1(b). For example, in the case of lip makeup, applying makeup based on a pixel-wise segmentation mask creates an unnatural look due to irregular filling of segments. These irregularities can be addressed by utilizing prior knowledge of an object's template shape, especially for the common content like face, and segments with accurate boundaries can be obtained. To address this shortcoming, we propose an unified object segmentation framework that utilizes the landmark points that best represent the template-shape of an object. We explicitly condition the encoder-decoder architecture to incorporate the template shape during training. Given any input image, the encoder first predicts its landmarks, which are then used by decoder to generate segments. Jointly training the encoder and decoder refines the encoder's predicted landmark points, which in turn conditions the decoder to generate template shape segments. We design our framework for the well-defined problem of lip segmentation due to its wide applications in fields such as face parsing [1–3], and discuss how our observations for lips extend to general objects.

The outline of this paper is as follows: Sect. 2 presents a brief review of the related works and solutions present in literature. Section 3 explains the proposed encoder-decoder architecture that utilizes underlying template shape of an object to perform segmentation. Section 4 is devoted to the details of implementation, while Sect. 5 presents our results. Finally, we present the summary and conclusion of the work in Sect. 6.

2   Related Work

Current object segmentation algorithms can be broadly classified into: 1) Contour-based methods [5–8]; 2) Landmark-point-based methods [9–12]; and 3) Semantic Segmentation methods [1,2,4,13–16]. Contour based methods, such as Active Contour Models (ACM) [5] use gradient information to fit contours to object boundaries. Although, these methods generate relatively smooth segment boundaries, they have other limitations including slow convergence, contour initialization. We address these issues by designing a lightweight network that requires neither contour initialization, nor complex metrics.

Many methods that localize landmarks for applications like facial feature detection are present in literature [5, 6, 8, 11, 12]. After landmark detection, these methods fit a polynomial curve and perform region filling to generate object segments [8]. The primary limitation with this approach is that landmarks have no notion of local inter-correspondence. We condition our landmark point detector on segments, thereby enforcing a representation that understands how these points 'stitch' together to form object shapes.

Recently, there has been a tremendous amount of study into semantic segmentation using Deep Neural Networks (DNN) [15–17]. Examples include U-Net based models [15], multi-scale CNN [16], and GAN based methods SegGAN [18]. In specific, face parsing solutions include exemplar based [3], hierarchical CNN based parsing [2] and multi-objective convolutional learning [1]. For example, [19] employs a residual encoder-decoder network. [17] proposed Normalized Receptive field and Statistical contextual loss to preform real-time face-parsing. While these methods achieve excellent pixel-wise accuracy, they often generate isolated *'islands'* of misclassified pixels in non-intuitive locations (Refer Fig. 1(c)). In applications like facial makeup, these kinds of errors generate unpleasant results. Our proposed method is robust to these kinds of errors as the landmark points generated are constrained by object shape.

To summarize, our main contributions are: 1) We propose a general model to segment objects via landmark points conditioned on the shape of the object's class; 2) Demonstrate the power of our lightweight architecture specifically for lip segmentation using DeepLab v3 [4], and demonstrate how it extends to other domains; 3) Achieve accurate and smooth segmentation results, and compare with existing state-of-the-art methods.

3   The Deep-Template Framework

We employ a CNN-based encoder-decoder (ENC-DEC) architecture for segmentation of the lip region into three classes: lip, inner-mouth and background. The encoder implements a mapping f from an RGB image x to 16 landmark points around the lip boundaries z. The decoder network g takes the predicted landmark points $f(x)$ and generates smooth segments $g(f(x))$ that adhere to the template shape of a lip. We have used an incremental training procedure wherein we first train the DEC and ENC separately, following which the ENC is trained under the guidance of the DEC in an end-to-end fashion. We explore the network architecture and implementation details in the following sections.

3.1   Decoder (DEC) Network

The task of the decoder module is to generate template-shaped segments $g(z)$ from 16 landmark points z. Conventional methods first create closed contours by fitting a polynomial to landmark points z [7], followed by region filling of these

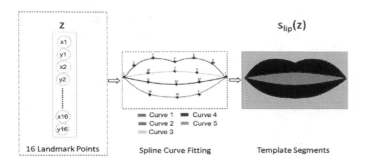

Fig. 2. Spline fitting for an example lip region

closed contours to generate smooth segments $s(z)$. These functions $s(z)$ often fail due to the ambiguity of the landmarks point in regions such as the corners of the lips and eyes. We discuss this in more detail in Sect. 3.3.

We use a CNN module g to mimic the behavior of conventional curve fitting functions s. The DEC architecture is inspired by the generator module of DCGAN [20]. The 16 lip landmark points are flattened to a single 32-dimensional vector z, and input to DEC. The network is fully convolutional with fractional-strided convolutions. Each convolution layer, except the output layer, is followed by a batch normalisation and a ReLU activation layers. The logits are bi-linearly up-sampled by a suitable factor to match the spatial resolution of label image. The output of the network is a $512 \times 512 \times 3$ map, where each channel represents the pixel-wise probability map of lip, inner-mouth and background classes.

To generate the ground truth template segments for DEC training, we designed a Spline Module (SM) $s_{lip}(z)$ [21], a subclass of $s(z)$, as illustrated in Fig. 2. Given 16 landmarks z, we first fit five cubic-spline curves to these points followed by region filling to create segments for inner mouth, lip and background. These segments are the $512 \times 512 \times 3$ ground-truth labels $s_{lip}(z)$ used for training. We have generated labels $s_{lip}(z_i)$ for all the z_i present in our training samples. The DEC was trained to optimize the following loss function:

$$L_{dec} = L_c\left[g\left(z\right), s_{lip}\left(z\right)\right] \tag{1}$$

where L_c is pixel-wise cross-entropy loss. Using DNN as a decoder has many advantages for the proposed framework. First, the differentiability of CNN architectures enables propagation of gradients from $g(z)$ back to z during end-to-end training. Furthermore, template segments created using s_{lip} have very sharp and unnatural corners where the spline curves intersect. Segments generated from our CNN architecture tend to average out these sharp details, resulting in more realistic segments with natural corners. This difference is further illustrated in Sect. 5.

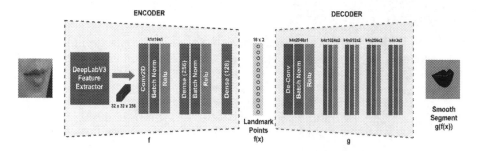

Fig. 3. Architecture for the Deep-Template system

3.1.1   Training the DEC

As $s_{lip}(z)$ has template-shaped segments, its use as ground truth while training the DEC is essentially an attempt to learn a mapping from $z_i \rightarrow s_{lip}(z_i)$ the DEC network is initialised with weights sampled from a Gaussian distribution with a mean of 0 and standard deviation of $2e-2$. The network is trained for 400 epochs with a batch size of 32 using Adam optimizer [22] and a learning rate of $2e-4$.

3.2   Encoder (ENC) Network

The ENC is a landmark-point detection network, which takes a $512 \times 512 \times 3$ RGB image x as input and predicts a 32 dimensional vector $f(x)$ consisting of (x,y) coordinate pairs of all 16 lip landmark points. Conventional landmark detection networks which directly aim to minimize the mean square error for the landmark points are not robust to variations in pose, expressions and illumination. To address this, we have used an incremental training procedure wherein we first train a state-of-the-art segmentation network [4] for face parsing; the features learnt here are then used to perform landmark detection. Using these learned weights as an initializer to train landmark detector provides the missing robustness to large variations in aforementioned facial conditions.

We use DeepLabV3 [4] as the backbone network to perform semantic segmentation. As observed, commonly deployed CNNs for the task of semantic segmentation make use of repeated combinations of max-pooling and down-sampling, which limits their capacity to hold accurate spatial information. These networks are not well suited for localisation tasks, which are essential for landmark detection. The architecture of DeepLabV3 is designed to retain these localisation cues in addition to rich semantic information by using Dilated convolutions instead of max-pooling.

Following the training for segmentation, we remove the layers after the Atrous Spatial Pyramid Pooling (ASPP) block [4] from the standard DeepLabV3 architecture. We add 1×1 convolutions to reduce the number of channels to 16, followed by two fully connected layers of 256 and 128 neurons to predict a 32 dimensional vector $f(x)$ in the final layer.

3.2.1   Training the ENC

We first train DeepLabV3 to segment an input image x into the lip, inner-mouth and background regions by minimizing cross entropy loss L_c between the ground truth labels y and the network's output $h(x)$.

$$L_{SEM} = L_c\left[h\left(x\right), y\right] \tag{2}$$

We utilize the above objective L_{SEM} to enforce the network to learn rich pose-invariant features that is used for landmark detection. The weights of the encoder are initialised by pre-trained weights from ImageNet classification [23]. We have trained the ENC for 150 epochs using Adam optimizer with a learning rate of $2e-4$ to optimize L_{SEM}. After the network learns semantics by optimizing L_{SEM}, we train our modified network to optimize the following objective:

$$L_{ENC} = L_{MSE}\left[f\left(x\right), z\right] \tag{3}$$

where z is the 32-dimensional vector representing the coordinates of lip landmarks and L_{MSE} is Mean-Square-Error loss.

3.3   End-to-End Network (E2E)

After we trained the ENC and DEC independently, we combined these modules to form our end-to-end encoder-decoder architecture (E2E), as illustrated in Fig. 3. Through joint training, we aimed to refine the predicted landmark points $f(x)$ to more accurate landmark points $f_0(x)$. This refinement was achieved by utilizing the template generation power of the DEC to guide the training of the ENC. More specifically, given an input image x, the ENC outputs landmarks $f(x)$. This $f(x)$ is then used by the DEC to create template shaped segments. To this end, we trained the ENC with a multi-objective loss, which contains two components: a cross entropy segmentation loss L_c and an MSE loss L_{MSE}. To train the E2E network, we kept the weights of DEC network fixed. This is because the DEC was already trained to generate template shaped segments from lip landmarks, and we did not want to change this behavior.

3.3.1   Training the E2E

The $f(x) \rightarrow f_0(x)$ refinement was carried out by gradient propagation from the DEC back to ENC to update the weights of the ENC. The following cost function was optimized to adjust the weights of ENC network:

$$L_{E2E} = L_c\left[g\left(f'\left(x\right)\right), y\right] + \lambda \ *L_{MSE}\left(f\left(x\right), z\right) \tag{4}$$

where y is the ground-truth segmentation mask and z is the ground-truth lip landmark point vector for the image x. The parameter λ is used to provide relative weight for the losses. For all our experiments we found the value $\lambda = 8.26$ worked best. Conventional landmark detector networks [9] use only L_{MSE} to train their networks, but having an additional loss term $L_c\left[g(f_0(x)); y\right]$ in our cost function provides additional information from the ground-truth segments y to increase the robustness and accuracy of predicted landmarks. Intuitively, we tried to refine points $f(x)$, so that they can be used by the DEC to create template shape segments $g(f(x))$ which simultaneously 1) best approximate the ground-truth mask y 2) enforce $f(x)$ to be close to ground-truth landmarks z. The complete E2E architecture was trained for 100 epochs with a lower learning rate of 2e-5 and a batch size of 32.

4   Implementation Details

4.1   Database Details

We use iBug 300W [24] and HELEN data set [3] for our training and testing as it contains face images with detailed landmark annotations and accurate segmentation maps for facial features like eyes, lips, etc. It also cover wide variations expressions, pose and illumination. On HELEN samples, we follow the mapping of (x, y, z), where x is the input image, y is the ground truth segmentation mask and z is the vector of ground truth landmarks, and use it for ENC training (2143 samples) and testing (187 samples). Likewise, we use iBug $300W$ to generate ground-truth upper lip, lower lip, and inside mouth segments by using slip as indicated in Sect. 3.1.

5   Results and Analysis

To evaluate our network, we performed an ablation study with various encoder decoder architectures. The Encoder module was chosen from 1) Dlib [9] landmark predictor 2) Ground-Truth landmarks 3) Our ENC. The decoder was chosen as our DEC or the spline module (SM) 3.1. Our ablation results demonstrate the importance of each module in our pipeline. We also compared the results of our final E2E architecture with Deeplab v3 (DLV3) [4], a state-of-the-art segmentation network, which does not follow a standard encoder-decoder framework. We evaluated these configurations with the mean Intersection Over Union (mIOU) and F-score metrics on HELEN's validation set as shown in Table 1 (Table 2).

Table 1. Performance Comparison with HELEN GT.

Method	Metric	Lip	Mouth	Background
DLV3	mIOU	0.695	0.412	0.989
	F-Score	0.809	0.476	0.994
DLIB + DEC	mIOU	0.679	0.399	0.990
	F-Score	0.798	0.481	0.995
E2E	mIOU	0.683	0.403	0.989
	F-Score	0.801	0.479	0.992

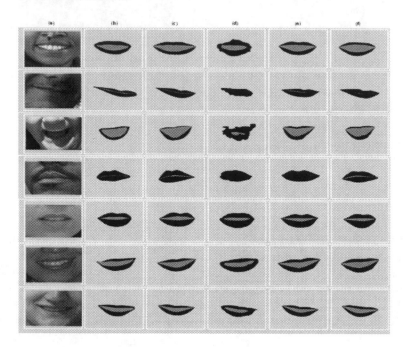

Fig. 4. Segmentation Results: a) RGB Image b) Ground Truth c) GTLSM d) DLV3 e) ENCSM f) E2E

Table 2. Performance Comparison with Spline GT.

Method	Metric	Lip	Mouth	Background
DLV3	mIOU	0.641	0.376	0.989
	F-Score	0.770	0.439	0.994
DLIB + DEC	mIOU	0.742	0.404	0.993
	F-Score	0.842	0.467	0.996
E2E	mIOU	**0.876**	**0.490**	**0.996**
	F-Score	0.933	**0.535**	**0.998**

We also evaluated the accuracy of our landmark point detector, the ENC, with the following three configurations: 1) Dlib [9], a state-of-the-art landmark predictor 2) Independently trained ENC 3) Refined ENC after E2E training. We used Mean-Square-Error (MSE) loss for evaluating all predictions, the results of which are presented in Table 3.

Table 3. Performance Comparison on Landmark Detection task.

	DLib [1]	ENC	E2E
MSE	54.91	36.31	34.26

We have shown visual outputs for the configurations evaluated in Table 1 in Fig. 4. The result for GT+SM configuration highlights the importance of the DEC module, as using SM to generate smooth segments results in sharp, unrealistic corners in its segments. ENC+SM generates template shape segments using the output from our ENC network. We observed that the generated segments were not as accurate as those from GT+SM. DLV3 was trained to minimize cross entropy loss, and it naturally scored highest in the mIOU and F-score metrics. Analyzing Fig. 4 confirmed our hypothesis that although this configuration achieved pixel-wise accuracy, it failed to provide smooth segmentation results overlooking boundary irregularities. The results for E2E indicated the most natural segmentation results, which were not only accurate, but closely resembled the template shape of a lip.

6   Conclusion and Future Work

We presented an object segmentation solution for an application of lip segmentation using a novel encoder-decoder architecture. Both subjective and quantitative evaluation of the proposed solution was demonstrated. The method is designed to suit applications that demand template-shape segments. Our method requires data sets with ground-truth landmark points and segmentation masks to support general object classes.

As an extension of this work, proposed method could be used to perform segmentation of various facial features as shown in Fig. 5(c) using template shapes from Fig. 5(b). This kind of segmentation can find use in applications like AR Makeup. Through improved segmentation, we can enhance the process of beautification as compared to traditionally employed pixel-based approaches and generate a result like shown in Fig. 5(d), which is closer to what is expected from beauty applications.

In the further works, current single-object specific network will we replaced with a universal architecture to support any type of objects.

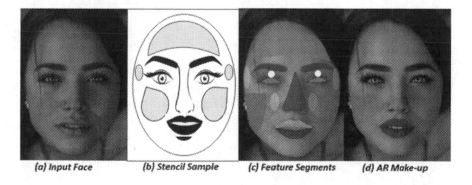

(a) Input Face   (b) Stencil Sample   (c) Feature Segments   (d) AR Make-up

Fig. 5. DeepTemplate based face parsing for improved AR Makeup

References

1. Liu, S., Yang, J., Huang, C., Yang, M.-H.: Multi-objective convolutional learning for face labeling. In: Proceedings of the IEEE Conference on Computer Vision and Pattern Recognition, pp. 3451–3459 (2015)
2. Luo, P., Wang, X., Tang, X.: Hierarchical face parsing via deep learning. In: IEEE Conference on Computer Vision and Pattern Recognition, pp. 2480–2487 (2012)
3. Smith, B.M., Zhang, L., Brandt, J., Lin, Z., Yang, J.: Exemplar-based face parsing. In: Proceedings of the IEEE Conference on Computer Vision and Pattern Recognition, pp. 3484–3491 (2013)
4. Chen, L.-C., Papandreou, G., Kokkinos, I., Murphy, K., Yuille, A.L.: Deeplab: semantic image segmentation with deep convolutional nets, atrous convolution, and fully connected CRFs. IEEE Trans. Pattern Anal. Mach. Intell. **40**(4), 834–848 (2017)
5. Cootes, T.F., Taylor, C.J., Cooper, D.H., Graham, J.: Active shape models-their training and application. Comput. Vis. Image Underst. **61**(1), 38–59 (1995)
6. Cootes, T.F., Edwards, G.J., Taylor, C.J.: Active appearance models. IEEE Trans. Pattern Anal. Mach. Intell. **23**(6), 681–685 (2001)
7. Lu, Y., Liu, Q.: Lip segmentation using automatic selected initial contours based on localized active contour model. EURASIP J. Image Video Process. **2018**(1), 1–12 (2018). https://doi.org/10.1186/s13640-017-0243-9
8. Milborrow, S., Nicolls, F.: Locating facial features with an extended active shape model. In: Forsyth, D., Torr, P., Zisserman, A. (eds.) ECCV 2008. LNCS, vol. 5305, pp. 504–513. Springer, Heidelberg (2008). https://doi.org/10.1007/978-3-540-88693-8_37
9. Kazemi, V., Sullivan, J.: One millisecond face alignment with an ensemble of regression trees. In: Proceedings of the IEEE Conference on Computer Vision and Pattern Recognition, pp. 1867–1874 (2014)
10. Le, V., Brandt, J., Lin, Z., Bourdev, L., Huang, T.S.: Interactive facial feature localization. In: Fitzgibbon, A., Lazebnik, S., Perona, P., Sato, Y., Schmid, C. (eds.) ECCV 2012. LNCS, vol. 7574, pp. 679–692. Springer, Heidelberg (2012). https://doi.org/10.1007/978-3-642-33712-3_49
11. Liang, L., Wen, F., Xu, Y.Q., Tang, X., Shum, H.Y.: Accurate face alignment using shape constrained Markov network. In: 2006 IEEE Computer Society Conference on Computer Vision and Pattern Recognition (CVPR 2006), vol. 1, pp. 1313–1319 (2006)
12. Liang, L., Xiao, R., Wen, F., Sun, J.: Face alignment via component-based discriminative search. In: Forsyth, D., Torr, P., Zisserman, A. (eds.) ECCV 2008. LNCS, vol. 5303, pp. 72–85. Springer, Heidelberg (2008). https://doi.org/10.1007/978-3-540-88688-4_6
13. Roy, A., Todorovic, S.: A multi-scale CNN for affordance segmentation in RGB images. In: Leibe, B., Matas, J., Sebe, N., Welling, M. (eds.) ECCV 2016. LNCS, vol. 9908, pp. 186–201. Springer, Cham (2016). https://doi.org/10.1007/978-3-319-46493-0_12
14. Zhou, Y., Hu, X., Zhang, B.: Interlinked convolutional neural networks for face parsing. In: Hu, X., Xia, Y., Zhang, Y., Zhao, D. (eds.) ISNN 2015. LNCS, vol. 9377, pp. 222–231. Springer, Cham (2015). https://doi.org/10.1007/978-3-319-25393-0_25
15. Long, J., Shelhamer, E., Darrell, T.: Fully convolutional networks for semantic segmentation. In: Proceedings of the IEEE Conference on Computer Vision and Pattern Recognition, pp. 3431–3440 (2015)

16. Yu, F., Koltun, V.: Multi-scale context aggregation by dilated convolutions. arXiv preprint, arXiv:1511.07122 (2015)
17. Wei, Z., Liu, S., Sun, Y., Ling, H.: Accurate facial image parsing at real-time speed. IEEE Trans. Image Process. **28**(9), 4659–4670 (2019)
18. Zhang, X., Zhu, X., Zhang, N., Li, P., Wang, L.: Seggan: semantic segmentation with generative adversarial network. In: 2018 IEEE Fourth International Conference on Multimedia Big Data (BigMM), pp. 1–5 (2018)
19. Guo, T., et al.: Residual encoder decoder network and adaptive prior for face parsing. In: Thirty-Second AAAI Conference on Artificial Intelligence (2018)
20. Radford, A., Metz, L., Chintala, S.: Unsupervised representation learning with deep convolutional generative adversarial networks. arXiv preprint, arXiv:1511.06434 (2015)
21. Reinsch, C.H.: Smoothing by spline functions. Numerische Mathematik **10**(3), 177–183 (1967)
22. Kingma, D.P., Ba, J.: Adam: a method for stochastic optimization. arXiv preprint, arXiv:1412.6980 (2014)
23. Krizhevsky, A., Sutskever, I., Hinton, G.E.: Imagenet classification with deep convolutional neural networks. In: Advances in Neural Information Processing Systems, pp. 1097–1105 (2012)
24. Sagonas, C., Antonakos, E., Tzimiropoulos, G., Zafeiriou, S., Pantic, M.: 300 faces in-the-wild challenge: database and results. Image Vis. Comput. **47**, 3–18 (2016)

Data-Centric Approach to SAR-Optical Image Translation

Paritosh Tiwari[1]([✉])[iD] and Muneendra Ojha[2][iD]

[1] IIIT -NR, Naya Raipur, CG 493661, India
paritosht@iisc.ac.in
[2] IIIT Allahabad, Prayagraj, UP 211015, India
muneendra@iiita.ac.in

Abstract. Image-to-image translation, especially from SAR to Optical domains, is of great importance in many Earth observation applications. However, the highly complex and unregularised nature of satellite images makes this problem challenging. Existing methods usually work on improving the underlying model to get better results and end up moving towards highly complex and unstable models tested on limited variations of the Earth's surface. In this paper, we propose a new data-centric approach toward SAR-Optical image translation. The methodology of segregating and categorising the data according different types of land surfaces leads to improvements in image quality and simplifies the task of scaling the model and improving the results. The model is able to effectively capture and translate features unique to different land surfaces and experiments conducted on randomised satellite image inputs demonstrate that our approach is viable in significantly outperforming other baselines.

Keywords: SAR · GAN · Sentinel-1 · Sentinel-2 · SAR-Optical · Data-Centric

1 Introduction

The task of translating an image from one domain to another is a fundamental research problem when it comes to reconstructing missing or contaminated information. In this case, we translate a satellite image from the Synthetic Aperture Radar (SAR) domain to the Optical (RGB) domain. SAR satellite images are useful because of their invariance towards weather conditions or the time of day. They fall under the category of active remote sensing, wherein the satellite generates the signal to capture images. Due to this, they are useful in a variety of applications such as sea monitoring (oil spills, ship activity etc.), land monitoring (agriculture, forestry etc.) and emergency responses to natural disasters.

On the other hand, images taken by satellites in the visual or other bands in the electromagnetic spectrum (multi-spectral images) are dependent on light received from the sun, categorised as passive remote sensing. They are useful in applications such as monitoring land cover change, observation of coastal zones, flood mapping, glacier monitoring etc. However, this method does not work in bad weather conditions, when the Earth's surface is obscured by clouds, or during night-time. Both of these obstacles are overcome by radar images, but they do not offer the detail that optical images provide. The idea of image translation is to leverage the information in radar images and use it to reconstruct optical images, which suffer from information contamination and loss due to previously mentioned obstacles.

Generative Adversarial Networks (GAN) are particularly useful for this task due to their ability to learn the pattern and distribution of an input dataset and generate new data points which are similar in nature to the input data but do not originally belong to it. Additionally, the possibility of passing a conditional input gives rise to Conditional Adversarial Networks (cGAN). This conditional input can be thought of as a reference to guide the network towards the kind of output it might generate. So, the SAR images act as a reference for the model to generate optical images.

A common trend in the deep learning research community is to improve the model to get better results. Increasing the network's size and tuning hyperparameters are some examples. In the case of GANs, this is a tedious task as they are notorious for their difficulty to train, remaining stable during training, and avoiding problems such as convergence failure and mode collapse.

We propose to engineer the data instead to improve the results. We take an already stable implementation of a conditional GAN and train it on a well-organised dataset to achieve desirable results during testing. Instead of supplying satellite images of the Earth's surface randomly from a collection, we first categorize them into four classes: barren lands, grasslands, agricultural lands, and urban areas. This type of land cover categorisation is based on our dataset survey, which points to these categories having the most varied levels of complexity and colour profiles. Thus, training separate generative models specialised for a category improves our results significantly. This also gives us the option to enhance or generalise the outputs of a specific category as desired without disturbing the stability of other categories. In order to facilitate randomised inputs during testing, we build a classifier trained to segregate the input SAR images into one of the four classes mentioned before so that they may be passed into the appropriate specialised cGAN for image translation.

In this paper, we first give a background on the various components of our model, starting with the conditional GAN, the chosen stable generative model, and finally, the classifier which segregates the input images. Next, we discuss our dataset, our approach towards curating it and its source vis the Sentinel 1 and 2 satellites. We then present our experimental setup, its subsequent results, and a comparison with the baseline model. Finally, we end with a critical discussion of our research and the future work that remains.

2 Related Work

The work done by Grohnfeldt et al. [4] has the closest relevance to ours. They have tried to address the problem of capturing multispectral (MS) images which suffer from the problems that come with spaceborne sensors that operate in the optical wave range, such as the weather. Their model is a modification of the original pix2pix model [6]. They also generate a multispectral output image with 10 channels instead of an optical image with 3 channels (RGB). Their conditional input has an additional entity, namely the contaminated multispectral image. With this feature heavy data comes the need for more memory in the network. Thus, they have scaled up the U-Net [13] generator and replaced the last 4 layers of the encoder and decoder, having 1024 instead of 512 units each. They have also included a batch normalisation layer in the bottleneck of the U-Net, which could cause the activations to be zeroed. To avoid this, we removed the batch normalisation layer, as was suggested by Isola et al. [6]. Their model needs the contaminated image as a conditional input to generate an output image of acceptable quality. Whereas we, have addressed the worst-case scenario when the cloud coverage is excessive, rendering the contaminated image useless.

Another paper along the same lines is by Meraner et al. [11]. Here, they have used a network of extensive residual blocks and trained the model in a non-adversarial way. The concept and leverage of skip connections remains the same. However, here too, they have had to use an additional contaminated image as an input, along with the SAR image. A long skip connection helps shuttle the useful information in the cloudy image to different layers of the network. The scene sites in their dataset are chosen randomly from two uniform distributions, one covering all landmasses and the other covering only populated areas. This creates a bias toward urban environments, which are often studied using remote sensing and include more complex patterns. Their model seems to perform fairly well, and they claim to have the added advantage of not dealing with the infamous training problems associated with GANs [3]. However, their showcased output images, too, suffer from blurry edges due to the clouds in the input and the lack of sharpness in the smaller objects and features.

Wang et al. [17] have used Cyclic Generative Adversarial Networks [19] to achieve SAR-Optical data fusion. However, the data they have used, although captured across different seasons, has been acquired on a specific region in China. This limits the model's generalisation, maybe not in the geographical features domain, but definitely in the colour profiles domain. Additionally, the use of Cyclic GAN is better in situations where we do not have a corresponding image set for the same image, and the second set does consist of images in the other domain. We do not think our dataset warrants a switch to Cyclic GANs since we already have corresponding image pairs.

Others have explored deep learning methods applied to SAR and remote sensing data viz Ma et al. [10] and Zhu et al. [20,21]. Although insightful, the information in the surveys did not particularly help our endeavour.

Another technique called progressive learning of GANs can be used here, which is covered by Karras et al. [7]. They force a stack of very simple generative adversarial networks to progressively learn features of an image dataset on increasing resolutions of said images. This lets the GAN focus on increasingly complex image features in a sequential manner instead of being presented with and trying to learn all of the features in single passes. We were unable to leverage this technique with our dataset, as we kept encountering mode collapses while training our GAN.

3 Model Components

3.1 Conditional Adversarial Network

Generative Adversarial Networks. GANs or Generative Adversarial Networks [3] are designed to learn the pattern or the distribution representative of the input dataset so as to generate new data points which could be thought of as having come from the original input dataset. The core 'adversarial' idea of GANs is to indirectly train them through a *Discriminator*, which is trained to distinguish between real (input data) and fake (generated) data. Thus, the generator does not try to minimise the distance to the real data, but instead tries to convince the discriminator to accept the generated data as part of the input dataset. The generator and the discriminator are trained alternatively until the generator is able to fool the discriminator half the time, i.e., the discriminator is able to classify images correctly 50% of the time.

Therefore, the goal of a GAN is to produce a new image x with a generator G parameterised by a latent variable z such that,

$$z \sim p_z(z) \rightarrow x = G(z) \sim p_G(x) \ \ s.t. \ \ p_G(x) \approx p(x) \tag{1}$$

where, z is sampled from a prior (unconditional) probability distribution $p_z(z)$, p_G is the generator probability, and $p(x)$ is the probability distribution of real data (our target estimation).

Thus, for generated images:

$$z \sim p_z(z) \rightarrow x = G(z) \sim p_G(x) \rightarrow p_D(x) = 0 \tag{2}$$

where, x is the fake image produced by the generator G, and $p_D(x) = 0$ is the probability value that x is classified as *fake* by the discriminator.

And for real images:

$$x \sim p(x) \rightarrow p_D(x) = 1 \tag{3}$$

where x is the training image sampled from the input data probability distribution (our target estimate), and $p_D(x) = 1$ is the probability value that x is classified as *real* by the discriminator.

The GAN optimisation problem can be stated as:

$$\min_{\theta} \ \max_{\phi} \ E_{x \sim p(x)} \left[\log p_{D_\phi}(x) \right] + E_{z \sim p_z(z)} \left[\log(1 - p_{D_\phi}(G_\theta(z))) \right] \tag{4}$$

where, $p_{D_\phi}(x)$ is the discriminator's estimate of the probability that the real data instance x is real, $E_{x \sim p(x)}$ is the expected value over all real data instances,

$G_\theta(z)$ is the generator's output given the latent variable (random noise vector) z, $p_{D_\phi}(G_\theta(z))$ is the discriminator's estimate of the probability that a fake data instance is real, and $E_{z \sim p_z(z)}$ is the expected value over all random inputs to the generator (the expected value over all generated fake instances $G_\theta(z)$).

The solution (Nash equilibrium) to Expression (4) is given by:

$$p_{G_\theta}(x) = p(x) \tag{5}$$

$$p_{D_\phi}(x) = \frac{p(x)}{p(x) + p_{G_\theta}(x)} = \frac{1}{2} \tag{6}$$

(5): Optimal generator for any discriminator
(6): Optimal discriminator for any generator

Conditional Adversarial Networks (cGAN). Generative adversarial nets can be augmented as conditional models [12] when the generator and discriminator are conditioned on some extra information y in addition to the latent vector z. This y could be anything, guiding the generator towards producing new data points from the mimicked input data distribution, conditioned on the newly added information.

Therefore expression (4) now changes to:

$$\min_\theta \max_\phi E_{x \sim p(x)} [\log p_{D_\phi}(x \mid y)] + E_{z \sim p_z(z)} [\log(1 - p_{D_\phi}(G_\theta(z \mid y)))] \tag{7}$$

The Pix2pix Model. For our purposes, we have made use of the *pix2pix* software [6] as a conditional adversarial network. It is considered as the benchmark, and in many cases, the baseline, when it comes to image-to-image translation. We train specialised pix2pix models for each of our categories. The following features distinguish the pix2pix model from traditional cGANs.

The *U-Net Generator* [13] in pix2pix looks like an auto-encoder. It takes the image to be interpreted and compresses it into a low-dimensional vector representation known as a 'bottleneck'. The Generator then upsamples the image to the required dimensions for output. The U-Net is identical to ResNets [5] in the way that information from earlier layers is passed into later layers.

The *PatchGAN Discriminator*. Instead of classifying the whole image as real or false, the PatchGAN/Markovian discriminator classifies particular $(N \times N)$ patches in the image as real or fake. According to the authors [6], this imposes more restrictions, which encourages sharp high-frequency detail.

3.2　CNN Classifier

We have employed a Convolutional Neural Network (CNN) (Fig. 1) to classify SAR images into appropriate categories so that they may be fed into their specialised, categorical, conditional generator networks.

The architecture:

$$\texttt{C32-R-C64-R-C128-R-C128-R-C256-R-D128-D4}$$

CX: represents a 2D convolutional layer with 'X' units.
R: represents a Rectified Linear Unit layer.
DX: represents a flattened Dense layer with 'X' units.

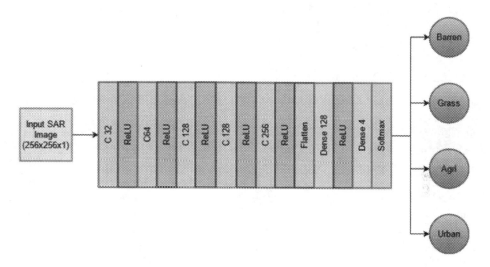

Fig. 1. SAR Classifier

All convolutional filters are of size 4×4 with a stride of 2, with the exception of the last convolutional layer (C256), which has a spatial filter of size 3×3 with a stride of 1. The last dense layer is followed by a softmax activation layer.

4   Data

The dataset we have curated and categorised is taken from a much larger collection of paired satellite images [14, 15]. These images, which are publicly available and free to use, are sourced from the Sentinel-1&2 earth observation missions of the Copernicus Programme, operated by the European Space Agency [1].

4.1   Sentinel Missions

The *Sentinel-1* mission is made up of two satellites, Sentinel-1A and Sentinel-1B, with identical orbital planes. Both of these satellites are equipped with a C-band Synthetic Aperture Radar (SAR) instrument that collects data in any weather condition and during any time of the day or night. The devices have a spatial resolution of 5 m and a swath of up to 400 kilometres. the satellites repeat their orbit every 12 d. The SAR images used in our work are a result of these satellites.

The optical images are taken by the *Sentinel-2* satellites. The constellation comprises of twin satellites, namely, Sentinel-2A and Sentinel-2B. They collect data at a spatial resolution ranging from 10 to 60 m. Although the data collected by the satellites is multi-spectral, ranging in the visible, near-infrared, and short-wave infrared regions of the spectrum with 13 bands, we have restricted ourselves to the Reg-Green-Blue (RGB) bands of the visual spectrum for the purpose of our work. Working in conjunction, the twin satellites cut down the revisit period from 10 to just 5 d.

4.2   Curated Dataset

The *original dataset* [14] is provided by the Technical University of Munich. It consists of 282,384 corresponding image pairs of Sentinel-1 SAR images and Sentinel-2 RGB optical images. These images have been captured over varied geographical locations during different seasons so as to have as much generalization introduced as possible. The entire dataset has been mainly segregated according to seasons: spring, summer, fall and winter. This was done to show the time-related generalisation on the scale of a year. However, we felt the need for another approach toward segregation. We decided to segregate the data into four classes and then train separate conditional GANs specifically on those classes.

We searched through images captured during the fall season in the original dataset and selected images which could belong to each of the four classes: *barren land, grassland, agricultural land, and urban areas.* Optical images shown in Fig. 2 give an idea of the type of images belonging to each class. We have tried to introduce as much variation as possible when selecting images for a class so that our specialised generator models do not suffer from a lack of generalisation. We have also intentionally added a bit of noise in the image sets, such as an image which should primarily belong to one class but is put in another. This was done in an effort to avoid over-fitting the specialised generators.

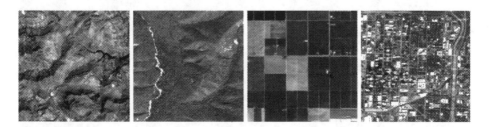

Fig. 2. Curated data: Barren Land (left-top), Grassland (right-top), Agricultural Land (left-bottom), Urban Area (right-bottom).

We selected 4,000 image pairs for each of the four classes, totalling 16,000 image pairs. We then randomly split them up into training and testing sets, 80%

of the images (3,200) in each class for training and the remaining 20% (800) for testing. We made 7 of these random splits using random seeds, trained and tested them, and then averaged out the results [16].

5   Experiments and Results

5.1   SAR Classifier

The model (Fig. 1) was trained and tested with an 80–20 train-test split on 16,000 SAR images from all of the classes for 15 epochs with a batch size of 1. Stochastic gradient descent was used as an optimiser, and categorical crossentropy as a loss function.

We got a test **accuracy of 84.16%** while refraining from over-fitting the model (Fig. 3).

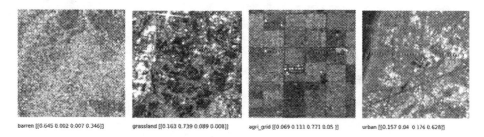

barren [[0.645 0.002 0.007 0.346]]   grassland [[0.163 0.739 0.089 0.008]]   agri_grid [[0.069 0.111 0.771 0.05]]   urban [[0.157 0.04 0 176 0.628]]

Fig. 3. SAR Classifier final model results (true class name) [barren land score, grass-land score, grid score, urban score]

5.2   Composite Model

Our final model (Fig. 4) comprises of the SAR image being fed into the SAR classifier and then the same image being fed into the appropriate cGAN for translation. Each cGAN specialises in translating its respective class of SAR images into optical images. The specialised models were trained for 100 epochs with a batch size of 1. They were trained and tested with an 80–20 split over each class.

The input SAR images have 3 channels which have redundant information. That is, the single channel information is repeated three times. This was done to ensure symmetry because the optical images have 3 channels as well, and for convenience while writing code for the project. The symmetry part comes into play during the downscaling and upscaling in the U-Net of the pix2pix model. It is better to ensure symmetry between the input and the output, in terms of dimensions.

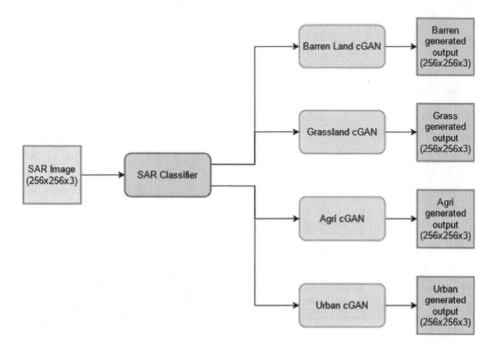

Fig. 4. Final Composite Model

We first tested the outputs of each of the generators separately, i.e., without using the SAR classifier to feed images. Each generator was fed images from their specialised class. The resultant images were compared with the ground truth images, i.e., the original Sentinel-2 optical images, and were scored using the Structured Similarity Index or SSIM [18]. The SSIM scores of the 800 test images were plotted using a violin plot to show the distribution of SSIM scores and their median. A score of over 0.65 is considered good enough for our model. The horizontal line in the middle of the plot represents the median of the distribution.

As we can see in Fig. 5, the SSIM distribution of urban areas is not desirable. This is because satellite images of urban areas (Fig. 2) have an increased amount of detail compared to other classes, with small objects and their boundaries. Not to mention, some urban areas contain elements of barren, grass and agricultural lands as well. In other words, the complexity of urban images is much more significant as compared to images of the rest of the classes. With the composite model (Fig. 4), our classifier outputs a probability vector with probabilities assigned to each class for the input SAR image. The image is then fed into the generator of whichever class received the maximum score. Subsequently, the SSIM scores and violin plots are generated as per the previous experiment.

Figure 6 shows the changes in plots. We observe that the ends are no longer tapering, and there is some bulge in the lower range. This is due to the fact that the SAR classifier's accuracy is 84.16%, and some of the images have been misclassified and ended up in the wrong generator. The most significant

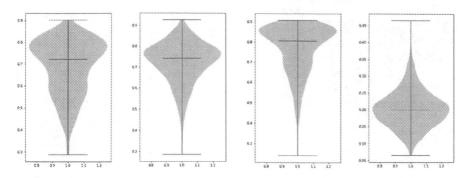

Fig. 5. Violin plots of SSIM scores without the classifier (left to right): barren land, grassland, agricultural land, urban areas.

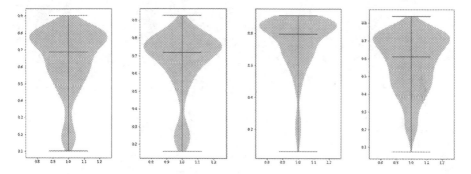

Fig. 6. Violin plots of SSIM scores with the classifier (left to right): barren land, grassland, agricultural land, urban areas.

observation, however, is that of the urban plot. Using the classifier has dramatically improved our result, with the median being just above 0.6. This might be a result of urban images having feature elements from other classes too. With this improvement, we do not deem it necessary to increase the complexity of the urban generator model. Although, this could also point towards the refinement of our urban dataset.

Figure 7 shows examples of the outputs generated with the composite model for each class.

5.3   Baseline Model Comparison

We took the pix2pix model and scaled it ×2, i.e., increased the number of units in the layers by two, which roughly follows the guidelines of this work by Grohnfeldt et al. [4]. After training and testing it on our dataset, the maximum median SSIM score we could achieve over all the classes was 0.45. Figure 8 shows some of the results.

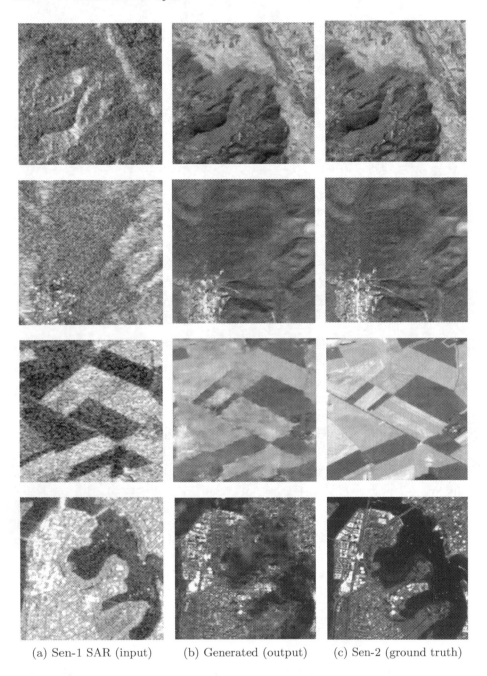

(a) Sen-1 SAR (input)   (b) Generated (output)   (c) Sen-2 (ground truth)

Fig. 7. Composite model output for (top to bottom) barren land, grassland, agricultural land, urban areas.

Since SAR images are captured using active signal generation and reflection, they easily emphasise geographical features like elevations, ridges, depressions, valleys etc. This technique is primarily sensitive to distances of objects from the source of emissions; rather than determining which wavelengths said objects are absorbing and which are being reflected, i.e., their colour. This also reflects in our results. The baseline model is easily able to recreate geographical features in the output optical images since they are in greater detail in the SAR images supplied to it. The reflectance textures for different land cover types are visible in the images. However, the model falls short of capturing this variation in land cover and colour profiles in detail. We could run the model for a greater number of epochs, but then we run the risk of memorisation and overfitting. Determining the threshold is challenging and has to be done experimentally through trial and error. However, this does not mean that land cover types cannot be distinguished at all in SAR images, as we clearly see different shades and reflection patterns representing various types of surfaces. But, what this also means is that surfaces with similar reflective properties will be indistinguishable in SAR images, such as soil with a thin layer of water over them and airport runways. The generated images also lack sharpness and clarity. This could be attributed to the distortions in the SAR images. We could benefit from increasing the sharpness of the input radar images and reducing their speckles.

These issues, combined with the varied colour profiles to learn, make it difficult for the model to learn the distribution. The problems stated above are generally not encountered when dealing with optical images, as the distinguishable colours, combined with geographical features, make it relatively easy for us to distinguish objects and land cover types in images. Another issue could be the complexity of the images themselves. As we have mentioned previously, satellite images are not regularised or normalised like benchmark datasets (CIFAR-10 [8], MNIST [9]) to fit specific criteria, so as to make sure that all images have a standard set of underlying characteristics on top of which the other characteristics are presented, which makes every image unique in its own way. While this does not make satellite images a good option to establish a baseline when trying out new architectures, they could come in handy when testing the robustness of a model.

6   Discussion

The intention behind the design of our model was to distribute the load. That is, to have specialised agents performing specialised tasks. We have included four major types of land cover that we encountered during our research. And in choosing images for those land cover classes, we have introduced some noise and intentionally misclassified data in order to avoid overfitting the model. Therefore, in this case, the aspect of generalisation, depends on the types of images we have at our disposal. That is to say, the exhaustive coverage of different land cover types in the dataset. And it all hinges on the process of classifying them accurately with some care taken to induce overfitting countermeasures. Even

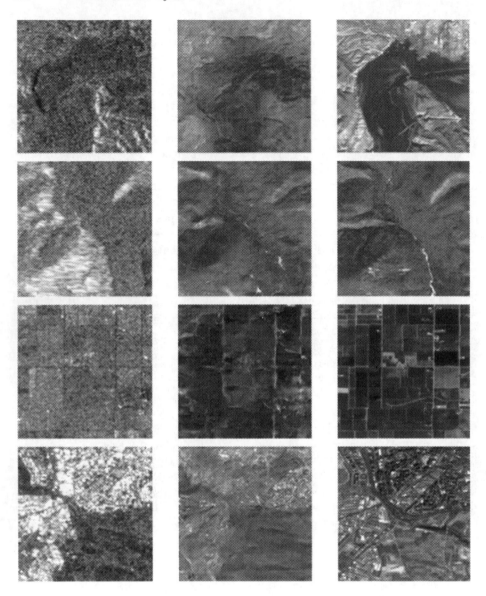

Fig. 8. Base model results: SAR (left), generated image (centre), ground truth (right)

though we have manually segregated the images for this study, when we attempt to automate the process, additional errors of such a process, whatever they may be, will seep into our results.

By virtue of the design of our model, we have also achieved *load distribution*. The generators in our architecture are only concerned with generating images from their domain or distribution. The classifier prior to this step takes care of that. Therefore, they can generate accurate colour profiles and images with increased sharpness. This also inherently takes care of the problem of improving our model via additional training. Suppose we feel that images of a particular class, say urban areas, are not being generated accurately. In that case, we only need to additionally train that separate generator and leave the other ones undisturbed since there is no intercommunication among them. This procedure will not disturb the learned weights of other classes, and we can surgically improve the results of a particular domain or distribution.

7 Future Work

The process of segregating images will eventually involve *unsupervised image classification*, which, even on structured data, is quite difficult. The process, when applied to images, gives no guarantees for being accurate, nor does it give us any hints towards improving its accuracy. The situation is bound to be worse when we supply it with highly complex and irregular images with no underlying geometric pattern, like satellite images. However, this paper by Gansbeke et al. [2] offers some insights into exploring this solution.

Our SAR classifier is a *bottleneck* towards the performance of our model. The accuracy and quality of the generated image depend on how accurately its SAR counterpart is classified and sent to the right generator. As of now, we are capable of getting decent results given our classifier accuracy of 85%. However, when the incoming data distribution eventually gets large, we will have to scale up our classifier, which might slow down our performance. It will also run a greater risk of misclassification. We might have to introduce multiple hierarchical layers of classifiers as the dataset grows more extensive, which would first classify incoming SAR images into a general domain and then classify them into a specialised domain for our multiple generators. Of course, this also means additional classification errors of those layers.

Additionally, instead of segregating our dataset based on land surfaces in optical images, we could also segregate it on the basis of SAR images having similar reflective properties. This makes sense because different surfaces that produce similar reflections will be indistinguishable to the classifier and generator anyway.

References

1. ESA: The sentinel missions. https://sentinels.copernicus.eu, Accessed 2 May 2022
2. Gansbeke, W.V., Vandenhende, S., Georgoulis, S., Proesmans, M., Gool, L.V.: Learning to classify images without labels. CoRR abs/2005.12320 (2020). https://arxiv.org/abs/2005.12320
3. Goodfellow, I.J., et al.: Generative adversarial networks. Adv. Neural Inform. Process. Syst. **3**(January), 2672–2680 (2014)
4. Grohnfeldt, C., Schmitt, M., Zhu, X.: A conditional generative adversarial network to fuse sar and multispectral optical data for cloud removal from sentinel-2 images. In: IGARSS 2018–2018 IEEE International Geoscience and Remote Sensing Symposium, pp. 1726–1729 (2018). https://doi.org/10.1109/IGARSS.2018.8519215

5. He, K., Zhang, X., Ren, S., Sun, J.: Deep residual learning for image recognition. CoRR abs/1512.03385 (2015). http://arxiv.org/abs/1512.03385

6. Isola, P., Zhu, J., Zhou, T., Efros, A.A.: Image-to-image translation with conditional adversarial networks. CoRR abs/1611.07004 (2016). http://arxiv.org/abs/1611.07004

7. Karras, T., Aila, T., Laine, S., Lehtinen, J.: Progressive growing of gans for improved quality, stability, and variation. arXiv pp. 1–26 (2017)

8. Krizhevsky, A., Nair, V., Hinton, G.: Cifar-10 (canadian institute for advanced research) http://www.cs.toronto.edu/ kriz/cifar.html

9. LeCun, Y., Cortes, C.: MNIST handwritten digit database (2010). http://yann.lecun.com/exdb/mnist/

10. Ma, L., Liu, Y., Zhang, X., Ye, Y., Yin, G., Johnson, B.A.: Deep learning in remote sensing applications: A meta-analysis and review (2019). https://doi.org/10.1016/j.isprsjprs.2019.04.015

11. Meraner, A., Ebel, P., Zhu, X.X., Schmitt, M.: Cloud removal in sentinel-2 imagery using a deep residual neural network and sar-optical data fusion, pp. 166, 333–346 (2020). https://doi.org/10.1016/J.ISPRSJPRS.2020.05.013

12. Mirza, M., Osindero, S.: Conditional generative adversarial nets. CoRR abs/1411.1784 (2014). http://arxiv.org/abs/1411.1784

13. Ronneberger, O., Fischer, P., Brox, T.: U-net: Convolutional networks for biomedical image segmentation. CoRR abs/1505.04597 (2015). http://arxiv.org/abs/1505.04597

14. Schmitt, M.: Sen1-2 (2018). https://mediatum.ub.tum.de/1436631

15. Schmitt, M., Hughes, L.H., Zhu, X.X.: The SEN1-2 dataset for deep learning in sar-optical data fusion. CoRR abs/1807.01569 (2018). http://arxiv.org/abs/1807.01569

16. Tiwari, P.: Sar-optical terrain segregated pairs, https://www.kaggle.com/datasets/requiemonk/sentinel12-image-pairs-segregated-by-terrain Accessed 2 May 2022

17. Wang, L.: SAR-to-optical image translation using supervised cycle-consistent adversarial networks. IEEE Access 7, 129136–129149 (2019). https://doi.org/10.1109/ACCESS.2019.2939649

18. Wang, Z., Bovik, A.C., Sheikh, H.R., Simoncelli, E.P.: Image quality assessment: from error visibility to structural similarity 13(4), 600–612 (2004). https://doi.org/10.1109/TIP.2003.819861

19. Zhu, J.Y., Park, T., Isola, P., Efros, A.A.: Unpaired Image-to-Image Translation Using Cycle-Consistent Adversarial Networks. In: Proceedings of the IEEE International Conference on Computer Vision 2017-Octob, pp. 2242–2251 (2017). https://doi.org/10.1109/ICCV.2017.244

20. Zhu, X.X., et al.: Deep Learning Meets SAR (jun 2020). https://arxiv.org/abs/2006.10027

21. Zhu, X.X., et al.: Deep learning in remote sensing: a review (december) (2017). https://doi.org/10.1109/MGRS.2017.2762307

Linear and Non-Linear Filter-based Counter-Forensics Against Image Splicing Detection

Debjit Das[1]([✉])[iD], Banalata Bhunia[2], Ruchira Naskar[1][iD],
and Rajat Subhra Chakraborty[3]

[1] Department of Information Technology, Indian Institute of Engineering Science
and Technology, Shibpur Howrah 711103, West Bengal, India
{debjit.rs2020,ruchira}@it.iiests.ac.in
[2] Vellore Institute of Technology, Vellore, Tamil Nadu, India
bhuniabanalata@gmail.com
[3] Department of Computer Science and Engineering, Indian Institute of Technology
Kharagpur, Kharagpur 721302, West Bengal, India
rschakraborty@cse.iitkgp.ac.in

Abstract. Digital images are widely used as primary sources of evidence in today's world, spanning security, forensics, and legal domains. However, image tampering poses a shallow technical skill barrier with the wide availability of sophisticated, easy-to-use image manipulation software. Tampered images are often used intentionally for unlawful and malicious purposes. One of the most common forms of image manipulation attack is image splicing, which is performed by combining regions from multiple source images to synthesize an artificial image that looks natural. Digital forensic measures have been widely explored in the literature to detect such type of image forgery. However, the recent growth of counter-forensics poses a threat to such forensic/security measures. Forensic techniques can be easily deceived by adopting counter-forensic manipulation of forged images. In this work, we explore different linear and non-linear filtering-based counter-forensic modifications to digital images and hence investigate the after-effects of those, in terms of severity of such manipulations in rendering state-of-the-art forensic splicing detection methods useless. In this paper, we implement two forensic image splicing detection techniques based on feature extraction from image along with machine learning and deep CNN with transfer learning. Then, different filtering techniques have been applied to the image dataset, investigating their effectiveness as a counter-forensic attack against image splicing detection. Experimental results show that the Gaussian filter and Average filter are the two most effective counter-forensic filtering methods against image splicing detection, suggesting the need for further strengthening the existing family of forensic techniques.

Keywords: Accuracy · Average filter · Counter forensic · Gaussian filter · Image splicing · Median filter · SSIM · VGG16

D. Gupta et al. (Eds.): CVIP 2022, CCIS 1776, pp. 261–275, 2023.
https://doi.org/10.1007/978-3-031-31407-0_20

1 Introduction

Due to the wide availability and extensive use of several ready-to-use, cost-effective tools and software, image manipulation has become very common nowadays. The associated risks are becoming more severe with each passing day, with more sophisticated image editing tools available to the common mass. Such image manipulations, when carried out with a malicious intention, mainly to assist any unlawful activity, pose a significant threat for society, many times, are threatening national security too. Hence, analysis, identification, and detection of image tampering plays an important role in conserving the law and security of any organization or nation as a whole.

Image splicing [9,17] is a very common form of image manipulation, which, when performed with malicious intent, poses a big threat since such type of image manipulation is difficult to be detected without sophisticated forensic measures. In image splicing, portions from different source images are intelligently composited together to constitute a natural-looking but artificially manipulated image. Due to this type of image synthesis, the resultant images exhibit extensive variation in image textures and features from one region to another. An example of an image splicing attack has been presented in Fig. 1.

Fig. 1. Splicing of a Digital Image: (*a*) Authentic Image 1, (*b*) Authentic Image 2, (*c*) Spliced Image - Composited of Authentic Image 1 and Authentic Image 2.

To make the forgery less detectable and more convincing, fraudsters may perform several enhancement operations [19] on the forged images . Among different enhancement techniques, noise removal or noise addition, edge enhancement, filtering, deblurring, compression, contrast enhancement, etc. are most common. In this work, we focus on different forms of image filtering (linear and non-linear) as counter forensic attacks against detection of spliced images.

In this work, first, two different forensic methods for detecting image splicing, based on *manual feature extraction from images with machine learning* and *deep*

Convolutional Neural Network (CNN) along with transfer learning, have been implemented and their results are recorded. Next, we investigate the effects of different image filtering techniques to render the above forensic measure unsuccessful in detecting splicing attacks. Through our experiments, we measure the success of a wide range of filtering operations on spliced images in fooling the forensic mechanisms. Experimental results show that for detection of image splicing, Gaussian filtering and Average filtering are the two most effective linear filtering-based counter forensic approaches. Among non-linear filters, Median filtering proves to be the most effective.

The rest of the paper is organized as follows. Section 2 provides a short overview of related research works, along with our contribution in this work. In Sect. 3, we discuss the adopted scheme for feature extraction based image splicing detection with machine learning in detail along with the result obtained. In Sect. 4, we discuss the adopted deep learning based scheme to detect image splicing along with the obtained result. In Sect. 5, we discuss linear and non-linear filters used in this work as counter forensic attacks against image splicing detection. In Sect. 6, we present and analyze the results of proposed counter forensic modifications with necessary discussion. Finally, in Sect. 7 we conclude the work with a discussion on its future scope.

2 Related Works and Our Contribution

In the present state-of-the-art, detection of image splicing is treated as a classification task in digital forensics. To hide any trace of image manipulation, different post-processing enhancement techniques such as filtering can be applied by the fraudsters as counter forensic attacks. This section provides a brief overview of recent notable research advancements in this domain.

Among the works related to image splicing detection, in [23], Walia et al. developed an effective scheme for image splicing detection and localization based on Gray Level Co-occurrence Matrix (GLCM). In [21], Shen et al. developed a splicing detection scheme with the help of textural features based on GLCM, named TF-GLCM. In [15], Pham et al. proposed a Markov feature-based method to detect image splicing. Islam et al. [8] developed an image tampering detection scheme based on DCT and LBP. In [6], Das et al. developed a model based on Gaussian blur to detect image splicing. In [9], Jaiswal et al. proposed a novel scheme for detecting image splicing using a hybrid feature set. In [1], Ahmed et al. proposed a blind image tampering detection method based on a deep learning neural network architecture named *ResNet-conv*. In [26], an image splicing detection mechanism was proposed with the help of adaptive clustering and Coarse-to-refined CNN (C2RNet). In [18], Rao et al. developed a model based on a local feature descriptor using a deep CNN to detect and localize spliced regions. In [24], the authors proposed an effective splicing detection scheme based on CNN and weight combination. Another novel method based on CNN and *illuminant maps* was proposed by Pomari et al. [17] for detecting spliced images.

Among the works related to counter forensic approaches, Ravi et al. [19] proposed a method to detect if an image had undergone any filtering enhancement to hide possible image forgery. In [3], Böhme et al. discussed counter forensic attacks against the forensic analysis of image forgery with a survey of counter forensic techniques. In [12], the authors discussed counter forensics approach-related to JPEG compression of digital images. In [5], median filtering was discussed, and a method was proposed to conceal the traces of image forgery using median filtering. In [20], a CNN-based model was presented to identify if an image has undergone any counter-forensic attack to mislead the forensic analysis of source identification.

2.1 Our Contribution

Most of the existing works discussed above majorly focus on image splicing detection. As per our knowledge, not many of these have probed into counter-forensic threats against splicing detection. Neither image enhancements have been explored as an area of counter forensic attacks; mostly, only a single counter forensic approach is presented. Concerning the above, in this paper, our significant contributions are:

- Initially, we employ a simple forensic technique to detect spliced images based on a homogeneous feature set of image texture features derived from GLCM. Then, we also employ another splicing detection model based on deep CNN and transfer learning.
- Next, different linear and non-linear image filters have been explored to be used as counter forensic attacks against the splicing detection methods mentioned above.
- Finally, we analyze the effect of the image filters through extensive experiments on both splicing detection mechanisms and prove that both of the splicing detection mechanisms are more robust toward non-linear filters as compared to linear.

In the next section, we present a homogeneous feature-based forensic model to detect spliced images and discussion on the feature sets utilized.

3   Feature Based Image Splicing Detection

In this method, we majorly work with *image textural features* calculated from corresponding GLCM [13,22,23]. We form the required feature matrix using only those textural features while preserving state-of-the-art performance for splicing detection.

In this scheme, each input image first undergoes the required pre-processing from the image dataset. Each color image is first converted to grayscale, and then, for each image, the GLCM is computed at different distances and in different directions. Then, different textural features from the GLCM are extracted for each input image. The feature sets that we work within particular have been discussed in the next section. Next, the feature sets are combined, and the target label is also stored based on forged and authentic images to form the complete feature matrix. Finally, the feature matrix is fed to an SVM classifier to identify the spliced images. A 10-fold cross-validation has been performed for validation check.

3.1   Feature Sets Explored

This section provides an overview of the image feature sets explored in this work, including the GLCM based texture feature sets.

Gray Level Co-occurrence Matrix (GLCM). GLCM [13, 22, 23] has been extensively used for texture analysis in images. It is a second-order statistical texture feature analysis method [13]. It deals with the spatial relationship of pixels in a grayscale image. The GLCM is formed from a grayscale image by calculating how often different combinations of pair of pixel values appear in a grayscale image together. Two essential parameters of GLCM are distance and direction. For a 2-dimensional image, the direction can be horizontal, vertical, right diagonal, and left diagonal based, i.c., the angles are $0°$, $45°$, $90°$, and $135°$ [21]. The distance value can be set as 1 for the nearest neighbor pixel, or it can be set as a higher value for finding the correlation between distant pixels. By default, the spatial relationship in GLCM is set as distance 1, and direction $0°$. In GLCM, if the value at location (i, j) is k, it indicates that the pixel pair (i, j) appears k times in the given grayscale image with the specific spatial relationship of a certain distance and direction. GLCM produces a square matrix of dimension $M \times M$ where M is the number of different gray levels. Usually, the input image is scaled down, and the gray level value is changed from 256 to 8 [22] to make the GLCM smaller in size.

In this paper, we have extracted five different texture features from each GLCM: energy, correlation, dissimilarity, homogeneity and contrast. These texture features are defined below.

Energy: Energy calculates the sum of squared elements in GLCM. The value of Energy lies between 0 to 1. If G_{ij} is the element at position (i, j) in the normalized symmetrical GLCM, and N denotes the number of gray-levels, then Energy can be calculated as follows:

$$Energy = \sum_{i,j=0}^{N-1} (G_{ij})^2 \tag{1}$$

Correlation: It measures how a pixel value is correlated to its neighbor pixel over the entire image. A high value in correlation means the elements in GLCM are uniform [21]. The range of value of correlation is -1 to 1. If μ represents the GLCM mean and σ^2 represents the variance of intensities in the GLCM, then the calculation of correlation will be:

$$Correlation = \sum_{i,j=0}^{N-1} G_{ij} \cdot \frac{(i-\mu)\cdot(j-\mu)}{\sigma^2} \qquad (2)$$

Dissimilarity: Dissimilarity uses weight as $|i-j|$, so when a pixel moves away from the diagonal, the weights in dissimilarity increase linearly. Therefore, if G_{ij} is the element at position (i,j) in the GLCM, and N represents the number of gray-levels, then formulation of dissimilarity is:

$$Dissimilarity = \sum_{i,j=0}^{N-1} G_{ij} \cdot |i-j| \qquad (3)$$

Homogeneity: It measures the similarity of the distribution of GLCM elements to the diagonal of GLCM. The homogeneity range is 0 to 1, and it is formulated as:

$$Homogeneity = \sum_{i,j=0}^{N-1} \frac{G_{ij}}{1+(i-j)^2} \qquad (4)$$

Contrast: It measures the difference of intensity between a pixel to its neighborhood over the whole image. If contrast is high, it indicates that the image is visually more clear [21] and sharp. It is formulated as follows:

$$Contrast = \sum_{i,j=0}^{N-1} G_{ij} \cdot (i-j)^2 \qquad (5)$$

3.2   Adopted Model for Feature-based Splicing Detection in Images

First, we have converted each color image to grayscale, by the following weighing formula: $I = 0.299 \times R + 0.587 \times G + 0.114 \times B$ where R, G and B represent *Red, Green* and *Blue* color components of the image, respectively, and the gray scale intensity of the converted image is represented by I. As stated previously, in this work, we adopt the features described in Sect. 3.1, viz. GLCM based texture features, as these proved to be the most effective sets in our experiments. We compute the Gray Level Co-occurrence Matrix (GLCM) of each gray image at three different distances and with four different angles. We have taken distances as 1, 3, and 5, and angles as $0°$, $45°$, $90°$, and $135°$. Each GLCM is calculated after the grayscale image is scaled down to gray level 8 for the region of interest. Therefore, an overall total $3 \times 4 = 12$ different GLCMs are calculated for each image. From each of the twelve calculated GLCMs, we have extracted five different GLCM texture features, which are-energy, correlation, dissimilarity, homogeneity and contrast (discussed above in Sect. 3.1). So, all total $3 \times 4 \times 5 = 60$ numbers of GLCM texture features are extracted from each input image. The target label is appended with all the above features to form the complete feature matrix. Finally, it is fed to an SVM classifier for supervised learning and classification of spliced images. The feature set is decomposed into two subsets after shuffling: $\frac{7}{8}$ of this is used for training and the rest $\frac{1}{8}$ for testing purposes. We have also performed a 10-fold cross-validation for accurate performance estimation of the proposed model.

3.3 Splicing Detection Result

Our adopted model based on textural features calculated from GLCM received an overall accuracy of 75.36% for successful detection of image splicing. Further, we have applied cross-validation on the test dataset and received an average accuracy of 73.03% for image splicing detection.

4 Deep Learning Based Image Splicing Detection

In this work, we implement an effective splicing detection method based on deep CNN and transfer learning. The initial convolution layers of this model are replaced with a pre-trained network known as VGG-16.

Transfer learning is a machine learning-based technique where the model trained on one task can be reapplied on another new task. The knowledge gained during training one model can be applied again to solve a new related problem which makes it very helpful in deep learning to reduce the training time and cost.

VGG-16 [2, 25]is a 16-layer deep CNN model trained with more than a million of images from the ImageNet dataset [11]. It is a publicly available pre-trained network that can classify the images of the ImageNet dataset into 1000 different classes.

4.1 Adopted Model for Deep Learning-based Image Splicing Detection

We have implemented a CNN model to detect image splicing where the pre-trained VGG-16 network replaces the initial layers of the CNN. We have explored the Columbia Image Splicing Detection Evaluation Dataset [14] for our experiments. We have sub-divided the dataset into three parts, where 80% of the data are taken for training, 10% for validation, and the rest 10% for testing purposes. The layers of the VGG-16 network are set as non-trainable as the model is already pre-trained on the ImageNet dataset with optimum weights. The final output layer of the VGG-16 has been removed and altered as the existing output layer has 1000 nodes to classify the images of ImageNet into 1000 categories. Instead, here we have applied the Global Average Pooling layer followed by six fully connected dense layers, where in each case, the activation function is used as ReLU. Finally, the output layer is added, having a single node and Sigmoid activation function, as our model is designed for binary classification. During the compilation of the model, we have selected an "Adam" optimizer with a learning rate of 0.0001, the "binary crossentropy" is taken as the loss parameter, and "accuracy" is selected as the performance metric. We have trained our model with training data for 50 epochs along with the provision of early stopping. Finally, the model's performance has been evaluated based on the test accuracy of the test dataset.

4.2   Result for Splicing Detection

Our adopted model based on pre-trained CNN model VGG-16 and transfer learning achieved an accuracy of 90.32% for successful detection of image splicing. The accuracy of both of these two adopted methods is shown in Table 1.

Table 1. Accuracy of Adopted Splicing Detection Models

Model	Accuracy (%)
Feature-based	73.03
Deep Learning-based	90.32

5   Counter Forensic Analysis on Adopted Model

Image filtering refers to a process of image modification through retaining and enhancing some of its features while removing or obscuring others. This is done with the intention of emphasizing the retained features of the image or suppressing some others. This might include suppressing high frequency components of an image, known as *smoothing*, or suppressing the low frequencies for *image enhancement* or *edge detection*. Such filtering is performed either in the frequency domain or spatial domain of an image.

Image filtering can be either *linear* or *non-linear*, depending on whether the filtered image is obtained through a sequence of linear or non-linear operations on the source image pixels, respectively.

5.1   Linear Filtering

In linear filtering, the output pixel value is calculated based on the linear combinations of the neighboring input pixel values. It is usually performed with convolutions. Usually, these filters are shift-invariant. Among different linear filtering techniques, the two most effective ones are Gaussian filter [7] and Average (Mean) filter [10].

Gaussian Filtering. Gaussian filtering [7] is used to remove noise and image detailing to blur the image. Using Gaussian filtering, the input signal is modified by convolution with a Gaussian function. In one dimension, a Gaussian function is shown in Eq. 6 where σ represents the standard deviation of Gaussian distribution, and x is the horizontal distance from the origin.

$$G(x) = \frac{1}{\sqrt{2\pi\sigma^2}} \cdot e^{-\frac{x^2}{2\sigma^2}} \tag{6}$$

Gaussian filtering is very useful for image smoothing but it can not remove salt and pepper noise. It has very minimum group delay.

Average (Mean) Filtering. This linear filtering method [10] is also effective to smooth an image. It is a windowed low-pass filter of linear class. Using this filter, an input image is modified pixel by pixel, where the value of each pixel is replaced with the average of all neighboring pixel values to reduce the intensity variance among adjacent pixels.

5.2 Non-Linear Filtering

In non-linear filtering [16], the output pixel value is not a linear combination or linear function of the input pixel values. It can not be performed with convolution. Non-linear filters may or may not be shift-invariant. We have adopted the following non-linear filters here: Median filtering [4,5], Min, Max and Mode filtering [16].

Median Filtering. This non-linear filtering [4,5] is widely used to remove unwanted noise from image, especially the salt and pepper noise. It is mainly used for image denoising, removing outliers, and image smoothing. It eliminates the effect of noise with huge magnitudes. An advantage of median filtering is that it can remove noise from the image while preserving the edges of the image.

Min Filtering. In this case, each pixel of the image is replaced by the minimum of all neighboring pixel values, i.e., the darkest pixel. It can remove positive outlier noise from the image.

Max Filtering This shift-invariant filtering replaces each image pixel with the maximum pixel value from its neighboring pixels. It is helpful to remove negative outliers from the image.

Mode Filtering. In mode filtering, the center pixel value of the window is replaced with the pixel value that appears most frequently within the window. It is useful for smoothing of image while preserving the edges.

We have experimented with all six filters discussed above. Next, we present our results of counter-forensics.

6   Experiments and Results of Counter Forensics

6.1   Dataset and Implementation

In this work, we have used the Columbia Image Splicing Detection Evaluation Dataset [14] that consists of 1845 number of 128×128 grayscale image blocks. Out of these 1845 image blocks, 933 are of authentic type and the remaining 912 image blocks are of spliced category. Authentic and spliced image blocks are further subdivided into five subcategories based on textured region, smooth region, and position of an object boundary between two regions. In our experiment, we have used this entire dataset without any further modification.

We have implemented this work with Python 3.7.6, Jupyter notebook IDE, Keras, and TensorFlow library. This experiment is executed on a workstation with an 8th generation Intel i7-8700 CPU with processor base frequency 3.20 GHz and 8 GB RAM.

6.2   Performance Evaluation Metrics

In our experiment, we have used the Accuracy and Structural Similarity Index Measure (SSIM) as the performance evaluation metric. Accuracy provides a measure of the overall correctness of the forensic detection model; it is computed as follows:

$$Accuracy\ (\%) = \frac{TP + TN}{TP + TN + FP + FN} \times 100\% \tag{7}$$

where, $TP = No.\ of\ True\ Positives$, $TN = No.\ of\ True\ Negatives$, $FP = No.\ of\ False\ Positives$, and, $FN = No.\ of\ False\ Negatives$.

Structural Similarity Index Measure (SSIM) tells how similar two images are. It is a metric to determine the similarity of two images. It takes the reference of the original image (say X) to determine the similarity between the processed image (say X') and the original unaltered image.

SSIM of X' with respect to X, is computed as:

$$SSIM(X, X') = \frac{(2\mu_X \mu_{X'} + C_1)(2\sigma_{XX'} + C_2)}{(\mu_X^2 + \mu_{X'}^2 + C_1)(\sigma_X^2 + \sigma_{X'}^2 + C_2)} \tag{8}$$

where μ_X and $\mu_{X'}$ represent the mean value of X and X' respectively, the standard deviations of X and X' are represented by σ_X and $\sigma_{X'}$ respectively, $\sigma_{XX'}$ denotes the covariance between X and X', and, C_1 and C_2 are two constants, used to avoid the instability when $(\mu_X^2 + \mu_{X'}^2)$ and $(\sigma_X^2 + \sigma_{X'}^2)$ are close to zero.

6.3   Experimental Results

We have adopted different kernel sizes (3×3, 5×5, 7×7, and 9×9) for the aforementioned filters in this work. *Kernel size* affects the quality of smoothing achieved by a specific filter on an input image. We have also reported the average and best SSIM value for each case. The performance analysis of counter forensic

Table 2. Results of Linear and Non-linear Filtering based Counter Forensic Attacks on Feature based Image Splicing Detection

Filter	Kernel Size	Accuracy (%)	Drop in Accuracy (%)	SSIM (Best)	SSIM (Average)
Gaussian Filtering	3 × 3	64.01	9.02	0.9959	0.9435
	5 × 5	65.78	7.25	0.9926	0.8958
	7 × 7	60.20	12.83	0.9882	0.8362
	9 × 9	60.08	12.95	0.9851	0.8196
Average (Mean) Filtering	3 × 3	67.24	5.79	0.9981	0.9078
	5 × 5	66.72	6.31	0.9963	0.8023
	7 × 7	65.82	7.21	0.9938	0.7116
	9 × 9	65.09	7.94	0.9926	0.6514
Median Filtering	3 × 3	69.39	3.64	0.996	0.9214
	5 × 5	68.97	4.06	0.991	0.8198
	7 × 7	69.61	3.42	0.9885	0.749
	9 × 9	68.90	4.13	0.9842	0.6946
Min Filtering	3 × 3	72.15	0.88	0.9889	0.8634
Max Filtering	3 × 3	71.63	1.40	0.9865	0.8923
Mode Filtering	3 × 3	71.23	1.80	0.9924	0.8831

attacks based on filtering on feature based image splicing detection is presented in Table 2. Here, we have reported the average accuracy of splicing detection by the adopted model after applying 10-fold cross-validation for each case.

The average accuracy of the adopted feature based image splicing detection model is 73.03% without filtering or any modification (from Sect. 3.3). So, to find out the drop in accuracy after applying each filtering, the corresponding accuracy needs to be subtracted from the original accuracy of 73.03%. It can be observed from Table 2 that Gaussian and Average filtering are the most effective ones as counter forensic attacks against feature-based splicing detection, as in these two cases, the accuracy drop is maximum. Median filtering is the most effective among the non-linear filters. We also consider the similarity of two images using SSIM before and after the counter forensic modifications. Since Min, Max, and Mode filters do not perform that great, compared to the others, we have included only a single kernel size of 3 × 3 for those in Table 2.

The performance analysis of filtering based counter forensic attacks on the adopted deep learning based image splicing detection method is presented in Table 3. The splicing detection accuracy of the adopted deep learning based model is 90.32% without any filtering or post-processing (from Sect. 4.2). So, here also, to find out the drop in accuracy after applying each type of filtering, the

Table 3. Results of Linear and Non-linear Filtering based Counter Forensic Attacks on Deep Learning based Image Splicing Detection

Filter	Kernel Size	Accuracy (%)	Drop in Accuracy (%)	SSIM † (Best)	SSIM † (Average)
Gaussian Filtering	3 × 3	84.40	5.92	0.9959	0.9435
	5 × 5	76.88	13.44	0.9926	0.8958
	7 × 7	72.72	17.60	0.9882	0.8362
	9 × 9	74.19	16.13	0.9851	0.8196
Average (Mean) Filtering	3 × 3	80.64	9.68	0.9981	0.9078
	5 × 5	78.49	11.83	0.9963	0.8023
	7 × 7	77.41	12.91	0.9938	0.7116
	9 × 9	76.88	13.44	0.9926	0.6514
Median Filtering	3 × 3	84.95	5.37	0.996	0.9214
	5 × 5	83.33	6.99	0.991	0.8198
	7 × 7	84.40	5.92	0.9885	0.749
	9 × 9	82.79	7.53	0.9842	0.6946
Min Filtering	3 × 3	86.02	4.30	0.9889	0.8634
Max Filtering	3 × 3	85.48	4.84	0.9865	0.8923
Mode Filtering	3 × 3	88.70	1.62	0.9924	0.8831

†SSIM values are same as it is reported in Table 2

corresponding accuracy needs to be subtracted from the initial accuracy of 90.32%. Here also, we can observe from Table 3 that Gaussian and Average filtering are the two most effective counter forensic attacks against deep learning-based image splicing detection, as in these two cases, the accuracy drop is maximum. Among the non-linear filters, the Median filtering is the most effective one. Here also, we consider the similarity of two images, before and after the counter forensic modifications using SSIM which is same as it is reported in Table 2.

The most effective counter forensic attack is supposed to be the one that drops the detection accuracy maximally while preserving the SSIM between actual and filtered images. Therefore, we aim to find the best trade-off between accuracy drop and average SSIM in our work. From the Table 2, we can observe that Gaussian filter with kernel size 3 × 3 is the most effective counter forensic attack. In this case, the average accuracy drop is 9.02%, and the average SSIM is as high as 94.35% (best SSIM 99.59). This is closely followed by the performance of the Average filter 3 × 3, where the average accuracy drop is 5.79% and average SSIM is 90.78 (best SSIM 99.81). Similarly, from Table 3, we can observe that Gaussian filtering and Average filtering are the two most effective counter forensic attacks against deep learning based image splicing detection, as here also, these two linear filtering achieved the best trade-off between accuracy drop and average SSIM. Our results prove that both feature based and deep learning based image splicing detection model are comparatively more robust to non-linear filters and are more vulnerable to linear filters. This suggests the need for further research towards enhancing the domain of image splicing detection, hence making it robust towards filtering based counter forensic attacks.

7   Conclusion and Future Work

In this paper, we presented linear and non-linear filtering-based counter forensic attacks and their effects on feature extraction-based and deep learning-based image splicing detection. Experimental results show that linear filtering attack is more potent against both of these image splicing detection models. Our findings are based on the suitable trade-off gained between the highest drop in splicing detection accuracy and gaining the best average SSIM. Future work will be directed towards developing an anti-counter-forensic framework to resist varied forms of filtering-based counter forensic modifications to digital images, hence enhancing the domain of image splicing detection about resisting counter-forensic attacks.

Acknowledgment. This work is partially supported by Department of Science and Technology (DST), Govt. of India, under Grant No.: DST/ICPS/Cluster/CS Research/2018 (General), dated: 13.03.2019.

References

1. Ahmed, B., Gulliver, T., alZahir, S.: Image splicing detection using mask-rcnn. Signal, Image and Video Processing, pp. 1–8 (2020)
2. Almawas, L., Alotaibi, A., Kurdi, H.: Comparative performance study of classification models for image-splicing detection. Procedia Comput. Sci. **175**, 278–285 (2020)
3. Böhme, R., Kirchner, M.: Counter-forensics: Attacking image forensics. In: Digital image forensics, pp. 327–366. Springer (2013). https://doi.org/10.1007/978-1-4614-0757-7_12
4. Cao, G., Zhao, Y., Ni, R., Yu, L., Tian, H.: Forensic detection of median filtering in digital images. In: 2010 IEEE International Conference on Multimedia and Expo, pp. 89–94. IEEE (2010)
5. Dang-Nguyen, D.T., Gebru, I.D., Conotter, V., Boato, G., Natale, F.G.: Counter-forensics of median filtering. In: 2013 IEEE 15th International Workshop on Multimedia Signal Processing (MMSP, pp. 260–265. IEEE (2013)
6. Das, A., Medhi, A., Karsh, R.K., Laskar, R.H.: Image splicing detection using gaussian or defocus blur. In: 2016 International Conference on Communication and Signal Processing (ICCSP), pp. 1237–1241. IEEE (2016)
7. Deng, G., Cahill, L.: An adaptive gaussian filter for noise reduction and edge detection. In: 1993 IEEE Conference Record Nuclear Science Symposium and Medical Imaging Conference, pp. 1615–1619. IEEE (1993)

8. Islam, M.M., Karmakar, G., Kamruzzaman, J., Murshed, M., Kahandawa, G., Parvin, N.: Detecting splicing and copy-move attacks in color images. In: 2018 Digital Image Computing: Techniques and Applications (DICTA), pp. 1–7. IEEE (2018)

9. Jaiswal, A.K., Srivastava, R.: A technique for image splicing detection using hybrid feature set. Multimedia Tools Appl. **79**(17), 11837–11860 (2020). https://doi.org/10.1007/s11042-019-08480-6

10. Kong, L., Wen, H., Guo, L., Wang, Q., Han, Y.: Improvement of linear filter in image denoising. In: International Conference on Intelligent Earth Observing and Applications 2015. vol. 9808, p. 98083F. International Society for Optics and Photonics (2015)

11. Krizhevsky, A., Sutskever, I., Hinton, G.E.: Imagenet classification with deep convolutional neural networks. In: Advances in Neural Information Processing Systems, vol. 25 (2012)

12. Lai, S.Y., Böhme, R.: Countering Counter-Forensics: The Case of JPEG Compression. In: Filler, T., Pevný, T., Craver, S., Ker, A. (eds.) IH 2011. LNCS, vol. 6958, pp. 285–298. Springer, Heidelberg (2011). https://doi.org/10.1007/978-3-642-24178-9_20

13. Mohanaiah, P., Sathyanarayana, P., GuruKumar, L.: Image texture feature extraction using glcm approach. Int. J. Sci. Res. Public. **3**(5), 1–5 (2013)

14. Ng, T.T., Hsu, J., Chang, S.F.: Columbia Image Splicing Detection Evaluation Dataset. Columbia Univ CalPhotos Digit Libr, DVMM lab (2009)

15. Pham, N.T., Lee, J.W., Kwon, G.R., Park, C.S.: Efficient image splicing detection algorithm based on markov features. Multimedia Tools Appl. **78**(9), 12405–12419 (2019)

16. Mildenhall, B., Srinivasan, P.P., Tancik, M., Barron, J.T., Ramamoorthi, R., Ng, R.: NeRF: representing scenes as neural radiance fields for view synthesis. In: Vedaldi, A., Bischof, H., Brox, T., Frahm, J.-M. (eds.) ECCV 2020. LNCS, vol. 12346, pp. 405–421. Springer, Cham (2020). https://doi.org/10.1007/978-3-030-58452-8_24

17. Pomari, T., Ruppert, G., Rezende, E., Rocha, A., Carvalho, T.: Image splicing detection through illumination inconsistencies and deep learning. In: 2018 25th IEEE International Conference on Image Processing (ICIP), pp. 3788–3792. IEEE (2018)

18. Rao, Y., Ni, J., Zhao, H.: Deep learning local descriptor for image splicing detection and localization. IEEE Access **8**, 25611–25625 (2020)

19. Ravi, H., Subramanyam, A.V., Emmanuel, S.: Forensic analysis of linear and nonlinear image filtering using quantization noise. ACM Trans. Multimedia Comput., Commun. Appl. (TOMM) **12**(3), 1–23 (2016)

20. Sameer, V.U., Naskar, R., Musthyala, N., Kokkalla, K.: Deep learning based counter–forensic image classification for camera model identification. In: Kraetzer, C., Shi, Y.-Q., Dittmann, J., Kim, H.J. (eds.) IWDW 2017. LNCS, vol. 10431, pp. 52–64. Springer, Cham (2017). https://doi.org/10.1007/978-3-319-64185-0_5

21. Shen, X., Shi, Z., Chen, H.: Splicing image forgery detection using textural features based on the grey level co-occurrence matrices. IET Image Process. **11**(1), 44–53 (2017)

22. Thakur, A., Aggarwal, A., Walia, S., Saluja, K.: Localisation of spliced region using pixel correlation in digital images. In: 2019 International Conference on Signal Processing and Communication (ICSC), pp. 153–157. IEEE (2019)

23. Walia, S., Kumar, K.: Characterization of splicing in digital images using gray scale co-occurrence matrices. In: 2019 Twelfth International Conference on Contemporary Computing (IC3). pp. 1–6. IEEE (2019)
24. Wang, J., Ni, Q., Liu, G., Luo, X., Jha, S.K.: Image splicing detection based on convolutional neural network with weight combination strategy. J. Inform. Secur. Appl. **54**, 102523 (2020)
25. Wilscy, M., et al.: Pretrained convolutional neural networks as feature extractor for image splicing detection. In: 2018 International Conference on Circuits and Systems in Digital Enterprise Technology (ICCSDET), pp. 1–5. IEEE (2018)
26. Xiao, B., Wei, Y., Bi, X., Li, W., Ma, J.: Image splicing forgery detection combining coarse to refined convolutional neural network and adaptive clustering. Inform. Sci. **511**, 172–191 (2020)

Ischemic Stroke Lesion Segmentation in CT Perfusion Images Using U-Net with Group Convolutions

Chintha Sri Pothu Raju[1](✉), Anish Monsley Kirupakaran[1],
Bala Chakravarthy Neelapu[2], and Rabul Hussain Laskar[1]

[1] National Institute of Technology, Silchar, Assam, India
{chintha_rs,anish_rs,rhlaskar}@ece.nits.ac.in
[2] National Institute of Technology, Rourkela, Odisha, India
neelapubc@nitrkl.ac.in

Abstract. Ischemic stroke is a cerebrovascular disease caused by a blockage in blood vessels of the brain. The early detection of the stroke helps in preventing the penumbra from turning into the core. So, early detection is essential. But the variability of the stroke lesion in size, location, and appearance makes the automatic segmentation of the stroke lesion difficult. Computed Tomography Perfusion (CTP) is more suitable because of its wide availability and the less acquisition time as compared to Magnetic Resonance Imaging (MRI). CTP parameter maps include Cerebral Blood Volume (CBV), Cerebral Blood Flow (CBF), Mean Transit Time (MTT), and Time to Peak (Tmax). In this paper, we propose a deep learning model derived from U-Net that can process all the perfusion parameter maps parallelly at the same time independently. This architecture helps in avoiding the necessity of developing and training different models to process the perfusion maps independently. The significant modifications in the proposed model are i) incorporation of group convolutions to process the parameter maps separately and ii) introduced element-wise summation of feature maps instead of concatenation. Also, the class imbalance problem in medical datasets makes the segmentations more challenging. This is overcome by employing a loss that is a combination of cross entropy and soft dice loss. The model is trained from scratch. We performed a 5-fold cross-validation on the data. The proposed model achieves the highest 0.441 as the dice coefficient in one fold and the average dice score is 0.421. The experimentation is conducted on Ischemic Stroke Lesion Segmentation Challenge (ISLES) 2018 dataset.

Keywords: Ischemic stroke · Segmentation · CT perfusion · Deep learning

1 Introduction

According to the WHO, stroke is one of the big threats to human life worldwide [1]. It causes severe disabilities and sometimes it may even lead to fatality in worst-case scenarios. A stroke can either be an ischemic stroke or a hemorrhage stroke, and the ischemic stroke is responsible for a mammoth portion of about 87% of all stroke cases

© The Author(s), under exclusive license to Springer Nature Switzerland AG 2023
D. Gupta et al. (Eds.): CVIP 2022, CCIS 1776, pp. 276–288, 2023.
https://doi.org/10.1007/978-3-031-31407-0_21

[1]. For the people affected by stroke, the time is the brain. The ischemic stroke territory has two parts referred to as core and penumbra. The core is a brain tissue where the brain cell death occurs within significantly less time after the stroke onset, and the tissue suffers from irreversible damage in the absence of blood flow to the tissue. The cells in the surrounding core region have a blood supply from the collateral circulation. The survival time of the cells depends on several factors including the reperfusion status and the time required for reperfusion. This region is termed the penumbra, where the cell dies slowly compared to the core region [2]. As time lasts long, the penumbra will be converted into the core. The quantification of the penumbra and core is very essential for treating patients. Based on the penumbra region, radiologists can make the right decision regarding reperfusion therapy and the benefits of the reperfusion of blood flow to the penumbra. But currently, manual delineation of the stroke is a gold standard which is a time-demanding and laborious process [3]. So, automatic detection and segmentation of stroke algorithms are in demand.

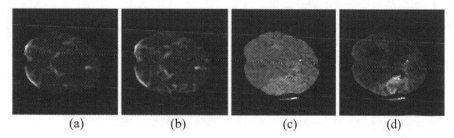

(a)   (b)   (c)   (d)

Fig. 1. (a) CBF, (b) CBV, (c) MTT, (d) Tmax are the perfusion parameter maps of an example from the ISLES 2018 dataset

Magnetic Resonance Imaging (MRI) and Computed Tomography (CT) are the most important modalities for assessing stroke lesions. The Diffusion Weighted Imaging (DWI), T-1 weighted and Fluid Attenuated Inversion Recovery (FLAIR) are the MRI sequences that have several advantages in terms of the resolution of an image and responsiveness to stroke lesions, but the most significant challenges are the wide availability, cost, and time required to acquire the images. Whereas the CT has no issue with the availability, cost, and acquiring times which is very important in stroke cases.[4] The soft tissues in the penumbra area are not observable clearly in MRI sequences which is a disadvantage. Radiologists are already using CT to quantify stroke lesions. However, the detection of core tissue is challenging in CT since the early necrotic changes in CT are very difficult to find. This results in underestimating the core region [5]. A more suitable modality to quantify the stroke is utilizing Computed Tomography Perfusion (CTP). CTP is a technique that can assess cerebral hemodynamics. To acquire these perfusion data a series of scans are performed at predefined intervals. These scans provide the necessary information to derive the perfusion parameter maps such as Cerebral Blood Flow (CBF), Cerebral Blood Volume (CBV), Mean Transit Time (MTT), and time of peak (Tmax) using deconvolution methods. Figure 1 shows all CT perfusion parameter maps of one case as an example. It can be observed from the parameter maps that in the CBF and CBV the stroke lesion area is dark whereas in MTT and Tmax the stroke lesion area is appearing as brighter.

Most researchers are motivated towards the application of CTP maps in the detection and quantification of stroke lesions because of its capabilities to provide better segmentation at early stages. However, the automatic segmentation of stroke lesions has several challenges. First, the irregular shapes and boundaries of the stroke lesion. Secondly, wide variability in the size, location, and lesion appearance. Finally, the scarcity of data is a major concern for any medical-related task.

The Ischemic Stroke Lesion Segmentation (ISLES) challenges [15] encouraged researchers worldwide to develop algorithms for the automation segmentation of stroke lesions. ISLES 2015 to ISLES 2017 have majorly concentrated on the MR imaging and MR Perfusion image datasets. Whereas, ISLES 2018 challenge was released with a new dataset of CT perfusion data. This publicly available dataset made the researchers work on CT perfusion for the detection and segmentation of stroke lesions.

In earlier times, features were manually extracted and used some algorithms to segment stroke lesions. But, during last few years, deep learning applications stepped into every possible field. Moreover, Convolutional Neural Networks (CNNs) are well-known and promising technique in image processing applications. Extensively, these are useful in medical imaging, particularly for segmentation tasks and classification tasks. U-Net has provided the best promising results in medical-related segmentation tasks.

Some of the recent literature related to ischemic stroke lesion segmentation is discussed. A U-shaped network with dilated convolutions to increase the field of view of the network has been proposed for the segmentation of stroke lesions [6]. G R Pinheiro et al. [7] have proposed the two U-Nets with different depths and the deeper U-Net has outperformed the shallower U-Net at the expense of computational cost. Dolz et al. developed the multipath network consists of hyper-dense connectivity to perform the stroke lesion segmentation on the CTP data [8].

Researchers also used generative models to segment stroke lesions [9, 10]. The benefits of utilizing the GAN networks are enforcing the spatial continuity and comparing the higher level inconsistencies between the predictions and reference [9]. In this paper also U-Net has been used as a backbone in the GAN network. The disadvantage of this network is, it need to be trained twice. At first, the weights are modified according the back propagation of gradients of segmentation loss then again the weights are updated during the backpropagation of gradients of adversarial loss. T. Song et al. [10] also used the generative model to segment the lesion. But instead of using a GAN these researchers used a U-Net-based generator to generate the DWI from the CT perfusion parameter maps. Then the generated DWI is segmented by using a segmentor network.

Researchers have also explored the adaption of the pre-trained networks which were developed to work on natural images for extracting the features from the parameters maps to segment the medical images [11, 12]. S. Abulnaga et al. [11] made use of a PSP network which was trained with the natural images and fine-tuned it further with the ischemic stroke data to segment the stroke lesions. PSP network extracts the local feature as well as global features for better segmentation and focal loss has been used which can classify the hard to detect samples. In the paper [12] published by V.K. Anand et al., the features were extracted by using the DenseNet-121 which is pre-trained on the ImageNet database.

In the paper [13], the author proposed a model with multiple parallel U-Nets for processing different parameter maps simultaneously. The four output maps from all models were given to the pixel classifier for the final location of the lesion. The disadvantage of the model is it requires the training of four different models and an external classifier to get the final segmentation output.

From the literature, it is observed that each parameter map is contributing differently to the segmentation of stroke lesions. However, most of the researchers adopted the processing of the parameter maps together at early stages instead of processing and extracting individual features. Hence, there is a scope for processing these parameter maps independently. There is a need to investigate and examine whether processing these parameter maps individually may give better segmentation results. To achieve this, U-Net has been adopted and modified to process the maps in parallel and separately in the same network. The main contribution of this paper is developing a U-Net with group convolution to segment stroke lesions using all CTP maps. The proposed deep learning model is trained and validated on the ISLES-2018 CT perfusion dataset.

2 Materials and Methods

2.1 Dataset

The ISLES 2018 dataset includes four CT Perfusion parameter maps such as CBF, CBV, MTT, and Tmax, along with the CT, which serve as the inputs for the deep learning model. In this paper, the model is fed with the four parameter maps only. It consists of the data from 156 patients. It consists of 94 cases in train data used for training the network and 62 cases in the test data used for testing the model. The resolution of voxels of a slice in a case lies anywhere between 0.785 and 1.086 mm. The thickness of the slice varies from 4.0 to 12mm across the slices. The stroke lesions are labelled on the DWI acquired after the CT scan is performed. It is provided for the training cases. The labelled data for the test cases were not provided for the public. The resolution of each parameter map is 256 X 256. The number of 2D slices in each scan varies from 2 to 22. Hence the extraction of 3D information is complicated. The training data is divided into 80% and 20% for training the network from scratch and validating the network respectively.

2.2 Pre-processing and Data Augmentation

The only pre-processing step performed on the data is intensity normalization. After this step the data is normalized to zero mean and unit variance. The intensity normalization is performed according to the given Eq. (1) in which I represents data, I_{norm} represents the normalized data, μ is the mean and σ is the variance of the data. It is very difficult to acquire the medical data and more over getting the annotated data in huge amount is laborious. On the other way deep learning architectures are data driven and requires a enormous amount of data for training the model. To overcome this problem, data augmentation is performed. This paper employs the techniques such as random rotation, random horizontal flip, and random vertical flip while training the model. The random rotation of $-45°$ to $+45°$ with a probability of 0.5 is applied on the data. The horizontal and vertical flips are also applied to data with a probability of 0.5. Generally, creating several images from the same image by using different augmentation techniques and saving the images locally, has a problem with the storage. So, to avoid this issue, the "On the fly" data augmentation technique is adopted. Moreover, the advantage of this technique is in every epoch the model is inputted with the same data but in a different way of representation. Data augmentation helps in preventing the model from overfitting.

$$I_{norm} = \frac{I - \mu}{\sigma} \tag{1}$$

2.3   Proposed Model

The U-Net [14] is developed by Olaf Ronneberger et al. The architecture of the U-Net includes a contracting path that extracts the features from the input channels and an expanding path that localizes the detected abnormalities. The encoder starts with 64 features in the first stage and ends with 1024 features and the number of feature maps at every step is doubled. Similarly, the decoder starts with 1024 features and ends with 64 features, and the number of feature maps is halved at every step. At each step in both encoder and decoder, two 3×3 convolutional layers, each layer followed by a rectified linear unit (ReLU) are employed. The features from the contracting path are concatenated with the features in the expanding path for more precise localization of abnormalities through skip connections. In the final stage of the decoder, 64 feature maps are decreased to two feature maps using a convolutional layer with a 1×1 kernel to get the final foreground and background segmentation output. The proposed model is derived from the U-Net.

The proposed modified U-Net architecture is shown in Fig. 2. The proposed model incorporates three alternations in the base U-Net. The first significant modification is the adaption of group convolutions instead of conventional convolutions. This helps the network to process the parameter maps parallelly at the same time independently. In the case of conventional convolutions, all the parameter maps are fused at the input of the network itself. Thus, fusing at early stages makes it difficult for the model to learn the complex relations between the parameter maps. The mentioned problem can be overcome by processing and extracting the features from the maps independently. This also helps in learning the complex features from the different parameters maps. This can be achieved by using group convolutions. The incorporation of group convolutions in U-Net made the network process the input channels given to the network separately as though these inputs are being processed in four different networks. The feature maps from a particular group are related only to the particular input.

The second modification is related to skip connections. Instead of concatenating the features from the encoding path to the decoding path, the elementwise summation is performed. This provides the isolation of features extracted from the different perfusion parameter maps from beginning to end. The usage of group convolutions in the encoder

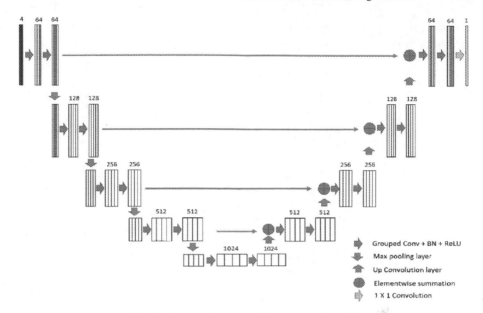

Fig. 2. The architecture of the proposed model

extracts the features from the parameter maps separately. A group of channels in the group convolution belongs to a particular parameter map contains the features derived only from that map. This avoids the fusion of features together throughout the model. But, a concatenation operation of feature maps from the encoder to the decoder through skip connections fuses the information that is derived independently from the feature maps. In order to avoid the feature fusion, instead of concatenation operation we used an elementwise summation operation. In elementwise summation, the feature maps on the contracting side are added with the feature maps on the expanding side. Now, features related to a particular group will be added to the features derived from the same group. With the inclusion of group convolution and elementwise summation, feature isolation among the feature derived from perfusion parameter maps is possible.

The third modification is adding a batch normalization layer after every convolution layer. These batch normalization layers regularize the model while training by reducing the covariance shift. The last stage of base U-Net has two feature maps for two class classification problem. But here instead of two feature maps, only one feature map is used because the background feature map is not used for further processing. The model is designed to accept four channels one for each parameter map as inputs. The threshold was set at 0.5 for converting the feature maps into the final segmentation result.

Group Convolutions. In the base U-Net, all the standard convolutions are replaced by the grouped convolutions. The grouped convolutions are shown in Fig. 3. The black box represents a group and the rectangular boxes with different colours represent channels in the group. Generally, in the standard convolution layers, the output channel depends on the all channels in the previous layer. Whereas in the grouped convolution layers, the output channel depends on the all channels in a particular group to which group it belongs. In this experiment, all the convolution layers are divided into four different groups to process four perfusion parameter maps independently.

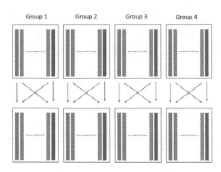

Fig. 3. Group convolutions

2.4 Loss Function

Lesions are very small in comparison with the normal tissue in the medical images. Thus, all the datasets in the medical imaging field suffer from a high class imbalance problems. Several techniques were adapted in the literature for dealing with imbalanced data and one of them is utilizing a proper loss function. The Eq. 2 represents the loss function that is used while training the model. In this paper, a hybrid loss function that incorporates both cross entropy loss and soft dice loss is used. In the Eq. 2, P_i represents a set of pixels in the predicted result and T_i represents the set of pixels in the ground truth.

$$\text{Loss (P, T)} = 0.5 * \text{BCE Loss} + 0.5 * \frac{2 * \sum_i (P_i, T_i) + 1}{\sum_i (P_i, P_i + T_i, T_i) + 1} \tag{2}$$

3 Results and Discussion

3.1 Experimental Configurations

The model is implemented using PyTorch library in a jupyter notebook. The hardware configuration of the system used for implementation is the NVidia (Tesla-T4) with 16G of memory. In this experiment, the network is trained from scratch (epochs: 200). The hyper-parameters are set as learning rate = 0.0001, batch size = 4, and Adam is used as an optimizer for updating the weights during the backpropagation. We used a loss function that incorporates both cross entropy and soft dice loss for training the network.

The following metrics were used for evaluation: Dice Coefficient (DC), Precision, Recall, Relative Absolute Volume Difference (RAVD), Hausdorff Distance (HD), and Average Symmetric Surface Distance (ASSD). DC is a measure of overlap between the detected region and the reference region. HD represents the largest distance between the pixels in the predicted result and the pixels in the reference. ASSD gives the average surface distance between the predicted result and the reference. The AVD indicates the absolute volume difference between the predicted volume and actual volume of the lesion. But RAVD computes the relative absolute volume difference between the detected region and reference region. It indicates whether the volume is underestimated or overestimated in comparison with the reference. The negative value indicates the detected lesion is a smaller lesion than the actual lesion and the positive value indicates the detected lesion is larger than the actual lesion. But, for better comparison purposes, the absolute values are taken into account to consider the overall performance irrespective of overestimation or underestimation. The performance evaluation of the deep learning model is performed based on the validation results. The dice score is calculated after every epoch on the validation images and saving the model which has best validation dice score. The validation results are obtained from the model saved.

3.2   Experimental Results

All the experiments were performed under the same conditions mentioned in Sect. 3.1. In this paper, a base U-Net has experimented with the perfusion parameter maps as inputs along with the proposed model. For comparison of results, all the models were trained and validated on same data. Table 1 shows the comparison of results obtained from the U-Net model and the proposed model and all values are average values of the corresponding metrics. The performance evaluation is done on the ISLES 2018 dataset.

Table 1. Comparison of results of the proposed model with the U-Net model. Best values are shown in bold

Model	Dice	Precision	Recall	HD	RAVD
U-Net	0.405	**0.452**	0.4264	23.27	0.7365
Proposed	**0.427**	0.443	**0.4360**	**20.30**	**0.4817**

In Table 1, the second column denotes the dice score achieved from the proposed model is increased by around 5.5% when compared with the base U-Net with standard convolutions. On average, the proposed model achieves better overlapping of predicted regions and references. The proposed model achieves a higher recall. HD is a distance-related metric that denotes the maximum distance between two segmentations. This value should be as low for a better performance indication of the model. The HD is decreased by 12% for the proposed model. The RAVD is a volume-related metric. The RAVD is decreased by around 35% which is a great improvement. From the RAVD it can be inferred that the proposed model is predicting the lesion more accurately without much deviation from the ground truth. From the results Table 1, it is observed that proposed model outperform the base U-Net.

To validate the results further, we performed the 5-fold cross-validation with an 80:20 ratio of train data and validation data of ISLES 2018 training data. The results obtained are shown in Table 2. It is observed that (i) the dice coefficient is consistent across the different folds; (ii) the average of the dice coefficient across different folds is 0.4204 which is closer to dice coefficient observed in Table 1; (iii) the maximum dice coefficient is obtained in the fold 3 i.e. 0.4401.

Table 2. Results of k fold cross validation.

Folds	Dice coefficient
Fold 1	0.4274
Fold 2	0.4134
Fold 3	0.4401
Fold 4	0.4057
Fold 5	0.4156

Figure 4 shows the prediction result of both the U-Net and the proposed model for the three different-sized lesions. In the larger-sized lesion case, both models performed in the same way which results in almost similar predictions also. But in the case of the medium-sized lesion, the U-Net underestimated the actual lesion whereas the proposed model predicted very accurately which is almost equal to the actual lesion volume. In the case of the small-sized lesion, the U-Net model overestimated the smaller lesion resulting in showing a larger volume than the actual volume whereas the proposed model predicts which is very close to the actual volume. Here, the proposed model is predicting the lesions more accurately in comparison with the U-Net in most of the cases.

In addition to the results mentioned above, a few notable observations related to the pixel-wise metrics such as true positives, false negatives, and false positives. The number of true positive pixels across all the validation images increased by 11.68% when compared with the performance of U-Net model. The false negatives are reduced by about 24% but there is a slight increase in the false positives by about 10%. True negatives are approximately the same since so many pixels are related to the background.

Due to large variations in the volumes of the lesions, the precision and recall values may not reflect the actual performance of the model. In medical image applications, pixel-wise metrics are also important for determining the performance of the model in the segmenting of the lesions. Hence, we introduced precision and recall which are directly calculated from the true positives, false positives, and false negatives of all the validation images together. We consider this is also a better representation to evaluate the model performance. The precision achieved for the proposed model is 65.4% which is similar to the U-Net model. The recall is increased to 75.08% when it is compared with the U-Net precision which stood at 65.23%.

Table 3 shows the comparison results with existing models from the literature. The proposed model achieved the highest dice score among all the existing models stated in the above table. The precision is when compared to all the models while the recall shows a better improvement over all the other models.

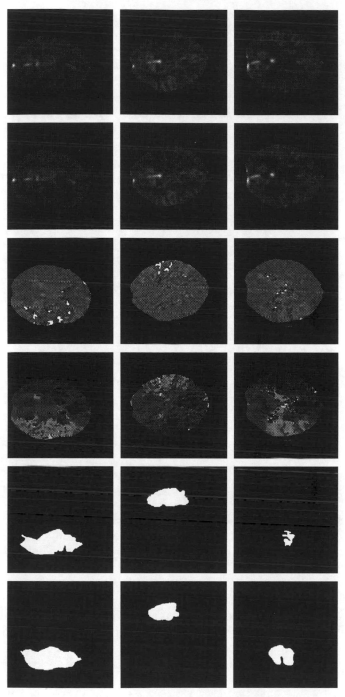

Fig. 4. Comparison of the proposed model performance with the U-Net in three different examples. From left to right, example cases for large-sized, medium-sized, and small-sized lesions. From top to bottom, CBF, CBV, MTT, Tmax, Ground truth, predicted result of U-Net, and predicted result of the proposed model.

Fig. 4. (*continued*)

Table 3. Comparison of results with the existing models

Model	Dice	Precision	Recall
Parallel U-Net	0.384	0.5017	0.3582
X- Net	0.39	0.5067	0.3714
HD-Net	0.418	**0.5355**	0.3842
Proposed	**0.427**	0.4430	**0.4360**

Table 4. Parameters comparison with existing models

Model	Parameters
U-Net	31.04M
Parallel U-Net	20.35M
X- Net	9.14M
HD-Net	20.69M
Proposed model	**6.99M**

The advantage of the proposed model is that it needs to be trained only once whereas the existing model which uses late fusion needs to be trained four different models. This proposed architecture helps to avoid the requirement of separate algorithms to fuse the four segmented outputs from the four models.

Table 4 shows the comparison of parameters with the existing deep learning models. The total parameters are also reduced to a great extent compared to all the models. The number of parameters in the proposed model is approximately 7 million. In comparison with the U-Net the parameters are reduced around 75%. In the same way, 65% of parameters are lesser when compared with parallel U-Net and HD-Net. 25% of lesser parameters in comparison with the X-Net. The proposed model is very less computational complexity. The inference time is also very less in comparison with the U-Net. The average inference time of the U-Net is 2.4 s. The average inference time of the proposed U-Net is 1.36 s. This has been improved by 43%.

4   Conclusion and Future Scope

In this paper, we developed a modified U-Net deep learning model using the group convolutions for processing the parameter maps independently. The element-wise summation implemented in skip connections helped the features to be isolated from each other. In addition to this, we utilized a batch normalization layer after every convolution layer to reduce the covariance shift. These modifications to the base U-Net helped in extracting the features from all the parameter maps for better segmentation of the stroke lesion. Results show that our proposed model performs better over the U-Net and other existing networks on the ISLES 2018 dataset. Results also show that the model is more robust to large as well as small lesions also. In the future, there is a scope for exploring different multimodal fusion strategies to carefully fuse the features extracted from the different modalities at different stages and analyze how these fusion strategies are affecting the final segmentation results.

References

1. Saini, V., Guada, L., Yavagal, D.R.: Global Epidemiology of Stroke and Access to Acute Ischemic Stroke Interventions. Neurology **97**, S6 LP–S16 (2021). https://doi.org/10.1212/WNL.0000000000012781
2. González, R.G., Hirsch, J.A., Lev, M.H., Schaefer, P.W., Schwamm, L.H.: Ischemic stroke: basic pathophysiology and neuroprotective strategies. Acute Ischemic Stroke Imaging Interv. 1–297 (2011). https://doi.org/10.1007/978-3-642-12751-9
3. Liu, Z., Cao, C., Ding, S., Liu, Z., Han, T., Liu, S.: Towards clinical diagnosis: automated stroke lesion segmentation on multi-spectral MR image using convolutional neural network. IEEE Access. **6**, 5706–57016 (2018). https://doi.org/10.1109/ACCESS.2018.2872939
4. Liu, P.: Stroke lesion segmentation with 2D novel CNN pipeline and novel loss function. In: Crimi, A., Bakas, S., Kuijf, H., Keyvan, F., Reyes, M., van Walsum, T. (eds.) BrainLes 2018. LNCS, vol. 11383, pp. 253–262. Springer, Cham (2019). https://doi.org/10.1007/978-3-030-11723-8_25
5. Fieselmann, A., Kowarschik, M., Ganguly, A., Hornegger, J., Fahrig, R.: Deconvolution-based CT and MR brain perfusion measurement: Theoret. Model Revisit Practical Implementation Details. J. Biomed. Imaging **2011** (2011)
6. Tureckova, A., Rodríguez-Sánchez, A.J.: ISLES challenge: U-shaped convolution neural network with dilated convolution for 3D stroke lesion segmentation. In: Crimi, A., Bakas, S., Kuijf, H., Keyvan, F., Reyes, M., van Walsum, T. (eds.) BrainLes 2018. LNCS, vol. 11383, pp. 319–327. Springer, Cham (2019). https://doi.org/10.1007/978-3-030-11723-8_32
7. Pinheiro, G.R., Voltoline, R., Bento, M., Rittner, L.: V-Net and U-Net for ischemic stroke lesion segmentation in a small dataset of perfusion data. In: Crimi, A., Bakas, S., Kuijf, H., Keyvan, F., Reyes, M., van Walsum, T. (eds.) BrainLes 2018. LNCS, vol. 11383, pp. 301–309. Springer, Cham (2019). https://doi.org/10.1007/978-3-030-11723-8_30
8. Dolz, J., Ben Ayed, I., Desrosiers, C.: Dense multi-path U-Net for ischemic stroke lesion segmentation in multiple image modalities. In: Crimi, A., Bakas, S., Kuijf, H., Keyvan, F., Reyes, M., van Walsum, T. (eds.) BrainLes 2018. LNCS, vol. 11383, pp. 271–282. Springer, Cham (2019). https://doi.org/10.1007/978-3-030-11723-8_27
9. Yang, H.-Y.: Volumetric adversarial training for ischemic stroke lesion segmentation. In: Crimi, A., Bakas, S., Kuijf, H., Keyvan, F., Reyes, M., van Walsum, T. (eds.) BrainLes 2018. LNCS, vol. 11383, pp. 343–351. Springer, Cham (2019). https://doi.org/10.1007/978-3-030-11723-8_35

10. Song, T.: Generative Model-Based Ischemic Stroke Lesion Segmentation. (2019)
11. Abulnaga, S.M., Rubin, J.: ischemic stroke lesion segmentation in CT perfusion scans using pyramid pooling and focal loss. In: Crimi, A., Bakas, S., Kuijf, H., Keyvan, F., Reyes, M., van Walsum, T. (eds.) BrainLes 2018. LNCS, vol. 11383, pp. 352–363. Springer, Cham (2019). https://doi.org/10.1007/978-3-030-11723-8_36
12. Anand, V.K., Khened, M., Alex, V., Krishnamurthi, G.: Fully automatic segmentation for ischemic stroke using CT perfusion maps. In: Crimi, A., Bakas, S., Kuijf, H., Keyvan, F., Reyes, M., van Walsum, T. (eds.) BrainLes 2018. LNCS, vol. 11383, pp. 328–334. Springer, Cham (2019). https://doi.org/10.1007/978-3-030-11723-8_33
13. Soltanpour, M., Greiner, R., Boulanger, P., Buck, B.: Ischemic stroke lesion prediction in CT perfusion scans using multiple parallel u-nets following by a pixel-level classifier. In: 2019 IEEE 19th International Conference on Bioinformatics and Bioengineering. BIBE 2019, pp. 957–963 (2019). https://doi.org/10.1109/BIBE.2019.00179
14. Ronneberger, O., Fischer, P., Brox, T.: U-Net: convolutional networks for biomedical image segmentation. In: Navab, N., Hornegger, J., Wells, W.M., Frangi, A.F. (eds.) MICCAI 2015. LNCS, vol. 9351, pp. 234–241. Springer, Cham (2015). https://doi.org/10.1007/978-3-319-24574-4_28
15. ISLES Homepage, https://www.isles-challenge.org/. Accessed 14 May 2022

Multi-generator MD-GAN with Reset Discriminator: A Framework to Handle Non-IID Data

Bharat Jain[1]([⊠])[iD] and W. Wilfred Godfrey[2][iD]

[1] Samsung R&D Institute India-Bangalore, Bengaluru, Karnataka, India
b.jain@samsung.com
[2] ABV-Indian Institute of Information Technology and Management, Gwalior,
Madhya Pradesh, India
godfrey@iiitm.ac.in

Abstract. Federated Learning is a machine learning concept that allows the training of machine learning models in a collaborative fashion by many users or devices, keeping the user data decentralized, thus providing data security and privacy. It focuses on optimal utilization of resources to train a machine learning model without accessing the user's private data. One of the main challenges in federated learning is to train a federated machine learning model with Non-IID (Non-Identically Independently Distributed) client/User Data. In this paper, we introduce a novel federated architecture, Multi-Generator MD-GAN (Multi-Discriminator Generative Adversarial Networks) with Reset Discriminator (MG-GAN-RD), to tackle one of the major challenges in federated learning, i.e., to train a federated model with Non-IID client image data. Our model learns the joint distribution of the Non-IID client image dataset and trains a global classifier without accessing the client's private dataset. Our approach uses label-specific generators at the server, and each client consists of a single discriminator with a reset property. We will show that our global classifier trained using our approach performs consistently well and provides accuracy in competing with the state-of-the-art federated learning algorithms.

Keywords: Federated Learning · Generative Adversarial Networks · Multi-Discriminator GAN · Non-IID

1 Introduction

Federated learning is a machine learning paradigm that allows the training of a global machine learning model using multiple users/devices without accessing the private data of the users/devices. The idea of federated learning was proposed by McMahan et al. 2017 [12], in which each client in a client-server architecture

Supported by organization Atal Bihari Vajpayee Indian Institute of Information Technology and Management, Gwalior.

has a local model which trains on the local data for some epochs and then sends the model hyper-parameter to the server. The server then averages the hyper-parameters and sends them back to the client's local models. The Federated algorithm is called FedAvg. Since it does not access the client's private dataset, it provides the client with data privacy. Many more federated algorithms have been developed, e.g., FedProx [11], SCAFFOLD [5], FedNova [18], and FedSplit [14], as an improvement over FedAvg and provide better convergence rates in different heterogeneous settings. Despite many improvements, the challenge of learning from Non-IID (Non-Identically Independently Distributed) clients [4] persists. Many novel federated schemes still face deterioration in performance in different heterogeneous settings (Statistical Heterogeneity) [9]

Goodfellow et al. 2014 [2] introduced a new machine learning framework known as Generative Adversarial Networks (GANs), which can generate samples by learning the distribution of the original dataset. It consists of two parts - a generator and a discriminator. The generator tries to generate samples similar to the training dataset, and the discriminator tries to differentiate between the generated samples and the original samples. The two participate in a min-max two-player game. Over time, many improvements have been made to increase the quality of generated samples [17]. Many recent works in federated learning have utilized GANs for data augmentation purposes. Majoritatively, the works either involves the usage of GANs for data privacy and malicious privacy threat attacks [1] or training a global GAN model to generate samples from the joint distribution of the client datasets [3,13,16,20]. This property of GAN to learn the joint distribution of client datasets can be very useful for developing a solution to handle Non-IID client datasets.

In this work, we propose a novel architecture Multi-Generator MD-GAN [3] with Reset Discriminator inspired by MD-GAN [3] to train a federated classifier that can learn from Non-IID clients and provide a consistent accuracy without any deterioration in performance in the different heterogeneous settings. Our model uses label-specific generators to learn the joint distribution of the Non-IID client dataset. With each client having a local discriminator with reset property, we avoid creating and training multiple discriminators, thus, reducing computation complexity at the client-side. We use the data generated by our label-specific generators to create the training dataset for our global federated classifier. With our framework, we try to bridge the gap between IID and Non-IID clients so that, no matter what type of client it is, our model can learn the joint distribution of the client dataset.

2   Key Related Research

McMahan et al. 2017 [12] defines the federated scheme FedAvg, which involves different clients sending their local machine learning model hyper-parameters to the server for aggregation. The server then provides the aggregated hyper-parameter to each client. Over time, many federated schemes have been introduced as an improvement over FedAvg to tackle different systems and statistical heterogeneity and provide better accuracy. FedProx [13] is an optimized framework over FedAvg that aims to tackle highly heterogeneous settings (system and statistical heterogeneity) and provides a better convergence rate. It defines a proximal term that can account for statistical heterogeneity and system heterogeneity occurring due to a non-uniform amount of local work. SCAFFOLD [14] can provide better convergence rates in a lesser number of communication rounds by using control variates to correct the client drift and overcome gradient dissimilarity. FedNova [18] reduces objective inconsistency by correctly normalizing local updates during model averaging. The survey [9] of various state-of-the-art federated schemes in Non-IID conditions shows that there is still some performance deterioration and inconsistent model accuracy in different Non-IID scenarios. Thus, the challenge of handling Non-IID data is still relevant [23,24].

GANs have seen a lot of usage in federated learning in domains of data privacy, privacy threat attacks involving data augmentation [17], and learning and generating samples from the joint distribution of the client dataset. Private FL-GAN [22] is a differentially private GAN model in a federated learning setting that can generate high-quality samples without compromising data privacy. FedGAN [16] proposes a framework to train a federated GAN using updates from local generators and local discriminators. It has a better convergence rate and performs similarly to distributed GAN but with less communication cost. Follow-up work [13] aims to reduce bias in FedGAN in a Non-IID setting. MD-GAN [3] proposes a system with a single global generator at the server, which takes updates from the local discriminator at each client. It removes redundant generators and can achieve better performance. FedCG [20] proposes a novel federated learning method that uses conditional GANs to protect data privacy while maintaining competitive performance.

3   Proposed Methodology

The proposed method takes inspiration from the MD-GAN [21] model, and define a novel framework which is a client-server architecture, as shown in Fig. 1. Instead of a single global generator at the server, a generator pool which consists of label-specific generators is present at the server and a global federated classifier. The aim of MD-GAN [21] is to train a global generator that can learn the image data distribution of all client's non-IID data. The property of generators learning the underlying image data distribution is used to create synthetic samples from the joint image data distribution of all clients to train the global classifier. Each client contains a local dataset, non-IID in nature, and a local discriminator. With the local discriminator, a local weight storage unit is also present. The weight storage unit contains saved discriminator weight for different labels presented to their respective clients. Each client decides the label it wants to train with and couples it with the generator for that specific label at the server. This is called **Coupling**. The generator for that specific label is now coupled with the client. The generator sends generated samples to the client. The local discriminator takes the generated samples original samples from the local dataset and gives outputs for the same. The client sends the discriminator output to the server for the coupled generator in the generator pool to update its weights. The local discriminator also updates its weight based on its output. Once the training with the label is complete, the client chooses the next label for training. The discriminator resets its model weights with the help of the weight storage unit for that specific label. This is called **Resetting**

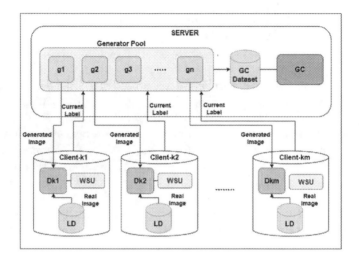

Fig. 1. MG-GAN-RD Architecture. (GC - Global Classifier, WSU - Weight Storage Unit, LD - Local Dataset)

3.1   Training Generator Pool

At the server, we have a generator pool G = {g_1, g_2, g_3, ..., g_N } containing N generators equal to the number of labels present in the dataset. Each generator provides generated samples to the one or more clients K = {k1, k2, ..., kM} to which the generator is coupled with and receives the discriminator output from all of the clients coupled with the generator. For each generator g_i, loss L_{g_i} is calculated and gradients are calculated using ADAM optimizer. The weights of each g_i are then updated (Fig. 2).

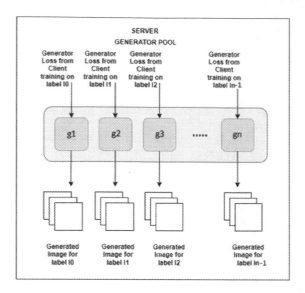

Fig. 2. Generator Pool at the Server.

Algorithm 1. Training of generators of Generator Pool G

1: **Inputs**: Client set K, Number of communication rounds R, Number of labels N
2: **procedure** TRAIN_GEN_POOL(K, R, N)
3:     Initialize weights w_i for each generator g_i
4:     **for** R communication rounds **do**
5:         **for** each i ← 1 to N **do**
6:             j = index of client with label i
7:             Generate and send fake samples $X_i \sim \mathcal{N}(0, 1)$ using g_i to client K_j
8:             Receive discriminator output O_{D_j} from K_j
9:             Calculate generator g_i loss L_{G_i} from O_{D_j}
10:            Calculate Δ_{wi} from L_{G_i}
11:            Update generator g_i
12:            $w_{i+1} \leftarrow w_i + \text{ADAM}(\Delta_{wi})$
13:        End for
14:    End for

3.2   Training Local Discriminator

Each client(j) decides on the label(i) it wants to train and is coupled with that label's generator at the server (Fig. 3). The discriminator D_{kj} initializes its weight θ_j with the help of weight storage unit and receives generated samples X_i from the server. The discriminator calculates discriminator loss L_{Dkj} based on its output for both real samples, O_{Dkj}^R, and fake samples O_{Dkj}^F, and update its weights. The client then sends the discriminator output for fake samples, O_{Dkj}^F, back to the server.

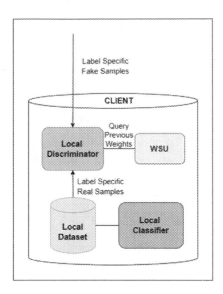

Fig. 3. Discriminator at Client.(WSU - Weight Storage Unit)

Algorithm 2. Training of local discriminator

1: **procedure** TRAIN_LOCAL_DISC(i, X_i)
2:     j = index of client with label i
3:     Initialize weights θ_j for the discriminator D_{Kj} with the help of weight storage unit for label i
4:     Receives generated samples X_i from server.
5:     **for** each sample in X_i **do**
6:         Calculate and send discriminator output $O^F_{D_{kj}}$ for fake sample to the server.
7:         Calculate discriminator output for both fake samples, O^F_{Dkj}, and real samples, O^R_{Dkj}.
8:         Calculate discriminator loss $L_{D_{kj}}$ from O^F_{Dkj}, and O^R_{Dkj}.
9:         Calculate $\Delta_{\theta i}$ from L_{Dkj}
10:        Update Discriminator D_{Kj}.
11:        $\theta_{j+1} \leftarrow \theta_j + \text{ADAM}(\Delta_{\theta j})$
12:     End For

3.3   Training Global Classifier

Once all the generator in the generator pool G are trained, they are then used to generate the training dataset for global classifier. Since the generators are label specific, we do not need to label generated samples. The global classifier is then trained on the generated training dataset.

3.4   Analytical Validation

The proposed model for solving the learning of the non-IID dataset is based on the fact that GAN models trained for specific labels produce much better results. Since the GAN has only to learn one label, it can learn the underlying distribution of the images of the same label. The MG-GAN-RD model removes the non-IID effect on the training process by training individual GAN for each label and perform consistently well whether the client data is IID or non-IID.

Training of GAN per label is better because images of the same label are more similar to each other than the images from the other label (see Fig. 4). Instead of learning the joint distribution, the proposed model learns individual distributions of the labels, and it seems that the whole architecture has learned the joint distribution.

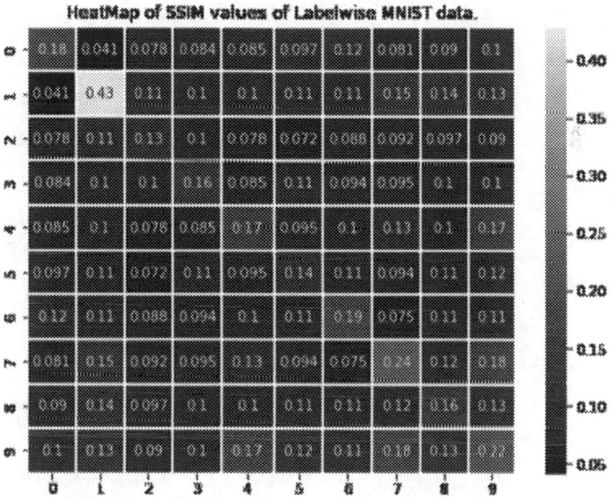

Fig. 4. Heatmap of SSIM values for label-wise MNIST data.

This is also supported by the fact that GANs learning individual labels have faster convergence rate (see Fig. 5 & 6). Figure 5 shows that label-specific generators have better convergence rates than a single global generator that learn all labels. The proposed federated architecture was able to take benefit of this fact and was able to learn the joint distribution of the dataset by learning the individual distribution of the labels without any redundant generators or discriminators. In fact, with limited number of generators, it can accommodate large number of clients.

NOTE : In Fig. 6 the discriminator loss is increasing because the discriminator loss here is the sum of real loss and fake loss. Thus, increase in discriminator loss is due to increase in fake loss. Increase in fake loss indicates that the fake image is much closer to the real image.

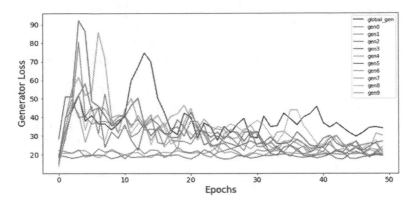

Fig. 5. Generator Loss vs Epochs.

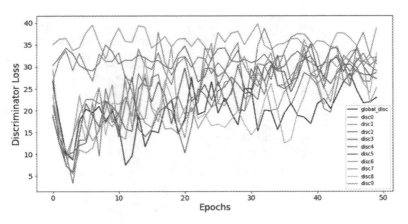

Fig. 6. Discriminator Loss vs Epochs.

3.5   Evaluation Metrics

1. **Accuracy:** Accuracy refers to total number of samples predicted correctly out of all the available samples.

$$\text{Accuracy} = \frac{\text{Number of correct predictions}}{\text{Total number of predictions}} \quad (1)$$

2. **Structural Similarity Index (SSIM):** SSIM [19] is an image quality metrics which can be useful for determining the fake images generated by generator model in GAN. It computes the image difference based on 3 characteristics - Luminance, Contrast, and Structure of the images. The formula for SSIM is given by-

$$\text{SSIM} = \frac{(2\mu_x\mu_y + C_1)(2\sigma_{xy} + C_2)}{(\mu_x^2 + \mu_y^2 + C_1)(\sigma_x^2 + \sigma_y^2 + C_2)} \quad (2)$$

where μ_x, μ_y represents the average of all pixel values of the two images that are being compared, namely, X and Y, σ_x, σ_y represents the standard deviation of all pixel values of the two images X and Y resp., σ_{xy} represents standard deviation of joint distribution of images X and Y, and C_1 & C_2 are constants.

4 Experiments

4.1 Dataset

Two datasets are used for experimentation - 1) MNIST (dataset containing images of handwritten digits from 0–9.) [8] and 2) Fashion-MNIST (dataset containing images of apparels categorized into 10 classes.) [21]. The dataset description is provided in Table 1.

Table 1. Dataset Description

S.No.	Dataset Name	Training Strength	Testing Strength	Number of Features	Number of Classes
1	MNIST	60000	10000	28*28(=784)	10
2	FMNIST	60000	10000	28*28(=784)	10

4.2 Models

1. **CNN Architecture:** A Convolutional Neural Network (modification of AlexNet [7]) model is used to classify images. It consists of 3 convolutional blocks. Each Convolutional Block consist of the following:

   (a) Convolutional Layer with 64 filters, kernel of size (5,5), with stride length of 1.
   (b) It consists of ReLu activation.
   (c) MaxPooling2D layer with pool size (2,2) and stride length of 1.

   Next, it consists of a Flatten Layer, 2 Dense Layers with 64 hidden units and ReLu activation and lastly the output layer with 10 hidden units corresponding to the number of labels. We compile the model using Adam optimizer (learning rate=0.001) and Sparse Categorical Cross Entropy as the loss function. The CNN architecture description is provided in Table 2.

Table 2. CNN Architecture.

Layer	Description	Hyper-Parameters
1	Conv2D	(64, (5,5))
2	MaxPooling2D	((2,2))
3	Conv2D	(64, (5,5))
4	MaxPooling2D	((2,2))
5	Conv2D	(64, (5,5))
6	MaxPooling2D	((2,2))
7	Dense	(64)
8	Dense	(64)
9	Dense	(10)

2. **Generator**: The generator inspired from DCGAN [15] contains one Dense block, Reshape layer, 2 Conv2DTranspose Block, and one Conv2DTranspose layer (see Table 3).

   (a) The Dense block contains a Dense layer followed by a Batch Normalization Layer and a Leaky ReLu Activation Layer.

   (b) The Conv2DTranspose Block contains one Conv2DTranspose Layer followed by a Batch Normalization Layer and a Leaky ReLu Activation Layer.

Table 3. Generator Architecture

Layer	Description	Hyper-Parameters
1	Dense Block	((7*7*256))
2	Reshape Layer	((7*7*256))
3	Conv2DTranspose Block	(128, (5,5), (1,1))
4	Conv2DTranspose Block	(64, (5,5), (2,2))
5	Conv2DTranspose Layer	(1, (5,5), (2,2))

3. **Discriminator**: The Discriminator inspired from DCGAN [15] contains 2 Conv2D Blocks, a Flatten Layer and a single Dense Layer (see Table 4).

   (a) The Conv2D block contains a Conv2D layer followed by a Leaky ReLu Activation Layer and a Dropout Layer with the dropout rate of 0.3.

   We compile the discriminator using Adam optimizer with learning rate of value 0.0002 and beta_1 of value 0.5. We use Binary Cross entropy as loss function.

Table 4. Discriminator Architecture

Layer	Description	Hyper-Parameters
1	Conv2D Block	(64, (5,5), (2,2))
2	Conv2D Block	(128, (5,5), (2,2))
3	Dense Layer	(1)

4.3 Baselines for Comparison

The proposed model is compared with 7 baseline federated algorithms. This includes FedAvg [12], FedProx [10], FedSplit [14], SCAFFOLD [5], FedNova [18], FedCG [20] whose results are referenced from [9,20] for different non-IID settings and also MD-GAN.

4.4 Experiment Results

The experiments are performed for MD-GAN and MG-GAN-RD for different number of labels. The number of clients is fixed to 10. All the clients are assumed to be participating in the federated learning. For all the experiments and all the algorithms, the data distribution is Non-IID. The experiments are performed for each client, having 1,2, and 3 labels of data. Each experiment is carried out, for about 150 communication rounds, for both MD-GAN and MG-GAN-RD with both the MNIST [12] and the FMNIST [13] data. The Accuracy of all models is tabulated in Table 5. The quality of images generated by MD-GAN and the proposed MG-GAN-RD models are compared by calculating SSIM values given in Table 6. The visual representation of image quality of MNIST and FMNIST images generated by our (MG-GAN-RD) model and the MD-GAN model is depicted in Fig. 7.

The results in Table 5 show that the state-of-the-art federated schemes in some Non IID conditions perform well. However, there is some deterioration in performance with varying Non-IID settings. Since algorithms like FedAvg, FedProx, and FedNova require updates from the local models, statistical heterogeneity and federated model performance are inversely proportional. As the number of labels per client increases, the local dataset becomes statistically similar to the original dataset reducing the statistical heterogeneity and increasing federated model performance. This does not affect the proposed model because the generator pool at the server trains label-specific generators irrespective of which client the label data comes from. The proposed model provides consistent accuracy and can successfully bridge the gap between IID and Non-IID client settings. Thus, it can be concluded that in some cases, the proposed model may not provide the best accuracy, but in different Non-IID scenarios, it performs consistently well without any sharp decline in model accuracy. From Table 6 and Fig. 7 show that the images generated by the proposed model (MG-GAN-RD) are of much better quality than MD-GAN.

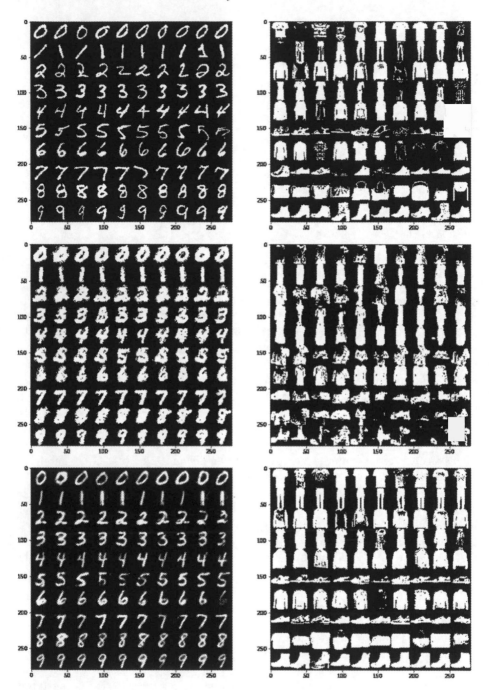

Fig. 7. First row of images contains original MNIST(left) and FMNIST(right) dataset images. Second row of images contains MD-GAN generated MNIST(left) and FMNIST(right) images. Third row of images contains MG-GAN-RD generated MNIST(left) and FMNIST(right) images

Table 5. Comparison of MG-GAN-RD with baseline federated algorithms in terms of top-1 test accuracy in Non-IID client data setting. - means no performance measured.

Model	Labels	MNIST	FMNIST
FedAvg [6]	1	29.8% ± 7.9%	11.2% ± 2.0%
	2	97.0% ± 0.4%	77.3% ± 4.9%
	3	98.0% ± 0.2%	80.7% ± 1.9%
FedProx [6]	1	40.9% ± 2.31%	28.9% ± 3.9%
	2	96.4% ± 0.3%	74.9% ± 2.6%
	3	97.9% ± 0.4%	82.5% ± 1.9%
FedSplit [22]	3	82.9% ± 0.4%	-
SCAFFOLD [6]	1	9.9% ± 0.2%	12.8% ± 4.8%
	2	95.9% ± 0.3%	42.8% ± 28.7%
	3	96.6% ± 1.5%	77.7% ± 3.8%
FedNova [6]	1	39.2% ± 22.1%	14.8% ± 5.9%
	2	94.5% ± 1.5%	70.4% ± 5.1%
	3	98% ± 0.3%	78.9% ± 3.0%
FedCG [22]	3	84.8% ± 0.4%	-
MD-GAN	1	80.38% ± 2.81%	32.80% ± 3.09%
	2	81.95% ± 2.05%	34.94% ± 0.96%
	3	84.00% ± 1.87%	32.42% ± 3.48%
MG-GAN-RD (ours)	1	91.60% ± 1.95%	82.21% ± 2.3%
	2	91.42% ± 3.5%	82.56% ± 1.5%
	3	92.0% ± 3.67%	81.60% ± 1.83%

Table 6. Evaluation of Quality of Images (SSIM Values)

Model	MNIST	FMNIST
MD-GAN	0.3064	0.1587
MG-GAN-RD (ours)	0.3421	0.2314

5   Conclusion and Future Scope

Our proposed federated architecture bridges the gap between the IID and Non-IID datasets and gives consistent accuracy. Since our model learns label-specific distribution, it will perform consistently well, and its performance will not deteriorate. It can handle many clients without the increasing model complexity at the server. The number of generator instances in the generator pool depends upon the number of classifications in the dataset. So, with a finite amount of generator instances, the proposed architecture can train with a large number of clients.

Label Privacy: Since before training, each client gets coupled with a generator instance by providing the label to the server the client is currently training on, it can lead to leakage of label data. However, the labels can be replaced with an arbitrarily generated random id and use that for coupling the client with the generator instance because the labels are unimportant.

For future works, more complex GAN models like WGAN, CGAN, etc., can be used to train the generator pool for better accuracy and performance of the model, and also improve the quality of the image generated at the server. It can be made more scalable and generic for different datasets with a different number of labels.

References

1. Cai, Z., Xiong, Z., Xu, H., Wang, P., Li, W., Pan, Y.: Generative adversarial networks: a survey toward private and secure applications. ACM Comput. Surv. (CSUR) **54**(6), 1–38 (2021)
2. Goodfellow, I., et al.: Generative adversarial nets. In: Advances in Neural Information Processing Systems, vol. 27 (2014)
3. Hardy, C., Le Merrer, E., Sericola, B.: MD-GAN: multi-discriminator generative adversarial networks for distributed datasets. In: 2019 IEEE International Parallel and Distributed Processing Symposium (IPDPS), pp. 866–877. IEEE (2019)
4. Kairouz, P., et al.: Advances and open problems in federated learning. Found. Trends® Mach. Learn. 14(1–2), 1–210 (2021)
5. Karimireddy, S.P., Kale, S., Mohri, M., Reddi, S., Stich, S., Suresh, A.T.: Scaffold: stochastic controlled averaging for federated learning. In: International Conference on Machine Learning, pp. 5132–5143. PMLR (2020)
6. Khan, L.U., Saad, W., Han, Z., Hossain, E., Hong, C.S.: Federated learning for internet of things: recent advances, taxonomy, and open challenges. IEEE Commun. Surv. Tutorials (2021)
7. Krizhevsky, A., Sutskever, I., Hinton, G.E.: ImageNet classification with deep convolutional neural networks. In: Advances in Neural Information Processing Systems, vol. 25 (2012)
8. LeCun, Y., Bottou, L., Bengio, Y., Haffner, P.: Gradient-based learning applied to document recognition. Proc. IEEE **86**(11), 2278–2324 (1998)
9. Li, Q., Diao, Y., Chen, Q., He, B.: Federated learning on non-IID data silos: an experimental study. arXiv preprint: arXiv:2102.02079 (2021)
10. Li, T., Sahu, A.K., Talwalkar, A., Smith, V.: Federated learning: challenges, methods, and future directions. IEEE Signal Process. Mag. **37**(3), 50–60 (2020)
11. Li, T., Sahu, A.K., Zaheer, M., Sanjabi, M., Talwalkar, A., Smith, V.: Federated optimization in heterogeneous networks. Proc. Mach. Learn. Syst. **2**, 429–450 (2020)
12. McMahan, B., Moore, E., Ramage, D., Hampson, S., y Arcas, B.A.: Communication-efficient learning of deep networks from decentralized data. In: Artificial Intelligence and Statistics, pp. 1273–1282. PMLR (2017)
13. Mugunthan, V., Gokul, V., Kagal, L., Dubnov, S.: Bias-free FedGAN: a federated approach to generate bias-free datasets. arXiv preprint: arXiv:2103.09876 (2021)
14. Pathak, R., Wainwright, M.J.: FedSplit: an algorithmic framework for fast federated optimization. In: Advances in Neural Information Processing Systems, vol. 33, pp. 7057–7066 (2020)

15. Radford, A., Metz, L., Chintala, S.: Unsupervised representation learning with deep convolutional generative adversarial networks. arXiv preprint: arXiv:1511.06434 (2015)

16. Rasouli, M., Sun, T., Rajagopal, R.: FedGan: federated generative adversarial networks for distributed data. arXiv preprint: arXiv:2006.07228 (2020)

17. Salimans, T., Goodfellow, I., Zaremba, W., Cheung, V., Radford, A., Chen, X.: Improved techniques for training GANs. In: Advances in Neural Information Processing Systems, vol. 29 (2016)

18. Wang, J., Liu, Q., Liang, H., Joshi, G., Poor, H.V.: Tackling the objective inconsistency problem in heterogeneous federated optimization. In: Advances in Neural Information Processing Systems, vol. 33, pp. 7611–7623 (2020)

19. Wang, Z., Bovik, A.C., Sheikh, H.R., Simoncelli, E.P.: Image quality assessment: from error visibility to structural similarity. IEEE Trans. Image Process. **13**(4), 600–612 (2004)

20. Wu, Y., Kang, Y., Luo, J., He, Y., Yang, Q.: FedCG: leverage conditional GAN for protecting privacy and maintaining competitive performance in federated learning. arXiv preprint: arXiv:2111.08211 (2021)

21. Xiao, H., Rasul, K., Vollgraf, R.: Fashion-MNIST: a novel image dataset for benchmarking machine learning algorithms. arXiv preprint: arXiv:1708.07747 (2017)

22. Xin, B., Yang, W., Geng, Y., Chen, S., Wang, S., Huang, L.: Private FL-GAN: differential privacy synthetic data generation based on federated learning. In: ICASSP 2020–2020 IEEE International Conference on Acoustics, Speech and Signal Processing (ICASSP), pp. 2927–2931. IEEE (2020)

23. Zhao, Y., Li, M., Lai, L., Suda, N., Civin, D., Chandra, V.: Federated learning with Non-IID data. arXiv preprint: arXiv:1806.00582 (2018)

24. Zhu, H., Xu, J., Liu, S., Jin, Y.: Federated learning on Non-IID data: a survey. Neurocomputing **465**, 371–390 (2021)

Video Colorization Using Modified Autoencoder Generative Adversarial Networks

Rishesh Agarwal[1], Manisha Das[1]([✉]) [iD], Deep Gupta[1] [iD], and Petia Radeva[2] [iD]

[1] Department of Electronics and Communication Engineering, VNIT Nagpur,
Nagpur, India
das.manisha1989@gmail.com
[2] Universitat de Barcelona and Computer Vision Center, Barcelona, Spain

Abstract. Colorization is a visual tool to convey ideas and emotions, especially when it comes to entertainment or film making. It is easy to perceive information from colored images rather than black and white or grayscale images. In the modern digitization era, colorization is even more important, because it helps in-person tracking, objects detection and provides an edge to the new state-of-the-art technologies. This paper presents a method for colorizing grayscale videos using Modified Autoencoder Generative Adversarial Network. The proposed generative model uses modified autoencoders by embedding a DenseNet based architecture. Its property of concatenation of all previous layers helps to increase the color consistency with the increase in the selection of color for an object. Subjective and quantitative results analysis is done using several performance measures. Experimental results show that the proposed model provides an improved and consistent mapping of colors on the video dataset.

Keywords: GANs · Autoencoder · DenseNet · Convolution · CIELAB

1 Introduction

Nowadays, the idea of monochrome video colorization has emerged a lot after the recent advancement in image processing and computer vision techniques. Video colorization has become a keen interest of many researchers because each frame of a colored video is represented in three channels, i.e. red, green, and blue. In contrast, the monochromatic images are represented using a single channel based on different gray shades. Therefore, mapping a single value to three different values or one-to-many mapping is not unprecedented; hence the colorization process becomes often ambiguous. Earlier provided solutions consist of user guidance-based systems that scribble some colors to some regions of a grayscale image and later provide a function to colorize the whole region by itself [15, 19, 20, 22, 27, 29]. Another method is by giving sample reference images to a system, where the user selects some colored reference image for the grayscale image that is needed for color similarly [9, 10, 12, 16, 21, 24, 26].

Some recent approaches show the use of deep convolutional networks based on learning different color relationships on a large dataset. Rao et al. [25] presented

D. Gupta et al. (Eds.): CVIP 2022, CCIS 1776, pp. 304–315, 2023.
https://doi.org/10.1007/978-3-031-31407-0_23

a method that takes into account the Most Informative (MI) frame containing maximum objects. After selecting the MI frame, a scribble-based colorization process is utilized for colorization of the MI frame. Akimoto et al. [5] proposed a reference-based video colorization with Spatio-temporal correspondence to color the grayscale images using some colored reference images. Kiani et al. [17] presented a method using Generative Adversarial Networks (GANs), Convolutional Neural Networks (CNNs) and a concept of hypercolumn [13]. Zhang et al. [28] proposed a CNN-based colorization method, which determines every possible color for each pixel using a probability distribution. Baldassarre et al. [6] provide a method by combining a dense convolutional neural network and the Inception-ResNet-v2 [23] pre-trained model and provides the high-level features to the model.

This paper presents a novel video colorization model using a Modified Autoencoder Generative Adversarial Network (MAE-GANs) and DenseNet based architecture. The proposed model assumes that every video frame is different, therefore flickering of colors can be observed in the resulted videos. For performance evaluation, several experiments are performed on high frame rate videos. Rest of the paper is structured as follows: Sect. 2 gives a brief of different methodologies which are used to implement the proposed video colorization model. Section 3 provides the detailed implementation of the proposed architecture. Section 4 presents experimental results and discussion followed by the conclusions in Sect. 5.

2 Methodology

2.1 Generative Adversarial Networks

GANs are a deep learning-based generative model [11] consisting of two networks that compete with each other to generate variations in the data. The two sub-models are known as the generator model (G) and the discriminative model (D). The generator task is to generate fake data with the help of input data. In contrast, the discriminator network decides whether the data is generated or taken from the original samples. GANs are trained in a repeated manner. After the training process, the generator is forced to create data similar to the original data distribution, which maximizes the probability of the discriminator making a mistake. This process The mathematical equation is as follows:

$$
\mathcal{L} = \min_G \max_D \left[\, E_{x \sim p_{data}(x)} log(D(x)) + \right.
$$
$$
\left. E_{z \sim p_z(z)} log(1 - D(G(z))) \, \right]
\tag{1}
$$

where E denotes the expectation, x is a sample from the real data, z is a sample from the generated data, $p_{data}(x)$ is the probability of the real data and $p_z(z)$ is the probability distribution of the generated data.

2.2 Autoencoders

An Autoencoder [7] is an unsupervised deep learning model that uses backprop-agation to set the output values same as the inputs with the minimum error. There are three main layers which are: encoder, bottleneck region, and decoder. The first component i.e. the encoder compresses the input into a latent space representation i.e. in a reduced dimensional space. The bottleneck layers repre-sents a compressed image which is the encoded version of the input image. Next, the decoder decodes the encoded image and generates a lossy reconstruction of the input image having the original dimension.

2.3 DenseNet Architecture

The connectivity pattern is the main idea behind DenseNets where the next layer's input is generated by a concatenation of all the previous layer inputs. For example, if the x_0 is the input layer and x_1, x_2, and x_3 are the first, second and third layer of the network, then layer x_3 will take output of layer x_1 and x_2 as input along with the original input x_0. All inputs are concatenated to make a real deep feature map with the same spatial resolution. By adding dense blocks all in a row connected to each other in this way they get really deep.

The DenseNet model [14] breaks up the dense blocks such that it can use a one-by-one convolution because it preserves the spatial resolution, but it shrinks the depth of the feature map, followed by a max-pooling to reduce the feature map size. This model is more parameter efficient because in some models a decision has to be made which information should be preserved from the previ-ous layer. However, in the DenseNet, since the information is just concatenated ahead, it does not need to have information preservation functions; it is just about adding new information.

3 Proposed Model

The main pipeline of the proposed model is summarized in Fig 1. The proposed model assumes every frame of the video to be different from one another. In the proposed model, a GAN is utilized as a base architecture whose generative model is autoencoder-based architecture shown in Fig. 2. The encoder architecture is modified by embedding a DenseNet architecture proposed by Gao Huang et al. [14] in every encoder block. The encoder architecture network is designed to downsample the image. The four layers are considered in the dense block followed by the same translational network layers as described similarly [14]. The encoder contains a total of 5 blocks, in which every block of the encoder consists of a strided convolutional layer (stride = 2), dense block, translation layer, rectified linear unit (ReLU) activation layers, and batch normalization shown in Fig. 3(a).

The decoder architecture network is designed to upsample the image. It also contains 5 decoder blocks shown in Fig. 3(b) in which every block contains a strided convolution/deconvolutional layer (stride = 2), and a batch normaliza-tion with concatenation from the symmetric opposite encoder block within the generator architecture (refer Fig 2).

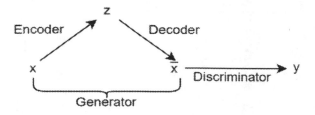

Fig. 1. Overall architecture flow of our proposed model. x is the input grayscale image, $\bar{x}$ is the generated image in CIELAB colorspace, and y is the probability of an image to be fake or real

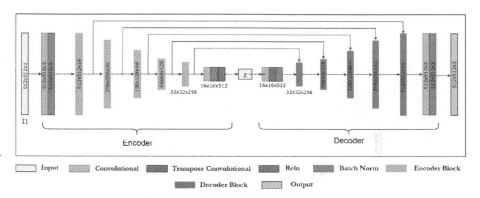

Fig. 2. The architecture of the generator model. It consists of encoder and decoder networks. Every encoder and decoder networks consist of five sub encoder and decoder blocks, shown in the Fig. 3. The output of each encoder block is forwarded to a similar size decoder block. Dimensions at each layer are given by W × H× C , where W and H refer to the width and height, respectively, and C is the number of channels at that layer. The output is the CIELAB colorspace consisting of all layers (l, a, b).

3.1 Model Workflow

For training, the original dataset in the RGB colorspace is divided into mini-batches of size 16. Before passing to the model, each minibatch is transformed into two datasets: grayscale and CIELAB color versions of ground truth images of the respective mini-batches. The grayscale version is provided to the generator, whereas the CIELAB version is provided to the discriminator. After feeding the grayscale image to the generator, its input image starts getting downsampled using the encoder network. After going from each encoder block, the image size is reduced to half; in contrast, the number of channels becomes double the previous ones. At the last encoder block's output, the image is converted into a single dimension vector, where it will be passed to the decoder network. After passing the vector through each decoder block, the image starts upsampling. The size becomes twice after each pass, and no channels start decreasing by a factor of 2. At the end of the decoder network, it generates an image having the

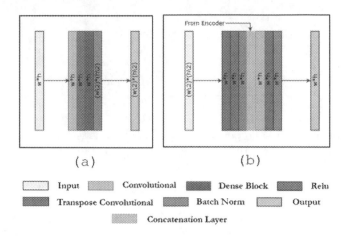

(a)   (b)

	Input		Convolutional		Dense Block		Relu
	Transpose Convolutional		Batch Norm		Output
	Concatenation Layer

Fig. 3. The architecture of the encoder (a) and the decoder (b) blocks. Both block architectures were designed using strided convolutional/deconvolutional layers, an activation layer, a dense block, and a batch normalization layer. The dimension of every layer is given by its width (W) and height (H). At the output layer, the vector dimension gets reduced by half. The number of channels gets twice as compared to the input layer.

same size as the ground truth image. Here, the generated image is assumed to be in CIELAB colorspace and passed to the discriminator model.

The discriminator consists of a series of encoder blocks for both the inputs, as shown in Fig. 4. The image is flattened into a single dimension vector, followed by a dropout layer and a sigmoid activation layer at the end of the discriminator model. The sigmoid function output will give the desired probability. Higher probability refers to higher the ability to mimic the original dataset images. The produced error and losses are back-propagated to update the kernel weights. This process is repeated until the termination criterion is not achieved.

To optimize the generation of images, the standard GAN loss function, and custom loss function are estimated as given below:

$$\mathcal{L} = (CS + 1) * MSE + MAE, \tag{2}$$

where CS stands for cosine similarity. MSE and MAE refer to the mean square error and mean absolute error. For testing purposes, the proposed generative model is required. The colored frame datasets are converted into the grayscale dataset, and mini-batches of size 16 of the dataset are generated which are given to the generative model in an orderly manner. Since the generative model's output is assumed to be in CIELAB colorspace, the generated images are again converted to RGB colorspace images. Later, to form a colored video, all the frames are recombined in the same frames as in the original video.

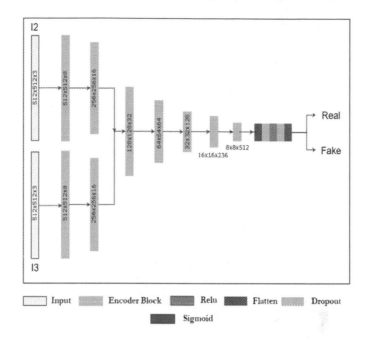

Fig. 4. The architecture of the discriminator model. I2 is the image from the generator output, and I3 is the ground truth image in the CIELAB colorspace. It consists of several encoder block architectures shown in Fig. 3(a). At each layer, the vector dimension gets reduced by half, and the channel size becomes twice. The dimensions at each layer are given by W× H × C, where W and H refer to the width and height, respectively and C is the number of channels at that layer. At the end of the architecture, the vector is flattened into a single dimension. The output is obtained using a sigmoid layer, which is 0 or 1, corresponding to being fake or real.

4   Experimental Results and Discussion

4.1   Dataset and Implementation

To evaluate the colorization performance of the proposed model, several sets of videos such as movies, a sitcom (a) "Dial M for Murder" (Movie, USA, 1954, 63,243 frames, directed by Alfred Hitchcock, 8.2 IMDB rating) [1], (b) "3 idiots" (Movie, INDIA, 2009, 246,385 frames, directed by Rajkumar Hirani, 8.4 IMDB rating) [3], (c) "Tarak Mehta ka Ulta Chashma," Ep3065 (Sitcom, Ep3065, India, 2020, 32,487 frames, directed by Asit Kumarr Modi, 8.0 IMDB rating) [2], and (d) "Kota Factory" Episode 3 (web series, INDIA, 2019, 55276 frames, directed by Raghav Subbu, 9.0 IMDB rating) [4] are used for training and testing purposes. These datasets are selected based on the number of characters and color variation. For example, in dataset (a), the number of characters is small, and there is not much color variation in the video, whereas, in dataset (c), the number of characters and the color variations is high.

For training and testing purposes, each dataset is divided into a 4:1 ratio.

Table 1. Adam parameter used in the proposed model

Parameter	value
L2	1e−4
β_1	0.9
β_2	0.999
ϵ	1e−8

The data augmentation is also done on the training dataset (horizontal flips, rotation at $\pm 15°$). The first three datasets, i.e. (a), (b), and (c), are used for both training and testing, whereas dataset (d) is originally in a black and white version and ground truth is also not available used for testing using proposed and other various trained models.

Table 1 presents four different parameters of Adam optimizer [18] used in the proposed model. L2 represents a regularizer parameter and β_1 is the first moment. β_2 and ϵ are kept small to prevent any division by zero in the implementation. 180–200 epoch is considered for testing for getting enhanced image quality. Excessive training causes color spilling at the object edges which decreases the performance of the model.

4.2 Performance Measures

In addition to the visual analysis of the results evaluated by the proposed model, quantitative evaluation is equally important. Borji et al. [8] proposed several measures to evaluate GAN models. The followings are the measures used for performance analysis of the proposed model.

1. *Peak Signal-to-Noise Ratio:* Peak Signal-to-Noise Ratio (PSNR) is determined between the generated image and the original image as it measures the quality between two images. This ratio should be as high as possible cause the higher the PSNR higher is the quality of the generated image.

$$PSNR(X,Y) = 10\log_{10}(\frac{MAX_X^2}{MSE}) \qquad (3)$$

where

$$MSE_{X,Y} = \frac{1}{mn}\sum_{i=0}^{m-1}\sum_{j=0}^{n-1}(X(m,n) - Y(m,n))^2 \qquad (4)$$

and MAX_X is the maximum possible pixel value of the image, in this case 255.

2. *Structural Similarity Index:* Structural Similarity Index (SSIM) is used to test the quality and the similarity between the original and the generated

images. By doing comparing of luminance (I), contrast (C) and structure (S) of images, SSIM between images can be determined.

$$I(x,y) = \frac{2\mu_x\mu_y + C_1}{\mu_x^2 + \mu_y^2 + C_1},$$

$$C(x,y) = \frac{2\sigma_x\sigma_y + C_2}{\sigma_x^2 + \sigma_y^2 + C_2}, \tag{5}$$

$$\& \ S(x,y) = \frac{\sigma_{xy} + C_3}{\sigma_x\sigma_y + C_3}$$

$$SSIM(x,y) = I(x,y)^\alpha C(x,y)^\beta S(x,y)^\gamma \tag{6}$$

where μ_x, μ_y, σ_x, σ_y and σ_{xy} denote the mean, standard deviations of pixel intensity in a local image patch and the sample correlation coefficient between the corresponding pixels in the patches centered at either x or y, respectively. C_1, C_2 and C_3 are small values added to ensure numerical stability.

3. *Sharpness Difference:* Sharpness Difference (SD) is the measurement of loss in sharpness in the generated images as compared to the original image. It is generally used for a comparison method between various GAN models.

$$SD(X,Y) = 10\log_{10}(\frac{MAX_X^2}{GRADS_{X,Y}}) \tag{7}$$

where

$$GRADS_{X,Y} = \frac{1}{N}\sum_i\sum_j(\|(\nabla_i X + \nabla_j X)$$
$$- (\nabla_i Y + \nabla_j Y)\|) \tag{8}$$

and

$$\nabla_i I = |I_{i,j} - I_{i-1,j}|, \ \nabla_j I = |I_{i,j} \quad I_{i,j-1}|. \tag{9}$$

4.3   Results and Discussions

To assess the performance of the proposed model, three different frames out of the dataset are shown in Fig. 5(a), and the trained results of the proposed model are presented in Fig. 5(c). The proposed model assumes that the generated image from the generative model to be in CIELAB colorspace. Earlier it was assumed to be in the RGB colorspace for performance analysis during different experiments, but the visual quality of the images (One can have a look at the dataset presented in Fig. 5(c)) is not so good and the quantitative measures as PSNR (21.07 dB) and SSIM (92%) are also lower sides. In the second experiment, CIELAB colorspace is used because it provides better human vision in four unique colors: red, green, blue, and yellow. The unique feature of the CIELAB colorspace provides a significant improvement in the performance of the proposed

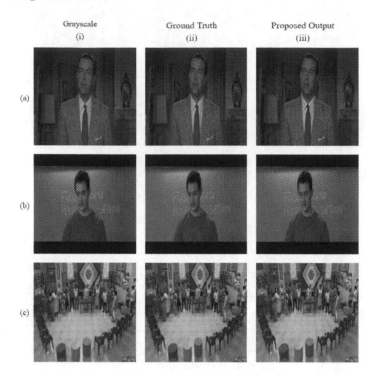

Fig. 5. Visual results of the training dataset i.e. (a) "Dial M for Murder," (b) "3 idiots", and (c) "Tarak Mehta ka Ulta Chashma" are shown here. The rows (a), (b), and (c) belong to the respected datasets. Columns (i), (ii) and (iii) represent the grayscale version, the ground truth, and the generated (proposed) images of the respected datasets.

model. Table 2 shows the quantitative performance measures evaluated for all datasets processed by the proposed model. All the measures are computed on the 5–6 mini-clips of size 2 min each over a particular out of the complete dataset. Higher values of PSNR, SSIM, and SD indicate higher quality of the generated video clips.   Based on the experimental results, it is observed that the proposed model produces appropriate colorization results when tested against the colored dataset video. The average accuracy of the proposed model is also evaluated by setting the average PSNR as standard over all the datasets (a), (b), and

Table 2. Average quantitative measures evaluated for all datasets

Video Set	PSNR (in dB)	SSIM (in %)	SD
(a)	40.02	98	41.20
(b)	35.37	93	40.34
(c)	28.09	97	30.96

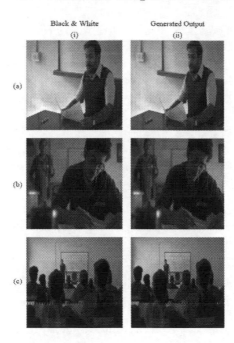

Black & White   Generated Output
(i)   (ii)

Fig. 6. Visual results of the testing dataset (d) "Kota Factory" are shown here. Column (i) represents the original black and white frames from the dataset, and column (ii) represents the generated images when the frames are passed through the proposed model.

(c), respectively, which is 97.41%. From Table 2, it can be observed that in the dataset (a) having less variation of colors and less number of characters give the high PSNR (40.02 dB) and SSIM (98%) values when compared to the ground truth, whereas in the dataset (c) having more variation of colors and more number of characters gives less PSNR (28.09 dB) and SSIM (97%). The use of DenseNet in the encoder architecture has increased the color consistency in various frames, which helps to improve the model performance. The trained model's performance is tested against the original black and white/grayscale video for which colored ground truth is not available. However, considerable colorization results can be observed in the generated outcomes as shown in Fig. 6. The predicted colors in the black and white images for any object are random. However, the color mapping is consistent with some flickering which may be observed under conditions such as the fast motion of objects between the frames or the random introduction of new objects.

5 Conclusions

In this paper, a novel model is proposed for video colorization using a modified autoencoder generative adversarial-based architecture embedded with the DenseNet in an encoder framework. The proposed architecture improves the consistent mapping of colors in all the video frames considered for experimentation purposes. The use of CIELAB colorspace also helps to enhance the visual quality of the generated images. Furthermore, another model can be developed to deal with consistent color mapping of fast-moving objects between different video frames in our next work.

References

1. Dial M for Murder (1954). https://www.imdb.com/title/tt0046912
2. Taarak Mehta Ka Ooltah Chashmah (2008-present). https://www.imdb.com/title/tt1708446
3. 3 Idiots (2009). https://www.imdb.com/title/tt1187043
4. Kota Factory (2019). https://www.imdb.com/title/tt9432978
5. Akimoto, N., Hayakawa, A., Shin, A., Narihira, T.: Reference-based video colorization with spatiotemporal correspondence. ArXiv Preprint ArXiv:2011.12528 (2020)
6. Baldassarre, F., Morín, D.G., Rodés-Guirao, L.: Deep koalarization: image colorization using CNNs and inception-ResNet-v2. ArXiv Preprint ArXiv:1712.03400 (2017)
7. Bank, D., Koenigstein, N., Giryes, R.: Autoencoders. ArXiv Preprint ArXiv:2003.05991 (2020)
8. Borji, A.: Pros and cons of GAN evaluation measures. Comput. Vis. Image Underst. **179**, 41–65 (2019)
9. Charpiat, G., Hofmann, M., Schölkopf, B.: Automatic image colorization via multimodal predictions. In: Forsyth, D., Torr, P., Zisserman, A. (eds.) ECCV 2008. LNCS, vol. 5304, pp. 126–139. Springer, Heidelberg (2008). https://doi.org/10.1007/978-3-540-88690-7_10
10. Chia, A.Y.S., et al.: Semantic colorization with internet images. ACM Trans. Graph. (TOG) **30**(6), 1–8 (2011)
11. Goodfellow, I., et al.: Generative adversarial nets. In: Advances in Neural Information Processing systems, vol. 27 (2014)
12. Gupta, R.K., Chia, A.Y.S., Rajan, D., Ng, E.S., Zhiyong, H.: Image colorization using similar images. In: Proceedings of the 20th ACM International Conference on Multimedia, pp. 369–378 (2012)
13. Hariharan, B., Arbeláez, P., Girshick, R., Malik, J.: Hypercolumns for object segmentation and fine-grained localization. In: Proceedings of the IEEE Conference on Computer Vision and Pattern Recognition, pp. 447–456 (2015)
14. Huang, G., Liu, Z., Van Der Maaten, L., Weinberger, K.Q.: Densely connected convolutional networks. In: Proceedings of the IEEE Conference on Computer Vision and Pattern Recognition, pp. 4700–4708 (2017)
15. Huang, Y.C., Tung, Y.S., Chen, J.C., Wang, S.W., Wu, J.L.: An adaptive edge detection based colorization algorithm and its applications. In: Proceedings of the 13th Annual ACM International Conference on Multimedia, pp. 351–354 (2005)
16. Ironi, R., Cohen-Or, D., Lischinski, D.: Colorization by example. Rendering Tech. **29**, 201–210 (2005)
17. Kiani, L., Saeed, M., Nezamabadi-pour, H.: Image colorization using generative adversarial networks and transfer learning. In: International Conference on Machine Vision and Image Processing, pp. 1–6. IEEE (2020)

18. Kingma, D.P., Ba, J.: Adam: A method for stochastic optimization. ArXiv Preprint ArXiv:1412.6980 (2014)
19. Levin, A., Lischinski, D., Weiss, Y.: Colorization using optimization. In: ACM SIGGRAPH 2004 Papers, pp. 689–694 (2004)
20. Luan, Q., Wen, F., Cohen-Or, D., Liang, L., Xu, Y.Q., Shum, H.Y.: Natural image colorization. In: Proceedings of the 18th Eurographics Conference on Rendering Techniques, pp. 309–320 (2007)
21. Morimoto, Y., Taguchi, Y., Naemura, T.: Automatic colorization of grayscale images using multiple images on the web. In: SIGGRAPH 2009: Talks, p. 1 (2009)
22. Qu, Y., Wong, T.T., Heng, P.A.: Manga colorization. ACM Trans. Graph. (TOG) **25**(3), 1214–1220 (2006)
23. Szegedy, C., Vanhoucke, V., Ioffe, S., Shlens, J., Wojna, Z.: Rethinking the inception architecture for computer vision. In: Proceedings of the IEEE Conference on Computer Vision and Pattern Recognition, pp. 2818–2826 (2016)
24. Tai, Y.W., Jia, J., Tang, C.K.: Local color transfer via probabilistic segmentation by expectation-maximization. In: IEEE Computer Society Conference on Computer Vision and Pattern Recognition (CVPR 2005), vol. 1, pp. 747–754. IEEE (2005)
25. Veeravasarapu, V.R., Sivaswamy, J.: Fast and fully automated video colorization. In: International Conference on Signal Processing and Communications, pp. 1–5. IEEE (2012)
26. Welsh, T., Ashikhmin, M., Mueller, K.: Transferring color to greyscale images. In: Proceedings of the 29th Annual Conference on Computer Graphics and Interactive Techniques, pp. 277–280 (2002)
27. Yatziv, L., Sapiro, G.: Fast image and video colorization using chrominance blending. IEEE Trans. Image Process. **15**(5), 1120–1129 (2006)
28. Zhang, R., Isola, P., Efros, A.A.: Colorful image colorization. In: Leibe, B., Matas, J., Sebe, N., Welling, M. (eds.) ECCV 2016. LNCS, vol. 9907, pp. 649–666. Springer, Cham (2016). https://doi.org/10.1007/978-3-319-46487-9_40
29. Zhang, R., et al.: Real-time user-guided image colorization with learned deep priors. ArXiv Preprint ArXiv:1705.02999 (2017)

Real-Time Violence Detection Using Deep Neural Networks and DTW

U. Rachna[1], Varsha Guruprasad[1], S. Dhruv Shindhe[2], and S. N. Omkar[2]($\boxtimes$) (iD)

[1] PES University, Bangalore, India
[2] ARTPARK, Indian Institute of Science, Bangalore, India
omkar@iisc.ac.in

Abstract. With the increased coverage of CCTV cameras across major metropolitan cities, there has been an increased need to continuously monitor these video feeds for them to be effective, this incurs human labor which is prone to boredom and flaws. We propose a system that can augment the capabilities of surveillance systems by automatically tagging sequences of violence in real-time. Instead of relying on a bigger network like CNN-LSTM, our system uses DTW to measure the similarity between two sequences of body joint angles over time and uses this feature as an input to different classifiers, thus reducing the need for a big video dataset to perform action recognition. For person detection on the individual frames we employ YoloV3 and then DeepSort is used to track different individuals over time then use this as an input to OpenPose to obtain the key points, the obtained key points are used to calculate different joint angles. The joint angles can be seen as temporal signals which can be compared with different joint angle signals over time and find the similarity measure and use this as a feature to classifiers like SVM, KNN, and Random forests. The results are at par with the ones that use CNN-based classifiers trained on larger data.

Keywords: Action recognition · DTW · Pose Estimation

1 Introduction

There is a growing awareness among the public about the importance of having CCTV cameras, as crime rates continue to rise across the country, and with the invention of Artificial Intelligence(AI) and the Internet of Things(IoT), there is an aggressive increase in the demand for smart security systems. As of Jan 2021, India reported having 274,784 surveillance cameras over nine metropolises. The top three cities with the highest number of CCTV cameras reported were New Delhi, Chennai, and Pune. According to the statistics as seen in Aug 2021, New Delhi is reportedly the city with the highest number of CCTV cameras globally. The Karnataka government in December 2020 started a Rs.620-crore initiative to increase CCTV coverage by tenfold in Bengaluru to ensure the safety of women, and identify crime-prone areas and miscreants across the city. These systems are

D. Gupta et al. (Eds.): CVIP 2022, CCIS 1776, pp. 316–327, 2023.
https://doi.org/10.1007/978-3-031-31407-0_24

mainly installed for public safety. Monitoring the actions of people helps prevent theft, collect evidence of crime scenes, protect against violent activities, curb sexual harassment and monitor general actions of the public.

Over the last few decades, there have been huge advancements in computer vision algorithms concerning object detection and pose estimation, these can be combined with the plethora of publically available datasets to incorporate intelligence onto surveillance systems. We propose an AI CCTV camera that can tag individuals engaging in violent actions autonomously, thereby assisting law enforcement, security personnel, and other departments to take swift and timely action by providing real-time alerts on the scene being surveillance. Most surveillance systems need a human operator to make decisions which decreases their reliability and increases their cost by incurring human labor. This can be mitigated by having automatic systems in place that can monitor the surveillance footage in real-time and alert the security personnel if something suspicious was noticed by the system. Having intelligent surveillance systems can assist law enforcement agencies in apprehending criminals, reducing staffing requirements, and getting alerts even in the absence of an operator. The goal of our paper is to propose a simple system that would detect violent activities like punching and kicking in real-time under well-lit conditions through video obtained from surveillance whilst keeping both computational time and complexity at a bare minimum.

2 Related Work

With the increased interest in action recognition, there have been numerous pipelines proposed to tag individuals engaging in violent actions. The methods proposed either use handcrafted features or implement various deep learning based architectures, with the inputs being surveillance videos, audio, or both. Cheng et al. [1] and Giannakopoulos et al. [2] implemented audio features to identify violence in videos. Most of the methods that use handcrafted features implement optical flow to obtain motion descriptors of moving objects. Lertniphonphanet al. [3] used both horizontal and vertical optical flow histograms as features, Zhou et al. [4] computed LHOG(Local histogram of oriented gradients) and LHOF (Local histogram of optical flow) on RGB and optical images as descriptors and used an SVM classifier to perform the classification. Hassner et al. [5] focused on monitoring crowd violence in real-time where they used the flow vector magnitude over time; later an SVM was used to perform the classification. Xu et al. [6] employed Motion SIFT (MoSIFT) to obtain low-level features and the important features were obtained by implementing the Kernel Density Estimation(KDE) and Bag of Words(BoW) was used for encoding the features obtained.

Carlos et al. [7] proposed a CNN-LSTM neural network to create a video action recognition system. Here, a VGG16 extracts the features later an LSTM is used to classify the scene into the appropriate category. Mahmoud et al. [8] proposed that Data Bus Networks (DBNs) trained with Restricted Boltzmann Machines(RBMs) can be used to recognize human actions in pictures.

Sumon et al in [9], developed a video dataset from extracts from movies and used them to train a CNN-LSTM model to form a classification between violent and non-violent videos. Amarjoth et al. [10] proposed a ScatterNet Hybrid Deep Learning (SHDL) to perform human pose estimation on aerial imagery. The framework initially employed a Feature Pyramid Network(FPN) for the detection of humans from drone images, following which it employed the proposed SHDL network to assess the stance of each individual. Finally, an SVM is used to estimate poses and identify violent persons. Dhruv et al. [11] proposed a lightweight system for identifying violence in real-time which used OpenPose for estimation of 2D key points of individuals, YoloV3 for identifying humans, and a CNN to categorize actions into kicking, punching, and non-violent activities. The system works well under good lighting conditions however, it fails to take into account the temporal nature of the data which may lead to inaccurate results.

Violence detection in real-time is extremely vital and difficult, in the proposed method we focus on solving problems lines - 1)Reduce the reliance on big video datasets to obtain accurate systems, 2)Keep the entire pipeline real-time and 3)Employ the temporal nature of actions by using video segments instead of individual frames.

3   Methodology

Fig. 1. Pipeline of the proposed methodology

3.1   Overview

The pipeline is as shown in Fig. 1. The video feed is first obtained from the CCTV camera and the obtained video is divided into frames and passed onto YoloV3 for human detection. YoloV3 is a fast object detection algorithm suitable for real-time applications which can detect objects present in a frame in a single pass. To track each individual in the frame, deep sort is employed. Deepsort is a real-time object tracking algorithm that when combined with YoloV3 performs efficient object detection and tracking across a series of frames. After each person has been tracked for a certain amount of frames, the pose of each individual is estimated through Openpose, which is a bottom-up pose estimation algorithm. Post this, the Dynamic Time Warping(DTW) scores for the joint angles obtained while performing different actions are calculated and used as a feature for the classifier. DTW is used as a similarity measure between two temporal data sequences. The dataset consists of several videos each of walking, punching, and kicking taken from several sources and recorded during a mock trial of violence. Three classifiers namely, K-Nearest Neighbors, Random forest, and Naive Bayes have been made use of with the features being the minimum DTW scores obtained for all angles (right neck, left neck, right shoulder, left shoulder, right hip, left hip, right elbow, left elbow, and left knee). The minimum DTW scores were calculated between the resulting angles between walking videos, walking and punching videos, and walking and kicking videos. These scores were then labeled for their respective classes and passed to all the classifiers for training and testing.

3.2   YoloV3

YoloV3 [12] is one of the fastest object detection algorithms out there, where it takes in the input image and outputs the bounding box coordinates along with the confidence scores of all the objects in that image by just using one neural network. The confidence score value is the IoU of the bounding box predicted by the network with the ground truth bounding box annotated by a person (i.e, the closest position to the ground truth center) and zero for a negative position. Yolo V3 network consists of a 53-layer CNN called darknet53, feature extraction is done at three different scales using a feature pyramid network, and also it employs residual networks to avoid the vanishing gradients problem. The most notable feature of YoloV3 is that it performs object detection at three distinct scales. The challenge of recognizing small objects is addressed by using three different levels of detection. The concatenation of upsampled layers with prior layers helps maintain fine-grained characteristics that aid in the detection of smaller objects. The input image is divided into S × S grid cells. For each object, the grid cell containing the center of the bounding box is responsible for prediction. Each cell will be responsible for predicting B bounding boxes, so the predictions will be of the size as follows:

$$S * S * B * [5 + C] \tag{1}$$

where the number of classes is given by C (80 in the case of the COCO dataset) and 5 corresponds to x, y (center of the bounding boxes) w, h (width and height), and the confidence score.

When two bounding boxes share the same center we use anchor boxes which are a predefined set of bounding boxes of fixed height and width. The ground truth boxes are approximated by the predefined anchors as closely as possible. Yolo also implements multi-scale training. Multi-scale training entails extending the dataset to include objects of many sizes. Because a neural network operates with pixels, scaling the images in the dataset at different sizes allows learning model objects at different scales. Anchor sizes will never be relative to the input image width or height to facilitate multi-scale training, as the goal of multi-scale training is to change the ratio between the input dimensions and anchor sizes. YoloV3 uses 9 anchor boxes to perform detections at each scale.

3.3 Deepsort

We must combine our understanding of detecting objects in static images with
the ability to analyze temporal information and use it to best anticipate trajectories to track objects in a video. An object tracking algorithm is essential
not just to analyze each frame separately and recognize objects present in that
frame, but to track every object present across a sequence of frames where each
object is given a unique tracking ID. Occlusion in images is one of the most
common hurdles to smooth object tracking. The tracker aims to recognize the
same individual in a later frame and link his past track and attributes. Most
trackers utilize the properties of an object to keep track of it. Such a tracker
may fail in instances when the item seems different owing to camera movements.
Deepsort [13] is one such algorithm that when combined with YoloV3 performs
efficient real-time object detection and tracking.

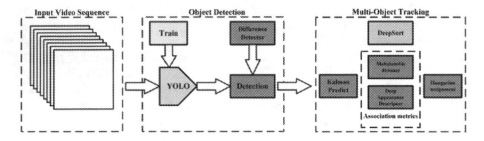

Fig. 2. Multi-target tracking using YoloV3 and Deepsort [14]

Figure 2 summarizes the workflow. YoloV3 is first used to detect all the
objects in a frame. These objects are then tracked in the subsequent frames
and matched with the predicted ones. The target state is updated using a typical Kalman filter with constant velocity motion and a linear observation model.
The premise of the Kalman filter is to keep track of the estimated state of the
object and the uncertainty of the estimate and to minimize the error between
the estimate and observation. The state describes variables namely - (u, v, a, h,
u', v', a', h') where (u, v) are bounding box centers, a denotes aspect ratio, and
h denotes the height of the image, the rest of the variables denotes velocities.

By factoring in noise and calculating an appropriate fit for bounding boxes
based on the past state, the Kalman filter enhances detection. The Kalman filter
gives us the position of the bounding box in the consecutive frame. From the
detection obtained in the t+1 frame and the bounding box predictions for the
t+1 frame, an appearance descriptor is computed for each bounding box with
L2 normalization, which is a feature vector obtained from the second last layer

of a pre-trained neural network. To track the association between the predicted and the detected bounding boxes, the Mahalanobis distance between the two appearance descriptors(cost function) to include uncertainties from the Kalman filter is used as a distance metric and the Hungarian assignment problem is used to sort out the detections and the prediction.

3.4 OpenPose

Most pose estimation algorithms employ a person detector first and then perform keypoint detection. This solution has some drawbacks, such as no resource to recover from when the human detection fails and a runtime that is proportional to the number of persons. OpenPose [15] is a multi-person bottom-up pose estimation algorithm instead of the detection-based top-down approach resulting in a runtime that is not dependent on the number of individuals in the frame. First feature extraction is performed using the first 10 layers of the VGG-19 model. The Part Affinity Fields (PAFs) and Confidence maps are generated using these features. The unstructured pairwise associations between joints are encoded by PAFs, which are a collection of 2D vector fields i.e., the position and orientation of the limbs. OpenPose generates 38 PAFs and these are further used to weigh the connection between each joint. PAF establishes a link between body parts that belong to the same individual. A stronger PAF relationship between body parts indicates that those body parts are likely to belong to the same individual. They come in pairs i.e one in the 'x-direction and one in the 'y' direction for each joint. Each of the pairings has 38 PAFs linked with it and indexed as follows:

$$the\ set\ L = (L_1, L_2, ..., L_C)\ where\ L_c \in R^{wxhx2}, c\ \epsilon 1, ...C \tag{2}$$

Each value is a list of the specific limb type found along with the ID of the source and target joints and their connection score. To connect the body parts, bipartite graphs are generated. A Confidence Map depicts the confidence that a specific body component may be located in the given pixel. Each body part is represented on a single map hence, there are 18 (+1) heatmaps associated with each one of the parts and are indexed as follows:

$$the\ set\ S = (S_1, S_2, ..., S_J)\ where\ S_j \in R^{wxhx2}, c\ \epsilon 1, ...J \tag{3}$$

The set contains a list of joints obtained by applying nonmaximal suppression to the generated heatmaps and their respective locations and probability scores. An L2 loss function is used to determine the difference between the predicted Confidence Maps and Part Affinity Fields and the ground truth maps and fields. Finally, to parse poses of numerous persons, Confidence Maps are used to locate all joint positions, PAFs to find joints that go together to construct limbs, and a final list of human poses to connect limbs that belong to the same person are estimated.

3.5   Dataset

There are several datasets available for action recognition like UCF101 [16] which is a collection of realistic action videos from YouTub with 101 action classes for action recognition. With a total of 7,000 clips divided across 51 action classes, the HMDB51 [17] dataset is a big collection of realistic videos from diverse sources, including movies and web videos. KTH [18] is a non-trivial and publicly available action recognition dataset that consists of six categories of human actions (walking, jogging, running, boxing, hand waving, and hand clapping). The UCF Sports dataset [19] is made up of a collection of actions from a variety of sports that are commonly seen on broadcast television. The Hollywood2 dataset [20] consists of two video classification problems: Actions and Scenes, which has 12 human action classes and 10 scene classes. Berkeley Multimodal Human Action (Berkeley Mhad) [21] consists of eleven different actions, and the Motion Capture HDM05 dataset [22]includes almost three hours of motion capture data that has been methodically captured and well-documented to give free motion capture data.

The data used to train the classifier came from a variety of places, including Youtube, stock films, and self-recorded mock violent videos. The data was divided into three different classes - walking, kicking, and punching. It consisted of 40 videos for walking, 33 videos for punching, and 33 videos for kicking. These video feeds are sent into Yolo + DeepSort to retrieve the bounding box coordinates, post which OpenPose estimates the poses of each cropped individual for further processing. These data were hand-labeled for training and testing the classifiers. Figure 3 shows snippets of the generated dataset.

Fig. 3. Dataset snippets used to train the classifier

3.6   DTW

Euclidean distance is used very widely as a distance metric however, it only performs one-to-one matching while making calculations. Dynamic time warping [23] on the other hand is used in time-series analysis, for comparing the similarity of two temporal sequences that may differ in speed. It develops a one-to-many match so that the troughs and peaks with the same pattern are perfectly matched and finally determines the best match between the two sequences. This can be visualized in Fig. 4(a) and Fig. 4(b)

(a) Euclidean matching.   (b) DTW matching.

Fig. 4. Time series matching patterns.

DTW has been used to calculate the similarity in the joint angles observed while performing specific actions. The coordinates obtained for the poses of each individual are used to calculate all 18 joint angles for walking, kicking, and punching. The angles obtained for walking are used as a reference to further distinguish the different actions by calculating the DTW scores between walking and punching and walking and kicking. These scores are again calculated for each joint for all the videos and passed as features to the classifier.

3.7   Classifier

Three distinct classifiers were trained and tested for detecting violent activities of punching and kicking. These classifiers were each chosen as they demand extremely little processing power, are easy to build, and provide simple and quick processing of the datasets.

K-Nearest Neighbours. The K-Nearest Neighbours(KNN) algorithm is a machine learning algorithm mostly used for classification. It's a method of lazy learning because it requires no training and instead uses all of the data for testing and classification. Data points that are similar are clustered together. The KNN algorithm relies on this assumption being true in order to work. By computing the Euclidean distance between points on a graph, KNN incorporates the concept of similarity. The KNN algorithm predicts the category of new data points based on similarity, which in our case is the Euclidean distance between the DTW scores obtained. This implies that the new data point will be assigned a class based on its' k-most closest neighbors. In our implementation, a value of 5 has been assigned to 'k' i.e., the chosen number of neighbors along with a 5-fold cross-validation split.

Naive Bayes. The Naive Bayes classifier uses Bayes Theorem based on conditional probabilities given by Eq. 4 to classify data from a sample. Using Bayes' theorem, we may determine the odds of A occurring if B has previously occurred. The hypothesis is A, and the proof is B. In this situation, the traits are believed to be independent. That is, one attribute's presence has no influence on the other. As a result, it is said to be naïve. Another assumption is that all of the features have the same impact on the result. The Naive Bayes is a fast and easy algorithm to implement that performs classification by calculating the probabilities of each data point belonging to a particular class and finally assigns the data point to the class with the highest probability.

$$P(A/B) = \frac{P(B/A)P(A)}{P(B)} \tag{4}$$

Random Forests. The Random Forest classifier uses decision trees as its building blocks. For each data sample, a decision tree is created. Any decision to be taken is done collectively by all the decision trees for each sample hence leading to strong and accurate decisions of classification for every data point. The predictions made are said to be correct when the decision trees are uncorrelated. They also incorporate bagging and feature randomness which makes them a robust and efficient method for classifying data.

Random forests are also a strong predictor of feature selection. With the model, Scikit-learn adds a new variable that displays the relative relevance or contribution of each feature to the prediction. It automatically generates the relevance score of each feature during the training phase. The importance is then reduced till the overall score is one. This score will assist in selecting the most critical characteristics for model construction and eliminating the less important ones. The relevance of each feature vector, which in our case are the DTW scores between joint angles obtained for punching and kicking with respect to walking, can be visualised in Fig. 5(a) And Fig. 5(b) respectively.

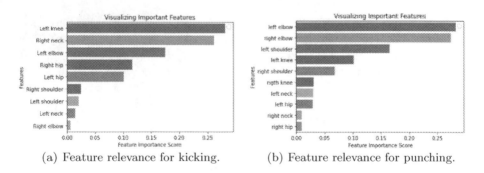

(a) Feature relevance for kicking.   (b) Feature relevance for punching.

Fig. 5. Feature relevance plots using Random forest classifier.

4   Results

Three different classifiers have been used to detect violent activities such as punching and kicking from non-violent activities such as walking. The results obtained are shown in Table 1.

Table 1. Accuracies achieved on test data.

Classifier	Punching - %Accuracy	Kicking - %Accuracy
KNN	0.95	0.862
Naive Bayes	0.947	0.90
Random Forest	0.10	0.857

The accuracy of each classifier is good and can be extended to additional violent activity detection, such as identifying pushing and stabbing actions from walking. Despite the small size of the dataset, the accuracies of the classifiers obtained for punching are good. Quantitative analysis proves that the model shows superior performance compared to the work done previously whilst taking into account the temporal nature of the data and achieves faster runtime as can be seen in Table 2.

These recorded accuracies are beneficial for a real-time set-up. This can be accounted for by the fact that the model is extremely light-weight without much requirement for a large training data. The mock videos in the dataset for kicking, punching and walking were taken from an inclination mimicking video feeds from CCTV cameras, implying that the entire pipeline can be used in real-time to detect different violence activities from a live CCTV video feed. These detections can further be used to alert the security personnel of violent activities.

Table 2. Average accuracies achieved on test data for DSS [10], CNN [11], and Proposed method.

Method	Punching %Average accuracy	Kicking %Average accuracy
DSS [10]	0.89	0.94
CNN [11]	0.95	0.862
Proposed method	0.966	0.873

5   Conclusion

The paper proposes a real-time violence detection pipeline that makes use of OpenPose, YoloV3 combined with Deepsort, DTW and three separate classifiers namely KNN, Random Forests and Naive Bias to detect and classify violent actions of punching and kicking from non-violent actions like walking. Openpose being a bottom-up pose estimation algorithm performs fast pose estimation of individuals as compared to other top-down approaches. YoloV3 combined with Deepsort performs efficient real-time person detection and tracking throughout a sequence of frames. Angles of each joint are then obtained for walking, punching and kicking post which the DTW scores between the same are calculated and passed into the classifier. In comparison to earlier work, the suggested approach further considers the temporal character of the data while maintaining a lower comput cost. Because an action like kicking or punching involves sequential data, implementing the suggested approach increases the overall system's reliability and reduces false alarms and since LSTM need more data to be accurate our proposed system that uses DTW scores as features can be more effective for action recognition with minimal data.

The system mainly focuses on detecting violent activities of punching and kicking from walking in well-lit areas with full body visibility. The setup is beneficial for real-time employment due to the model's lightweight nature as the system does not have a high computational cost and does not require large datasets for training. By integrating more videos in the dataset, the system's accuracy may be increased even further.

References

1. Cheng, W.H, Chu, W.T, Ling, J.L.: Semantic context detection based on hierarchical audio models. In: Proceedings of the ACM SIGMM Workshop on Multimedia Information Retrieval, pp. 109–115 (2003)
2. Giannakopoulos, T., Kosmopoulos, D., Aristidou, A., Theodoridis, S.: Violence content classification using audio features. In: Antoniou, G., Potamias, G., Spyropoulos, C., Plexousakis, D. (eds.) SETN 2006. LNCS (LNAI), vol. 3955, pp. 502–507. Springer, Heidelberg (2006). https://doi.org/10.1007/11752912_55
3. Lertniphonphan, K., Aramvith, S., Chalidabhongse, T.H.: Human action recognition using direction histograms of optical flow. In: 2011 11th International Symposium on Communications & Information Technologies (ISCIT), 2011, pp. 574–579. https://doi.org/10.1109/ISCIT.2011.6089701
4. Zhou, P., et al.: Violence detection in surveillance video using low-level features. PLoS one **13**(10), e0203668 (2018)
5. Hassner, T., Itcher, Y., Kliper-Gross, O.: Violent flows: real-time detection of violent crowd behavior. In: 2012 IEEE Computer Society Conference on Computer Vision and Pattern Recognition Workshops, pp. 1–6. IEEE (2012)
6. Xu, L., Gong, C., Yang, J., Qiang, W., Yao, L.: Violent video detection based on MoSIFT feature and sparse coding. In: 2014 IEEE International Conference on Acoustics, Speech and Signal Processing (ICASSP), pp. 3538–3542 (2014)
7. Orozco, C.I., et al.: Human action recognition in videos using a robust CNN LSTM approach. Ciencia y Tecnología, 23–36 (2020)
8. Al-Faris, M., et al.: A review on computer vision-based methods for human action recognition. J. Imag. **6**(6), 46 (2020)
9. Sumon, S.A., et al.: Violence detection by pretrained modules with different deep learning approaches. Vietnam J. Comput. Sci. **7**(01), 19–40 (2020)

10. Singh, A., Patil, D., Omkar, S.N.: Eye in the sky: real-time drone surveillance system (DSS) for violent individuals identification using ScatterNet hybrid deep learning network. In: Proceedings of the IEEE Conference on Computer Vision and Pattern Recognition Workshops (2018)

11. Dhruv Shindhe, S., Govindraj, S., Omkar, S.N.: Real-time violence activity detection using deep neural networks in a CCTV camera. In: 2021 IEEE International Conference on Electronics, Computing and Communication Technologies (CONNECT). IEEE (2021)

12. Redmon, J., Farhadi, A.: Yolov3: an incremental improvement. arXiv preprint: arXiv:1804.02767 (2018)

13. Wojke, N., Bewley, A., Paulus, D.: Simple online and realtime tracking with a deep association metric. In: 2017 IEEE International Conference on Image Processing (ICIP). IEEE (2017)

14. Zhang, X., et al.: Multi-target tracking of surveillance video with differential YOLO and DeepSort. In: Eleventh International Conference on Digital Image Processing (ICDIP 2019), vol. 11179. International Society for Optics and Photonics (2019)

15. Cao, Z., et al.: OpenPose: realtime multi-person 2D pose estimation using part affinity fields. IEEE Trans. Pattern Anal. Mach. Intell. **43**(1), 172–186 (2019)

16. Soomro, K., Zamir, A.R., Shah, M.: UCF101: a dataset of 101 human actions classes from videos in the wild. arXiv preprint: arXiv:1212.0402 (2012)

17. Kuehne, H., Jhuang, H., Garrote, E., Poggio, T., Serre, T.: HMDB51: a large video database for human motion recognition. In: Proceedings of the IEEE International Conference on Computer Vision, pp. 2556-2563 (2011). https://doi.org/10.1109/ICCV.2011.6126543

18. Schuldt, C., Laptev, I., Caputo, B.: Recognizing human actions: a local SVM approach. In: Proceedings of the 17th International Conference on Pattern Recognition, ICPR 2004, Cambridge, UK, 23–26 August 2004, vol. 3, pp. 32–36. IEEE, Piscataway, NJ, USA (2004)

19. Soomro, K., Zamir, A.R.: Action recognition in realistic sports videos. In: Moeslund, T.B., Thomas, G., Hilton, A. (eds.) Computer Vision in Sports. ACVPR, pp. 181–208. Springer, Cham (2014). https://doi.org/10.1007/978-3-319-09396-3_9

20. Laptev, I.: Hollywood2: human actions and scenes dataset, November 2011. http://www.irisa.fr/vista/actions/hollywood2/

21. Ofli, F., Chaudhry, R., Kurillo, G., Vidal, R., Bajcsy, R.: Berkeley MHAD: a comprehensive multimodal human action database. In: Proceedings of the 2013 IEEE Workshop on Applications of Computer Vision (WACV), pp. 53–60. Clearwater Beach, FL, USA, 15–17 January 2013

22. Müller, M., Röder, T., Clausen, M., Eberhadt, B., Krüger, B., Weber, A.: Documentation Mocap Database hdm05. University of Bonn, Bonn, Germany (2007)

23. Müller, M.: Dynamic time warping. In: Information Retrieval for Music And Motion, pp. 69–84 (2007). https://doi.org/10.1007/978-3-540-74048-3_4

Skin Disease Detection Using Saliency Maps and Segmentation Techniques

Rishit Toteja[✉][iD], Dhruv Gupta[iD], Vibhor Gautam[iD],
and Dinesh Kumar Vishwakarma[iD]

Delhi Technological University, Shahbad Daulatpur, Main Bawana Road, Delhi
110042, India
totejarishit262@gmail.com, dinesh@dtu.ac.in

Abstract. Skin diseases are the most common disease on the planet. When detecting skin diseases, dermatologists must have a high degree of expertise and precision, which is why computer-aided diagnosis is so helpful. An approach for detecting skin diseases has been presented to give more information. Several investigations have been carried out to aid in diagnosing skin disorders such as skin cancer and skin tumours. However, exact identification of skin disease is challenging to cure because of the following factors: visual likeness, little contrast in-between the lesions and skin that is between the affected and non-diseased areas, etc. In this paper we propose a model that uses an image set which is pre-processed by various techniques like deblurring, noise reduction, and then enhanced. The images are then segmented using U-Net and MobileNetV2 is used for classification. The disease is detected at the output for a corresponding input image based on the definite pattern pertaining to a dispersant in the processed image. Then, we compute a class saliency map for the provided image and class. We demonstrate how ConvNets may classify and segment skin diseases using such maps.

Keywords: Dermatology · Skin disease · Image segmentation · Saliency maps · Classification

1 Introduction

Due to a lack of understanding and ignorance, skin disorders are known to be quite widespread and are also considered complex diseases to diagnose. People contact dermatologists for skin problems and preventative measures in numerous developing countries. The medical recommendations that dermatologists issue are still fraught with uncertainty. According to studies, most people have skin disorders as a result of their work/job, hereditary, lack of nutrition, regular environments, chemical exposure, and so on. Skin illnesses are influenced by environmental factors such as climate, summer, and winter seasons. As a result, detecting and diagnosing the skin illness at an early stage is critical. As a result, illness analysis using image processing-based approaches is in demand, as it provides accurate results in less time, and as a result of the proliferation of electronic devices such as smartphones. A person can submit the input image using their smartphone camera, and the skin illness linked with the image is discovered and diagnosed using machine learning and image processing algorithms. A two-staged approach can be used to accomplish the input analysis or main analysis of the image. The input image is first enhanced with image processing techniques to improve its characteristics and quality, and then the treated image is classified using deep learning and machine learning techniques. Because the characteristics and properties of various skin diseases differ, the machine learning algorithm must be taught in order to make an accurate forecast. Skin cancer can develop if skin problems are not taken seriously and disregarded at an early stage. The increased skin disease infection is found subsequently using a biopsy in the current approach. This inspection is normally done by hand, taking into account a variety of histopathological features. Because this technique is done by hand, it is prone to human error, and the biopsy results take about 1–2 days to receive. Furthermore, a physician may find it difficult to diagnose the type of skin illness and, as a result, may prescribe the wrong treatment to the patient. To solve this issue, a deep learning methodology can be used to examine microscopic images of skin conditions.

In this research paper we have proposed a deep learning based model, for identification of skin diseases and classification using Mobile Net, a popular convolutional neural network architecture. Before the input images were passed to train the model, the images were first preprocessed using Gaussian and Median filters and converted into segmented images using U-Net Architecture. We used data augmentation in order to increase the dataset size since publicly available data was relatively less.

2   Related Work

Skin diseases are often characterized as disorders that happen inside the body or the skin and are visible to the naked eye. Some diseases are either uncommon, i.e., do not have the proper treatment, or some are commonly occurring. Dermatologists guarantee that many skin diseases are manageable with proper medications if they are diagnosed decisively. To reduce the workload on dermatologists, there is a need to design an automated skin disease detection system. The recent works have shifted the focus to neural networks to have a more effective and more robust system of skin disease detection.

Jessica Velasco et al. [17] used Mobile Net convolutional neural networks to classify seven classes with 94.4% accuracy on an unbalanced dataset. They also used various sampling approaches such as data augmentation. To categorise four classes and produce state-of-the-art results, Kyamelia Roy et al. [13] used several segmentation approaches. The described methods are applied to photographs of the four skin illnesses, and the differences in the dataset findings are seen. K.Melbin et al. [10] proposed an improved deep neural network model for identifying skin diseases. Using GLCM algorithm, feature extraction was performed on all of the segmented images which were then used to recover the feature vectors. Finally, a deep neural network with dragonfly optimization was used to classify skin disorders. To demonstrate the model's efficiency, the proposed algorithm, dragonfly-based DNN was tested against known machine learning models such as Artificial Neural Networks and Support Vector Machines using several evaluation metrics such as specificity, sensitivity and accuracy. Alaa Haddad et al. [7] set out to classify skin diseases from a skin lesion image and analyse it by adding filters to remove noise and unnecessary elements, as well as transforming the image to grayscale to aid processing and extract any useful/meaningful information. This helps to provide evidence for any type of skin lesion and illustrate the emergency orientation. The analysis result obtained from this study can be used to support doctors to assist them in primary diagnoses and know the kind of disease. Jianpeng Zhang et al. [19] used a synergic deep learning (SDL) model and achieved state-of-the-art results. The model uses two deep convolutional neural networks (DCNNs) which enables both of them to learn from each other mutually. They have concatenated learnt representation of the skin disease image representation by both DCNNs. This is provided as input to the proposed synergic model, which consists of fully connected layers which then tries to predict whether the pair of input images belong to the same class. The Synergic Deep Learning model was trained in an end-to-end manner and achieved state-of-the-art results. V.R. Balaji et al. [1] have implemented a state-of-the-art dynamic graph cut algorithm for segmentation of skin disease images. The segmented images are then used as input to a Bayes classifier for skin lesion classification purposes. For the dataset, they used the International Skin Imaging Collaboration (ISIC) 2017 dataset for testing their proposed model and found that their results surpassed many state-of-the-art machine learning models that includes models like FCN and SegNet by 6.5% and 8.7%, respectively. Anurag Kumar Verma et al. [18] have developed a model which comprised of four types of classification methods. They have used a commonly used open-source skin lesion dataset for testing the accuracy of different machine learning models to classify various classes of skin diseases. The results of base learners that are implemented in the paper are shown to be more accurate than the results which were obtained by previous studies. Parvathaneni Naga Srinivasu et al. [14] have proposed an automated skin disease classification through deep learning-based MobileNet V2 architecture and using a Long Short-Term Memory Network (LSTM). MobileNet V2 model achieved higher accuracy and proved to be efficient since it could work considerably well on lightweight computational devices. The model proposed in the paper was efficient in remembering stateful information used for precise predictions. The model performance was compared against many other state-of-the-art models. These findings have suggested that the proposed model can be used by general practitioners for efficient and effective diagnosis of skin diseases, and thus reducing further complications and morbidity. Chang et al. [2] used a U-Net convolutional neural network to segment melanoma dermoscopy images. The original dermoscopic images along with segmented images from the U-Net model were then fed as input into a deep skin lesion classification network consisting of two Inception V3 networks. When the segmentation and classification models were tested with the International Skin Imaging Collaboration (ISIC) dataset it achieved state-of-the-art results. Lin et al. [8] compared the performance of two approaches for skin lesion segmentation, i.e., K-Means based algorithm and U-net. When tested with the ISIC skin lesion dataset, the Dice coefficients for the U-net and K-Means were 0.78 and 0.62 respectively. These findings revealed that U-net performed better than the clustering approach. For segmentation of skin disease images, Codella et al. [4] created a convolutional neural network based on U-Net architecture with mixed HSV and RGB inputs of the channel. According to experimental results, the suggested technique performed comparably to the state-of-the-art models in segmentation and the results were in agreement with the ground truth which was within the spectrum of human specialists. Zhiwei Qin et al. [12] tried to increase the training dataset by using StyleGAN to generate synthetic lesion images. They carried out transfer learning for training the model and used ResNet50 model with pre-trained weights. Tschandl et al. [16] used the HAM10000 dataset to train VGG and ResNet networks and then placed the necessary layers into a U-Net architecture as encoders. On the official International Skin Imaging Collaboration (ISIC) 2017 challenge dataset [3], the deep learning model was trained in order to perform binary segmentation. Liu et al. [9] built a multiple branch system based on such an encoder-decoder network with two other components for segmentation of Cutaneous T-cell lymphomas into four classes. The first module, Lesion Area Learning, produces an attention map based which was based on the lesion edge characteristics and a binary segmentation outcome. The Feature Co-Learning module produces an attention map for every branch. Zhang et al. [20] proposed a metric-inspired loss function based on the Kappa index and utilised a simplified U-net to segment skin lesions. Cui et al. [5] presented an ensemble transductive learning technique for the purpose of segmentation to overcome this issue. The suggested method effectively reduces the difference between training and testing sets by directly inferring from U-Net. As a result, existing segmentation models generalization performance is improved significantly.

3   Methodology

The flow chart of the proposed deep learning model implemented in this paper is described in the Fig. 1. The methodology consists of various techniques, which include data augmentation, U-Net segmentation technique for segmentation of images, and MobileNetV2 classifier for detection and classification of the classes we used.

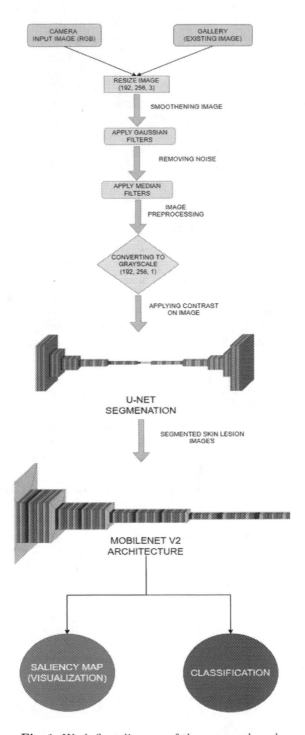

Fig. 1. Work flow diagram of the proposed work

3.1 Datasets

PH2 Dataset. The PH2 dataset [11] is an open-source dataset that has been developed for use in research and benchmarking purposes. It has been used widely by researchers for performing studies on segmentation and classification techniques of dermoscopic images. This PH^2 dataset consists of 200 skin lesion images of various skin diseases, i.e., melanocytic lesions, atypical nevi, common nevi, and melanomas. The PH^2 dataset also consists of segmented images of skin diseases, and histological and clinical diagnoses.

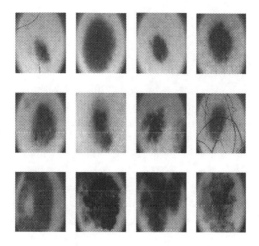

Fig. 2. PH2 Dataset

HAM10000. The HAM10000 dataset [15] is another open-source dataset consisting of 10015 dermatoscopic images, which can be used in training and testing of several deep learning algorithms. The dataset comprises images of all commonly occurring major skin diseases: (a) Actinic keratoses and intraepithelial carcinoma/Bowen's disease; (b) basal cell carcinoma; (c) benign keratosis-like lesions; (d) dermatofibroma; (e) melanoma; (f) melanocytic nevi; (g) vascular lesions (Fig. 3).

3.2 Data Augmentation

Data Augmentation comes into play when the available data for training is in limited amount. Augmentation helps to increase the amount of data available and thus helping to implement more accurate machine learning algorithms. Here, we increased the size of the PH2 dataset from two hundred to four hundred images by performing augmentation techniques on the skin lesion images such as horizontal flip, vertical flip, and random rotation (rotating the image at a specified angle). The size of each image in the dataset is 192 x 256 x 3.

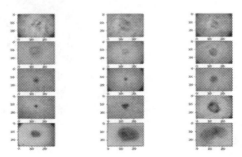

Fig. 3. HAM 10000

3.3   Preprocessing

The enhancement method entails using a modification filter called a Gaussian filter to smoothen the picture, whether it was acquired recently or from a database. In the proposed model, we have uses a median filter to eliminate undesired elements from the skin lesion images, such as noise. First, the image is resized into the shape of 360 x 360 x 3. Then the lesion image is transformed into grayscale image from RGB (Red, Green, Blue). For obtaining better performance, the quality of skin lesion images was improved by using contrast enhancement techniques. It is necessary to remove hair from a skin scan in order to properly evaluate the lesion image for accurate results (Fig. 4).

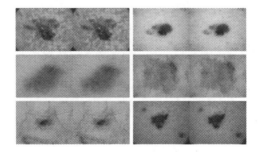

Fig. 4. Deblurring and Denoising of Skin Lesion Images

3.4   Image Segmentation

U-Net segmentation provides state-of-the-art results and is getting admired in the area of Bio-Medical Image segmentation. It is very promising and segmented images from U-Net are often used as input for training and testing various machine learning models. In our proposed classification model, we used the original and segmented masks of the Ph2 Dataset for trained the U-Net model.

Image augmentation was also used to increase the dataset size. The training was done for a hundred epochs, and stochastic gradient descent was used as the optimizer for the model. Equation 1 is the general formula of the Stochastic Gradient Descent (SGD) optimizer:

$$\omega := \omega - \frac{\eta}{n} \sum_{i=1}^{n} \nabla J_i (\omega) \tag{1}$$

where,

ω = parameter, i.e., weights and biases,

η = learning rate,

n = number of images in dataset,

J_i = value of loss function at i-th example

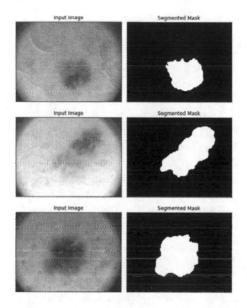

Fig. 5. U-Net generated segmented masks for skin lesion images from HAM10000

3.5   Classification

Apart from the fact that MobileNetV2 seeks to perform well on mobile devices, it gives highly accurate results nonetheless. We used the MobileNetV2 CNN architecture to classify and detect skin diseases. We trained the model on the HAM 10000 dataset with all seven classes, and the categorical cross-entropy loss function was used alongside the Adam optimizer for gradient descent. Imagenet [6] weights were used as the initial point for the MobileNetV2 model. We were able to achieve over 92% accuracy on the test dataset. Loss Function used is given in Eq. 2:

$$L = \frac{1}{M} \sum_{p}^{M} -\log\left(\frac{e^{s_p}}{\sum_{j}^{C} e^{s_j}}\right) \tag{2}$$

where,
M = Number of positive classes
C = Number of classes
s_p = CNN score for the positive class,
s_j = CNN scores obtained by the net for each class in C

3.6 Visualization Using Saliency Maps

Saliency maps find the regions that are most prominent or caught by the naked eye at all location points in the visual field. They help in guiding the selection of specific regions/locations based on the spatial distribution of saliency. In general, we require only a certain number of pixels to classify the classes used in training the machine learning model while doing image classification. In other words, the whole input is not significant for predicting the output class. Therefore, we have used saliency maps for highlighting the critical and important location points of the image and then only processing the highlighted parts. Saliency maps can be beneficial to get an estimate of the pixels in the image where the model is focusing while making predictions. Saliency maps are a great tool to inspect the model before training it on a large dataset. It helps decrease the computational burden massively and gives accurate image classification results. We used saliency maps while training to visualize the pixels the model was using for prediction, which helped in changing and fine-tuning the hyper-parameters.

4   Experimental Results

The HAM10000 dataset was split into two parts: eighty percent for training and twenty percent for testing and validation. A typical dataset of original images and their segmented masks as given in Fig. 5, was created and used for the experimental study. We used a variety of metrics to assess the performance of our model, including accuracy, precision, recall, and F1-score. Table 1 shows the calculated precision, recall, and F1-scores for all the seven classes available in the HAM10000 dataset. The computed class saliency maps for the skin disease images are shown in Fig. 6. Visualization using saliency maps helped immensely in checking the model's performance and fine-tuning the hyperparameters. The U-Net model used for training the PH2 dataset achieved a test-set accuracy of 98%. The results of segmented images generated by U-Net on the HAM10000 dataset are shown in Fig. 2. Segmentation produces a validation accuracy of 99% on the final processed dataset. We attained state-of-the-art results by introducing the segmented masks into the classification model. The classification model had

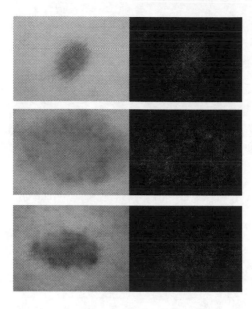

Fig. 6. Plots of Saliency Maps for various skin diseases

a precision and recall score of 0.91 each, with an accuracy of above 92%. The model outperformed the models indicated in Table 2 by a significant margin (Fig. 7).

Table 1. Precision, Recall and F1 Score for different classes in the dataset

Diseases	Precision	Recall	F1-Score
Actinic keratoses	0.92	0.82	0.87
Basal cell carcinoma	0.99	0.99	0.99
Benign keratosis	0.92	0.85	0.89
Dermatofibroma	0.94	0.92	0.93
Melanoma	0.86	0.92	0.89
Melanocytic nevi	1.00	1.00	1.00
Vascular lesions	0.76	0.95	0.80

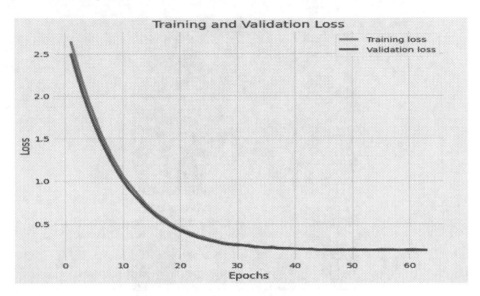

Fig. 7. Training Loss vs Number of Epochs

Table 2. Comparison of proposed model with existing models

Models	Accuracy	Precision	Recall
BILSK	91.21%	0.92	0.93
ResNet-50	84.42%	0.83	0.87
EfficientNet	87.91%	0.88	0.88
Mask-RCNN	88.50%	0.89	0.86
Proposed Model	92%	0.91	0.91

5   Conclusion

To demonstrate the effectiveness of the suggested system, it was utilized to diagnose skin disorders automatically and compared to existing methodologies. The evaluation metrics stated above were estimated for several parameters. The presented method's accuracy for segmentation task was 99%. When classifying the skin dataset images into the types of skin diseases for various metrics, the segmented images achieved nearly 92% accuracy.

After applying noise reduction improvements, two noise reduction approaches were examined. To enhance computational efficiency and the quality of training images, noise reduction filters such as the Gaussian filter and the median filter were used, as well as four colour spaces: RGB, YUV, HSV, and YCbCr for skin lesion and feature extraction. Saliency maps were used to depict the regional support of a certain class in the skin illness images for better visualization. We used segmented images for classification rather than the raw image data.

References

1. Balaji, V., Suganthi, S., Rajadevi, R., Krishna Kumar, V., Saravana Balaji, B., Pandiyan, S.: Skin disease detection and segmentation using dynamic graph cut algorithm and classification through Naive Bayes classifier. Measurement **163**, 107922 (2020). https://doi.org/10.1016/j.measurement.2020.107922. https://www.sciencedirect.com/science/article/pii/S0263224120304607

2. Chang, H.: Skin cancer reorganization and classification with deep neural network. CoRR abs/1703.00534 (2017). http://arxiv.org/abs/1703.00534

3. Codella, N.C.F., et al.: Skin lesion analysis toward melanoma detection: a challenge at the 2017 international symposium on biomedical imaging (ISBI), hosted by the international skin imaging collaboration (ISIC). In: 2018 IEEE 15th International Symposium on Biomedical Imaging (ISBI 2018), pp. 168–172 (2018). https://doi.org/10.1109/ISBI.2018.8363547

4. Codella, N.C.F., et al.: Deep learning ensembles for melanoma recognition in dermoscopy images. CoRR abs/1610.04662 (2016). http://arxiv.org/abs/1610.04662

5. Cui, Z., Wu, L., Wang, R., Zheng, W.-S.: Ensemble transductive learning for skin lesion segmentation. In: Lin, Z., et al. (eds.) PRCV 2019. LNCS, vol. 11858, pp. 572–581. Springer, Cham (2019). https://doi.org/10.1007/978-3-030-31723-2_49

6. Deng, J., Dong, W., Socher, R., Li, L.J., Li, K., Fei-Fei, L.: Imagenet: a large-scale hierarchical image database. In: 2009 IEEE Conference on Computer Vision and Pattern Recognition, pp. 248–255 (2009). https://doi.org/10.1109/CVPR.2009.5206848

7. Haddad, A., Hameed, S.A.: Image analysis model for skin disease detection: Framework. In: 2018 7th International Conference on Computer and Communication Engineering (ICCCE), pp. 1–4 (2018). https://doi.org/10.1109/ICCCE.2018.8539270

8. Lin, B.S., Michael, K., Kalra, S., Tizhoosh, H.: Skin lesion segmentation: U-nets versus clustering. In: 2017 IEEE Symposium Series on Computational Intelligence (SSCI), pp. 1–7 (2017). https://doi.org/10.1109/SSCI.2017.8280804

9. Liu, Z., et al.: Multi-class skin lesion segmentation for cutaneous T-cell lymphomas on high-resolution clinical images. In: Martel, A.L., et al. (eds.) MICCAI 2020. LNCS, vol. 12266, pp. 351–361. Springer, Cham (2020). https://doi.org/10.1007/978-3-030-59725-2_34

10. Melbin, K., Raj, Y.V.: An enhanced model for skin disease detection using dragonfly optimization based deep neural network. In: 2019 Third International conference on I-SMAC (IoT in Social, Mobile, Analytics and Cloud) (I-SMAC), pp. 346–351 (2019). https://doi.org/10.1109/I-SMAC47947.2019.9032458

11. Mendonça, T., Celebi, M., Mendonca, T., Marques, J.: Ph2: A public database for the analysis of dermoscopic images. Dermoscopy Image Anal. (2015)

12. Qin, Z., Liu, Z., Zhu, P., Xue, Y.: A GAN-based image synthesis method for skin lesion classification. Comput. Methods Programs Biomed. **195**, 105568 (2020). https://doi.org/10.1016/j.cmpb.2020.105568. https://www.sciencedirect.com/science/article/pii/S0169260720302418

13. Roy, K., Chaudhuri, S.S., Ghosh, S., Dutta, S.K., Chakraborty, P., Sarkar, R.: Skin disease detection based on different segmentation techniques. In: 2019 International Conference on Opto-Electronics and Applied Optics (Optronix), pp. 1–5 (2019). https://doi.org/10.1109/OPTRONIX.2019.8862403

14. Srinivasu, P.N., SivaSai, J.G., Ijaz, M.F., Bhoi, A.K., Kim, W., Kang, J.J.: Classification of skin disease using deep learning neural networks with mobilenet v2 and LSTM. Sensors **21**(8) (2021). https://doi.org/10.3390/s21082852. https://www.mdpi.com/1424-8220/21/8/2852

15. Tschandl, P., Rosendahl, C., Kittler, H.: The ham10000 dataset, a large collection of multi-source dermatoscopic images of common pigmented skin lesions. Sci. Data **5**(1), 1–9 (2018)

16. Tschandl, P., Sinz, C., Kittler, H.: Domain-specific classification-pretrained fully convolutional network encoders for skin lesion segmentation. Comput. Biol. Med. **104**, 111–116 (2019). https://doi.org/10.1016/j.compbiomed.2018.11.010. https://www.sciencedirect.com/science/article/pii/S001048251830372X

17. Velasco, J., et al.: A smartphone-based skin disease classification using mobilenet CNN. CoRR abs/1911.07929 (2019). http://arxiv.org/abs/1911.07929

18. Verma, A.K., Pal, S., Kumar, S.: Prediction of different classes of skin disease using machine learning techniques. In: Tiwari, S., Trivedi, M.C., Mishra, K.K., Misra, A., Kumar, K.K., Suryani, E. (eds.) Smart Innovations in Communication and Computational Sciences, pp. 91–100. Springer, Singapore (2021)

19. Zhang, J., Xie, Y., Wu, Q., Xia, Y.: Skin lesion classification in dermoscopy images using synergic deep learning. In: Frangi, A.F., Schnabel, J.A., Davatzikos, C., Alberola-López, C., Fichtinger, G. (eds.) MICCAI 2018. LNCS, vol. 11071, pp. 12–20. Springer, Cham (2018). https://doi.org/10.1007/978-3-030-00934-2_2

20. Zhang, J., Petitjean, C., Ainouz, S.: Kappa loss for skin lesion segmentation in fully convolutional network. In: 2020 IEEE 17th International Symposium on Biomedical Imaging (ISBI), pp. 2001–2004 (2020). https://doi.org/10.1109/ISBI45749.2020.9098404

An Alternate Approach for Single Image Haze Removal Using Path Prediction

Divyansh Agarwal and Amitesh Singh Rajput[✉]

Birla Institute of Technology and Science, Pilani, India
{f20180791,amitesh.singh}@pilani.bits-pilani.ac.in

Abstract. Haze removal is an important problem that existing studies have addressed from slight to extreme levels. It finds wide application in landscape photography where the haze causes low contrast and saturation, but it can also be used to improve images taken during rainy and foggy conditions. In this paper, considering the importance of haze removal and possible limitations of a well-known existing method, DehazeNet, we propose an alternate end-to-end method for single image haze removal using simple yet efficient image processing techniques. DehazeNet is among well performing haze removal schemes in the literature, however the problem of coloration and artifacts being produced in the output images has been observed for a certain set of images. Addressing this problem, the proposed solution is devised by taking advantage of the color features of the three color channels of an image to establish a decision criteria. Based on that, a suitable dehazing method for an input hazy image is selected. Removing the problem of poor coloration in output images, we have come up with an alternate method to remove the haze while retaining the visual and perceived quality of the image. The experimental results show that the proposed method yields better structural restoration, reduces haze content significantly, and does not cause any artifacts in the output image.

Keywords: DehazeNet · CLAHE · Gamma Correction · Single image haze removal

1 Introduction

Dust, smoke, and other dry particles can cause haze, a common atmospheric phenomena that reduces the clarity of the air. Haze significantly degrades visibility and causes many computer vision systems to fail. It poses problems for terrestrial photography since it may be necessary to penetrate large amounts of dense atmosphere to capture images of distant subjects. Due to light dispersion via the haze particles, this causes a visual illusion of a lack of contrast in the subject. The task of dehazing images for better visual clarity and information retrieval is a very utilitarian yet important problem in the industry. It also has a huge potential for use in security camera footage and video surveillance for identification of objects and people from clear images. It is a significant subject that has gotten a lot of global interest in the field of computer vision.

© The Author(s), under exclusive license to Springer Nature Switzerland AG 2023
D. Gupta et al. (Eds.): CVIP 2022, CCIS 1776, pp. 341–350, 2023.
https://doi.org/10.1007/978-3-031-31407-0_26

Due to the use of better assumptions and priors, single image haze removal has made significant progresses recently. The issue of reducing haze from a single image has been addressed using a variety of image enhancing techniques, including contrast or histogram-based, physics or nature model-based, and deep learning-based. Zhiyuan Xu et al. [1] proposed a Contrast Limited Adaptive Histogram Equalization (CLAHE) - based method to improve the poor contrast of images suffering from haze. This method establishes a maximum value to clip the histogram and redistributes the clipped pixels equally to each gray-level. In [2], Independent Component Analysis (ICA) based on minimal input is introduced to remove the haze from color images, but the method is time-consuming and unable to handle dense-haze images.

Narasimhan et al. [3] presented a model inspired from physics that describes the appearances of outdoor scenes in consistently poor weather conditions. The model includes a weather removal technique to restore scene contrast that does not need any prior knowledge of the specific weather state, scene structure, or distributions of scene reflectances. Park et al. [4] proposed a single dehazing algorithm through the estimation of local atmospheric light and transmission using a modified saturation evaluation metric and intensity difference. But this method fails to produce good results in low-light conditions. In [5], a technique to enhance night-time hazy scenes is proposed that builds on multi-scale fusion approach using several inputs derived from the original image. Night-time haze is estimated by computing the airlight component on image patch and not on the entire image.

Boyi Li et al. [6] proposed an image dehazing model called AOD-net which is based on a re-formulated atmospheric scattering model. Instead of estimating the transmission matrix and atmospheric light separately, it generates a clean image through a light-weight CNN. He Zhang et al. [7] proposed a densely connected pyramid dehazing network which jointly optimizes transmission map, atmospheric light and dehazed image. In [8], a convolutional neural network based architecture is proposed to estimate the transmission map of the hazy scene, so that the haze-free image can be reconstructed. The proposed network takes the hazy image as an input and extracts the haze relevant features using RNet and YNet, and generates two TrMaps. For the elimination of haze from a single image, Akshay et al. [9] suggested an end-to-end generative adversarial dehazing network. The Residual Inception GAN (RI-GAN) generating network is created using residual and inception concepts, and the Dense Residual Module (DRM) discriminator network is suggested to distinguish between fake and real data.

DehazeNet, a trainable CNN-based end-to-end system for medium transmission, is one of the deep learning-based techniques for removing haze. It emphasises that recovering an accurate medium transmission map is essential to achieving haze removal. In the design of DehazeNet, the feature extraction layer and the non-linear regression layer are distinguished from classical CNNs. Instead of ReLU or Sigmoid, a new activation function termed BReLU is employed to maintain bilateral constraint and local linearity for picture restoration. This lightweight architecture enables DehazeNet to exceed state-of-the-art methods in terms of efficiency and dehazing outcomes. However, apart from its significant performance, we found that DehazeNet still suffers from certain limitations for a specific category of images. Upon performing the haze removal computations on a standard dataset of hazy images (part of the standard RESIDE [10] dataset) using DehazeNet, we made an observation in the output images as - For some input images, after the image was passed through the DehazeNet, the output image produced coloration in some portions of the image. This significantly caused degradation in the image quality and in some cases caused certain white and grey areas of the original image to get overly saturated. In this paper, we address these problems by deriving a statistical measure from color features of the underlying image. The artifacts observed with the DehazeNet in the output images and improvements achieved by the proposed method are shown in Fig. 1.

(a) Hazy input (b) DehazeNet output (c) Our result

Fig. 1. Coloration observed in DehazeNet [11]

The main contributions of this paper are described as follows.

1. An end-to-end method for single image haze removal using simple yet efficient image processing techniques is proposed that aim to rectify the problem of coloration in output images.
2. A decision criteria is established by utilizing pixel intensity values of the three channels of the underlying image for choosing a suitable dehazing method for an input hazy image.
3. An alternate method using novel image processing techniques to dehaze an image and achieve appreciable image qualities in the output is proposed.
4. The proposed method is assessed by evaluating scores for several standard image evaluation metrics and comparing them against other existing methods.

The proposed method is an improvement over other methods for images which show coloration and artifacts, especially in day light scenario where poor exposure is observed and coloration is a problem. Our method solves this problem by achieving better results while also maintaining an appreciable image quality. The dehazing method proposed can be utilised in improving visibility of surveillance footage since the method is fast and efficient and can also assist drivers in poor weather conditions.

2   Proposed Work

The primary objective of the proposed method is to overcome the problem of coloration and artifacts while processing some input hazy images with the DehazeNet. To accomplish this, a statistical decision criteria for choosing a suitable method to dehaze the image is derived after performing rigorous experimentation on the input images. The initial experiments are conducted by considering images from Outdoor SOTS data which is part of the standard RESIDE dataset [10]. We considered 500 outdoor hazy images, synthesized artificially from natural images since naturally occurring hazy image training data is not very abundant. The coloration or artifacts in the output images from DehazeNet were observed only for a subset of input images which led to the investigation into the characteristic properties of the underlying input images.

The primary objective of the proposed approach is to predict upfront whether an input image would produce coloration or not after processing through the DehazeNet. This would help us in choosing an alternate and a more appropriate path for removing haze from that particular image and to obtain better visual output. We propose a simple yet efficient method utilizing image processing techniques for haze removal that solves these two problems by (1) Establishing a decision criteria and model to predict coloration upfront for input hazy images; (2) Proposing an alternate and a better method to remove haze from such images without compromising on the visual quality and visibility.

2.1   Color Class Labeling for Path Prediction

The first step accumulates finding the best color class and labelling it accordingly so that a decision criteria for image haze removal can be established. To predict the coloration path, initially, all images are labeled for their respective color classes. This is achieved by passing all the hazy images present in the dataset through the DehazeNet model for haze removal and observing the outputs visually. Based on whether or not artifacts or coloration was visible in the output, correct class label $C \in \{C_1, C_2\}$ is given to the input image. The images that produce coloration after processing through DehazeNet are labeled to class C_1, whereas images belonging to class C_2 are clean and do not produce any coloration after processing through DehazeNet. These class labels are also used to confirm the results of our established decision model and test the prediction accuracy of the model (explained later in the paper).

Once class labeling is done, two possible paths are established for dehazing an input image, namely P_1 and P_2. The proposed decision model predicts the suitable path for dehazing a particular image, which is then chosen to dehaze that image. The two paths are described as follows -

- P_1 : Input is passed through DehazeNet to obtain the Output.
- P_2 : Input is processed through Gamma Correction and then CLAHE to obtain the Output.

The **Input** is the hazy image passed to the model and **Output** is the dehazed image that we get as output from the model. The P_1 is the suitable path for dehazing images that do not show coloration when passed through DehazeNet, whereas P_2 is the alternate method that we propose in this paper to dehaze those images which would otherwise show artifacts or coloration in the output if they were passed through DehazeNet. This is a simple yet efficient method that utilizes a combination of image processing techniques - *Gamma Correction* and *Contrast Limited Adaptive Histogram Equalization (CLAHE)*. It reduces haze content of the image and at the same time does not degrade the visual quality or visibility of the elements of the image.

2.2   Predicting Coloration

To establish a decision criteria, the mean pixel intensity values for hazy images are employed for predicting coloration upfront. The images which show coloration suggest some mean value for pixel intensity for the three channels that was noticeably higher than the mean pixel intensity value for images that do not show coloration. In accordance with this observation, we establish two different classification functions, $f_1(x), f_2(x)$, to predict the appropriate path for dehazing an image. Their functioning is described in Algorithms 1 and 2 respectively, where R, G, and B (Red, Green, and Blue) are the three color channels of the underlying image. The $S_m^R(x), S_m^G(x), S_m^B(x)$ are the mean pixel intensity values of the input image x, for the three channels respectively. The function

---

Algorithm 1. Classification function 1: $f_1(x)$

    Input: Input hazy image x, Pixel threshold value t
    Output: Suitable dehazing path $\rightarrow path$
Compute $count = N(S_m^R(x), S_m^G(x), S_m^B(x), t)$
if $count = 3$ **then**
    $path \leftarrow P1$
else
    $path \leftarrow P2$
end if
Return $path$

Algorithm 2. Classification function 2: $f_2(x)$

    Input: Hazy image x, Pixel threshold value t
    Output: Suitable dehazing path $\rightarrow path$
Compute $count = N(S_m^R(x), S_m^G(x), S_m^B(x), t)$
if $count = 2$ or 3 **then**
    $path \leftarrow P1$
else
    $path \leftarrow P2$
end if
Return $path$

$N(S_m^R(x), S_m^G(x), S_m^B(x), t)$ gives a count of the number of channels which have mean pixel intensity value greater than a threshold value of t.

To arrive at the optimal value of pixel threshold t which gives the best accuracy, the two classification functions $f_1(x)$ and $f_2(x)$ are evaluated for a range of values of t and their path classification accuracies are compared. Figure 2 shows a comparison of classification accuracies for a range of t values where it has been found that the first classification function $f_1(x)$ gives the best possible results for predicting the suitable path to dehaze an image with a path prediction accuracy of **84.10%** (accuracy was computed by comparing the actual dehazing path for an image with the path predicted by the classification function). The corresponding optimal pixel threshold value t came out to be **117**, as observed from the graph in Fig. 2.

2.3 Alternate Method for Haze Removal

The images for which $f_1(x)$ predicted the suitable dehazing path as P2 were processed by our proposed alternate method for haze removal. We experimented with a number of novel image processing techniques in an attempt to come up with an alternate and a better method for dehazing images. This method does not produce any coloration in the output and also reduces the haze content. Some of the methods that we combined and experimented with were CLAHE, Gamma Correction, Adaptive Gamma correction, Adaptive CLAHE, and other notable methods for color correction, color restoration and contrast enhancement.

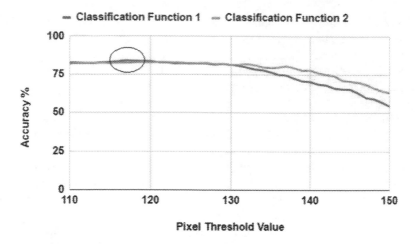

Fig. 2. Classification Accuracies v/s Pixel Thresholds

Visual observation of the results from the different image processing techniques shows that doing a gamma correction processing on the input image followed by CLAHE (Contrast Limited Adaptive Histogram Equalization) produces the best output results both in terms of visual quality as well as in terms of the various image evaluation metrics. In contrast to conventional histogram equalisation techniques, CLAHE employs a number of ways, each of which corresponds to a different area of the image, to disperse the image's brightness value. This improves the visibility level of foggy photos. It is a variant of Adaptive Histogram Equalization (AHE) which takes care of over-amplification of the contrast and preserves the visual quality of the image. Gamma correction is an exponential operation used to encode and decode luminance or tristimulus values in images and we tuned it for our use case of removing haze from images. The technique regulates the overall brightness of the image, and changing the gamma correction's quantity alters not just the brightness but also the proportions of red, green, and blue in the image. Ultimately, our algorithm is summarised in Algorithm 3.

3   Results

In this section, we analyze the proposed method, its inner components, and the DehazeNet. Every experiment is run on a computer with an Intel Core i7 8th Gen 8750,H processor running at 2.2 GHz using 8 GB of RAM, with a dedicated GPU of Nvidia GeForce GTX 1050 Ti, with the machine running a Windows 10 operating system. The experiments are performed over outdoor hazy images from the SOTS dataset which is part of the standard RESIDE dataset [10]. We considered a pool of 500 outdoor hazy images to run our experiments efficiently. For assessment, five diverse metrics - UQI (Universal Quality Index),

SSIM (Structural Similarity Index Measure), TMQI (Tone Mapped image Quality Index), FADE (Fog Aware Density Evaluator) and PSNR (Peak Signal to Noise Ratio) are used. The metrics can be grouped into three categories - to measure the haze content in the image (FADE), to measure the structural quality of the image (SSIM) and, to measure the visual and perceived quality of the image (UQI, PSNR, TMQI). FADE is an absolute computation over the dehazed image and low FADE score means low haze content in the image. SSIM is computed as a comparison between the dehazed image and the ground truth and high SSIM score means high similarity between the two images. UQI is an absolute computation over the dehazed image and higher the UQI score, better the image quality. PSNR computes the peak signal-to-noise ratio, in decibels, between two images and higher the PSNR, the better the quality of the reconstructed image. TMQI is an absolute computation over the dehazed image for an objective quality assessment and high TMQI means better image quality. Since the overall appearance of an image should be appreciable, we considered all five metrics during the experimentation and compared our results with the ground truth, wherever possible.

Considering the path prediction for the underlying images and processing them as per the suggestion by the proposed method, it has been found that no coloration is produced in the output images. Moreover, the haze content in the underlying image is reduced while maintaining its overall visual quality. We compare our approach with existing dehazing techniques in order to show the efficiency of our proposed method. Table 1 shows a comparison of the performance of the various methods and the values for different metrics. When analyzing Table 1, it has been found that the proposed method achieves best dehazing effects and visual perceived quality while maintaining decent structural properties of the underlying image. We compare the proposed method with the below four approaches on the hazy images that were challenging to dehaze from the dataset. The results are shown in Fig. 3.

Algorithm 3. Proposed Model

    Input: Hazy image x

    Output: Dehazed image y

Evaluate Dehazing path from function: $path \leftarrow f_1(x)$

if $path = P1$ **then**

    Obtain output y by processing input x with DehazeNet

    $y = DehazeNet(x)$

else if $path = P2$ **then**

    Obtain output y by processing input x with Gamma Correction followed by CLAHE

    $y = CLAHE(GammaCorrection(x))$

end if

Table 1. Quantitative Evaluation. Comparison of different metric scores for output images across various methods

Methods	UQI	SSIM	TMQI	FADE	PSNR
CLAHE	0.79	0.81	0.22	0.88	16.39
Gamma Correction	0.83	0.86	0.225	0.97	19.72
CLAHE + Gamma	0.81	0.78	0.226	0.59	17.41
DehazeNet	0.76	0.77	0.221	0.63	19.72
Proposed Method	0.86	0.82	0.227	0.58	18.87

Fig. 3. Results. (a) is the input hazy image **(b)** is the output produced by DehazeNet which shows coloration and artifacts in the output **(c)** is the output produced by our method which is free from any artifacts and has a better image quality and visibility than DehazeNet output.

4 Conclusion

We have introduced a simple yet effective model to remove haze from images by using well known image processing techniques. Our method not only removes the haze content from the image, but also maintains the visual quality of the image and overcomes the coloration problem observed in DehazeNet for the outdoor SOTS dataset. We use the mean pixel intensities of the images to derive a path prediction function for the input image which gives the suitable path through which the image should pass for haze removal. The function has a prediction accuracy of 84.10% on the outdoor SOTS dataset. Final subjective and objective results show that our method outperforms DehazeNet and other image processing techniques because it does not cause coloration or show artifacts in the outputs. Our method achieves best or second-best results for all the image evaluation metrics. In the future, there is still scope to improve the proposed method by enhancing the color intensities in the output image and making them more prominent.

References

1. Xu, Z., Liu, X., Ji, N.: Fog removal from color images using contrast limited adaptive histogram equalization. In: 2009 2nd International Congress on Image and Signal Processing, pp. 1–5 (2009)
2. Fattal, R.: Single image dehazing. ACM Trans. Graph. SIGGRAPH **27**, 1–9 (2008)
3. Narasimhan, S.G., Nayar, S.K.: Contrast restoration of weather degraded images. IEEE Trans. Pattern Anal. Mach. Intell. **25**(6), 713–724 (2003)
4. Park, H., Park, D., Han, D.K., Ko, H.: Single image haze removal using novel estimation of atmospheric light and transmission. In: 2014 IEEE International Conference on Image Processing (ICIP), pp. 4502–4506 (2014)
5. Ancuti, C., Ancuti, C.O., De Vleeschouwer, C., Bovik, A.C.: Night-time dehazing by fusion. In: 2016 IEEE International Conference on Image Processing (ICIP), pp. 2256–2260 (2016)
6. Li, B., Peng, X., Wang, Z., Jizheng, X., Feng, D.: AOD-Net: all-in-one dehazing network. In: 2017 IEEE International Conference on Computer Vision (ICCV), pp. 4780–4788 (2017)
7. Zhang, H., Patel, V.M.: Densely connected pyramid dehazing network. In: 2018 IEEE/CVF Conference on Computer Vision and Pattern Recognition, pp. 3194–3203 (2018)
8. Dudhane, A., Murala, S.: RYF-Net: deep fusion network for single image haze removal. IEEE Trans. Image Process. **29**, 628–640 (2020)
9. Dudhane, A., Singh Aulakh, H., Murala, S.: RI-GAN: an end-to-end network for single image haze removal. In: 2019 IEEE/CVF Conference on Computer Vision and Pattern Recognition Workshops (CVPRW), pp. 2014–2023 (2019)
10. Li, B., Ren, W., Dengpan, F., Tao, D., Feng, D., Zeng, W., Wang, Z.: Benchmarking single-image dehazing and beyond. IEEE Trans. Image Process. **28**(1), 492–505 (2019)
11. Cai, B., Xiangmin, X., Jia, K., Qing, C., Tao, D.: Dehazenet: an end-to-end system for single image haze removal. IEEE Trans. Image Process. **25**(11), 5187–5198 (2016)

Detecting Tropical Cyclones in INSAT-3D Satellite Images Using CNN-Based Model

Soumyajit Pal[1,2]([⊠]) [iD], Uma Das[1] [iD], and Oishila Bandyopadhyay[1] [iD]

[1] Indian Institute of Information Technology Kalyani, Kalyani, West Bengal 741235, India
{soumyajit_phd21,uma,oishila}@iiitkalyani.ac.in
[2] St. Xavier's College (Autonomous), Kolkata, West Bengal 700016, India

Abstract. The devastation caused by a natural disaster like tropical cyclone (TC) is beyond comprehension. Livelihoods are damaged and take years on end to fix. An automated process to detect its presence goes a long way in mitigating a humanitarian crisis that is waiting to occur. With the advent of deep learning techniques, Convolutional Neural Network (CNN) has had significant success in solving image-related challenges. The current study proposes a CNN based deep network to classify the presence or absence of TC in satellite images. The model is trained and tested with multi-spectral images from INSAT-3D satellite obtained from Meteorological & Oceanographic Satellite Data Archival Centre (MOSDAC) of Indian Space Research Organization (ISRO), Government of India, and an average accuracy of 0.99 is obtained with the proposed architecture. The number of parameters trained are only 1.9 million, which is far less than earlier studies. The detection process described in this study can serve as the first step in better predicting TC tracks and intensity for disaster management and to minimize the impacts on human lives and economy of the country.

Keywords: Tropical Cyclone · Convolutional Neural Network · Cross-entropy loss · MOSDAC · Remote Sensing

1 Introduction

Cyclones are an occasional severe weather phenomenon and are being recorded for a long time in human history [1]. However, their impact is being felt on a large scale in the past few decades [2]. According to the World Meteorological Organization Atlas of Mortality and Economic Losses [2], the years from 1970 to 2019 saw the second largest loss of human lives due to tropical cyclones (TCs), extra-tropical storms and convective storms. The article [2] also elucidates that the top ten storms are all TCs, not only in terms of maximum economic damage but also loss of human lives. Depending upon the region of occurrence, these storms take on different names. In the Indian Ocean, this phenomenon is called TC, and in other parts of the world, it is known as hurricane or typhoon. The year 2017 alone saw the formation and subsequent destruction caused by three of the deadliest storms in the Atlantic Ocean - hurricanes Harvey, Maria and Irma. These three storms together accounted for 35% of the total economic losses caused

© The Author(s), under exclusive license to Springer Nature Switzerland AG 2023
D. Gupta et al. (Eds.): CVIP 2022, CCIS 1776, pp. 351–363, 2023.
https://doi.org/10.1007/978-3-031-31407-0_27

by natural disasters from 1970 to 2019 [2]. Many researchers [3, 4] argue that climate change has had a lot to do with the growth of intensity of these storms and is often attributed to human activities. Authors in [3, 4] explore how the man-made activities are contributing to the formation of cyclones and find merit in the claim. Thus, it would not be factually incorrect to arrive at a seemingly alarming conclusion that anthropogenic activities are indirectly contributing to the increasing devastation that is being caused by cyclones. Thus, the importance of TC prediction as a pressing problem of social and economic impacts can be established without a shadow of a doubt for appropriate mitigation activities.

Current data-driven era is the best time to investigate this cataclysmic weather phenomenon because of the abundance of data that is available at the disposal of researchers and the industry, alike. Satellites are now being launched on a more frequent basis than ever in order to monitor weather, climate change, human settlements and other related phenomena. Coupled with this is the availability of massive computational power in the form of sophisticated Graphics Processor Units (GPUs) and abundant primary and secondary storage devices. Furthermore, deep learning frameworks such as Keras and Tensorflow [5, 6] are enabling the rapid development of new algorithms and architectures to solve real-world challenges faster. The confluence of data availability, modern hardware and powerful algorithms make deep learning an ideal choice to address big-data problems. Convolutional Neural Networks (CNNs) have proven to be very effective [7] in the recent past for image related studies. As data is available for investigations of TCs, the current study focuses on building a custom CNN architecture to perform a binary classification to detect the presence or absence of a TC in a given satellite image.

Extensive research on TCs has been taking place for the past many years. Cyclones tend to be a very complex weather phenomenon and are hard to quantify. There are many aspects of TCs that can be investigated from the perspective of research. TC track prediction is one such challenge. To predict the track of the storm, authors in [8] explore the features extracted from clouds found in National Oceanic and Atmospheric Administration-Advanced Very High Resolution Radiometer (NOAA-AVHRR) satellite images. The shape and other relevant features of clouds surrounding the TC are automatically learnt using an Artificial Neural Network (ANN). These features govern the direction in which the cyclone would move, thereby giving an automated way to predict its future track. A 3-stage track prediction model is proposed in [9]. In the first stage, inputs from the satellite image dataset and cyclone track dataset are analyzed to keep only those variables which are highly correlated with the target variable of cyclone track. This is followed by stage two, where the selected inputs are passed to a CNN model for feature extraction. Finally, a Gated Recurrent Unit (GRU) layer is used to predict the track of the TC at the next instant of time. In [10], the cyclone track is estimated in terms of latitude and longitude by using a window that moves over the central region of the storm over a time interval of 24 h. A combination of past trajectory data from NOAA International Best Track Archive for Climate Stewardship (IBTrACS), three dimensional atmospheric images of wind and three-dimensional atmospheric images of pressure from European Centre for Medium-Range Weather Forecasts (ECMWF) Re-Analysis (ERA)-Interim is used for developing the neural network model, which can generate results rapidly. There also exists work on the detection of TC intensity. In [11], a deep convolutional neural network is developed to automatically extract features from cyclonic clouds which are then used to estimate the intensity of the storm. A Long Short Term Memory (LSTM) model is developed in [12] to predict the intensity. Satellite images from Meteosat 5 (2001 to 2007) and Meteosat 7 (2007 to 2016), sampled at a 6-h frequency, were used in [13] to build an automated 3-stage deep learning model (mask region-CNN) with high precision and true negative rate to classify images over the North Indian Ocean as cyclonic or non-cyclonic with an accuracy of 0.86. An ensemble CNN which can balance the disparity between the number of cyclonic and non-cyclonic images [14] to detect not only TCs but also their precursors over western North Pacific Ocean, using simulated Outgoing Longwave Radiation (OLR) data collected over a time span of 20 years has also been developed and implemented with an accuracy of 0.9.

The objectives and contributions of the current work can be summarized as follows:

- to detect the presence / absence of cyclones in multi-spectral images of Indian National Satellite System 3D series (INSAT-3D) provided by the Meteorological & Oceanographic Satellite Data Archival Centre (MOSDAC) with a 30-min cadence, using a deep learning-based approach.
- to develop a CNN architecture with fewer number of parameters to be trained in comparison to earlier studies
- scalability of the model architecture across various sizes of datasets; going from as small as 200 images to over 6000 images.

This is the first step in the investigations of TC genesis, development and landfall to enable its track and intensity prediction for developing data driven forecast models and capability for the Bay of Bengal (BoB) region.

In the rest of the paper, the data used for the study is discussed in Sect. 2, methodology in Sect. 3, analysis in Sect. 4, results in Sect. 5 and conclusions in Sect. 6.

2   Data

INSAT-3D multi-spectral images of Asian sector are obtained from MOSDAC for four TCs in BoB region – PHAILIN, FANI, AMPHAN, and YAAS. To label the images as cyclonic or non-cyclonic, storm bulletin reports from the Indian Meteorological Department (IMD) are relied upon [15–18] as reference points and the timestamp found in the image files are used to automate the labeling process. Also, the number of non-cyclonic images far exceeds the number of cyclonic images in all the four storm datasets. To keep the dataset balanced and allow the neural network to learn the underlying features in a systematic manner, only a subset of the non-cyclonic images is chosen. For AMPHAN, the timeline considered for gathering the cyclonic satellite images is May 16, 2020, UTC – 00:00 to May 21, 2020, UTC – 12:00 [15], whereas the timeline for gathering the non-cyclonic satellite images is May 10, 2020, UTC – 00:00 to May 15, 2020, UTC – 23:30 [15]. Similar approach is adopted for YAAS, FANI, and PHAILIN and the details are given in Table 1.

All satellite images are obtained from the MOSDAC portal, which is maintained by ISRO, Government of India. INSAT-3D, commissioned in 1983, generates these images using the IMAGER payload [19]. It images the Earth from geostationary altitude across six bands of the electromagnetic spectrum. One of these lies in the visible band (VIS) in the wavelength range of 0.52 to 0.72 μm. The remaining five bands are spread across the infrared region – 1.55 μm to 1.70 μm for shortwave infrared (SWIR), 3.80 μm to 4.00 μm for mid wave infrared (MIR), 6.50 μm to 7.00 μm for water vapor (WV), 10.2 μm to 11.2 μm for the first split band of thermal infrared (IR1) and 11.5 μm to 12.5 μm for the second split band of thermal infrared (IR2). The resolution of these bands varies from 1 km for VIS and SWIR to 4 km and 8 km for MIR and IR1, IR2, respectively. In the current study, images in MIR, WV, IR1 and IR2 bands are investigated and the numbers of images considered for each band are also summarized in Table 1.

Table 1. Details of images investigated in the current study

TC	Timeline for Cyclone Images	Timeline for N-Cyclone Images	Band	Images (no.)	Cyclone	N-Cyclone
AMPHAN [15]	May 16 2020, UTC 0000 – May 21, 2020, UTC 1200	May 10 2020, UTC 0000- May 15 2020, UTC 2330	IR1	512	247	265
			IR2	511	246	265
			MIR	510	245	265
			WV	510	245	265
YAAS [18]	May 23 2021, UTC 0029 - May 28, 2021, UTC 2130	June 1 2021, UTC 0000 - June 6 2021, UTC 2000	IR1	534	265	269
			IR2	537	267	270
			MIR	537	267	270
			WV	537	267	270
FANI [16]	April 29, 2019, UTC 0500 - May 3, 2019, UTC 1700	May 4, 2019, UTC 0200 - May 8, 2019, UTC 1430	IR1	375	185	190
			IR2	375	185	190
			MIR	375	185	190
			WV	375	185	190
PHAILIN [17]	October 9, 2013, UTC 1200 - October 13, 2013, UTC 1200	October 1, 2013, UTC 0000 to October 8, 2013, UTC 0330	IR1	217	107	110
			IR2	217	107	110
			MIR	217	107	110
			WV	217	107	110

For experimentation purpose, the four bands IR1, IR2, WV and MIR are considered. In Table 1, the column header Cyclone refers to the number of cyclonic images that have been used. Similarly, N-Cyclone refers to the total number of non-cyclonic images considered.

3   Methodology

The study is performed in three stages – data acquisition, design of deep learning model and analysis. In the first stage, INSAT-3D satellite multi-spectral image data are obtained from MOSDAC [19] for the four storms for the durations detailed in Table 1. The number of N-Cyclone images far exceeds the count of Cyclone images for each storm. N-Cyclone images are sampled to keep the overall dataset perfectly balanced or nearly balanced. Stratified K-fold cross validation with K = 5 is used for evaluating the models. The first K-1, i.e., four folds are used for training, and the remaining fold is used for testing. This is repeated for K, i.e., five folds. The mean of accuracy, precision, recall and f-score for all five folds are recorded.

The proposed CNN architecture is based on the sequential model where the input for the ith layer is the output of the $(i-1)^{th}$ layer. Grayscale images are used for experimentation having a single channel and a uniform height and width of 201 pixels each. The first layer in the proposed CNN is the input layer which is responsible for generating the satellite image. This is followed by a series of alternating convolution and pooling layers as illustrated in the architecture in Fig. 1.

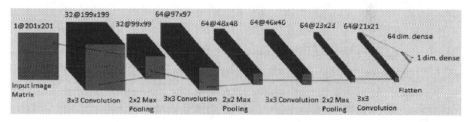

Fig. 1. The used CNN Architecture

The CNN model is designed using a combination of convolution layers and max pooling layers followed by two fully connected layers (Fig. 1). The pooling layers in between two consecutive convolutional layers ensure that the input features to be learnt are within computational limits and the model that is being proposed is not overfitted. This is ensured by downsizing the dimensions of the image in a consistent manner. To obtain a 1-D tensor which would be used for classification, flattening of the output tensor generated from the final convolution layer is carried out. Lastly, the output of the flattening operation is fed to the fully connected layer which predicts the presence or absence of TC in the input satellite image.

Barring the first convolutional layer (conv1) that consists of 32 filters, the remaining three convolutional layers (conv2, conv3, conv4) are made up of 64 kernels each. All the convolution layers have a filter size of (3 x 3) while the pooling operations (maxpool1, maxpool2, maxpool3) use a 2 × 2 kernel in each case. A uniform stride (denoted by s) of one is applied for all convolution and pooling layers. No padding (denoted by p) is applied to the feature maps. The first dense layer (fc1) is made up of 64 neurons while the second dense layer (fc2) has exactly 1 neuron. This configuration is given in Table 2 and the number of parameters to be learnt by each layer are shown in the last column. The entire architecture learns about 1.9 million parameters.

Table 2. Configuration of the proposed CNN model

Network Layer	Shape	Output Size	Parameter Shape	Parameters
Input	1@201 × 201			
conv1	32@3 × 3, s = 1, p = 0	199 × 199	(32, 1, 3, 3)	320
maxpool1	2 × 2, s = 1, p = 0	99 × 99		
conv2	64@3 × 3, s = 1, p = 0	97 × 97	(64, 32, 3, 3)	18496
maxpool2	2 × 2, s = 1, p = 0	48 × 48		
conv3	64@3 × 3, s = 1, p = 0	46 × 46	(64, 64, 3, 3)	36928
maxpool3	2 × 2, s = 1, p = 0	23 × 23		
conv4	64@3 × 3, s = 1, p = 0	21 × 21	(64, 64, 3, 3)	36928
fc1	64		(64, 28224)	1806400
fc2	1		(1, 64)	65
Total number of parameters				1899137

Rectified Linear Unit (ReLu) was the activation function of choice for all the layers except the last fully connected layer, which uses sigmoid, to generate a probabilistic output for a binary classification problem. The binary cross-entropy loss function is used for error estimation and Adam optimizer is used for optimizing the weights during training. The training of the model is carried out with a learning rate of 0.0001 in 8 iterations. Accuracy, along with precision, recall and f-score, are used as metrics for performance evaluation.

4   Analysis

The satellite images considered for experimentation are from four spectral bands, namely, IR1, IR2, MIR and WV. A sample of images from each band for the storm AMPHAN are shown in Fig. 2. Figure 3 gives a visual overview of the obtained results in the classification and misclassification of both cyclonic as well as non-cyclonic images. With the help of stratified K-fold cross validation, the entire dataset for each band and storm is considered for the purpose of evaluation.

The architecture of the proposed CNN along with the dataset for a TC from a particular band makes up a model. For example, a model is trained and tested for YAAS IR1 images. This implies the existence of a total of 16 models (4 bands for each storm). Also, for each storm, all image bands are combined to produce a new dataset, hereinafter referred to as ALL models. This leads to the creation of another 4 models. This is followed by taking into account images from all four storms in a given band leading to the creation of 4 more models, hereinafter referred to as MERGED models. Finally, images from all four bands of all four storms are combined to generate the largest dataset for the final model referred to as MERGED-ALL model. For each of these 25 models, the size of the dataset is highly varying.

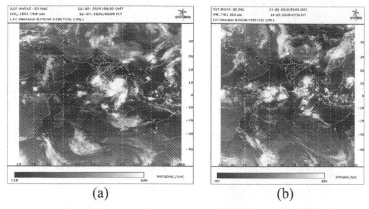

Fig. 2. Sample INSAT-3D satellite images a) during and b) before AMPHAN obtained from MOSDAC

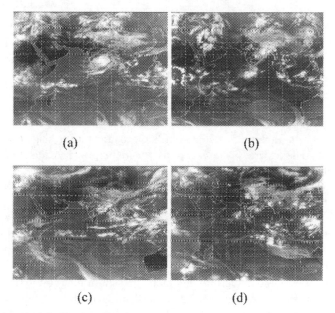

Fig. 3. Sample visual results (a) cyclonic image classified as cyclonic (b) cyclonic image misclassified as non-cyclonic (c) non-cyclonic image classified as non-cyclonic (d) non-cyclonic image misclassified as cyclonic

5   Results

Evaluation of each model is carried out based on four parameters – accuracy, precision, recall and F1-Score, which are defined as follows:

$$Accuracy = \frac{Number\ of\ correctly\ classified\ satellite\ images}{Total\ number\ of\ satellite\ images\ considered} = \frac{TP + TN}{TP + FP + FN + TN} \tag{1}$$

$$Precision = \frac{Number\ of\ correctly\ classified\ cyclonic\ images}{Total\ number\ of\ cyclone\ images\ considered} = \frac{TP}{TP + FP} \tag{2}$$

$$Recall = \frac{Number\ of\ correctly\ classified\ cyclonic\ images}{Total\ number\ of\ images\ which\ are\ actually\ cyclonic} = \frac{TP}{TP + FN} \tag{3}$$

$$F - Score = Harmonic\ Mean\ of\ Precision\ and\ Recall = \frac{2 * Recall * Precision}{Recall + Precision} \tag{4}$$

TP = True Positive = Cyclones correctly predicted as cyclones by the CNN.
FP = False Positive = Non-cyclones incorrectly predicted as cyclones by the CNN.
FN = False Negative = Cyclones incorrectly predicted as non-cyclones by the CNN.
TN = True Negative = Non-cyclones correctly predicted as non-cyclones by the CNN.

The cross validation (CV) scores for average accuracy (Avg. Acc.), average precision (Avg. Pr.), average recall (Avg. Recall) and average f-score (Avg. F-Score) for all 25 models are shown in Table 3. Selected confusion matrices from the testing phase are shown in Fig. 4. The accuracy and loss plots for training and validation for the ALL models are shown in Fig. 5.

The average accuracy obtained in the current study is 0.99. The lowest accuracy value is close to 0.94 for the MIR band of images for FANI. Consistently high values for all metrics are obtained regardless of the size of the dataset. For instance, the dataset for PHAILIN contains only 217 images. Nonetheless, the CNN reports at least 94% f-score for all bands. On the other hand, the MERGED model makes use of a total of 6556 images for cross validation. It also reports very high measures of precision and recall among other metrics without overfitting, which is a sign of the proposed architecture's power of scalability across various sized datasets. The curves for training and validation accuracy almost coincide at the eighth epoch, which denotes the absence of overfitting (Fig. 6). This also indicates that the model has high generalization.

The proposed method is a light-weight, energy-saving CNN with fewer number of parameters. It outperforms the existing TC detection methods [13, 14] and the details are summarized in Table 4.

6   Summary and Conclusion

INSAT-3D images are analyzed for binary classification to detect presence/absence of cyclone. The objective is successfully achieved with an average accuracy of 0.99. This is verified through the high measures of accuracy, precision, recall and f1-score, which

Table 3. Performance summary of all models

Storm	Band	Avg. Acc CV Score	Avg. Pr CV Score	Avg. Recall CV Score	Avg. F-Score CV Score
AMPHAN	IR1	0.979	0.986	0.965	0.975
	IR2	0.998	0.994	0.984	0.989
	WV	0.974	0.979	0.986	0.982
	MIR	0.967	0.948	0.979	0.963
	ALL	0.994	0.996	0.983	0.989
FANI	IR1	0.997	0.997	0.983	0.990
	IR2	0.971	0.989	0.973	0.981
	WV	0.992	0.993	0.989	0.991
	MIR	0.937	0.911	0.961	0.935
	ALL	0.996	0.986	0.978	0.982
YAAS	IR1	0.998	0.999	0.989	0.994
	IR2	0.998	0.998	0.993	0.995
	WV	0.997	0.996	0.992	0.994
	MIR	0.923	0.914	0.945	0.929
	ALL	0.998	0.994	0.983	0.988
PHAILIN	IR1	0.991	0.986	0.991	0.988
	IR2	0.996	0.998	0.992	0.995
	WV	0.948	0.996	0.991	0.993
	MIR	0.943	0.892	0.998	0.942
	ALL	0.998	0.995	0.981	0.988
MERGED	IR1	0.993	0.990	0.981	0.985
	IR2	0.997	0.993	0.997	0.995
	WV	0.992	0.991	0.997	0.994
	MIR	0.998	0.991	0.976	0.983
	ALL	0.991	0.998	0.989	0.993

have been obtained on the MOSDAC dataset. Thus, it can be concluded that the INSAT-3D satellite images worked upon can be harnessed further to extract useful details such as future track and intensity of storms.

Although the results obtained are promising, more investigations are required to investigate the process of automatic feature extraction. This will help in better understanding of the architecture, thereby leading to the development of more robust prediction models.

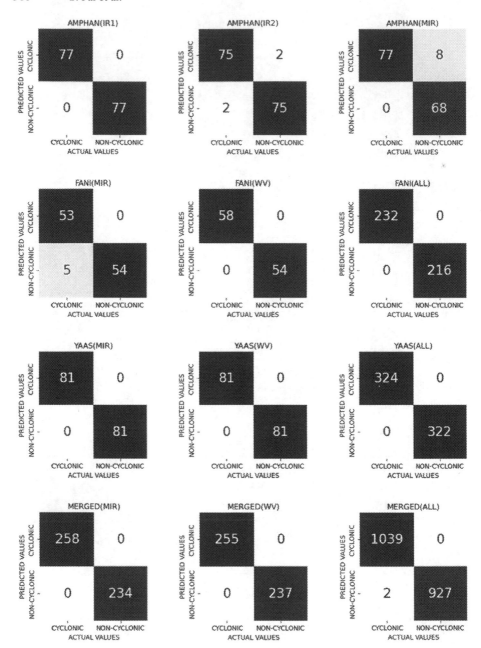

Fig. 4. Confusion matrices for a few models

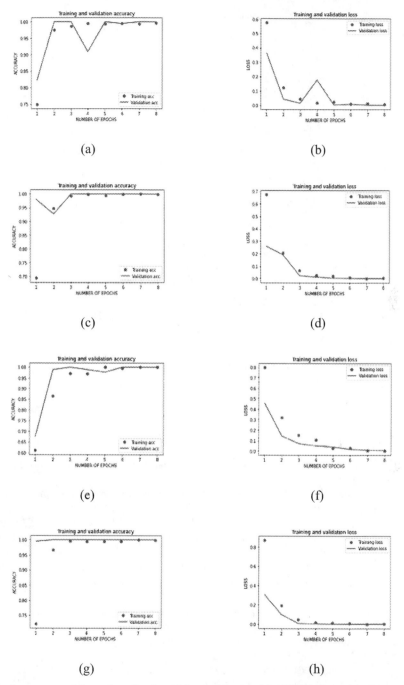

Fig. 5. Accuracy and loss plots for the ALL models: (a)-(b) AMPHAN, (c)-(d) FANI, (e)-(f) PHAILIN, (g)-(h) YAAS

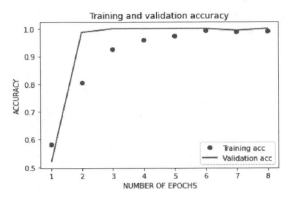

Fig. 6. Plot of Accuracy v/s Number of Epochs for the MERGED model

Table 4. Comparison with existing models

Work	Technique	Number of parameters	Region	Accuracy
Nair et al. 2022 [13]	Mask-region CNN	25.4 million	North Indian Ocean	0.86
Matsuoka et al. 2018 [14]	Ensemble CNN	> 2 billion	North Pacific Ocean	0.9
Current Study	**2-D CNN**	**1899137**	**BoB**	**0.99**

References

1. Emanuel, K.: Tropical cyclones. Annu. Rev. Earth Planet. Sci. **31**, 75–104 (2003). https://doi.org/10.1146/annurev.earth.31.100901.141259
2. Smith, A.: The Atlas of Mortality and Economic Losses from Weather, Climate and Water Extremes (1970–2019) (2021)
3. Knutson, T., et al.: Tropical Cyclones and Climate Change Assessment: Part I. Detection and Attribution. Bull. Am. Meteorol. Soc. **100**. (2019). https://doi.org/10.1175/BAMS-D-18-0189.1
4. Knutson, T., et al.: Tropical cyclones and climate change assessment: part ii. projected response to anthropogenic warming. Bull. Am. Meteorol. Soc. **101**. (2019). https://doi.org/10.1175/BAMS-D-18-0194.1
5. Abadi, M., et al.: TensorFlow: Large-scale machine learning on heterogeneous systems, Software (2015). tensorflow.org
6. Chollet, F., et al.: Keras (2015). https://keras.io.software
7. Deng, J., Dong, W., Socher, R., Li, L.-J., Li, K., Li, F.-F.: ImageNet: a large-scale hierarchical image database. In: IEEE Conference on Computer Vision and Pattern Recognition, pp.248–255 (2009).https://doi.org/10.1109/CVPR.2009.5206848
8. Kovordányi, R., Roy, C.: Cyclone track forecasting based on satellite images using artificial neural networks. ISPRS J. Photogramm. Remote. Sens. **64**, 513–521 (2009). https://doi.org/10.1016/j.isprsjprs.2009.03.002

9. Lian, J., Dong, P., Zhang, Y., Pan, J., Liu, K.: A novel data-driven tropical cyclone track prediction model based on CNN and GRU with multi-dimensional feature selection. IEEE Access **8**, 97114–97128 (2020). https://doi.org/10.1109/ACCESS.2020.2992083
10. Giffard-Roisin, S., Yang, M., Charpiat, G., Bonfanti, C., Kegl, B., Monteleoni, C.: Tropical cyclone track forecasting using fused deep learning from aligned reanalysis data. Frontiers Big Data. **3**, 1 (2020). https://doi.org/10.3389/fdata.2020.00001
11. Pradhan, R., Aygun, R.S., Maskey, M., Ramachandran, R., Cecil, D.J.: Tropical cyclone intensity estimation using a deep convolutional neural network. IEEE Trans. Image Process. **27**(2), 692–702 (2018). https://doi.org/10.1109/TIP.2017.2766358
12. Li, Y., Yang, R., Yang, C., Yu, M., Hu, F., Jiang, Y.: Leveraging LSTM for rapid intensifications prediction of tropical cyclones. ISPRS Ann. Photogramm. Remote Sens. Spatial Inf. Sci. **IV-4/W2**, 101–105 (2017). https://doi.org/10.5194/isprs-annals-IV-4-W2-101-2017
13. Aravind Nair, K.S.S., et al.: A deep learning framework for the detection of tropical cyclones from satellite images. IEEE Geosci. Remote Sens. Lett. **19**, 1–5 (2022). https://doi.org/10.1109/LGRS.2021.3131638
14. Matsuoka, D., Nakano, M., Sugiyama, D., Uchida, S.: Deep learning approach for detecting tropical cyclones and their precursors in the simulation by a cloud-resolving global nonhydrostatic atmospheric model. Prog. Earth Planet Sci. **5**(1), 1–16 (2018). https://doi.org/10.1186/s40645-018-0245-y
15. India Meteorological Department (IMD) Report on Amphan, May 16, 2020 - May 21, 2020. https://internal.imd.gov.in/press_release/20200614_pr_840.pdf. Accessed 5 Nov 2022
16. India Meteorological Department (IMD) Report on Fani, April 26, 2019 - May 4, 2019. https://reliefweb.int/sites/reliefweb.int/files/resources/fani.pdf. Accessed 5 Nov 2022
17. India Meteorological Department (IMD) Report on Phailin, October 8, 2013 - October 14, 2013. https://nwp.imd.gov.in/NWP-REPORT-PHAILIN-2013.pdf. Accessed 5 Nov 2022
18. India Meteorological Department (IMD) Report on Yaas, May 25, 2021. https://mausam.imd.gov.in/Forecast/marquee_data/10.%20National_Bulletin_20210524_1800UTC.pdf. Accessed 5 Nov 2022
19. 19038/SAC/10/3DIMG_L1C_SGP, MOSDAC. (https://mosdac.gov.in). Accessed 5 Dec 2022

Two Stream RGB-LBP Based Transfer Learning Model for Face Anti-spoofing

Aashania Antil and Chhavi Dhiman[(✉)]

Delhi Technological University, Delhi, India
`chhavi.dhiman@dtu.ac.in`

Abstract. Face spoofing detection has enthralled attention due to its requirement in face access control-based systems. Despite the recent advancements, existing traditional and CNN-based face authentication algorithms are still prone to a variety of presentation attacks, especially those unknown to the training dataset. In this work, we propose a robust transfer learning-based face anti-spoofing framework to boost the generalization by considering both RGB images and Local Binary Patterns (LBPs). The presented methodology fuses the distinct features of RGB images with texture features of LBP images, encrypted as pre-trained Xception network-based features for anti-spoofing. Performance of the proposed framework is evaluated on two public database- CASIA-FASD and Replay-Attack under both intra and inter-dataset test conditions. The proposed work is compared with other state-of-the-art methods and shows improved generalization, achieving HTER of 13.3% and 11.9% in cross-dataset testing on CASIA-FASD and Replay-Attack respectively.

Keywords: Transfer Learning · Local Binary Patterns (LBPs) · Presentation Attack Detection · Face Anti-Spoofing

1 Introduction

Biometrics for authentication have gained widespread acceptance in recent years. Face recognition is silent and contactless during information capture compared to other biometric-based techniques. This has made facial recognition ubiquitous in authentication application such as device unlocking (Apple FaceID, Window Hello, Face Unlock in android), payment authentication, access control, immigration, etc. However, the easy availability of face samples from social media renders facial recognition vulnerable to presentation attacks. A physical-layer attack known as Presentation attack, sometimes also referred to as spoofing attack, targets the input channel of id verification systems. To prevent unauthorized access, most devices incorporate additional modalities. These come at the expense of increasing hardware and computation costs, as well as user discomfort. Thus, curtailing reliable deployment for general use.

Traditionally, PAD has been reliant on manual methods for feature extraction and attack detection. These methods are very sensitive to environmental and lighting changes. In the past decade, significant research and developments in deep learning has paved

© The Author(s), under exclusive license to Springer Nature Switzerland AG 2023
D. Gupta et al. (Eds.): CVIP 2022, CCIS 1776, pp. 364–374, 2023.
https://doi.org/10.1007/978-3-031-31407-0_28

the way for software-based PAD techniques. This stems from the ability of the deep neural architectures to capture high-level details from images or video frames. A robust model which can adapt to environment and other changes can be trained and deployed faster than creating entirely novel solutions on a case-to-case basis. This will result in increased stability, reliability, and scalability for commercial use.

Motivated from above discussion, a frame-level transfer learning-based framework has been proposed for PAD. The proposed network uses the Xception model [1] as backbone for the feature extraction pipeline as the separable depth wise convolutions in the architecture result in lighter model with smaller no. of parameters. Also, it has been reported in ILSVRC competition [1] that the design of Xception model has achieved superior performance over InceptionV3 architecture for ImageNet dataset. We estimate the efficacy of our methodology by experimenting on two public datasets, namely, CASIA-FASD [2] and Replay-Attack [3].

2 Related Works

Traditional Methods. Earlier, many traditional methodologies were brought forward as countermeasures for face authentication systems such as texture-based [4], image quality based [5], recapturing based [6], liveness detection [7], and hybrid based-methods [8]. These methods require rich prior knowledge of the researcher for algorithm design and deployment. The extracted features were passed to supervised classifiers (e.g., SVM, LDA) [9] for binary classification. To extract discriminative and generalized patterns, definite data domains have also been exploited, beginning from GLCMs [10] and later shifting to RGB, HSV, and YCbCr. Frequency domain and temporal features have also been utilized in many works [11] to differentiate between bonafide and fake faces. For instance, few authors [6] observed abnormal movements such as hand-holding to catch spoof attacks. While some researchers focused on some types of distortions such as deformation of faces, color analysis, blurriness, etc. [5],to differentiate between authentic and spoof faces. Despite numerous proposals, the lack of a general solution, sensitivity to environmental changes has these methods strenuous to implement.

Deep Learning Methods. Deep learning FAS/PAD methodologies have received an increased focus from research communities in recent year. Deep learning approaches consider FAS/PAD a binary classification problem and thus opt for binary supervision. In contrast to traditional methods, deep methods learn mapping functions automatically from an input with the help of advanced architectures [12] and regularization techniques [13]. Thus, leading to continuous, gradual, yet compounding improvements as the models and techniques mature with newer datasets. This, coupled with continuous efforts by researchers has led deep learning-based approaches to dominate the FAS field. Works such as Lucena et al. [14] and Chen et al. [15] considered pre-trained VGG16 and ResNet18 models for face countermeasure whereas, in [16], Mobile level network is utilized. For temporal clues aggregation, [17] [18] have cascaded frame-level CNN features with LSTM. Apart from CNNs, a pre-trained vision transformer based approach is reported in [19] for end-to-end FAS/PAD.

Additionally, fusion-based methods have also been explored in recent studies. These methods fuse features extracted from traditional based methods and CNNs. CNNs tend to extract high-level features from images, whereas, traditional based methods extract low-level features, fusing these, may result in increased robustness of FAS/PAD systems [20].

Limitations. From the recent literature, it's evident that deep methods have surpassed traditional-based approaches. There's a lack of large scale, publicly available, diverse datasets for FAS. Thus, CNN-based methods tend to suffer from overfitting, end-up learning unfaithful patterns, and even resulting in performance degradation for some architectures. Hybrid methods (deep learning + traditional methods) have been explored [20] to overcome such issues but the increased modalities in some methods may result in increased computational cost, severely restricting deployment feasibility to real world. In addition, another drawback is exploiting videos in many algorithms. In the cell phone authentication scenario, presentation attack detection decisions time is momentary. Hence, frame-based face PAD may be beneficial from a usability point of view.

3 Proposed Work

Hybrid networks provide better stability and achieve robustness when facing distinct type of attacks. Thus, a frame-level deep learning-based method is proposed for recognizing face presentation and spoofing attacks, using both manual and deep network features analysis. Both RGB and LBP frames are employed as simultaneous inputs into the Xception backbone. Discriminative local features for different portions of image obtained from LBP operation as frames are fed into an Xception network for high-level feature extraction. The output of this pipeline is then concatenated with high level RGB features to increase the robustness of the FAS framework. The resulting feature set is used by fully connected layers for anti-spoofing.

3.1 Xception Model

The Xception model [1] consists of three modules, each called as a 'flow'. As shown in Fig. 1, these three modules are labelled as Entry flow, Middle flow and Exit flow. Unlike inception model, Xception relies solely on depth-wise separable convolution layers and residual connections. The residual connections prevent the gradient from disappearing during the training, while depth-wise separable convolution reduces the number of parameters. Moreover, it learns channel correlation and spatial correlation separately. This methodology makes it comparatively efficient from other backbone networks by reducing computational complexity [1]. Thus, making it an appropriate baseline feature extraction network for our proposed architecture.

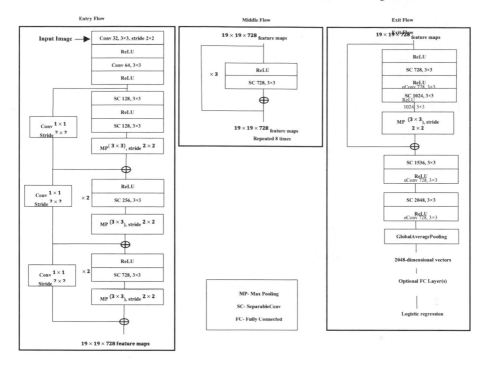

Fig. 1. Basic Xception model [1]

3.2 Local Binary Patterns (LBP)

The local binary pattern (LBP) [3] is a computationally simple, efficient non-parametric operator used to describe of local image features. A per-pixel binary code is obtained by comparing its 8 neighbor pixels with the value of the center pixel, resulting in an ordered binary set. The LBP can thus be expressed as the decimal equivalent version of an octet binary integer. The classic LBP descriptor for a pixel P is mathematically given by:

$$LBP_{IJ}(P_c) = \sum_{j=0}^{J-1} G(P_j - P_c)2^j, \tag{1}$$

In Eq. (1), P_c represents the gray level of center pixel, P_j the gray level of jth neighbor pixel and G is a thresholding function defined as:

$$G(x) = \begin{cases} 0, & x < 0 \\ 1, & otherwise \end{cases} \tag{2}$$

These per-pixel labels generated by LBP can be converted to an equivalent LBP frame. The computational simplicity and robustness of LBP towards illumination changes, makes it suitable for face PAD techniques. As shown in Fig. 2, there is a visible difference in LBP of real and spoofed samples as LBP is very sensitive to local features such as illumination changes.

Figure 3 shows the overall proposed architecture. For each branch, different Xception models were utilized, one taking RGB frames as input while other accepting LBP frames. To acquire more precise and consistent features for representation, the outputs of two streams were combined into one and routed to the three consecutive dense layers of dimensions [128 × 1], [64 × 1] and [2 × 1]. The final output is the actual face presentation attack prediction probability.

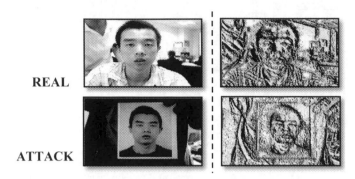

Fig. 2. Real and spoof sample images from CASIA-FASD datasets and their corresponding LBP features

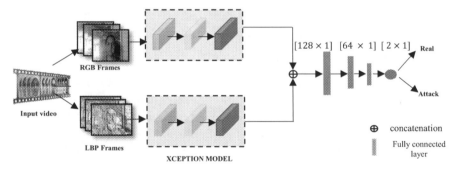

Fig. 3. The overall proposed framework with two stage architecture. Stage 1 takes pre-processed input frames fed into pretrained Xception models individually for feature extraction. RGB stream extracts high level features and LBP stream extracts low-level features. Extracted features are fused and fed into the Stage 2 for distinguishing attack and bonafide samples. The latter part of model is trained simultaneously for LBP and RGB frames.

4 Experimental Analysis

Here, we estimate the performance of our proposed work by experimenting on Replay-Attack and CASIA-FASD, for both intra-database and inter-database scenarios. A fair comparison has been made with existing state-of-the-art.

Datasets. Replay-Attack (RA) consists of video and photo samples for 50 clients under different illumination conditions for a total of 1300 clips. The dataset has been split into 4 sub-groups: test data for error reporting, development data for threshold estimation, enroll data and training data. Since our work is a face anti-spoofing-based experiment, enrolment samples take no notice.

CASIA-FASD (CF) dataset holds images of 50 distinct subjects with 5105 client images and 7509 imposter images. CASIA-FASD as available, is split into 2 subsets-test-set and train-set. We further split the train samples into two sub-parts in 70:30 ratio for validation data. It includes three types of spoofing images i.e., warping the photo, cutting photo, and displaying on an electronic screen attack in varying qualities, respectively. For each subject, 3 real and 9 fake (spoofing attempt) sequences are provided.

Evaluation Metrics. Our evaluation is in accordance with the associated protocols for each dataset. Since CF doesn't provide a 'dev' set, we only considered the EER (equal error rate) parameter of the test set. For RA dataset, both EER and HTER (half total error rate) of the testing set have been computed. EER is referred to a point on ROC or DET curve where FAR (false acceptance rate) and FRR (false rejection rate) are equal.

$$EER = (FAR = FRR) \tag{3}$$

HTER is the point at which the average of false acceptance rate (FAR) and false rejection rate (FRR) is lowest.

$$HTER = \frac{FAR + FRR}{2} \tag{4}$$

Additionally, ROC curves and confusion matrices for the experiments have also been displayed in Figs. 4 and 5 respectively. ROC curve stands for receiver operating characteristics and represents TPR and FPR pairs for different decision thresholds.

Data Pre-Processing. Processing complete video files is computationally expensive, and frame by frame, the change in a video is very minimal. Thus, videos were sampled at interval of ten frames and then resized to 299x299. To raise the numeral of the specimen, random horizontal flips (probability = 0.5) were implemented while training. LBP for each sampled frame was calculated for immediate neighbor ($R = 1$, $P = 8$). Pixel wise representation of LBP was used.

Training. The proposed network was implemented with tensor-flow and the experiment was performed on 'Google Colab Pro' with GPU runtimes using Nvidia P100 GPU with 16GB RAM. The pre-trained Xception models were fine-tuned on RGB and LBP data individually with a batch size set to 16 for 5 epochs. As the amount of training data is limited, 5 number of epochs are used to avoid overfitting. The outputs of resulting models were fused and further trained on both RA and CF datasets. The model was optimized with Adam optimizer with learning rate set at 0.0001. Callbacks were employed to select the best model with lowest validation loss for the dev set.

Intra-Database Testing. Intra-test was performed on CF and RA dataset to evaluate our proposed network. Table 1 reports results on CF while RA results are covered in Table 2.

Table 1. Intra-database testing comparison results on CF dataset

Methods	EER (%)
Fine-tune VGG face [21]	5.2
Attention [15]	3.14
LiveNet [22]	4.59
DPCNN [21]	4.5
Dropblock [23]	1.12
Ours	**12.34**

Table 2. Intra-database testing comparison results on RA dataset

Methods	HTER (%)	EER (%)
CompactNet [24]	0.7	0.8
Fine-tune VGG face [21]	4.3	8.4
Attention [15]	0.25	0.13
LiveNet [22]	5.74	-
DPCNN [21]	6.1	2.9
Dropblock [23]	0.29	0.00
Ours	**4.58**	**9.69**

The proposed framework when trained and tested on CASIA-FASD, the model yielded a similar HTER of 4.8% but with a higher EER at 12.34%. Whereas, on Replay-Attack dataset, performed satisfactorily with an HTER of 4.6% and EER of 9.69%. These results are on par as reported by similar works.

Inter-Database Testing. To exemplify the strong generalization of our approach, we perform the inter-database testing and compared our results with other state-of-arts. We preferred the most widely used inter-testing cases: CF *vs* RA dataset. The results are reported in Table 3. The proposed approach obtains the lowest HTER (11.9% and 13.3%) for both datasets among other state-of-arts. This shows our model is capable enough to learn more generalized features. Figure 4 shows the ROC curve obtained for intra and inter-dataset whereas, Fig. 5 presents the confusion matrix for both intra and inter datasets. It's clearly visible from ROC curve that the model when trained on RA dataset has better generalization performance as compared to CF.

Table 3. Comparison of Inter-Testing on CF and RA datasets

Methods	Training: CASIA-FASD Testing: Replay-Attack		Training: Replay-Attack Testing: CASIA-FASD	
	HTER (%)	EER (%)	HTER (%)	EER (%)
Attention [15]	30	-	33.4	-
SfSNet [25]	29.8	-		-
Anomaly [26]	25.00	-	16.74	-
KSA [27]	33.1	-	32.1	-
Deep Learning [28]	48.2	-	45.4	-
Color texture [4]	30.3	-	37.7	-
Motion Mag [29]	50.1	-	47	-
Ours	**11.9**	**51.4**	**13.3**	**27.8**

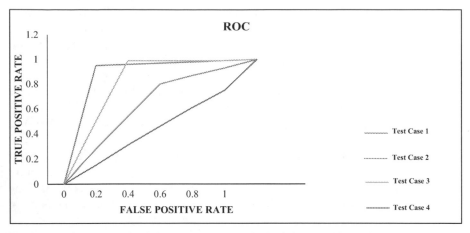

Fig. 4. ROC curves obtained for proposed work for both intra and inter-database testing conditions. *Test case1*: Train and Test with Replay Attack; *Test Case 2:* Train with Replay-Attack, Test with CASIA FASD; *Test Case 3:* Train and test with CASIA FASD, *Test Case 4:* Train with CASIA FASD, Test with Replay Attack

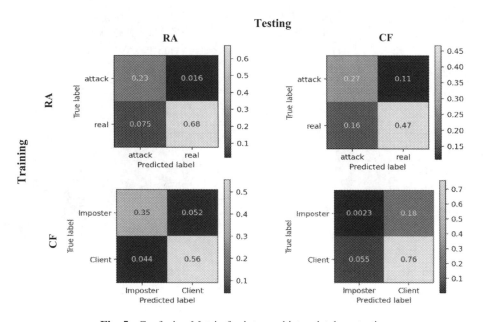

Fig. 5. Confusion Matrix for intra and inter-database testing

5   Conclusion

In this research, a novel architecture is proposed for face spoofing detection using Xception model backbone for feature extraction. Models trained on simple RGB input tend to suffer from lack of enough discriminant features for robust detection and are not very resilient towards illumination changes. Comparatively, LBPs are very sensitive to texture information in images. LBP generation is, fast, computationally cheap, doesn't require any additional hardware and can be implemented independent of any input stream. RGB stream extracts large scale features from images which is complimented with local features extracted by the LBP stream. Aggregation of these features enhances accuracy and reliability over using deep learning-based models individually. With our proposed work, we obtained promising results on par with other state-of-arts. The intra-dataset testing reports satisfactorily show the capabilities of our approach for face anti-spoofing. The inter-dataset testing achieves better HTER (11.9% and 13.3%) for both CASIA-FASD and replay-attack datasets representing better generalization capability of our architecture.

References

1. Chollet, F.: Xception: deep learning with depthwise separable convolutions. In: IEEE Conference on Computer Vision and Pattern Recognition (CVPR), Honolulu, HI, USA (2017)
2. Zhang, Z., et al.: A face antispoofing database with diverse attacks. In: 5th IAPR International Conference on Biometrics (ICB), New Delhi, India (2012)
3. Chingovska, I., Anjos, A., Marcel, S.: On the effectiveness of local binary patterns in face anti-spoofing. In: BIOSIG - Proceedings of the International Conference of Biometrics Special Interest Group (BIOSIG), Darmstadt, Germany (2012)
4. Boulkenafet, Z., Komulainen, J., Hadid, A.: Face spoofing detection using color texture analysis. IEEE Trans. Inf. Forens. Secur. **11**(8), 1818–1830 (2016)
5. Boulkenafet, Z., Komulainen, J., Hadid, A.: Face antispoofifing using speeded-up robust features and fisher vector encoding. IEEE Signal Process. Lett. **24**(2), 141–145 (2017)
6. Akhtar, Z., Foresti, G.L.: Face spoof attack recognition using discriminative image patches. J. Elcct. Comput. Eng. **2016**, 14 (2016)
7. Tirunagari, S., Poh, N., Windridge, D., Iorliam, A., Suki, N., Ho, A.T.S.: Detection of Face Spoofing Using Visual Dynamics. IEEE Trans. Inf. Forensics Secur. **10**(4), 762–777 (2015)
8. Chingovska, I., Anjos, A.R.: On the use of client identity information for face anti-spoofing. IEEE Trans. Inf. Forensics Secur. **10**(4), 787–796 (2015)
9. Raghavendra, R.J., Kunte, R.S.: A Novel Feature Descriptor for Face Anti-Spoofing Using Texture Based Method. Cybern. Inf. Technol. **20**(3), 159–176 (2020)
10. Pinto, A., Schwartz, W.R., Pedrini, H., Rocha, R.: Using visual rhythms for detecting video-based facial spoof attacks. IEEE Trans. Inf. Forensics Secur. **10**(5), 1025–1038 (2015)
11. Das, D., Chakraborty, S.: Face liveness detection based on frequency and micro-texture analysis. In: International Conference on Advances in Engineering and Technology Research (ICAETR), Unnao, India (2014)
12. Huang, G., Liu, Z., Maaten, L.V.D., Weinberger, K.Q.: Densely connected convolutional networks. In: IEEE Conference on Computer Vision and Pattern Recognition (CVPR) (2017)
13. Ioffe, S., Szegedy, C.: Batch normalization: accelerating deep network training by reducing internal covariate shift. In: 32nd International Conference on Machine Learning, PMLR, Lille, France (2015)
14. Lucena, O., Junior, A., Moia, V., Souza, R., Valle, E., Lotufo, R.: Transfer learning using convolutional neuralnetworks for face anti-spoofing. In: International Conference Image Analysis and Recognition, Montreal, Canada (2017)
15. Chen, H., Hu, G., Lei, Z., Chen, Y., Robertson, N.M., Li, S.Z.: Attention based two-stream convolutional networks for face spoofing detection. IEEE Trans. Inf. Forensics Secur. **15**, 578–593 (2019)

16. Heusch, G., George, A., Geissbuhler, D., Mostaani, Z., Marcel, S.: Deep Models and Shortwave Infrared Information to Detect Face Presentation Attacks. arXiv:2007.11469 (2020)
17. Yang, X., et al.: Face anti-spoofing: model matters, so does data. In: IEEE/CVF Conference on Computer Vision and Pattern Recognition (CVPR), Long Beach, CA, US (2019)
18. Muhammad, U., Holmberg, T., Melo, W.C., Hadid, A.: Face antispoofing via sample learning based recurrent neural network. In: The British Machine Vision Conference(BMVC), Cardiff, UK (2019)
19. George, A., Marcel, S.: On the Effectiveness of Vision Transformers for Zero-shot Face Anti-Spoofing arXiv:2011.08019
20. Cai, R., Chen, C.: Learning deep forest with multi-scale Local Binary Pattern features for face anti-spoofing. arXiv:1910.03850 (2019)
21. Li, L., Feng, X., Boulkenafet, Z., Xia, Z., Li, M., Hadid, A.: An original face anti-spoofing approach using partial convolutional neural network. In: Sixth International Conference on Image Processing Theory, Tools and Applications (IPTA), Oulu, Finland (2016)
22. Rehman, Y.A.U., Po, L.M., Liu, M.: Livenet: Improving features generalization for face liveness detection using convolution neural networks. Expert Syst. Appl. 108(15), 159–169 (2018)
23. Wu, G., Zhou, Z., Guo, Z.: A robust method with dropblock for face anti-spoofing. In: International Joint Conference on Neural Networks (IJCNN), Shenzhen, China (2021)
24. Li, L., Xia, Z., Jiang, X., Roli, F., Feng, X.: Compactnet: learning a compact space for face presentation attack detection. Neurocomputing. **409**(7), 191–207 (2020)
25. Pinto, A., Goldenstein, S., Ferreira, A., Carvalho, T., Pedrini, H., Rocha, A.: Leveraging shape, reflectance and albedo from shading for face presentation attack detection. Trans. Inf. Forens. Secur. **15**, 3347–3358 (2020)
26. Perez-Cabo, D., Jimenez-Cabello, D., Costa-Pazo, A., Lopez-Sastre, R.J.: Deep anomaly detection for generalized face anti-spoofing. In: CVPR, Long Beach, CA (2019)
27. Benlamoudi, A., Aiadi, K.E., Ouafi, A., Samai, D., Oussalah, M.: Face antispoofing based on frame difference and multilevel representation. J. Electron. Imaging. **26**(4) (2017)
28. Menotti, D., et al.: Deep Representations for Iris, Face, and Fingerprint Spoofing Detection. IEEE Trans. Inf. Forens. Secur. **10**(4), 864–879 (2015)
29. Li, H., Li, W., Cao, H., Wang, S., Huang, F., Kot, A.C.: Unsupervised domain adaptation for face anti-spoofing. TIFS **13**(7), 1794–1809 (2018)
30. Baweja, Y., Oza, P., Perera, P., Patel, V.M.: Anomaly Detection-Based Unknown Face Presentation Attack Detection. arXiv:2007.05856 (2020)

Logarithmic Progressive-SMOTE: Oversampling Minorities in Retinal Fundus Multi-disease Image Dataset

Sachin Panchal$^{(\boxtimes)}$ (ID) and Manesh Kokare (ID)

Shri Guru Gobind Singhji Institute of Engineering and Technology,
Nanded, Maharashtra, India
{2021pec202,mbkokare}@sggs.ac.in

Abstract. Multiple retinal diseases co-occur more frequently. It is extremely challenging to effectively diagnose several diseases in an image and provide appropriate treatment for those diseases with high accuracy. The performance of such an imbalanced dataset, which has minority classes, can be enhanced. The Retinal Fundus Multi-Disease Image Dataset (RFMiD) is a collection of 3200 Multi-labeled Imbalanced Dataset (MLID) marked with 46 different disease labels. The suggested Logarithmic Progressive Synthetic Minority Oversampling Technique (LP-SMOTE) is intended to oversample the minority classes in imbalanced dataset. The Imbalance Ratio Per Label (IRPL) and Mean Imbalance Ratio (MeanIR) are used and assessed to distinguish the minority and majority classes. The logarithmic progressive sampling per label is applied to minority classes. The Oversampling is implemented to level up the samples in minority classes. The proposed technique improved the overall minority class samples by 5.4 times. After employing LP-SMOTE technique, the overall validation accuracy and test accuracy is improved by 2.81% and 4.53% respectively on VGG19 pre-trained model.

Keywords: Oversampling · Transfer Learning · Data Analysis

1 Introduction

1.1 Motivation

Near or far vision impairment affects at least 2.2 billion individuals worldwide. One billion people have moderate to severe distance vision impairment or blindness. However, as per WHO report of 2019, 88.4 million people had uncorrected refractive error, 94 million had cataracts, 7.7 million had glaucoma, and 3.9 million had diabetic retinopathy [1,2]. As per the recent fact sheet of WHO, Diabetes caused 1.5 million fatalities in 2019, with 48% of all diabetes-related deaths occurring before the age of 70. In Southeast Asia, diabetic retinopathy (DR) is a leading cause of vision loss and blindness. In 2015, diabetic retinopathy (DR) caused 1.07% of blindness and 1.25% of mild to severe visual impairment [3].

D. Gupta et al. (Eds.): CVIP 2022, CCIS 1776, pp. 375–389, 2023.
https://doi.org/10.1007/978-3-031-31407-0_29

Age-related macular degeneration and glaucoma afflicted 195.6 and 76 million persons in 2020, respectively, with a projected increase to 243.4 and 95.4 million by 2030. Major cause of eye diseases includes lifestyle and ageing population [4]. Aside from common disorders, there are several unusual conditions that can damage vision.

It is challenging to design and develop an algorithm for MLID datasets. The data cleaning and data processing aid to improve the performance of the model. The data cleaning is used to detect insufficient data and process on it accordingly. The data processing is needed after data cleaning operation that includes dimensionality reduction. MLID datasets require resampling of data to balance all classes present in datasets. SMOTE is used to over-sample the minority class using data augmentation techniques [5]. The amount of over-sampling on different classes is depend upon the amount of samples available in a class. Some researchers worked on RFMiD dataset to balance datasets by oversampling minority classes like MLSMOTE, Multi-label Tomek Link, DeepSMOTE, ensembling learning etc. Even though there is tremendous growth in technology, imbalanced dataset remains a fundamental challenge for modern machine learning models. Imbalanced dataset consists of undersampled or minority classes. The data augmentation is used to level up the number of samples in uniform manner. Moreover, the main drawback of data augmentation is data bias, which means that the augmented data distribution may differ significantly from the original. Because of this data bias, traditional data augmentation methods perform poorly [6].

On the original dataset, many data cleaning techniques were carried out to remove labels with few samples while ensuring that the overall quality of the images was acceptable for model development. Furthermore, new custom dataset MuReD was created to overcome the deficiencies in the publicly available datasets [7,8].

1.2   Related Work

Synthetic Minority Over-Sampling Technique is used to oversample the minority class. Synthetic samples are generated by employing k closest neighbour with present samples to resample the minority class [5]. Tomek link is determined as the hamming distance between two instances. Generating Tomek links is based on finding similarity features with distinct labels at the same time. Pereira et al. [9] proposed Multi-label Tomek Link, which makes use of the undersampling and cleaning methods. Majority classes are recognized in undersampling by comparing the IRPL to the meanIR. The adjusted hamming distance (ADH) is used to find the nearest neighbour in majority courses. The cleaning methods involves ADH and threshold value for cleaning the labels in dataset. This proposed technique down-samples the majority classes. F. charte et al. [10] developed Multilabel Synthetic Minority Over-Sampling Technique (MLSMOTE) in four aspects of data processing. This method involves identification of minority classes, nearest neighbor search, generation of feature map, and synthetic labelset production. Minority classes are identified by comparing IRPL and meanIR, if IRPL is greater than meanIR, then labelset is identified as minority. Nearest neighbor search is carried out by using Euclidean distance measurement between to samples. For resampling the labelset, the ranking method was found to be more efficient than the intersection and union methods. Imbalance level is improved to 14% to 43% after preprocessing.

Now a days several researchers are focusing on the preprocessing of data. The data preprocessing, cleaning, and processing operations are performed on dataset to achieve desired structure and result. The deep learning approach is introduced for SMOTE technique on image database. Dablain et al. [11] proposed the deep learning technique to oversample the labelset. The DeepSMOTE uses autoencoder to encode and decode the images batchwise. The encoder represents the sampled images to a lower dimensional feature, whereas decoder reconstructs the encoded images. The variance is introduced in encoded and decoded images by changing the sequence in the process. The variance is known as penalty term, which is mean squared error between sampled images. In DeepSMOTE, the permutation is used to order the sampled images. Müller, et al. [12] have implemented ensembling learning approach with stacking using existing deep learning models on RFMiD dataset, however authors have considered only 27 diseases for classification and remaining rare diseases have been categorized under 'OTHER' class. The AUCROC is reported as 0.95 for binary classification.

1.3 Summary of Major Contributions

We have proposed a oversampling technique on data pre-processing. The proposed method oversamples the minority classes present in dataset. LP-SMOTE involves minority class selection and Logarithmic progressive Oversampling technique for finding Oversampling factor. The proposed technique for data processing is validated by comparing existing methods. VGG19 and MobileNetV2 pre-trained models are used in combination with proposed oversampling technique in data processing, superior results are produced, including enhanced classification accuracy on the validation data. On the other hand, The InceptionResNetV2 model has very less impact on findings.

The rest part of the paper is carried out as follows: In Sect. 2, related work of some researcher on RFMiD datasets has been summarized. The RFMiD datasets are described and their analysis is shown in a table in Sect. 3. Section briefly explains the proposed method, which includes selecting minority classes, calculating the oversampling factor, and applying data augmentation to perform the oversampling technique. Section 3 contains the experimental results of the proposed methods as well as a performance comparison. The future scope is mentioned in Sect. 4. The proposed work is concluded in the last section of this paper.

2   Proposed Method

2.1   Material

RFMiD dataset was created to provide a collection of retinal images for research and diagnosis system development [13]. The RFMiD is a set of 3200 images that includes a set of 1920 samples for training, 640 samples for validation, and 640 samples for testing. The training, validation and testing ration is maintained at 60:20:20 respectively. The dataset includes images with three distinct image sizes presented in Table 1.

Table 1. RFMiD Dataset analysis: Image dimensions, training, validation and testing sets for model building.

Dimensions of images	Training Set	Validation Set	Testing Set	Total
2144×1424	1493	495	439	2427
4288×2848	277	92	128	497
2048×1536	150	53	73	276
Total	1920	640	640	3200

The RFMiD is labelled with 46 diseases. Each class represents a disease that has been diagnosed and annotated by medical professionals. Moreover, ODPM and HR class suffered from insufficient information for training model. Figure 1 illustrates how the dataset is severely unbalanced [13].

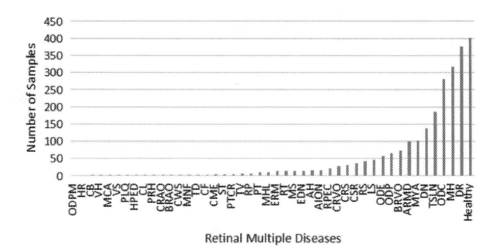

Fig. 1. RFMiD Multi-labeled Imbalanced Dataset (MLID) with imbalance per label presentation.

2.2 Logarithmic Progressive Synthetic Minority Oversampling Technique (LP-SMOTE)

Resampling methods refers to under-sampling, oversampling or both. Under-sampling techniques reduces the size of majority class by removing number of samples, whereas the oversampling technique improvise the size of minority class by generating new samples [14,15]. The flow of implementation of logarithmic progressive SMOTE technique is presented in Fig. 2. Implementation of proposed technique includes minority classes selection and Logarithmic progressive Oversampling technique for finding Oversampling factor.

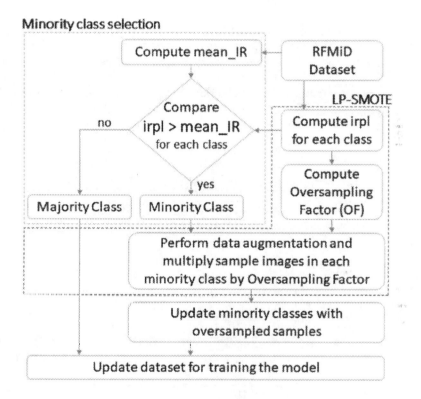

Fig. 2. The flow of implementation of LP-SMOTE technique on RFMiD Dataset.

Minority Class Selection. Imbalance ratio per label (IRPL) represents the level of frequency of labels in dataset. Majority and minority classes are often seen in MLDs. Majority classes have a larger frequency of labels, whereas minority classes have a lower frequency. Imbalance ratio (IRPL) and Mean Imbalance

Ration (mean_IR) are computed and compared to categorize the classes. IRPL can be calculated as follows [16,17].

$$IRPL = \frac{\max_{\lambda \epsilon L}(\sum_{i=1}^{m} h(\lambda_i', Y_i))}{\sum_{i=1}^{m} h(\lambda, Y_i)} \qquad (1)$$

where L is the set of labels in given dataset, Y_i is the actual labelset for the sample. λ is a label in labelset.

MeanIR is the ratio of summation of IRPLs to the number of labels.

$$MeanIR = \frac{\sum_L IRPL}{L} \qquad (2)$$

Equation 1 determines the imbalance ratio per label. Number of classes with sample size computes IRPL and meanIR. The IRPL represents the level of imbalance in dataset. Minority classes are being selected by comparing IRPL with meanIR. If IRPL of any class is greater than the calculated value of meanIR, then this class is classified as minority class. The samples size in minority class is less than other majority class [18]. Chart in Fig. 3 illustrates the minority class selection. By using Eq. 1, we have calculated the meanIR for RFMiD dataset as 101.74 for selection.

Minority Class Selection Based on IRPL and MeanIR

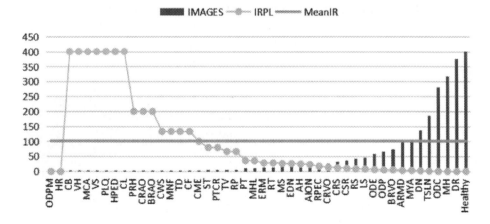

Fig. 3. Selection of classes based on the value of IRPL and MeanIR

Logarithmic Progressive Oversampling Technique for Finding Oversampling Factor. It is observed from Fig. 1 that the plot follow an exponential fit, which is significantly more challenging than a linear fit, while analysing multi-labeled imbalanced datasets. In this scenario, logarithms are frequently used to linearize exponential functions. The oversampling technique improves the class size with significant amount. The proposed method chooses minority classes,

Table 2. Selection of Majority, Minority, and null classes based on the value of IRPL.

Labels	No. of Images	IRPL	Class Selection
CWS: Cotton-wool spots	3	133.7	Minority Class
CB: Coloboma	1	401.0	Minority Class
PRH: Preretinal hemorrhage	2	200.5	Minority Class
MNF: Myelinated nerve fifibers	3	133.7	Minority Class
CRAO: Central retinal artery occlusion	2	200.5	Minority Class
TD: Tilted disc	3	133.7	Minority Class
CF: Choroidal folds	3	133.7	Minority Class
VH: Vitreous hemorrhage	1	401.0	Minority Class
MCA: Macroaneurysm	1	401.0	Minority Class
VS: Vasculitis	1	401.0	Minority Class
BRAO: Branch retinal artery occlusion	2	200.5	Minority Class
PLQ: Plaque	1	401.0	Minority Class
HPED: hemorrhagic pigment epithelial detachment	1	401.0	Minority Class
CL: Collateral	1	401.0	Minority Class
Healthy	401	1.0	Majority Class
DR: Diabetic Retinopathy	376	1.1	Majority Class
ARMD: Age-related macular degeneration	100	4.0	Majority Class
MH: Media Haze	317	1.3	Majority Class
DN: Drusens	138	2.9	Majority Class
MYA: Myopia	101	4.0	Majority Class
BRVO: Branch retinal vein occlusion	73	5.5	Majority Class
TSLN: Tessellation	186	2.2	Majority Class
ERM: Epiretinal membrane	14	28.6	Majority Class
LS: Laser scars	47	8.5	Majority Class
MS: Macular scar	15	26.7	Majority Class
CSR: Central serous retinopathy	37	10.8	Majority Class
ODC: Optic disc cupping	282	1.4	Majority Class
CRVO: Central retinal vein occlusion	28	14.3	Majority Class
TV: Tortuous vessels	6	66.8	Majority Class
AH: Asteroid hyalosis	16	25.1	Majority Class
ODP: Optic disc pallor	65	6.2	Majority Class
ODE: Optic disc edema	58	6.9	Majority Class
ST: Optociliary shunt	5	80.2	Majority Class
AION: Anterior ischemic optic neuropathy	17	23.6	Majority Class
PT: Parafoveal telangiectasia	11	36.5	Majority Class
RT: Retinal traction	14	28.6	Majority Class
RS: Retinitis	43	9.3	Majority Class
CRS: Chorioretinitis	32	12.5	Majority Class
EDN: Exudation	15	26.7	Majority Class
RPEC: Retinal pigment epithelium changes	22	18.2	Majority Class
MHL: Macular hole	11	36.5	Majority Class
RP: Retinitis Pigmentosa	6	66.8	Majority Class
CME: Cystoid macular edema	4	100.3	Majority Class
PTCR: Post-traumatic choroidal rupture	5	80.2	Majority Class
ODPM: Optic disc pit maculopathy	0	0	Null Class
HR: Hemorrhagic retinopathy	0	0	Null Class

and the number of samples in that class will be boosted to a set quantity. The improved minority class size is combined effect of oversampling and data augmentation technique. The level of oversampling is determined by oversampling factor, which is computed by taking natural logarithm of IRPL as expressed in Eq. 3 (Table 2).

$$OF[i] = log_e IRPL \qquad for\ i = 1\ to\ m \qquad (3)$$

Furthermore, sample images in each minority class are augmented by OF amount using data augmentation technique. Data augmentation is employed to increase samples in a class. Furthermore, we obtained logarithmic equivalent of each size of each class. The logarithmic function provides us the range of 0.0 to 6.0 Oversampling factor.

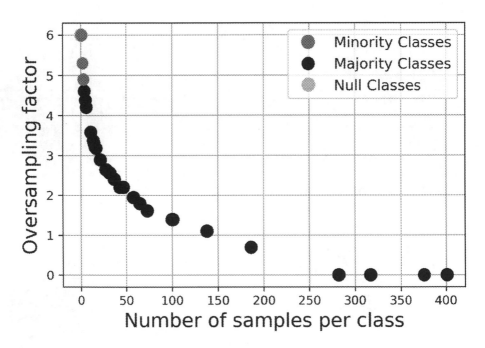

Fig. 4. Minority, Majority and null classes are represented with respective oversampling factor.

The following are the steps for computing and comparing the IRPL and meanIR to choose minority classes, as well as computing the Oversampling Factor to increase the amount of samples available to minority classes.

Step 1: Initialize an array for the total number of samples in each class.
Step 2: Append number of samples for each class in an array.
Step 3: Initialize an array for IRPL.
Step 4: Compute IRPL for each class and append calculated value to IRPL array.

Step 5: Compute Mean Imbalance Ratio (MeanIR) by taking average of IRPL of all classes.

Step 6: Compare IRPL with MeanIR to separate the minority classes.

Step 7: If IRPL greater than MeanIR of a class then, the class is recognized as minority class.

Step 8: Else, the given class is majority class.

Step 9: Store all Minority classes in a array for further processing

Step10: Find Logarithmic equivalent value for IRPL of each class.

Step11: Store the Logarithmic equivalent i.e. Oversampling Factor (OF) into array (Y).

Step12: Using Data augmentation, multiply number of samples in minority class by OF amount to reproduce modified version of dataset.

Algorithm 1. Algorithm for LP-SMOTE

Data: Dataset (D) with imbalanced classes (c0, c1, c2, ...cn), Array of class sizes (X), Number of classes (N)

Result: Minority classes, Oversampling Factor (OF)

  for classes (c0, c1, c2,....cn) in Dataset (D) **do**
    $irpl\_class \leftarrow append(class\_size)$
  end for
  $max\_class = max(irpl\_class)$
  for classes (c0, c1, c2,....cn) in Dataset (D) **do**
    if $irpl\_class \neq 0$ **then**
      $irpl\_class = max\_class/irpl\_class$
    else
      $irpl_class = 0$
    end if
  end for
  $MeanIR \leftarrow sum(irpl_class)$
  $MeanIR \leftarrow \frac{MeanIR}{N}$

  for classes (c0, c1, c2,....cn) in Dataset (D) **do**
    if $irpl\_class \geq meanIR$ **then**
      $minority\_class \leftarrow append(class\_name)$
    end if
  end for
  for each irpl_class in Y **do**
    $temp = \log_e irpl$
    $OF \leftarrow append(temp)$
  end for
  Initialize Data_Generator as datagen using rotation_range, zoom_range, horizontal_flip, brightness_range
  for batch, image in datagen: **do**
    apply data_augmentation
  end for

The number of samples get multiplied with the oversampling factor obtained from the above algorithm. Since the oversampling factor is a float value, the integer component is used to significantly boost entire sample size in a class, while the fractional part is utilized to take random samples from the same dataset for data generation. The oversampling factor for each sample size i.e. number of images per class is illustrated in Fig. 4. Depending on the class sample size, the classes are separated into majority, minority, and null classes. Finally, the minority classes are updated with increased number of samples to the dataset.

3   Experimental Results and Discussion

The proposed method improves the quantity in dataset by applying data augmentation technique. The original number of samples present in minority classes get multiplied by amount of oversampling factor and new samples are generated using data augmentation. The fractional amount of samples are taken and augmented on random basis from the class. Data augmentation includes zoom, horizontal flip, 20° rotation, and brightness transformations. The classes with number of samples before and after oversampling are shown in Table 3 and the graphical representation is given in Fig. 5. The modified samples are added in respective classes in the dataset. Selected minority classes having 1, 2, and 3 sample sizes are improved to 6, 11, and 15 respectively. Minority selection block selects 12 classes as minority classes for oversampling. The overall samples of minority classes are raised from 25 to 135.

Table 3. LP-SMOTE approach to enhance the number of samples from the minority classes in the dataset.

Labels	No of samples	Increased No of samples
CWS	3	15
CB	1	6
PRH	2	11
MNF	3	15
CRAO	2	11
TD	3	15
CF	3	15
VH	1	6
MCA	1	6
VS	1	6
BRAO	2	11
PLQ	1	6
HPED	1	6
CL	1	6
Total Minority class samples	25	135

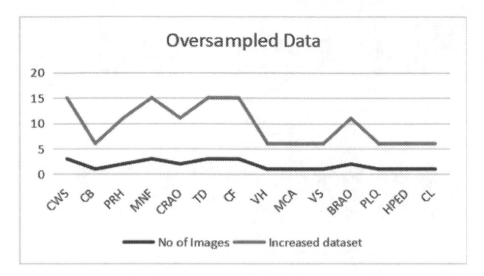

Fig. 5. The oversampling of the minority classes from the dataset using LP-SMOTE technique.

The proposed method allows dataset to pass through minority class selection and Oversampling phases. Pictorial representation of obtained results by implementing proposed method is shown in Fig. 6.

The proposed Oversampling technique updated the dataset by improving sample size in minority classes. This upgradation leads to increase in overall size of dataset. The number of samples per class are improvised by amount of oversampling factor. The pre-trained models are employed on this updated dataset with new sample size. VGG19, MobileNetV2, InceprionResNetV2 performs differently on same dataset. We find improvements in classification accuracy when we apply VGG19 and MobileNetV2. However, the results show no significant changes in accuracy for InceptionResNetV2. Table 4 shows the classification accuracy of pre-trained models on a validation and testing set using SMOTE, and LP-SMOTE techniques. We have the original RFMiD dataset as well as a modified version of it. Using the proposed technique, the modified version of dataset is obtained by oversampling the minority classes.

The models are trained on these dataset. Futhermore, the trained models are saved and evaluated on the RFMiD dataset, including the original and modified versions. Two varients of MobileNetV2, InceptionResNetV2, and VGG19 have been created and tested. Models trained on the modified RFMiD dataset outperform models trained on the original dataset as shown in Table 5 (Fig. 7).

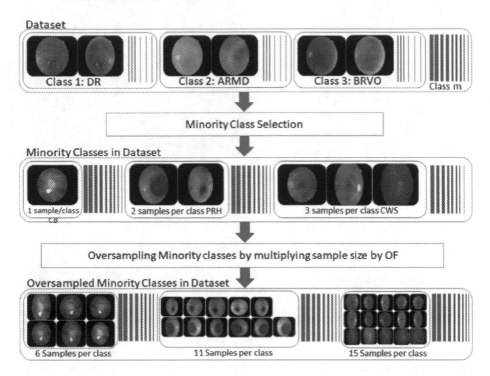

Fig. 6. Pictorial representation of the results obtained by employing the LP-SMOTE technique.

Table 4. Comparison of the model performance with SMOTE, LP-SMOTE technique.

Architecture of model	Performance Metric	Original	SMOTE	LP-SMOTE
VGG19	Val_ACC	0.5328	0.5500	**0.5609**
	Test_ACC	0.5250	0.5697	**0.5703**
MobileNetV2	Val_ACC	0.5671	0.5859	**0.5875**
	Test_ACC	0.5653	0.5422	**0.5813**
InceptionResNetV2	Val_ACC	0.6109	0.5812	0.6063
	Test_ACC	0.6172	0.6046	0.6125

Table 5. The results obtained after testing models on training set and modified training set of RFMiD datasets.

Architecture of model	ACC on Modified RFMiD Dataset	ACC on RFMiD Dataset
VGG19	**0.908**	0.9015
MobileNetV2	**0.8988**	0.8917
InceptionResNetV2	**0.907**	0.9005

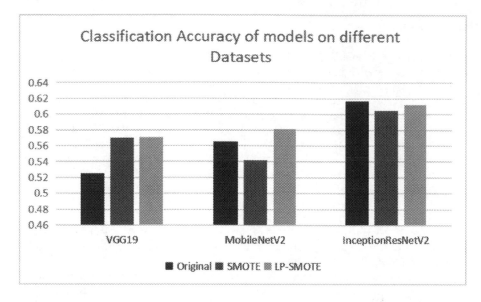

Fig. 7. Comparison of classification accuracy on Test set of RFMiD Dataset using pre-trained models.

4   Conclusion and Future Work

In spite of significant advancements in technology, imbalanced datasets remain a major difficulty for current machine learning models. The proposed method involves the improved data augmentation which, ensures that the model is unbiased and progressive resampling prevents minority class over-fitting. The more data you provide to the machine-learning model, the faster it can learn and improve performance. So, for improved accuracy, sufficient data should be supplied to the training model. The proposed method is useful in boosting the overall minority samples in RFMiD dataset by 5.4 times.

Data processing techniques can be developed to improve the performance of classification. To increase overall performance, classes with fewer samples are oversampled in Multi-Labelled Dataset (MLID). We can implement this technique on other datasets for object detection and image segmentation. The object detection algorithms such as YOLO [20], RCNN can be employed on the modified dataset.

Acknowledgements. We extend out thanks Technical Education Quality Improvement Program (TEQIP), the World Bank project, for providing a state of the art Center of Excellence in Signal and Image Processing research lab. Also, we thank the authors of "Retinal Fundus Multi-Disease Image Dataset (RFMiD): A Dataset for Multi-Disease Detection Research" for making their dataset RFMiD publicly available.

References

1. World Health Organization, 14 October 2021. https://www.who.int/news-room/fact-sheets/detail/blindness-and-visual-impairment. Accessed 22 Mar 2022
2. Vision Loss Expert Group of the Global Burden of Disease Study: Causes of blindness and vision impairment in 2020 and trends over 30 years: evaluating the prevalence of avoidable blindness in relation to "VISION 2020: the Right to Sight". Lancet Glob. Health (2020). https://doi.org/10.1016/S2214-109X(20)30489-7
3. WHO Publishes SEAsia-Specific DR Guidelines - The International Agency for the Prevention of Blindness. https://www.iapb.org/news/who-publishes-seasia-specific-dr-guidelines. Accessed 05 Mar 2022
4. World report on vision, World Health Organization (2019). https://cdn.who.int/media/docs/default-source/infographics-pdf/world-vision-infographic-final.pdf?sfvrsn=85b7bcde_2. Accessed 22 Mar 2022
5. Chawla, N.V., Bowyer, K.W., Hall, L.O., Kegelmeyer, W.P.: SMOTE: synthetic minority over-sampling technique. J. Artif. Intell. Res. **16**, 321–357 (2002). https://doi.org/10.1613/jair.953
6. Xu, Y., Noy, A., Lin, M., Qian, Q., Li, H., Jin, R.: WeMix: how to better utilize data augmentation. arXiv (2020). https://doi.org/10.48550/arxiv.2010.01267
7. Rodriguez, M.A., AlMarzouqi, H., Liatsis, P.: Multi-label retinal disease classification using transformers. arXiv (2022). https://doi.org/10.48550/arXiv.2207.02335
8. Rodriguez, M., AlMarzouqi, H., Liatsis, P.: Multi-label retinal disease (MuReD) dataset. IEEE DataPort (2022). https://doi.org/10.21227/7fx7-8q47
9. Pereira, R.M., Costa, Y.M.G., Silla, C.N., Jr.: MLTL: a multi-label approach for the Tomek Link undersampling algorithm. Neurocomputing **383**, 95–105 (2020). https://doi.org/10.1016/j.neucom.2019.11.076
10. Charte, F., Rivera, A.J., del Jesus, M.J., Herrera, F.: MLSMOTE: approaching imbalanced multilabel learning through synthetic instance generation. Knowl.-Based Syst. **89**, 385–397 (2015). https://doi.org/10.1016/j.knosys.2015.07.019
11. Dablain, D., Krawczyk, B., Chawla, N.V.: DeepSMOTE: fusing deep learning and SMOTE for imbalanced data. IEEE Trans. Neural Netw. Learn. Syst. 1–15 (2022). https://doi.org/10.1109/TNNLS.2021.3136503
12. Müller, D., Soto-Rey, I., Kramer, F.: Multi-disease detection in retinal imaging based on ensembling heterogeneous deep learning models, March 2021. arXiv:2103.14660. https://doi.org/10.48550/arXiv.2103.14660
13. Pachade, S., et al.: Retinal fundus multi-disease image dataset (RFMiD): a dataset for multi-disease detection research. Data **62** (2021). https://doi.org/10.3390/data6020014
14. Castellanos, F.J., Valero-Mas, J.J., Calvo-Zaragoza, J., Rico-Juan, J.R.: Oversampling imbalanced data in the string space. Pattern Recogn. Lett. (2018). https://doi.org/10.1016/j.patrec.2018.01.003
15. Liu, X.Y., Wu, J., Zhou, Z.H.: Exploratory undersampling for class-imbalance learning. IEEE Trans. Syst. Part B Cybern. (2009). https://doi.org/10.1109/TSMCB.2008.2007853
16. Charte, F., Rivera, A., del Jesus, M.J., Herrera, F.: A first approach to deal with imbalance in multi-label datasets. In: Pan, J.-S., Polycarpou, M.M., Woźniak, M., de Carvalho, A.C.P.L.F., Quintián, H., Corchado, E. (eds.) HAIS 2013. LNCS (LNAI), vol. 8073, pp. 150–160. Springer, Heidelberg (2013). https://doi.org/10.1007/978-3-642-40846-5_16

17. Charte, F., Rivera, A.J., del Jesus, M.J., Herrera, F.: Addressing imbalance in multilabel classification: measures and random resampling algorithms. Neurocomputing **163**, 3–16 (2015). https://doi.org/10.1016/j.neucom.2014.08.091
18. Tarekegn, A.N., Giacobini, M., Michalak, K.: A review of methods for imbalanced multi-label classification. Pattern Recogn. **118** (2021). https://doi.org/10.1016/j.patcog.2021.107965
19. Bernardo, A., Della Valle, E.: An extensive study of C-SMOTE, a continuous synthetic minority oversampling technique for evolving data streams. Expert Syst. Appl. **196**, 116630 (2022)
20. Bochkovskiy, A., Wang, C.Y., Liao, H.Y.M.: YOLOv4: optimal speed and accuracy of object detection. arXiv (2020). https://doi.org/10.48550/arxiv.2004.10934

Sequence Recognition in Bharatnatyam Dance

Himadri Bhuyan⬤, Rohit Dhaipule(✉)⬤, and Partha Pratim Das⬤

Indian Institute of Technology Kharagpur, Kharagpur 721302, West Bengal, India
himadribhuyan@gmail.com, rohit1045d@gmail.com, ppd@cse.iitkgp.ac.in

Abstract. *Bharatanatyam* is the oldest Indian Classical Dance (ICD) which is learned and practiced across India and the world. *Adavu* is the core of this dance form. There exist 15 *Adavus* and 58 variations. Each *Adavu* variation comprises a well-defined set of motions and postures (called dance steps) that occur in a particular order. So, while learning *Adavus*, students not only learn the dance steps but also take care of its sequence of occurrences. This paper proposed a method to recognize these sequences. In this work, firstly, we recognize the involved Key Postures (KPs) and motions in the *Adavu* using Convolutional Neural Network (CNN) and Support Vector Machine (SVM), respectively. In this, CNN achieves 99% and SVM's recognition accuracy becomes 84%. Next, we compare these KP and motion sequences with the ground truth to find the best match using the Edit Distance algorithm with an accuracy of 98%. The paper contributes hugely to the state-of-the-art in the form of digital heritage, dance tutoring system, and many more. The paper addresses three novelties; (a) Recognizing the sequences based on the KPs and motions rather than only KPs as reported in the earlier works. (b) The performance of the proposed work is measured by analyzing the prediction time per sequence. We also compare our proposed approach with the previous works that deal with the same problem statement. (c) It tests the scalability of the proposed approach by including all the *Adavu* variations, unlike the earlier literature, which uses only one/two variations.

Keywords: Adavu · Bharatanatyam · Key posture · Motion · SVM · CNN · HOG · MHI

1 Introduction

Bharathanatyam, Kuchipudi, Kathak, Manipuri, and Kathakali are the most famous ICDs. *Bharatanatyam* is a significant ICD form with a perplexing mix of visual and audio data. To analyze *Bharatanatyam* dance, one must analyze *Adavu*, the basic building blocks. The *Adavus* is the collection of postures and movements. There are 15 classes of *Adavus* having 58 variations.

The visual data comprises of key postures, motions, and trajectories. A key posture (KP) in which the dancer remains stationary for a while. A motion is

D. Gupta et al. (Eds.): CVIP 2022, CCIS 1776, pp. 390–405, 2023.
https://doi.org/10.1007/978-3-031-31407-0_30

a part of the dance from one KP to the accompanying KP. Motions (M) and KP occur alternately and may repeat in a performance. Figure 1 shows this. The audio data is known as *Sollukattu* which comprises of Bols, Beats, and tempo. In this work, we only deal with the visual information of the *Adavus*.

Fig. 1. An example showing the sequence of KPs and motion in *Natta-1*

In this work, we use the Key Posture and Motion information and train a model to recognize the *Adavus* using Edit Distance algorithm. We first solve the sub-problems of recognizing the KP and Motion classes which will be used to recognize the Adavu class.

The data set is created by [13], where the RGB, Depth, and Skeleton videos of dance performances have been captured using Kinect V1. The videos are then manually segmented into Key Frames (KF) sequences corresponding to the expected KPs and Motions. To recognize the KPs in the segmented KFs, we follow two approaches - SVM and CNN. SVM uses HOG as a feature between these two approaches, and CNN takes the raw KPs for classification. Similarly, for motions, we first merge all the key frames related to a particular motion and generate Motion History Images (MHI), from which HOG features are extracted. SVM uses these features to build the trained model.

2   Related Work

The recognition of *Adavu* is based on recognizing the KPs and motions involved. So, the given problem is divided into three sub-problems that are be solved: (a) KP recognition, (b) Motion recognition, and (c) *Adavu* recognition as a sequence of KPs and Motions. Hence a survey is conducted on the recent works related to the mentioned sub-problems.

2.1   Recognition of Key Postures

Over time, many authors have worked in the area of posture recognition. [7,14] classify eight different ICDs based on different postures as input and recognize the type of ICD to that posture belongs. [14] use ResNet50 whereas, [7] use and VGG16 & VGG19 (pre-trained) as classifier. A similar work is reported in [24], which tries to classify five ICDs based on postures using CNN. In all these works, authors work on recognizing the body postures. Authors in [27] design a framework to classify different foot postures using Naive Bayes classifier. [23] recognize the ICD postures using CNN. The data set comprises 26 postures where Kinect captures 12 postures in a controlled environment, and 14 are taken from YouTube videos. [26,29] include recognition of Key Postures in ICD using SVM and obtain good results.

CNN, SVM, and GMM were used by [21] with RGB and Skeleton-Angle as input to recognize the KPs in *Bharatanatyam's Natta Adavus*. The best result (99.56%) has been obtained using ResNet (32 CV Layers, 2 FC Layers) for 23 classes with RGB data, whereas SVM with RGB-HOG also does relatively well (97.95%). They also used GMM with skeleton angle as features, resulting in an accuracy of 83.04%.

Further, authors in the paper [13] use SVM for KP recognition in ICD. The authors use two approaches to classify key postures. In the first approach, angles of skeleton bones are used as features, whereas in the second approach, HOG features from the RGB frames are used as features. In both the approaches, SVM has been used to recognize the Key postures and achieve 93.36% and 94.15% respectively. Using this model and the Edit Distance Algorithm, the *Adavus* are recognized and classified. This has been performed only on two *Adavus*, *Natta* and *Mettu* and report 99.38% accuracy. However, the authors do not consider motion aspects during this recognition.

2.2   Recognition of Motion

Motion Recognition has been one of the most famous and worked problems in recent years. Worldwide many researchers propose different machine learning and deep learning techniques to solve it.

In [9], with Spacetime interest point (STIP) and Histogram of optical flow (HOOF) as features, motion information has been extracted from the dance movements. KNN, Neural network, and Tree bagger classifier are explored. Here, the Treebagger classifier gives a maximum accuracy of 92.6% with N = 150 trees as a parameter. Similarly, in [6], the velocities of skeleton joints have been used as features, and methods like dynamic time warping (DTW) and the kNN algorithm are explored, resulting in the best accuracy of 85%.

The growth of Deep Learning models has helped researchers work with the motions effectively. In [19], a new segmentation model is developed using discrete wavelet transform, and local binary pattern (LBP) features. This is combined with an AdaBoost multi-class classifier that was used to classify the dance actions. The Indian classical dance datasets used by the authors consist of performances on 'Bharatanatyam' and 'Kuchipudi' from online YouTube videos and offline dance videos recorded in a controlled environment at K.L. University, cams department studio.

Symmetric Spatial Transformer Networks (SSTN) were constructed by the authors of [16] to recognize the ICD dance forms' sequences. They used the postures as features based on skeletal joints and 3D CNN as a classifier. In [17] they use CNN to recognize or classify dance actions based on posture.

Motion History Image (MHI) has been a simple, effective, and robust approach to recognizing human actions. Several works based on MHI have been reported in the article [1]. In this paper, we use HoG of MHI as a feature in motion recognition.

2.3   Recognition of *Adavus*

While performing an *Adavu*, the dancers follow a predetermined sequence and mix of Postures and Motions in sync with the musical beats. The dancer needs to ensure that the rules adapted to change from a KP to a Motion and back to another KP are followed. The classifier we build needs to ensure those rules are adhered to while recognizing a particular *Adavu*.

One of the first works on *Adavu* recognition [28] was reported based on the posture sequence, without considering the temporal information. Authors of [15] used RGB-D data which was captured using Kinect to recognize the Adavu. They get 73% recognition accuracy. Later, authors of [21] used RGB-HOG data in Hidden Markov Model (HMM) to recognize only 8 *Adavus*, resulting in an accuracy of 94.64% which is a significant improvement when compared to [15]. Recently, in [13], the authors use the posture information to recognize all the variations of *Mettu* and *Natta Adavus*. In this, they recognize the occurrence of the postures using SVM in a given *Adavu* and use the Edit Distance algorithm to find the best match among the *Adavu* dictionary. Here, 12 *Adavus* are considered and achieved an accuracy of 99%.

The **research gaps** identified in the literature survey are summarised as: (a) The earlier works [13,15,21,28] consider only KPs in the *Adavu* recognition. However, the involved motions are not included. It may be due to the complexity of the motion recognition. (b) Most of the earlier works [13,15,21,28] include only one or two *Adavus*. However, there exist 58 *Adavu* variations. (c) Instead of the classical ML technique, an effective deep learning approach is yet to be explored. (d) The time complexity of the different approaches is yet to be analyzed.

In this paper, we address the above gaps as the **contribution of the paper**: (a) The *Adavu* recognition considers both motions and postures rather than only postures. (b) We take 13 *Adavus* and 51 sub-classes into consideration which tests the robustness of the approach. (c) The paper designs an effective CNN which takes less time (d) The performance of the proposed approaches is analyzed based on the time complexity.

3   Data Set

We record all the *Adavus* using Microsoft Kinect V1 [22] in a controlled environment as followed in [2]. The Kinect captures three streams of data; RGB, Depth, and Skeleton. We use the RGB stream. The paper tries to recognize the *Adavus* by considering both the KP and motion aspects. So, the dataset should include both of these attributes. Table 1 shows the *Adavu*, its variants, the involved KPs, and motions. Though there exist 15 *Adavus* and 58 variations, by discarding the erroneous data (error in data extraction), the entire data set boils down to 13 *Adavus* and 51 variations. There are 184 KPs and 334 motion classes. However, all the motions reported in the Table 1 are not used due to their sample size. We only consider the motions having # of samples more than 12 to avoid the biases of the motion recognizer. Similarly, Two KPs (P67 & P69) are ignored. So, 182 classes of KPs are considered for recognition. [3] shows the KPs and its Train-Test split. Table 1 shows one of the annotations as an example. It gives information about the duration of the occurrence of the motions and KPs in a given *Adavu*.

Table 1. Involved KPs & Motions in the *Adavus* and Annotations

Adavu	Variant	Total KPs	Unique KPs	Total Motions	Unique motions
Joining	3	1350	13	78	14
Katti_kartari	1	258	2	23	4
Kuditta_Nattal	6	5861	28	231	51
Kuditta_tattal	5	3914	32	616	61
Mandi	2	4525	18	192	27
Mettu	4	4573	25	238	32
Natta	8	9449	19	410	54
Paikkal	3	1620	12	72	14
Sarika	4	2720	8	191	25
Tatta	8	6920	1	264	2
TeiTei_Dhatta	9	1262	9	96	15
Trimana	3	1973	14	149	31
Uttasanga	1	278	3	24	4
Total	51	44703	184	2584	334

(a) Motion annotation			(b) KP annotation		
Motion ID	Start-Frame	End-Frame	KP ID	Start-Frame	End-Frame
M219	103	123	P134	124	134
M220	135	205	P135	206	225
M221	226	307	P136	308	330
M222	331	403	P28	404	416
..	..	..	..	..	..
M224	701	780	P32	781	805

3.1 Data Set for *Adavu*

A particular *Adavu* includes a sequence of motions and KPs as addressed in the annotation, Table 1. Each KP and motion comprises a set of frames. The set of frames involved with KPs is momentarily stationary. However, in motion, these frames are dynamics. To identify an *Adavu*, we need to recognize the KPs and motions that occur in a definite sequence. For a KP, there exist several candidate key frames (KP implies a set of momentarily stationary frames). However, for motion, it is not. So, for a given *Adavu*, we can have several sequences of KPs and motions.

Let us consider *Paikkal-1 Adavu* as an example to construct such candidate sequences. Note that a set of motion frames gives rise to a single motion. However, each key frame is treated as KP in a video. So we can not count the number of valid sub-sequences based on motions. The number of valid sub-sequences will be restricted by the KP containing the smallest number of KFs. For *Paikkal-1 Adavu*, there will be 11 valid sub-sequences, which are restricted by 'P134' (see Table 1) which has only 11 frames. That means $n = min(\#$ of frames of a $KP \in$ given Adavu) = 10. Therefore, the 1st sequence is: M219 – P124 – M220 – P206 – M221 – P308 – M222 – P404 – .... – M224 – P781 and the last sub-sequence of *Paikkal-1* is: M219 – P134 – M220 – P216 – M221 – P318 – M222 – P414 – .... – M224 – P791. Using this strategy, we create sub-sequences from the videos in the data set that can be used as data instances for the classifiers. The number of possible sequences associated with each *Adavu* variant is shown in Table 2. Here, we should remember that a given sequence always starts with a KP. Before starting the dance, the dancer takes a random posture which denotes that the dancer is ready to dance, but this start KP may not appear further in the given sequence. So, during the sequence annotation, we discard this start KP.

Table 2. The number of Sequences associated with each Adavu variant

Adavu	Sequneces	Adavu	Sequneces	Adavu	Sequneces	Adavu	Sequneces	Adavu	Sequneces	Adavu	Sequneces
Joining_1	33	Tatta_6	67	Natta_7	38	Kuditta_Nattal_4	11	Mandi_2	11	Tei_Tei_Dhatta_2	50
Joining_2	55	Tatta_7	70	Natta_8	24	Kuditta_Nattal_5	13	Paikkal_1	48	Tei_Tei_Dhatta_3	16
Joining_3	23	Tatta_8	22	Mettu_1	33	Kuditta_Nattal_6	58	Paikkal_2	44	Tirmana_1	17
Kartari_1	63	Natta_1	56	Mettu_2	34	Kuditta_Tattal_1	13	Paikkal_3	44	Tirmana_2	13
Tatta_1	79	Natta_2	66	Mettu_3	25	Kuditta_Tattal_2	20	Sarika_1	15	Tirmana_3	9
Tatta_2	90	Natta_3	45	Mettu_4	19	Kuditta_Tattal_3	13	Sarika_2	34	Utsanga_1	25
Tatta_3	60	Natta_4	41	Kuditta_Nattal_1	10	Kuditta_Tattal_4	5	Sarika_3	16		
Tatta_4	41	Natta_5	36	Knditta_Nattal_2	11	Kuditta_Tattal_5	21	Sarika_4	12		
Tatta_5	20	Natta_6	30	Kuditta_Nattal_3	10	Mandi_1	17	Tei_Tei_Dhatta_1	19	Total	1645

4   Workflow

Figure 2 shows the workflow of the proposed approach. In this recognition process, We give an *Adavu* video as an input along with the annotation file (Refer Table 1). We convert each video frame into a gray frame using the equation $GrayFr_i(x,y) = 0.299*Fr_i(x,y)_{Red}+0.587*Fr_i(x,y)_{Green}+0.144*Fr_i(x,y)_{Blue}$ and subtract the background using the binary mask, $D_i(x,y) = Fr_i(x,y) * Mask_i(x,y)$ that can identify the dancer in a frame using depth information (captured by Kinect v1) as reported in [4]. Where, $Mask_i(x,y) = 1$ if there exist dancer in $Fr_i(x,y)$ otherwise $Mask_i(x,y) = 0$.

After the grayscale conversion and background removal, we extract the feature for KPs and motions that occur in the given video separately. The feature extraction is discussed in Sect. 5. Using the required feature, our trained ML model identifies the KP and motion in the *Adavu*. For KP recognition, CNN uses background subtracted frames and automatic feature extraction in convolutional layers. Whereas, for motion, the HOG-MHI feature is extracted by us and given as an input to SVM for classification. The recognized KP and motion sequences are fed to the *Adavu* Recogniser to recognize the *Adavu*. We use Edit distance for this *Adavu* classification.

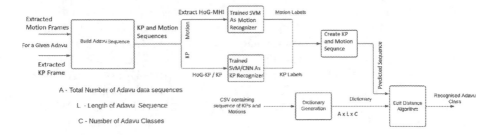

Fig. 2. *Adavu* Recognition Workflow

5   Feature Extraction

The resultant frames are used for feature extraction after the grayscale conversion and background removal. The frames are of size 480×640 given as an input to compute the feature. We can use the annotation to distinguish KP and motion frames in a given *Adavu*. As we use CNN for KP recognition, CNN takes care of feature extraction in its convolutional layers. So, here we discuss only the motion feature extraction technique.

5.1   Feature Extraction for Motion

First, for the motion frames, a matrix MHI of size 480×640 is initialized to zeros. After that, (a) The contours of each gray-scale frame are computed, (b) the Difference of contours between the two frames is computed, (c) A threshold will be applied now to create a binary image, and (d) The MHI will be updated with the values of differential binary frames, and (e) This process continues until the last frame of a particular motion instance resulting in an MHI. Figure 1 shows the motion MHI of M165, M166, and M167.

After the above process, we resize the MHI image from 480×640 to 120×160 and compute the HOG [10] resulting in a feature vector of size 9576. These features will be used for Motion Recognition.

5.2   Feature for *Adavu*

An *Adavu* comprises two basic attributes; KP and motion. The KPs and motions appear in a definite order within a given *Adavu*. We call it as *Adavu* sequence. To recognize an *Adavu* we need to identify the KPs and motions involved. That means, in an *Adavu*, we will have the sequence of the feature of KPs and motions. From these features, our machine learning (ML) models will predict the KPs and motions that occur in an *Adavu*. For example, Let us consider a segment of *Natta-1 Adavu*. It comprises of the KPs and motions as: P3 – M165 – P8 – M166 – P3 – M167 – P11 (Refer Fig. 1). A given sequence contains $|P|$ and $|M|$ number of KPs and Motions, respectively. On replacing the features (f) in this sequence we get a matrix of size $|P| \times |M| \times f$. Now, this feature is given as an input to the classifiers to recognize the individual KPs and motions, generating a sequence. This sequence helps us to recognize an *Adavu*.

6   KP Recognition

This section discusses KP recognition, one of the attributes in the *Adavu*. Here, we use CNN as classifier and background subtracted frame as input. CNN compute the feature of each KP in its feature extraction layer. Input to the CNN is the background subtracted KP. Figure 3 shows the CNN architecture used for KP Recognition. The given CNN uses two convolutional (CV) layers and three fully connected (FC) layers.

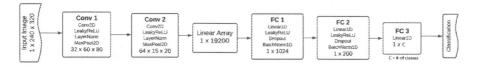

Fig. 3. CNN architecture for KP Classification

We use 32 and 64 channels in two CV layers, respectively, with required padding in the input. We do apply layer normalization to normalize the feature. Finally, max-pooling is applied with the window 2×2 and stride two. The output of each CV layer is shown in the Fig. 3

The operations involved in each FC layer are shown in Fig. 3. To handle the overfitting, we apply *drop out* and limit the number of epochs to 15. The decision on the number of the epoch is taken by analyzing the train test accuracy (beyond 15, it is moving towards overfitting). Both techniques help prevent CNN from memorizing the data and driving towards learning. We use *Leaky ReLu* instead of *ReLu* to prevent the "Dead ReLu", since no learning happens for negative input in *ReLu*. Moreover, as reported in [11], Leaky ReLu also performs better than *ReLu*. The last FC layer's output is 182 feature arrays corresponding to 182 KP classes. These features are converted into class scores using the *softmax* layer and label the unknown KPs.

Using CNN, out of 8943 test samples 8895 predicted correctly, that is, we get a recognition accuracy of 99.46% along with the average Precision = 99.95%, Recall = 99.15% and F1 Score = 99.51%. This good F1 Score shows the robustness of the result and classifier. Moreover, 158 KPs achieve 100% accuracy and the rest score more than 95% except for a few. Table 4 shows the test result and misclassification details.

We also try the two popular CNN models, AlexNet [18] and VGG16 [25] for the KP recognition to learn the behavior of the models with different numbers of CV and FC layers. Finally, we reach our proposed CNN model with two CV and three FC layers. With the increase in depth (more number of CV and FC layers) the execution time for training and testing increases [12]. The execution time for training and testing is shown in Table 3. Again, after looking at the accuracy, precision, recall, and F1 score, we reported our CNN model as the best performer on the given data set. Table 3 shows the result comparison among the proposed model, AlexNet, VGG16, and ResNet. The robustness of the proposed CNN architecture is yet to be tested with the different types of data.

Table 3. Result & Time Comparison of different CNN Models

CNN Type	Precision (%)	Recall (%)	F1 Score (%)	Accuracy (%)	# of KPs with Accuracy = 100%	Training Time (s)	Test Time(s)
AlexNet [18]	79.62	80.35	79.14	94.14	99	7415.60	41.97
VGG16 [25]	90.06	88.54	88.86	95.73	92	9393.10	72.10
ResNet [21]	99.27	98.77	98.97	99.54	164	6410.02	58.43
Our Model	99.95	99.15	99.51	99.46	158	4672.75	36.37

6.1   KP Recognition: Result Discussion

Table 4 shows the result. CNN achieves 99.46% accuracy. In this, only 48 samples are mispredicted out of 8,895 test samples.

Most of the misclassifications are well expected. In P8, the dancer stretches their right leg. When these stretches are insignificant, it resembles P3 just as bending. So, in some cases, P8 is mispredicted as P3. In P94 and P95, postures are very much similar. The only difference is there in the leg position. In P94, the foot is grounded, whereas, in P95, the dancer stands on the toes. Though P28 seems very dissimilar from P3, some samples of P28 are mispredicted as P3. Sometimes in P3 and P28, the dancer's hand could not be tracked by Kinect while stretching the left hand towards the left or raising the hand upward. So, in that scenario, P28 becomes similar to P3 and gets mispredicted. Figure 4 shows the mispredictions KPs.

Table 4. KP Recognition Test Result using CNN

Class #	Test Sample	Accuracy (%)	Miss Predictions	Class #	Test Sample	Accuracy (%)	Miss Predictions	Class #	Test Sample	Accuracy (%)	Miss Predictions
P3	1134	99.91	P11(1)	P46	110	99.09	P3(1)	P89	5	80	P183(1)
P8	413	98.06	P3(8)	P49	46	97.82	P48(1)	P94	14	57.14	P95(6)
P11	406	99.75	P3(1)	P52	67	98.50	P3(1)	P100	161	99.37	P103(1)
P23	40	97.5	P52(1)	P74	12	91.66	P60(1)	P103	111	99.09	P100(1)
P26	16	93.75	P17(1)	P75	9	88.88	P54(1)	P109	33	96.96	P125(1)
P28	47	87.23	P3(6)	P78	58	98.27	P76(1)	P163	10	90	P3(1)
P42	14	92.85	P46(1)	P79	154	99.35	P77(1)	P173	64	95.31	P6(1), P3(2)
P43	43	97.67	P48(1)	P84	44	95.45	P3(2)	P181	12	91.66	P52(1)

*The KP classes attending < 100% accuracy are reported in this table

Fig. 4. Most misclassified KPs–P3, P8, P28, P94 and P95 as reported in CNN

7 Motion Recognition

In *Adavu* each KP is followed by a motion. To recognize an *Adavu*, we also need to recognize the motion. Here, we use SVM to recognize the motion. SVM uses HoG of MHI as an input for the classification [5]. The dance motion recognition comes up with several challenges, such as (a) Motions' complexity, (b) Occlusion due to the dressing style that is being followed in any Indian classical dance, and (c) Uneven frames involved with each motion. Even the same motion may not have the same number of frames, making it challenging to generate an equal-sized feature vector for any ML model. We try to handle these challenges and can classify the motion.

As discussed in Sect. 5.1, we create MHI for a given motion which is a 2D vector of size 120×160. Now, this MHI is given as an input to the HOG generator to generate the HOG of MHI image. For each motion, it yields a feature vector of size 9576 (Refer Sect. 5). It is used as a feature in SVM.

We use SVM [8] of One-Vs-One for this classification. Here, we choose only those motion classes with samples ≥ 12, since most of the motions have very few samples. By this, 54 motion classes are left; that is, out of 334 motions, only 54 are chosen. Of 320 motion samples, 271 predicted correctly, resulting in an overall 84.08% accuracy. In most of the classes, one or two samples are wrongly predicted.

7.1 Motion Recognition – Result Discussion

During motion recognition, following observations are made:

- The quantum of misclassifications is not high since most of the mispredictions occur for one or two samples. The mispredictions of zero, one, and two/three are 22, 20, and 12, respectively. That implies, 22 motion classes reach 100% accuracy.
- The motions having similar characteristics are getting misclassified, which is well expected. For example, M72 as M73, M74 as M75, and M75 as M74. In M72, with the help of toes, the body is raised, and then the body comes down. However, In M73, the body weight is given to the right foot, and the left foot is tapped. So, the MHI of M72 becomes very close to M73, and

some samples of M72 are misclassified as M73. A similar pattern is observed between M74 and M75. Here, M74 and M75 are mirror images of M72 and M73, respectively.

- Sometimes, motion in the leg remains unrecognizable due to occlusion (the dress in the lower body part). It implies that the MHI can not give us the expected result and may be a reason for mispredictions. For Example, M110 is misclassified as M112 and vice versa.
- There is misclassification of the motions M287 & 86 and M244 & M334. In M287, the dancer takes a half circular anti-clockwise movement from a side view (the left side towards the camera), faces the camera, and then taps the left foot. In contrast, the M86 motion is only taping the left foot. Here, the half circular motion around the torso may not be recorded by MHI, making M287 and M86 the same kind of motion.

  M244 and M334 are minimal motion, that is, these motions occur for a very small number of frames. In M244, the dancer stands on the heels making tows up, and then taps the tows on the floor. However, M334 is just opposite M244. In this, dancer stands on its tows by taking the body slightly up and then comes down by striking the heel on the floor. These two motions are hardly distinguishable and get misclassified. The MHI of the feet is hardly recognized. However, the slight change of MHI is visible on the hand due to the vertical movement of the body.
- When we restrict the number of samples ≥ 25, the SVM shows a good recognition accuracy, 95.58% over 12 classes. Again the accuracy of SVM also goes up compared to the SVM with # of samples ≥ 12. It implies that the more samples, the classifiers' performance improves.
- SVM can cover 54 motion classes when # of samples ≥ 12 with an accuracy 84.86%. So, we use this trained SVM during *Adavu* recognition.

8   *Adavu* Recognition

To recognize an *Adavu*, we need to recognize the KPs and motions involved. The recognized sequence (i.e., KPs and motions) is matched with the dictionary of the *Adavus* using Edit Distance algorithm. This algorithm computes the best match and recognizes the *Adavu*. Figure 2 shows the workflow. In this, we use the trained models to recognise the KP (Using CNN) and motion (using SVM) as discussed in Sect. 6 and 7.

First, we need to create a dictionary that keeps the ground truth of the *Adavu* [3]. This ground truth is nothing but the labeling of an *Adavu* and the occurrence of KPs and motion IDs involved in that. This dictionary is used in Edit Distance algorithm to predict the best match.

8.1   Result Discussion

This section discusses the prediction accuracy using Edit Distance algorithm. The inputs to this algorithm are an unknown sequence, and a dictionary denotes the *Adavu sequences* labeled with the *Adavu* name. The algorithm computes the distance score of the given unknown sequence with each of the *Adavu* sequences in the dictionary. The least score is treated as the best match. If it gives the same distance score for multiple *Adavu* sequences in the dictionary of an unknown sequence, then the first matched sequence's label name in the dictionary is given to the unknown one. We try two approaches for the *Adavu* recognition.

Approach-1: In this, only KP sequences are considered to recognise the *Adavu* as in [13, 15, 21, 28].

Approach-2: For a given *Adavu*, the motions that do not participate in the recognition are predicted correctly in the given sequence of an *Adavu*. It is because, out of 334 motions, we consider only 54 during the recognition due to the lack of data. With this approach, we can include all the *Adavus* during the *Adavu* recognition. So, a total 1645 number of sequences need to be predicted in this approach (Refer Table 2).

In **Approach-1**, 1275 sequences are predicted correctly out of 1645. That is, the recognition accuracy is 77.51%. In this, the wrongly predicted 370 sequences belong to *Tatta_2* to *Tatta_8* (For sequence count refer Table 2). These are misclassified with *Tatta_1* since the sequence of KPs in all these *Tatta Adavus* are the same (Refer [3]). The KP sequence of all these *Tatta*: [P153 – P153 – P153 – P153 – ..... – P153]. As we can see, these *Adavus* only comprises one KPs. Hence, the cross misclassifications occur within the *Tatta*. By considering only *Natta* and *Mettu Adavus* as considered in [13], we achieve 100% accuracy.

Approach-2 attends an accuracy of 98.66%. Here, out of 1645 *Adavu* sequences, 1623 predicted correctly. Here, 22 sequences of *Tatta-8 Adavu* are mispredicted as *Tatta-1* since These two *Adavus* share common KPs and motions which follow the same order (Refer [3]). The sequence of *Tatta-1* and 8 is: [M257 – P153 – M258 – P153 – M257 – P153 – M258 – P153 – M257 – P153 – M258 – P153 – M257 – P153 – M258 – P153]. These two *Adavus* are performed by two different *Sollukattus* (Refer [20]). So they only can be distinguished by the audio beats, not by the video analysis.

In both of these approaches, except *Tatta* the rest of the *Adavus'* accuracy is 100%. Though, in some cases, the KPs or motions may get mispredicted in an *Adavu*, the *Adavu* recognizer is still able to predict the correct *Adavu*. It is because, none of the motions or KPs are repeated in higher density (Refer [3]) in any of the *Adavu* sequences (except *Tatta*).

Due to the non-overlapping sequences, the cross misclassifications are taken care by Edit Distance algorithm in both approaches. Now, let us take an example to understand this. The example is based on only KP sequences, and the same applies to KP and motions. Table 5 shows the sequence of KPs (ground truth sequences) involved in *Mettu Adavus*. In these four *Mettus*, all the KPs are unique, except P12 and P9. For *Mettu-1*, CNN predicts the KP sequence as P2–P1–P4–P1–P5–P6–P4–P1–P7–P8–P4–P8–P5–P6–P4–P3

Here, red shows mispredicted KPs. When this predicted sequence is compared with the ground truth (Table 5), Edit Distance algorithm yields distance values

3, 16, 16, and 16 with respect to *Mettu-1*, 2, 3, and 4. So, the predicted sequence matches with *Mettu-1*, even with three KP misclassifications.

Table 5. Ground Truth KP Sequences in *Mettus*

Mettu	KPs
1	P2–P3–P4–P1–P5–P6–P4–P1–P7–P8–P4–P1–P5–P6–P4–P1
2	P10–P11–P12–P9–P10–P11–P12–P9–P10–P11–P12–P9–P10–P11–P12–P9
3	P14–P15–P16–P13–P14–P15–P16–P13–P18–P19–P20–P17–P18–P19–P20–P17
4	P21–P22–P12–P9–P23–P24–P12–P9–P25–P26–P27–P28–P29–P30–P31–P32

Table 6 shows the result comparison of the contemporary approaches. As we can observe that the current approaches outperform the earlier ones, [13,21], and [28].

Table 6. Adavu Recognition Result Comparison

Approach	*Adavu* Attributes		# of	# of	Accuracy
	KP	Motion	*Adavus*	Sequences	(%)
SVM & ED [13]	✓	–	12	326	99.38
HMM [21]	✓	–	8	56	94.64
HMM [28]	✓	–	12	–	80.55
CNN & ED * (Approach-1)	✓	–	12	447	100
CNN, SVM & ED* (Approach-2)	✓	✓	51	1645	98.66

* mark denotes the proposed approaches

Execution time Comparison – [13] Vs Proposed Approaches

Time	SVM & ED [13]	Approach-1	Approach-2
Prediction time (P_rT)	21182 (s)	278 (s)	519 (s)
Average Prediction Time ($AvgP_rT$)	12.88 (s)	0.169 (s)	0.316 (s)

8.2 Performance Analysis Based on Time

We compute and compare the time complexity (Execution time) between the current approaches and earlier work [13]. Table 6 shows the comparison. Here, the prediction time (P_rT) implies the total time incurred to recognize all the *Adavu* sequences. Similarly, average prediction time ($AvgP_rT = P_rT/\gamma$) is the approximate prediction time per sequence. Here, The number of Sequences $\gamma = 1645$,

Refer Table 2. The training time or model building time for SVM-KP, CNN-KP, and SVM-Motion recognition are 5121(s), 5472(s), and 1788(s), respectively. We carry the experiment on a system with Windows-10 OS, Intel Xeon Silver 4110 CPU, 32 GB DDR4 RAM, and NVIDIA GeForce RTX 2080 Ti GPU with 11 GB of GDDR6 RAM. In this system, Approach-1 is ≈ 76 times faster than [13], whereas Approach-2, is ≈ 40 times faster. While comparing the performance of the two proposed approaches, we find that Approach-1 is ≈ 2 times faster than Approach-2.

9 Conclusion

The proposed approach recognizes the *Adavu* based on KP and motion rather than considering only KPs as in [13, 21, 28]. This is the novelty of the work. Again, most of the earlier works use classical machine learning algorithms, whereas we use an effective deep learning technique, which gives a comparatively better result in less time. However, the robustness of the proposed CNN model is yet to be tested with the other data sets. The recognition accuracy (98.66%) of the proposed one outperforms the previous approaches looking at the quantum of data. Though we try more sequences, we still achieve good accuracy. Again, the KP recognition uses CNN which is better than the SVM as reported in [13, 21, 28]. Moreover, the paper also explores and analyzes the performance of the proposed approaches based on prediction time. The same is also compared with the earlier similar work [13] and found that the performance/efficiency of the proposed work is better than the earlier ones. For future work, we may try RNN for this sequence recognition since the occurrence of KPs and motions are the time series data, and RNN can handle this. In RNN, we can directly train the sequences (comprises of KPs and MHIs) and test the same for recognition.

References

1. Ahad, M.A.R., Tan, J.K., Kim, H., Ishikawa, S.: Motion history image: its variants and applications. Mach. Vis. Appl. **23**(2), 255–281 (2012). https://doi.org/10.1007/s00138-010-0298-4
2. Aich, A., Mallick, T., Bhuyan, H.B.G.S., Das, P.P., Majumdar, A.K.: *NrityaGuru*: a dance tutoring system for *Bharatanatyam* using kinect. In: Rameshan, R., Arora, C., Dutta Roy, S. (eds.) NCVPRIPG 2017. CCIS, vol. 841, pp. 481–493. Springer, Singapore (2018). https://doi.org/10.1007/978-981-13-0020-2_42
3. Bhuyan, H., Mallick, T., Das, P.P., Majumdar, A.K.: Annotated Bharatanatyam data set, May 2022. https://hci.cse.iitkgp.ac.in/Miscellaneous.html
4. Bhuyan, H., Das, P.P., Dash, J.K., Killi, J.: An automated method for identification of key frames in Bharatanatyam dance videos. IEEE Access **9**, 72670–72680 (2021)
5. Bhuyan, H., Killi, J., Das, P.P., Dash, J.: Motion recognition in Bharatanatyam. IEEE Access (2022). https://doi.org/10.1109/ACCESS.2022.3184735
6. Bhuyan, H., Roy, M., Das, P.P.: Motion classification in *Bharatanatyam* dance. In: Babu, R.V., Prasanna, M., Namboodiri, V.P. (eds.) NCVPRIPG 2019. CCIS, vol. 1249, pp. 408–417. Springer, Singapore (2020). https://doi.org/10.1007/978-981-15-8697-2_38

7. Biswas, S., Ghildiyal, A., Sharma, S.: Classification of Indian dance forms using pre-trained model-VGG. In: 2021 Sixth International Conference on WiSPNET, pp. 278–282. IEEE (2021)
8. Chang, C.C., Lin, C.J.: LIBSVM: a library for support vector machines. ACM Trans. Intell. Syst. Technol. (TIST) **2**(3), 1–27 (2011)
9. Chaudhry, H., Tabia, K., Rahim, S.A., BenFerhat, S.: Automatic annotation of traditional dance data using motion features. In: ICDAMT, pp. 254–258. IEEE (2017)
10. Dalal, N., Triggs, B.: Histograms of oriented gradients for human detection. In: 2005 IEEE Computer Society Conference on Computer Vision and Pattern Recognition (CVPR 2005), vol. 1, pp. 886–893. IEEE (2005)
11. Dubey, A.K., Jain, V.: Comparative study of convolution neural network's relu and leaky-relu activation functions. In: Mishra, S., Sood, Y.R., Tomar, A. (eds.) Applications of Computing, Automation and Wireless Systems in Electrical Engineering. LNEE, vol. 553, pp. 873–880. Springer, Singapore (2019). https://doi.org/10.1007/978-981-13-6772-4_76
12. He, K., Sun, J.: Convolutional neural networks at constrained time cost. In: Proceedings of the IEEE Conference on Computer Vision and Pattern Recognition, pp. 5353–5360 (2015)
13. Bhuyan, H., Das, P.P.: Recognition of *Adavu*s in *Bharatanatyam* dance. In: Singh, S.K., Roy, P., Raman, B., Nagabhushan, P. (eds.) CVIP 2020. CCIS, vol. 1378, pp. 174–185. Springer, Singapore (2021). https://doi.org/10.1007/978-981-16-1103-2_16
14. Jain, N., Bansal, V., Virmani, D., Gupta, V., Salas-Morera, L., Garcia-Hernandez, L.: An enhanced deep convolutional neural network for classifying Indian classical dance forms. Appl. Sci. **11**(14), 6253 (2021)
15. Kale, G., Patil, V.: Bharatnatyam Adavu recognition from depth data. In: 2015 Third ICIIP, pp. 246–251. IEEE (2015)
16. Kaushik, V., Mukherjee, P., Lall, B.: Nrityantar: pose oblivious Indian classical dance sequence classification system. In: 11th ICVGIP, pp. 1–7 (2018)
17. Kishore, P., et al.: Indian classical dance action identification and classification with convolutional neural networks. Adv. Multimedia **2018** (2018)
18. Krizhevsky, A., Sutskever, I., Hinton, G.E.: ImageNet classification with deep convolutional neural networks. In: Advances in Neural Information Processing Systems, vol. 25 (2012)
19. Kumar, K., Kishore, P., Kumar, D.A., Kumar, E.K.: Indian classical dance action identification using adaboost multiclass classifier on multifeature fusion. In: 2018 Conference on SPACES, pp. 167–170. IEEE (2018)
20. Mallick, T., Bhuyan, H., Das, P.P., Majumdar, A.K.: Annotated Bharatanatyam data set, May 2017. https://hci.cse.iitkgp.ac.in/Audio%20Data.html
21. Mallick, T., Das, P.P., Majumdar, A.K.: Posture and sequence recognition for Bharatanatyam dance performances using machine learning approaches. J. Vis. Commun. Image Represent. **87**, 103548 (2022)
22. Microsoft: Microsoft kinect sensor v1 to capture RGB, depth, and skeleton stream, November 2010. https://msdn.microsoft.com/en-us/library/hh438998.aspx
23. Mohanty, A., et al.: Nrityabodha: towards understanding Indian classical dance using a deep learning approach. Sig. Process. Image Commun. **47**, 529–548 (2016)
24. Naik, A.D., Supriya, M.: Classification of Indian classical dance images using convolution neural network. In: ICCSP, pp. 1245–1249. IEEE (2020)
25. Russakovsky, O., et al.: ImageNet large scale visual recognition challenge. Int. J. Comput. Vis. **115**(3), 211–252 (2015). https://doi.org/10.1007/s11263-015-0816-y

26. Saha, S., Ghosh, S., Konar, A., Nagar, A.K.: Gesture recognition from Indian classical dance using kinect sensor. In: 5th International Conference on CICSN, pp. 3–8. IEEE (2013)
27. Shailesh, S., Judy, M.: Computational framework with novel features for classification of foot postures in Indian classical dance. Intell. Decis. Technol. **14**(1), 119–132 (2020)
28. Sharma, A.: Recognising Bharatanatyam dance sequences using RGB-D data. IIT, Kanpur, India (2013)
29. Venkatesh, P., Jayagopi, D.B.: Automatic Bharatnatyam dance posture recognition and expertise prediction using depth cameras. In: Bi, Y., Kapoor, S., Bhatia, R. (eds.) IntelliSys 2016. LNNS, vol. 16, pp. 1–14. Springer, Cham (2018). https://doi.org/10.1007/978-3-319-56991-8_1

Multi-modality Fusion for Siamese Network Based RGB-T Tracking (mfSiamTrack)

A. V. Chithra[✉] and Deepak Mishra

Indian Institute of Space Science and Technologies,
Thiruvananthapuram, Kerala, India
chithra.av@gmail.com

Abstract. Object tracking in thermal imagery is a challenging problem relevant to more and more growing applications. By fusing the complementary features of RGB and thermal images, the object tracking algorithms can be enhanced to give better outputs. mfSiamTrack (Multi-modality fusion for Siamese Network based RGB-T Tracking) is a dual-mode STSO (Short Term Single Object) tracker. The tracker works in Thermal Mode and Multi-modality fusion mode (RGBT mode). The RGBT mode gets activated if the dataset contains the Thermal Infrared and the corresponding RGB sequences. The complementary features from both RGB and Thermal Imagery are fused, and tracking uses fused sequences. If only thermal sequences exist in the dataset, the tracker works in thermal tracking mode. An auto-encoder (AE) based fusion network is proposed for multi-modality fusion. The Encoder decomposes the RGB and thermal images into the background and detail feature maps. The background and detail feature maps of the source images are fused by the Fusion Layer and the Decoder reconstructs the fused image. For handling objects at different scales and viewpoints, mfSiamTrack introduces a Multi-Scale Structural Similarity (MS-SSIM) based reconstruction method. mfSiamTrack is a fully convolutional-siamese network based tracker which also incorporates a semi-supervised video object segmentation (VOS) for pixel-wise target identification. The tracker was evaluated on the VOT-RGBT2019 dataset with Accuracy, Robustness, Expected Average Overlap (EAO) and Average IoU as performance evaluation measures. It is observed that mfSiamTrack outperforms the state-of-the-art.

Keywords: Visual Object Tracking (VOT) · Multi-modality fusion · Siamese Network · Image Fusion · Auto-Encoder · Video Object Segmentation (VOS)

1 Introduction

Visual Object tracking is one of the challenging areas in Computer Vision. The aim is to find the trajectory of an object over time. The tracker locates a specific object in all frames, given the location of the object in the initial frame.

© The Author(s), under exclusive license to Springer Nature Switzerland AG 2023
D. Gupta et al. (Eds.): CVIP 2022, CCIS 1776, pp. 406–420, 2023.
https://doi.org/10.1007/978-3-031-31407-0_31

Object Tracking has been a vibrant research area in recent years due to its applications in many domains, like robotics, surveillance, self-driving cars, and human-machine interface. Object tracking can be formulated as a problem of similarity measurement, correlation, correspondence, matching, or data association between objects in adjacent frames. Various algorithms were proposed in the area of Object Tracking, based on handcrafted features and deep features. Deep learning-based trackers get good tracking results by exploiting Convolutional Neural Networks' (CNN) strong feature representation ability. In this paper, object tracking is considered as a problem of similarity measurement with the help of the Siamese Network. The Siamese network based trackers are considered as the most promising architectures because of their balance between performance and accuracy.

A lot of tracking algorithms are available for tracking objects in the visible spectrum. Even though RGB tracking has dominating status in the tracking community, it faces many problems, particularly tracking target objects in darkness, poor light conditions, and difficult weather conditions (rain, fog, snow, smog, etc.). Tracking in Thermal Imaging is an effective alternative for these situations. By combining thermal and visible spectrum data, tracking performance can further be improved. They complement each other and contribute to visual object tracking in various aspects. mfSiamTrack is a siamese network based dual mode tracker which operates in both thermal and RGBT mode (This paper uses the terms RGBT mode and multi-modality fusion mode interchangeably). It also incorporates a semi-supervised video object segmentation (VOS) for pixel wise target identification.

2   Key Contributions

The major contributions of this paper are given below:

- **A multi-modal fusion network:** A fusion network with auto-encoder is proposed for RGB and thermal modality fusion. Multi scale structural similarity (MS-SSIM) based image reconstruction is proposed, which is suitable for handling image details at different resolutions and viewing distances.
- **A Dual mode Object Tracker:** The tracker is designed to work in dual mode. It tracks objects on thermal data if the corresponding RGB modality is not available. The tracker works on the fused data if both modalities are available.
- **Short-Term Single-Object tracking (STSO) on fused sequences:** The Object Tracking algorithm is designed to work on the fused sequences, which is the output of a multi-modal fusion network.
- **Performance comparison with SSIM and MS-SSIM:** Carried out comparative study of tracking performance on SSIM based and MSSSIM based fused sequences.
- **Comparison of tracking performance on different modalities:** Compared the tracking performance on RGB, thermal, and fused image sequences.

3   Related Work

3.1   Tracking in Thermal Imagery

TIR tracking sequentially locates an object in an infrared video similar to RGB tracking. There are two frequent misconceptions about tracking of objects in thermal infrared imagery [1]. The first assumption is that thermal object tracking means hotspot tracking (tracking warm objects over cold backgrounds) This is valid only for some applications, such as tracking aircraft on a cool sky, but the situation is more complicated in most other cases. A surveillance application can be taken as an example: at starting the object can be warmer compared to the background, but as day progresses, due to the increase in sunlight the surrounding can be hotter than the object. The second widespread misconception is that thermal infrared tracking is the same as tracking in gray-scale. As a result, a good tracker designed for object tracking in visual imagery should also perform good in thermal infrared imagery. But, this is not the case because different trackers produce distinct result on RGB and thermal sequences. Thermal object tracking is not the same as tracking in visual grayscale imagery.

- Since thermal infrared imagery has various noise characteristics, such as lower resolution and more blooming, a tracker relies primarily on high resolution is likely to be inadequate.
- Because there are no shadows, a tracker which considers shadows may be ineffective for thermal infrared imaging.
- Color patterns are noticeable in the infrared imagery if they relate to variations in temperature or material.
- Re-identification and addressing occlusions may require distinct approaches. (Two people with differently patterned dresses may appear same in thermal imagery).
- The most evident thing is that thermal infrared imagery has no color. Therefore trackers that rely on colour are not ideal for thermal imagery.

3.2   Image Fusion

Image fusion combines information, specifically complementary, from different images into a single image. This fused images provide a better data source for applications. In general, infrared images can avoid visually cognitive obstacles created by illumination variations, but they have poor texture detail information and low spatial resolution. On the other hand, visible images have high spatial resolution and rich knowledge of appearance but are easily affected by hinders and light reflections. Therefore, a good image fusion architecture that combines complementary information from both modalities can make tracking easier.

3.3   Semi-supervised Video Object Segmentation

Semi-supervised video object segmentation is the process of segmenting objects in all the frames of a video. Currently, deep learning approaches made the research to achieve remarkable results. Mainly, video object segmentation methods comes under two categories, detection-based methods and propagation-based methods. In detection-based methods [2,3], the representations of the object is learned from the initial frame and perform pixel-wise detection in the continuous frames. In propagation-based methods [4,5], segmentation task is formulated as a tracking problem and try to propagate the mask to fit the object over time.

4   Methodology

4.1   Siamese Network

Bromley and LeCun first introduced Siamese networks in 1994 to solve signature verification as a problem of image matching [6]. A Siamese neural network is an artificial network containing two or more identical subnetworks. These subnetworks have the same configuration along with the same parameters and weights. We need to train one of the subnetworks and use the same configuration for other sub-networks. By comparing the feature vectors of inputs, these networks can find the similarity of the inputs. These networks can be trained with triplet loss [7], contrastive loss [8] or binary cross-entropy loss. The anchor image is compared with a positive and negative image vector for learning by triplet loss. The positive vector functions as a regularizer, whereas the negative vector forces learning in the network. In the case of contrastive loss function, parameters are learned by the concept that the neighbors are pulled together and non-neighbors are pushed apart.

4.2   Siamese Networks for Visual Object Tracking

Tracking with Siamese networks is an effective way to handle varying challenges. For doing tracking, one input of the network is taken as the target/exemplar image and the other input as a search image or the current frame. The network is responsible for locating target image inside of search images. By assessing the similarity between the target and each part of the search image, the tracker generates a map of the similarity score. The location with the highest similarity score may contain the target (See Fig. 1).

Siamese-FC (Fully-Convolutional Siamese Networks) is one of the first Siamese network-based trackers to achieve high accuracy and speed [9]. Siamese-RPN, followed by the idea of Siamese-FC, uses Siamese networks for feature extraction and an additional region proposal network for proposal refinement [10]. For learning more discriminative feature representation, DaSiamRPN (distractor-aware Siamese networks) introduces an effective sampling strategy for training and a distractor-aware module for inference [11]. As the backbone of Siamese networks, all of the above trackers employ a five convolutional-layer AlexNet-like design. SiamRPN++ [12] uses ResNet [13] as the backbone and uses a spatial aware sampling strategy to accomplish better performance using a fusion of feature maps. SiamMask [14] proposes a unifying approach for Tracking the objects along with semi-supervised Video Object Segmentation (VOS).

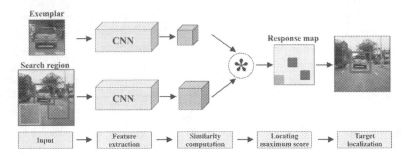

Fig. 1. Fully Convolutional Siamese Network: Target and Current frames are the two inputs to the network, and target localization is based on the score in the response map

4.3 Multi-modality Fusion Networks

Image fusion combines information, specifically complementary information, from different images into a single image. This fused image can provide more information for applications. Various algorithms were introduced under pixel-level, feature-level and decision level fusion. In VGG-ML [15], the image decomposition method decomposes the source images into a base and details parts. The base parts of both images are then fused by a weighted average strategy and the details part with a pre-trained VGG19. DenseFuse [16] is pre-trained on MS-COCO and utilizes addition and L1-norm for fusion. ResNet-ZCA [17] employs ResNet for extracting deep features from source images. DIDFuse [18] is an auto-encoder (AE) based fusion network. The encoder decomposes background and detail feature maps from the source images, and the decoder reconstructs the image after fusion. DIDFuse is taken as the base work for multi-modality image fusion in this paper.

4.4 mfSiamTrack

mfSiamTrack is an STSO tracker designed to track objects in thermal imagery and RGBT domain depending on the availability of type of sequences. The tracker consists of two major modules, viz., multi-modality fusion and object tracking, as shown in Fig. 2.

If the dataset contains only thermal images, the multi-modality fusion module gets exempted, and object tracking is enabled for thermal imagery. If the dataset contains RGB images of corresponding thermal images, the complementary benefits of both the modalities are getting fused using the multi-modality fusion module, and the object tracking works on the fused images. The tracker also incorporates a semi-supervised video object segmentation (VOS) for pixel-wise target identification.

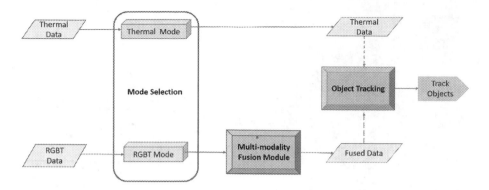

Fig. 2. mfSiamTrack: Operates in RGBT Mode if thermal and RGB sequences are available, and in Thermal mode if only thermal sequences are available

Modality Fusion Module: We propose An auto-encoder (AE) based fusion network similar to [18] for fusing the RGB and Thermal modalities. A Multi-Scale Structural Similarity (MS-SSIM) based loss function is proposed to handle image details at different resolutions and viewing distances. The network works with an encoder and a decoder. With the help of frequency information (low or high), the encoder decomposes the images into feature maps of background and detail. Then concatenation happens through the channels. The decoder is responsible for reconstructing the fused images from the concatenated feature maps.

During the training phase, the encoder is taught to breakdown the source images and the decoder to rebuild them. The loss function encourages the base feature maps to be similar and the detail feature maps to be distinct during the decomposition stage. During the reconstruction step, the loss function preserves pixel intensities among source and rebuilt images, as well as visible image gradient information. The structural similarity of images are also considered for getting better reconstruction results. During the test phase, the feature maps of background and detail are fused separately using a specified fusion method, and the decoder can then acquire the fused image. The architecture of multi-modality fusion module is shown in Fig. 3.

Image Decomposition: The background feature maps contain the similar features and the detail feature maps contain the distinguishing features from thermal and visible images. The network aims to make the distance of background feature maps small, and that of detail feature maps more during image decomposition. Therefore, the loss function creates the background feature maps similar and detail feature maps dissimilar.

$$L_1 = \phi(||B_V - B_T||_2^2) - \alpha_1\phi(||Dv - D_T||_2^2) \tag{1}$$

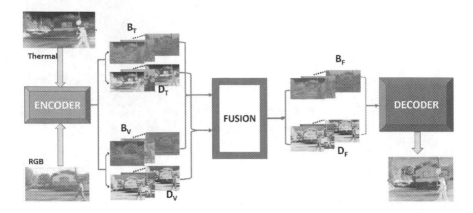

Fig. 3. Multi-modality fusion module: Encoder decomposes source images, Fusion module concatenate backgrounds and details, and Decoder reconstruct the fused images

where B_V is the background feature map, D_V is the detail feature map of RGB Images and, B_T and D_T are that of Thermal Images. $\phi()$ is the Tanh function.

Image Reconstruction: The concatenated feature maps of both background and detail images go through the decoder. Both pixel-intensity wise and structural similarity wise checking is carried out in the loss function. L2-norm estimates the intensity of pixel between reconstructed and original images, and structural similarity measures image similarity in respect of contrast, brightness and structure.

The Structural Similarity (SSIM) [19] between the samples $a\&b$ can be calculated based on the comparison measurements: structure (s), luminance (l) and contrast (c). SSIM is the weighted combination of these and it can be calculated as:

$$SSIM(a,b) = \left[l(a,b)^\alpha \cdot c(a,b)^\beta \cdot s(a,b)^\gamma \right] \tag{2}$$

In [18], SSIM [19] was used for structural similarity calculation which is a single-scale approach. The single-scale method may be suitable only for specific settings. To incorporate image details at different resolutions and viewing distance, multi-scale method is a convenient way. In this paper, MSSSIM (Multi-Scale Structural Similarity) [20] based image reconstruction is proposed. The system considers the original image at scales 1 and M as the largest scale. At the j-th scale, the contrast comparison $(c_j(a,b))$ and structure comparison $(s_j(a,b))$ are calculated. The luminance comparison is calculated at scale M $(l_M(a,b))$. The total MS-SSIM value is calculated by combining the values at each scale.

$$\text{MSSSIM}(\mathbf{a},\mathbf{b}) = [l_M(\mathbf{a},\mathbf{b})]^{\alpha_M} \cdot \prod_{j=1}^{M} [c_j(\mathbf{a},\mathbf{b})]^{\beta_j} [s_j(\mathbf{a},\mathbf{b})]^{\gamma_j} \tag{3}$$

Loss Function: The multi-scale similarity between the original and reconstructed image can be formulated as:

$$L_{MSSSIM}(X, X_R) = \frac{1 - MSSSIM(X, X_R)}{2}, \tag{4}$$

where X and X_R are the Input and reconstructed images. The similarity calculation is like

$$f(X, X_R) = ||X - X_R||_2^2 + \lambda L_{MSSSIM}(X, X_R), \tag{5}$$

The loss function for reconstruction phase is represented as

$$L_2 = \alpha_2 f(T, T_R) + \alpha_3 f(V, V_R) + \alpha_4 ||\nabla V - \nabla V_R||, \tag{6}$$

where T- Thermal Image Input, T_R - Reconstructed Thermal Image, V - Visible image input, V_R - Reconstructed Visible Image, ∇ - the gradient operator. Combining equations, the final loss, L_{tot} can be calculated as

$$L_{tot} = \phi(||B_V - B_T||_2^2) - \alpha_1\phi(||Dv - D_T||_2^2 + \alpha_2 f(T, T_R) + \alpha_3 f(V, V_R) + \alpha_4 ||\nabla V - \nabla V_R|| \tag{7}$$

where α s are the tuning parameters.

During Fusion, the background and detail feature maps are fused separately,

$$B_F = Fusion(B_T, B_v), D_F = Fusion(D_T, D_V) \tag{8}$$

where B_F and D_F are the fused feature maps of background and detail.

$$BF = B_T \oplus B_V, DF = D_T \oplus D_V \tag{9}$$

where the symbol $\oplus$ indicates element-wise addition.

Object Tracking Module: Siamese network-based object tracking module is proposed as in [14] with an enhanced dual-mode input module. The input pipeline is designed to accept the fused exemplar and search images if the dataset contains both thermal and RGB images. It accepts only thermal images if the RGB version is absent. The fundamental building block of tracking system is adopted as proposed by Bertinetto et al. [9]. The Schematic diagram of the tracking module is given in Fig. 4.

The fused exemplar image (target) and search image (current frame) is given as the input to the network. The backbone network (Resnet-50) extracts features from both targets and search images and creates feature maps. The response map is created with a size of $17 \times 17 \times 256$ after the depth-wise cross-correlation operation (channel by channel basis). The response of a candidate window(RoW) is considered to be $1 \times 1 \times 256$, and Classification, regression and segmentation branches are enabled for it.

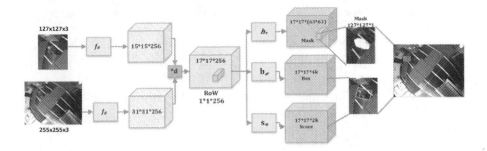

Fig. 4. Schematic diagram of Object Tracking module: Inputs are target image ($127 \times 127 \times 3$) and Search Image (Current frame - $255 \times 255 \times 3$), d is the depth wise cross-correlation operation on feature maps. It contain three branches for classification, bounding box regression and segmentation

Classification Loss: In the classification branch, the training is carried out using logistic loss:

$$l(y, n) = log(1 + exp(-yn)) \tag{10}$$

where n is the score of a target window and $y(+1 or - 1)$ the corresponding ground truth. The entire score map's loss:

$$L(y, m) = \frac{1}{|D|} \sum_{m \in D} l(y[m], n[m]) \tag{11}$$

for each position $n \in D$ in the score map. In this work each spatial element of the response map is considered as the response of a candidate window(RoW). For getting richer information about each RoW, the cross-correlation operation is replaced with depth-wise cross-correlation [12] which produces multi channel response map.

Regression Loss: For improving the performance, Region Proposal Network is included in the siamese network as per SiamRPN [10]. So for each RoW, a set of k anchor box proposals are encoded. If there are k anchors, network need to produce $2k$ channels for foreground/background classification and $4k$ channels for regression.

$$A_{w \times h \times 2k}^{classification} = [\phi(x)]_{classification} * [\phi(z)]_{classification} \tag{12}$$

$$A_{w \times h \times 4k}^{regression} = [\phi(x)]_{regression} * [\phi(z)]_{regression} \tag{13}$$

During training, Smooth $L1$ loss with normalized coordinates is used.

$$L_{reg} = \sum_{i=0}^{3} smooth_{L1}(dt[i], \sigma) \tag{14}$$

where $dt[i]$ is the normalized distance.

Segmentation Loss: In addition to the bounding box prediction, per-frame binary segmentation is also used during tracking as in [14]. For each RoW, there are ground-truth label $y_n \in \pm 1$ and a ground truth mask (pixel-wise) c_n with size wxh. The mask prediction loss:

$$L_{mask}(\theta, \phi) = \sum_n (\frac{1 + y_n}{2wh} \sum_{ij} log(1 + e^{-c_n^{ij} m_n^{ij}})) \qquad (15)$$

where $c_n^{ij} \in \pm 1$ is the ground truth of pixel (i, j) of $n - th$ RoW and m_n^{ij} be the prediction.

Final Loss: The final loss can be formulated as

$$L = \lambda_1.L_{mask} + \lambda_2.L_{score} + \lambda_3.L_{box} \qquad (16)$$

where λ_1, λ_2 and λ_3 are the hyper parameters.

In Thermal mode mfSiamTrack do tracking on thermal sequences as shown in Fig. 4. In the multi-modality fusion mode, the fusing of RGB and Thermal frames happens first, and tracking work on the fused sequences. The architecture of mfSiamTrack-RGBT mode is shown in Fig. 5

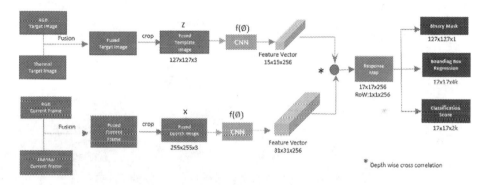

Fig. 5. mfSiamTrack-RGBT Mode: In RGBT mode, fusion of RGB and Thermal versions of target and search frames happens prior to tracking

5   Experiments and Results

Experimental Setup: The multi-modality fusion module was trained and tested with FLIR, TNO, NIR and VOT-RGBT2019 dataset. The network is trained for 120 epochs. The batch size was 24 and the optimizer was Adam. Initial learning rate was taken as 10^{-3} and is reduced by ten times after each 40 epochs. The object tracking module is trained with COCO [21], Imagenet-VID [22], Youtube-VOS [23] datasets. The target image was set to $127 \times 127 \times 3$ and search image to $255 \times 255 \times 3$. The backbone network is Resnet-50, which has been pre-trained using the Imagenet dataset. Stochastic Gradient Descent (SGD) was used for optimization with an initial learning rate of 10^{-3}.

Performance Evaluation: VOT-RGBT-2019 dataset is considered for performance evaluation in this work. There are a total of 234 sequences in this collection, on an average 335 frames per sequences. [24]. Out of that, 60 video pairs are used for performance evaluation. Each sequence contains multiple frames with RGB and Thermal versions. Three key indicators are used to examine the short-term tracking performance according to the benchmark VOT-2019: A-Accuracy, R-Robustness and EAO-Expected Average Overlap. Accuracy is measured as the average overlap between the predicted bounding boxes and ground truth bounding boxes in the successful tracking period. Robustness is inversely proportional to the failure rate. EAO combines accuracy and robustness by averaging the overlaps for different sequence lengths. Average Intersection over union (IoU) was also evaluated which is the overlap between the predicted and the ground-truth bounding boxes.

5.1   Experimental Results

mfSiamTrack contains a Multi-modality fusion and an Object Tracking module. In the fusion module, experiments were conducted on FLIR, TNO, NIR and VOT-RGBT2019 datasets. The sample of fusion result obtained from VOT-RGBT2019 dataset is given in Fig. 6. An example of tracker performance is illustrated with the help of sequence 'fog' (shown in Fig. 7).

Fig. 6. Image fusion on VOT-RGBT2019 dataset: From left to right: Thermal, RGB and Fused version of sequence dog11 and car10

For evaluating the performance of mfSiamTrack, the experiments were conducted on all the validation sequences (in Thermal, RGB and fused sequences separately) from VOT-RGBT2019. IoU was calculated for each frame with the predicted and ground-truth bounding boxes. The mean IoU (from all the frames)

RGB   Thermal   Fused

Fig. 7. Object Tracking in sequence 'fog' (VOT-RGBT2019): Ground truth in green and prediction in blue (Color figure online)

was taken for all the sequences. From the summary of IoU score, it is observed that in most of the cases, fused sequences gave better IoU score compared to RGB and Thermal sequences.

mfSiamTrack proposes the multi-modality fusion module with Multi-scale structural similarity (MS-SSIM). For reaching a conclusion about MS-SSIM based fusion architecture, experiments were conducted on both SSIM and MS-SSIM based fused sequences. For both the versions, IoU was calculated. In terms of IoU, Tracking on MSSSIM-based fused sequences gave better results compared to SSIM-based sequences. Out of 60 validation sequences, MS-SSIM based fused sequences came with top IoU score for 15 sequences compared to RGB and Thermal sequences. 34 sequences were in second position and 11 were in third. The Accuracy, Robustness, EAO and Average IoU were calculated for evaluating the tracker. The results are given in the Table 1. The MS-SSIM version of tracker came with accuracy 0.615, Robustness 0.533 and EAO 0.339 which is better compared to other versions of sequences. Comparison of both the versions of mfSiamTrack (mfSiamTrack-SSIM and mfSiamTrack-MSSSIM) with the state-of-the-art has been carried out. Table 2 shows the comparison of performance with respect to EAO, Accuracy, and Robustness on the VOT-RGBT2019 benchmark. In VOT Challenges, EAO is taken as the critical measure to identify the winner. In case of Accuracy, FSRPN is in first, SiamDW-T in second and JMMAC in third positions. But, in terms of Robustness and EAO these three trackers are not performing well. MANet came in last position in all the criteria.

Table 1. Performance Evaluation based on Accuracy, Robustness, EAO and Average IoU (Compared Thermal, RGB, SSIM based fusion and MS-SSIM based fusion sequences and observed better performance on MS-SSIM based fused sequences)

Sequence	Accuracy	Robustness	EAO	Average IoU
RGB	0.593	0.448	0.323	0.4599
Thermal	0.603	0.398	0.315	0.4297
Fused-SSIM	0.604	0.513	0.326	0.4603
Fused-MSSSIM	0.615	0.533	0.339	0.4643

Table 2. Comparison with the state-of-the-art on the VOT-RGBT2019 benchmark (Red indicates first, blue indicates second and green indicates third positions)

Tracker	EAO	Accuracy	Robustness
mfDimp [25]	0.2347(3)	0.6133	0.3160(3)
SiamDW-T [26]	0.2143	0.6515(2)	0.2714
MANet [27]	0.2041	0.5784	0.2592
JMMAC [28]	0.2037	0.6337(3)	0.2441
FSRPN [24]	0.1873	0.6561(1)	0.1755
mfSiamTrack-SSIM	0.326(2)	0.604	0.513(2)
mfSiamTrack-MSSSIM	0.339(1)	0.615(4)	0.533(1)

mfDimp reached third position in terms of Robustness and EAO. The SSIM version of mfSiamTrack came in the second position interms of Robustness and EAO. Eventhough in terms of Accuracy, mfSiamTrack-MSSSIM was in third position, interms of Robustness and EAO, the tracker was giving best performance. Thus it is concluded that, mfSiamTrack outperforms the state-of-the-art in terms of EAO measure.

6   Conclusion

In this paper, a dual mode object tracking method is proposed which is termed as mfSiamTrack. Both RGB and Thermal modalities have its own advantage and disadvantage. mfSiamTrack tries to take advantage of both the modalities and combine them using a multi-modality fusion module. In the absence of RGB data, the tracker works in Thermal mode. When both RGB and Thermal versions of sequences are supplied as input to the tracker, the multi-modality fusion module gets enabled and tracking works on the fused sequences. An auto-encoder based fusion network is used for fusing RGB and Thermal data. The tracker is constructed with a fully convolutional siamese network. SSIM and MS-SSIM based image reconstruction methods were experimented and concluded that MS-SSIM version is giving better performance on tracking objects, especially in varying view points. The performance of the tracker was evaluated on the basis of Accuracy, Robustness, EAO and average IoU. VOT-RGBT2019 dataset was used for the evaluation purpose. A comparitive study has been done with state-of-the-art and it is observed that mfSiamTrack outperforms. Currently, the tracker focuses more on improving the robustness. It is intended to enhance the image fusion module in the future, so that accuracy can also be improved.

References

1. Berg, A., Ahlberg, J., Felsberg, M.: A thermal object tracking benchmark. In: 2015 12th IEEE International Conference on Advanced Video and Signal Based Surveillance (AVSS), pp. 1–6. IEEE (2015)

2. Caelles, S., Maninis, K.-K., Pont-Tuset, J., Leal-Taixé, L., Cremers, D., Van Gool, L.: One-shot video object segmentation. In: Proceedings of the IEEE Conference on Computer Vision and Pattern Recognition, pp. 221–230 (2017)

3. Chen, Y., Pont-Tuset, J., Montes, A., Van Gool, L.: Blazingly fast video object segmentation with pixel-wise metric learning. In: Proceedings of the IEEE Conference on Computer Vision and Pattern Recognition, pp. 1189–1198 (2018)

4. Ci, H., Wang, C., Wang, Y.: Video object segmentation by learning location-sensitive embeddings. In: Ferrari, V., Hebert, M., Sminchisescu, C., Weiss, Y. (eds.) ECCV 2018. LNCS, vol. 11215, pp. 524–539. Springer, Cham (2018). https://doi.org/10.1007/978-3-030-01252-6_31

5. Hu, P., Wang, G., Kong, X., Kuen, J., Tan, Y.-P.: Motion-guided cascaded refinement network for video object segmentation. In: Proceedings of the IEEE Conference on Computer Vision and Pattern Recognition, pp. 1400–1409 (2018)

6. Bromley, J., Guyon, I., LeCun, Y., Säckinger, E., Shah, R.: Signature verification using a "siamese" time delay neural network. In: Advances in Neural Information Processing Systems, vol. 6 (1993)

7. Hoffer, E., Ailon, N.: Deep metric learning using triplet network. In: Feragen, A., Pelillo, M., Loog, M. (eds.) SIMBAD 2015. LNCS, vol. 9370, pp. 84–92. Springer, Cham (2015). https://doi.org/10.1007/978-3-319-24261-3_7

8. Wu, Z., Xiong, Y., Yu, S.X., Lin, D.: Unsupervised feature learning via non-parametric instance discrimination. In: Proceedings of the IEEE Conference on Computer Vision and Pattern Recognition, pp. 3733–3742 (2018)

9. Bertinetto, L., Valmadre, J., Henriques, J.F., Vedaldi, A., Torr, P.H.S.: Fully-convolutional siamese networks for object tracking. In: Hua, G., Jégou, H. (eds.) ECCV 2016. LNCS, vol. 9914, pp. 850–865. Springer, Cham (2016). https://doi.org/10.1007/978-3-319-48881-3_56

10. Li, B., Yan, J., Wu, W., Zhu, Z., Hu, X.: High performance visual tracking with siamese region proposal network. In: Proceedings of the IEEE Conference on Computer Vision and Pattern Recognition, pp. 8971–8980 (2018)

11. Zhu, Z., Wang, Q., Li, B., Wu, W., Yan, J., Hu, W.: Distractor-aware siamese networks for visual object tracking. In: Ferrari, V., Hebert, M., Sminchisescu, C., Weiss, Y. (eds.) ECCV 2018. LNCS, vol. 11213, pp. 103–119. Springer, Cham (2018). https://doi.org/10.1007/978-3-030-01240-3_7

12. Li, B., Wu, W., Wang, Q., Zhang, F., Xing, J., Yan, J.: SiamRPN++: evolution of siamese visual tracking with very deep networks. In: Proceedings of the IEEE/CVF Conference on Computer Vision and Pattern Recognition, pp. 4282–4291 (2019)

13. He, K., Zhang, X., Ren, S., Sun, J.: Deep residual learning for image recognition. In: Proceedings of the IEEE Conference on Computer Vision and Pattern Recognition, pp. 770–778 (2016)

14. Wang, Q., Zhang, L., Bertinetto, L., Hu, W., Torr, P.H.: Fast online object tracking and segmentation: a unifying approach. In: Proceedings of the IEEE/CVF Conference on Computer Vision and Pattern Recognition, pp. 1328–1338 (2019)

15. Li, H., Wu, X.-J., Kittler, J.: Infrared and visible image fusion using a deep learning framework. In: 2018 24th International Conference on Pattern Recognition (ICPR), pp. 2705–2710. IEEE (2018)

16. Li, H., Wu, X.-J.: DenseFuse: a fusion approach to infrared and visible images. IEEE Trans. Image Process. **28**(5), 2614–2623 (2018)

17. Li, H., Wu, X.-J., Durrani, T.S.: Infrared and visible image fusion with ResNet and zero-phase component analysis. Infrared Phys. Technol. **102**, 103039 (2019)

18. Zhao, Z., Xu, S., Zhang, C., Liu, J., Li, P., Zhang, J.: DIDFuse: deep image decomposition for infrared and visible image fusion. arXiv preprint arXiv:2003.09210 (2020)

19. Wang, Z., Bovik, A.C., Sheikh, H.R., Simoncelli, E.P.: Image quality assessment: from error visibility to structural similarity. IEEE Trans. Image Process. **13**(4), 600–612 (2004)

20. Wang, Z., Simoncelli, E.P., Bovik, A.C.: Multiscale structural similarity for image quality assessment. In: The Thrity-Seventh Asilomar Conference on Signals, Systems & Computers 2003, vol. 2, pp. 1398–1402. IEEE (2003)

21. Lin, T.-Y., et al.: Microsoft COCO: common objects in context. In: Fleet, D., Pajdla, T., Schiele, B., Tuytelaars, T. (eds.) ECCV 2014. LNCS, vol. 8693, pp. 740–755. Springer, Cham (2014). https://doi.org/10.1007/978-3-319-10602-1_48

22. Russakovsky, O., et al.: ImageNet large scale visual recognition challenge. Int. J. Comput. Vis. **115**(3), 211–252 (2015). https://doi.org/10.1007/s11263-015-0816-y

23. Xu, N., et al.: YouTube-VOS: sequence-to-sequence video object segmentation. In: Ferrari, V., Hebert, M., Sminchisescu, C., Weiss, Y. (eds.) ECCV 2018. LNCS, vol. 11209, pp. 603–619. Springer, Cham (2018). https://doi.org/10.1007/978-3-030-01228-1_36

24. Kristan, M., et al.: The seventh visual object tracking VOT2019 challenge results. In: Proceedings of the IEEE/CVF International Conference on Computer Vision Workshops (2019)

25. Zhang, L., Danelljan, M., Gonzalez-Garcia, A., van de Weijer, J., Shahbaz Khan, F.: Multi-modal fusion for end-to-end RGB-T tracking. In: Proceedings of the IEEE/CVF International Conference on Computer Vision Workshops (2019)

26. Zhang, Z., Peng, H.: Deeper and wider siamese networks for real-time visual tracking. In: Proceedings of the IEEE/CVF Conference on Computer Vision and Pattern Recognition, pp. 4591–4600 (2019)

27. Li, C.L., Lu, A., Zheng, A.H., Tu, Z., Tang, J.: Multi-adapter RGBT tracking. In: 2019 IEEE/CVF International Conference on Computer Vision Workshop (ICCVW), pp. 2262–2270. IEEE (2019)

28. Zhang, P., Zhao, J., Bo, C., Wang, D., Lu, H., Yang, X.: Jointly modeling motion and appearance cues for robust RGB-T tracking. IEEE Trans. Image Process. **30**, 3335–3347 (2021)

Automated Detection of Changes in Built-Up Areas for Map Updating: A Case Study in Northern Italy

Mattia Stasolla[1] and Fabio Dell'Acqua[2,3]([⊠]) [iD]

[1] Royal Military Academy, Brussels, Belgium
mattia.stasolla@rma.ac.be
[2] Department of Electrical, Computer, Biomedical Engineering,
University of Pavia, Pavia, Italy
fabio.dellacqua@unipv.it
[3] CNIT, Pavia Unit, Pavia, Italy

Abstract. Keeping track of changes in urban areas on a large scale may be challenging due to fragmentation of information. Even more so when changes are unrecorded and sparse across a region, like in the case of long-disused production sites that may be engulfed in vegetation or partly collapse when no-one is witnessing. In Belgium the Walloon Region is leveraging Earth observation satellites to constantly monitor more than 2200 redevelopment sites. Changes are automatically detected by jointly analysing time series of Sentinel-1 and Sentinel-2 acquisitions with a technique developed on Copernicus data, based on ad-hoc filtering of temporal series of both multi-spectral and radar data. Despite different sampling times, availability (due to cloud cover, for multispectral data) and data parameters (incidence angle, for radar data), the algorithm performs well in detecting changes. In this work, we assess how such technique, developed on a Belgian context, with its own construction practices, urban patterns, and atmospheric characteristics, is effectively reusable in a different context, in Northern Italy, where we studied the case of Pavia.

Keywords: Spaceborne Remote Sensing · Built-up detection · Time series

1 Introduction

Urban areas can drastically change over the years, due to urbanization trends, relocation to places of greater comfort, shifts in citizens' mindsets and habits, and even de-industrialization. This is visible both in large cities and small town, and may involve even sparse settlements where former industries clutter the countryside. In regards to this, the Walloon Region of Belgium is managing an inventory

This work was partly supported by the European Commission under H2020 project "EOXPOSURE", GA number 734541, and partly supported by BELSPO (Belgian Science Policy Office) in the frame of the STEREO III programme, project "SARSAR" (SR/00/372).

of more than 2,200 abandoned sites, called "Redevelopment sites" (RDS), which are former industrial, commercial, social, real estate areas, excluding housing. While the presence of RDSs has a generally negative impact on the urban fabric, it also represents an opportunity for sustainable urban planning. The Walloon Region needs up-to-date information about the sites that have been regenerated and those that are still in disuse. The full update of this inventory, with its 2,200 sites spread over nearly 17,000 km^2, is costly and time consuming, but is essential to provide updated information to the different actors involved. The database is accessible to the public, and used by several institutions; it is thus of paramount importance that it constantly reflects the actual situation.

The inventory is updated through field campaigns and/or manual analysis of aerial orthophotos. Since only a single-digit percentage of the sites are estimated to change from one year to the next, to optimize available resources the field visits should be prioritized according to actual needs. This led to the development of SARSAR, a new EO service that exploits the Sentinel-1 synthetic aperture radar (SAR) and Sentinel-2 multi-spectral images made available through the European Copernicus programme for the automatic monitoring of the RDSs. Its main goal is to provide the Walloon administration with a shortlist of the sites that are likely to have changed and for which an on-field visit would be required. For all the details about SARSAR and its implementation the reader can refer to [14]. Although SARSAR was devised to specifically solve a regional administrative problem, it has a general-purpose formulation and is intended to be used in various applications and geographical areas, provided that some of its parameters are suitably modified. The goal of this paper is precisely to test the software using a different dataset and evaluate which are the key parameters to be tuned for optimizing the performance. This paper is organized as follows: the next Section presents the state of the art, Sect. 3 introduces the method used. Section 4 describes the test sites and their mutual differences, whereas Sect. 5 describes the data and the tools used to process them, including a discussion on the combinations of parameters tested, while Sect. 6 presents and discusses results. Section 7 draws some conclusions and presents future avenues of development.

2   State of the Art

Large-scale change detection is one of the key applications where satellite-based remote sensing can play a unique role. Due to the limited availability of data, for several years the standard processing scheme has been based on a bi-temporal approach, where a pair of images would be analyzed and compared in order to establish if any changes between the two acquisition dates had occurred. Amongst the most common methods, we can mention image differencing, principal component analysis, post-classification comparison, and change vector analysis [1]. With the launch of the Copernicus satellites, an unprecedented amount of free satellite data has been made available to the general public and a great deal of new possibilities has opened up. Besides machine learning techniques [2], which can be very powerful but require a large number of training data, the attention of researchers has been recently drawn to changepoint detection methods, a family of techniques that have been developed since the 1950 s to solve the problem of finding changes in the underlying model of a signal or time series and have been used in a variety of applications, ranging from economics to climatology [3]. As far as satellite-based remote sensing is concerned, although a few attempts have been made in the past, mainly involving the analysis of MODIS and Landsat images for vegetation monitoring [4,5], it is thanks to Sentinel-1 and Sentinel-2 data that changepoint detection methods can now start to play a more important role. Given their spatial and temporal resolution, the Sentinel satellites can enable a more detailed and accurate tracking of changes both at local and regional scale and can therefore be suitable for a variety of applications. Vegetation monitoring is one of these. Only to mention a few examples, in [6], the Bayesian estimator of abrupt change, seasonal change, and trend (BEAST) and the continuous change detection and classification (CCDC) are leveraged to monitor forest windstorm damage areas by means of Sentinel-2 time series, whereas in [7], the authors use Sentinel-1 time series in combination with a method based on continuous wavelet transform and mathematical morphology to detect and estimate harvest dates in sugarcane fields. Land monitoring is another application that could benefit from changepoint analysis, as shown in [8], where a statistical approach is employed to detect offsets and gradient changes in InSAR time series. The potential of changepoint detection has been also demonstrated when both SAR and multi-spectral time series are used, such as in [9], whose goal was to automatically derive the phenological development of winter wheat and winter barley from Sentinel-1 and Sentinel-2 images, or in [10], where the two sensors were used to assess land degradation in South Africa by measuring the number of breakpoints occurring in the areas of interest. Within this context, the SARSAR service, which is based on the Pruned Exact Linear Time (PELT) [11], a well-known changepoint detection method, can be seen as one of the first examples of how this type of approach could be successfully applied also to the detection of changes in an urban environment, even at the operational level.

3 The *cpd4sits* Routine

As described in [14], the SARSAR service is composed of two main processing blocks: (a) the change detection module, whose task is to flag a site as changed/unchanged and to provide an estimate of the possible change dates; and (b) the change classification module, which is in charge of classifying the changes. As an initial step to evaluate the transferability of the approach to other areas of interest, for this paper we decided to focus solely on the change detection module, the *cpd4sits* routine, leaving the study of the change classification module to a future work.

The main processing steps of the *cpd4sits* routine are shown in Fig. 1 and can be itemized as follows:

- the software takes as input a combination of temporal signatures of the sites of interest. These are obtained by computing the average value (over the full site) of suitable features extracted from the input data.
- the time series are normalized;
- data gaps are filled by interpolation, so that the time series contain one value per day of the year;
- the time series are smoothed by applying a Gaussian filter;
- the obtained temporal signature (or a combination of them) for each site is segmented via the Pruned Exact Linear Time (PELT) algorithm [11], which enables the exact segmentation of the time series with a linear time complexity.

Given a time series $s_{1:k} = (s_1, ..., s_k)$, the number n of the changepoints and their time positions $t_{1:n} = (t_1, ..., t_n)$ are obtained by solving the penalized minimization problem:

$$Q_n(s_{1:k}, p) = \min_{n, t_{1:n}} \left\{ \sum_{i=1}^{n+1} \left[C\left(s_{(t_{i-1}+1):t_i}\right) \right] + p \right\} \tag{1}$$

where C is a segment-specific cost function, and p a penalty term to control overfitting. For our analysis, we have used the following cost function:

$$C(s_{a:b}) = \sum_{i=a+1}^{b} \|s_i - \bar{s}_{a:b}\|_2^2 \tag{2}$$

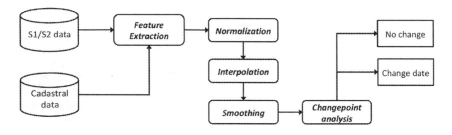

Fig. 1. Processing steps of the *cpd4sits* routine.

4   Test Sites

4.1   The Pavia, Italy Test Site

Pavia is a small town in Northern Italy, whose municipality covers just above 63 km^2 and hosts about 71,000 inhabitants. Several disused industrial sites are located within the urban area and in close proximity; since the beginning of the Sentinel missions (years 2014–15), several demolitions and new constructions have been witnessed in the area. This site was selected because it is where the institution of one author is located, which made generation of ground reference data much easier and cheaper. In the next subsection, the differences with respect to the Belgian test site will be discussed.

4.2 Differences with Belgian Test Site

One important difference is in terms of weather. Both the inland Walloon Region and the Pavia area are far enough from the sea, so that their climate can be considered continental. Pavia, however, features a greater annual temperature range (-1° to 30° C vs. 1° to 24° C). The mean annual precipitation is around 900 mm in both places, far more evenly distributed in Liège (a representative place in the Walloon Region) than in Pavia; on the other hand, summer humidity level is far higher in Pavia. Fog is reported 40 days a year in Belgium, but in Pavia it is even more frequent, i.e. 59 days a year. Another important aspect that should be considered is air pollution: $PM_{2.5}$ and PM_{10} concentrations can severely impact optical satellite measurements. Recent yearly averages of such concentrations are much higher for Pavia (71 and 26 $\mu g/m^3$ respectively) than for Liège (39 and 18 $\mu g/m^3$).

Whereas differences in weather patterns impact on preservation of man-made structures, including how fast abandoned sites are incorporated by vegetation, fog and particulate generate disturbances during acquisition of multispectral data that may be impossible to fully compensate with atmospheric correction.

Another important difference concerns construction practices. Accurate comparisons are out of the scope of this paper, however a few qualitative comments can be made. Residential houses in Belgium typically feature a steep-sloping roof, and narrow and tall facades, whereas North-Italian houses have flatter roofs and broad shapes [12]. Differences in shape of the observed objects typically reflect into differences in radar response. Redeveloping sites, such as ex-factories and warehouses, however, involve construction practices that are largely similar across Europe.

Considering all of the above, some adjustment of parameters is expected to optimize performance when moving from one context to the other. This subject will be investigated in the rest of the paper.

5 Tools and Data

5.1 Ground Reference Data

Google Earth Pro (GEP) [15] was used as a tool for generating ground reference data on changes in the test site of Pavia. Historical images of Pavia and the surrounding municipalities between 2015 and 2021 were inspected, seeking changes in buildings, construction sites and abandoned places, leveraging personal knowledge and interviewing locals when appropriate.

At the time of experiments, GEP made available a mosaic of satellite and aerial images, captured about once a year. This frequency is not sufficient for accurate change analysis, yet it was considered an acceptable starting point to build on.

50 polygons featuring at least one significant change between Jan 2017 - Dec 2020 (*change* polygons), and 50 more polygons without changes (*no-change* polygons) were identified and labeled as such. A selection of the polygons is presented in red in Fig. 2. The resulting 100 polygons were then partitioned into a *test30* set with 30 polygons and a *test70* set with 70 polygons; *change* and *no-change* polygons were evenly distributed among the two test sets.

For each *No-change* polygon a land cover class was assigned, and for each *change* polygon a land cover *change* class was defined, according to the type of change observed. In Fig. 3, it is provided an example that shows the construction of new residential buildings. In this work, however, the specific class information was not used, as the focus was on the class change taking place rather than on what class has changed into what other class. Still, this information has been retained for future use.

Fig. 2. A sample of the ground reference data on the Pavia site shown as red polygons on a Google Earth Pro background. (Color figure online)

All polygons were exported as KMZ files from Google Earth Pro and a bash routine using the Geospatial Data Abstraction Library (GDAL) was used to batch-convert these many KMZ files into a single *.shp* shapefile containing all

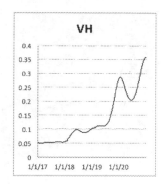

Fig. 3. Example of change (construction of residential buildings): a) 2007; b) 2021; c) Corresponding time series (average of VH bands). Background satellite images from Google Earth.

ground reference information; the shapefile was then imported into Google Earth Engine (GEE) to use polygons as *features* within the GEE environment.

5.2   Satellite Data

Once imported into GEE, the shapefile becomes a Feature Collection (FC). For each of the features (polygons), two Image Collections were created, *s1* and *s2*, using calibrated, orthorectified Sentinel-1 and Sentinel-2 data, respectively. To this end, the images were first filtered based on three parameters: initial and final date of analysis, and maximum cloud coverage percentage allowed for each image.

As shown in Fig. 4, Pavia falls in the bottom-left corner of a Sentinel-2 tile (*T32TNR*). Each tile covers an area of $110 \times 110 \ km^2$, with a 10-km overlap in both dimensions. This implies that some fringe polygons are shared with other tiles: *T32TMR* to the West, *T32TMQ* to the South-West, *T32TNQ* to the South. Therefore, the same acquisition may appear twice, or even up to four times, in the same time series, as the swath is broken down into partly overlapping tiles. Additional filtering was introduced that removed duplicates with same acquisition times.

Sentinel-2 data was further filtered based on cloud percentage using the *COPERNICUS/S2_CLOUD_PROBABILITY* collection, containing a single band expressing pixel cloudiness as computed by the *Microsoft Light Gradient Boosting Machine (LightGBM)* framework [13]. For each polygon, acquisitions with cloud coverage exceeding 30% over the considered polygon were discarded.

Sentinel-1 data were instead split based on relative orbit number, in 3 or 4 collections depending on the location, each with homogeneous incidence angles. The involved orbits are numbers 15, 66, 88 and 168, shown in Fig. 5.

For each orbit of Sentinel-1 and for the whole Sentinel-2 imagery, a new Feature Collection was defined, containing date and time of acquisition, the mean of the computed index over the polygon, and the size of the polygon.

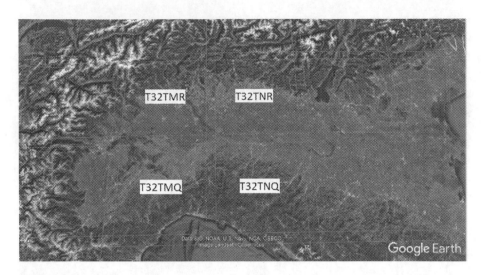

Fig. 4. Sentinel-2 tiling grid of the North Italian territory, with the indication of the four tiles of our interest; Pavia is located in correspondence of the red dot. Background from Google Earth Pro, KML overlay from Copernicus Hub [15,16] (Color figure online).

Data tables are finally exported into Google Drive as *.csv* files and downloaded to be used as input for the *cpd4sits* code running on a local machine.

5.3   Parameters and Testing Combination

The *cpd4sits* routine accepts a set of different input parameters that can be tuned based on the user's needs. A summary of the parameters used in this paper follows:

1. Features:
   - VH: cross-polarization backscatter coefficients by all Sentinel-1 orbits (maximum temporal frequency);
   - VH_{66}: cross-polarization backscatter coefficients for orbit 66 only (maximum homogeneity);
   - VV: co-polarization backscatter coefficients by all Sentinel-1 orbits;
   - VV_{66}: co-polarization backscatter coefficients for orbit 66 only;
   - NDVI, the Normalized Difference Vegetation Index computed on Sentinel-2 data;
   - NDBI, the Normalized Difference Built-up Index computed on Sentinel-2 data;
   - SBI, the Soil Brightness Index computed on Sentinel-2 data.

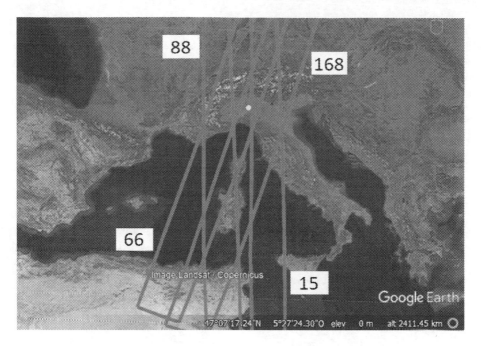

Fig. 5. Sentinel-1 relative orbits covering the test site of Pavia, marked with a yellow dot. Background from Google Earth Pro, KML overlay from Copernicus Hub [15,16] (Color figure online).

2. Length of the time series: in terms of time interval, the investigation started from Jan 2017 to ensure maximum temporal frequency (Sentinel-2B became operational in Mar 2017) and ended on Dec 2020 to reduce the risk of multiple changes on the same polygon.
3. Maximum time gap between two adjacent valid samples: due to the higher cloudiness of the considered site with respect to Belgium, this parameter had to be adjusted consequently, with a maximum gap that was increased to 150 days (instead of 120 days).
4. Cost function: least squared deviation (see Eq. 2).
5. Penalty term: the higher it is, the more significant a change needs to be for it to be detected. We tested the values [3, 5, 7, 10].
6. Smoothing window: the previously set value for the Belgian context was 61, and we tried the following values [1, 31, 61, 91].

All possible combinations of the above values and selections of the input parameters were tested on *test30*. Of these, the ones with F1-score below 0.8 were filtered out, leaving 57 supposedly best combinations on the table. The last phase involved cross-checking the identified parameter combinations by testing them on the 70 remaining polygons.

In order to identify the best possible set of parameters for the considered case study, the focus was placed on the ability of detecting *at least* one change, neglecting the change date, which would be ambiguous in many cases anyway. This transformed the experiment into a binary classification problem (*change* vs. *no change*). Assessing the accuracy of results for every possible combination of parameters on each of the 30 training polygons (the *test30* set) should offer clues on the best settings, and on the impact of each parameter.

6   Experimental Results

As stated in the previous Section, of all the parameter combinations analysed, only 57 featured F_1-score ≥ 0.80; these were then applied to the polygons in the *test70* set, and their metrics were placed alongside the results from *test30*. 24 out of 57 combinations (corresponding to 42%) confirmed an F1-score ≥ 0.80, while the others sunk below; however, of the 24, only 2 were below 0.7, confirming a certain degree of general robustness of the parameter selection.

In Table 1 below, an overview of the average metrics resulting from the analysis of *test30* and *test70* is presented.

Table 1. Average metrics results from the experiments.

Average	TPR	FPR	F_1-score
Test30	84%	21%	0.82
Test70	78%	22%	0.78

More clues can be extracted by examining how frequently each value of the parameters appears in the "winning" combinations. In Fig. 6, 7 and 8, the percentages are shown for the 57 above-threshold results.

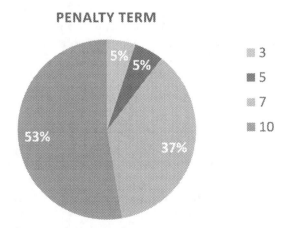

Fig. 6. Values of the penalty parameter in best-performing combinations.

Results suggest that the *window size* parameter has little impact, whereas higher *penalty* values lead to better performance, with values 7 and 10 covering 90% of the best combination set. From the graph in Fig. 8, reporting the frequency of appearance of each feature in the best combinations, it can be noticed that NDVI appears in nearly 90% of cases. Moreover, the performance depends more on the selection of parameters than on the number of parameters used; among the 57 combinations with a good F_1-score, about half use 3 features, and only one uses all the features at disposal (see Fig. 9).

Further, specific investigation of classification errors was carried out by visually interpreting time series of optical, high-res images from Google Earth Pro. This permitted us to identify some possible causes:

– long renovation work, which leads to continuous, distributed change in the parameters along the time series result into false negatives;
– piece-wise construction work (e.g. rows of terraced houses built incrementally) also lead to continuous change in parameters, preventing identification of a single change point and again resulting into false negatives;
– thin clouds, which go unidentified by the cloud masking algorithm but still generate perceivable shadows, have been observed introducing perceptible changes in multispectral indexes. These changes can be accounted for as changes in land cover and trigger false positives;
– in period of frequent cloud cover, a single, clear-sky image affected by e.g. atmospheric correction error can be identified as a change, generating a false positive.

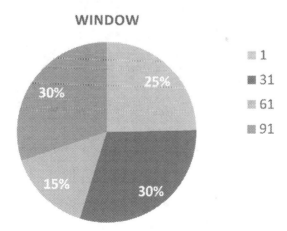

Fig. 7. Values of the window size parameter in best-performing combinations.

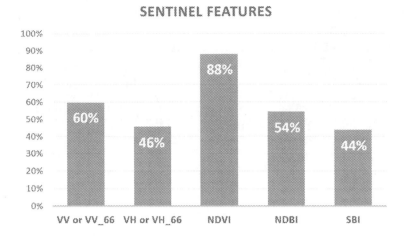

Fig. 8. Frequency of features resulting in best-performing combinations.

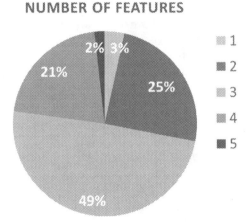

Fig. 9. Number of Sentinel-1 and -2 features used in the 57 best combinations.

Suitable solutions are being devised for each of the above listed causes of false classification. Outlining individual buildings in hi-res optical data, for example, may help in isolating and detecting individual changes [17,18].

7   Conclusions

In this paper, we proposed a case study aimed at assessing how well an existing method for urban change detection, developed for a specific context, can be re-used in a different one.

The method is based on the Pruned Exact Linear Time method and uses data from the *Copernicus* ESA missions Sentinel-1 and Sentinel-2, and was developed originally to cover the Belgian context, where it featured good change point detection performance. The case study proposed here focused on the area of Pavia in Northern Italy.

Differences between the two contexts were identified, including weather (fog, rain patterns), air pollution, and building practices, that could reflect on data features.

The work focused on finding the combinations of parameters that provide the best change point detection results for our area of interest in terms of True Positive and False Positive Rates, and F_1-score.

More than 900 combinations of parameters were tested on an initial "learning set" of 30 elements, and 57 combinations turned out to work nicely, so that they were counter-tested on the remaining 70 polygons (the validation set) from the ground truth. This latter outcome was further analyzed.

A list of 24 combinations confirmed to maintain F_1-score ≥ 0.80 in the validation set, and can be considered the optimal combinations for our case study. Most of these combinations make use of three features, originating from Sentinel-1 and -2 sensors, and NDVI performed best. While the window term seems not to be critical, on the other side the penalty term impacts significantly, with higher values performing better.

A further investigation was performed on False Negative and False Positive results. False Negatives are often generated by extensive and long-lasting construction work, that presents no single, well-defined change point. This can be improved by defining small polygons, where stages of construction may generate more definite, local changes. False Positives turned out to often relate with frequently cloudy weather; inspection of Sentinel-2 imagery revealed that Copernicus datasets sometimes struggle with correctly identifying thin clouds and cloud boundaries and this contributes to the generation of "fake" changes. The new 's2cloudless' tool, presented by the Earth Engine Team in November 2020, could more effectively cater for this need [19].

All in all, we believe the proposed method can be fruitfully reused in other context provided that more general criteria to adjust parameters can be determined. Further analysis is required to link local features with optimal parameters.

Acknowledgements. The authors wish to thank Andrea Fecchio for generating the ground reference data and code and for carrying out the experiments described in this paper in the framework of his final graduate thesis work.

References

1. Wu, L., et al.: Multi-type forest change detection using BFAST and monthly landsat time series for monitoring spatiotemporal dynamics of forests in subtropical wetland. Remote Sens. **12**, 341 (2020). https://doi.org/10.3390/rs12020341
2. Anantrasirichai, N., et al.: Detecting ground deformation in the built environment using sparse satellite InSAR data with a convolutional neural network. IEEE Trans. Geosci. Remote Sens. **59**, 2940–2950 (2021). https://doi.org/10.1109/TGRS.2020.3018315

3. Truong, C., Oudre, L., Vayatis, N.: Selective review of offline change point detection methods. Signal Proc. **167**, 107299 (2020). https://doi.org/10.1016/j.sigpro.2019.107299

4. Kennedy, R.E., Yang, Z., Cohen, W.B.: Detecting trends in forest disturbance and recovery using yearly Landsat time series: 1. LandTrendr - Temporal segmentation algorithms. Remote Sens. Environ. **114**, 2897–2910 (2010). https://doi.org/10.1016/j.rse.2010.07.008

5. Rahman, A.F., Dragoni, D., Didan, K., Barreto-Munoz, A., Hutabarat, J.A.: Detecting large scale conversion of mangroves to aquaculture with change point and mixed-pixel analyses of high-fidelity MODIS data. Remote Sens. Environ. **130**, 96–107 (2013). https://doi.org/10.1016/j.rse.2012.11.014

6. Giannetti, F., et al.: Estimating VAIA windstorm damaged forest area in Italy using time series sentinel-2 imagery and continuous change detection algorithms. Forests **12**, 680 (2021). https://doi.org/10.3390/f12060680

7. Stasolla, M., Neyt, X.: Applying sentinel-1 time series analysis to sugarcane harvest detection. https://doi.org/10.1109/IGARSS.2019.8898706

8. Hussain, E., Novellino, A., Jordan, C., Bateson, L.: Offline-online change detection for sentinel-1 InSAR time series. Remote Sens. **13**, 1656 (2021). https://doi.org/10.3390/rs13091656

9. Harfenmeister, K., Itzerott, S., Weltzien, C., Spengler, D.: Detecting phenological development of winter wheat and winter barley using time series of sentinel-1 and sentinel-2. Remote Sens. **13**, 5036 (2021). https://doi.org/10.3390/rs13245036

10. Urban, M., et al.: Sentinel-1 and sentinel-2 time series breakpoint detection as part of the south african land degradation monitor (SALDi). In: 2021 IEEE International Geoscience and Remote Sensing Symposium IGARSS, Brussels, Belgium, pp. 1997–2000 (2021). https://doi.org/10.1109/IGARSS47720.2021.9553331

11. Killick, R., Fearnhead, P., Eckley, I.A.: Optimal detection of changepoints with a linear computational cost. J. Am. Stat. Assoc. **107**, 1590–1598 (2012). https://doi.org/10.1080/01621459.2012.737745

12. De Decker, P.: Facets of housing and housing policies in Belgium. J. Hous. Built Environ. **23**, 155–171 (2008)

13. Microsoft Corporation, Light Gradient Boosting Machine. https://lightgbm.readthedocs.io/en/latest/

14. Petit, S., Stasolla, M., Wyard, C., Swinnen, G., Neyt, X., Hallot, E.: A new earth observation service based on Sentinel-1 and Sentinel-2 time series for the monitoring of redevelopment sites in Wallonia, Belgium. Land **11**, 360 (2022). https://doi.org/10.3390/land11030360

15. Google LLC, Google Earth Pro. https://www.google.com/earth

16. European space agency, Copernicus: Europe's eyes on earth. https://www.copernicus.eu/en

17. Pasquali, G., Iannelli, G., Dell'Acqua, F.: Building footprint extraction from multispectral, spaceborne earth observation datasets using a structurally optimized u-net convolutional neural network. Remote Sens. **11**, 2803 (2019). https://www.mdpi.com/2072-4292/11/23/2803

18. Ferrari, L., Dell'Acqua, F., Zhang, P., Du, P.: Integrating EfficientNet into an HAFNet structure for building mapping in high-resolution optical earth observation data. Remote Sens. **13**, 4361 (2021). https://www.mdpi.com/2072-4292/13/21/4361

19. Braaten, J., Schwehr, K., Ilyushchenko, S.: More accurate and flexible cloud masking for Sentinel-2 images. (Earth Engine Data, 2020,9,9), https://medium.com/google-earth/more-accurate-and-flexible-cloud-masking-for-sentinel-2-images-766897a9ba5f

Adaptive Learning for Leather Image Pre-processing Using GAN

Anjli Varghese[1], Malathy Jawahar[2], Prajjwal Gupta[1],
and A. Amalin Prince[1(✉)]

[1] Birla Institute of Technology and Science, Pilani, K K Birla Goa Campus,
Zuarinagar, Goa, India 403726
amalinprince@goa.bits-pilani.ac.in
[2] Central Leather Research Institute, Chennai 600020, India

Abstract. Computer vision and image processing advancements contribute to an automated leather species identification technique. In the novel leather image data, hair pores are the key to distinguishing among species. However, non-pore regions append the uncertainty and complexity in determining the distinct pore patterns. Hence, this paper proposes a generative adversarial network (GAN) as an automatic leather image pre-processing tool. It is chosen to adaptively learn the leather-image-specific pore and non-pore regions in a supervised manner. It adversarially updates to synthesize an image with more plausible pore pixels. Thus, the proposed method effectively pre-processed the leather images by removing the undesirable non-pore regions and enhancing the pore pixels. The experimental results with NIQE, entropy, SSIM, and PSNR objectively prove the effect of GAN-based leather image pre-processing. The adaptive and supervised learning with an adversarial update makes the proposed GAN unbounded. Thus, unlike the traditional methods, the proposed method promotes effective leather image pre-processing. Thereby facilitating further pore segmentation and classification.

Keywords: Adaptive learning · generative adversarial network (GAN) · image pre-processing · image quality evaluator · leather image · species identification

1 Introduction

Leather is the most durable commodity used for everyday life. The animal skins of buffalo, cow, goat, and sheep are the permissible materials. However, leather from exotic animal skin and synthetic materials is marketed in the leather industry. Leather species identification is a necessary medium to detect such non-permissible materials. It plays a vital role in biodiversity preservation and consumer protection. The existing leather species identification techniques are theoretical, supervised, and subjective. Digital leather image analysis can drive species identification from the human-to-automated technique.

D. Gupta et al. (Eds.): CVIP 2022, CCIS 1776, pp. 436–447, 2023.
https://doi.org/10.1007/978-3-031-31407-0_33

The leather surface of each species possesses a unique hair-pore arrangement. The buffalo hide has the sparsely distributed largest pores, while in the cow hide, the medium-sized pores are densely packed. The pores are arranged in a trio-cluster in the goat skin and a wavery pattern in sheep skin. A digital microscope is an economically efficient imaging device capable of acquiring the pore pattern variability [8]. However, the digital microscopic leather images include both desirable pore and undesirable non-pore regions. The animal birthmarks, skin damages, stretch marks, wrinkles, etc., form the non-pore regions. In addition, the surface damage and stretchy-pores during the leather manufacture, the illumination effects and motion blur during the image capturing processes cause the undesirable artifacts. Figure 1 illustrates the examples of undesirable non-pore regions. These non-pore regions make the leather image analysis more complex and challenging. Hence, this paper aims to pre-process the leather images by suppressing the non-pore regions and highlighting the desirable pore regions. The main objective is to design an automatic and unbounded pre-processing technique generic to any leather image type.

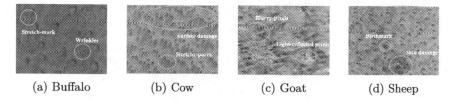

(a) Buffalo   (b) Cow   (c) Goat   (d) Sheep

Fig. 1. Example of leather images with undesirable non-pore regions.

In leather images, the pore patterns and noise vary both within and between species. The traditional image pre-processing methods are bounded and tedious. Finding an appropriate pre-processing method suitable for all the four species' leather images is challenging. A deep learning method trained with highlighted pore regions can solve this issue. In this work, a generative adversarial network (GAN) is adopted and proposed as the leather image pre-processing tool. The GAN is trained with the two sets of images: raw and manually pre-processed leather images. The network learns the relationship between the images and automatically generates an output image with highlighted pores alone. The performance of the proposed GAN-based leather image pre-processing is compared and analyzed with the traditional methods. Unlike the traditional methods, the proposed method is unbounded and automatic. In this paper, the image quality evaluators such as Natural Image Quality Evaluator ($NIQE$), entropy, peak-signal-to-noise ratio ($PSNR$), and Structural Similarity Index Measure ($SSIM$) are estimated. The estimated values objectively validated the leather image quality improvement in terms of highlighted pore regions. Thus, the proposed work designed an automatic leather image pre-processing method for effective leather image analysis.

The outline of this paper is as follows: Sect. 2 reviews the traditional image pre-processing methods for the leather images. The methodology of the proposed GAN-based leather image pre-processing is presented in Sect. 3. The experimental procedure for subjective and objective validation of the proposed work is described in Sect. 4. Followed by conclusion in Sect. 5.

2   Review on Image Pre-processing

In the leather image analysis, hair pores are the medium to differentiate among the leather species. But the non-pore regions corrupt the pore pixels causing inaccurate species identification. Pre-processing the leather images can benefit the hair-pore analysis for precise segmentation and classification.

In recent years, several pre-processing techniques have evolved. The techniques generally involve image enhancement, smoothing, and sharpening [1,2,9]. Contrast stretching and histogram equalization are the common enhancement techniques. Low pass and high pass filters are generally used to smoothen/blur and sharpen the images, respectively. These global techniques improve the quality of visibility of the leather images. Although the thresholds are bounded and hence encounter over, or under-smoothing [12]. To deal with varied pore patterns, instead of global techniques, local methods can be used for leather images. They allow the flexibility to pre-process the pore pixels on a windowing basis. However, they involve high computational time and human-intervention.

Image pre-processing using deep learning algorithms can build automated and optimized methods. The existing deep convolutional neural networks automatically learn the variability between the image features and noise. They extensively remove general image noise and deal with lower resolution images to reduce the computational time [3]. However, due to unsupervised learning, they fail to remove the microscopic leather image noise/non-pore regions. Instead, tend to produce blurry images. In addition, the desirable pore features are lost while converting the image resolution from high to low. This leather image resizing can also affect the further classification process. Hence, a deep supervised learning algorithm is proposed for leather image pre-processing. The objective is to design an adaptive and automated leather image pre-processing model.

3   GAN-based Pre-processing

The generative adversarial network (GAN) is an adaptive model that learns in a supervised manner. Unlike convolutional neural networks (CNN), GAN learns the loss function from the given data [3]. Recently, GAN is enormously studied for different applications such as, image-to-image translation [3], data augmentation [6], image segmentation [11], etc. In this study, GAN is proposed to design an automatic leather image pre-processing model. The objective is to adaptively learn the uncertain and ambivalent pore pattern from the given leather image data. Further, to generate an output image with desirable pore regions alone.

3.1 Data Used

This paper employs the novel digital microscopic leather image data comprising 1200 images [8]. The data is grouped into four different permissible leather species. Each image is acquired at $47 \times$ magnification and 1024×1280 image resolution. The acquisition is assisted by the Central leather research institute (CLRI) leather experts. Based on the leather expertise knowledge, each raw image is pre-processed to generate images with pore pixels. That is, manually, through several iterations, each image is fine-tuned with pore regions alone. The manually pre-processed leather images act as a reference. The raw and reference image data are fed to GAN to learn the leather-image-specific pore and non-pore regions.

3.2 Methodology

In this study, the GAN is proposed as the pre-processing model on the customized data. A conditional GAN (cGAN) is adopted to synthesize a pre-processed image (I_p) based on the given raw (I_r) and reference image (I_{ref}) data. Equation 1 mathematically represents the cGAN for generating I_p.

$$cGAN : \{I_r, I_{ref}\} \rightarrow I_p \tag{1}$$

Figure 2 illustrates the methodology behind cGAN generating the preprocessed leather image. It is comprised of a generator and a discriminator model. The generator is implemented with a basic U-net to generate a synthetic leather image. Firstly, it finds the relationship between the pore and non-pore regions from the raw and reference images. Secondly, it learns the unique nonpore regions as noise. Thirdly, it synthesizes an image with pore regions and feeds it to the discriminator.

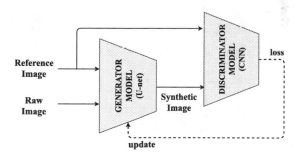

Fig. 2. The framework of GAN-based leather image pre-processing (The dotted line indicate the updation in the entire process).

The CNN-based discriminator is trained to determine the likelihood between the synthetic and reference images. It estimates the loss/mean absolute error between the synthetic and reference image. Accordingly, the generator is adversarially updated to synthesize the image with more plausible pixels. That is, the generator is updated to minimize the loss predicted by the discriminator. The update remains unchanged if the synthetic image is closer to the reference image. In the entire process, the generator tries to fool the discriminator, while the latter tries to counterfeit it.

Table 1. Example of raw, reference, and GAN leather images.

3.3   Implementation

The following work is implemented using Keras Python Library. The GAN model pre-trained for image-to-image translation in [3] is adopted for the present work.

The 1200 raw and reference images are randomly divided into 960 training and 240 testing samples. The adopted GAN model is then re-trained for the raw and reference training samples. The number of epochs and the batch-size are 100 and 1, respectively. The trained weights are saved to automatically pre-process the raw test samples. Thus, unlike the traditional applications, the GAN is proposed to implement an automatic leather image pre-processing model. In this study, prior to training, the input images are converted to gray-scale. Trained GAN thus generates pre-processed images in gray levels.

4 Experimental Procedure

The test samples are used to evaluate the performance of the proposed GAN-based leather image pre-processing model. The experimental procedure involves both subjective and objective validation. The results are discussed in the following Sects. 4.1 and 4.2, respectively.

4.1 Subjective Validation

The objective of this paper is to learn the leather-image-specific pore regions and remove the non-pore regions automatically. In subjective validation, the GAN-generated leather images are perceptually analyzed to visualize the pre-processing effect [8]. The non-pore regions such as wrinkles, skin damage, light reflections, and image blur are considered for perceptual analysis. Table 1 and 2 illustrates the effect of non-pore regions after GAN-based pre-processing. Each tabular column indicates four respective species images. From Table 1, the GAN generated images (I_p) are perceptually similar to manually generated images (I_{ref}). Table 1 row 1 to row 3 convey that, compared to I_r, most of the wrinkles are removed in I_p. At the same time, from row 4 to row 6, a portion of skin damage is retained in I_p. This is because they are retained in I_{ref}, and GAN generated similar images with less effect. Since skin damage affects only a portion of higher resolution image pixels, this error can be avoided. While in Table 2, the light-reflected and blurry pixels are removed effectively by retaining the desirable pore pixels. The tabulated results show that GAN has effectively learned the species as well as the leather-image-specific pore features. Thus, subjective validation proved the significance of GAN in generating pre-processed images as similar to the reference images. It also visually confirmed that the non-pore regions in raw images are removed in GAN-based pre-processed images.

4.2 Objective Validation

For objective validation, various image quality evaluation metrics are estimated. The evaluation is carried out in the MATLAB R2018a platform. Natural Image Quality Evaluator (NIQE) is the first metric to validate the GAN-based pre-processed leather images. It statistically measures the naturalness of an image [5, 11]. In the leather images, NIQE measures the variability between the pore and

Table 2. Example of raw, reference, and GAN leather images.

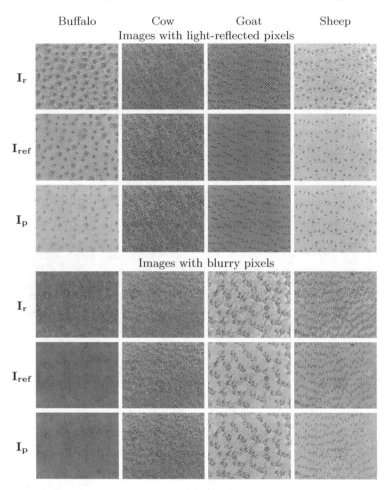

non-pore regions. Lower NIQE implies less variability indicating fewer non-pore regions. Figure 3 graphically represent the NIQE values estimated for raw (I_r), reference (I_{ref}), and GAN-based pre-processed (I_p) images (on test samples). The four graphs are respectively for each of the four leather species: buffalo, cow, goat, and sheep. The graphs clearly show that the NIQE curve of I_r is the highest. This is because the presence of non-pore regions increases the variability. Whereas the NIQE curves of I_{ref} and I_p are smooth, indicating the variability is reduced. Also, I_p with the lowest NIQE curve satisfied in achieving GAN-based leather image pre-processing.

Secondly, entropy of I_r, I_{ref} and I_p are estimated to measure the randomness due to non-pore regions [4]. Figure 4 depicts the entropy curves generated over test leather images. I_p possess the lowest entropy curves for buffalo, goat, and

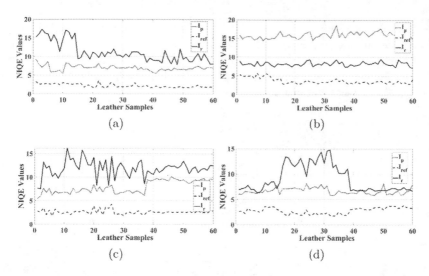

Fig. 3. NIQE value comparison between raw, reference, and GAN-based pre-processed leather images of (a) Buffalo, (b) Cow, (c) Goat, and (d) Sheep.

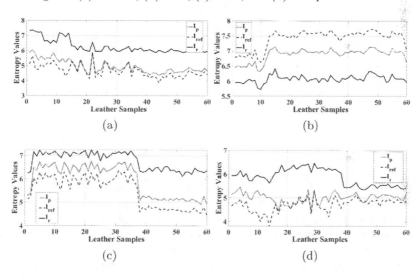

Fig. 4. Entropy value comparison between raw, reference, and GAN-based pre-processed leather images of (a) Buffalo, (b) Cow, (c) Goat, and (d) Sheep

sheep samples. This validates that the effect of randomly distributed non-pore regions is suppressed in I_p. Due to the dense pore pattern, this effect is mis-interpreted in the case of cow leather samples. However, I_p with lower entropy proved the efficacy of GAN in suppressing the non-pore pixels.

In this study, peak-signal-to-noise ratio $(PSNR)$ [7] is estimated to measure the contrast between the pore and leather surface. The pore over the leather surface exhibits a sudden intensity variation. The pre-processed image is expected to have the highest intensity variation. Figure 5 shows the PSNR values estimated between $[I_p, I_r]$, and $[I_{ref}, I_r]$. As expected, $[I_p, I_r]$ has the lowest curve indicating highly contrast pore pixels. Thus, PSNR proved the efficiency of GAN in performing image enhancement.

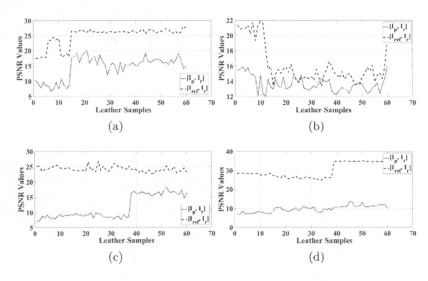

Fig. 5. PSNR value comparison between raw, reference, and GAN-based pre-processed leather images of (a) Buffalo, (b) Cow, (c) Goat, and (d) Sheep.

The dissimilarity between the raw, reference, and pre-processed images are evaluated in terms of the Structural Similarity Index Measure (SSIM) [7,10]. SSIM close to 1 indicates similarity, and -1 indicates dissimilarity. Figure 6 shows the similarity curve evaluated between $[I_p, I_r]$, and $[I_{ref}, I_r]$. Among the curves, the former is more close to -1, indicating the dissimilarity between the raw and GAN-based pre-processed image. This objectively validate that the non-pore regions present in I_r are absent in I_p. Thus ensuring the efficiency of GAN in pre-processing the leather images. The third curve (bold curve) in Fig. 6 represent the similarity curve between $[I_p, I_{ref}]$. The I_p of buffalo and a few samples of goat are almost similar to the corresponding I_{ref}. While I_p of sheep and a few samples of goat are comparatively similar and the cow samples result in dissimilarity. The effect of dissimilarity due to the dense pore can be avoided, as only a portion of the high-resolution image is affected. On average, GAN can generate the pre-processed leather images more similar to the reference images.

The NIQE and entropy values of the GAN-based pre-processed leather images are compared with the recent work. In [8], scale and shifted image enhancement, followed by Gaussian filtering, is applied for leather image pre-processing. Table 3 tabulates the NIQE and entropy values of I_r, I_p from the proposed GAN method, I_p from the existing method. In comparison, the existing method offered lower

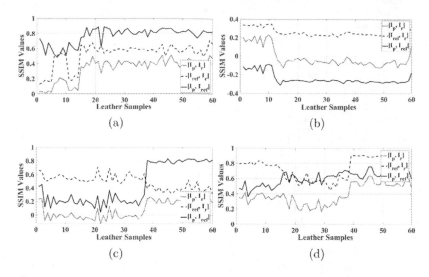

Fig. 6. SSIM value comparison between raw, reference, and GAN-based pre-processed leather images.

values for cow and goat samples. Although, the scaling and shifting parameters and Gaussian kernel size are bounded. Thus, the proposed GAN method is objectively efficient in pre-processing the complex leather image data.

Table 3. NIQE and Entropy comparison between the proposed and existing leather image pre-processing methods.

		Buffalo	Cow	Goat	Sheep
NIQE	I_r	23.1264	15.0178	19.6310	18.0353
	$I_{p_{GAN}}$	2.0494	3.3862	2.6251	2.2952
	$I_{p_{exist}}$	3.0928	2.8812	2.5741	2.5836
Entropy	I_r	7.1288	7.3392	7.1647	6.4179
	$I_{p_{GAN}}$	4.9466	6.8765	5.9289	5.0065
	$I_{p_{exist}}$	5.7361	5.4224	4.7502	2.9299

Thus, from the experimental procedure, the lower NIQE and entropy values confirmed the efficiency of GAN-based pre-processing in removing the non-pore regions. The lower PSNR values objectively validated the image-enhancement offered by GAN. Finally, SSIM affirmed the efficiency of GAN in synthesizing images similar to the reference images. Therefore, unlike the traditional methods, the proposed method offered an automatic and leather-image-specific pre-processing method. The proposed GAN efficiently dealt with the complex leather image data for adequate pre-processing.

5   Conclusion

This paper discussed the significance of efficient leather image pre-processing for accurate species identification. In turn, it assisted in biodiversity preservation and consumer protection. The generative adversarial network (GAN) is proposed to automatically pre-process the unique leather image data. The proposed GAN is fed with the novel leather images and their corresponding reference images. The manually generated reference images offered supervised learning. GAN effectively learned the difference between the desirable pore and undesirable non-pore regions through adaptive learning. Thus, GAN resulted in an unbounded pre-processing with leather-image-specific pore pixels. The image quality evaluators objectively proved the efficacy of the proposed GAN-based leather image pre-processing. The estimated NIQE, entropy, and PSNR values confirmed the non-pore filtration and pore enhancement applied by the proposed GAN. The SSIM values affirmed that the proposed method synthesized the pre-processed image with plausible pore pixels similar to the reference image. Thus, GAN is efficiently proposed for automatic and unbounded leather image pre-processing with adaptive learning.

Acknowledgments. The authors are pleased to thank the leather experts in Central Leather Research Institute CLRI, Adyar, Chennai, India, (CSIR-CLRI Communication No. 1731) for providing the permissible leather samples necessary for image data acquisition. The authors are also contented with Tata Consultancy Services TCS, India, for their support in carrying out the research through the TCS-RSP fellowship.

References

1. Gonzalez, R.C., Woods, R.E.: Digital Image Processing. Pearson Education, London (2009)
2. Gopi, E.S.: Digital Image Processing using Matlab. Scitech, Sriperumbudur (2007)
3. Isola, P., Zhu, J.Y., Zhou, T., Efros, A.A.: Image-to-image translation with conditional adversarial networks. In: 2017 IEEE Conference on Computer Vision and Pattern Recognition (CVPR), pp. 5967–5976 (2017). https://doi.org/10.1109/CVPR.2017.632
4. Li, C., Ju, Y., Bovik, A.C., Wu, X., Sang, Q.: No-training, no-reference image quality index using perceptual features. Opt. Eng. **52**(5), 057003 (2013). https://doi.org/10.1117/1.oe.52.5.057003
5. Mittal, A., Soundararajan, R., Bovik, A.C.: Making a "completely blind" image quality analyzer. IEEE Sig. Process. Lett. **20**(3), 209–212 (2013). https://doi.org/10.1109/LSP.2012.2227726
6. Morís, D.I., de Moura Ramos, J.J., Buján, J.N., Hortas, M.O.: Data augmentation approaches using cycle-consistent adversarial networks for improving COVID-19 screening in portable chest X-ray images. Expert Syst. Appl. **185** (2021). https://doi.org/10.1016/j.eswa.2021.115681
7. Pinki, Mehra, R.: Estimation of the image quality under different distortions. Int. J. Eng. Comput. Sci. **5**(7), 17291–17296 (2016). https://doi.org/10.18535/ijecs/v5i7.20

8. Varghese, A., Jain, S., Prince, A.A., Jawahar, M.: Digital microscopic image sensing and processing for leather species identification. IEEE Sens. J. **20**(17), 10045–10056 (2020). https://doi.org/10.1109/JSEN.2020.2991881

9. Wang, A., Zhang, W., Wei, X.: A review on weed detection using ground-based machine vision and image processing techniques. Comput. Electr. Agric. **158**, 226–240 (2019) https://doi.org/10.1016/j.compag.2019.02.005

10. Wang, Z., Bovik, A.C., Sheikh, H.R., Simoncelli, E.P.: Image quality assessment: From error visibility to structural similarity. IEEE Trans. Image Process. **13**(4), 600–612 (2004). https://doi.org/10.1109/TIP.2003.819861

11. Zhang, C., et al.: MS-GAN: GAN-based semantic segmentation of multiple sclerosis lesions in brain magnetic resonance imaging. In: 2018 Digital Image Computing: Techniques and Applications (DICTA), pp. 1–8. IEEE (2018). https://doi.org/10.1109/DICTA.2018.8615771

12. Zhang, C., Cheng, W.: Corrupted reference image quality assessment of denoised images. IEEE Trans. Image Process. **28**(4), 1732–1747 (2019)

Automated Sulcus Depth Measurement on Axial Knee MR Images

Ridhma[1]([envelope]), Manvjeet Kaur[2], Sanjeev Sofat[1], Devendra K. Chouhan[3], and Mahesh Prakash[4]

[1] Department of Computer Science and Engineering, Punjab Engineering College, Sector-12, Chandigarh, India
ridhmakhokhar@gmail.com
[2] Cyber Security Research Center, Punjab Engineering College, Sector-12, Chandigarh, India
[3] Department of Orthopaedics, Post Graduate Institute of Medical Education and Research, Sector-12, Chandigarh, India
[4] Department of Radio Diagnosis and Imaging, Post Graduate Institute of Medical Education and Research, Sector-12, Chandigarh, India

Abstract. Patellofemoral instability is a knee disorder in which the patella, slips out of its usual placement leading to knee pain. The patella may displace from its position due to abnormality in the shape of patellar surface on femur bone. The orthopaedic experts manually measure certain parameters from the available axial knee scans for the patellar instability diagnosis, which is labor-intensive and susceptible to inter- and intra-observer variations. The automated segmentation of femur region in knee magnetic resonance (MR) image can help in easily identifying the abnormality in the patellar surface. Therefore, in this paper, the femur bone in the axial knee MR scans has been segmented using two variants of U-Net: basic U-Net and U-Net++ and the results have been compared and visualized. The validation dice similarity coefficient (DSC) and accuracy of 89.62% and 94.05% were obtained, respectively, for U-Net. For U-Net++, the validation DSC of 95.04% and validation accuracy of 94.91% were obtained. Further, in this paper, the sulcus depth measurement has been automated using basic image processing techniques. A mean error of 0.565 mm was obtained when tested on 20 axial knee MR images. The T2-weighted knee MRI dataset of 55 patients has been acquired from Post Graduate Institute of Medical Education and Research (PGIMER), Chandigarh for training and testing of the proposed approach.

Keywords: Patellar Instability · Femur · Image Segmentation · Deep Learning · U-Net · MRI

1 Introduction

Musculoskeletal disorders are common in human population. Knee joint, which is one of the most complex joint, is prone to several disorders especially in athletes, military personnel and adolescents due to involvement of rigorous physical activities. Patellar instability with an annual incidence rate of 5.8 in 1,00,000 human population is one such knee disorder, where the patella or kneecap moves from its normal position, leading to knee pain [1]. The patellar surface on femur bone, also known as trochlear groove, becomes shallow, flat, convex or there is a formation of cliff which leads to dislocation or instability of patella as presented in Fig. 1(b). The diagnosis of patellar instability involves the manual measurement of certain parameters such as sulcus depth, facet asymmetry, patellar tilt angle, sulcus angle, etc. [2]. The manual measurement requires human-effort and time and it is also subject to inter-observer and intra-observer variations. Therefore, an automated approach for the measurement of these parameters can assist the experts in clearly identifying the level of abnormality in the patellar surface.

An axial knee joint magnetic resonance (MR) slice contains two bones: femur and patella, as shown in Fig. 1. The patellar surface on femur bone (trochlear groove) and the femoral condyles in a knee MRI are of importance for the measurement of various parameters for diagnosis of patellar instability. Therefore, it is significant to segment the femur bone precisely from the axial knee MRI. The segmentation of region of interest (ROI) has been performed to automate the measurement process in various medical areas, such as, the diagnosis of spinal disorders [3–6], fetal growth and age estimation [7] and the diagnosis of patellar dislocation [8]. For patellar instability diagnosis, sulcus depth is one of the parameters which is measured on the axial images of knee joint as shown in Fig. 2. The depth is calculated by first taking average of perpendicular distances of lateral and medial femoral condyles from the line parallel to the posterior ends of the femoral condyle. The perpendicular distance of the deepest part of the trochlear groove from the line parallel to posterior end of femoral condyle is then subtracted from the average distance calculated to obtain the value of sulcus depth [9]. As per Fig. 2, trochlear depth is calculated as $[((a+b)/2)\text{-}c]$. A sulcus depth of less than 3 mm is considered to be pathologic and therefore the subject may have dysplastic trochlea [10].

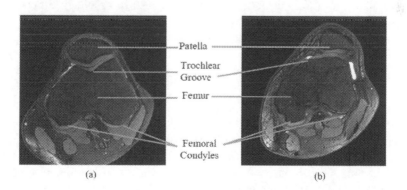

Patella

Trochlear
Groove

Femur

Femoral
Condyles

(a)   (b)

Fig. 1. Axial knee MRI with: (a) Normal trochlear groove and (b) Flat trochlear groove

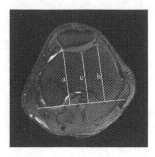

Fig. 2. Sulcus depth measurement on axial knee MRI [((a+b)/2)-c]

Medical image segmentation has remained an interesting area of research. The knee image segmentation techniques have evolved from the classical approaches, such as, thresholding, region-growing, level-set method, graph-cuts, model-based approaches, etc. to the complex deep learning based approaches with a drastic improvement in the performance [11]. In this paper, the most popular deep-learning based model known as U-Net and its improvement i.e. U-Net++ have been applied to the available knee MRI dataset owing to their remarkable results in medical image segmentation. The segmentation results obtained using U-Net++ are further used to automate the sulcus depth measurement on axial knee MR images.

To the best of our knowledge, no attempt has been made to automate the sulcus depth measurement from the knee MR images. Therefore, this work is focused upon the measurement of sulcus depth which can assist the orthopedic experts in faster diagnosis of patellar instability

The rest of the article is divided into four sections. In Sect. 2, a discussion of the related work on various knee image segmentation techniques has been carried out. The details of the dataset, the image segmentation models used and the automated approach for sulcus depth measurement are provided in Sect. 3. The experimental results obtained are presented and discussed in Sect. 4. Further, the paper has been concluded in Sect. 5.

2   Related Work

The knee image segmentation has been a frequently studied research problem in literature for the detection of knee joint pathologies. The major image segmentation techniques included thresholding, graph-based methods, deformable models, model-based methods, atlas-based methods and deep learning models [11]. The knee MRI scans have intensity inhomogeneties due to the presence of complex structures and artifacts, therefore, the thresholding based and region-growing methods do not perform very well on them [12]. The graph-based segmentation technique uses the graph-cut algorithm where the pixels of an image are considered as the vertices of the graph. The vertices are connected via edges having weights allocated to them based on the intensity differences among the pixels.

As compared to thresholding, the graph-cut method performed well, but it is still prone to the problem of boundary leakages [13]. The atlas-based segmentation methods require human effort and time for the atlas construction and performs moderately well [14]. The deformable models use the concept of partial differential equations to segment the ROI and they performed quite well on knee MRIs [15,16]. The model-based methods work on the basis of the appearance and shape of the structures to be segmented. They performed remarkably well on the knee MRI datasets [17,18].

With the accessability to high-end computing resources, the attention has shifted from traditional segmentation approaches to machine learning (ML) based segmentation approaches. K-nearest neighbor (KNN), decision trees, support vector machine (SVM) and random forests are the most commonly used ML based approaches for knee image segmentation [19–21]. The major drawback of ML based segmentation is the manual feature extraction. However, to eliminate the effort of manual feature extraction, the deep learning (DL) based segmentation approaches have been developed. The performance of the DL based segmentation models on knee images has been comparable to the human expert annotations [22–25]. There exist various DL based models, such as U-Net [26], SegNet [27], fully convolutional networks (FCN) [28], which have been frequently used for medical image segmentation. The only limitation of ML and DL based methods is the need of large volume of data which is not always feasible in medical domain. Therefore, to deal with the limited dataset, different data augmentation techniques have been developed. The basic operations of rotation, flip, zoom and shear are applied to the available medical datasets for increasing the dataset size. Another way is to use the synthetically generated dataset using Generative Adversarial Networks (GANs) designed by Goodfellow [29].

Although the DL based segmentation models need high-end computational resources and time for training, these are often used in medical domain due to their high accuracy in comparison to other segmentation techniques.

3 Methodology

3.1 Dataset Used

The knee MRI scans of 55 patients were acquired from Post Graduate Institute of Medical Education and Research (PGIMER), Chandigarh. The dataset of randomly selected 35 patients have been used for training the segmentation models. The knee scan of a single patient contains multiple axial slices covering the cross-sectional area of knee joint. From every patient's MRI, four axial slices are used where the femur region is clearly visible. A total of 140 grayscale MR images of size 320×320 have been used for training, validating and comparing the segmentation models. Data augmentation has been performed using geometric transformations to further increase the size of dataset for training. The remaining dataset of 20 patients has been used to test the precision of the automated approach for sulcus depth measurement. The ground truth annotations are validated by the experts in the domain.

3.2 Data Augmentation

Although the U-Net and U-Net++ perform well even with the smaller training set, still data augmentation can be performed to further obtain good segmentation results. Therefore, the popular data augmentation techniques such as flipping, rotation with range of 15°, zooming with range of 0.2 and shearing with range of 50° have been applied to the available knee MRI dataset. A few augmented images are presented in Fig. 3 which help in improving the model generalizability.

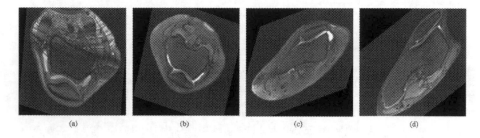

Fig. 3. Data Augmentation:(a), (b) Vertical flip and rotation and (c), (d) Shear

3.3 Segmentation Models Used

For bio-medical image segmentation, Olaf Ronneberger proposed a DL based network known as U-Net [26] which has performed exceptionally well. Another variant of U-Net named as U-Net++ was proposed with an architectural enhancement to improve the performance of U-Net model [30]. U-Net architecture consists of a downsampling path which is responsible for capturing the context information. An upsampling path helps in maintaining the resolution of the output along with the spatial information obtained from the corresponding symmetric downsampling unit using shortcut connections. In this work, U-Net and U-Net++ has been used for femur bone segmentation from the axial knee MR images as they perform well even on limited dataset. Also, data augmentation has been performed to increase the dataset size. The architectural details of these models are discussed below.

U-Net. Each downsampling unit contains two convolution layers, where each convolution layer includes a convolution operation of size 3×3, batch normalization, activation (rectified linear unit) followed by dropout operation. After two convolution layers, 2×2 max pooling operation with a stride of 1 is applied.

In the middle inut, there are two convolutional layers followed by an upsampling operation. The upsampling unit takes the upsampled input from the previous unit and concatenates it with the output of corresponding downsampling using shortcut connections. In the last upsampling unit, the output obtained after two convolution layers is passed through 1×1 convolution operation with sigmoid activation function to produce the final binary segmentation mask. The U-Net architecture has been presented in Fig. 4.

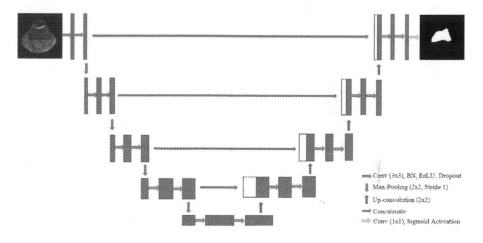

Fig. 4. U-Net Architecture

U-Net++. U-Net++ is an enhancement of basic U-Net model. It follows the DenseNet architecture to achieve higher performance accuracy [31]. Instead of using shortcut connections directly, every corresponding downsampling and upsampling unit in U-Net++ is connected via nested dense connections. The dense connections allow the encoder feature maps to be as closer to the semantic level of feature maps expected in the decoder. A detailed architecture of U-Net++ is presented in Fig. 5. The red structures in the figure represent the basic U-Net architecture. Each square block represents two consecutive convolutional layers. The downward arrows represent max pooling operation and the upward arrows depict the upsampling operation. The dotted arrows represent the skip connections.

3.4   Model Training

For model implementation, the Keras library has been used with Tensorflow at the backend. The model has been trained using Nvidia K80 GPU with memory of 12GB. Data augmentation has been applied to the available 140 grayscale axial knee MR images each of size 320×320. The images are then fed to the

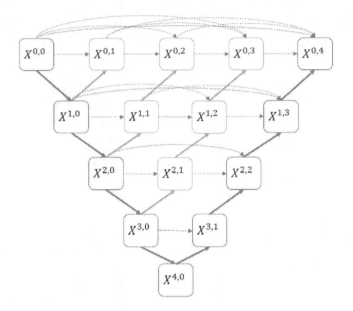

Fig. 5. U-Net++ Architecture

segmentation models for training and validation. The training and validation split of 80:20 has been performed. Both the models have been trained for 150 epochs using Adam optimizer with learning rate set to 0.0001. The binary cross entropy loss function has been used to compute the difference between predictions and ground truth. The initial number of kernels is set to 64 which are doubled in every downsampling unit. Batch normalization has been performed for standardizing the input passed to each layer. A dropout value of 0.2 has been used. Rectified Linear Unit (ReLU) activation function has been used as it is not compute-intensive and converges faster as compared to sigmoid and tanh functions. As the output required is a binary segmentation mask, therefore, the sigmoid activation function has been used at the output layer.

3.5 Automated Sulcus Depth Measurement

The predicted segmentation masks are subjected to basic image processing operations to obtain the landmark points lying on the patellar surface and femoral condyles for sulcus depth measurement. Figure 6 presents the steps followed to automate the measurement of sulcus depth. The boundary of the predicted segmentation mask is extracted using sobel edge detection operation. The resulting image has been further divided into two equal halves, both vertically as well as horizontally. From these halves, the highest points A and C and the lowest points D and E are obtained. The valley point B is the lowest point lying between A and C. Using all the landmark points, the sulcus depth is computed using basic geometrical formulas. The symbol H in Fig. 6 represents the height of the image in cm, which is important to find the relationship between pixel and measurement unit. The height varies for every axial knee MR image.

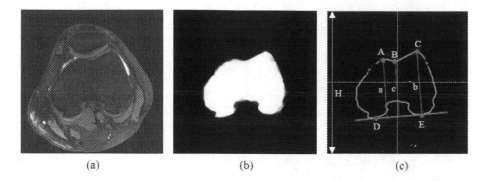

(a)   (b)   (c)

Fig. 6. Automated sulcus depth measurement: (a) Original Image (b) Predicted segmentation Mask (c) Landmark point detection and measurement

4   Experimental Results

4.1   Performance Metrics for Image Segmentation

The performance of the segmentation models used has been evaluated using two metrics: accuracy and dice similarity coefficient (DSC). The accuracy also takes into account the background information i.e. true negatives (TN), therefore, we also considered DSC as it is a more accurate measure for reporting the segmentation performance. To calculate these metrics, the entities from the confusion matrix are used. The pixels which are correctly identified as foreground pixels represent the true positives (TP). True negatives (TN) indicate the correctly identified background pixels. The pixels which belong to the background, but are predicted as foreground represent false positives (FP). The pixels belonging to foreground but are identified as background are known as false negatives (FN).

Accuracy. Accuracy is the ratio of the correctly segmented pixels to the total number of the pixels in an image given in Eq. (1).

$$Accuracy = \frac{TP + TN}{TP + TN + FP + FN} \qquad (1)$$

Dice Similarity Coefficient. Dice similarity coefficient (DSC) depicts the amount of spatial overlap among the expert annotations and the automated segmentation results which is computed as per Eq. (2).

$$DSC = \frac{2*TP}{2*TP + FP + FN} \tag{2}$$

4.2 Segmentation Results

The difference in the segmentation results of U-Net and U-Net++ on few validation images can be easily visualized in Fig. 7. The quantitative segmentation results obtained for U-Net and U-Net++ on training and validation dataset are presented in Table 1. It has been observed that U-Net++ performs well on comparison with U-Net due to the application of nested dense connections. The corresponding graphs for accuracy, DSC and binary cross entropy loss with respect to number of epochs are shown in Fig. 8, 9 and 10, respectively.

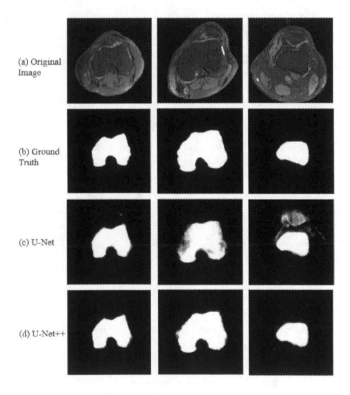

Fig. 7. Validation results: (a) Axial knee MR image; (b) Expert annotations; (c) U-Net results; and (d) U-Net++ results

Table 1. Quantitative Segmentation Results

	Train Set		Validation Set	
	Accuracy	DSC	Accuracy	DSC
U-Net	94.46%	95.75%	94.05%	89.63%
U-Net++	94.55%	96.44%	94.91%	95.04%

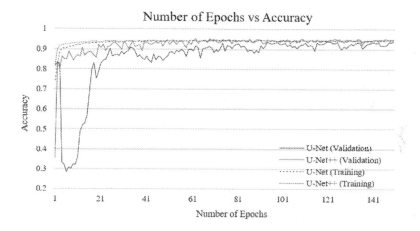

Fig. 8. Epochs vs Accuracy for U-Net and U-Net++

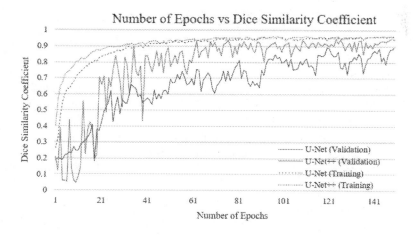

Fig. 9. Epochs vs DSC for U-Net and U-Net++

The validation accuracy of U-Net and U-Net++, as observed in Fig. 8, is almost same. Accuracy is not considered a very relevant metric for evaluating the segmentation model performance in case there are large number of true negatives. Therefore, DSC has been computed at every epoch for U-Net and U-Net++ models. From Fig. 9, it can be analyzed that the U-Net++ model performs better than U-Net.

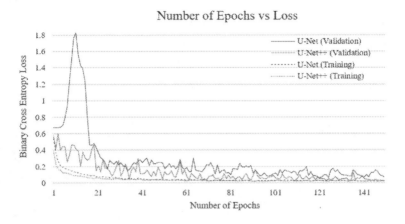

Fig. 10. Epochs vs Loss for U-Net and U-Net++

It can be observed in Fig. 10 that the validation loss for U-Net++ is slightly less as compared to U-Net model, therefore, producing good segmentation results.

4.3   Automated Results of Sulcus Depth Measurement

The automated measurement approach has been tested on the axial knee MR images of 20 patients. Since, U-Net++ model provided significantly correct segmentation results as compared to U-Net model, it has been used for automated sulcus depth measurement. The results obtained are presented in Table 2. A mean error of 0.565 mm has been produced for 20 cases. From case number 16 to 20 in Table 2, the error is greater than 1 mm which does not fall within the acceptable error range. The error occurs due to the inaccurate segmentation results produced which further leads to incorrect landmark point detection. However, the proposed approach performed well for 75% of the cases with an average error of 0.315 mm.

Table 2. Comparison of manual (M) and automated (A) sulcus depth measurement

S.No	Sulcus Depth(M,mm)	Sulcus Depth(A,mm)	Height of image(cm)	Error, |M-A|(mm)
1	4.68	4.702	16	0.022
2	5.05	5.014	16	0.036
3	4.67	4.736	13	0.066
4	5.05	5.142	15	0.092
5	7.25	7.349	13	0.099
6	4.27	4.134	16	0.136
7	7.5	7.332	16	0.168
8	7.33	7.066	13	0.264
9	5.4	5.687	13	0.287
10	6.35	5.9	16	0.45
11	5.85	5.398	13	0.452
12	5.17	5.766	14	0.596
13	4.4	3.78	13	0.62
14	5.1	4.435	14	0.665
15	5.95	5.176	14	0.774
16	5.5	4.484	13	1.016
17	6.75	5.603	16	1.147
18	6.23	7.424	13	1.194
19	4.07	2.567	16	1.503
20	6.5	4.777	14	1.723
	Mean Error			0.565

5   Conclusion

Patellar dislocation is associated with the abnormality in the shape of patellar surface. Therefore, in this work, the automated femur bone segmentation from the axial knee MRI has been carried out which can clearly help in identifying the abnormality in the shape of patellar surface. Further, the segmentation results produced are used for automated measurement of sulcus depth. Two famous biomedical image segmentation networks, U-Net and U-Net++ have been deployed for the purpose. Due to the usage of dense connections in U-Net++ which help in preserving and transferring the expected feature maps from encoder to decoder, it performed well when compared with U-Net model. The predicted segmentation results obtained using U-Net++ model, produced the automated sulcus depth measurements which were comparable to the expert readings. Therefore, the proposed approach can be used to provide a second opinion or assist the experts in patellar instability diagnosis.

References

1. Fithian, D.C., Paxton, E.W., Stone, M.L., et al.: Epidemiology and natural history of acute patellar dislocation. Am. J. Sports Med. **32**(5), 1114–21 (2004)
2. Diederichs, G., Issever, A.S., Scheffler, S.: MR imaging of patellar instability: injury patterns and assessment of risk factors. Radiographics **30**(4), 961–981 (2010)
3. Horng, M.H., Kuok, C.P., Fu, M.J., et al.: Cobb angle measurement of spine from X-ray images using convolutional neural network. Comput. Math. Methods Med. **2019** (2019)
4. Masad, I.S., Fahoum, A.A., Qasmieh, I.A.: Automated measurements of lumbar lordosis in T2-MR images using decision tree classifier and morphological image processing. Eng. Sci. Technol. Int. J. **22**(4), 1027–1034 (2019)
5. Caesarendra, W., Rahmaniar, W., Mathew, J., et al.: Automated cobb angle measurement for adolescent idiopathic scoliosis using convolutional neural network. Diagnostics **12**(2), 396 (2022). https://doi.org/10.3390/diagnostics12020396
6. Zhang, K., Xu, N., Guo, C., et al.: MPF-net: an effective framework for automated cobb angle estimation. Med. Image Anal. **75**, 102277 (2022)
7. Prieto, J.C., Shah, H., Rosenbaum, A.J., et al.: An automated framework for image classification and segmentation of fetal ultrasound images for gestational age estimation. In: Proceedings of SPIE-The International Society for Optical Engineering 2021, Bellingham, Washington, PMC (2016). https://doi.org/10.1117/12.2582243
8. Sun, L., Kong, Q., Huang, Y., et al.: Automatic segmentation and measurement on knee computerized tomography images for patellar dislocation diagnosis. Comput. Math. Methods Med. **2020** (2020)
9. Pfirrmann, C.W., Zanetti, M., Romero, J., Hodler, J.: Femoral trochlear dysplasia: MR findings. Radiology **216**(3), 858–64 (2000)
10. Osman, N.M., Ebrahim, S.M.B.: Patellofemoral instability: quantitative evaluation of predisposing factors by MRI. Egypt. J. Radiol. Nuclear Med. **47**(4), 1529–1538 (2016)
11. Ridhma, Kaur, M., Sofat, S., et al.: Review of automated segmentation approaches for knee images. IET Image Process. **15**(2), 302–324 (2021)
12. Kang, Y., Engelke, K., Kalender, W.A.: A new accurate and precise 3-D segmentation method for skeletal structures in volumetric CT data. IEEE Trans. Med. Imaging **22**(5), 586–598 (2003)
13. Wu, D., Sofka, M., Birkbeck, N., Zhou, S.K.: Segmentation of multiple knee bones from CT for orthopedic knee surgery planning. In: Golland, P., Hata, N., Barillot, C., Hornegger, J., Howe, R. (eds.) MICCAI 2014. LNCS, vol. 8673, pp. 372–380. Springer, Cham (2014). https://doi.org/10.1007/978-3-319-10404-1_47
14. Dam, E.B., Lillholm, M., Marques, J., et al.: Automatic segmentation of high- and low-field knee MRIs using knee image quantification with data from the osteoarthritis initiative. J. Med. Imaging **2**(2), 024001 (2015)
15. Gandhamal, A., Talbar, S., Gajre, S., et al.: Fully automated subchondral bone segmentation from knee MR images: data from the osteoarthritis initiative. Comput. Biol. Med. **88**(1), 110–125 (2017)
16. Chen, H., Sprengers, André M.J., Kang, Y., et al.: Automated segmentation of trabecular and cortical bone from proton density weighted MRI of the knee. Med. Biol. Eng. Comput. **57**(5), 1015–1027 (2019)
17. Driban, J., Fripp, J., Tamez-Pena, J., et al.: On the use of coupled shape priors for segmentation of magnetic resonance images of the knee. IEEE J. Biomed. Health Inform. **19**(3), 1153–1167 (2015)

18. Fripp, J., Crozier, S., Warfield, S.K., et al.: Automatic segmentation of the bone and extraction of the bone-cartilage interface from magnetic resonance images of the knee. Phys. Med. Biol. **52**(6), 1617–1631 (2007)

19. Yin, Y., Zhang, X., Williams, R., et al.: LOGISMOS-layered optimal graph image segmentation of multiple objects and surfaces: cartilage segmentation in the knee joint. IEEE Trans. Med. Imaging **29**(12), 2023–2037 (2010)

20. Prasoon, A., Igel, C., Loog, M., et al.: Femoral cartilage segmentation in Knee MRI scans using two stage voxel classification. In: Proceedings of the Annual International Conference of the IEEE Engineering in Medicine and Biology Society (EMBS), Osaka, Japan, pp. 5469–5472 (2013)

21. Pang, J., Li, P.Y., Qiu, M., Chen, W., Qiao, L.: Automatic articular cartilage segmentation based on pattern recognition from Knee MRI images. J. Digit. Imaging **28**(6), 695–703 (2015). https://doi.org/10.1007/s10278-015-9780-x

22. Ambellan, F., Tack, A., Ehlke, M., et al.: Automated segmentation of knee bone and cartilage combining statistical shape knowledge and convolutional neural networks: Data from the osteoarthritis initiative. Med. Image Anal. **52**, 109–118 (2019)

23. Burton, W., Myers, C., Rullkoetter, P.: Semi-supervised learning for automatic segmentation of the knee from MRI with convolutional neural networks. Comput. Methods Programs Biomed. **189**, 105328 (2020)

24. Gaj, S., Yang, M., Nakamura, K., et al.: Automated cartilage and meniscus segmentation of knee MRI with conditional generative adversarial networks. Magn. Reson. Med. **84**(1), 437–449 (2020)

25. Deng, Y., You, L., Wang, Y., Zhou, X.: A coarse-to-fine framework for automated knee bone and cartilage segmentation data from the osteoarthritis initiative. J. Digit. Imaging **34**(4), 833–840 (2021). https://doi.org/10.1007/s10278-021-00464-z

26. Ronneberger, O., Fischer, P., Brox, T.: U-Net: convolutional networks for biomedical image segmentation. In: Navab, N., Hornegger, J., Wells, W.M., Frangi, A.F. (eds.) MICCAI 2015. LNCS, vol. 9351, pp. 234–241. Springer, Cham (2015). https://doi.org/10.1007/978-3-319-24574-4_28

27. Badrinarayanan, V., Kendall, A., Cipolla, R.: SegNet: a deep convolutional encoder-decoder architecture for image segmentation. IEEE Trans. Pattern Anal. Mach. Intell. **39**(12), 2481–2495 (2017)

28. Shelhamer, E., Long, J., Darrell, T.: Fully convolutional networks for semantic segmentation. IEEE Trans. Pattern Anal. Mach. Intell. **39**(4), 640–651 (2017)

29. Goodfellow, Ian J., Pouget-Abadie, J., Mirza, M., et al.: Generative adversarial nets. In: Ghahramani, Z., Welling, M., Cortes, C., et al. (eds.) Advances in Neural Information Processing Systems, vol. 27. Curran Associates, Inc. (2014)

30. Zhou, Z., Rahman Siddiquee, M.M., Tajbakhsh, N., Liang, J.: UNet++: a nested U-net architecture for medical image segmentation. In: Stoyanov, D., et al. (eds.) DLMIA/ML-CDS -2018. LNCS, vol. 11045, pp. 3–11. Springer, Cham (2018). https://doi.org/10.1007/978-3-030-00889-5_1

31. Huang, G., Liu, Z., Van Der Maaten, L., Weinberger, K.Q.: Densely connected convolutional networks. In: IEEE Conference on Computer Vision and Pattern Recognition (CVPR) 2017, pp. 2261–2269 (2017). https://doi.org/10.1109/CVPR.2017.243

LiSHT: Non-parametric Linearly Scaled Hyperbolic Tangent Activation Function for Neural Networks

Swalpa Kumar Roy[1], Suvojit Manna[2], Shiv Ram Dubey[3(✉)], and Bidyut Baran Chaudhuri[4,5]

[1] Department of Computer Science and Engineering, Jalpaiguri Government of Engineering College, Jalpaiguri, West Bengal, India
swalpa@cse.jgec.ac.in
[2] CureSkin, Bengaluru, Karnataka, India
suvojit@heallo.ai
[3] Computer Vision and Biometrics Lab, Indian Institute of Information Technology, Allahabad, Allahabad, Uttar Pradesh, India
srdubey@iiita.ac.in
[4] Techno India University, Kolkata, India
[5] Indian Statistical Institute, Kolkata, India

Abstract. The activation function in neural network introduces the non-linearity required to deal with the complex tasks. Several activation/non-linearity functions are developed for deep learning models. However, most of the existing activation functions suffer due to the dying gradient problem and non-utilization of the large negative input values. In this paper, we propose a Linearly Scaled Hyperbolic Tangent (LiSHT) for Neural Networks (NNs) by scaling the Tanh linearly. The proposed LiSHT is non-parametric and tackles the dying gradient problem. We perform the experiments on benchmark datasets of different type, such as vector data, image data and natural language data. We observe the superior performance using Multi-layer Perceptron (MLP), Residual Network (ResNet) and Long-short term memory (LSTM) for data classification, image classification and tweets classification tasks, respectively. The accuracy on CIFAR100 dataset using ResNet model with LiSHT is improved by 9.48, 3.40, 3.16, 4.26, and 1.17% as compared to Tanh, ReLU, PReLU, LReLU, and Swish, respectively. We also show the qualitative results using loss landscape, weight distribution and activations maps in support of the proposed activation function.

Keywords: Activation Function · Convolutional Neural Networks · Non-Linearity · Tanh function · Image Classification

1 Introduction

The deep learning method is one of the breakthroughs which replaced the hand-tuning tasks in many problems including computer vision, speech processing, natural language

---

S. R. Dubey—Work done while at IIIT Sri City.

D. Gupta et al. (Eds.): CVIP 2022, CCIS 1776, pp. 462–476, 2023.
https://doi.org/10.1007/978-3-031-31407-0_35

processing, robotics, and many more [4,8,9,28,29]. In recent times, the deep Artificial Neural Networks (ANNs) have shown a tremendous performance improvement due to existence of larger datasets as well as powerful computers [12]. Various types of ANN have been proposed for several problems such as Multilayer Perceptron (MLP) [17] to deal with the real vector R-dimensional data [18]. Convolutional Neural Networks (CNN) are used to deal with the image and videos [14]. Recurrent Neural Network (RNN) like Long-Short Term Memory (LSTM) are used for the sentiment analysis [30]. The main aim of different type of neural networks is to transform the input data in abstract feature space. In order to achieve it, all the neural networks rely on a compulsory unit called the activation function [1]. The activation functions bring the non-linear capacity in the network to deal with the complex data [7].

The $Sigmoid$ activation function was mostly used in the at the inception of neural networks. It is a special case of the logistic function. The $Sigmoid$ function squashes the real-valued numbers into 0 or 1. In turn, the large negative number becomes 0 and large positive number becomes 1. The hyperbolic tangent function $Tanh$ is the another popular activation function. The output range of $Tanh$ is defined with -1 as lower limit and 1 as upper limit. The vanishing gradient in both positive as well as negative directions is one of the major problems with both $Sigmoid$ and $Tanh$ activation functions. The Rectified Linear Unit ($ReLU$) activation function was proposed in recent past for training deep networks [22]. $ReLU$ is a breakthrough against vanishing gradient. It is a zero function (i.e., the output is zero) for the negative inputs and an identity function for the positive inputs. The $ReLU$ is very simple, hence became very popular and mostly used in different deep models. The diminishing gradient for the inputs less than zero can be seen as primary bottleneck with $ReLU$ leading to dying gradient problem.

Several researchers have proposed the improvement on $ReLU$ such as Leaky ReLU ($LReLU$) [25], Parametric ReLU ($PReLU$) [13], $Softplus$ [26], Exponential Linear Unit (ELU) [3], Scaled Exponential Linear Unit ($SELU$) [20], Gaussian Error Linear Unit ($GELU$) [16], Average Biased ReLU ($ABReLU$) [5], Linearized sigmoidal activation ($LiSA$) [2] etc. The $ReLU$ is extended to $LReLU$ by allowing a small, non-negative and constant gradient (such as 0.01) for the negative inputs [25]. The $PReLU$ makes the slopes of linear function for negative inputs (i.e., leaky factor) as trainable [13]. The $Softplus$ activation function tries to make the transition of $ReLU$ (i.e., at 0) smooth by fitting the log function [26]. Otherwise, the $Softplus$ activation is very similar to the $ReLU$ activation. The ELU function is same as $ReLU$ for positive inputs and exponential for negative inputs [3]. The ELU becomes smoother near zero. For positive inputs, the ELU [3] can blow up the activation, which can lead to the gradient exploding problem. The $SELU$ adds one scaling parameter in ELU, which makes it better against weight initialization [20]. The $GELU$ uses a Gaussian approach to apply the zero/identity map to the input of a unit randomly [16]. The $ABReLU$ utilizes the representative negative values as well as representative positive values by shifting rectification based on the average of activation values [5]. The $ABReLU$ also could not utilize all the negative values due to trimming of values at zero, similar to $ReLU$. Most of these existing activation methods are sometimes not able to take the advantage of negative values which is solved in the proposed $LiSHT$ activation.

Recently, Xu et al. have performed an empirical study of rectified activations in CNNs [31]. Very recently, a promising $Swish$ activation function was introduced as sigmoid-weighted linear unit, i.e., $f(x) = x \times sigmoid(\beta x)$ [27]. Based on the value of the learnable β, $Swish$ adjusts the amount of non-linearity.

In this paper, a linearly scaled hyperbolic tangent activation function ($LiSHT$) is proposed to introduce the non-linearities in the neural networks. The $LiSHT$ scales the $Tanh$ function linearly to tackle its gradient diminishing problem.

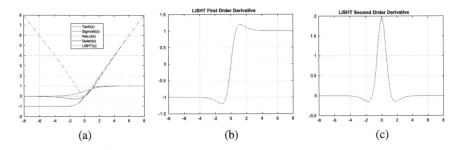

Fig. 1. (a) The characteristics of the *LiSHT* activation function along with $Tanh$, $Sigmoid$, $ReLU$, and $Swish$. (b) The 1st order Derivative of proposed *LiSHT* activation. (c) The 2nd order Derivative of the proposed *LiSHT* activation.

The contributions of this paper are as follows,

– A new activation function named non-parametric Linearly Scaled Hyperbolic Tangent ($LiSHT$) is proposed by linearly scaling the $Tanh$ activation function.
– The increased amount of non-linearity of the proposed activation function is visualized from its first and second order derivatives curves (Fig. 1).
– The proposed $LiSHT$ activation function is tested with different types of neural networks, including Multilayer Perceptron, Residual Neural Network, and Long-Short Term Memory based networks.
– Three different types of experimental data are used 1) $\mathbb{R}$-dimensional data, including Iris and MNIST (converted from image) datasets, 2) image data, including MNIST, CIFAR-10 and CIFAR-100 datasets, and 3) sentiment analysis data, including twitter140 dataset.
– The impact of different non-linearity functions over activation feature maps and weight distribution has been analyzed.
– The activation maps, weight distributions and optimization landscape are also analyzed to show the effectiveness of the proposed $LiSHT$ activation function.

This paper is organized as follows: Sect. 2 outlines the proposed $LiSHT$ activation; Sect. 3 presents the mathematical analysis; Sect. 4 describes the experimental setup; Sect. 5 presents the results; and Sect. 6 contains the concluding remarks.

2   Proposed LiSHT Activation Function

A Deep Neural Network (DNN) comprises of multiple hidden nonlinear layer. Let an input vector be $x \in \mathbb{R}^d$, and each layer transforms the input vector followed by a nonlinear mapping from the lth layer to the $(l+1)^{th}$ layer as follows:

$$\left.\begin{aligned} \tau^0 &= x \\ s_i^{l+1} &= \sum_{j=1}^{N^l} w_{ij}^l \tau_j^l + o_i^l \\ \tau_i^{l+1} &= \phi(s_i^{l+1}) \end{aligned}\right\} \tag{1}$$

Here, τ represents the activation volume of any given layer, s_i^l, w_{ij}^l, o_i^l, and N^l represent the vectors of output, weights, biases and number of units in the hidden l^{th} layer, respectively, and a non-linear activation mapping $\phi(x)$. Looking for an efficient and powerful activation function in DNN is always demanding due to the overabundance by the *saturation* properties of existing activation functions. An activation function $\phi(x)$ is said to be saturate [10], if its derivative $\phi'(x)$ tends to zero in both directions (i.e., $x \to \infty$ and $x \to -\infty$, respectively). The training of a deep neural networks is almost impossible with of $Sigmoid$ and $Tanh$ activation functions due to the gradient diminishing problem when input is either too small or too large [12]. For the first time, the Rectified Linear Unit ($ReLU$) (i.e., $\phi(x) = max(0, x)$) became very popular activation for training the DNN [22]. But, $ReLU$ also suffers due to the gradient diminishing problem for negative inputs which lead to the dying neuron problem.

Hence, we propose a non-parametric linearly scaled hyperbolic tangent activation function, so called $LiSHT$. Like $ReLU$ [22] and $Swish$ [27], $LiSHT$ shares the similar unbounded upper limits property on the right hand side of activation curve. However, because of the symmetry preserving property of $LiSHT$, the left hand side of the activation is in the upwardly unbounded direction, hence it satisfies non-monotonicity (see Fig. 1(a)). Apart from the literature [3,27] and to the best of our knowledge, first time in the history of activation function, $LiSHT$ utilizes the benefits of positive valued activation without identically propagating all the inputs, which mitigates gradient vanishing at back propagation and acquiesces faster training of deep neural network. The proposed activation function $LiSHT$ is computed by multiplying the $Tanh$ function to its input x and defined as,

$$\phi(x) = x \cdot g(x) \tag{2}$$

where $g(x)$ is a hyperbolic tangent function and defined as,

$$g(x) = Tanh(x) = \frac{exp^x - exp^{-x}}{exp^x + exp^{-x}}. \tag{3}$$

where x is the input to the activation function and exp is the exponential function.

For the large positive inputs, the behavior of the $LiSHT$ is close to the $ReLU$ and $Swish$, i.e., the output is close to the input as depicted in Fig. 1(a). Whereas, unlike $ReLU$ and other commonly used activation functions, the output of $LiSHT$ for negative inputs is symmetric to the output of $LiSHT$ for positive inputs as illustrated in Fig. 1(a). The 1st order derivative (i.e., $\phi'(x)$) of $LiSHT$ is given as follows,

$$\begin{aligned} \phi'(x) &= x[1 - Tanh^2(x)] + Tanh(x) \\ &= x + Tanh(x)[1 - \phi(x)]. \end{aligned} \tag{4}$$

Similarly, the 2nd order derivative (i.e., $\phi''(x)$) of $LiSHT$ is given as follows,

$$
\begin{aligned}
\phi''(x) &= 1 - Tanh(x)\phi(x) + [1 - \phi(x)](1 - Tanh^2(x)) \\
&= 2 - Tanh(x)\phi'(x) - \phi(x) - Tanh(z)[\phi'(x) - x] \\
&= 2[1 - Tanh(x)\phi'(x)].
\end{aligned}
\tag{5}
$$

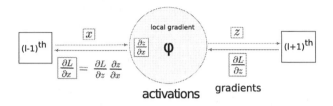

Fig. 2. Flow of gradients through any activation layer.

The 1st and 2nd order derivatives of the proposed $LiSHT$ are plotted in Fig. 1(b) and Fig. 1(c), respectively. An attractive characteristic of the $LiSHT$ is *self-stability* property, the magnitude of derivatives is less than 1 for $x \in [-0.65, 0.65]$. It can be observed from the derivatives of $LiSHT$ in Fig. 1 that the amount of non-linearity is very high near to zero as compared to the existing activations which can boost the learning of a complex model. As described in Fig. 1(c) that the 2nd order derivative of proposed $LisHT$ activation function is similar to the opposite of the Laplacian operator (i.e., the 2nd order derivative of Gaussian operator) which is useful to maximize a function. Thus, due to opposite nature of Gaussian operator, the proposed $LiSHT$ activation function boosts the training of the neural network for the minimization problem of the loss function.

We understand that being unbounded for both negative and positive inputs, smooth, and non-monotonicity are the advantages of the proposed $LiSHT$ activation. The complete unbounded property makes $LiSHT$ different from all the traditional activation functions. Moreover, it makes use of strong advantage of positive feature space. $LiSHT$ is a smooth, symmetric w.r.t. y-axis and non-monotonic function and introduces more amount of non-linearity in the training process than $Swish$.

3   Mathematical Analysis

In this section we show mathematically that $LiSHT$ actively solves the vanishing gradient problem of $Tanh$. The flow of gradient through any activation function is depicted in Fig. 2. Let ϕ is an activation function given as $z = \phi(x)$, where x is the input and z is the output. Let L is the final objective function and the running gradient $\frac{\partial L}{\partial z}$ is the input to ϕ during back-propagation. The running gradient output of ϕ is $\frac{\partial L}{\partial x} = \frac{\partial L}{\partial z} \cdot \frac{\partial z}{\partial x}$ using chain rule, where $\frac{\partial z}{\partial x}$ is the local gradient of ϕ.

Theorem 1. *If $\phi = Tanh$ then it leads to the gradient diminishing problem.*

Proof.

$$z = Tanh(x) \tag{6}$$

The local gradient for $Tanh$ activation is given as,

$$\frac{\partial z}{\partial x} = 1 - Tanh^2(x) \approx \begin{cases} 0, & x < -2 \\ \frac{\partial z}{\partial x}, & -2 \le x \le 2 \\ 0, & x > 2 \end{cases} \tag{7}$$

where $Tanh^2(x) \approx 1$ for $-2 < x < 2$. It can be noticed that for smaller and larger inputs the local gradient $\frac{\partial z}{\partial x}$ of $Tanh$ is very close to zero which makes the running gradient $\frac{\partial L}{\partial x}$ also close to zero, thus leading to the gradient diminishing problem.

Theorem 2. *If $\phi = LiSHT$ then the local gradient $\frac{\partial z}{\partial x} = 0$ iff $x = 0$.*

Proof.

$$z = LiSHT(x) = x.Tanh(x) \tag{8}$$

The local gradient for LiSHT activation is given as,

$$\frac{dz}{dx} = x + Tanh(x)[1 - xTanh(x)] \tag{9}$$

For $x < -2$, $Tanh(x) \approx -1$, thus $\frac{\partial z}{\partial x} \approx -1$. For $x > 2$, $Tanh(x) \approx 1$, thus $\frac{\partial z}{\partial x} \approx 1$. For $-2 \le x \le 2$, $-1 \le Tanh(x) \le 1$, thus $2x - 1 \le \frac{\partial z}{\partial x} \le 2x + 1$. The $LiSHT$ can lead to gradient diminishing problem iff $\frac{\partial z}{\partial x} = x + Tanh(x)[1 - xTanh(x)] = 0$. It means $x = \frac{Tanh(x)}{Tanh^2(x) - 1}$ which is only possible iff $x = 0$. It can be also visualized in Fig. 1(b). Thus, the $LiSHT$ activation function exhibits non-zero gradient for all positive and negative inputs and solves the gradient diminishing problem of $Tanh$ activation function.

4 Experimental Setup

In this section, first, six datasets are described in detail, then the three types of networks are summarized, and finally the training settings are stated in detail.

4.1 Datasets Used

We evaluate the proposed *LiSHT* activation function on five benchmark databases, including Iris, MNIST, CIFAR-10, CIFAR-100 and twitter140. The **Fisher's Iris Flower dataset**[1] [32] consists three Iris species (i.e., Versicolor, Virginica and Setosa) with a total of 150 examples. Each example of Iris dataset is represented by four characteristics, including length and width of petal and sepal, respectively. The **MNIST dataset** is a popular dataset to recognize the English digits (i.e., 0 to 9) in images. It consists of 60,000 and 10,000 images in the training and test sets, respectively [23]. The

---

[1] C. Blake, C. Merz, UCI Repository of Machine Learning Databases.

CIFAR-10 dataset is an object recognition dataset with 10 categories having images of resolution 32×32 [21]. The 50,000 and 10,000 images are available in the training and test sets, respectively. All the images of the CIFAR-10 dataset are also present in the **CIFAR-100 dataset** dataset (i.e., $50K$ for training and $10K$ for testing), but categorized in 100 classes. The training and testing test sets contain 100 classes in CIFAR-100 dataset. The **twitter140 dataset** [11] is used to perform the classification of sentiments of Twitter messages by classifying as either positive, negative or neutral with respect to a query. In this dataset, we have considered 1,600,000 examples, where 85% are used as training set and the rest 15% as validation set.

Table 1. The classification accuracy on Iris and MNIST datasets using different activation functions for MLP model.

Dataset	Activation Functions						
	Sigmoid	Tanh	ReLU [22]	PReLU [13]	LReLU [25]	Swish [27]	LiSHT
Iris	96.23	96.26	96.41	97.11	96.53	96.34	**97.33**
MNIST	98.43	98.26	98.48	98.34	97.69	98.45	**98.60**

Table 2. The classification accuracy on MNIST and CIFAR-10/100 datasets using different activation functions for ResNet model.

Dataset	ResNet Depth	Activation Functions					
		Tanh	ReLU [22]	PReLU [13]	LReLU [25]	Swish [27]	LiSHT
MNIST	20	99.48	99.56	99.56	99.52	99.53	**99.59**
CIFAR-10	164	89.74	91.15	92.86	91.50	91.60	**92.92**
CIFAR-100	164	68.80	72.84	73.01	72.24	74.45	**75.32**

4.2   Tested Neural Networks

We use three models, including a Multi-layer Perceptron (MLP), a widely used Pre-activated Residual Network (ResNet-PreAct) [15]), and a Long-Sort Term Memory (LSTM) to show the performance of activation functions. These architectures are explained in this section. The **Multi-layer Perceptron (MLP)** with one hidden layer is used in this paper for the classification of data. The internal architecture in MLP uses input, hidden and final $softmax$ layer with 6, 5, and 4 nodes for the Car evaluation dataset. For Iris Flower dataset, the MLP uses 4, 3, and 3 nodes in the input, hidden and final $softmax$ layer, respectively. The MNIST dataset samples are converted into 1-D vectors when used with MLP. Thus, for MNIST dataset, the MLP uses 784 neurons in the input layer, 512 neurons in the hidden layer, and 10 neurons in the last layer. The **Residual Neural Network (ResNet)** is a very popular CNN model for the image classification task. We use the Pre-activated ResNet [15] for image classification experiments in this paper. The ResNet-PreAct is used with 164-layer (i.e., very deep network) for CIFAR-10 and CIFAR-100 datasets, whereas it is used with 20-layer for MNIST dataset. The channel pixel mean subtraction is used for preprocessing over image datasets with this network as per the standard practice being followed by most image classification neural networks. In this paper, the **Long Short Term Memory (LSTM)** is used as the third type of neural network, which basically belongs to the Recurrent Neural Network (RNN) family. A single layered LSTM with 196 cells is used for sentiment analysis over twitter140 dataset. The LSTM is fed with 300 dimensional word vectors trained with FastText Embeddings.

4.3 Training Settings

We perform the implementation using in the Keras deep learning framework. Different computer systems, including different GPUs (such as NVIDIA Titan X, Pascal 12GB GPU and NVIDIA Titan V 12GB GPU) are used at different stages of the experiments. The $Adam$ optimizer [6, 19] is used for the experiments in this paper. The batch size is set to 128 for the training of the networks. The learning rate is initialized to 0.1 and reduced by a factor of 0.1 at 80th, 120th, 160th, and 180th epochs during training. For LSTM, after 10625 iteration on 128 sized mini-batches, the learning rate is dropped by a factor of 0.5 up to 212, 500 mini-batch iterations.

Table 3. The classification accuracy on twitter140 dataset using different activation functions for LSTM model.

Dataset	Activation Functions				
	Tanh	ReLU [22]	LReLU [25]	Swish [27]	LiSHT
Twitter140	82.27	82.47	78.18	82.22	**82.47**

5   Results and Analysis

We investigate the performance and effectiveness of the proposed $LiSHT$ activation and compare with state-of-the-art activation functions such as $Tanh$, $ReLU$, and $Swish$.

5.1   Experimental Results

The results on Iris and MNIST datasets using MLP model are reported in Table 1. The *categorical cross-entropy* loss is used to train the models for 200 epochs. In order to run training smoothly in both the dataset, 80% of samples were randomly chosen for training and remaining 20% are used for validation. The proposed $LiSHT$ activation achieves outperforms the existing activation functions. The top accuracy on Iris and MNIST datasets are achieved by LiSHT as 97.33% and 98.60%, respectively.

Table 2 shows the validation accuracies on MNIST, CIFAR-10 and CIFAR-100 datasets for different activations with pre-activation ResNet. The depth of ResNet is 20 for MNIST and 164 for CIFAR datasets. We train the model for 200 epochs using the cross-entropy objective function. It is observed that $LiSHT$ outperforms the other activation functions on MNIST, CIFAR-10 and CIFAR-100 datasets, and achieves 99.59% and 92.92%, and 75.32% accuracy, respectively. Moreover, a significant improvement has been shown by $LiSHT$ on CIFAR datasets. The unbounded, symmetric and more non-linear properties of the proposed $LiSHT$ activation function facilitates better and efficient training as compared to the other activation functions such as $Tanh$, $ReLU$ and $Swish$. The unbounded and symmetric nature of $LiSHT$ leads to the more exploration of weights and positive and negative gradients to tackle the gradient diminishing and exploding problems.

The sentiment classification performance in terms of the validation accuracy is reported in Table 3 over twitter140 dataset with LSTM for different activations. It is observed that the performance of proposed $LiSHT$ activation function is better than $Tanh$ and $Swish$, whereas the same as $ReLU$. It points out one important observation that by considering the negative values as negative by $Swish$ degrades the performance because it leads the $Swish$ activation more towards the linear function as compared to the $ReLU$ activation.

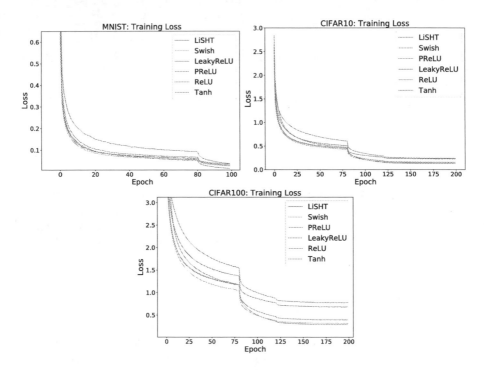

Fig. 3. The convergence curves in terms of loss for training sets using the $LiSHT$ and state-of-the-art $Tanh$, $ReLU$, and $Swish$ activations with ResNet model over MNIST (upper row, left column), CIFAR-10 (upper row, right column) and CIFAR-100 (lower row) datasets.

5.2 Result Analysis

The convergence curve of losses is also used as the metric to measure the learning ability of the ResNet model with different activation functions. The training and validation loss over the epochs are plotted in Fig. 3 and 4 for MNIST, CIFAR-10 and CIFAR-100 datasets using ResNet. It is clearly observed that the proposed $LiSHT$ boosts the convergence speed. It is also observed that the $LiSHT$ outperforms the existing non-linearities across several classification tasks with MLP, ResNet and LSTM networks.

5.3 Analysis of Activation Feature Maps

In deep learning, it is a common practice to visualize the activations of different layer of the network. In order to understand the effect of activation functions over the learning of important features at different layer, we have shown the activation feature maps for different non-linearities at 2nd layer of the pre-activation ResNet of MNIST digit 7 in Fig. 5. The number of activation feature maps in 2nd and 11th layers are 64 (each having the 32×32 spatial dimensions) and 128 (each having the 16×16 spatial dimensions), respectively. It can be seen from Fig. 5 that the images looking deeper blue are due to the dying neuron problem caused by the non-learnable behavior arose due to the

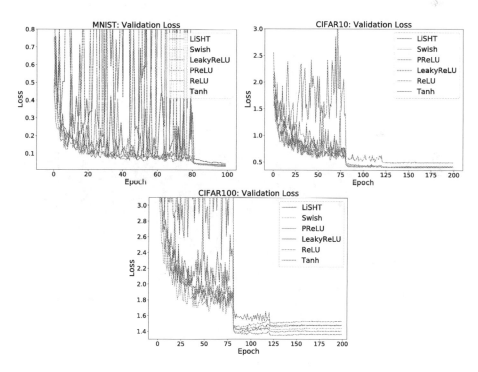

Fig. 4. The convergence curves in terms of loss for validation sets using the $LiSHT$ and state-of-the-art $Tanh$, $ReLU$, and $Swish$ activations with ResNet model over MNIST (upper row, left column), CIFAR-10 (upper row, right column) and CIFAR-100 (lower row) datasets.

improper handling of negative values by the activation functions. The proposed $LiSHT$ activation consistently outperforms other activations. It is observed that the $LiSHT$ generates the less number of non-learnable filters due to the unbounded nature in both positive and negative scenarios which helps it to overcome from the problem of dying gradient. It is also observed that some image patches contain noise in terms of the Yellow color. The patches corresponding to the $LiSHT$ contain less noise. Moreover, it is uniformly distributed over all the patches, when $LiSHT$ is used, compared to other activation functions. It may be also one of the factors that proposed $LiSHT$ outperforms other activations.

5.4   Analysis of Final Weight Distribution

The weights of the layers are useful to visualize because it gives the idea about the learning pattern of the network in terms of 1) the positive and negative biasedness and 2) the exploration of weights caused by the activation functions. We have portrayed the weight distribution of final $Conv$ layer in Fig. 6 for pre-activation ResNet over the MNIST dataset using $Tanh$, $ReLU$, $Swish$ and $LiSHT$ activations. The weight distribution for $Tanh$ is limited in between -5 and 4 (see Fig. 6(a)) due to its bounded nature in both negative and positive regions. Interestingly, as depicted in Fig. 6(b), the weight distribution for $ReLU$ is biased towards the positive region because it converts all negative values to zero which restricts the learning of weights in the negative direction. This leads to the problems of dying gradient as well as gradient exploding. The $Swish$ tries to overcome the problems of $ReLU$, but unable to succeed due to the bounded nature in negative region (see Fig. 6(c)). The above mentioned problems are removed in the $LiSHT$ as suggested by its weight distribution shown in Fig. 6(d). The $LiSHT$ activation leads to the symmetric and smoother weight distribution. Moreover, it also

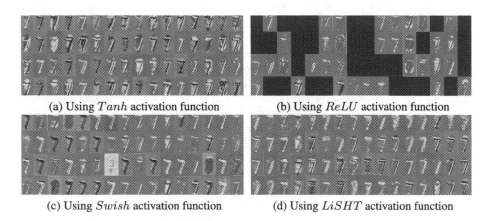

(a) Using $Tanh$ activation function   (b) Using $ReLU$ activation function

(c) Using $Swish$ activation function   (d) Using $LiSHT$ activation function

Fig. 5. Visualization of MNIST digit 7 from the 2nd $conv$ layer activation feature maps without feature scale clipping using a fully trained pre-activation ResNet model using the (a) $Tanh$ (b) $ReLU$ (c) $Swish$ and (d) $LiSHT$ activation, respectively. Note that there are 64 feature maps of dimension 32×32 in the 2nd layer, represented in 4 rows and 16 columns. (Color figure online)

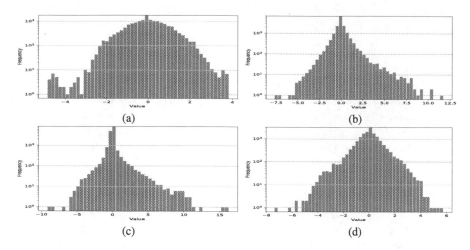

Fig. 6. Visualizations of the distribution of weights from the final $Conv$ layer of pre-activation ResNet over MNIST dataset for the (a) $Tanh$ (b) $ReLU$ (c) $Swish$ and (d) $LiSHT$ activations, respectively.

allows the exploration of weights in the higher range (i.e., in between -8 and 6 in the example of Fig. 6).

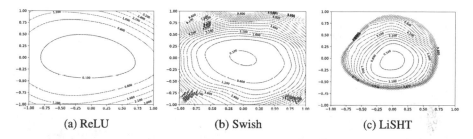

(a) ReLU   (b) Swish   (c) LiSHT

Fig. 7. The visualization of 2D Loss Landscape plot of CIFAR-10 shown using ReLU, Swish and LiSHT, respectively.

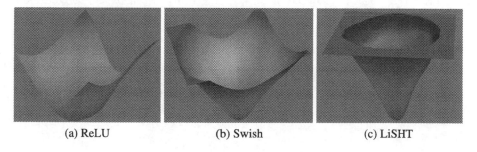

(a) ReLU   (b) Swish   (c) LiSHT

Fig. 8. The visualization of 3D Loss Landscape plot of CIFAR-10 shown using ReLU, Swish and LiSHT, respectively.

5.5 Analysis of Loss Landscape

The training ability of DNN is directly and indirectly influenced by the factors like network architecture, the choice of optimizer, variable initialization, and most importantly, what kind of non-linearity function to be used in the architecture. In order to understand the effects of network architecture on non-convexity, we trained the ResNet-152 using $ReLU$, $Swish$ and proposed $LiSHT$ activations and try to explore the structure of the neural network loss landscape. The $2D$ and $3D$ visualizations of loss landscapes are illustrated in Fig. 7 and 8 by following the visualization technique proposed by Li et al. [24].

As depicted in the $2D$ loss landscape visualizations in Fig. 7(a)–(c), the $LiSHT$ makes the network to produce the smoother loss landscapes with smaller convergence steps which is populated by the narrow, and convex regions. It directly impacts the loss landscape. However, $Swish$ and $ReLU$ also produce smooth loss landscape with large convergence steps, but unlike $LiSHT$, both $Swish$ and $ReLU$ cover wider searching area which leads to poor training behavior. In $3D$ landscape visualization, it can be seen in Fig. 8(a)–(c), it can be observed that the slope of the $LiSHT$ loss landscape is higher than the $Swish$ and $ReLU$ which enables to train deep network efficiently. Therefore, we can say that, the $LiSHT$ decreases the non-convex nature of overall loss minimization landscape as compared to the $ReLU$ and $Swish$ activation functions.

6 Conclusion

A novel non-parametric linearly scaled hyper tangent activation function ($LiSHT$) is proposed in this paper for training the neural networks. The proposed $LiSHT$ activation function introduces more non-linearity in the network. It is completely unbounded and solves the problems of diminishing gradient problems. Other properties of $LiSHT$ are symmetry, smoothness and non-monotonicity, which play an important roles in training. The classification results are compared with the state-of-the-art activation functions. The efficacy of LiSHT is tested on benchmark datasets using MLP, ResNet and LSTM models. The experimental results confirm the effectiveness of the unbounded, symmetric and highly non-linear nature of the proposed $LiSHT$ activation function. The importance of unbounded and symmetric non-linearity in both positive and negative regions are analyzed in terms of the activation maps and weight distribution of the learned network. The visualization of loss landscape confirms the effectiveness of the proposed activations to make the training more smoother with faster convergence.

Acknowledgments. We gratefully acknowledge the support of NVIDIA Corporation with the donation of the GeForce Titan X Pascal GPU used partially in this research.

References

1. Agostinelli, F., Hoffman, M., Sadowski, P., Baldi, P.: Learning activation functions to improve deep neural networks. arXiv preprint arXiv:1412.6830 (2014)

2. Bawa, V.S., Kumar, V.: Linearized sigmoidal activation: a novel activation function with tractable non-linear characteristics to boost representation capability. Expert Syst. Appl. **120**, 346–356 (2019)
3. Clevert, D.A., Unterthiner, T., Hochreiter, S.: Fast and accurate deep network learning by exponential linear units (ELUs). arXiv preprint arXiv:1511.07289 (2015)
4. Dubey, S.R.: A decade survey of content based image retrieval using deep learning. IEEE Trans. Circuits Syst. Video Technol. **32**(5), 2687–2704 (2021)
5. Dubey, S.R., Chakraborty, S.: Average biased RELU based CNN descriptor for improved face retrieval. Multimedia Tools Appl. **80**(15), 23181–23206 (2021)
6. Dubey, S.R., Chakraborty, S., Roy, S.K., Mukherjee, S., Singh, S.K., Chaudhuri, B.B.: diffgrad: an optimization method for convolutional neural networks. IEEE Trans. Neural Netw. Learn. Syst. **31**(11), 4500–4511 (2019)
7. Dubey, S.R., Singh, S.K., Chaudhuri, B.B.: Activation functions in deep learning: a comprehensive survey and benchmark. Neurocomputing (2022)
8. Dubey, S.R., Singh, S.K., Chu, W.T.: Vision transformer hashing for image retrieval. In: 2022 IEEE International Conference on Multimedia and Expo (ICME), pp. 1–6. IEEE (2022)
9. Garcia-Garcia, A., Orts-Escolano, S., Oprea, S., Villena-Martinez, V., Garcia-Rodriguez, J.: A review on deep learning techniques applied to semantic segmentation. arXiv preprint arXiv:1704.06857 (2017)
10. Glorot, X., Bordes, A., Bengio, Y.: Deep sparse rectifier neural networks. In: Proceedings of the Fourteenth International Conference on Artificial Intelligence and Statistics, pp. 315–323 (2011)
11. Go, A., Bhayani, R., Huang, L.: Twitter sentiment classification using distant supervision. Technical report, Stanford (2009)
12. Goodfellow, I., Bengio, Y., Courville, A., Bengio, Y.: Deep Learning, vol. 1. MIT Press, Cambridge (2016)
13. He, K., Zhang, X., Ren, S., Sun, J.: Delving deep into rectifiers: surpassing human-level performance on imagenet classification. In: Proceedings of the IEEE International Conference on Computer Vision, pp. 1026–1034 (2015)
14. He, K., Zhang, X., Ren, S., Sun, J.: Deep residual learning for image recognition. In: Proceedings of the IEEE Conference on Computer Vision and Pattern Recognition, pp. 770–778 (2016)
15. He, K., Zhang, X., Ren, S., Sun, J.: Identity mappings in deep residual networks. In: Leibe, B., Matas, J., Sebe, N., Welling, M. (eds.) ECCV 2016. LNCS, vol. 9908, pp. 630–645. Springer, Cham (2016). https://doi.org/10.1007/978-3-319-46493-0_38
16. Hendrycks, D., Gimpel, K.: Bridging nonlinearities and stochastic regularizers with gaussian error linear units. arXiv preprint arXiv:1606.08415 (2016)
17. Hornik, K., Stinchcombe, M., White, H.: Multilayer feedforward networks are universal approximators. Neural Netw. **2**(5), 359–366 (1989)
18. Kim, L.W.: Deepx: deep learning accelerator for restricted Boltzmann machine artificial neural networks. IEEE Trans. Neural Netw. Learn. Syst. **29**(5), 1441–1453 (2018)
19. Kingma, D.P., Ba, J.: Adam: a method for stochastic optimization. arXiv preprint arXiv:1412.6980 (2014)
20. Klambauer, G., Unterthiner, T., Mayr, A., Hochreiter, S.: Self-normalizing neural networks. In: Advances in Neural Information Processing Systems, pp. 971–980 (2017)
21. Krizhevsky, A.: Learning multiple layers of features from tiny images. Technical report, Citeseer (2009)
22. Krizhevsky, A., Sutskever, I., Hinton, G.E.: Imagenet classification with deep convolutional neural networks. In: Advances in Neural Information Processing Systems, pp. 1097–1105 (2012)

23. LeCun, Y., Bottou, L., Bengio, Y., Haffner, P.: Gradient-based learning applied to document recognition. Proc. IEEE **86**(11), 2278–2324 (1998)
24. Li, H., Xu, Z., Taylor, G., Studer, C., Goldstein, T.: Visualizing the loss landscape of neural nets. In: Advances in Neural Information Processing Systems, pp. 6389–6399 (2018)
25. Maas, A.L., Hannun, A.Y., Ng, A.Y.: Rectifier nonlinearities improve neural network acoustic models. In: Proceedings of ICML, vol. 30, no. 1, p. 3 (2013)
26. Nair, V., Hinton, G.E.: Rectified linear units improve restricted Boltzmann machines. In: Proceedings of the 27th International Conference on Machine Learning (ICML 2010), pp. 807–814 (2010)
27. Ramachandran, P., Zoph, B., Le, Q.V.: Swish: a self-gated activation function. arXiv preprint arXiv:1710.05941 (2017)
28. Schmidhuber, J.: Deep learning in neural networks: an overview. Neural Netw. **61**, 85–117 (2015)
29. Voulodimos, A., Doulamis, N., Doulamis, A., Protopapadakis, E.: Deep learning for computer vision: a brief review. Comput. Intell. Neurosci. **2018** (2018)
30. Wang, Y., Huang, M., Zhao, L., et al.: Attention-based LSTM for aspect-level sentiment classification. In: Proceedings of the 2016 Conference on Empirical Methods in Natural Language Processing, pp. 606–615 (2016)
31. Xu, B., Wang, N., Chen, T., Li, M.: Empirical evaluation of rectified activations in convolutional network. arXiv preprint arXiv:1505.00853 (2015)
32. Zhang, L., Suganthan, P.N.: Random forests with ensemble of feature spaces. Pattern Recogn. **47**(10), 3429–3437 (2014)

Plant Disease Classification Using Hybrid Features

Vamsidhar Muthireddy$^{(\boxtimes)}$ and C. V. Jawahar

International Institute of Information Technology, Hyderabad, India
vamsidhar.muthireddy@research.iiit.ac.in

Abstract. Deep learning has shown remarkable performances in image classification, including those of plants and leaves. However, high-performing networks in terms of accuracy may not be using the salient regions for making the prediction and could be prone to biases. This work proposes a neural network architecture incorporating handcrafted features and fusing them with the learned features. Using hybrid features provides better control and understanding of the feature space while leveraging deep learning capabilities. Furthermore, a new IoU-based metric is introduced to assess the CNN-based classifier's performance based on the regions focused on making predictions. Experiments over multiple leaf disease datasets demonstrate the performance improvement with the model using hybrid features. Classification using hybrid features performed better than the baseline models in terms of P@1 and also on the IoU-based metric.

Keywords: Hybrid Network · Plant disease classification · PlantVillage

1 Introduction

Agriculture has been a vital pillar in sustaining civilizations. It plays an irreplaceable role not just in feeding the populace but also in generating economic value. In recent times, the agricultural yield has declined [1]. There is a growing interest in Precision Agriculture (PA) to maintain sufficient conditions of the farm during the growth phase of the crop [8, 36] and the imaging tools for tracking the growth of the harvest and early detection of the crop diseases [28]. Effective designing of these tools leveraging Image processing techniques and machine learning algorithms for plant disease detection is an active research problem.

Traditional plant disease recognition algorithms used handcrafted features containing a combination of shape, colour, and texture-based features. A shallow classifier is subsequently used for the classification task [19]. Disease recognition systems built on such algorithms were difficult to scale and generalize due to the requirement of specific domain knowledge. Moreover, any change in imaging conditions would impact the efficiency of the systems. On the other hand, neural networks are capable of learning a data-specific feature space. Convolutional neural networks have been used for plant disease recognition [25]. However, to improve the baseline performance of the neural networks for a particular task, either a large amount of data or a change in architectural design is needed.

D. Gupta et al. (Eds.): CVIP 2022, CCIS 1776, pp. 477–492, 2023.
https://doi.org/10.1007/978-3-031-31407-0_36

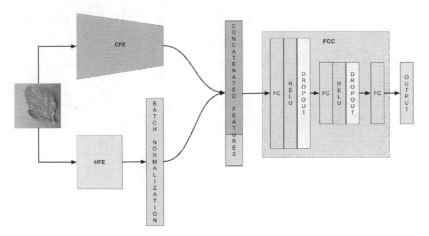

Fig. 1. This figure shows our proposed hybrid network. Convolutional block of Inception-V3 network is used as CFE. Features from the HFE block are concatenated and fed into FCNN for predicting output softmax scores.

Data fusion is a methodology where designed neural networks contain an architectural provision to inject additional features at different layers of the network [9]. We propose one such architecture to leverage handcrafted features in the training process of the CNN. We compare the efficacy of our designed network against other CNNs for plant disease classification. In addition, we compare the performance of our network against the baseline networks on similar datasets to show its efficacy on plant disease classification.

In a classification task, the algorithms are evaluated based on their ability to predict an accurate label for a given input [14]. This is in contrast to object detection tasks, where the algorithms are evaluated on their ability to localize the predicted label in the input image along with their ability to predict an accurate label. In this work, the necessity to integrate the localization capacity of the CNN while assessing its efficacy on the task of object classification is presented. In traditional classification algorithms, handcrafted features are designed to primarily encode the foreground object. This ensures that the shallow classifiers built using such features would be using encoded foreground objects in their task. However, CNN classifiers would select the feature space optimal for the classification task. With no restrictions in place to regulate or assess this behaviour, these classifiers might select a significant portion of the feature space from the background objects [31]. Coupled with the tendency to generate train, validation, and test sets to follow a similar data distribution would make it relatively complicated to diagnose this issue unless tested on real-world data. Therefore, CNNs trained on the classification task should be assessed on their ability to select the feature space from the foreground object. Employing visualization techniques could alleviate this issue by providing a gateway to understanding the feature space of the neural network with respect to an input image. We utilize one such approach to analyze our CNN-based classifiers trained on the Plant disease recognition task [35]. Further, we generate quantitative results to assert the importance of integrating the localization capacity of the network while assessing its classification performance.

The contributions of this work can be summarized as follows:

- We propose a hybrid CNN architecture for plant disease recognition which utilizes the data fusion technique to inject handcrafted features into the first FC layer, allowing the CNN to learn the complimentary feature space to improve the classification accuracy.
- We provide the quantitative and qualitative experimental results that show the importance of assessing CNN classifiers on their ability to learn the feature space from the foreground object, along with the accuracy of predicting labels.

2   Related Works

Earlier works on plant disease detection performed the task by selecting the features by Molecular techniques [24,32,34]. These methods did not provide real-time feedback on the health of the plant. Features extracted from non-invasive methods like spectroscopy, and imaging techniques [6,29,33] have provided an opportunity to develop and deploy systems that can be used to assess the health of a plant in real-time. While able to identify plant diseases in real-time, these techniques have a heavy cost factor associated with the equipment needed to collect the data. A picture-based analysis has been proposed to identify plant diseases that have visible parts of the symptoms. These approaches usually collect image data using mobile phones [17]. Hand-crafted features are extracted from the images using classical image-processing techniques. These features in general are comprised of colour, shape, texture [27], a combination of the above [19,30,38,41]. These features are combined with shallow discriminative classifiers to perform plant disease recognition [18,19,30,38].

The classification pipelines built with hand-crafted features rely heavily on the prior knowledge of the task and dataset. Selecting a task-specific feature space or a classification algorithm takes tedious effort. To tackle these constraints, convolutional neural networks have been used for plant disease recognition [4,5,25,39]. CNNs optimally select the feature space specific to the task, hence alleviating the task of feature selection [23]. In addition, when integrated with the training pipeline, the data augmentation framework increases the generalizability of the network [13,21].

Although CNNs can learn optimal feature space, outperforming shallow classifiers built on hand-crafted features, they still lack the controllability of such learned space. Ensemble networks tackle this issue by combining the features extracted from the FC layer of the CNN with the hand-crafted features and feeding them into a shallow classifier [10]. However, in these types of architectures, CNNs do not learn a feature space that works along with the hand-crafted features since the network weights are not optimized after data fusion. To address this, data fusion techniques have been proposed that concatenate the hand-crafted features with the FC layers of a CNN at different levels of abstraction [9]. We propose a network along a similar approach to show the efficacy of the data fusion techniques for leaf disease recognition.

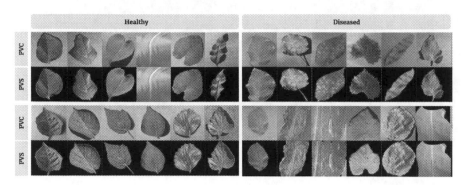

Fig. 2. This figure shows images of leaves belonging to 12 healthy plant species. Rows 1, 3 show the images from PlantVillage Colour (PVC) and rows 2, 4 show their counterparts from PlantVillage Segmented (PVS) dataset

Accuracy, Precision@K, F score are some of the metrics used to obtain the efficacy of the models trained on the classification task [14]. Contrarily, models trained on object detection tasks include IoU to assess the localization behaviour of the model along with its classification capability. Enhancements have been made to the evaluation metrics of the object detection task [15,42]. During inference, these methods return a confidence score by weighing classification accuracy with an IoU score. We propose using a similar metric for evaluating the models trained on the classification task. For a generation of the object mask to calculate IoU, we use the class-activated mapping obtained by Grad-CAM [35] to identify the salient regions in an image for a prediction. These salient regions are then thresholded at different values to obtain the object masks [3,43]. In order to establish the necessity of modifying the evaluation methodology of classifiers, we provide qualitative and quantitative results demonstrating the utility of the proposed metrics.

3 Dataset

To validate the efficacy of the proposed hybrid pipeline, we compare its performance over datasets that are composed of images of diseased leaves. These datasets are described below.

PlantVillage Dataset: The PlantVillage dataset is a corpus containing 54K images of healthy and unhealthy plant leaves. The dataset is divided into 38 different plant-disease pairs. Images in these classes belong to 16 plant species and contain 26 leaf diseases. Every image in the PlantVillage dataset contains a single leaf in three different configurations, *Color, Segmented,* and *Grayscale.*

Plant Pathology: Plant Pathology Dataset [7] contains leaf images of twelve plants in healthy and diseased conditions. It consists of 4503 images (2278 healthy; 2225 diseased). Overall, a total of 22 classes are available for a classification task. All the leaf images were collected from March to May in a controlled environment.

PlantDoc: PlantDoc [37] is a publically available dataset introduced in 2020. It covers 13 plant species through 2,598 images across 27 classes (10 healthy; 27 diseased) for image classification and object detection tasks. In contrast to the Plant Village dataset and Plant Pathology Dataset, where the images are taken in a controlled environment, the images in PlantDoc are curated from natural settings containing multiple leaves against different backgrounds and varying light conditions.

DiaMOS Plant: DiaMOS Plant [11] is a dataset of images of an entire growing season of pear trees (Cultivar: Septoria Piricola), from February to July, under realistic field conditions in Itlay. It comprises 3505 images, including 499 fruit images and 3006 leaves images.

4   Methods

Our proposed hybrid network utilizes data fusion techniques between two components - a convolutional neural network and a handcrafted feature extractor. In this section, we use the term Convolutional Feature Extractor (CFE) for the convolutional block of the neural network. The handcrafted feature block that extracts a set of pre-defined features from an input image is termed Handcrafted Feature Extracter (HFE). The fully connected block of the neural network is referred to as FCNN.

An overview of the hybrid network is given in Fig. 1. Features obtained from CFE and HFE are concatenated into a feature vector for an input image. This feature vector is fed into FCNN to obtain the classification result.

4.1   Handcrafted Feature Extractor (HFE)

For an input image, 258 features are extracted by the HFE. They contain 120 colour, 54 morphological, and 84 texture features. These features are concatenated to obtain a 258-dimensional feature vector. A batch normalization layer normalizes this feature vector.

Colour features are obtained by processing each channel of the RGB and HSI colour space. Each color channel's mean, standard deviation, minimum, and maximum intensity values are computed. Each channel is further processed to obtain a 16 binned histogram from 256 gray levels. All the obtained features are united to generate a 120-dimensional colour feature vector.

Morphological features include area, perimeter, major axis length, minor axis length, minimum radius, seven Hu moments, area of the convex hull, solidity, and Fourier descriptor composed of 20 harmonics. Fourier descriptor was obtained on the contour of the binary image. All the obtained features are united to generate a 54-dimensional morphological feature vector.

Texture features are extracted from the image's Red, Green, Blue, and Grayscale channels. They are composed of properties of gray level co-occurrence matrix (GLCM) and 13 Harlick features. Each of the channels is quantized to 32 intensity levels prior to the extraction of features. From the GLCM obtained for each channel, mean, standard deviation, contrast, correlation, homogeneity, dissimilarity, energy, and Angular Second Moment(ASM) are extracted. All these obtained features are united to generate an 84-dimensional texture feature.

4.2 Convolutional Feature Extractor (CFE)

We use the Inception-v3 [40] to build our CFE. We remove the final FC layer of the Inception-v3 to obtain the feature vector. This 2048 dimensional feature vector is extracted after the Average pooling layer. We use the PlantVillage dataset to explore plant disease recognition in this work. The disease parts in the images are not restricted to a particular size. Multi-scale convolutions in Inception-v3 will encode these regions for better classification. Further, CFE composed of convolutional blocks of Inception-v3 will better establish the efficacy of our proposed hybrid model against the baseline.

4.3 Fully Convolutional Neural Network (FCNN)

Features extracted from the CFE and HFE are concatenated to form a 2316 dimensional feature vector. This feature is fed into FCNN to obtain the classification prediction. Our designed FCNN is composed of three Fully-Connected layers. The first and second FC layers are composed of 256 and 128 neurons, respectively, while the third FC layer is composed of c neurons, where c denotes the count of unique class labels in the classification task. Each of the first two FC layers is followed by a ReLU activation layer and a dropout layer for regularization. A softmax layer follows the third FC layer to perform classification.

4.4 Model Validation

We validate the models trained for Plant disease classification using P@K and IoU. After the convolutional networks are trained, we use GradCAM [35] to obtain the heatmaps. These heatmaps are used as the predicted localization masks for the foreground objects. The localization mask is thresholded at k where $k \in (0, 1)$ to convert into the binary mask. The obtained binary mask is used to compute Intersection over Union (IoU) scores at a threshold of k. We evaluate the performance of the classification model using IoU based on the underlying assumption that the features used in a classification task should be obtained from the foreground objects in an image.

5   Experimental Setup

Our experiments are composed of two tasks: finding an optimal network for the classification of plant diseases and evaluating the trained network using the gradient-activated heatmaps. To find the optimal network, first, we compare the classification performance of the proposed Inception-V3 hybrid network with the baseline Inception-V3 network. Further, we experimented with networks belonging to the ResNet family. All these networks are trained on the PlantVillage

Table 1. The table shows the P@1 values of different models on the two configurations of PlantVillage dataset. Resnet152 outperforms the rest of the models in the PVC configuration with P@1 of 99.742. Inception-V3 Hybrid outperforms the rest of the models in the PVS configuration with P@1 of 99.558

Model	P@1	
	PVC	PVS
Inception-V3(baseline)	99.3400	99.2500
Resnet18	99.5672	99.3463
Resnet34	99.4383	99.2600
Resnet50	99.6133	99.3739
Resnet101	99.7145	99.4568
Resnet152	**99.7422**	99.3463
Inception-V3 hybrid	*99.7330*	**99.5580**

Table 2. P@1 values obtained by other works on PlantVillage dataset. [12] has reported the highest test accuracy of 99.53.

Model	P@1 - PVC
AlexNet [12]	99.44
VGG [12]	99.53
MobileNet [20]	98.65
EfficientNet B5 [2]	98.42
CNN-RNN [22]	98.77

datasets (PVC, PVS) and pre-trained on the ImageNet dataset. Moreover, to further validate the proposed approach, multiple other datasets curated for plant diseases were used for experimentation. To explore the significance of in-domain dataset, the pretraining was done on the Imagenet or PVC dataset.

The datasets are split into train, validation, and test sets by keeping their ratio at 60:20:20. The batch size across all the experiments is set to 24. We use Stochastic Gradient Descent (SGD) as an optimizer with a momentum of 0.9. We keep the learning rate as 0.01 for networks belonging to ResNet architecture while we keep the learning rate of 0.005 for the Inception-V3 hybrid network. The learning rate is decayed by a factor of 0.1 for no improvement in validation loss for ten consecutive epochs.

We evaluate the trained networks under the fair assumption that a neural network needs to look at the foreground object of interest while classifying an image into a particular class. We generate the gradient-activated heatmaps utilizing the GradCAM network. These heatmaps represent the areas of interest in an input image identified by a network for a predicted class label. To obtain the binary masks, we threshold these gradient activations at bins ranging from 0 to 1. These binary maps are used to generate IoU scores across the multiple threshold values. We use this metric to evaluate the focus of the network. The results generated are presented in Table 4 and are further discussed in the following section.

6   Results

To show the efficacy of the proposed hybrid model, we compared it with different classification networks. Table 1 shows the obtained P@1 scores for the classification part of the experiments. All the tested models have a better P@1

Table 3. The table shows the P@1 values obtained on multiple plant disease datasets using Inception-V3 (baseline) and Inception-V3 hybrid (proposed) networks. It can be noted that our proposed hybrid methodology outperforms the baseline reported. Pretraining on the domain specific PlantVillage dataset (PVC) improves the P@1 of the models

Dataset	Pre-trained	Model	
		Inception-V3	Inception-V3 hybrid
Diamos	ImageNet	82.72 [11]	88.52
	ImageNet + PVC	89.02	**89.33**
plantDoc	ImageNet	41.10	51.69
	ImageNet + PVC	29.73	**53.81**
plantDocDetection	ImageNet	46.67 [37]	61.5
	ImageNet + PVC	62.06 [37]	**67.92**
Plant Leaves	ImageNet	94.55 [16]	98.56
	ImageNet + PVC	98.82	**99.16**

compared to the baseline model in both configurations of the dataset. Resnet-152 has the best top P@1 accuracy in the PVC configuration of the dataset (P@1 = 99.74). Inception-V3 hybrid has the best accuracy in the PVS configuration of the dataset (P@1 = 99.56). Models trained on PVC configuration have higher P@1 when compared to their counterparts trained on PVS configuration of the dataset by a considerable margin.

The comparison between the baseline Inception-V3 architecture with the proposed Inception-V3 hybrid approach across multiple plant disease datasets is presented in Table 3. It can be observed that our proposed hybrid model outperforms the baseline model for all the datasets. The difference in performance for the plantDoc and plantDocDetection detection datasets is most pronounced. Pretraining on the domain-specific dataset PVC yielded much better results than the pretraining on the ImageNet dataset.

Models trained on both dataset configurations are further interpreted using GradCAM architecture. Figure 5 shows the results obtained on healthy and unhealthy leaves. These heatmaps are generated from the last convolutional layer of each trained network in Table 1. This is done under the fair assumption that these layers feed directly into the softmax layer, which acts as a final classifier. The figure contains six rows of sub-figures; the odd positioned rows (1, 3, 5) have images from PVC configuration, while the even positioned rows (2, 4, 6) have their counterparts from the dataset's PVS configuration. These results were obtained to infer the model behaviour with respect to a classification; to find the parts of the leaf which the network is using to identify a particular plant-disease combination.

The heatmaps generated by Grad-CAM are used to convert the obtained qualitative results in the Fig. 5 into quantitative results. These results are pre-

Table 4. The table shows the IoU values obtained between heatmaps generated by Grad-CAM with foreground binary mask. IoU@0.5 represents the scores when the Grad-CAM is thresholded at 0.5. Mean IoU scores are obtained by taking the mean of IoU across different threshold values. In both PVC, and PVS configuration of the data, Inception-V3 hybrid outperforms all other models in IoU@0.5 and mean IoU scores.

Model	PVC		PVS	
	IoU@0.5	**meanIoU**	**IoU@0.5**	**meanIoU**
Resnet18	0.5125	0.3801	0.4747	0.3715
Resnet50	0.0666	0.1016	0.0919	0.1223
Resnet101	0.2174	0.2204	0.2905	0.2646
Resnet152	0.2572	0.2433	0.2821	0.2627
Inception-V3 hybrid	**0.5468**	**0.3986**	**0.5031**	**0.3771**

sented in Table 4. For a particular classification task, we assess the performance of the classification model based on the percentage of foreground regions chosen to classify an image. The Grad-CAM heatmaps are converted into binary masks at ten threshold ranges from 0 to 1. These are treated as the predicted binary masks. For the ground truth, we utilize the PVS configuration of the dataset to generate binary masks. We calculate IoU scores at each of these thresholds for different networks on both dataset configurations. Figure 3 shows the obtained results across different threshold values. We use the obtained IoU values to quantify the model performance in two ways. First, we measure the $IoU@k$ to show the network performance in being able to identify the foreground with higher values. Following the standard norms, we select $k = 0.5$. Second, we calculate the mean IoU values obtained by averaging the IoU at different threshold values to evaluate the model performance across the range of 0 to 1. From Table 4, it is evident that the Inception-V3 hybrid network outperforms all other networks across $IoU@k$ and $meanIou$ metrics. For PVC dataset configurations, Inception-V3 hybrid has $IoU@0.5$ of 0.5468 and $meanIoU$ of 0.3998. For PVS dataset configurations, Inception-V3 hybrid has $IoU@0.5$ of 0.5031 and $meanIoU$ of 0.3771. Both $IoU@0.5$ and $meanIoU$ values of the Inception-V3 hybrid network are higher for PVC when compared with the PVS configuration of the dataset.

We conducted the above analysis on the scan-like plant leaf datasets, Swedish-leaf, Flavia, Leafsnap, MEW-2012, and MEW-2014 datasets reported in [26]. We use the ResNet-101 trained on these datasets and Grad-CAM methodology to obtain the foreground heatmaps. By following the above-explained procedure, we generate $IoU@0.5$ and $meanIoU$ scores. The results obtained are reported in Table 5 and Fig. 4. Swedish-leaf, Flavia, and Leafsnap have $IoU@0.5 \leq 0.06$. The IoU of the MEW-2014 dataset is 0.24, which is more significant in comparison to its subset, MEW-2012, having an IoU of 0.20. It should be noted that the ResNet-101 models used to generate the heatmaps are trained individually on each dataset. The accuracy of each of these models is above 97%.

6.1   Discussion

Different models are trained on both PVC and PVS configurations of the datasets. ResNet-152 in the PVC configuration and Inception-V3 hybrid in the PVS configuration outperform the rest of the models. We observe that all the models that we trained outperform the baseline model. It can also be noted that the Inception-V3 hybrid underperforms ResNet-152 in PVC configuration by a margin of 0.009%. The same network outperforms the second-best ResNet-101 on PVS by a margin of 0.1%, which hints at the efficacy of our hybrid model in the datasets having a similar structure to PVS.

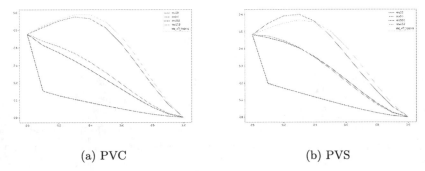

(a) PVC   (b) PVS

Fig. 3. This figure shows the IoU scores for ResNet-18, 50, 101, 152, Inception-V3 hybrid networks on threshold values ranging from 0-1. In PVS configuration, Inception-V3 hybrid has higher IoU scores across all threshold values. In PVS configuration, At lower threshold(≤ 0.5) ResNet-18 has higher IoU scores whereas at higher threshold(≥ 0.5), Inception-V3 hybrid has higher IoU scores.

To validate this, the Inception-V3 hybrid is tested on the plant disease datasets against the baseline Inception-V3 architecture as shown in Table 3. The hybrid model outperforms the baseline model in each of the datasets. Moreover, the improvement of P@1 when the models are pre-trained on PVC indicates that domain-specific initialization of the weights is a suitable way to obtain performance gains during training. The obtained results outline the efficacy of the proposed methodology over plant disease datasets.

It should also be noted that models trained on PVC outperform their counterparts trained on PVS, as shown in Table 1. Figure 2 shows the key difference between both configurations to be the presence of non-zero valued background in PVC and zero-valued background in PVS. Stating that the background is helping the network in making better classifications would be a fair conclusion in this scenario where the classifiers trained on the PVC outperform their counterparts trained on PVS. To verify this claim, Grad-CAM was used in further experiments. Using Grad-CAM, heatmaps were generated from the final convolutional layer of the networks trained on PVS and PVC configurations for each input image. Figure 5 shows the heatmaps overlapped with their respective input

Table 5. IoU@0.5 and meanIoU values are obtained for Swedish-leaf, Flavia, Leafsnap, MEW-2012, and MEW-2014 datasets for the models reported in [26]. ResNet-101 is used too obtain the Grad-CAM heatmaps used to generate the foreground binary mask.

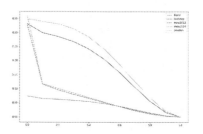

Dataset	IoU@0.5	meanIoU
Swedish	0.0535	0.0784
Flavia	0.052	0.0743
Leafsnap	0.0481	0.0410
MEW-2012	0.2052	0.1790
MEW-2014	0.2413	0.2057

Fig. 4. This figure shows the IoU scores for ResNet-101 on threshold values ranging from 0–1 on Swedish-leaf, Flavia, Leafsnap, MEW-2012, and MEW-2014 datasets

images for healthy and unhealthy leaves in the same order. A series of observations were made by analyzing these images. Firstly, each network identifies a specific part of an image for classifying an image. This region of interest varies from network to network. Secondly, some networks have chosen a significant part of the background as the region of interest for making a classification. This can be observed for outputs of ResNet-50, ResNet-101, and ResNet-152 on PVC, as shown in Fig. 5. Thirdly, the regions of interest identified by some of the networks contain parts of the background in a significant majority. This could be interpreted as networks correctly classifying the input image by heavily relying on the background rather than the foreground, as shown in Fig. 5(a–g). Extreme cases such as Fig. 5(e) were observed where ResNet-50 generated heatmap has an uncanny resemblance to the shape of the leaf in the image; only, in this case, it appears to have learned it from the background. ResNet 18 seems to work as expected but shows inferior performance in terms of accuracy. The inception V3 hybrid network consistently showed better heatmaps where the major focus of the network was on the foreground. Fourthly, across all the networks, it is evident that the generated region of interest overlaps more with the foreground object in the case of PVS rather than PVC.

A series of experiments were conducted to verify the claims mentioned above and to identify the overlap between the generated heatmaps and foreground objects in each input image. The ground truth for these foreground objects was generated using the PVS version of the dataset. We binarize the obtained heatmaps by thresholding at $k \in (0, 1)$ and compute the IoU@k for the models in the Table 1. The results are presented in the Table 4. $k = 0.5$ is selected for a fair comparison of networks as the halfway point in its range. Inception-V3 outperforms other networks in both these metrics across PVC and PVS. ResNet-18 outperforms the rest of the deeper architectures with more convolutional layers among the ResNet family. It is rather surprising that deeper ResNets

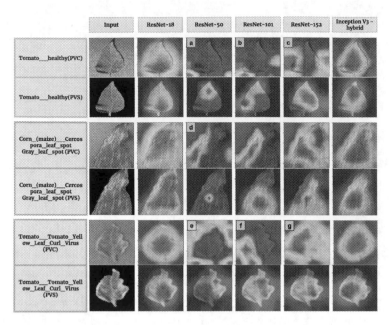

Fig. 5. This figure shows Grad-CAM heatmaps overlapped with their respective images. These heatmaps are obtained for healthy and unhealthy leaves from models specified in Table 1. Although all the images were correctly classified, the focussed regions by the different models vary.

that outperform their shallow counterparts with respect to the accuracy underperform when it comes to IoU. It is to be noted that, even though these networks vary in terms of their depth, their architecture is similar with respect to ResNet blocks and their usage of skip connections.

Deeper networks with more trainable parameters have a higher capacity for selecting features from an image. They would identify and extract these features from the input image irrespective of whether they belong to the foreground or background object. When texture in the background is removed to make it a constant value, as in PVS, these same architectures tend to look more at the foreground object. In essence, ResNet-50, 101, and 152 have higher IoU in PVS when compared to PVC as seen in Table 4 and Fig. 5. In contrast, ResNet-18 and Inception-V3 hybrid perform better in PVC when compared to PVS. Figure 3 shows IoU@k for different models for $k \in (0, 1)$. As noted, the Inception-V3 hybrid outperforms every network in PVC configuration across all the values of k. In the PVS configuration, it outperforms other networks for $k \geq 0.5$. This indicates that the Inception-V3 hybrid has better success in identifying important areas of the foreground as regions of interest for making a classification decision when compared with other networks. The graph also shows that ResNet-50, 101, 152 have degrading IoU for an increase in threshold value. This also supports our claim that these networks have identified more parts of the background than the foreground as the region of interest for classifying an image.

To validate our findings, we conducted our recommended IoU based evaluation on the models trained on Swedish-leaf, Flavia, Leafsnap, MEW-2012, and MEW-2014 reported in [26]. Each of the ResNet-101 configurations used in the assessment has $P@1 \geq 0.97$. Swedish, Flavia, and Leafsnap have $IoU@0.5$ scores within a range of ~ 0.06 from each other. They have a difference in the number of classes and total images. The low IoU obtained on these datasets hints at the lack of direct correlation between dataset size and the focus of the neural network. However, there is an improvement in IoU from 0.20 in MEW-2012 to 0.24 in MEW-2014. MEW-2014 is an upgraded version of MEW-2012 containing more classes and images than its past subset. Introducing inter-class variability along with an increase in the size of the dataset has improved the focus of the neural network. The results obtained in Table 5 strengthen our claim of having an IoU based assessment that can also determine the focus of the network w.r.t the foreground object.

6.2   Conclusion

This paper presents an approach for image classification by including handcrafted features in deep learning. We propose a hybrid network that fuses the handcrafted features with the learned features from the neural network. This architecture utilizes the generalization capacity of the neural networks and its ability to select an optimal feature space while giving more control over the learned feature space. We demonstrate the superior results from our approach on different datasets and the improvement with pretraining on domain-specific datasets.

On evaluating the classification model, we have highlighted an unexplored problem in neural network based architectures while training on datasets like PVC. It is a reasonable expectation that the high-performing neural networks for classification learn the feature space from the foreground object. Our analysis demonstrates that this is not always the case. Therefore, it is necessary to further analyze a trained classification model for the regions it focuses on for predicting the label. A properly trained model is the one that not only gives high classification performance in terms of conventional metrics but also has significantly identified the salient regions of the image for making the prediction. We proposed an evaluation methodology based on IoU for quantifying the network's focus on the salient regions. Our proposed hybrid network performed the best in terms of accuracy and the IoU based evaluation. Though the experiments have been done on leaf datasets, the methods are general and can be applied to other domains.

References

1. Alexandratos, N., Bruinsma, J.: World agriculture towards 2030/2050: the 2012 revision (2012)
2. Atila, Ü., Uçar, M., Akyol, K., Uçar, E.: Plant leaf disease classification using efficientNet deep learning model. Eco. Inform. **61**, 101182 (2021)

3. Bae, W., Noh, J., Kim, G.: Rethinking Class Activation Mapping for Weakly Supervised Object Localization. In: Vedaldi, A., Bischof, H., Brox, T., Frahm, J.-M. (eds.) ECCV 2020. LNCS, vol. 12360, pp. 618–634. Springer, Cham (2020). https://doi.org/10.1007/978-3-030-58555-6_37
4. Barbedo, J.G.: Factors influencing the use of deep learning for plant disease recognition. Biosys. Eng. **172**, 84–91 (2018)
5. Brahimi, M., Boukhalfa, K., Moussaoui, A.: Deep learning for tomato diseases: classification and symptoms visualization. Appl. Artif. Intell. **31**(4), 299–315 (2017)
6. Chaerle, L., Lenk, S., Hagenbeek, D., Buschmann, C., Van Der Straeten, D.: Multicolor fluorescence imaging for early detection of the hypersensitive reaction to tobacco mosaic virus. J. Plant Physiol. **164**(3), 253–262 (2007)
7. Chouhan, S.S., Singh, U.P., Kaul, A., Jain, S.: A data repository of leaf images: Practice towards plant conservation with plant pathology. In: 2019 4th International Conference on Information Systems and Computer Networks (ISCON), pp. 700–707. IEEE (2019)
8. Cisternas, I., Velásquez, I., Caro, A., Rodríguez, A.: Systematic literature review of implementations of precision agriculture. Comput. Electron. Agric. **176**, 105626 (2020)
9. Cruz, A.C., Luvisi, A., De Bellis, L., Ampatzidis, Y.: X-FIDO: An effective application for detecting olive quick decline syndrome with deep learning and data fusion. Front. Plant Sci. **8**, 1741 (2017)
10. Çuğu, İ., et al.: Treelogy: A novel tree classifier utilizing deep and hand-crafted representations. arXiv preprint arXiv:1701.08291 (2017)
11. Fenu, G., Malloci, F.M.: DiaMos plant: a dataset for diagnosis and monitoring plant disease. Agronomy **11**(11), 2107 (2021)
12. Ferentinos, K.P.: Deep learning models for plant disease detection and diagnosis. Comput. Electron. Agric. **145**, 311–318 (2018)
13. Fujita, E., Kawasaki, Y., Uga, H., Kagiwada, S., Iyatomi, H.: Basic investigation on a robust and practical plant diagnostic system. In: 2016 15th IEEE International Conference on Machine Learning and Applications (ICMLA). pp. 989–992. IEEE (2016)
14. Hossin, M., Sulaiman, M.N.: A review on evaluation metrics for data classification evaluations. Int. J. Data Min. knowl. Manag. Process **5**(2), 1 (2015)
15. Huang, Z., Huang, L., Gong, Y., Huang, C., Wang, X.: Mask scoring r-CNN. In: Proceedings of the IEEE/CVF Conference on Computer Vision and Pattern Recognition, pp. 6409–6418 (2019)
16. Huertas-Tato, J., Martín, A., Fierrez, J., Camacho, D.: Fusing CNNS and statistical indicators to improve image classification. Information Fusion **79**, 174–187 (2022)
17. Hughes, D., Salathé, M., et al.: An open access repository of images on plant health to enable the development of mobile disease diagnostics. arXiv preprint arXiv:1511.08060 (2015)
18. Islam, M., Dinh, A., Wahid, K., Bhowmik, P.: Detection of potato diseases using image segmentation and multiclass support vector machine. In: 2017 IEEE 30th Canadian Conference on Electrical and Computer Engineering (CCECE), pp. 1–4. IEEE (2017)
19. Johannes, A., Picon, A., Alvarez-Gila, A., Echazarra, J., Rodriguez-Vaamonde, S., Navajas, A.D., Ortiz-Barredo, A.: Automatic plant disease diagnosis using mobile capture devices, applied on a wheat use case. Comput. Electron. Agric. **138**, 200–209 (2017)
20. Kamal, K., Yin, Z., Wu, M., Wu, Z.: Depthwise separable convolution architectures for plant disease classification. Comput. Electron. Agric. **165**, 104948 (2019)

21. Kawasaki, Y., Uga, H., Kagiwada, S., Iyatomi, H.: Basic study of automated diagnosis of viral plant diseases using convolutional neural networks. In: Bebis, G., Boyle, R., Parvin, B., Koracin, D., Pavlidis, I., Feris, R., McGraw, T., Elendt, M., Kopper, R., Ragan, E., Ye, Z., Weber, G. (eds.) ISVC 2015. LNCS, vol. 9475, pp. 638–645. Springer, Cham (2015). https://doi.org/10.1007/978-3-319-27863-6_59

22. Kaya, A., Keceli, A.S., Catal, C., Yalic, H.Y., Temucin, H., Tekinerdogan, B.: Analysis of transfer learning for deep neural network based plant classification models. Comput. Electron. Agric. **158**, 20–29 (2019)

23. LeCun, Y., Bengio, Y., Hinton, G.: Deep learning. Nature **521**(7553), 436–444 (2015)

24. Li, W., Abad, J.A., French-Monar, R.D., Rascoe, J., Wen, A., Gudmestad, N.C., Secor, G.A., Lee, M., Duan, Y., Levy, L.: Multiplex real-time PCR for detection, identification and quantification of 'Candidatus liberibacter solanacearum'in potato plants with zebra chip. J. Microbiol. Methods **78**(1), 59–65 (2009)

25. Mohanty, S.P., Hughes, D.P., Salathé, M.: Using deep learning for image-based plant disease detection. Front. Plant Sci. **7**, 1419 (2016)

26. Muthireddy, V., Jawahar, C.V.: Computer vision for capturing flora. In: Mukhopadhyay, J., Sreedevi, I., Chanda, B., Chaudhury, S., Namboodiri, V.P. (eds.) Digital Techniques for Heritage Presentation and Preservation, pp. 245–272. Springer, Cham (2021). https://doi.org/10.1007/978-3-030-57907-4_12

27. Ojala, T., Pietikainen, M., Maenpaa, T.: Multiresolution gray-scale and rotation invariant texture classification with local binary patterns. IEEE Trans. Pattern Anal. Mach. Intell. **24**(7), 971–987 (2002)

28. Patrício, D.I., Rieder, R.: Computer vision and artificial intelligence in precision agriculture for grain crops: A systematic review. Comput. Electron. Agric. **153**, 69–81 (2018)

29. Purcell, D.E., O'Shea, M.G., Johnson, R.A., Kokot, S.: Near-infrared spectroscopy for the prediction of disease ratings for fiji leaf gall in sugarcane clones. Appl. Spectrosc. **63**(4), 450–457 (2009)

30. Qin, F., Liu, D., Sun, B., Ruan, L., Ma, Z., Wang, H.: Identification of alfalfa leaf diseases using image recognition technology. PLoS ONE **11**(12), e0168274 (2016)

31. Ribeiro, M.T., Singh, S., Guestrin, C.: " why should i trust you?" explaining the predictions of any classifier. In: Proceedings of the 22nd ACM SIGKDD International Conference on Knowledge Discovery and Data Mining. pp. 1135–1144 (2016)

32. Ruiz-Ruiz, S., Ambrós, S., del Carmen Vives, M., Navarro, L., Moreno, P., Guerri, J.: Detection and quantitation of citrus leaf blotch virus by taqman real-time rt-PCR. J. Virol. Methods **160**(1–2), 57–62 (2009)

33. Sankaran, S., Mishra, A., Maja, J.M., Ehsani, R.: Visible-near infrared spectroscopy for detection of huanglongbing in citrus orchards. Comput. Electr. Agric. **77**, 127–134 (2011)

34. Saponari, M., Manjunath, K., Yokomi, R.K.: Quantitative detection of citrus tristeza virus in citrus and aphids by real-time reverse transcription-PCR (Taqman®). J. Virol. Methods **147**(1), 43–53 (2008)

35. Selvaraju, R.R., Cogswell, M., Das, A., Vedantam, R., Parikh, D., Batra, D.: Grad-cam: Visual explanations from deep networks via gradient-based localization. In: Proceedings of the IEEE International Conference on Computer Vision, vol. 128, pp. 336–359 (2017)

36. Shafi, U., Mumtaz, R., García-Nieto, J., Hassan, S.A., Zaidi, S.A.R., Iqbal, N.: Precision agriculture techniques and practices: From considerations to applications. Sensors **19**(17), 3796 (2019)

37. Singh, D., et al.: Plantdoc: a dataset for visual plant disease detection. In: Proceedings of the 7th ACM IKDD CoDS and 25th COMAD, pp. 249–253 (2020)
38. Singh, V., Misra, A.K.: Detection of plant leaf diseases using image segmentation and soft computing techniques. Information processing in Agriculture 4(1), 41–49 (2017)
39. Sladojevic, S., Arsenovic, M., Anderla, A., Culibrk, D., Stefanovic, D.: Deep neural networks based recognition of plant diseases by leaf image classification. Computational intelligence and neuroscience 2016 (2016)
40. Szegedy, C., Vanhoucke, V., Ioffe, S., Shlens, J., Wojna, Z.: Rethinking the inception architecture for computer vision. In: Proceedings of the IEEE conference on computer vision and pattern recognition. pp. 2818–2826 (2016)
41. Wang, H., Li, G., Ma, Z., Li, X.: Image recognition of plant diseases based on backpropagation networks. In: 2012 5th International Congress on Image and Signal Processing. pp. 894–900. IEEE (2012)
42. Wu, S., Li, X., Wang, X.: Iou-aware single-stage object detector for accurate localization. Image Vis. Comput. 97, 103911 (2020)
43. Ye, W., Yao, J., Xue, H., Li, Y.: Weakly supervised lesion localization with probabilistic-cam pooling. arXiv preprint arXiv:2005.14480 (2020)

Analyzing Hydro-Estimator INSAT-3D Time Series with Outlier Detection

Neha Sisodiya[1]([⊠]) [iD], Keshani Vyas[2], Nitant Dube[3], and Priyank Thakkar[1]

[1] Department of Computer Science, Nirma University, Ahmedabad, Gujarat, India
{17ptphde169,priyank.thakkar}@nirmauni.ac.in
[2] Department of IT, LD College, Ahmedabad, Gujarat, India
[3] SAC-ISRO, Ahmedabad, Gujarat, India
ndube@sac.isro.gov.in

Abstract. Precipitation plays an important role in various applications like agriculture, health care, disaster management, forest health and others. These applications are directly or indirectly affected by precipitation. In order to predict precipitation, it becomes important to analyze the pattern followed by the event. The generated pattern should be accurate to obtain the prediction at par. Presence of outliers in any data significantly affects the generated pattern, time required and accuracy in prediction. Treating missing values is not sufficient to get higher accuracy in prediction. In this paper, we present the performance evaluation of Support vector regression (SVR), Seasonal auto regressive integrated moving average (SARIMA), and Bi-directional LSTM (Bi-LSTM) for prediction of hydro estimator values (HEM), in domain of machine learning, statistical and deep learning approaches respectively. We have made a comparison between the generated pattern and prediction with and without outliers. We have identified a suitable outlier detection technique by comparing the performance of Cluster Based Local Outlier Factor (CBLOF), Histogram based outlier Detection (HBOS), K nearest neighbour (KNN), Isolation Forest for detecting outliers. The performance on prediction techniques are compared using RMSE and MAE measures. The implementation is done over a big data architecture, since the data is, Big data'.

Keywords: Precipitation (HEM) · Big EO Data · Outlier detection · Machine Learning · Deep Learning

1 Introduction

Time series data prediction is an important and critical application for years in many application domains such as finance, marketing, earth science, etc. It becomes even more important when earth observation data is concerned [8]. There are two major challenges that need to be addressed, first one is the gathered data is large in volume and second one is, the suitable choice of prediction algorithm. For handling huge amounts of data for access and retrieval, we have a number of distributed architectures available. But the problem here is not only with the volume

© The Author(s), under exclusive license to Springer Nature Switzerland AG 2023
D. Gupta et al. (Eds.): CVIP 2022, CCIS 1776, pp. 493–508, 2023.
https://doi.org/10.1007/978-3-031-31407-0_37

of data, there are other aspects that need to be considered like veracity, variety and velocity, that qualifies the type of data we are handling here as "Big data" [5]. We have proposed an architecture keeping in mind all the requirements to handle Big Earth Observation Data (BEOD), which is geospatial in nature. The format in which the data is available is also complex to understand and process. So, we have provided a unified platform for BEOD to store, retrieve, process and analyze this data at scale. To deal with the second challenge, a suitable prediction algorithm with higher accuracy and capability to handle data at scale is required. Since there are many algorithms like, ARIMA, SARIMA, SVR, Random forest, Holt Winter, LSTM, BiLSTM and many more [17], it is important to find the one with significant improvement in the performance as compared to all others. As time series data forecasting requires higher accuracy in mining the patterns, since the prediction or forecast depends on the obtained patterns. The accuracy in prediction fairly depends on the mined patterns. The noise points or outliers are responsible for inaccuracy in pattern detection and subsequently in prediction. We in our work [18] [17], have explored a few machine learning, forecasting techniques and deep learning models, for time series prediction of rainfall data. Also, have identified the algorithms with high accuracy.

In this work, we have considered SARIMA, which is a well established and popular statistical approach for time series prediction. SVR is a well suited combination of SVM and linear regression, a well known machine learning approach with considerable good performance for prediction problems. BiLSTM, a deep learning architecture for time series prediction, as its learning strategy follows in both the directions that produces better learning than that of traditional LSTM [15]. To enhance the performance of these algorithms at scale, we have tried to preprocess the data in such a way that prediction can be made with large amounts of data as well as the improvement in accuracy can also be done. There are two problems that are present in the data, missing values and the observed values moving out of trend, called as anomaly or outliers. The outliers are detected with four different methods namely, Cluster Based Local Outlier Factor (CBLOF), Histogram based outlier Detection (HBOS), K nearest neighbour (KNN), Isolation Forest. The outlier detection techniques are compared, and best among all is considered in time series pattern detection and prediction. The mentioned prediction algorithms are also compared for reduced error rate. Contributions to the paper includes:

- Treating missing values and outliers for enhancing accuracy in prediction and handling data at scale.
- Identification of suitable outlier detection algorithm.
- Improvement in time complexity and accuracy in prediction.
- Compared traditional prediction algorithms with deep learning architecture utilizing big data architecture.

This paper is organized in five sections, Sect. 1 comprises the literature review done for the problem, Sect. 2 represents the dataset and the methodology used. In Sect. 3 we have shown results and analysis of the proposed work. We have concluded our work and discussed future scope, in Sect. 4.

2   Related Work

Monsoon prediction is the most challenging task, especially when geographic areas like states in India are concerned. We have a wide variation in rainfall pattern being observed over the years due to drastic climatic changes and dependency of rainfall on various parameters. Also, the pattern to be mined for prediction requires a lot of data to make prediction more accurate. Based on this, prediction on precipitation is difficult to make with actual data without preprocessing it. Preprocessing the data includes handling of missing values in some geographic locations and also eliminating the values, which are unconventionally falling-off from the trend, called as outliers.

Rainfall trend of Kerala state of India, is obtained using the data collected by the Indian Meteorological Department (IMD) and Ministry of Earth and Science (MoES) over 100 years. Authors [11] have used Mann-Kendall test, which is a statistical method for estimating rainfall trend. Mann Kendall test is not suitable for handling seasonal effects showing one of its limitations. Secondly, the test in this work, is applied on district levels or for specific predefined regions only. Visualizing rainfall trends has not portray improper and inaccurate trends. Bayesian theory for rainfall prediction [12] analyzed over Indian Meteorological Department (IMD) data with a reported accuracy of 90 % over three cities Delhi, Mumbai and Pune. But, with an increase in the amount of data, the accuracy will not persist. Also, the classifier considers the value as zero in presence of missing values, leading to incorrect prediction.

Similar approach for crop suitability analysis in India, through regression analysis on rainfall with various attributes affecting rainfall is considered [14]. The rainfall variation from one state to another has not been considered in this analysis. The authors haven't performed any data preprocessing. So, eliminating noise form the data and treating missing values will also be helpful.

The authors [19] have used various classifiers such as, Support Vector Machine (SVM), Naive Bayes, Neural Network, Decision Tree (DT), and Random Forest (RF) for prediction on the rainfall data and identified the suitable technique for classification of rainfall data. Data gathered from various weather stations in Malaysia for January 2010 to April 2014, by Malaysia Drainage and Irrigation Department and Malaysia Meteorological Department. Cleaning and preprocessing is done followed by, filling of missing values by mean average technique and data is normalized for bringing the data values into a specific range. Random forest is the most suited classifier for their data. The result of the best suited technique will vary with the ratio of train test split. Correlation between features is not considered. The authors [6] have used decision trees for predicting fog, rainfall, cyclones and thunderstorms. Data collected from National Climatic Data Center (NCDC)-NOAA for year 2013 to 2014, is used. Data contains 20 attributes but the authors have considered only 12 attributes.

In [9], authors have proposed hybrid clustering by combining the advantages of k-means and hierarchical clustering methods on mapreduce framework and compared the result of hybrid clustering with k-means and hierarchical clustering. K-means takes least time to cluster, than hybrid on the data from NCDC, which contains the world's largest active archive of weather data.

The advantages and disadvantages of the various existing approaches used for precipitation prediction are summarized in Table 1.

Initially, we were dependent on statistical models and methods for precipitation prediction. With advancement in machine learning approaches and introduction of deep learning architectures [17], prediction over time-series data using deep learning architectures like LSTM and Bi-LSTM [15] are gaining popularity. A hybrid model [10], that uses LSTM deep learning model, both parameterized and time series model for rainfall prediction with some other attributes like maximum temperature, minimum temperature, and visibility, etc. Data is collected from the coastal region of Andhra Pradesh during a Hud-Hud cyclone. In a parameterized prediction approach, wind speed, pressure, humidity, and temperature, etc. attributes, will work as input, and rainfall will work as an output value. Time series prediction approach is used with 12 neurons in the hidden layer for wind, max temperature, min temperature, pressure, and visibility attributes. Results can be improved by considering more neurons. Only cyclone dataset is considered. Authors [13] have compared the performance of Bi-LSTM and 1D-CNN for precipitation nowcasting by considering multiple variables. The accuracy result of the Bi-LSTM model for the Indian weather dataset and Kaggle dataset is 93.7 % and 89.8 % respectively. The accuracy result of CNN for the Indian weather dataset is 93.2 % and for the Kaggle dataset, it is 84.9 %. A compilation of progressive contributions, made in the past few years, for prediction of time series data with large amounts of data handling capability, is presented in Table 2.

We have used outlier detection techniques, Cluster Based Local Outlier Factor (CBLOF), Histogram based outlier Detection (HBOS), K nearest neighbour (KNN) and Isolation Forest and compared the results as a preprocessing step, to get higher accuracy in prediction. Most of the prediction algorithms mentioned earlier in this section, have been applied for predicting precipitation directly on the data or have treated the missing values as a preprocessing. But, outliers greatly affect the prediction accuracy and also the prediction time especially, when we have large amounts of data. So, we in this work have made an attempt to improve these parameters by handling both missing values and outliers.

3   Proposed Approach

HEM is product derived from raw EO obtained from an Indian satellite called INSAT-3DR. This represents the value of precipitation over the area of observation. With the drastic changes in climate, we have deviation in the recorded observations given by the satellites involved in it. This leads to error in the prediction and also, the presence of abnormal values adds on to the processing time. In order to get more accuracy in prediction, we need to identify the values that are moving off trend and either have to remove it, or try to make out whether it is contributing to some disastrous event.

Table 1. Compilation of popular approaches in precipitation prediction.

Method	Advantage	Disadvantage
Decision Tree	Easy to understand. Useful in Data exploration. Requires relatively little effort from users for data preparation i.e, less data cleaning required	Overfitting, not fit for continuous variables, complex calculations when there are multiple class label. Information gain in a decision tree with categorical variables gives a biased response for attributes with greater no. of categories
Naive Bayes	If assumption of independent predictors holds true, Naive Bayes classifier performs better. Small amount of training data required to estimate test data. Easy to implement	Practically, it is impossible to get all features are independent from each other. If categorical variable has category which isn't visible while training them, model will assign it zero and will be unable to make a prediction
SVM	Handles non-linear data efficiently. Solves both Classification and Regression problems. Stability remains with small changes	Selecting appropriate kernel function. Feature scaling required. More time required to train large databases. Difficult to interpret when applied to Multidimensional space
KNN	Handles non-linear data efficiently. Solves both Classification and Regression problems. Stability remains with small changes.	Does not work well with large dataset and high dimensions. Complex to find value of K. Standardization and normalization before applying KNN algorithm to any dataset. Sensitive to noisy data, missing values and outliers
Linear Regression	Linear Regression performs well when the dataset is linearly separable. Linear Regression is easier to implement, interpret and very efficient to train. It is prone to over-fitting but it can be easily avoided using some dimensionality	Assumption of linearity between the dependent variable and the independent variables. Prone to noise and overfitting. Prone to outliers
K means	Computationally faster than hierarchical clustering, if we keep k smalls. Tighter clusters than hierarchical clustering	Difficult to predict K-value. Different initial means points results in different final clusters
Association Rule Mining	simple and easy-to-understand algorithm It doesn't require labeled data as it is fully unsupervised; as a result, you can use it in many different situations	It is limited to only one item in the consequent. Requires Multiple passes over the database

Table 2. Compilation of progression of popular approaches in precipitation prediction.

Contribution year	Data	Approach	Gap
2013 [12]	Indian Meteorological Department (IMD) data for three cities Pune, Mumbai and Delhi	Bayesian theory	Unable to persist the accuracy, with data amount up-scaled and in presence of missing values. Preprocessing on the data is not done
2014 [11]	Ministry of Earth and Science (MoES) and Indian Meteorological Department (IMD) (100 years)	Mann-Kendall test	Unable to seasonal effects. Applied to a specific region, Kerala for trend estimation. Results are not accurate
2014 [6]	National Climatic Data Center (NCDC)-NOAA	Decision tree	Considered data for one year
2016 [14]	Indian Meteorological Department (IMD) and Open Government Data (OGD)	Regression analysis	Inter-state variation of rainfall is not considered
2016 [19]	Malaysia Meteorological department and Malaysia Drainage and Irrigation Department	Compared different classifiers and reported Random forest as most suitable	Missing values are treated with mean-average mechanism. Ignored the correlation between features
2018 [18]	Indian Meteorological Department (IMD), Pune	Compared machine learning and forecasting techniques, over estimated weather parameters. Estimation is made individually	Outliers were not treated. Have not handled data at scale
2018 [10]	Hud-Hud cyclone data, Indian Meteorological Department (IMD)	Hybrid model, a combination of parameterized and time series (regression model)	LSTM provides better results but, multiple weather parameters are predicted with time series model
2018 [13]	Indian weather data and Kaggle dataset	Bi-LSTM and 1D-CNN	Bi-LSTM results in higher accuracy. But, have not handled the big data characteristics of weather data
2019 [9]	National Climatic Data Center (NCDC)-NOAA	Hybrid model, a combination of k-means and hierarchical clustering, on mapreduce framework	Mapreduce is slow. Hybrid clustering takes time even more than k-means and hierarchical clustering individually. The amount of data have been used, is not specified
2020 [17]	Variety of EO data including, weather data from heterogeneous sources	Statistical, machine learning and deep learning models	Reviewed recent trends

3.1   Dataset

Data from INSAT 3D IMAGER satellite used in this work. INSAT3D IMAGER data is divided into LEVEL 1 and LEVEL 2 products based on bandwidth of the channels. In this work, we have used LEVEL 2 product- HEM (Hydro estimator for precipitation), which is a derived product from TIR1, TIR2 and Water Vapour (WV) products of LEVEL1. HEM product has latitude, longitude, date, time and HEM value as attributes in it. HEM product has both spatial and temporal attributes in it. So, our data fall into the category of spatio-temporal data. Acquired data is archived in HDF5 format and generated at the rate of every half an hour. We have used HEM data over the year 2015 to 2018.

Preprocessing. In the preprocessing phase, we have removed noisy values from latitude, longitude and HEM value attributes. Storing data in HDF5 format may consume less memory but it is not an efficient way for analyzing the huge amount of data. Additionally, Geomesa HBase provides support for ingesting data, in csv, tsv and geojson formats. Considering these factors, we have converted hdf5 data into csv data, for ease of analysis and ingestion. Raw HEM data occupies almost 500GB memory in hdf5 format. The converted csv file size for HEM data products is around 900GB for the year 2015 to 2018.

3.2   Big Data Techniques for Geo-Spatial Data Handling

As the data is growing larger day by day, we are required to use big data handling approaches [8]. The authors [7] have compared two big data frameworks mapreduce and Apache spark with performance analysis using k-means. Performance of k-means on both mapreduce and Apache spark are compared. K-means is implemented using MLlib (Apache spark) and Mahout (mapreduce). Apache spark requires 85 s and mapreduce requires 163 s for executing k-means. But, a very small amount of data have been used for processing. Also, proper description of which data is taken as key and value from the sensor data, is not there. Additionally, the feature on which k-means applied is also not mentioned. Data preprocessing may help to improve performance. The authors [16] have presented a scalable cloud based architecture named SMASH. It contains various components like Hadoop Distributed File System (HDFS), which is used for storing huge amounts of data. Apache spark is used for performing aggregation, statistics, machine learning and many other computations. As traffic data is geospatial in nature, indexing is implemented using Geomesa Accumulo, and Geoserver [1] is used for visualization of data in various maps. The authors have used geoserver for visualization of data, for every request there has to publish a layer for visualization which is not a feasible approach. If a user wants to store the analyzed data, there is no provision for the users to do so. Also, user is not able to select specific regions and visualize results.

We have used a big data architecture for handling this data. The storage part is handled by Hadoop HDFS and is accessed through Geomesa Hbase. Geomesa HBase on top of Hadoop provides many features for handling spatio-temporal data. It gives spatio-temporal data type support for polygon, point and line strings. It also provides spatio-temporal indexing for the data. Geomesa HBase uses Hadoop for storing data in distributed manner and Hbase for storing data in column oriented way. Geomesa also has support for Apache Spark for analyzing data and geoserver for visualization of raster and vector data by publishing different layers.

Master-Slave Architecture. A distributed big data architecture comprises of one master and five slaves. The system configuration of this master slave system is having Redhat 7.4 based operating system with three of the systems including master, are of following specification: 32 GB RAM, 2.1 TB Hard disk, 1.86 GHz processor. The rest of the slave systems are having a configuration of, 16 GB RAM, 2.3 TB Hard disk and 2.67 GHz processor. The architecture has Hadoop 2.7.3 as base which provides distributed storage for handling huge amounts of spatio-temporal data then on top of Hadoop, Hbase 1.3.5 has been used for converting raw data into some column oriented format for ease of access and query. On top of Hbase, we have used Geomesa Hbase 2.3.1 for ingestion of data into Hbase and Hadoop and indexing on spatio-temporal data. On top of Geomesa, Geoserver 2.11 is used for publishing data in various formats and creating datastores for different kinds of vector and raster data. Apache spark 2.3.4 is also used with Geomesa Hbase which provides us capability to read and write data through Geomesa Hbase, query for spatio-temporal data and perform various analysis on data. Django is used here for interfacing the user with the backend. Openlayer is also used on top of all tools for providing interactive user interfaces to users. This architecture works for different data mining algorithms. We have discussed time series analysis for this work. Also, a comparison between various forecasting algorithms with outlier removal and without outlier removal have been done.

3.3 Time Series Forecasting

The frequency of earth observations obtained through INSAT-3D IMAGER satellite, is 30 min. That is, to every 30 min, we will have an image from the satellite. As we are analyzing the HEM product, which deals with precipitation values, it is important to identify the pattern followed at a spatial location over a period of time. In order to get the pattern, we need to analyze the past values obtained, and based on that, we can make a decision on whether the outlier detected is an indication of an extreme event or is contributing to noise in the observation. The noise content will affect the accuracy of forecasting, and hence required to be removed. There are several statistical, machine learning and deep learning do exists for forecasting. We have applied the most popular ones in each category and compared the results on our dataset. We have also identified and compared most widely used outlier detection techniques and chosen the best among all based on the number of actual outliers detected.

Outlier Detection and Removal. The points or collection of points in the dataset possess significant different properties are known as Outliers or Anomalies. Outliers in rainfall data are the unconventional pattern observed in the rainfall trend over the time and /or over a specific location. We have considered and compared three types of Outlier Detection (OD) techniques: k-nearest neighbors (KNN) Detector, isolation forest and histogram-based OD. ARIMA, SARIMA, Support vector regression and LSTM models are used for time series forecasting. Here, we have data on a daily basis and seasonality on a yearly basis. As our data is not continuous, we have grouped data into weeks for maintaining more continuity of the data. We have used weekly data with two attributes: date and HEM values.

SARIMA. SARIMA [3] stands for Seasonal Auto Regressive Integrated Moving Average is a combination of, auto regressive (AR) model represents the number of lags observations we are considering for model estimation and intercept term and moving average (MA) model represents lagged forecast errors. These error terms are the errors of respective lags observation in the AR model.

$$Z_t = \alpha + \beta_1 Z_{t-1} + \beta_2 Z_{t-2} + ... + \beta_p Z_{t-p} + \phi_1 \epsilon_{t-1} + ... + \phi_q \epsilon_{t-q} \quad (1)$$

SARIMA has defined by seven parameters: p & P is the order of the AR term, d represents differencing that must be required for converting non stationary series to stationary series, D represents seasonal differencing that must be required for converting non stationary series to stationary series, q & Q is the order of the MA term, m represents the number of time steps in a single seasonal period.

Time Series Analysis on Actual Data. Before applying SARIMA time series forecasting algorithms on the data we need to check the stationarity of the time series, therefore we have used two tests ADF and KPSS. Here, ADF acronym stands for augmented Dickey-Filler test and KPSS acronym stands for Kwiatkowski-Phillips-Schmidt-Shin test. If the time series is not stationary then we have to perform differentiation, log transform and few methods for converting it into stationary. ACF and PACF plots are also used for verifying stationarity of time series data. Our dataset contains trend and seasonality both so to remove trends we have applied differentiation and to remove seasonality we have applied seasonality differences. The results of the adf, kpss test and plots for ACF and PACF are shown in Fig. 1(a)–(d).

Stationarity Check After Converting Non Stationary to Stationary. After submitting the parameters from users, the data of selected regions with date range is stored in spark dataframe. Group by operation is performed on the dates with sum of HEM values and date is selected as index. For checking the stationarity of the series adf and kpss test have been applied on time series data.

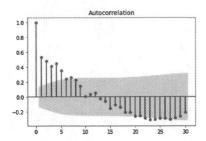

(a) Auto correlation on actual data.

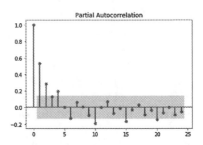

(b) Partial Auto correlation on actual data.

```
Results of ADF test:
Test Statistic                  -3.263561
p-value                          0.016588
#Lags Used                       3.000000
Number of Observations Used    197.000000
Critical Value (1%)             -3.463987
Critical Value (5%)             -2.876326
Critical Value (10%)            -2.574652
dtype: float64
```

(c) Result of ADF test on actual data.

```
Results of KPSS Test:
Test Statistic                  0.156894
p-value                         0.100000
Lags Used                      15.000000
Critical Value (10%)            0.347000
Critical Value (5%)             0.463000
Critical Value (2.5%)           0.574000
Critical Value (1%)             0.739000
dtype: float64
```

(d) Result of PACF test on actual data.

Fig. 1. Stationarity check after converting non stationary to stationary.

Convert it into stationary series, if it is not stationary. For checking seasonality of series check seasonal decomposition of the dataset and conclude whether the seasonality is on a monthly basis or yearly basis. Apply the auto ARIMA method for finding out the best suited parameters such as p, q, seasonal P, and seasonal Q for the model. Divide the data into train and test data and train the model with the best parameters. Prediction is performed by giving testing data as input to the model. Evaluated the model by considering different error metrics such as root mean squared error, mean absolute error etc.

We can get an idea about the seasonality and trend of the dataset the plot of data. We have to set our m according to seasonal patterns. Here, as per weekly data and yearly seasonality our m will become 52.

For weekly data: (3,1,1) x (1,1,1), 53 becomes the best suitable parameters for SARIMA model.

Result and Analysis

We have applied outlier detection algorithms by over date and consider outlier fraction=0.01. The results reveal that the CBLOF and KNN result in the same number of inliers and outliers. Isolation forest and HBOD have false inliers in the data. With graphical representation for plot patterns, we have observed that the CBLOF and KNN algorithms show true outliers and inliers (Fig. 2).

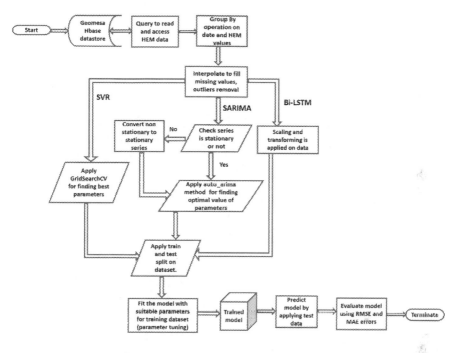

Fig. 2. Time series analysis flow chart.

Table 3. Performance of prediction algorithms evaluated without outlier removal.

Name of method	Outliers	Inliers
Cluster Based Local Outlier Factor (CBLOF)	15	1446
Histogram based outlier Detection (HBOD)	7	1454
K nearest neighbour (KNN)	15	1446
Isolation Forest	9	1452

3.4 SARIMA

SARIMA model is [3] combination of two terms seasonal moving average that defines p order in the series, integration term that defines the q order and d is seasonal differences, as described in related work. It is applicable stationary data. We have applied three tests for checking stationarity of the time series data in both scenarios: Auto-correlation (ACF) and Partial auto-correlation PACF plots, Augmented Dickey Fuller test (ADF) and Kwiatkowski-Phillips-Schmidt-Shin (KPSS) test. Seasonal decomposition plot is used for identifying the seasonality. Seasonality and trend removal in the data, using differentiation have been done. Results of ADF and KPSS test statistics are lower than all critical values and p-value is also lower than 0.05.

3.5 SVR

SVR [4] is a combination of SVM and linear regression. C, gamma, and kernel functions as parameters where, C is kernel coefficient, gamma is penalty parameter that controls the smoothness of decision boundaries, type kernel defined the type of hyperplane to fit in. Radial basis function (RBF) kernel is used. By experimentation the best suited parameters for data after applying Grid-SearchCV method are observed to be: C=1, kernel= rbf, gamma=0.0001.

3.6 Bi-LSTM

Bidirectional LSTM (Bi-LSTM)

LSTM model is an improved RNN model with the memory cell. The memory cell contains an input gate, forget gate, and an output gate. Equation for input, forget and output gates in LSTM model are as follow:

$$Input gate : i_t = \sigma(W_{ix}x_t + W_{ih}h_{t-1} + b_i \tag{2}$$

$$Forget gate : f_t = \sigma(W_{fx}x_t + W_{fh}h_{t-1} + b_f) \tag{3}$$

$$Output gate : o_t = \sigma(W_{ox}x_t + W_{oh}h_{t-1} + b_o) \tag{4}$$

$$Cell state : c_t{}' = tanh(W_{cx}x_t + W_{ch}h_{t-1} + b_c)c_t = f_t * c_{t-1} + i_t * c_t \tag{5}$$

$$Output gate : h_t = o_t * tanh(c_t) \tag{6}$$

Bi-LSTM [2, 10, 13] layer considers both forward and backward hidden sequences at a time. So final output is a concatenation of both sequences, $c_t = [\overrightarrow{h_t}, \overleftarrow{h_t}]$.

$$\overrightarrow{h_t} = \sigma(W_{\overrightarrow{h}x}x_t + W_{\overrightarrow{h}\overrightarrow{h}}\overrightarrow{h}_{t-1} + b_{\overrightarrow{h}}) \tag{7}$$

$$\overleftarrow{h_t} = \sigma(W_{\overleftarrow{h}x}x_t + W_{\overleftarrow{h}\overleftarrow{h}}\overleftarrow{h}_{t-1} + b_{\overleftarrow{h}}) \tag{8}$$

$$y_t = W_{y\overrightarrow{h}}\overrightarrow{h_t} + W_{y\overleftarrow{h}}\overleftarrow{h_{t-1}} + b_y \tag{9}$$

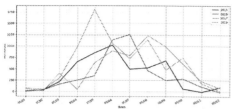

(a) Combined trend on actual data.

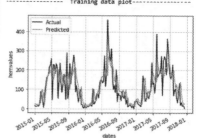

(b) Training data after outliers removal.

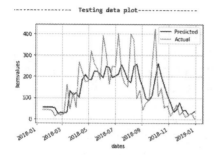

(c) Bi-LSTM test data plot after outliers removal.

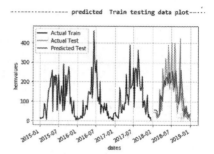

(d) Bi-LSTM train and test data plot after outliers removal.

Fig. 3. Results of Bi-LSTM on HEM training and testing data.

Table 4. Performance of prediction algorithms evaluated without outlier removal.

Prediction Algorithm	RMSE	MAE
Support Vector Regression (SVR)	160.29	111.40
Seasonal ARIMA (SARIMA)	138.60	84.25
Bidirectional LSTM (BiLSTM)	128.58	83.91

Here, $y = (y_1, y_2, \ldots\ldots, y_t, \ldots\ldots y_n)$) is the output sequence of the first hidden layer. $\overrightarrow{h_t}$ represents forward pass and $\overleftarrow{h_t}$ represents a backward pass sequence.

We have applied bidirectional LSTM with following parameters in both the case of with outliers and without outliers: Neurons=30, optimizer= adam, batch size=10, epochs=70, activation function= relu. We have trained our model for 2015 to the 2017 year data and give 2018 year data as testing. The results are shown in Fig. 3(a)–(d). Results reveal that the BiLSTM algorithm outperforms SARIMA and SVR both with outliers and without outliers.

Comparison of RMSE and MAE errors for all three prediction algorithms such as SVR, SARIMA, and Bi-LSTM without and with outliers removal is

Table 5. Performance of prediction algorithms evaluated with outlier removal.

Prediction Algorithm	RMSE	MAE
Support Vector Regression (SVR)	121.27	91.92
Seasonal ARIMA (SARIMA)	92.94	66.14
Bidirectional LSTM (BiLSTM)	89.84	64.15

shown in Table 3, Table 4 and Table 5 respectively. We have observed considerable improvement in RMSE and MAE after removal of outliers. In both cases, BiLSTM performs well and shows better RMSE and MAE as compared to the other two.

4   Conclusion and Future Work

Hydro estimator Derived Precipitation (HEM) has been considered for experimentation in this work. We have implemented the K-means data mining (clustering) technique on HEM data values and provide an effective visualization of it on the interactive map interface. Other data mining techniques can easily be integrated into this system using the plugin feature of the system.

The prediction capability of data mining is used for rainfall prediction. We have used two approaches, in the first approach, the prediction is applied to the raw data, and in the second we have removed outliers after pre-processing steps. We have considered these two approaches and compared the RMSE errors and MAE errors for support vector regression, seasonal ARIMA, and long short term memory algorithms. We can conclude that after outlier removal, RMSE error is reduced by 24.34%, 32.94%, and 30.13% for SVR, SARIMA, and Bi-LSTM respectively, and MAE error is reduced by 17.48%, 21.49%, and 23.54% for SVR, SARIMA, and Bi-LSTM respectively. Although Bi-LSTM outperforms the other two, but SARIMA shows competitive performance in both with and without outliers.

In the future, we would like to extend our work over datasets such as, Land Surface Temperature (LST), Sea Surface Temperature (SST), and Upper Troposphere Humidity (UTH) and other LEVEL1B standard products. We are also planning to extend our work by integrating different deep learning models in the architecture in order to improve the capability of the architecture when data scales.

References

1. The mouse tumor biology database, https://www.osgeo.org/projects/geoserver
2. Cai, L., Zhou, S., Yan, X., Yuan, R.: A stacked BILSTM neural network based on coattention mechanism for question answering. Comput. Intell. Neurosci. 1–12 (2019). https://doi.org/10.1155/2019/9543490
3. Chen, P., Niu, A., Liu, D., Jiang, W., Ma, B.: Time series forecasting of temperatures using SARIMA: an example from nanjing. In: IOP Conference Series: Materials Science and Engineering, vol. 394, 052024p (August 2018). https://doi.org/10.1088/1757-899X/394/5/052024
4. Drucker, H., Burges, C.J.C., Kaufman, L., Smola, A., Vapnik, V.: Support vector regression machines. In: Proceedings of the 9th International Conference on Neural Information Processing Systems, pp. 155–161. NIPS 1996, MIT Press, Cambridge, MA, USA (1996)
5. ESA: Newcomers EO guide (newcomers-earth-observation-guide). https://business.esa.int, Accessed 20 Mar 2022
6. Geetha, A., Nasira, G.M.: Data mining for meteorological applications: decision trees for modeling rainfall prediction. In: 2014 IEEE International Conference on Computational Intelligence and Computing Research, pp. 1–4 (2014). https://doi.org/10.1109/ICCIC.2014.7238481
7. Gopalani, S., Arora, R.: Comparing apache spark and map reduce with performance analysis using k-means. Int. J. Comput. Appl. **113**, 8–11 (2015). https://doi.org/10.5120/19788-0531
8. Guo, H., Wang, L., Liang, D.: Big earth data from space: a new engine for earth science. Sci. Bull. **61**(7), 505–513 (2016). https://doi.org/10.1007/s11434-016-1041-y
9. Kumar, S., Singh, M.: A novel clustering technique for efficient clustering of big data in Hadoop ecosystem. Big Data Min. Anal. **2**(4), 240–247 (2019). https://doi.org/10.26599/BDMA.2018.9020037
10. M. Swapnaa, N.S.: A hybrid model for rainfall prediction using both parametrized and time series models. Int. J. Pure Appl. Math. **119**(14), 1549–1556 (2018)
11. Nair, A., Ajith Joseph, K., Nair, K.: Spatio-temporal analysis of rainfall trends over a maritime state (Kerala) of India during the last 100 years. Atmospheric Environment **88**, 123 132 (2014). https://doi.org/10.1016/j.atmosenv.2014.01.061, https://www.sciencedirect.com/science/article/pii/S1352231014000867
12. Nikam, V.B., Meshram, B.: Modeling rainfall prediction using data mining method: A Bayesian approach. In: 2013 Fifth International Conference on Computational Intelligence, Modelling and Simulation, pp. 132–136 (2013). https://doi.org/10.1109/CIMSim.2013.29
13. Patel, M., Patel, A., Ghosh, R.: Precipitation nowcasting: Leveraging bidirectional LSTM and 1d CNN. CoRR abs/1810.10485 (2018), http://arxiv.org/abs/1810.10485
14. Rao, P., Sachdev, R., Pradhan, T.: A hybrid approach to rainfall classification and prediction for crop sustainability. In: Thampi, S.M., Bandyopadhyay, S., Krishnan, S., Li, K.C., Mosin, S., Ma, M. (eds.) Advances in Signal Processing and Intelligent Recognition Systems, pp. 457–471. Springer, Cham (2016)
15. Shi, J., Jain, M., Narasimhan, G.: Time series forecasting (TSF) using various deep learning models (2022). https://doi.org/10.48550/ARXIV.2204.11115, https://arxiv.org/abs/2204.11115

16. Sinnott, R.O., Morandini, L., Wu, S.: Smash: a cloud-based architecture for big data processing and visualization of traffic data. In: 2015 IEEE International Conference on Data Science and Data Intensive Systems, pp. 53–60 (2015). https://doi.org/10.1109/DSDIS.2015.35

17. Sisodiya Neha, Dube Nitant, T.P.: Next-Generation Artificial Intelligence Techniques for Satellite Data Processing, pp. 235–254 (January 2020). https://doi.org/10.1007/978-3-030-24178-11

18. Urmay, S., Sanjay, G., Neha, S., Nitant, D., Shashikant, S.: Rainfall Prediction: Accuracy Enhancement Using Machine Learning And Forecasting Techniques, pp. 776–782 (December 2018). https://doi.org/10.1109/PDGC.2018.8745763

19. Zainudin, S., Jasim, D., Abu Bakar, A.: Comparative analysis of data mining techniques for Malaysian rainfall prediction. Int. J. Adv. Sci. Eng. Inf. Technol. 6, 1148 (2016). https://doi.org/10.18517/ijaseit.6.6.1487

Scalable Architecture for Mining Big Earth Observation Data: SAMBEO

Neha Sisodiya[1]($\boxtimes$)(iD), Keshani Vyas[2], Nitant Dube[3], and Priyank Thakkar[1]

[1] Department of Computer Science, Nirma University, Ahmedabad, Gujarat, India
{17ptphde169,priyank.thakkar}@nirmauni.ac.in
[2] Department of IT, LD College, Ahmedabad, Gujarat, India
[3] SAC-ISRO, Ahmedabad, Gujarat, India
ndube@sac.isro.gov.in

Abstract. Variety of sensors present in the satellites revolving around the earth, generates a huge amount of raw data called Big Earth Observation Data (BEOD). The data collected by the sensors contains the information important to various applications. There are a number of architectures proposed for processing earth observation (EO) data by the people working in the relevant areas. The spatio-temporal nature of data poses a variety of challenges in terms of storage and archival, retrieval, processing, analysis, visualization. A scalable solution is required for handling exponential rise in data.

In order to address the scalability issues, recent well known distributed architectures to process spatio-temporal data are, HadoopGIS, SpatialSpark, STARK, Sedona, Geomesa and Geowave. In this paper, we present an architecture for mining BEOD to provide scalability in every phase, from storage to analysis. Also, the architecture is equipped with the capability of analyzing the data through machine learning and deep learning models. We also present the comparison based on the performance on different types of spatial queries involved in effective accessing of data, that utilizes spatial indexing techniques for the data stored in a distributed environment. We also have demonstrated the performance of proposed architecture on EO data obtained through INSAT-3D Imager.

Keywords: EO data processing · Big EO Data Mining · Scalable Distributed Architecture · INSAT-3D

1 Introduction

Earth observations are gathered from different heterogeneous sources, resulting from advances in technologies. The data acquired from satellites, is huge in volume and dynamic in nature, which qualifies it as "Big Data". As big data is characterized majorly with 4 Vs: volume, variety, velocity and value, it is to be handled through big data techniques. Every organizations are processing and analyzing big data now. Especially for space agencies, the huge amount of data

D. Gupta et al. (Eds.): CVIP 2022, CCIS 1776, pp. 509–523, 2023.
https://doi.org/10.1007/978-3-031-31407-0_38

is a matter of concern. With the rapid advancements in Remote Sensing (RS) strategies, EO is creating a colossal volume of RS data continuously. The data acquired is usually in the form of digital imagery. Majorly we have two different types of Earth Observation imagery, named as active and passive, based on the nature of sensing instruments involved in acquiring the images [5]. Passive imagery are results of observations made by passive sensors, which depend on the illumination by the sun to capture the reflection. The emissions by earth surface and atmosphere are in the form of electromagnetic radiation. Panchromatic, Pan-sharpened, Microwave Radiometry, Multi-spectral (MS), and Hyperspectral (HS) imagery fall under the category of passive imagery. Active imagery on the other hand, is independent of sunlight. Active sensors have light emitting units installed in them, and the sensor receives and observes the interactions between signal and surface of earth. Synthetic aperture radar (SAR), LiDAR, Radar Altimetry, GNSS-R, Scatterometry imagery are the examples of imagery by active sensors. A number of sensors are involved in observation of different kinds of data to capture the earth's surface. They also differ in resolution which can be categorized as spatial (surface covered by a pixel (from 300m to few tens of centimetres)), spectral (number of spectral information (from blue to infrared) corresponding to the number of sensors) and radiometric (linked to the ability to recognize small brightness variations (from 256 to 64000 level) resolutions. The details are presented in the next subsequent subsections.

1.1 Big Earth Observation Data

Remote sensing data sets are stored in the form of raster or vector data. Files can be stored in variety of standard formats, including ASCII, HDF, FAST, Geo-TIFF, netCDF, and so on [13]. Stages for processing of satellite images are: acquisition at ground stations, storage at data centre, processing through database analysis; usually at web servers, visualization at client side, dissemination at web portals. We have restricted the scope of the paper to storage & archival, retrieval, processing, analysis and visualization of earth observation data, dissemination of EO data is beyond scope of this work. The big data acquired by the satellites are required to be stored for different stages of processing, that involve uncovering the hidden information [12]. It becomes even more challenging, when it comes to archival i.e., for long term storage. Storage of EO data has its own challenges whether it may have to store to on-board devices or ground stations. Processing the Big EO data requires storage, which is expected to be fault tolerant and time efficient in terms of retrieval and access. There are some distributed architectures like Google Earth Engine (GEE) which is considered a standout among all. It is most effective, easy to understand and provides great performance analysis. But, it has to make additional efforts for the data, which cannot fit in a very popular mapreduce model.

We, in this work have made an effort to provide a time efficient and scalable system that can help the space agencies and researchers working in the area of earth observation data mining at scale. Moreover, a variety of applications can be derived from the BEOD by using different data mining algorithms. We have to come up with a solution which has a capability of providing all types of analytics on one single platform, that can be extended with ease and will be a user friendly system. So, the architecture we have proposed here, is capable of handling these issues with the help of big data techniques and incorporating a deep learning interface to it.

This paper is organized in five sections.In Sect. 2, we have discussed a few existing architectures and their gaps with respect to the processing stages of big EO data. Section 3 represents the challenges presented in the prevailing architectures. The architecture we have proposed is presented in Sect. 4. We have shown few results obtained through experimenting with the architecture in Sect. 5. We have concluded our work in Sect. 6, with possible future directions.

2   Prevailing Architectures for Big Earth Observation Data Mining

The processing of satellite data involves stages for processing of satellite images: Acquisition, Storage, Processing, Analysis, Visualization, Dissemination as shown in Fig. 1. With the advent of technology, we have ample of tools and technologies available for each stage of processing, which are suitable in different aspects.

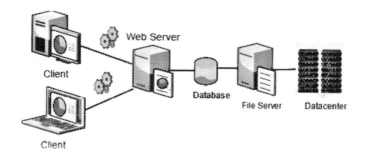

Fig. 1. Processing stages for mining EO data

2.1   Storage and Archival

There various factors affecting the storage and archival of EO data for different storage devices have been compared on costs and operations.

It is being observed that, with the limited capacity, these devices are unable to handle the dynamic data rate and volume of the data generated by the sensors on board storage as well as for secondary storage. The authors in [9] have explained a new system called Integrated Multi-mission Ground Segment for Earth Observation Satellites (IMGEOS) established long back for storage with consideration of the major factors like accessibility, protection of data for long term, availability, manageability and scalability.

They have discussed a few aspects of remote sensing data processing but it does not provide a customized and user friendly solution for processing. A distributed system for storage, processing, three-dimensional visualization and basic analysis of EO data is proposed in [20]. The system is based on the MEAN stack for high performance web applications. Data used is in NetCDF format, from Michelson Interferometer for Passive Atmospheric Sounding on the ESA's Envisat satellite. This approach is bound to a specific data type and satellite. One of the most successful an popular infrastructure among all, for Big Data computing and cloud is, Hadoop and its entire ecological environment [10]. has become one of the most successful infrastructure for Cloud and also for Big Data computing. By open source implementation of MapReduce framework, Hadoop enables distributed, data-intensive and parallel applications. Inside the Hadoop ecology, the distributed File System (HDFS) is a large distributed file system with strategic layouts and data replication for fault tolerance and better accessing performance. In recent time, Yahoo has deployed its search engine on the Hadoop cluster, Facebook and eBay also develop its large applications at a scale of exabyte with Hadoop. In addition, the Hadoop-GIS [1] system for large-scale spatial data processing, search and accessing is also built upon the Hadoop system. A modification over Hadoop to address the problem of preprocessing of image data on HDFS is presented in [19]. SAR image data for two standard formats were taken into consideration Committee on Earth Observation Satellites (CEOS) and Geotiff, and modified the splitting technique along with the data read interface in recording on top of hadoop.

Hadoop-GIS [1] is a data warehousing system, which is scalable and claims to provide considerable high performance for spatial data, for large scale spatial queries on Hadoop. So, by looking at the existing storage solutions for big data, Hadoop based storage seems to be most feasible and versatile to handle data with big data characteristics.

Retrieval Techniques. Traditional databases are being replaced with NoSQL databases for retrieving big data. Earlier, probabilistic approach for retrieval of similar spatio-temporal structures learned by unsupervised models using graph trajectories. Later content based image retrieval for satellite images using MapReduce model on cloud computing was proposed.

A high performance and scalability is achieved using MongoDb for sharding and node scala for horizontal scalability is presented in [19]. Architecture consists of the implementation of quad-trees for storing data into Hbase on top of hadoop [11]. The metadata is accessed using traditional PostgreSQL. PostgreSQL is time inefficient as compared to NoSQL databases. A proposed Node Scala [14] leads to efficient usage of available computing resources in addition to allowing the system to scale simply by adding new workers.

2.2 Accessing Techniques

RS applications also perform a small non-contiguous input/output, as most of the scientific applications do. But still, by these type of applications we only can achieve one tenth of performance of the peak input/output. This is because most of the widespread parallel file systems (PFSs) are optimized for contiguous data access. Basically, the parallel input/output interfaces and physical data organization over storage do not meet the expectations of these application's data access patterns.

Present implementations of MPI does not support well, the interactions of this complex RS data structures over processing nodes. Which results in, frequent calls to lower level MPI send/receive communication APIs is made, with substantial performance degradation [13]. Indexing schemes that is efficient in processing large raster data. Also provides effective computation of multiple spatio-temporal aggregates in single query over raster streams. The raster streams are location and size variants. Authors have taken NOAA's GOES satellite data for experimentation and reported the result. These can be made more easier, efficient and effective by introducing big data components.

2.3 Processing

With the rapid growth of data volume diversity and complexity is also increasing. Several high performance platforms are employed to make sense of these Big RS datasets. The most prominent and popular among the high performance computing (HPC) platforms, are cloud based, cluster based HPC and supercomputers. Optimization and transformation effort for tools, techniques and system is also been attempted in this work.

Sharing the data globally and providing inter-operation capability requires this massively distributed data to be well managed and easily accessible. This also indicates the requirements for large number of storage devices for this distributed remote sensing "Big Data". To cope with these challenges, it is critically important to make revolutionize the traditional processing architectures and devices for data storage [17]. Presently, the cluster based platforms are the established architectures for HPC. A NEX system build by NASA has a cluster of 16 computers employed for processing remote sensing data [8,13].

Scalability on pre-processing on SAR and MS data are used in a distributed environment [19]. This architecture is also confined to specific data and type of processing. Authors in [16] integrated R with hadoop in different ways in order to get advantages of hadoop as a distributed environment along with statistical analysis using R. They reported that the utility of mapreduce jobs is limited to text input but the Rhipe or Rhadoop can be used for complex inputs also. HPCs are expensive and not meant to provide customized processing. It would be much more beneficial to make use of available commodity hardwares, that can be customized as per requirement.

2.4 Analysis

Physical Analytics Integrated Repository and Services (PAIRS) has capability of that enables faster data realization by automatic joins, updating, and integrating data layers in time and space. Presented model for: vegetation monitoring and

high resolution evapo-transpiration for agriculture and hyperlocal weather forecasting through machine learning for forecasting renewable energy [11] have been
introduced. Dataset by Data Assimilation for Agro-Modeling (ADAM) project
has been used earlier for mining of the information associated with satellite
images time series. Database to store spatio-temporal dataset as a part of infrastructure, termed as spatial data infrastructure (SDI), is being proposed in [6].
They have used an open source extension to PostgreSQL known as PostGIS,
that can efficiently handle a huge amount of vector data. BigDL [3] is a platform
that makes use of a spark cluster on top of hadoop, to analyze the data through
deep learning models.

2.5   Visualization

Visual representation gives a better understanding and insights of the data to
be processed and analyzed. There is a lot of research done in the area of spatio-
temporal visualization, especially for earth observations. The rendering of spatial
and temporal data is presented in [2] by a software called Openspace. 3D points
coordinates representation of selected observables, on virtual globe, through a
data browser called KAGLV, is proposed in [20]. A web-based scalable platform
called Node Scala [14], that is capable of splitting and handling requests on a
parallel distributed system. Raster data visualization through maps generated
from the three-dimensional data in space and time, as web services on top of
SciDB is used in [6]. Authors also presented the type of users associated with the
database to store access, manage, retrieve, visualize and validate data, depending
on the way of accessing the database directly and via web services. But, the
intermediate results on which users may further wish to do some analytics are
not available.

An application in [7] has been developed which is capable of representing
vector and raster geospatial data representing various events, with the help of a
slider. Also facilitate the user to customize their visualization to extract information associated with the data. A detailed survey of the most recent tools
and technologies capable of handling big data dealing with earth observations is
presented. There are algorithms trending in the area of processing earth observations with statistical, machine learning and deep learning [12].

We also have a few analytical architectures, based on the general processing
stages of RS data in a distributed environment. Distributed analytical architecture with three layers in [18] is being proposed.

The architecture is not capable of handling the geo-spatial queries, process a
data from geographic areas of interest. There are a number of architectures proposed on top of the most popular distributed architecture in big data processing
known as Hadoop distributed environment. The data is required to be stored,
and can be handled by a Hadoop based, distributed file system. Rather than
traditional databases, NoSQL databases like, Accumulo, Hbase, and Cassandra,
on top of it are responsible for querying and manipulation of big data. There are
a few multidimensional data infrastructure such as MD-Hbase and Accumulo,
that provide scalable solutions for big geospatial data (vector and/or raster).

These technologies are available open source. Similar techniques that implement SQL-type queries over OpenStreetMap (OSM) vector data using Hadoop are introduced as Hadoop-GIS [1]. A modification on Hadoop, incorporating capability of spatial query processing both in uncompressed and compressed data form is given as SpatialHadoop [4]. Authors have mentioned a few others as well, that have capability of implementing, querying and visualizing text, vector and raster data. ADAM [15] and SpatialSpark [21] employed on Apache Spark for analyzing big geospatial raster and vector data respectively.

An infrastructure for spatial data called PAIRS, has been introduced [11]. This platform serves real time data with accelerated access and analysis using HBase on top of Hadoop.

Authors have compared the query results with conventional python library GDAL, but there are several other geospatial support available open source, that can have even much better performance than this. Generally, Hadoop based architectures use mapreduce model for processing. Due to data replication and processing through disk interaction and serialization, mapreduce models are slow. Processing spatio-temporal data applications requires faster execution. A faster processing platform STARK [9] is being proposed. It is based on spark that uses RDDs for processing and is much faster than mapreduce. As compared to other platforms like, GeoSpark [6] and SpatialSpark that are specifically introduced to process geospatial data, STARK have a wide range of spatial operation sets, indexing schemes and partitioning schemes, that are better than others.

3   Challenges in Prevailing Architectures

- Capability of handling diversity in data and applications.
- Data independence for processing algorithms to be used.
- Making robust architecture for end to end processing.
- Customizing the architecture for different applications.
- Capability to scale the architecture with rise in data volume.
- Performance optimization in terms of time.
- Memory efficient geospatial big data representation for processing.
- Integration of big data techniques to machine learning and deep learning frameworks.
- Training and model optimization for big geospatial data with deep learning models.

4   Proposed Architecture

We have proposed an architecture that provides a user-friendly environment for analyzing BEOD. A Hadoop cluster is employed for handling the storage of data. In this architecture, on top of Hadoop, geomesa is utilized for storage, processing and analysis. Visualization of the resultant data is made available to the user, either through geoserver or Django and is displayed to openlayers. Hadoop HDFS is the foundation of the storage stage of architecture where the data is physically present. It provides fault tolerance, data availability and replication of data. The stage above storage is NoSQL database, we have used geomesa-hbase for ingesting the data into HDFS. Although accumulo has shown competent performance in the processing geoserver, Hbase has been chosen, because of its in-memory capabilities. HBase filters and co-processors are pretty great as well, which is not present in any other NoSQL based datastore with geospatial support. These are important parameters to be taken under consideration when scalability is concerned. Accumulo datastore is claimed to be most robust and well established among all the other datastores available on geomesa. Whereas, geomesa-hbase is the one which is just a prototype. We have observed that there are many version compatibility issues while setting-up the architecture with Accumulo datastore. We have compared the datastores supported by geomesa on a few parameters in Table 1. We have used the prototype for our architecture and have observed an acceptable performance. Moreover, we have set up a new machine to expand our cluster and found that geomesa-hbase in terms of cluster configuration is much more robust than acuumulo. The ingested data is made available through SQL query, a capability by SparkSQL. Users can interact through the interface developed with help of HTML5, javascript and openlayers. The architecture leverages the ability to analyse the data with deep learning models with BigDL on top of spark. The proposed architecture is shown in Fig. 2.

Table 1. Parameter comparison for different supported database for Geomesa

Database	Availability	Server side scripts	Data schema	In-memory capabilities	ACID
Hbase	Open source	Co-processors and filters	Schema free (definition is possible)	Yes	Single row ACID
Accumulo	Open source	No	Schema free	No	Supports isolation.
Cassandra	Open source	No	Schema free (definition is possible)	No	Atomicity and isolation.
Google Bigtable	Hosted	No	Schema free	No	Atomicity

4.1   Cluster Specifications

The configuration of the nodes used to set up the cluster is shown in Table 2. As mentioned earlier in this section, the proposed architecture is built on the top of Hadoop distributed storage structure. A hadoop based cluster supports master-slave architecture. A cluster with one master and five slave nodes is established in order to store the data. Master is responsible for communication to all slave nodes, also known as data nodes in a hadoop environment. The application will submit the job to hadoop master containing namenode and will further distribute the task among the data nodes in the cluster. In case of failure of the namenode, secondary namenode will take care of the assigned processing.

Table 2. Specification of nodes in Hadoop Master-Slave Architecture

	Master	Slave1	Slave2	Slave3	Slave4	Slave5
OS	Redhat 7.4	Redhat 7.4	Redhat 7.4	Redhat 7.4	Redhat 7.4	Redhat 7.4
RAM	32 GB	32 GB	32 GB	16GB	16GB	16GB
Hard-Disk	2.1 TB	2.1 TB	2.1 TB	2.3 TB	2.3 TB	2.3 TB
CPU	1.86 GHz	1.86 GHz	1.86 GHz	2.67 GHz	2.67 GHz	2.67 GHz

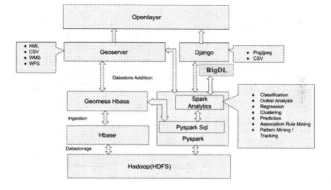

Fig. 2. Proposed Architecture: Scalable Architecture for Mining Big Earth Observation Data (SAMBEO).

Network architecture for the cluster is represented in Fig. 3. The raw data received from the satellite to ground station, is stored in some external storage after transforming it into some standard format and archived subsequently, in order to further analyze it. Majority of the EO data is mostly archived in H5 files, nc file, geotiff and img formats. The native storage format for hadoop is comma separated values (csv). In order to store the data in the hadoop cluster, we convert the existing format of the data to csv.

4.2   Features of Proposed Architecture

The proposed architecture is capable of handling spatio-temporal big data with key features like, it is scalable, robust, user friendly, efficient and provides end to end processing at one platform. The key contributions we have made in the work is enlisted and described in the subsequent subsections below.

Key contributions of the proposed architecture:

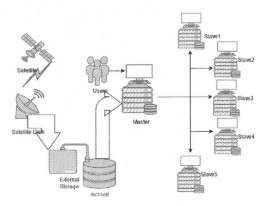

Fig. 3. Network architecture for EO data mining

Scalable. The proposed architecture is scalable horizontally. We can add on the slaves to the cluster and ingest the data with rise in volume. Further, time required to access the data is close to linear, when we scale the data. The scalability is constrained by the replication factor we have used, in terms of capacity of data that can be stored. Further at the time of processing part scalability is taken care of by the intermediate representation of the data.

Robust. The robustness of the architecture is presented as the ability to process all formats of data. As the data has been ingested in the datastore in unified format irrespective of the original format of observation. Any kind of required analysis on the earth observation data can be done. We also have the data availability and no single point failure, as the data is replicated with on slaves with factor of two.

Efficient. Efficiency is majored in terms of amount of data being processed and time required to process. The architecture shows consistent rise in time requirement with increase in data.

Analysis. We have identified a set of algorithms that works efficiently in analyzing earth observations. Among all the seven categories of data mining, we have explored that works well with the ingested data. The ingested data can be analyzed through the listed algorithms.

User Friendly. The architecture we have proposed here is very user friendly. The end user just has to inject the data that needs to be analyzed, rest all will be given by an interactive interface. It provides end to end processing through this architecture right from storing, accessing, processing to visualization.

5 Experimentation and Results

The performance of the architecture of different shape geometries, like point and polygon are evaluated. We have presented the result for different regions and for different tenures i.e., varying spatial and temporal ranges.

5.1 Spatial Query Performance

The temporal range is kept fix from January-December, 2018 for different spatial locations. The spatial points are considered for one of the states in India with different time ranges. Here, we have shown the results of spatial bounds of Kerala, Gujarat (GJ), Madhya Pradesh (M.P), Maharastra (MH), Rajasthan (RJ) state and with all locations in India. We have observed that, with around 4 million points the spatial query took approximately 42 min to get the result. But, as we have increased the number of points slightly above it (nearly 76 lac points), we are getting a substantial decrease in the query time. Further, the increase in geom points to around four times in the previous query, we have observed that, still the query time is decreased by approximately three minutes. The result of spatial query is shown in Table 3.

Table 3. Spatial query performance

Spatial Bounds	Number of points (geom count)	Time (in sec)
Kerala	4146512	2490.3927
Gujarat	4762868	964.99
Madhya Pradesh, Maharastra	24721645	826.82
Rajasthan, Gujarat, Madhya Pradesh, Maharastra	36934409	768.41
India	137696326	45261.42

5.2 Temporal Query Performance

The results of spatial bounds of Kerala state with varying temporal ranges are considered. Similarly, we have considered, few other spatial bounds like, considering multiple states with same temporal ranges. We have started with one monsoon season in 2018 for all of the spatial bounds and then we have increased the temporal range from one season to multiple years. We have considered the temporal range of four years as per the data ingested to our proposed architecture, January 2015 to December 2018. The results reveal that, as and when we increase the number of geom points in a specific spatial range, there is a gradual increase in query time. In fact, in some cases like the bounds of Rajasthan, Gujarat, Madhya Pradesh and Maharashtra, we are getting an improved query time with rise in geom point even better than the spatial bounds with lesser number of geom point. The result of temporal query is shown in Table 4.

Table 4. Temporal query performance

Spatial Bounds	Temporal Bounds	Number of points (geom count)	Time (in sec)
Kerala	Jun-Dec, 2018	3299783	1058.2838
	Jan-Dec, 2018	4146512	2490.39
	Jan, 2017 to Dec 2018	8488653	2534.84
	Jan, 2016 to Dec 2018	11875397	3571.25
	Jan, 2015 to Dec 2018	14518107	2959.22
M.P, MH	Jan-Dec, 2018	24721645	826.82
	Jan, 2017 to Dec 2018	53612353	1494.47
	Jan, 2016 to Dec 2018	94162365	4126.74
	Jan, 2015 to Dec 2018	121508669	3230.52
RJ., GJ., M.P, MH	Jan-Dec, 2018	36934409	768.41
	Jan, 2017 to Dec 2018	80168187	3148.96
	Jan, 2016 to Dec 2018	140751424	2745.14
	Jan, 2015 to Dec 2018	181653140	5523.81
India	Jan-Dec, 2018	137696326	4561.43
	Jan, 2017 to Dec 2018	321803727	10870.41
	Jan, 2016 to Dec 2018	502758082	13238.34
	Jan, 2015 to Dec 2018	657922166	25093.92

5.3 Spatio-Temporal Query Performance

HEM data for Jun-Dec, from 2015 to 2018 is considered for different spatial locations. Kerela, Gujarat and India are compared as they have wide variation in geom points. We have observed that, in spite of the large number of geom points in Gujarat we get less time to get query results. The spatial temporal range for India is large as we have considered four years and geom count is also considerably large, but there is a linear rise in query time which is acceptable. Table 5 presents the result of spatio-temporal query, where different spatial bounds for different time periods have been observed.

Table 5. Spatial-Temporal query performance

Spatio-Temporal Range	Number of points (geom count)	Time (in sec)
Kerala	11875397	4928.2425
Gujarat	17207586	2245.5868
India	434804384	9187.2165

The time complexity of the query performance shown by the architecture against the number of geom points is represented in Fig. 3. We have observed that the time complexity is nearly linear with an increase in the number of geom points. This shows that the architecture is a time efficient system, as the linear rise with rise in data along with replication in storage and retrieval is considered as acceptable performance (Fig. 4).

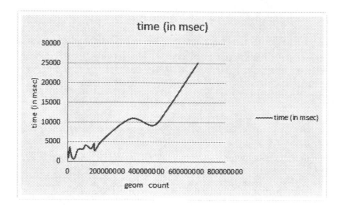

Fig. 4. Time complexity trend for number of geom points processed.

6   Conclusions and Future Scope

EO data comprises the characteristics of big data and also contains both spatial and temporal components. Due to the complexity contents, EO data has to be handled with a big data technological stack. We have proposed an architecture that is capable of handling the big data in an effective way. Storage, access and retrieval of spatio-temporal data is taken care of by a distributed file system provided by Hadoop and NoSQL databases, Hbase here. Geomesa Hbase gives spatio-temporal support for processing EO big data in accessing, retrieving and analyzing it. A web interface for interactively selecting the region of interest on map, in order to investigate different products ingested, is also provided. Around 4TB of EO data, HEM, LST and SST, has been ingested without facing any performance degradation in the clustered setup. In this paper, we have evaluated the performance of our architecture on different types of queries. The trend in the spatial, temporal and spatio-temporal queries on different geom points, is observed. The time complexities for queries with different spatial and temporal ranges also presented. Accessing the spatio-temporal data associated with complex events required to be accessed through spatial queries with interaction to the data stored in a distributed environment is still challenging and requires further advancement against the scope of improvement. Memory footprints require to be reduced for effective and expedite processing. As the EO data is associated with lots of metadata which requires handling of overheads results in access latency. Also, the architecture is capable of leveraging deep learning models, to analyse large scale data. The proposed architecture has a wide scope to explore a number of deep learning models. Deep learning models are in general slow, while training. The future scope is to execute different deep learning models to expedite the training process, with less expense and fewer resources, without compromising accuracy.

References

1. Aji, A., et al.: Hadoop-GIS: a high performance spatial data warehousing system over MapReduce. In: Proceedings of the VLDB Endowment International Conference on Very Large Data Bases, vol. 6, August 2013
2. Bladin, K., et al.: Globe browsing: contextualized spatio-temporal planetary surface visualization. IEEE Trans. Visual Comput. Graphics **24**(1), 802–811 (2018). https://doi.org/10.1109/TVCG.2017.2743958
3. Dai, J.J., et al.: BigDL: a distributed deep learning framework for big data. In: Proceedings of the ACM Symposium on Cloud Computing, pp. 50–60. SoCC 2019, Association for Computing Machinery (2019). https://doi.org/10.1145/3357223.3362707, https://arxiv.org/pdf/1804.05839.pdf
4. Eldawy, A., Mokbel, M.: Spatialhadoop: a mapreduce framework for spatial data. In: Proceedings - International Conference on Data Engineering 2015, pp. 1352–1363, May 2015. https://doi.org/10.1109/ICDE.2015.7113382
5. ESA: Newcomers EO guide (newcomers-earth-observation-guide). https://business.esa.int. Accessed 8 Jan 2022
6. Ferreira, K.R., et al.: Towards a spatial data infrastructure for big spatiotemporal data sets. In: Proceedings of 17th Brazilian Symposium on Remote Sensing (SBSR), 2015, pp. 7588–7594 (2015)
7. Griffith, D., Chun, Y., Dean, D.: Advances in Geocomputation: Geocomputation 2015–The 13th International Conference (2017). https://doi.org/10.1007/978-3-319-22786-3
8. Guo, H., Wang, L., Liang, D.: Big earth data from space: a new engine for earth science. Sci. Bull. **61**(7), 505–513 (2016). https://doi.org/10.1007/s11434-016-1041-y
9. Hagedorn, S., Götze, P., Sattler, K.U.: The stark framework for spatio-temporal data analytics on spark. In: Mitschang, B., et al. (eds.) Datenbanksysteme für Business, Technologie und Web (BTW 2017), pp. 123–142. Gesellschaft für Informatik, Bonn (2017)
10. Karun, A.K., Chitharanjan, K.: A review on hadoop - hdfs infrastructure extensions. In: 2013 IEEE Conference on Information and Communication Technologies, pp. 132–137 (2013)
11. Klein, L., et al.: Pairs: A scalable geo-spatial data analytics platform. pp. 1290–1298, Oct 2015. https://doi.org/10.1109/BigData.2015.7363884
12. Li, S., et al.: Geospatial big data handling theory and methods: a review and research challenges. ISPRS J. Photogramm. Remote. Sens. **115**, 119–133 (2016). https://doi.org/10.1016/j.isprsjprs.2015.10.012
13. Ma, Y., et al.: Remote sensing big data computing: Challenges and opportunities. Future Gener. Comput. Syst. **51**, 47–60 (2015). https://doi.org/10.1016/j.future.2014.10.029. (special Section: A Note on New Trends in Data-Aware Scheduling and Resource Provisioning in Modern HPC Systems)
14. Maatouki, A., Szuba, M., Meyer, J., Streit, A.: A horizontally-scalable multiprocessing platform based on node.js. CoRR abs/1507.02798 (2015). http://arxiv.org/abs/1507.02798

15. Nothaft, F.A., et al.: Rethinking data-intensive science using scalable analytics systems. In: Proceedings of the 2015 ACM SIGMOD International Conference on Management of Data, pp. 631–646. SIGMOD 2015, Association for Computing Machinery, New York, NY, USA (2015). https://doi.org/10.1145/2723372.2742787
16. Oancea, B., Dragoescu, R.: Integrating r and Hadoop for big data analysis. Roman. Statist. Rev. 83–94 (2014)
17. Oliveira, S.F., Fürlinger, K., Kranzlmüller, D.: Trends in computation, communication and storage and the consequences for data-intensive science. In: 2012 IEEE 14th International Conference on High Performance Computing and Communication 2012 IEEE 9th International Conference on Embedded Software and Systems, pp. 572–579 (2012). https://doi.org/10.1109/HPCC.2012.83
18. Raghavendra, M, A.U.: A survey on analytical architecture of real-time big data for remote sensing applications. Asian. J. Eng. Technol. Innov. **4**, 120–123 (2016)
19. Roy, S., Gupta, S., Omkar, S.: Case study on: scalability of preprocessing procedure of remote sensing in hadoop. Proc. Comput. Sci. **108**, 1672–1681 (2017). https://doi.org/10.1016/j.procs.2017.05.042
20. Szuba, M., Ameri, P., Grabowski, U., Meyer, J., Streit, A.: A distributed system for storing and processing data from earth-observing satellites: System design and performance evaluation of the visualisation tool. In: Proceedings of the 16th IEEE/ACM International Symposium on Cluster, Cloud, and Grid Computing, pp. 169–174. CCGRID 2016, IEEE Press (2016). https://doi.org/10.1109/CCGrid.2016.19
21. Yu, J., Wu, J., Sarwat, M.: Geospark: a cluster computing framework for processing large-scale spatial data, pp. 1–4, November 2015. https://doi.org/10.1145/2820783.2820860

An Efficient Deep Transfer Learning Approach for Classification of Skin Cancer Images

Prithviraj Purushottam Naik⑩, B. Annappa⑩, and Shubham Dodia$^{(\boxtimes)}$⑩

Department of Computer Science and Engineering,
National Institute of Technology Karnataka, Surathkal, India
prithvirajpurushottamnaik.213cs001@nitk.edu.in, annappa@ieee.org,
shubham.dodia8@gmail.com

Abstract. Prolonged exposure to the sun for an extended period can likely cause skin cancer, which is an abnormal proliferation of skin cells. The early detection of this illness necessitates the classification of dermatoscopic images, making it an enticing study problem. Deep learning is playing a crucial role in efficient dermoscopic analysis. Modified version of MobileNetV2 is proposed for the classification of skin cancer images in seven classes. The proposed deep learning model employs transfer learning and various data augmentation techniques to more accurately classify skin lesions compared to existing models. To improve the performance of the classifier, data augmentation techniques are performed on "HAM10000" (Human Against Machine) dataset to classify seven different kinds of skin cancer. The proposed model obtained a training accuracy of 96.56% and testing accuracy of 93.11%. Also, it has a lower number of parameters in comparison to existing methods. The aim of the study is to aid dermatologists in the clinic to make more accurate diagnoses of skin lesions and in the early detection of skin cancer.

Keywords: Transfer learning · EfficientNet · MobileNet · Data Augmentation · Deep learning · Skin cancer classification

1 Introduction

Skin cancer is the most often diagnosed type of cancer in the United States [1]. Avoiding lengthy exposure to the sun throughout the summer months can reduce the risk of developing skin cancer [2]. More than 5 million Americans are diagnosed with skin cancer each year, according to the National Cancer Institute. In 2022, around 99,780 people had a form of skin cancer that spreads rapidly, whereas 97,920 people had stage 0 melanoma (Melanoma in situ), and 7,650 people had a high risk of mortality from skin cancer. Women are more likely to develop skin cancer under 50 than men, but after that age, exposure to ultraviolet (UV) radiation puts men at greater risk for skin cancer. To better understand the type of cancer and its fatality rate, early detection would be quite beneficial [3].

© The Author(s), under exclusive license to Springer Nature Switzerland AG 2023
D. Gupta et al. (Eds.): CVIP 2022, CCIS 1776, pp. 524–537, 2023.
https://doi.org/10.1007/978-3-031-31407-0_39

Skin cancer screening via visual examination takes approximately 2–3 minutes. However, determining the type of skin cancer can be complex and time-consuming in the early stages, as it requires extensive knowledge and training. Skin cancer identification that is accurate and timely can significantly reduce mortality and can improve the 5-year survival rate of patients [4]. There is a dearth of professionals and medical equipment in rural and remote areas for skin cancer screening. Hence, there is a strong demand for computer-aided diagnosis (CAD) for detection of skin cancer. Early signs of skin cancer may appear as white scaly patches bordered by darker skin or little reddish or brown dots. Skin cancer detection can be performed accurately with a high success rate utilizing machine and deep learning techniques, as they have demonstrated remarkable success in recent years and there is an abundance of labeled data. When it comes to deep learning, artificial neural networks are employed to extract low-level information in the first layers and high-level features in the last or top layers. Convolutional neural networks have recently been used in deep learning to help solve classification and segmentation problems.

It is prohibitively expensive and exceedingly difficult to collect the training data and create the model frequently in real-world applications. As a result, the effort required to obtain the essential data for training by utilizing transfer learning to transfer knowledge between tasks can be reduced [5]. Transfer learning involves the transfer of information from a source task to a related target task and the subsequent fine-tuning of the target task using new data. This strategy can be quite beneficial for training deep learning models in order to reduce the amount of time required to train the target task.

Our proposed deep learning model is lightweight and employs transfer learning to classify seven different forms of skin cancer with good accuracy, aiding in early detection. The model is trained and tested using the Harvard Dataverse dataset HAM10000 ("Human Against Machine with 10,000 training images") [6]. Data augmentation techniques are applied to solve the data imbalance problem. The proposed model is compared to other network architectures such as ResNet152, DenseNet201, EfficientNetB7, and EfficientNetV2L in terms of various evaluation metrics.

2   Related Work

This section reviews previous work on classifying seven distinct forms of skin cancer using the HAM10000 benchmark dataset. In 2020, Syed Rahat Hassan et al. [7] proposed a fully convolutional deep learning model that gives 92% accuracy, 91% precision, and 91% recall. The model starts with a pre-trained Densenet121 [14] model that was trained on the ImageNet [19] dataset, followed by a Global Average pooling layer and Dropout. In 2020, Hari Kishan Kondaveetiet et al. [8] developed a convolutional neural network model using modified ResNet50 [13] This model gives 90% of accuracy. The model employs the transfer learning technique, with a pretrained ResNet50 base model trained on ImageNet. It is followed by the Global Average Pooling layer, the dense layer, and the dropout layer.

In 2020, Zillur Rahman et al. [9] proposed a model for classifying skin lesions utilising ResNet, Xception, and DenseNet, deep learning pre-trained models. During training and evaluation, the balanced accuracy of 78%, 82%, and 82% is achieved for three models, respectively. It is then combined with the weighted ensemble technique to attain an 85.8% balanced accuracy. In 2020, Satin Jain et al. [11] proposed a convolutional neural network model that achieved 90.48% accuracy using Xception. The model leverages the transfer learning technique using a pretrained base model trained on ImageNet. Normalization is performed at the preprocessing stage. Normalization was performed by calculating standard deviation and the mean of all photos and subtracting the mean of all images from the original images. Finally, the result was divided by the standard deviation of the distribution. In 2021, R Raja Subramanian et al. [10] have developed a custom convolutional neural network model. This model gives 83.04% of accuracy. The image is first sent to a convolution layer with 16 filters (with 3×3 kernel size each) and a ReLU activation function. This layer receives the image for the first two convolutions and feeds it to the max pooling layer. This is done four times with varying max pooling layers, activation functions, and filters. Finally, the final vector was flattened and given to fully connected later to get the result. Data augmentation was used in all of the works included in this section to address the problem of class imbalance.

3   Background

In this section, deep transfer learning and some pre-trained models are discussed as it is used in the study.

3.1   Deep Transfer Learning

The term "Transfer Learning" refers to an algorithmic approach in machine learning that transfers the knowledge gained from solving the first task to the second related task. By performing this technique, the model need not learn from scratch. The pre-trained model can be used, and it can be fine-tuned with new data. This can reduce a significant amount of time and help us to solve the problem with less training data [12], while performing the second related task such as classification and/or segmentation. This technique can be applied in deep learning by using the already trained deep learning models like ResNet50 on data such as Imagenet and can be finetuned with new data. This type of machine learning method only works if the source problem is related to the target problem. If there is a greater mismatch the pre-trained models may converge to a local minimum and would yield in degrading the performance.

3.2 Pre-trained Models

Four deep learning models were considered in this work: ResNet152, DenseNet201, EfficientNetB7 and EfficientNetV2L. The reason behind choosing these models is that these models performed well on the ImageNet dataset. To enhance the depth of a deep learning network, adding layers together would not work since this would result in a vanishing gradient issue. The vanishing gradient is a well-known issue in which repeated multiplication leads the gradient to become infinitely small, making the deep learning model more difficult to train. As a result, residual learning frameworks may aid in training deeper models. Without increasing complexity, this system may considerably enhance classification accuracy by using "identity short connections" that can flow over one or more layers [13]. Resnet152 was chosen because it has the highest accuracy among the Resnet family members.

Recent research has shown that convolutional neural networks (CNNs) are more efficient to train when the layers near the input and the output have shorter connections. Hence, each layer is linked in a feed-forward method in Dense Convolutional Networks (DenseNet). However, standard CNNs contain L connections for L layers, i.e., one connection between each layer and one between successive layers. There are direct $L(L+1)/2$ connections in DenseNet. Each layer provides input to all following layers through its feature maps and receives input from all prior layer's feature maps. DenseNet has several characteristics that contribute to its efficiency in training: it improves feature propagation, eliminates the vanishing gradient issue, minimizes the number of parameters, and supports feature reuse [14]. In this study, DenseNet201 is used.

EfficientNet uses compound coefficients to scale the dimensions. In conventional architecture, factors are freely scaled. However, EfficientNet employs predefined scaling coefficients to scale the network's depth, width, and resolution [15]. The number of computing resources available can be increased by increasing the network's depth, width, and image size while maintaining constant coefficients.

Many optimized convolutional neural networks use the MBConv Block, an Inverted Residual Block that employs an inverted structure for improved efficiency. A convolutional neural network called MobileNetV2 [16] have introduced the MBConv Block for the first time. Residual blocks often have a structure of wide-narrow-wide. Because of this, the construction of the MBConv Block follows a narrow-wide-narrow pattern. An initial 1×1 convolution, followed by 3×3 depth-wise convolutions, and eventually a 1×1 convolution, is used. Parameters and FLOPs (Floating point operations per second) can be improved by replacing all blocks with Fused-MBConv blocks, although this will slow down the training. A convolutional neural network's performance may be improved by finding the ideal mix of Fused-MBConv and MBConv. Figure 1 illustrates the structure of MBConv and Fused MBConv.

In order to function effectively on mobile devices, the MobileNetV2, a convolutional neural network, was invented. Compared to other architectures, it has lower number of parameters. Bottleneck layers are those with a low number of

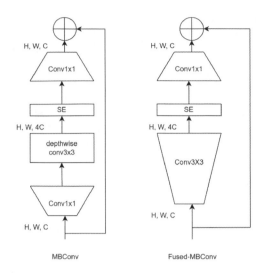

Fig. 1. MBConv and Fused-MBConv structure

nodes in comparison to the preceding ones. An inverted residual structure with residual connections between bottleneck layers is the structure's main component. There are 32 filters, with 19 remaining residual layers of the bottlenecks [16]. Figure 2 shows the architecture of MobileNetV2.

Input	Operator	t	c	n	s
$224^2 \times 3$	conv2d	–	32	1	2
$112^2 \times 32$	bottleneck	1	16	1	1
$112^2 \times 16$	bottleneck	6	24	2	2
$56^2 \times 24$	bottleneck	6	32	3	2
$28^2 \times 32$	bottleneck	6	64	4	2
$14^2 \times 64$	bottleneck	6	96	3	1
$14^2 \times 96$	bottleneck	6	160	3	2
$7^2 \times 160$	bottleneck	6	320	1	1
$7^2 \times 320$	conv2d 1x1	–	1280	1	1
$7^2 \times 1280$	avgpool 7x7	–	–	1	–
$1 \times 1 \times 1280$	conv2d 1x1	–	k	–	

Fig. 2. Architecture of MobileNetV2: t-expansion factor applied to input size, c-Number of output channels, n-Number of layers,s-strides

In terms of parameter efficiency and training time, EfficientNetV2 outperforms previous models. Because EfficientNetV2 is 6.8 times smaller, it can be trained more quickly by raising the image size during training. However, this reduces accuracy as the image size is increased. Regularisation and image size are both used to improve training accuracy. Thus, it outperforms the prior models on ImageNet [17]. Architecture of EfficientNetV2 is described in Fig. 3.

Stage	Operator	Stride	#Channels	#Layers
0	Conv3x3	2	24	1
1	Fused-MBConv1, k3x3	1	24	2
2	Fused-MBConv4, k3x3	2	48	4
3	Fused-MBConv4, k3x3	2	64	4
4	MBConv4, k3x3, SE0.25	2	128	6
5	MBConv6, k3x3, SE0.25	1	160	9
6	MBConv6, k3x3, SE0.25	2	256	15
7	Conv1x1 & Pooling & FC	-	1280	1

Fig. 3. EfficientNetV2 Architecture

4 Methodology

4.1 Dataset

This dataset, named HAM10000 ("Human vs. Machine with 10000 training pictures") [6], provided by Harvard Dataverse, is used in this study. It consists of 10015 lesion images. Each image has resolution of 600×450 pixel. It has seven different classes: Actinic Keratosis (AKIEC), Basal Cell Carcinoma (BCC), Benign Keratosis (BKL), Dermatofibroma (DF), Melanoma (MEL), Melanocytic Nevi (NV) and Vascular Skin Lesion (VASC). Figure 4 shows the sample images of these classes.

4.2 Preprocessing

The dataset is purged of any duplications. After the duplicate photos have been removed, the dataset is divided into two sets i.e. training set and a testing set. There are 9187 photos in the training set and 828 images in the test set. Figure 5 shows that the dataset is very imbalanced. As demonstrated in Table 1, increasing the number of training photos helps enhance the model's performance, so the data argumentation technique is used. Data augmentation techniques include height shift range, width shift range, horizontal flip, zoom, and shear range. As a result, training can be better with a larger amount of training image set. The training models require the images to be scaled from their original dimensions of 600*450 pixels to 224*224 pixels.

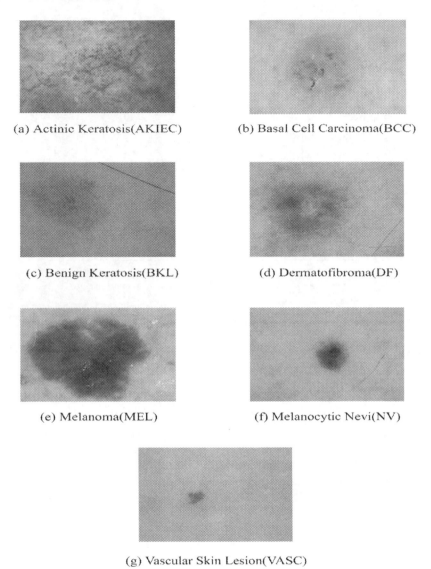

(a) Actinic Keratosis(AKIEC)   (b) Basal Cell Carcinoma(BCC)

(c) Benign Keratosis(BKL)   (d) Dermatofibroma(DF)

(e) Melanoma(MEL)   (f) Melanocytic Nevi(NV)

(g) Vascular Skin Lesion(VASC)

Fig. 4. Sample images of the HAM10000 dataset

4.3   Model Architecture and Training

Adamax is used as an optimization technique. It is an extension of Adam gradient descent technique based on the infinity norm, as it proves to be more successful in optimizing for specific conditions. The model is employed with a categorical cross-entropy loss function. The pooling layers of pre-trained MobileNetV2 are replaced with GlobalMaxPooling layers in the proposed model. Followed by the Modified pre-trained model, the GlobalAveragepooling layer is applied. The

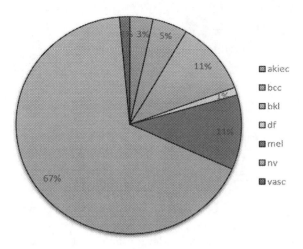

Fig. 5. HAM10000 data-set image distribution.

Table 1. Number of images in train and test set before data augmentation and after data augmentation

Class	Number of Train Images	Number of Train Images (After augmentation)	Number of Test Images
akiec	304	6992	23
bcc	488	7858	26
bkl	1033	7931	66
df	109	5877	6
mel	1079	7903	34
nv	6042	8042	663
vasc	132	7096	828

dropout layer is used with a value of 0.5 after the GlobalAveragepooling layer to prevent overfitting. The proposed model's design is shown in Fig. 6

The total number of parameters in the proposed model is 2,266,951. Out of which 2,232,839 are trainable parameters and 34,112 are non-trainable parameters. First few layers of pre-trained MobileNetV2 were frozen initially so that it could primarily focus on high-level features of skin cancer images and improve the speed of training and also reduce the efforts in terms of time and resources, but it was found that there was a drop in accuracy when layers were frozen [18].

The model was trained across 150 epochs, using a batch size of 16 and 100 iterations per epoch. The proposed model was run on a Google Colab Pro with an Nvidia Tesla P100 graphics card. In the training section, the proposed model took an average of 136.82 s per epoch. After completing the training phase, the proposed model was assessed using the remaining test dataset.

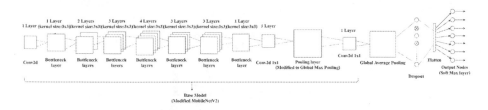

Fig. 6. Architecture of Proposed model

4.4 Evaluation Metrics

In this section, the evaluation metrics are discussed that were used to measure the performance of the proposed model.

Accuracy: An overall measure of the model's performance across all classes is called accuracy. When all classes are of similar importance, it is helpful. It can be defined as the ratio of accurate predictions(true positives) divided by the total number of predictions. This can be expressed mathematically as in Eq. 1.

$$Accuracy = \frac{TP+TN}{TP+TN+FP+FN} \tag{1}$$

Precision: It can be defined as the ratio of true positives divided by the total number of predicted positives.(i.e., true positives and false positives are summed together).This can be expressed mathematically as in Eq. 2.

$$Precision = \frac{TP}{TP+FP} \tag{2}$$

Recall: It can be defined as the ratio of true positives to sum of true positive and false negative.This can be expressed mathematically as in Eq. 3.

$$Recall = \frac{TP}{TP+FN} \tag{3}$$

F1 score: It can be defined as the harmonic mean of two evaluation metrics i.e precision and recall.This can be expressed mathematically as in Eq. 4.

$$F1score = \frac{2*Precision*Recall}{Precision+Recall} \tag{4}$$

5 Results and Discussion

Many pre-trained models have been developed using the ImageNet dataset, and few of them are evaluated and compared to the proposed model in terms of evaluation metrics. The classification report of the proposed model is given in Table 2. The weighted averaging method is considered when the average of mentioned metrics is considered. The result of all the tested models is shown in Table 3. The proposed model has been employed with an early stopping method that enables us to run a large number of epochs and then stop the training when the model's performance starts degrading. The model was trained with a patience value of 30 and stopped after 133 epochs with a training accuracy of 96.56% .

The proposed model that uses pre-trained MobileNetV2 achieved excellent accuracy of 93.11% and has a lower number of parameters i.e., around 2.3 million parameters, when compared to other existing models. In terms of accuracy, the ResNet152 model performed poorly. EfficientV2L performed well, but it has around 107 million parameters that are considered heavy. Having more parameters can slow down the training process and take more resources. Figure 7 shows the graph of training and validation loss. The limitation of the proposed model is that the validation loss is around 35% at 133 epoch. It can be reduced by training the model with a higher epoch value or experimenting with different optimization techniques. If EfficientNetV2L is used as the base model, the loss can be reduced, but the accuracy will be reduced too, and the training parameter will be huge. Figure 8 shows the graph of training and validation accuracy. Figure 9 shows the confusion matrix of the proposed model.

Table 2. Classification report of proposed model

Class	Precision	Recall	F1-score	Accuracy
akiec	0.84	0.91	0.87	**0.9311**
bcc	1.00	0.81	0.89	
bkl	0.86	0.64	0.73	
df	0.80	0.67	0.73	
mel	0.59	0.65	0.62	
nv	0.96	0.99	0.97	
vasc	1.00	0.70	0.82	
Weighted Average	0.93	0.93	0.93	

The comparison of previous related works with the current study is mentioned in Table 4. It is unfair to compare the proposed model to other systems in this domain since they all utilize different datasets and classify them into a different number of classes. In this study, classifying the HAM10000 dataset into seven classes is only focused, and the proposed model is compared with other models. In terms of accuracy, the proposed model has outperformed every other model.

Table 3. The Result of Tested Models

Model	Accuracy	Weighted Average Precision	Weighted Average Recall	Weighted Average F1-score
ResNet152	0.8212	0.8372	0.8212	0.82
DenseNet201	0.9082	0.9041	0.9082	0.91
EfficienetB7	0.9215	0.9195	0.9215	0.92
EfficienetV2L	0.9251	0.9303	0.9251	0.92
Proposed Model	**0.9311**	**0.9348**	**0.9311**	**0.93**

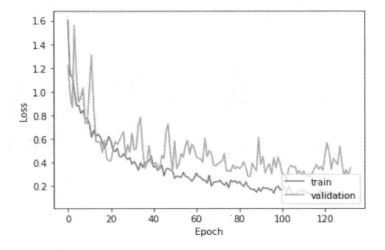

Fig. 7. Training and validation loss

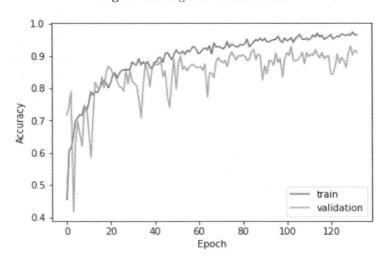

Fig. 8. Training and validation accuracy

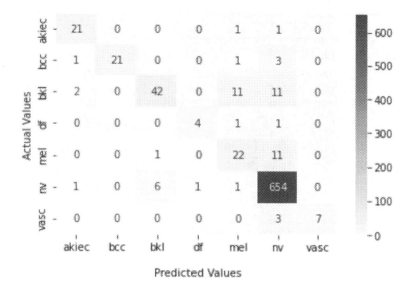

Fig. 9. Confusion matrix

Table 4. Comparison of previous related works with current study

Source	Year	Architectures used	Number of classes	Accuracy (in %)
[7]	2020	DenseNet121	Seven	92
[8]	2020	ResNet50	Seven	90
[9]	2020	ResNet, Xception, DenseNet	Seven	85.8
[11]	2020	Xception	Seven	90.48
[10]	2021	Custom Convolutional Neural Network	Seven	83.04
[20]	2021	Custom Convolutional Neural Network	Seven	75
-	**Current Study**	**Modified MobileNetV2**	**Seven**	**93.11**

6 Conclusion

Skin cancer is easily curable if identified early; however, early diagnosis has proved challenging. The proposed model was compared with the other pre-trained models such as ResNet152, DenseNet201, EfficientNetB7, and EfficientNetV2L. The proposed model outperformed the above-mentioned models, achieving 93.11% test accuracy. Convolutional neural networks process images and help us to build more accurate models for the given task. Neural networks are usually considered as black boxes incapable of deducing a precise cause for their behavior. They have the potential to be valuable for future study, especially in the medical area, if properly understood. To reduce noise in the input data, the use of segmentation is recommended which will in turn improve the model's performance for the classification task. The research may be enhanced with more computing and memory resources by studying different robust architectures and undertaking deeper fine-tuning.

References

1. Guy, G.P., Jr., Machlin, S.R., Ekwueme, D.U., Yabroff, K.R.: Prevalence and costs of skin cancer treatment in the US, 2002–2006 and 2007–2011. Am. J. Prev. Med. **48**(2), 183–187 (2015)
2. "Infographic: Don't Fry: Preventing Skin Cancer". American Cancer Society. Accessed 10 May 2022. https://www.cancer.org/healthy/be-safe-in-sun/skin-cancer-prevention-infographic.html
3. Cancer Facts & Figures 2022: American Cancer Society. Accessed 10 May 2022. https://www.cancer.org/research/cancer-facts-statistics/all-cancer-facts-figures/cancer-facts-figures-2022.html
4. Hill, L., Ferrini, R.L.: Skin cancer prevention and screening: summary of the American College of Preventive Medicine's practice policy statements. CA Cancer J. Clin. **48**(4), 232–235 (1998)
5. Pan, S.J., Yang, Q.: A survey on transfer learning. IEEE Trans. Knowl. Data Eng. **22**(10), 1345–1359 (2009)
6. Tschandl, P., Rosendahl, C., Kittler, H.: The HAM10000 dataset, a large collection of multi-source dermatoscopic images of common pigmented skin lesions. Sci. Data **5**(1), 1–9 (2018)
7. Hassan, S.R., Afroge, S., Mizan, M.B.: Skin lesion classification using densely connected convolutional network. In: 2020 IEEE Region 10 Symposium (TENSYMP), pp. 750–753, IEEE (2020)
8. Kondaveeti, H.K., Edupuganti, P.: Skin Cancer Classification using Transfer Learning. In: 2020 IEEE International Conference on Advent Trends in Multidisciplinary Research and Innovation (ICATMRI), pp. 1–4. IEEE(2020)
9. Rahman, Z., Ami, A.M.: A transfer learning based approach for skin lesion classification from imbalanced data. In: 2020 11th International Conference on Electrical and Computer Engineering (ICECE), pp. 65–68. IEEE (2020)
10. Subramanian, R.R., Achuth, D., Kumar, P.S., kumar Reddy, K.N., Amara, S., Chowdary, A.S.: Skin cancer classification using Convolutional neural networks. In: 2021 11th International Conference on Cloud Computing, Data Science & Engineering (Confluence), pp. 13–19. IEEE (2021)
11. Jain, S., Singhania, U., Tripathy, B., Nasr, E.A., Aboudaif, M.K., Kamrani, A.K.: Deep learning-based transfer learning for classification of skin cancer. Sensors **21**(23), 8142 (2021)
12. Tan, C., Sun, F., Kong, T., Zhang, W., Yang, C., Liu, C.: A Survey on Deep Transfer Learning. In: Kůrková, V., Manolopoulos, Y., Hammer, B., Iliadis, L., Maglogiannis, I. (eds.) ICANN 2018. LNCS, vol. 11141, pp. 270–279. Springer, Cham (2018). https://doi.org/10.1007/978-3-030-01424-7_27

13. He, K., Zhang, X., Ren, S., Sun, J.: Deep residual learning for image recognition. In: Proceedings of the IEEE Conference on Computer Vision and Pattern Recognition, pp. 770–778 (2016)
14. Huang, G., Liu, Z., Van Der Maaten, L., Weinberger, K.Q.: Densely connected convolutional networks. In: Proceedings of the IEEE Conference on Computer Vision and Pattern Recognition. pp. 4700–4708 (2017)
15. Tan, M., Le, Q.: Efficientnet: rethinking model scaling for convolutional neural networks. In: International Conference on Machine Learning. pp. 6105–6114. PMLR, (2019)
16. Sandler, M., Howard, A., Zhu, M., Zhmoginov, A., Chen, L.C: MobileNetV2: inverted residuals and linear bottlenecks. In: Proceedings of the IEEE Conference on Computer Vision and Pattern Recognition. pp. 4510–4520 (2018)
17. Tan, M., Le, Q.: EfficientNetV2: smaller models and faster training. In: International Conference on Machine Learning. pp. 10096–10106. PMLR (2021)
18. Taormina, V., Cascio, D., Abbene, L., Raso, G.: Performance of fine-tuning convolutional neural networks for HEP-2 image classification. Appl. Sci. **10**(19), 6940 (2020)
19. Deng, J., et al:. ImageNet: a large-scale hierarchical image database. In: IEEE Conference on Computer Vision and Pattern Recognition. pp. 248–255 (2009)
20. Huo, Y.: Full-stack application of skin cancer diagnosis based on CNN Model. In: 2021 IEEE International Conference on Computer Science, Electronic Information Engineering and Intelligent Control Technology (CEI). pp. 754–758. IEEE (2021)

Computer Vision Based Mechanism for Detecting Fire and Its Classes

Khushi Jashnani, Rishi Kaul, Arka Haldi$^{(\boxtimes)}$, and Anant V. Nimkar

Sardar Patel Institute of Technology, Andheri, Mumbai 400058, India
{khushi.jashnani,rishi.kaul,arka.haldi,anant_nimkar}@spit.ac.in

Abstract. Fire is an abnormal event that can cause significant damage to lives and property within a very short time. Furthermore, it is important to detect it as soon as it arises and prevent it from posing a threat and damage to society. This paper aims to build a fire detection model that can not only detect the fire in the video sequence but also determine the class it belongs to by considering the background where the fire is detected. This can prove to be beneficial for the first responders to determine the type of fire extinguisher to be used in order to subdue the fire. To achieve this, YOLOv5 is used, which helps in developing a fast, robust, lightweight model and can be deployed with ease in a real-time environment with CCTV surveillance.

Keywords: Fire Detection · Fire Classification · Real Time · IOU · Class Detection · Deep Learning · Convolutional Neural Networks · YOLOv5

1 Introduction

In 2019 alone, 9 million cases of fires were reported with 1.4 lakh fatalities worldwide according to a 195-nation analysis by Global Diseases Burden. The main causes of such disasters include human error or a system failure which results in severe loss of human life and proprietary damage. In order to avoid such a disaster, it is important to detect fire at an early stage, utilizing surveillance cameras, to create a robust fire detection system. Since traditional sensor-based detectors depend on factors like proximity, temperature, etc, there has been a rise in research in the Computer Vision (CV) domain as an alternative. Latest work in CV domain includes the use of Convolutional Neural Network (CNN); a deep learning method to get features and aid in object detection by applying convolution operation on the input image/video data [2].

The latest state-of-the-art techniques in computer vision and deep learning domain has made it possible to automatically detect the fire and prompt its location in real-time [1]. Moreover, the current state of the art techniques uses transfer learning, along with CNN in their methodology to achieve high accuracy in fire detection. The transfer learning approach with various parameters and the CNN based methods using the state-of-the-art object detection models such as YOLOv3 [4], outperforms the traditional fire detection methods from a decade earlier which included feature extractors like edge detector, color detector, etc

D. Gupta et al. (Eds.): CVIP 2022, CCIS 1776, pp. 538–553, 2023.
https://doi.org/10.1007/978-3-031-31407-0_40

to extract the features explicitly from the pixels [8]. But even by using the latest techniques of CNN, it is found that in many of the fire detection systems, the detection accuracy is high when the models are tested on a dataset which is similar to data it has been trained on, whereas the accuracy drops when the same model is being tested on a different dataset [11]. To the best of our knowledge, we observed that none of existing research has worked on discovering the source of the fire from video sequence in real time.

It is necessary that, on the onset of a fire, a corresponding extinguishing agent is used, not only for efficient firefighting but also because the wrong combination could be lethal. The incorrect type of extinguisher may cause electrical shock, explosion, or even contribute to the spread of fire. For example, a type K fire (also known as Kitchen fire) can lead to an explosion if water(class-A extinguisher) is used to eliminate it. Also, the impact of this research would allow common citizens to take appropriate action, with the knowledge of the source of fire which is needed to deal with fire disasters more effectively.

This paper investigates the different fire classes, chooses a standard, and aims to not only detect fire, but also classify the fire into it's fire classes in real time. This is achieved through the use of two different object detectors that are trained separately. First one is trained to detect fire, and second one is trained to detect different flammable objects in the surrounding. This helps to classify the fire into one of it's type, by following the US standard of fire classes. Thus, this paper proposes and tests the BackInTime system, consisting of two object detectors, a YOLOv5 based fire detector for localisation and detection of fire, and a YOLOv5 based object detector, that can detect sources of flammable objects in its surrounding, and classify the fire, based on the IoU scores of fire and the flammable objects. The scope of our research is limited to a single CCTV camera video, and fire classes belonging to A, C, and K.

In this paper, a YOLOv5 based fire detector first localises and detects fire, and sends the fire coordinates to the next phase. A YOLOv5 based object detector, then detects the sources of flammable objects, using the previous few frames of the video, according to their respective fire classes. For example curtain, couch, newspaper, laptop, tv, pot, bowl etc. are used to determine the class of fire, some of which are available already in COCO dataset. For this to work, a comprehensive dataset was made for each label, and YOLOv5 was further trained on these images to be able to identify them. The IOU scores over the frames was found and then a confidence score for each class was displayed at the end of the object detection phase, along with it's location.

This paper contains further 5 sections: Literature Survey (Sect. 2), Motivation (Sect. 3), Back in Time Model (Sect 4), System Implementation (Sect. 5), Results and Discussion (Sect. 6), Conclusion and Future Scope (Sect. 7). The Literature Survey discusses in detail about existing work, and their comparisons to highlight the need for our solution. The next section, talks about the Motivation behind this paper and the Problem statement in detail, about the fire classes. The Proposed Methodology discusses in detail about the two detectors and how they work together, followed by the Results and Discussion section where the results of the model training and testing on the final 150 video dataset is shown. Conclusion and Future Scope discusses about how our methodology can be extended to include more fire classes and multiple cameras.

2   Literature Survey

The objective of the survey was to find existing work on fire detection, compare their methodology, results, datasets used, and find the gaps and issues existing in them. Based on the gaps, research was also done to identify the different classes of fire.

2.1   Fire and Its Classes

This sub-section discusses the different fire classes in literature. According to [18], below are 5 major classes of fire depending on its flammable source/origin:

– Class A: Ordinary solid combustibles such as paper, wood, cloth, and some plastics.
– Class B: Flammable liquids such as alcohol, ether, oil, gasoline, and grease.
– Class C: Electrical equipment, appliances, and wiring in use.
– Class D: Certain flammable metallic substances such as sodium and potassium.
– Class K: Cooking fire involving combustion from liquids used in food preparation.

This is however based on the American standard on fire safety[1] released by US fire administration. Fire is classified on the basis of the kind of fuel it burns, and correspondingly there are different extinguishers to tackle different classes of fire. It is to be noted however that while many countries follow more or less the same convention, there are minor variations as to what each class stands for in some countries[2]. In the Indian context, the fire classes are slightly different[3], but since it lacks electrical fire category, the American class categorisation of fire is used for the purpose of our research.

2.2   Fire Detection Models

This section discusses about all the fire detection papers whose methodology was reviewed, studied, and compared. The earlier approaches that were explored, specifically P. Foggia's [8] model focused on having a Multi-Expert system that

---

[1] https://www.usfa.fema.gov/prevention/outreach/extinguishers.html.
[2] https://en.wikipedia.org/wiki/Fire_class.
[3] https://crpf.gov.in/writereaddata/images/pdf/95012020.pdf.

detects the color, shape, and motion of fire to develop a near-realtime (3 FPS for 352×288 resolution input images) model deployed on Raspberry PI, and demonstrated that there was potential in Computer Vision based Fire detection in real time.

A decade later saw the rise of transfer learning techniques (VGG16 and MobileNet [3]) in the space of fire detection which gave a better accuracy than conventional models at that time. There were also other models that proposed using transfer learning approach (eg. Resnet50 [6]) for feature extraction and used ML models like SVM for classification that provided better fire detection results (in terms of accuracy and no. of misclassifications). With the release of YOLOv3 model, there are many more papers that showed a much better accuracy than the models before, with some methods [14] using depth wise separable convolution and YOLOv3, and some [7] using background subtraction method to detect motion, distinguishing between fire and fire-like images.

One of the more notable works is that of B. Kim, J. Lee [10] who made a video based fire detection model and used Faster R-CNN to get features. It then applied LSTM on them and voted regions to detect fire, and gave fire decision i.e. fire or non-fire. They used datasets like the BowFire dataset, NIST dataset, YouTube clips, Flickr-fire dataset etc. The latest work done was on striking a balance between creating a light weight model and detecting fire relatively fast, maintaining the trade off between model size and accuracy, which they named FireNet [12]. This work created a custom neural network, and deployed it on Raspberry Pi. Here too they used datasets from multiple sources like Foggia's dataset [8], Sharma's dataset [12], and web scraped images.

A follow up paper KutralNet [11], proposed a very lightweight model that reduced FireNet's parameters by 71% and compared it against different datasets (FireNet [12], FiSmo [16], FiSmoA, FiSmoB, FiSmoBA). It also compared them against other models including FireNet, to find that KutralNet performed better in various scenarios. FireNet was very limited to the dataset it was trained on, and gave notably lesser accuracy on other datasets.

The detection accuracy is high on standard datasets individually for many models, whereas when comparative analysis is done using other datasets, one can observe a drop in testing accuracy [11]. Furthermore, since transfer learning approaches gives high computational complexity and results in lower fps rate, novelty in the space of developing lightweight CNN models is observed (FireNet [12] and KutralNet [11]). Also, there's research focusing on fire detection using LSTM [10] to give fire decision in real-time, but they tend to have more number of false alarms. On the other hand, a 2020 paper [2] conclusively establishes that single-stage CNNs like YOLOv3 can acheive a significantly high accuracy(83.7%) with a considerably high frame rate(28fps). While the state of the art in fire detection points to numerous methods that can "detect" fire, little to no work has been found that focuses on detecting the source of fire/ fire classes.

3 Motivation

As we know the importance of the classes of fire, a fire must be subdued by using its corresponding extinguisher. For example, if there is a kitchen fire involving oils (i.e class-K fire), and we use water (class-A extinguisher), there's a high chance of an explosion that spreads the fire even more. Knowing the type of fire, can thus help the first responders to better deal with the fire, and use an appropriate extinguisher (eg. Class A extinguisher on class A fire). The value generated by this research will enable common citizens to not make the mistakes of using the wrong extinguisher and guide the average person in real time to use the appropriate measures/extinguishers to deal with a particular class of fire.

Existing research work focused only on detection of fire, and no work has been found yet that detects the type of fire from its source. Looking at the potential of computer vision in this domain, YOLOv5 can be used to classify the fire in real time with high accuracy and high frame detection speed. As it was seen in the literature survey that YOLOv3 performed the best among other approaches. YOLOv5[4] being the latest version of the YOLO family, can prove to be promising in this proposed research.

This paper tackles the research problem of detection, localisation and classification of fire into it's classes, based on the source of fire in its surrounding in real time. The scope of this research is limited to a single CCTV camera, since there is lack of available data on multiple cameras monitoring the same room. But, our research methodology can be easily extended to accommodate the same. Further, this work is limited to classifying fire into classes A, C, and K, as Common fire, Electrical fire and Kitchen fire are the most commonly occurring fires. This research also requires the testing videos to be stable i.e. negligible movement throughout the duration of the footage, to effectively simulate the fire hazard in real life captured by a CCTV camera.

4 BackInTime

BackInTime is a system which takes input as a CCTV footage and outputs back an image which detects the location of fire and predicts the class of fire in real time. This helps in identifying the type of extinguisher to use and give valuable insights to the first responders to take the right action at the right time in order to subdue the fire. The proposed system has two major components:

– Fire Detection
– Source Detection

Through extensive experiments it was found that directly detecting the fire along with its class in one object detector makes it difficult to correctly predict the class and it turns out to be computationally inefficient. Hence, we propose a system with two object detectors. One for detecting the presence of fire and

---

[4] https://github.com/ultralytics/YOLOv5.

the second for detecting the type/class of fire. This approach reduces the overall computational power needed as the first detector only looks for one class i.e. fire and can thus be robust enough in identifying it. Below is the flow (Fig. 1) of our system:

Fig. 1. Flow of Back in Time

The Input module inputs the video frames. The preprocessing module converts the inputted frames into a 640×640 dimension image for detection by the model. The Fire Detector module analyses the patterns in video frames for fire. If fire is detected by the Fire Detector module, the frames are sent to the Source Detector module for analysis of the class. The output from both detectors is then shown by the output module.

4.1 Caching of Frames

As a CCTV video footage/sequence is sent as an input to our system, the fire detector detects the presence of fire in the footage, frame by frame and labels the frame as a fire or a non-fire frame. While doing so, the system also maintains a cache of alpha number of frames belonging to non-fire. This cache corresponds to the alpha (α) number of most recent non-fire frames (as mentioned in Fig. 2 and algorithm 1) in which the source of the fire can be clearly detected if a fire exists in the near future. This helps in better identifying the flammable objects in the surrounding which otherwise gets obstructed by the fire in the frame. Hence, the model inserts the frames of the incoming video into the cache in queue fashion; while constantly maintaining the size of the cache, till the ten frames of fire having more than 60% confidence are detected. Below is the pictorial representation of the above mentioned process:

4.2 Classifying the Fire

Once the fire is detected by the fire detector, the next step is to actually classifying the fire into its fire class. This is achieved by finding the Intersection over Union (IoU) of the fire with the objects detected in the surrounding. For this purpose, we use the frames stored in the cache and send it to the object detector for identifying the flammable objects in the frames. As the objects are getting detected, we calculate the IoU of the bounding box of the flammable object in the frame with the bounding box of the fire (averaged coordinates of 10 fire frames). Now to find out the most probable fire class, the confidence of

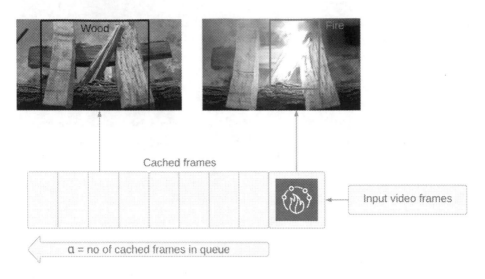

Fig. 2. Working of Back in Time System

each class is calculated by summing the IoU scores of the objects belonging to a particular fire class and then averaging it. Algorithm 1 refers to the psuedo code of the proposed methodology.

Algorithm 1. Back in Time Algorithm for Source Detection

Data: *video* (Input video stream), α (size of queue), *fireDetector*(fire detection function), *classDetector* (class detection function)

Result: *fire*(fire detection, and BBox coordinates), *class* (class wise confidence, and BBox coordinates)

$cache = queue(\alpha)$;   // Initialize queue of size α

for *frame in video* **do**

    $preprocessed = $ prePross $(frame)$ $cache$.enqueue($preprocessed$) ;

    // add the preprocessed frame to cache

    $fire = $ fireDetector $(preprocessed)$;   // fireDetector returns

    isfire True if fire is detected

    if *fire.isfire* **then**

        $class = $ classDetector $(cache, fire.coordinates)$;

        // classDetector returns class confidence

        return *fire, class*;

    end

end

As mentioned in the pseudo code, we have two functions fireDetector and classDetector that perform fire, and fire-class detection respectively. First a queue(cache) is created of α size, where the latest α frames are stored; and each new frame is enqueued after preprocessing. Then the frame is sent to the fire detector that detects if there's presence of fire, and if fire is detected, returns the bounding box coordinates of the region where the fire is detected (Fig. 3).

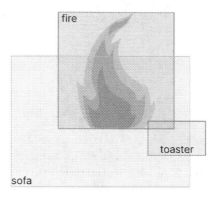

Fig. 3. Illustration of IoU score

This information along with the cache of past α frames is then sent to the object detector that detects the flammable objects in the surrounding. Now, according to the IoUs of different objects obtained in the alpha frames, the classDetector determines which class's objects are the most overlapping with fire, and returns the confidence of the respective fire classes along with the bounding box coordinates of the object having the highest IoU. This information is then returned by the fire-class detection algorithm and subsequent results are displayed with the fire detection frame and object detection frame along with their bounding boxes. For example, in Fig. 4, we can see that the bounding box that first detected fire, is then used with the previous frames which have various objects that are detected like sofa(class A fire source) and toaster(class C fire source) belonging to different fire classes, and is then used to give the confidence score using the IoU scores with corresponding fire source intersecting with the initial fire frame. In this case, BackInTime gives us high confidence(due to IoU) for class A as sofa causes class A fire.

5   System Implementation

Back in Time algorithm comprises of two object detectors namely a YOLOv5 based fire detector for localisation and detection of fire; and a YOLOv5 based object detector, that can detect sources of flammable objects, according to their respective fire classes. Below are the steps for implementation:

5.1   Requirements

For our implementation, we used a Google Colab Notebook using a dual core GPU as the hardware accelerator. The hardware specifications equivalent to this are mentioned below:

1. 12GB NVIDIA Tesla K80 GPU
2. Intel(R) Xeon(R) CPU @ 2.20GHz

Along with this, the following software requirements are recommended:

1. Python 3.8
2. Tensorflow 1.x
3. Keras 2.1.0
4. Jupyter Notebook

5.2   Data Collection and Preprocessing

For our problem statement, there was no dataset available , and hence created it ourselves. Videos were gathered, which were CCTV or CCTV like. The characteristics of these videos is that they are held in position by a stand or a mount i.e. the footage is stable without much movement.

1. **Fire dataset**: The fire dataset that was collected had 4200 images. The images were collected from publicly available datasets, Google Images and YouTube. However, the expected result could not be achieved with this dataset, and good fire detection rates cannot be expected in real scenarios. Hence various data augmentation operations like rotation (Between -20° and +20°), shear (±22° horizontal, ±22° vertical), saturation (between -30% and +30%), noise (upto 15% of pixels) were applied. This helped in increasing the size of the dataset to 15000 images. Along with these fire frames, we also added images that appear to be fire. This was done in order to reduce the number of false positives in the predictions.
2. **Object detection dataset**: For object detector, we chose two additional objects i.e. 'pot' and 'curtain' to be detected through the custom Object Detector. This was done to keep the training time within bounds, but can be extended to include more flammable objects belonging to different classes. For source object dataset, 5909 images through Google Images were collected, with 4404 images of both blurry and crisp pictures of 'pot' and 'curtain' object classes. The chosen images were consolidated into a dataset by hand annotating them for the objects in it, in a darknet txt format.[5] The dataset has a total of 7814 annotations, with 3525, 2687, and 1602 belonging to the 'curtain', 'pot' and 'toaster' classes respectively, of which curtain and pot were used for training. Also, the pre-trained weights of YOLOv5 were leveraged to detect the labels already present in the COCO Dataset. Thus, allowing us to detect 25 more flammable objects, and increasing the robustness of our system.

---

[5] The Object detection dataset: https://github.com/Arka-h/pot-curtain-toaster-object-etection-classes-datasethttps://github.com/Arka-h/pot-curtain-toaster-object-detection-classes-dataset.

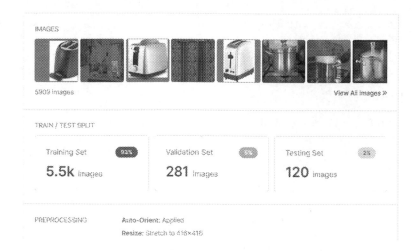

Fig. 4. The Object Detection Dataset

3. **Test dataset**: For testing purposes, we collected 150 youtube videos/ video
   snippets to be used for detecting fire and its class. 130 of the selected videos
   contained fire, and the rest non-fire videos were also added to detect false
   positives. The data collection was done in accordance to the criteria that the
   videos should be CCTV or CCTV like. The footage was selected to meet the
   following criteria:
   1. **Video stability**: The footage is stable without much movement/ zoom-
      ing
   2. **Video content**: Footage must not be too zoomed into the fire and cap-
      ture a room/facility/environment
   3. **Video angle**: Multiple room angles shouldn't be shown simultaneously;
      Also there shouldn't be sudden changes in view/zoom.
   4. **Fire evolution**: Footage must capture the start of the fire, and shouldn't
      start in the middle of a fire.
   The 130 videos collected, contained 49, 41, and 40 videos each of Class A,
   Class C and Class K respectively, to form the benchmark to test BackInTime
   and demonstrate it's performance in a real world scenario.

5.3   Training

After preprocessing the dataset for fire and source, we now move on to build
separate detectors for each as mentioned in the methodology. For training both
the detectors, we have used YOLOv5 architecture and used transfer learning to
extract the desired features of our custom dataset. The reason we selected YOLO
is because of the single stage detection architecture unlike the two stage detection
of Faster-RCNN technique. This allows YOLO to have a faster detection rate
which is crucial for our problem as our primary goal is to detect fire in real

time. Our dataset for both Fire and Source was split such that 70% was used for training, 20% for validation, and 10% for testing. We trained our models for 300 epochs using Google Colab Notebook with Tesla K80/P100 GPU.

5.4   Testing

After training, we tested both of the models on our test dataset, which contained a set of 150 CCTV like videos containing both fire and non-fire, with 130 fire, 20 non-fire videos. They were obtained from the internet through various datasets and YouTube clips of class A, C, and K fires that were found. This dataset acted as the benchmark to get an idea about how it will perform on real data. CCTV like data was prepared by selecting videos that are held in position by a stand or mount i.e. the footage is stable without much movement/ zooming. The final trained model with the best weights for both fire detection and object detection were used on the videos to evaluate the model performance in terms of confusion matrix, and accuracy measures.

6   Results and Discussion

Since we have 2 object detection models, we are evaluating them with Precision, Recall and Mean Average Precision.

Table 1. Fire and Source Detection Model Performance

Detector	Precision	Recall	mAP
Fire	0.902	0.903	0.929
Source	0.872	0.745	0.825

6.1   Fire Detection Results

From Table 1 we can observe all three metrics i.e. precision, recall and mAP@0.5 and say that the fire object detector performs well. A high precision value indicates that the number of false positives predicted are very few. We achieved this result by including several fire-like images such as sun, street lights, yellow halogen lights in both day and night scenarios. Moreover, a high recall value indicates that the number of false negatives are low. This shows that almost all the fire instances are getting detected.

Figure 5 refers to the Precision-Recall curve of fire object detector which is in agreement with the above interpretation (Table 1). Further, Table. 2 is the confusion matrix generated after testing 150 videos out of which 130 contained fire and 20 did not. By seeing the table, we can observe that number of true positives is 117, true negatives is 18, false positives is 2 and false negatives is 13. This shows that the testing results are in alignment with the precision and recall scores discussed above with 90% accuracy. Hence, we can conclude there are very few misclassification happening and the model is very robust in terms of detecting fire.

Table 2. Confusion Matrix of Fire Detector

Fire Detection Results		Actual	
		Fire	Non-Fire
Predicted	Fire	117	2
	Non-Fire	13	18

6.2 Source Object Detection Results

The objects that we have chosen for the custom purposes to be detected like pot and curtain, vary largely with respect to their shapes, sizes and colours and hence we can see from Table 1 that the custom source object detector i.e. Class Detector has a precision of 0.872, recall of 0.903 and mAP of 0.825. The lower values for curtain class can possibly be because the curtain dataset varies alot in terms of both shape and color whereas pot dataset varies majorly with color and less in terms of shape which can be seen in the real world too. Fig 5 refers to the Precision Recall curve for the same.

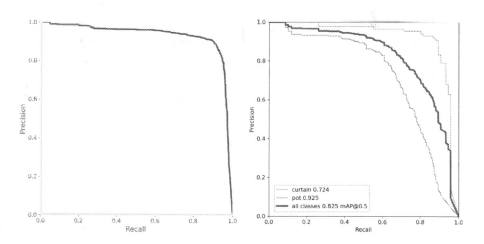

Fig. 5. Fire Detector Precision Recall Curve (left) and Source Detector Precision Recall Curve(right)

Since Class Detector will only work on the videos in which fire is getting detected. From the 117 correctly predicted fire videos, 46 belonged to Class A, 35 belonged to Class C and 36 belonged to Class K. Further, Table 3 shows the confusion matrix of number of videos in which the source i.e. Fire class is getting correctly predicted - 40 from class A, 31 from class C and 33 from class K. There have been videos in which the fire is not clearly visible or is not present in the frame which accounts for the number of videos in which the source is not predicted. Further, if the source object is not properly overlapping with the fire or if the source object is at a distance from the point where fire has been detected leads to misclassifications which also has been recorded in the same table.

Table 3. Confusion Matrix for 3 source classes A, C and K

Source Class		Actual		
		A	C	K
Predicted	A	40	2	3
	C	5	31	0
	K	1	2	33

The results were obtained using a cache size(α) of previous 70 frames as that was the optimum best out of the 3 tested values of frames cached at: 30, 50, and 70 frames. The model used in testing them, for the fire detector and the source detector are both yolov5x, that gave the best results out of the different available yolov5 nets (i.e yolov5s, yolov5m, yolov5x). The threshold for the bounding box was put to be 0.6, and the cumulative result of all the different bounding boxes made over the previous 70 frames were then weighed w.r.t their IoU scores (against the fire bounding box) into the different classes A, C, K in a percentage confidence score.

The figure shown below represents the system's final output for class A (Fig. 6).

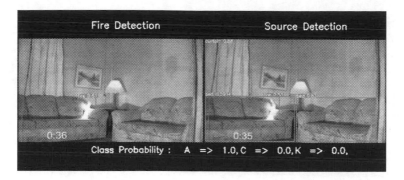

Fig. 6. The image shows the fire detector in action. After fire is detected, the cached frames are scanned where the class detector identifies objects around the fire and looks for the source, which in this case is the sofa. Since sofas belong to class A and there are no objects of other classes, the algorithm outputs a confidence score of 1 or 100% for class A.

The figure below shows the ability of our model to handle false positives (Fig. 7).

Fig. 7. Image of the sun (fire like) image, where the model correctly identifies the absence of fire

7   Conclusion and Future Scope

In order to tackle this problem of detecting fire and its classes, this research came up with the above discussed methodology which is efficient in detecting fire and its class from its surroundings. The two object detectors i.e. fire and source detector were extensively trained on large datasets which helped in achieving mAP of 0.929 and 0.825 respectively. Moreover, the proposed method - Back In Time, gave an accuracy of 86.95%, 88.57% and 91% for fire classes A, C and K respectively, after testing it on 150 CCTV videos. The approach of evaluating the IOU of the fire co-ordinates with the objects' co-ordinates in determining the source, works well.

Further, future work can be done to improve the object detector so that it can be helpful in detecting different kinds of flammable objects in the surrounding and can thus help in increasing the robustness of the solution. Also, this methodology can be extended by incorporating multiple camera angles and using their IOU scores to give a better prediction of the fire class.

References

1. Saponara, S., Elhanashi, A., Gagliardi, A.: Real-time video fire/smoke detection based on CNN in antifire surveillance systems. J. Real-Time Image Process. **18**(3), 889–900 (2021)
2. Li, P., Zhao, W.: Image fire detection algorithms based on convolutional neural networks. Case Stud. Thermal Eng. **19**, 100625 (2020)
3. Dua, M., Kumar, M., Charan, G.S., Ravi, P.S.: An improved approach for fire detection using deep learning models. In: 2020 International Conference on Industry 4.0 Technology (I4Tech). pp. 171–175. IEEE (2020)
4. Jiao, Z., et al.: A deep learning based forest fire detection approach using UAV and YOLOv3. In: 2019 1st International conference on industrial artificial intelligence (IAI). pp. 1–5. IEEE (2019)
5. Muhammad, K., Ahmad, J., Mehmood, I., Rho, S., Baik, S.W.: Convolutional neural networks based fire detection in surveillance videos. IEEE Access **6**, 18174–18183 (2018)
6. Kumar, C., Suhas G., Abhishek B.S., Gowda, K.A.D., Prajwal R.: Fire detection using deep learning. Int. J. Progress. Res. Sci. Eng. **1**(5), 1–5 (2020). https://journals.grdpublications.com/index.php/ijprse/article/view/141 Accessed: 28 May 2022
7. Wu, H., Wu, D., Zhao, J.: An intelligent fire detection approach through cameras based on computer vision methods. Process Safety Environ. Prot. **127**, 245–256 (2019)
8. Foggia, P., Saggese, A., Vento, M.: Real-time fire detection for video-surveillance applications using a combination of experts based on color, shape, and motion. IEEE Trans. Circuits Syst. Video Technol. **25**(9), 1545–1556 (2015)
9. Moumgiakmas, S.S., Samatas, G.G., Papakostas, G.A.: Computer vision for fire detection on UAVs–From software to hardware. Future Internet **13**(8), 200 (2021)
10. Kim, B., Lee, J.: A video-based fire detection using deep learning models. Appl. Sci. **9**(14), 2862 (2019)
11. Ayala, A., Fernandes, B., Cruz, F., Macêdo, D., Oliveira, A.L., Zanchettin, C.: KutralNet: portable deep learning model for fire recognition. In: 2020 International Joint Conference on Neural Networks (IJCNN). pp. 1–8. IEEE (2019)
12. Jadon, A., Omama, M., Varshney, A., Ansari, M.S., Sharma, R.: FireNet: a specialized lightweight fire & smoke detection model for real-time IoT applications (2019). arXiv preprint arXiv:1905.11922
13. Dubey, V., Kumar, P., Chauhan, N.: Forest Fire Detection System Using IoT and Artificial Neural Network. In: Bhattacharyya, S., Hassanien, A.E., Gupta, D., Khanna, A., Pan, I. (eds.) International Conference on Innovative Computing and Communications. LNNS, vol. 55, pp. 323–337. Springer, Singapore (2019). https://doi.org/10.1007/978-981-13-2324-9_33
14. Qin, Y.Y., Cao, J.T., Ji, X.F.: Fire detection method based on depthwise separable convolution and yolov3. Int. J. Autom. Comput. **18**(2), 300–310 (2021)

15. Sharma, J., Granmo, O.-C., Goodwin, M., Fidje, J.T.: Deep Convolutional Neural Networks for Fire Detection in Images. In: Boracchi, G., Iliadis, L., Jayne, C., Likas, A. (eds.) EANN 2017. CCIS, vol. 744, pp. 183–193. Springer, Cham (2017). https://doi.org/10.1007/978-3-319-65172-9_16

16. Cazzolato, M.T., et al.: Fismo: A compilation of datasets from emergency situations for fire and smoke analysis. In: Brazilian Symposium on Databases-SBBD. pp. 213–223. SBC (2017)

17. Muhammad, K., Ahmad, J., Lv, Z., Bellavista, P., Yang, P., Baik, S.W.: Efficient deep CNN-based fire detection and localization in video surveillance applications. IEEE Trans. Syst. Man Cyber. Syst. **49**(7), 1419–1434 (2018)

18. The Five Classes of Fires and the Fire Extinguishers that Stop Them, Strikefirstusa Article. https://www.strikefirstusa.com/news-articles/five-classes-of-fires-fire-extinguishers-stop-them Accessed: 18 Apr 2022

19. Choosing and using fire extinguishers, U.S. Fire Administration webpage. https://www.usfa.fema.gov/prevention/outreach/extinguishers.html Accessed: 18 Apr 2022

20. Fire class article, Wikipedia. https://en.wikipedia.org/wiki/Fire_class Accessed: 18 Apr 2022

21. Portable Fire Extinguishers - Performance and Construction - Specification, Central Reserve Police Force Website. https://crpf.gov.in/writereaddata/images/pdf/95012020.pdf Accessed: 18 Apr 2022

A Random Forest-based No-Reference Quality Metric for UGC Videos

Krishna Kumar[1], Pramit Mazumdar[1(✉)], Kamal Kishor Jha[1],
and Kamal Lamichhane[2]

[1] Indian Institute of Information Technology Vadodara, Gujarat, India
{202061004,pramit.mazumdar,kamal}@iiitvadodara.ac.in
[2] University of Roma Tre, Rome, Italy
kamal.lamichhane@uniroma3.it

Abstract. The images and videos randomly captured by people for sharing in social media or their own use are commonly termed as the user generated content. With the growing popularity of various social media and streaming platforms along with the availability of low-cost portable devices, the amount of such user generated content is exponentially increasing. Visual quality assessment of such user-generated contents is necessary for various purpose such as estimating how the distortions induced during media transmission effects the visual quality of the non-professionally captured image or video, the social media platforms to estimate quality of a media before it gets posted, assessing quality to evaluate performance of a handheld camera or mobile phone, etc. This is a very challenging task due to the fact that the user generated content significantly suffers from multiple artifacts and distortions during both the capturing and transmission pipeline stage that eventually hinder the visual quality. This work mostly deals with the artifacts induced during video capturing stage, and subsequently, use them for estimating visual quality. A random forest-based no-reference video quality assessment metric is proposed for user generated content videos. The proposed approach is divided into two steps. Firstly, the encoding and content-based features are extracted at the frame level. Secondly, an ensemble-based prediction model is employed to exploit the extracted frame-level features for estimating the visual quality score for each frame. Finally, max pooling is performed to estimate the final video level quality score. We also study various score predictors to eventually suggest the best performing ensemble-learning method for the proposed model. Experiments are performed on the benchmark ICME grand challenge dataset of user generated content videos. The model is compared with several state-of-the-art user generated content video quality metrics. The observed results indicate that the proposed no-reference model outperforms the existing approaches for quality estimation of user generated content videos.

Keywords: User Generated Content · Quality Metric · Feature Extraction · Random Forest Regressor

D. Gupta et al. (Eds.): CVIP 2022, CCIS 1776, pp. 554–566, 2023.
https://doi.org/10.1007/978-3-031-31407-0_41

1 Introduction

Recent years have witnessed significant increase in the usage of mobile handheld electronic devices such as mobile phones, tablets, digital cameras, etc. This in particular is enabling people to capture and share their content ubiquitously through various social network platforms such as Facebook, Instagram, YouTube, etc.[1]. Media content available at various social networking platforms which are either public or private to a specific user and media files randomly captured by people using their handheld smart devices are collectively known as the User Generated Content (UGC). Now with the increase of UGC for capturing, storing, and sharing via media platforms, it has become essential to assess quality of a media before it gets shared via a particular platform. Assessing quality of 2D images and videos have been an important field of research due to its multiple application oriented necessities [3,21]. However, the standard quality assessment metrics cannot be directly applied over UGC. This is due to the fact that UGC is neither a computer generated imagery nor a professionally generated content. UGC is typically generated from random photos/ videos captured by users using different devices having variable resolution, and with an obvious inclusion of artifacts while capturing. In addition to this, users tend to apply multiple filters on top of the captured media before they are transmitted and shared via a platform, this makes the visual quality assessment more challenging. It requires developing a quality metric, that could incorporate the specific properties related to an UGC media. In literature, the popularly used objective quality assessment approaches are Full Reference (FR) and No Reference (NR) [4]. Recently, the research community is more inclined towards developing NR objective quality metrics as it does not require the reference videos. Usually the low and high-level features, content-based features, etc. are considered as the identifiers for devising a NR metric [14,18]. Similarly, features that are specific to UGC content is also used for quality assessment [7,12].

This work focuses on visual quality assessment of random UGC videos captured using mobile phones. The Random Forest-based No-Reference Video Quality Assessment Metric (RFNQA) works in two steps; first, a feature extractor is used to identify the video encoding features, and the video content based features. Secondly, the features are combined together by average pooling. Subsequently, the visual quality predictor by employing an ensemble-based approach predicts the quality score. The score is predicted in accordance with the five-point Absolute Category Rating (ACR) scale where 1 indicates bad and 5 indicates excellent quality of UGC [5]. Further, a comprehensive analysis is performed by evaluating our model with the other state-of-the-art quality metrics. We also conduct extensive experiments to test performance of various predictors when used in our model, and subsequently, selected the best performing predictor for the given scenario.

The remainder of this paper is organized as follows; Sect. 2 presents the existing related works on quality assessment in UGC. Section 3 describes the proposed

---

[1] https://www.wyzowl.com/video-social-media-2020/.

methodology of RFNQA. The proposed RFNQA model is evaluated using the benchmark UGCVQA dataset[2] and the experimental results are presented in Sect. 4. Finally, we conclude in Sect. 5.

2 Related Works

Visual quality assessment have long been studied in literature and multiple FR and NR metrics for 2D images and videos are available [2,6,8,10,11,17,20]. Yao et al. in [20] proposed a no-reference visual quality assessment metric for videos by combining video bitrate and the visual perception of video contents. First the bitrate of the videos are selected as a feature. Second, the low-level features such as texture, contrast, and temporal information are extracted at frame level and subsequently, max pooling is performed for video level features. Finally, the bitrate and low-level features are combined, and weight coefficients are applied to predict the quality score. Similarly, in [6] the video quality metric is based on the idea of computing features in two levels; the low complexity features computed first for the entire sequence and subsequently, the high complexity features are extracted from a subset of representative video frames selected using the low complexity features. Chen et al. in [2] proposed a quality predictor that achieves a high-generalized capability in cross content, resolution, and frame-rate quality prediction. To address the observed differences in resolution and content of the videos, the metric applies Gaussian distribution restrictions to the quality features in spatial domain. Moreover, the unified distribution can greatly reduce the domain gap between the video samples, resulting in a more generalised representation of quality features.

Recent efforts have also been made to propose visual quality metrics designed specifically for the UGC scenario [7,13,14,17,22]. Zadtootaghaj et al. in [22] proposed a deep learning based quality assessment metric DEMI for both gaming and non-gaming videos. Distortion artifacts such as blurriness and blockiness are considered in the model and the extracted features are pooled using a random forest regressor. However, influence of the video encoders on visual quality and complexity of scenes are not considered in the DEMI metric. The ITU-T Rec. P.1203.1 presented a bitstream-based video quality model for streaming data [14]. The video resolution is considered as the influencing factor for quality score estimation. A short-term video quality estimator is devised which can act as an input to the P.1203 recommendation. In recent literature, there exists quality metrics that are typically developed for the UGC scenario. Zhengzhong et al. in [17] proposed a rapid and accurate video quality evaluator (RAPIQUE) which combines quality-aware scene statistics and semantic aware deep convolutional features for quality score estimation. RM3VQA [7] devised a convolutional neural network based framework which exploits the video content information such as Spatial Information (SI), Temporal Information (TI) and employ a support vector regressor for pooling the features. Similar to [17], RM3VQA also do not consider the video encoding technique as an influencing factor for quality

---

[2] http://ugcvqa.com/.

assessment. Recently, Nguyen et al. proposed an ensemble learning-based no reference metric (ELVQ) in [13]. ELVQ considers bit-stream level and packet-level information as well as various encoding parameters such as quantization parameter. In addition to this, the model also includes blurriness and different pooling approaches for quality assessment.

3 Proposed Methodology

The working of the proposed RFNQA model is primarily divided into two steps, first the feature extraction and second the quality score predictor. A detailed description of the individual blocks involved in the RFNQA model is presented in Fig. 1. The feature extractor module is capable of identifying the influencing factors from the UGC videos that affects the visual quality score. Subsequently, the visual quality predictor module uses an ensemble-based approach to predict the visual quality score.

3.1 Feature Extractor

There exists multiple influencing factors which drive the visual quality of a video. However, an UGC scenario differs from a normal professionally generated content. This is due to the fact that UGC is captured by amateur photographers, thus inducing distortion-based artifacts in the content. Considering this, the feature extractor module extracts two categories of features from the UGC videos; encoding-based features and content-based features.

Encoding-based Features. Video encoding-based features are often used for assessing quality of a media [19,21]. Features such as bitrate, resolution, quantization parameters, etc. impacts the visual quality. The proposed RFNQA combines two encoding and distortion related features, which are briefly described in the following:

– Bitrate (B) and Resolution (R): The bitrate and resolution both have important role in improving the visual quality of a video. In particular, bitrate of a video refers to the rate at which it is transferred at a given time. Whereas, resolution indicates the number of pixels that combines to form a video frame. Thus, with a high resolution UGC videos, it is believed to have a better visual quality.

Content-based Features. The content-based features can be divided into two categories; one that deals with features that are typically taken from the overall video, whereas the other category is the region-based features such as region-of-interests, position of objects, etc. The former category of features include colour information, edge, texture, etc. [20]. Moreover, artifacts present in a visual scene, position of the artifacts, etc. could also be considered as feature for estimating

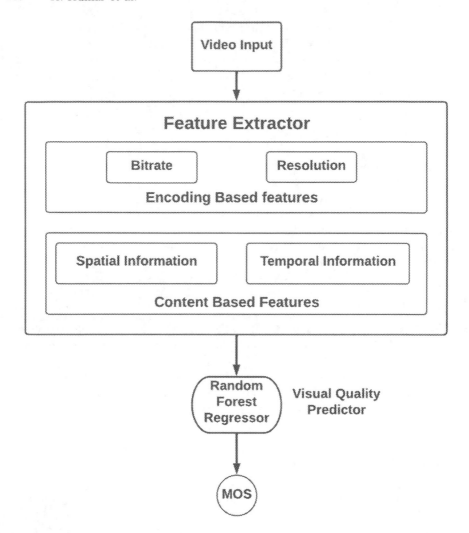

Fig. 1. The proposed Random Forest-based No-Reference video Quality Assessment model (RFNQA).

visual quality. These features are also very important when we are considering the UGC videos. This is due to the fact that the captured videos are from various domains as mentioned in Fig. 2, and eventually several distortions are induced as depicted in Fig. 3. The proposed RFNQA considers some of such content-based features which are briefly described in the following:

| (a) Food | (b) Landscape | (c) Person | (d) Game |

Fig. 2. Sample frames extracted from UGCVQA video dataset to show the different types of video contents.

– *Spatial Information* (SI): It is a standard approach to quantify the amount of spatial detail present in a frame. With videos having more complex scenes, it is observed that the average frame-level SI carries a higher value [1]. Typically the UGC videos are captured for public sharing. Thus one typical characteristic of UGC are the complex scenes. Therefore, SI is used in RFNQA to introduce a variation in the assessment based on complexity of scenes. Each frame extracted from a UGC video is filtered using the horizontal (*hor*) and vertical (*ver*) Sobel kernels to compute the signal strength at any one pixel p, where $p \in P$, set of all pixels in the extracted frame,

$$SI_p = \sqrt{hor^2 + ver^2} \tag{1}$$

Further, the SI mean and standard deviation is computed as follow,

$$SI_{mean} = \frac{1}{P} \sum SI_p \tag{2}$$

$$SI_{std} = \sqrt{\frac{1}{P} \sum (SI_p - SI_{mean})^2} \tag{3}$$

For each frame the SI_{std} is computed in accordance with the ITU-T Rec. P.910 [5]. Finally, the maximum SI_{std} over all the frames for the entire duration of the video is considered.

The natural images have a different distribution of pixel intensities than the deformed or distorted images. Therefore, to exploit the distortion level of the UGC we employ the Mean Subtracted Contrast Normalization (MSCN) approach. The MSCN coefficients changes along with the variation of distortion

(a) Blurring   (b) Filter   (c) Motion Blur   (d) Blocking

Fig. 3. Sample frames extracted from UGCVQA video dataset to show the different type of artifacts induced in a UGC video.

level of the images [11]. The probability density function (pdf) of histograms of the pixel values of MSCN coefficients are completely different compared to the video frame and adopts a Gaussian distribution as depicted in Figure 4. Hence, MSCN is considered in this work as important feature source. Eventually these coefficients are used as the features in the model RFNQA. Thus for each video, we obtained two spatial quality features using mean,μ, and standard deviation σ based on the MSCN coefficients.

Furthermore, User generated content are very prone to get blurred due to the fact that they are being recorded or captured by common users. Therefore, the blurring impacts the user experience in terms of quality and viewing. We extracted the blur value feature from the input videos in accordance with the approach proposed in [16]. The approach uses Haar wavelet transform to detect the edges and sharpness [15]. Finally, the ratio of blurred edges over the detected edges is used to represent the blurriness of the image.

– *Temporal Information* (TI): The TI is a similar parameter that can be used to measure complexity of a video, using the difference between pixel intensities of current frame (f) and the previous frame ($f - 1$). It is usually observed that Greater motion in between adjacent frames results in a higher TI. The TI feature can thus be computed as,

$$TI_v = \max_{time} \left(std\left[f - (f - 1) \right] \right) \tag{4}$$

Next, feature pooling is applied over the above extracted frame-level features. We employ four different pooling methods (average, minimum, maximum, and standard deviation) for all the above features except bitrate and resolution as

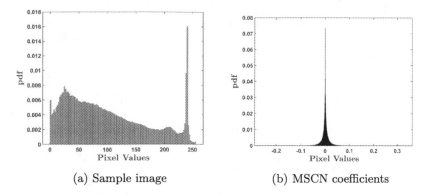

(a) Sample image   (b) MSCN coefficients

Fig. 4. Histogram plots of a sample frame taken from UGC0001_720x1280_30_crf_00.mp4 video of the UGCVQA dataset and its corresponding MSCN coefficients.

they can be directly obtained from a video. Finally, the set of extracted features are considered together as input to the following visual quality predictor module.

3.2 Visual Quality Predictor

The visual quality predictor module is devised to utilise the extracted features for predicting quality score for UGC videos. An ensemble-based learning approach is employed in this regard. The Ensemble learner combines all the predictions obtained from the multiple base learners to produce the final quality scores. We used the Random forest tree due to the fact that it performs better on data obtained from different sources and having less dependencies [9]. A random forest is a meta estimator that fits a number of decision tree on various sub-samples of the dataset and uses average pooling to improve the predictive accuracy. The predicted values from the multiple decision trees are combined together to obtain the final estimated quality score. Hereby, we briefly provide the training method used for RFNQA.

A random subset of the extracted features is used to generate the training data $X = (x_1, x_2, \ldots x_M)$ and their corresponding labels (Mean Opinion Score (MOS)) $Score = (s_1, s_2, \ldots s_M)$, where M is the training data size. The data is fitted to the decision trees which acts as the base indicator. The process is repeated N times which subsequently generates the set of N base quality scores. Further, to predict the quality score of an unknown sample v (UGC video) is computed by averaging the quality scores from all the decision trees.

$$Score(v) = \frac{1}{N} \sum_{n=1}^{N} P_n(x^{'}) \tag{5}$$

where, P_n denotes the prediction using the decision tree learned at the nth step.

Since each tree is trained with different set of samples, the variance is significantly decreased compared to that of a single tree, leading to better prediction performance.

4   Experimental Results

The performance of RFNQA is evaluated using the benchmark UGCVQA dataset[3] which was made publicly available during the ICME Grand Challenge on Quality Assessment of Compressed UGC videos, 2021[4]. The dataset consists of 7200 UGC videos obtained from multiple video sharing platforms. The reference videos are compressed with H.264 encoder with 7 different levels of compression. The dataset also consists of MOS for both the reference and compressed videos obtained through subjective tests. For training RFNQA we used 6400 videos and subsequently, tested on the rest 800 videos. RFNQA is evaluated in two parts; first, we study various regressing technique and their performance in our model. Subsequently, RFNQA is compared with 9 existing state-of-the-art metrics such as two baseline quality metrics, three quality metrics specific to natural scene, and also with four quality metrics that are specific to UGC videos. Furthermore, the performance of the proposed quality metric and the existing approaches are evaluated using Root Mean Square Error (RMSE), Pearson Linear Correlation Coefficient (PLCC), Spearman's Rank Order Correlation Coefficient (SROCC), and Kendall's Rank Order Correlation Coefficient (KROCC) which are considered as the standard approaches for evaluating a visual quality metric.

The SITI toolbox[5] is used to extract the SI and TI from videos, and the FFMPEG Toolbox[6] is used to find the bitrate and resolution of video frames. Blur values are obtained from OpenCV, which works using the total variance of the Laplacian of each frame[7].

We performed a study on how the different ensemble-based learners effect the overall performance of RFNQA. Experiments were performed using five different approaches for the visual quality predictor module in RFNQA; Linear Regressor (LNR), Support Vector Regressor (SVR), CatBoosting (CatBoost), Gradient Boosting (GBoost) and Random Forest Regressor (RFR). LNR is often used due to the fact that the approach is capable of handling overfitting during the learning process. Whereas, SVR predicts discrete values and is very much robust to outliers. We experimented multiple decision tree based score predictors as well. Such as the GBoost method is based on the intuition that when the best potential next model is coupled with prior models, the overall prediction error is minimised. In CatBoost the primary principle behind boosting is to successively

---

[3] http://ugcvqa.com/.
[4] http://2021.ieeeicme.org/2021.ieeeicme.org/conf_challenges.html.
[5] https://github.com/slhck/siti.
[6] https://github.com/FFmpeg/FFmpeg.
[7] https://github.com/WillBrennan/BlurDetection2.

integrate multiple weak models (models that perform marginally better) to generate a strong competitive prediction model using a greedy search. Finally, RFR creates decision tree for subset of data and combines the outcome of all such decision trees to make the final estimation. The approach is found to be good for handling overfitting and also works well for categorical data. Performance of proposed RFNQA using the six different predictors is presented in Table 1. It can be observed that our proposed model RFNQA performs better with the RFR approach in terms of the four performance metrics (RMSE, PLCC, SROCC, and KROCC). One probable reason for a better performance of RFR for our model is due to the fact that RFR combine results of multiple decision trees to find the optimal result. Additionally, the method is more robust to the overfitting problem.

In the following sub-section, we compare the proposed RFNQA with the existing video quality assessment metrics in literature.

Table 1. Performance analysis of the proposed RFNQA using different regressor models.

Regressor	RMSE↓	PLCC↑	SROCC↑	KROCC↑
CatBoost	0.365	0.957	0.896	0.721
GBoost	0.468	0.928	0.879	0.689
LNR	1.084	0.466	0.470	0.328
SVR	0.841	0.763	0.865	0.664
RFR	**0.359**	**0.959**	**0.938**	**0.783**

4.1 Comparative Study

The proposed RFNQA approach is compared with the quality metrics for natural scenes such as NIQE [10], BRISQUE [11], and VSFA [8]. Quality metrics ITU-T P.1203.1 [14] and DEMI [22] used for two use-cases streaming videos and gaming videos, are also included for comparison. Finally, the existing visual quality metrics specific to UGC videos such as RAPIQUE [17], RM3VQA_KNN [7], RM3VQA_SVR [7] and ELVQ [13] are also selected for comparison purpose. The performance of existing approaches and the proposed approach in terms of the standard metrics are depicted in Table 2. It can be noted here that the performance metric values of the existing approaches on UGC dataset are either directly taken from the published articles [8,13,14,17,22] or re-implemented using available online sources provided by the authors [7,10,11].

Table 2. Performance of the proposed RFNQA with existing video quality metrics.

Metrics	RMSE↓	PLCC↑	SROCC↑	KROCC↑
P.1203.1 [14]	0.550	0.918	0.875	0.694
DEMI [22]	0.992	0.676	0.686	0.496
NIQE [10]	0.976	0.597	0.592	0.417
BRISQUE [11]	0.558	0.888	0.834	0.647
VSFA [8]	0.346	0.959	0.892	0.728
RAPIQUE [17]	0.474	0.9247	0.864	0.689
RM3VQA_KNN [7]	0.490	0.932	0.870	0.695
RM3VQA_SVR [7]	**0.057**	0.936	0.881	0.705
ELVQ [13]	0.294	0.970	0.918	0.761
RFNQA	0.359	**0.959**	**0.938**	**0.783**

The typical quality metrics for natural scene is developed for the traditional video quality assessment where the content is usually generated by professionals. However, in UGC the captured contents are random, and is significantly affected with distortion based on how the media is captured, and also on the specifications of the capturing device. These are some of the probable reasons regarding the decrease in performance of traditional approaches when applied on UGC videos.

The RM3VQA metric mentioned in [7] propose two quality score prediction approaches. One using the support vector regressor, and the other using the K-nearest neighbour. In this work, we mentioned the later as RM3VQA_KNN and the former as RM3VQA_SVR. Although the score predicting method was different, they used the same set of features for quality assessment. It can also be noted here that the RMSE score of RM3VQA_SVR is significantly low in comparison to all the compared approaches including our approach RFNQA. One possible reason behind such an observation is the use of CNN architecture and training it with a fairly large natural image dataset. However, the distortions incorporated in the UGC videos and how they effect the overall visual quality is not considered in both the models of RM3VQA. In a similar direction, the ELVQ metric also uses both encoding and content-based features. However, ELVQ primarily focus on various encoding based features such as the QP value of UGC, and comparatively less towards the content of the videos. Similarly, the RAPIQUE approach do not utilise distortions as the influencing factor in quality assessment. It can also be noted here that the DEMI quality metric [22] which is specific to gaming videos did not perform good on the UGC videos. The gaming videos are computer generated imagery (CGI) and is believed to have real to natural scenes. Therefore, this is another indicator the existing metrics developed for the professionally developed contents fails to assess quality of the user-generated contents. In comparison to the existing approaches, our proposed approach considers more features which are based on the content captured in the videos. Moreover, the use of MSCN in our approach provides the statistical distribution (mean and standard deviation) of the distorted pixels in each extracted frame is believed to be a good indicator towards how distortion effects quality assessment.

5   Conclusion

Visual quality assessment of UGC videos is a challenging task due to the fact that the content is generated randomly, captured using different handheld devices, and having different resolution. Therefore, performance of the standard quality metrics for 2D videos is significantly degraded when used over UGC. In this direction, a random forest-based no-reference visual quality metric for UGC videos is proposed. The metric predicts quality score in two steps, feature extractor and visual quality predictor. In the first step, the video encoding and content based features are extracted and max pooled over each video. Secondly, a random forest regressor is used to predict the visual quality score of the input UGC video. We also study the impact of five different predictors for our proposed model. The observed results show that the random forest regressor is suitable for score predicting in a UGC scenario. Furthermore, the model is compared with nine existing quality metrics in literature. The obtained results depicts that the proposed quality assessment metric outperforms the state-of-the-art metrics considered in this work.

References

1. Barman, N., Khan, N., Martini, M.G.: Analysis of spatial and temporal information variation for 10-bit and 8-bit video sequences. In: International Workshop on Computer Aided Modeling and Design of Communication Links and Networks, pp. 1–6. IEEE (2019)
2. Chen, B., Zhu, L., Li, G., Lu, F., Fan, H., Wang, S.: Learning generalized spatial-temporal deep feature representation for no-reference video quality assessment. IEEE Trans. Circuits Syst. Video Technol. (2021)
3. Chen, Y., Wu, K., Zhang, Q.: From QoS to QoE: a tutorial on video quality assessment. IEEE Commun. Surv. Tutor. **17**(2), 1126–1165 (2014)
4. Chikkerur, S., Sundaram, V., Reisslein, M., Karam, L.J.: Objective video quality assessment methods: a classification, review, and performance comparison. IEEE Trans. Broadcast. **57**(2), 165–182 (2011)
5. ITU-T Recommendation, P.: 910: Subjective video quality assessment methods for multimedia applications (2008)
6. Korhonen, J.: Two-level approach for no-reference consumer video quality assessment. IEEE Trans. Image Process. **28**(12), 5923–5938 (2019)
7. Lamichhane, K., Mazumdar, P., Battisti, F., Carli, M.: A no reference deep learning based model for quality assessment of UGC videos. In: International Conference on Multimedia Expo Workshops, pp. 1–5 (2021)
8. Li, D., Jiang, T., Jiang, M.: Quality assessment of in-the-wild videos. In: ACM International Conference on Multimedia, pp. 2351–2359 (2019)

9. Mazumdar, P., Arru, G., Battisti, F.: Early detection of children with autism spectrum disorder based on visual exploration of images. Signal Process. Image Commun. **94**, 116184 (2021)
10. Mittal, A., Soundararajan, R., Bovik, A.C.: Making a "completely blind" image quality analyzer. IEEE Signal Process. Lett. **20**(3), 209–212 (2012)
11. Mittal, A., Moorthy, A.K., Bovik, A.C.: No-reference image quality assessment in the spatial domain. IEEE Trans. Image Process. **21**(12), 4695–4708 (2012)
12. Nguyen, D., Tran, H., Thang, T.C.: An ensemble learning-based no reference QOE model for user generated contents. In: International Conference on Multimedia Expo Workshops, pp. 1–6 (2021)
13. Nguyen, D., Tran, H., Thang, T.C.: An ensemble learning-based no reference QOE model for user generated contents. In: IEEE International Conference on Multimedia and Expo Workshops, pp. 1–6. IEEE (2021)
14. Raake, A., Garcia, M.N., Robitza, W., List, P., Göring, S., Feiten, B.: A bitstream-based, scalable video-quality model for http adaptive streaming: ITU-T, p. 1203.1. In: International Conference on Quality of Multimedia Experience, pp. 1–6 (2017)
15. Stanković, R.S., Falkowski, B.J.: The HAAR wavelet transform: its status and achievements. Comput. Elect. Eng. **29**(1), 25–44 (2003)
16. Tong, H., Li, M., Zhang, H., Zhang, C.: Blur detection for digital images using wavelet transform. In: IEEE International Conference on Multimedia and Expo, vol. 1, pp. 17–20. IEEE (2004)
17. Tu, Z., Yu, X., Wang, Y., Birkbeck, N., Adsumilli, B., Bovik, A.C.: Rapique: rapid and accurate video quality prediction of user generated content. IEEE Open J. Signal Process. **2**, 425–440 (2021)
18. Varga, D.: No-reference video quality assessment based on Bedford's law and perceptual features. Electronics. **10**(22) (2021). https://www.mdpi.com/2079-9292/10/22/2768
19. Wang, Y., et al.: Rich features for perceptual quality assessment of UGC videos. In: IEEE/CVF Conference on Computer Vision and Pattern Recognition, pp. 13435–13444 (2021)
20. Yao, J.Y., Liu, G.: Bitrate-based no-reference video quality assessment combining the visual perception of video contents. IEEE Trans. Broadcast. **65**(3), 546–557 (2018)
21. Yu, X., et al.: Subjective quality assessment of user-generated content gaming videos. In: IEEE/CVF Winter Conference on Applications of Computer Vision, pp. 74–83 (2022)
22. Zadtootaghaj, S., et al.: Demi: deep video quality estimation model using perceptual video quality dimensions. In: International Workshop on Multimedia Signal Processing, pp. 1–6. IEEE (2020)

Endmember Extraction with Unknown Number of Sources for Hyperspectral Unmixing

Gouri Shankar Chetia⬤ and Bishnulatpam Pushpa Devi$^{(\boxtimes)}$⬤

National Institute of Technology Meghalaya, Shillong 793003, Meghalaya, India
{p19ec010,bishnulatpam.pushpa}@nitm.ac.in

Abstract. Hyperspectral Unmixing requires a prior known number of endmembers present at the scene. Most blind hyperspectral unmixing methods perform the estimation of the number of endmembers as a separate step before extracting those endmembers. Recent approaches to bridge this gap and simultaneously count and extract endmembers increase accuracy of the overall unmixing process and promote the applicability of unsupervised unmixing. In this paper, we propose a new method to extract the endmembers without requiring a prior number of endmembers or a separate step to finding them. The method also attempts to address a few limitations of the existing methods which mainly follow distance-based linear mixing models. The proposed method is based on the fact that the non-endmembers are either linear combinations of the endmembers or a spectral variant of an endmember. The method follows a linear mixing model which imposes the non-negative and sum-to-one constraints on the abundances. Our method first violates the sum-to-one constraint and iteratively adds endmembers to reinforce the constraint. The method removes the redundant spectra by applying a redundancy reduction technique based on correlation. The iterative process and the optimization are applied to a few selected spectra leading to a much faster approach. The proposed method is compared with other competing methods and is found to be faster with increased accuracy.

Keywords: Hyperspectral unmixing · Endmember estimation · Endmember extraction · Spectral redundancy removal

1 Introduction

Hyperspectral Images(HSI) capture the reflectances across the electromagnetic spectrum in hundreds of continuous bands with narrow bandgap. Depending on the applications, HSI can be acquired by remotely sensed satellites (space-borne), air crafts (airborne), and field spectroscopy [1]. Remotely sensed HSI suffers the problem of mixed pixels due to lower spatial resolution [2]. The higher spectral resolution (numbers of bands) allows only a lower spatial resolution to maintain a trade-off between the data size and image information. The reflectances

© The Author(s), under exclusive license to Springer Nature Switzerland AG 2023
D. Gupta et al. (Eds.): CVIP 2022, CCIS 1776, pp. 567–578, 2023.
https://doi.org/10.1007/978-3-031-31407-0_42

reaching the HSI sensor may come from several distinct ground objects known as endmembers, resulting in a mixture of spectra from different endmembers. The pixels containing such mixtures of spectra are called mixed pixels. Thus, a model is required to unmix the mixed pixels to obtain the constituents of individual endmembers affecting the mixed pixels. In real HSI, the spectra of endmembers are not known a priori, thus leading to a much harder ill-posed problem. The unsupervised unmixing is essentially a blind source separation problem [3] and requires an estimated number of endmembers, to begin with. The unsupervised unmixing method is also known as Blind Hyperspectral Unmixing(BHU). BHU extracts the endmembers and calculates their fractional abundances per pixel. The process starts by estimating the number of endmembers at the scene. The signatures of endmembers are extracted using endmember extraction algorithm (EEA). Finally, the abundances of the found endmembers are calculated for each pixel to obtain the fraction of different endmembers at that pixel.

Unsupervised EEA can be categorized as geometrical and statistical approaches. The convex geometry-based approaches exploit certain geometrical properties of the HSI data, such as the convex hull of all the endmember signatures, denotes a $(1 - P)$ simplex (for p number of endmembers) [4] and the vertices of such simplex represent pure pixels. The fact that all endmember signatures are linearly independent also makes it affinely independent and thus forms a simplex [5]. Few algorithms based on this principle are vertex component analysis (VCA) [6], N-FINDR [7], simplex volume maximization and, minimization (SVMAX) [8]. Other geometrical methods which do not assume the presence of pure pixels are the minimum volume simplex analysis (MVSA) [9], minimum-volume enclosing simplex (MVES) [10] and the simplex identification via variable splitting and augmented Lagrangian (SISAL) [11]. The former methods (assuming pure pixel) are faster compared to the latter, but the availability of pure pixel in real data is a subjective condition. Thus under highly mixed pixel scenarios the latter outperforms the former.

Statistical methods perform better in terms of highly mixed scenarios and endmember variability but are computationally expensive. Based on such a model, the Non-Negative Matrix factorization(NMF) method decomposes image data into a set of non-negative matrices. With the known matrix X(image data), NMF reconstructs unknown matrices M and an (endmember matrix and abundance matrix respectively) by minimizing the reconstruction error which requires solving a non-convex optimization problem. Minimum volume constraint NMF(MVC-NMF) [12] is a BHU method that combines the concept of convex geometry and NMF to estimate endmembers and their abundances simultaneously. Although all the EEAs mentioned here can be used in different applications depending on their implications, all of them require a prior estimated number of endmembers. Estimation of the number of endmembers itself is a separate problem and can be approximated with approaches such as virtual dimensionality based Harsanyi-Farrand-Chang (HFC) method [13], subspace estimation [14], and geometry-based estimation of the number of endmembers (GENE) [15]. The accuracy of the EEA algorithm is highly affected by the number of estimated endmembers. Thus there is a need to simultaneously estimate and extract the endmembers. A few approaches that attempt to bridge this gap between the two independent processes are presented in the divergent sets method [16] and maximum distance analysis [17]. DS method attempts to find the pixels with the most discriminability from other pixels using distance-based criteria. The feature distance, Euclidean distance, and divergent degree between each pixel and each subset are calculated to select the most distinct pixels in the image. The pixel-wise calculations increase the time complexity and relying only on distance-based parameters can decrease accuracy in the case of real data due to the presence of spectral variabilities. [18]

MDA method is similar to the DS method and follows distance-based endmember estimation and extraction. It is based on the fact that the vertices of the simplex with maximum volume are endmembers. The method attempts to estimate the farthest pixel in the affine hull formed by already found endmembers. This approach is not suitable for highly mixed and noisy data and can be seriously affected by variabilities within endmembers.

In this paper, we propose an unsupervised method to estimate and extract endmembers based on both distance-based selection and abundance-based removal of mixed pixels. The method can be applied to a set of selected pixels that can be initialized by any EEA or based on spatial property. Thus improving computational cost and removal of redundancy and iterative endmembers selection enforcing abundance constraints improve the accuracy. The proposed method addresses the few drawbacks of simultaneously counting and extracting endmembers methods and promotes the applicability of such methods in real remotely sensed HSI data.

2 Methodology

The process of the proposed method is shown in Fig. 1. The method is initialized by extracting a set of an overestimated number of endmembers using any EEA. This overestimated set of spectral signatures is named as Candidate Endmembers (M_c). Assuming that the required final set of endmembers is contained within the set of candidate endmembers, the method proceeds to the next step of removing redundancy. The highly correlated spectra are a result of spectral variability which are eliminated to obtain only the distinct spectral signatures named as Reduced Endmembers (M_{re}). Although the number of candidate endmembers reduces significantly after eliminating the remaining redundant signatures but may still contain the mixed pixels which are essentially a linear combination of the pure pixels. The final step is to remove such mixed pixels by iteratively selecting and eliminating endmembers from M_{re}, and finally we obtain the set of final endmembers (M_f) after satisfying the ASC.

The Linear Mixing Model. The hyperspectral image cube contains reflectance values across the electromagnetic spectrum with a very narrow bandgap [19]. Thus it can be represented as a 3D matrix with reflectance values

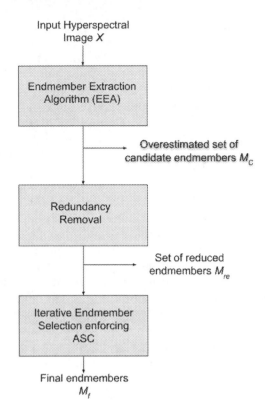

Fig. 1. Block diagram representation of the proposed method

along the third dimension. Let us consider an HSI X with L number of bands and N number of pixels. Suppose there are P numbers of endmember at the scene and their signatures are represented by M. Thus M is a matrix of size $P \times L$ containing $\{m_1, m_2, ..., m_p\}$ column vectors representing the endmembers signatures. The abundance matrix A is a $N \times P$ matrix containing the fractional abundances of the endmembers per pixel. Considering the noise and other reconstruction errors as n, the linear mixing model is given as:

$$X = MA + n \tag{1}$$

where X is subject to two constraints:

$$\forall \, a_{ij} >= 0 \tag{2}$$

and

$$\sum_{j=1}^{P} a_{ij} = 1 \tag{3}$$

where a_{ij} represents abundance of jth endmember present at i^{th} pixel. Using this model, the linear unmixing problem estimates the unknown abundances by solving the inverse of (1) subject to the constraints (2) and (3). Thus unmixing is an optimization problem given by

$$A = minimize||X - MA|| \tag{4}$$
$$s.t. \ (2) \ and \ (3)$$

Redundancy Removal. The candidate endmembers are over-estimated and may contain variants of the same endmembers and mixed pixels. Although the choice of EEA for initialization affects the presence of mixed pixels, but over-estimated candidate endmembers may include certain mixed pixels. For e.g. convex geometry-based EEA may include mixed pixels closer to the vertex. In this step, the highly correlated candidate signatures are grouped and the redundant signatures are removed. Let us consider the candidate endmembers as $M_c = \{m_{c1}, m_{c2}, ..., m_{cPO}\}$ where PO is the overestimated number of endmembers. The correlation matrix M_{CR} is given by:

$$M_{CR} = \begin{pmatrix} 1 & \rho(m_{c2}, m_{c1}) & \cdots & \rho(m_{cPO}, m_{c1}) \\ \rho(m_{c1}, m_{c2}) & 1 & \cdots & \rho(m_{cPO}, m_{c2}) \\ \vdots & \vdots & \ddots & \vdots \\ \rho(m_{c1}, m_{cPO}) & \cdots & \cdots & 1 \end{pmatrix} \tag{5}$$

After replacing the diagonal element with 0, from Eq. (5), the indices of row and column $M_{CR} > 0.95$ are extracted. The threshold value of 0.95 ensures that the signatures are highly correlated [20]. The indices are compared with each other to group them together such that every group contains indices that satisfy the above thresholding with at least one member of the group. The repeated indices are removed and the spectra corresponding to the indices for every group are extracted from the set of candidate endmembers. Since each group represents the same endmembers, one of them is to be selected as a reduced endmember for further processing. The euclidean distance (ED) based selection is performed to obtain the fastest pixel from origin. The pixel with maximum distance is more likely to be a pure pixel as compared to their correlated counterparts. Therefore the ED D_{ij} between i^{th} and j^{th} pixels of the HSI having L number of bands can be calculated as:

$$D(i,j) = \sqrt{\sum_{l=1}^{L} (x_{li} - x_{lj})^2} \tag{6}$$

Based on (6), the signature corresponding maximum D_{ij} from each group is selected to get the set of reduced endmembers M_{re}. The final endmembers are selected from the set of reduced endmembers by iteratively adding endmembers and enforcing the ASC constraint as described in the next section.

Iterative Endmember Selection Enforcing ASC. From the previous steps, we have the reduced endmembers M_{re} from which the final set of endmembers are to be extracted. This step eliminates the spectra which are linear combinations of other endmembers. The obtained reduced endmember matrix $M_{re} = \{M_{1re}, M_{2re}, ..., M_{kre}\}$, where M_{kre} is the column vector representing k^{th} reduced endmember signature. We select first two final endmembers from M_{re} using ED as given in (6). The first final endmember corresponds to the maximum ED from origin and the second final endmember is choosen to be the one farthest from the first endmember. Thus the first two final endmembers can be written as $M_f = \{M_{f1}, M_{f2}\}$.

Algorithm 1. Algorithm for Iterative Endmember Selection enforcing ASC

$Input : Reduced\ endmember\ matrix\ M_{re}$

$Find\ 1^{st}\ and\ 2^{nd}\ final\ endmember\ M_f\ using\ (6)$

while $cond = 1$ **do**
    for $i = 1\ to\ no.\ of\ columns\ in\ M_{re}$ **do**
        $solve\ (7)\ for\ every\ column\ in\ M_{re}$
        $find\ \alpha$
    end for
    $Diff \leftarrow abs(1 - sum(\alpha))$
    if $any\ 0.98 \geq \alpha \geq 1.02$ **then**   ▷ α not close to 1
        $cond \leftarrow 1$
        $find\ new\ M_f\ corresponding\ to\ max(Diff)$
    else
        $cond \leftarrow 0$
    end if
end while

To estimate the rest of the endmembers, each signatures in M_{re} are iteratively reconstructed using M_f to find the linear combination of M_f present in M_{re}. This is essentially a least-square optimization problem given by:

$$\alpha = minimize\ ||\alpha M_f - M_{rek}||$$
$$s.t.\ \forall\ \alpha >= 0\ and\ \sum \alpha = 1 \tag{7}$$

The ASC in (7) can be violated here (which will be enforced later) to make (7) a non negative least square problem. To make the range of α between 0 to 1, both M_f and M_{re} are multiplied by a value δ which is given by:

$$\delta_{M_f} = \frac{1}{max(M_f)} \tag{8}$$

$$\delta_{M_{re}} = \frac{1}{max(M_{re})} \tag{9}$$

After solving (7), the α values corresponding to each M_{re} column are added to detect whether the reduced signature M_{rek} can be reconstruced using linear combination of the final endmembers or not. The following condition is tested on every column vector of M_{rek}:

$$\sum \alpha \approx 1 \tag{10}$$

If Eq. (8) is satisfied for any M_{rek}, it will be removed and the M_{rek} corresponding to $max\{abs|1-\sum\alpha|\}$ will be considered as next endmember and will be added to M_f. The process continues until sum of all α is closer to 1. Finally we will obtain the set of final endmembers after simultaneously satisfying the ASC constraint.

3   Experimental Results

The proposed method is tested on both synthetic and real HSI data. The experiments are performed on Matlab-R 2019 on a 3.4 GHz CPU, and 8 GB RAM. The results of the number of endmember estimation are compared with HFC, Hysime, DS, and MDA methods. The accuracy of the extracted endmembers is compared with VCA+Hysime, DS, and MDA methods. The evaluation parameters for extracted endmembers are root mean squared error (RMSE) and spectral angle distance (SAD) [21] which are calculated by Eqs. (11) and (12) respectively. Let the actual endmembers be represented by matrix $\hat{M}$ and the estimated endmember is M_f with p number of endmembers. Therefore SAD and RMSE is between $\hat{M}$ and M_f is given by:

$$SAD = \sqrt{\frac{1}{p}\Sigma_{i=1}^{p}\left[arccos\left(\frac{\hat{M}_i^{T}M_{fi}}{||\hat{M}_i||||M_{fi}||}\right)\right]^2} \tag{11}$$

$$RMSE = \sqrt{\frac{1}{p}\Sigma_{i=1}^{p}\left(\frac{\hat{M}_i - M_{fi}}{L}\right)^2} \tag{12}$$

where L is the number of bands in $\hat{M}$ and M_f. The value of 0 for both SAD and RMSE means that both estimated and actual endmembers are the same. The values of SAD and RMSE closer to 0 indicate very good accuracy of extracted endmembers.

Synthetic HSI Data. The synthetic data are created using Hyperspectral Imagery Synthesis tools for MATLAB [22] and the endmembers are selected from the United States Geological Survey (USGS) spectral library. We create a synthetic image with size $128 \times 128 \times 431$ containing 5 endmembers using the Legendre method of the least square polynomial as provided in [22]. The true endmember spectral signatures of the generated image are shown in Fig. 2.

Our method is initialized by considering overestimated number of endmembers as 50 and extracting endmembers using the VCA algorithm. We considered VCA because of its fast computation and good accuracy. After performing the

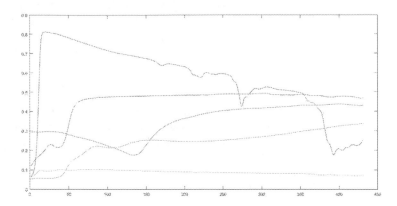

Fig. 2. True endmember signatures of the synthetic data. X-axis represents the band number ranging from 1 to 431 and Y-axis represents their respective reflectance values normalized between 0 to 1.

redundancy reduction and iterative endmember extraction enforcing ASC, we obtain 5 endmember spectra as our final endmembers. The number of columns in M_f is our estimated number of endmembers. The performance evaluation of the obtained final endmembers compared with VCA+Hysime, DS and MDA are illustrated in Table 1. A series of tests for all the methods were performed on the dataset and the best results obtained by each of the methods are evaluated.

Table 1. Comparison of the proposed method in terms of the counted number of endmembers, RMSE, SAD, and execution time (algorithm running time) with VCA+Hysime, DS, and MDA methods for the synthetic hyperspectral image of size128 × 128 × 431 containing 5 endmembers.

Method	Number of endmembers	RMSE	SAD	Execution time (sec)
VCA+Hysime	5	0.2828	17.144	3.498
DS	8	0.1989	14.51	1.618
MDA	5	0.242	19.3249	0.557
Proposed	5	0.216	18.87	0.340

All methods accurately counted the number of endmembers except for the DS method. To analyze the performance of extracted endmembers of the DS method, only the first 5 endmembers are considered. Although the estimated number of endmembers for the DS method is not accurate, the extracted endmembers have the highest accuracy among all methods. Our proposed method performs better than the MDA and VCA+Hysime methods and the results are comparable to the DS method. From the computational point of view, our method outperforms all the other methods.

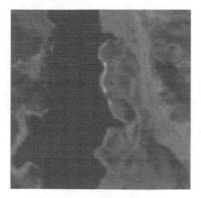

(a) Jasper Ridge Image

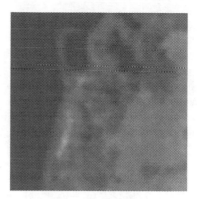

(b) Samson Image

Fig. 3. False color RGB image of the real HSI datasets

Real HSI Data. The real HSI Jasper Ridge dataset with resolution $100 \times 100 \times 198$ has four endmembers(Trees, Water, Road and Soil) and the Samson dataset with resolution $95 \times 95 \times 156$ has three endmembers(Trees, Water and Soil). These real datasets are subsets of original space-borne HSI which are atmospherically corrected and bad bands are removed. The false-color reconstructed image for Jasper Ridge and Samson datasets are shown in Figs. 3.a. and 3.b. respectively. The number of endmembers counted by the proposed method is dependent on the EEA used to initialize the overestimated set. Using VCA as our EEA, the initialized set becomes inconsistent, resulting in different sets on different runs. Thus the counted number of endmembers tends to vary on different runs. Therefore the obtained results are the average of the counted endmembers in 10 different runs for the algorithm. Table 2 shows the counted number of endmembers estimated by the proposed method as compared to other methods.

Table 2. Number of endmembers estimated by the proposed method as compared to other methods for Jasper Ridge dataset with 4 endmembers and Samson dataset with 3 endmembers. GT: Ground Truth

Method	Jasper	samson
HFC	9	9
Hysime	18	43
DS	08	06
MDA	–	–
Proposed	5	4
GT	4	3

For the HFC method, we have to provide a false alarm probability P_{fa} to find a threshold value corresponding to each band in the image. The value of P_{fa} is varied from 10^{-3} to 10^{-6} and the best results are considered for evaluation. The HFC method counted 9 endmembers for both Jasper Ridge and Samson datasets whereas Hysime counted 18 and 43 respectively. Hysime produces the most inaccurate results compared to all the methods. The MDA method, on the other hand, failed to estimate the number of endmembers, and the algorithm iterates till the maximum allowed endmembers. This proves the inability of distance-based criteria in the linear mixing model to estimate endmembers. The method also fails when pure pixels are not available or when the data is noisy. DS method performs better than HFC, Hysime, and MDA, and the counted endmembers are closer to the ground truth. Although the DS method when implemented with other EEAs to initialize can improve the estimation as presented in [16], but here only the VCA initialized DS method results are evaluated. Among all the compared methods, the accuracy of our method is the highest and the estimated number is close to the ground truth.

The accuracy of the estimated number of endmembers varies significantly and further affects the results of extracted endmembers. Therefore the performance evaluation for the real data is carried out by selecting the first P extracted endmembers for each method. Where P is the true number of endmembers in the dataset. Table 3 shows the performance comparison of the extracted endmembers for the proposed method as compared to other methods. For both real datasets, we can see that the extracted endmembers from the DS method are most accurate followed by our proposed method. Results of MDA are less accurate as compared to the other two.

Table 3. Performance comparison of the extracted endmembers for the proposed method as compared to other methods

Method	Jasper		Samson	
Parameters (horizontally)	RMSE	SAD	RMSE	SAD
DS	1.812	35.607	0.541	50.099
MDA	2.207	23.455	0.393	51.35
Proposed	1.632	12.63	0.412	51.86

The computational time to execute these methods for HSI of size $58 \times 58 \times 188$ and $100 \times 100 \times 198$ is shown in Table 4. HFC+VCA is the fastest method with slightly less computation time than our method. Hysime+VCA is the computationally most expensive. The DS method also has a high computational cost which is comparable with Hysime. MDA, on the other hand has a computational cost between DS and the proposed method.

The performance of methods discussed here depends on all three parameters: counting, extracting endmembers, and computational costs. Summarizing the performance for all three parameters we can conclude that our proposed method outperforms other methods in counting the endmembers and computational time with comparable accuracy in extracting endmembers.

Table 4. Comparison of execution time of the proposed method and the other competing methods

Method	Resolution of size $58 \times 58 \times 188$	Resolution of size $100 \times 100 \times 198$
HFC+VCA	0.122	0.243
Hysime+VCA	0.425	1.29
DS	0.837	1.55
MDA	0.432	0.495
Proposed	0.11	0.326

4   Conclusions

We have developed a new algorithm to extract endmembers when the number of sources is not available. Our method introduces an alternative approach to this relatively new field of simultaneously estimating and extracting endmembers and addresses the shortcomings of the existing distance-based methods. The algorithm is designed to eliminate redundancy and mixed pixels to tackle the spectral variabilities. Moreover, performing the optimization problem on a reduced set of selected pixels decreases the computational burden leading to a faster method. The method is tested on synthetic and real datasets and obtained better results than the existing state-of-the-art methods.

The method can be improved by selecting an EEA which does not assume the presence of pure pixels. The dependence of the initialized set of pixels on EEA can be regarded as a disadvantage of this method. An alternative to such limitation would be to involve spatial information-based selection of candidate pixels from the local neighborhood region of the image. Our future work will include the applicability of such approaches in highly mixed scenarios and real HSIs.

References

1. Ghamisi, P., et al.: Advances in hyperspectral image and signal processing: a comprehensive overview of the state of the art. IEEE Geosci. Remote Sens. Mag. **5**(4), 37–78 (2017)
2. Bioucas-Dias, J.M., et al.: Hyperspectral unmixing overview: geometrical, statistical, and sparse regression-based approaches. IEEE J. Sel. Top. Appl. Earth Observ. Remote Sens. **5**(2), 354–379 (2012)
3. Ma, W.-K., et al.: A signal processing perspective on hyperspectral unmixing: insights from remote sensing. IEEE Signal Process. Mag. **31**(1), 67–81 (2014)
4. Drumetz, L., Chanussot, J., Jutten, C., Ma, W.-K., Iwasaki, A.: Spectral variability aware blind hyperspectral image unmixing based on convex geometry. IEEE Trans. Image Process. **29**(1), 4568–4582 (2020)
5. Xu, H., Fu, N., Qiao, L., Peng, X.: Directly estimating endmembers for compressive hyperspectral images. Sensors **15**(4), 9305–9323 (2015)

6. Nascimento, J.M., Dias, J.M.: Vertex component analysis: a fast algorithm to unmix hyperspectral data. IEEE Trans. Geosci. Remote Sens. **43**(1), 898–910 (2005)
7. Winter, M.E.: N-FINDR: an algorithm for fast autonomous spectral end-member determination in hyperspectral data. In: Proceedings of SPIE Conference Imaging Spectrometry, Pasadena, CA, October 1999, pp. 266–275 (1999)
8. Chan, T.-H., Ma, W.-K., Ambikapathi, A., Chi, C.-Y.: A simplex volume maximization framework for hyperspectral endmember extraction. IEEE Trans. Geosci. Remote Sens. **49**(11), 4177–4193 (2011)
9. Li, J., Bioucas-Dias, J.: Minimum volume simplex analysis: a fast algorithm to Unmix hyperspectral data. In: Proceedings of IEEE International Conference Geoscience Remote Sensing (IGARSS) 2008, vol. 3, pp. 250–253 (2008)
10. Chan, T.H., Chi, C.Y., Huang, Y.M., Ma, W.K.: A convex analysis-based minimum-volume enclosing simplex algorithm for hyperspectral unmixing. IEEE Trans. Signal Process. **57**(1), 4418–4432 (2009)
11. Bioucas-Dias, J.M.: A variable splitting augmented Lagragian approach to linear spectral unmixing. In: Proceedings IEEE GRSS Workshop Hyperspectral Image Signal Process: Evolution in Remote Sensing (WHISPERS) 2009, pp. 1–4 (2004)
12. Miao, L., Qi, H.: Endmember extraction from highly mixed data using minimum volume constrained nonnegative matrix factorization. IEEE Trans. Geosci. Remote Sens. **45**(1), 765–777 (2007)
13. Chang, C.I., Du, Q.: Estimation of number of spectrally distinct signal sources in hyperspectral imagery. IEEE Trans. Geosci. Remote Sens. **42**(1), 608–619 (2004)
14. Bioucas-Dias, J.M., Nascimento, J.M.: Hyperspectral subspace identification. IEEE Trans. Geosci. Remote Sens. **46**(1), 2435–2445 (2008)
15. Ambikapathi, A., Chan, T.H., Chi, C.Y., Keizer, K.: Hyperspectral data geometry-based estimation of number of endmembers using p-norm-based pure pixel identification algorithm. IEEE Trans. Geosci. Remote Sens. **51**(1), 2753–2769 (2012)
16. Tao, X., Cui, T., Plaza, A., Ren, P.: Simultaneously counting and extracting endmembers in a hyperspectral image based on divergent subsets. IEEE Trans. Geosci. Remote Sens. **58**(12), 8952–8966 (2020)
17. Tao, X., Paoletti, M.E., Haut, J.M., Ren, P., Plaza, J., Plaza, A.: Endmember estimation with maximum distance analysis. Remote Sens. **13**(4), 713 (2021)
18. Veganzones, M.A., et al.: A new extended linear mixing model to address spectral variability. In: 6th Workshop on Hyperspectral Image and Signal Processing: Evolution in Remote Sensing (WHISPERS) 2014, pp. 1–4 (2014). https://doi.org/10.1109/WHISPERS.2014.8077595
19. Khan, M.J., Khan, H.S., Yousaf, A., Khurshid, K., Abbas, A.: Modern trends in hyperspectral image analysis: a review. IEEE Access. **6**(1), 14118–14129 (2018)
20. Du, W., Kirlin, R.L.: Correlation matrix estimation and order selection for spectrum estimation. In: IEEE Sixth SP Workshop on Statistical Signal and Array Processing, 1992, pp. 86–89 (1992). https://doi.org/10.1109/SSAP.1992.246854
21. Keshava, N.: Distance metrics and band selection in hyperspectral processing with applications to material identification and spectral libraries. IEEE Trans. Geosci. Remote Sens. **42**(7), 1552–1565 (2004)
22. Hyperspectral Imagery Synthesis (EIAs) toolbox, Grupo de Inteligencia Computacional, Universidad del Pat's Vasco/Euskal Herriko Unibertsitatea (UPV/EHU), Spain. https://www.ehu.es/ccwintco

Advancement in Spectrum Sensing Algorithms in Cognitive Radio Architecture

Tejal Shambharkar[1], Ila Sharma[1(✉)], and Shikha Maurya[2]

[1] Malaviya National Institute of Technology, Jaipur, India
ila.ece@mnit.ac.in
[2] National Institute of Technology, Patna, India

Abstract. Cognitive Radio Networks (CRNs) consider as one of the advanced and emerging technologies that can be employed in 5G/6G and beyond to satisfy the high data rate demand of wireless communication by reducing the channel scarcity problem. The objective of CRN is to permit the unlicensed/secondary users (SUs) to efficiently utilize the available licensed spectrum without affecting the operations of licensed/primary users (PUs). While implementing CRNs, SUs have to face several challenges such as the detection of PUs as well as resource allocation problems, which occur due to the interference between PU and SU, and between SU and SU. CRN faces problems like inter-symbol interference (ISI) and a lower data rate. Hence to reduce the problem of ISI and to achieve a higher data rate, the Orthogonal Frequency Division Multiplexing (OFDM) technique utilized in CRN. It proves advantageous since it lowers the ISI, pro-vides interoperability, and also improves spectrum sensing. However, OFDM exhibits a spectrum leakage problem. As a solution to this, Filter Bank based Multi-Carrier (FBMC) technique can be employed in the cognitive radio (CR) scenarios. In this paper, we explore different directions and applications where FBMC can be employed with CRNs.

Keywords: Cognitive radio · Spectrum sensing · FBMC

1 Introduction

As the number of wireless communication users continuously increases, each user needs more and more bandwidth. However, the available frequency range is limited. In a study published in early millennium [1], Mitola attempts to reconcile this conflict by introducing the idea of cognitive radio (CR). Primary users (PUs) as well as secondary users (SUs) are the two main entities introduced in CR. When the PUs are not transmitting or receiving data on the licensed spectrum or sections of it [2], SUs can send or receive signals on the licensed spectrum. SUs have ability to access the radio environment and utilize the unused licensed spectrum wisely and passing it over to PUs when they start transmitting [3]. It is needed to obtain information about radio environment and discover spectrum holes in order to run CR systems successfully. There is difficulty in identifying and detecting PU signals in a noisy and hostile channel environment.

Filter bank based multi-carrier (FBMC) is employed in CRN due to having the same flexibility as Orthogonal frequency division multiplexing (OFDM) in terms of using

D. Gupta et al. (Eds.): CVIP 2022, CCIS 1776, pp. 579–588, 2023.
https://doi.org/10.1007/978-3-031-31407-0_43

spectrum holes, but it is less susceptible to rapid time change of the timing offset and channel due to lack of synchronization [4]. In FBMC, there is no need of cyclic prefix (CP) extension and it is more resilient to frequency offsets than OFDM. As a result, FBMC is utilized in a spectrum sensing (SS) process to its lower cost and its excellent performance [2]. It has observed that with small spectral leakage of its prototype filter, the use of FBMC with CR networks can have a significant impact on the Inter-Channel Interference (ICI) caused by timing offset, which reduces the overall information rates of the system and interference between PUs and SUs [5]. Hence it is needed to explore more research and state of art on FBMC based CR methodologies for an efficient CRN.

In this paper, the benefits of FBMC in CR spectrum sensing has been studied. Spectrum sensing is essential functionality in CR to detect the spectrum holes efficiently at small signal to noise ratio (SNR) level. Thus, detection of PUs is the main challenge in CR technology. In literature, there are several techniques available for the detection of PUs in which energy detection based spectrum sensing is one of the most commonly used technique due to its lower computational complexity. However, it cannot detect PUs at low SNR. Therefore, FBMC can be used to detect PUs at low SNR.

The remaining paper is arranged as follows: Basic architecture of CR and its scenarios are discussed in Sect. 2 and Sect. 3, respectively, Sect. 4 discuss different spectrum sensing techniques. Further, advantages of FBMC in CR is discussed in Sect. 5. Some Challenges and future directions are also described in Sect. 6. Finally, conclusions are drawn in Sect. 7.

2   Cognitive Radio Architecture

2.1   Functionality of Cognitive Radio Networks (CRNs):

There are two main qualities of CR, i.e., cognitive capability and configurability. The ability to sense information from the environment is referred to as cognitive capability. Whereas, configurability enables the CR to continuously arrange its parameters in response to the environment [3]. As shown in Fig. 1, a cognitive cycle can be used to describe the basic functions of a CRN.

(a) **Spectrum Sensing (SS).** The fundamental property of SU in CR is to identify the presence of PU in the licensed spectrum and leave the spectrum as soon as PU starts its transmission to prevent the interference with PU. So, SS identifies and distributes available spectrum without interfering with other users

(b) **Spectrum Decision.:** CRs have the ability to choose the best available spectrum for the transmission of SUs in order to fulfill their quality-of-service (QoS) requirements without interfering with PUs.

(c) **Spectrum Sharing.** It is the technique in which CR shares the resources required for SUs.

(d) **Spectrum Mobility.** Whenever PU is available for transmission of data over the channel occupied by SU, SU will vacate that channel immediately so that smooth continuous transmission is sustained.

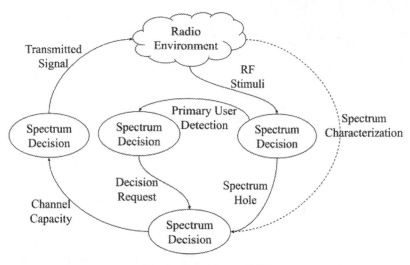

Fig. 1. Cognitive cycle [3]

CR can be mainly classified into two categories: available spectrum property, spectrum access technique.

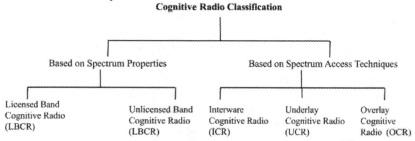

2.2 CRN Architecture

CRN architecture is made up of primary and secondary networks. A primary network includes one or more PUs and one or more primary base stations (BS). PUs can communicate among each other through BS only. A secondary network includes SUs which communicate with each other either directly or by using base station (BS). The licensed spectrum band can only be accessible by SUs when it is unused by PUs. Secondary BS can be referred to as hub for secondary network. When numerous secondary networks use a shared frequency band, a central network entity called a spectrum broker can correlate their spectrum consumption [4]. The spectrum broker collect data from the secondary network and applies it to spectrum sharing. In CR, SU can temporarily use the unoccupied licensed bands that are known as spectrum hole which belongs to the PUs [6] (Fig. 2).

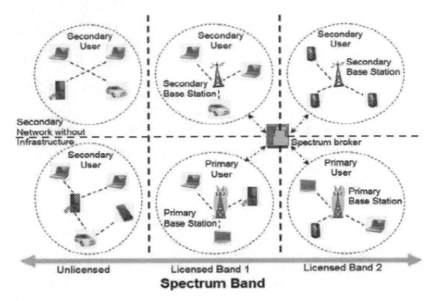

Fig. 2. CRN architecture [7]

3   Spectrum Sensing in Cognitive Radio

In this paper, we are focusing on interweave spectrum access mode of operation. The aim of CR is to increase spectrum efficiency by detecting the presence of spectrum holes and transmitting in it without any interference. Thus, SS is an important feature of CR for the identification of the spectrum holes and make sure that SU does not interfere with PU. SU must detect [8] the spectrum often, while reducing latency period which is spent sensing in order to make optimal use of the available spectrum opportunities. SS as a generic technique is difficult to put together, and particular approaches must be developed based on real applications. Detection of signal is based on two criteria: "probability of detection (Pd) and probability of false alarm (Pfa). Probability of detection denotes the probability of a cognitive radio user declaring that a primary user is present when the spectrum is indeed occupied by a primary user [5]. Probability of false alarm denotes the probability of a cognitive radio user declaring that a primary user is present when the spectrum is free [5]. A false alarm therefore signifies the reduction of the CR throughput (missing the spectrum holes)". Two hypothesis representation for spectrum sensing problem is given by

$$H_0 : Y[n] = W[n] \ (\textit{If PU is absent}) \tag{1}$$

$$H_1 : Y[n] = hS[n] + W[n] \ (\textit{If PU is present}) \tag{2}$$

where, Y is received signal at SU, S is signal from PU, h is the channel gain and W is additive white Gaussian noise(AWGN) signal. To evaluate the performance, result of test statistic (τ) is compared with predefined threshold value (λ). The result is given as:

$$\tau > \lambda \quad ' \quad \text{PU is present}$$
$$\tau > \lambda \quad \quad \text{PU is absent}$$

SS can be done by detecting the signal strength in the spectrum and for that different signal detection techniques can be used such as matched filter, energy detection, and cyclostationary feature detector [9–12] (Table 1).

Table 1. Features of spectrum sensing techniques [12].

Techniques	Advantages	Disadvantages
Matched Filter based Techniques	Optimal performance Least computation cost and quick sensing	primary user information required High power High complexity
Energy Detection based Techniques	Low complexity Independent of any prior information about primary signal Low computational cost	In noisy environment, can't distinguish between signal and noise
Cyclostationary Feature Detection based Techniques	Robust against noise interference and uncertainty Applicable to low signal to noise ratio	primary user information required High complexity Long sensing time

4   FBMC Based Spectrum Sensing in Cognitive Radio

FBMC has become a much better solution for overcoming the restrictions that exist in OFDM systems because of the lower guard bands between symbols and the absence of CP. When compared to OFDM with a cyclic prefix, FBMC has less spectrum leakage [13]. FBMC can detect multiple number of users having different center frequencies and also users with spectral holes. Farhang first developed the notion of FBMC in [2] for SS.

Cosine Modulated Multi-Tone (CMT), Offset Quadrature Amplitude Modulation (OQAM), and Filtered Multi-Tone (FMT) are three basic FBMC techniques that have been introduced. Unlike OFDM, which sends complex-symbols at constant data rate, it is feasible to accomplish baud rate spacing between consecutive subcarrier channels and retrieve the symbol by inserting delay in-between in phase and quadrature components of QAM signals, which does not have ISI and Inter-Carrier Interference. CMT [14] has a great bandwidth efficiency and the capacity to do blind detection [10] due to the underlying signals' unique structure. Because of CMT's reconstruction characteristic, overlapping neighboring bands may be separated precisely when numerous adjacent bands are utilized for transmission. Another FBMC method, FMT, was first developed for DSL applications [11]. When compared to CMT, it enables neighboring bands to overlap. In FMT, the subcarrier bands do not overlap. As a result, the main distinction between CMT and FMT is how the frequency band is employed. Distinct subcarrier signals in FMT can be split using traditional filtering. The overlapping subcarrier bands in CMT, on the other hand, need be separated by complex filtering design, i.e. FMT, which allows for straightforward and flexible signal processing at the receiver, may be appealing from an implementation standpoint. CMT, on the other side, can provide greater blind detection capabilities and bandwidth efficiency [15].

OQAM divides the channel into a number of sub channels, each of which overlaps exclusively with its neighbors [16].

FBMC contains the following distinct characteristics:

1. Because there is no requirement for a small guard bands and CP, they are adequate to prevent cross-channel interference, OQAM can handle the whole transmission bandwidth [17].
2. FBMC is significantly less susceptible to time offset than OFDM because of small side-lobe [18]. Furthermore, FBMC is less susceptible to frequency offset, indicating greater Doppler Effect resilience.
3. For CR systems high resolution spectrum analysis capabilities of filter banks is use as shown in[19], and filter banks can yield a considerably broader spectrum range than the traditional FFT. As a result, there are fewer unwanted collisions between secondary and primary users.

4.1 FBMC for Spectrum Sensing

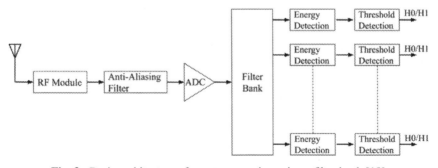

Fig. 3. Basic architecture of spectrum sensing using a filter bank [18].

The fundamental architecture of filter bank [18] for spectrum sensing is shown in Fig. 3. Following the radio frequency (RF) block, an analog to digital converter samples the RF signal, which is then sent to the filter bank [20]. Filter bank consists of analysis and synthesis filter bank. A low pass model filter is shifted to create these filter banks. The overall bandwidth is divided into linear non-overlapping sub-bands using several band pass filters. These sub-band signal is then fed to energy detector for energy detection. Energy detection is a widely used technique due to its lower computational complexity. Each sub-band's power is estimated and evaluated separately. By comparing the energy to a predefined threshold, the signal is recognized and classified as present or not. Energy detection is applied at the sub-band levels at analysis filter banks output, making filter bank based techniques robust and dynamic. The wideband signal is divided into narrowband signal by the analysis filter bank [21]. Challenges and Future Research Directions.

During SS, there should be higher likelihood of exact sensing and fewer chances of false alarm in order to decrease the impact of interference at PUs [22]. Existing sensing approaches have drawbacks. Such as weak signals that are below thermal noise are not detectable by energy detection. If specific signal information is familiar such as operational frequency, bandwidth, pulse shape, type of modulation type and frame structure of the PU, then matched filtering detection techniques with shorter detection times are preferable. The channel responsiveness has a big impact on this method's detection performance. To accomplish this, both the physical and media access control layers must be perfectly timed and synchronized and this adds to the calculations complexity. On the other hand cyclostationary detection is a technique for recognizing PUs transmission that takes use of the received signals' cyclostationarity [23]. The detector can then distinguish among PU, SU, and other interfering signals. However, the success of this strategy is based largely on the number of samples, which rises the complexity. Furthermore, cyclostationary features need a significant amount of computing power, which is not desired in portable systems [24]. Another challenge in SS is to deal with noise uncertainty [15]. The majority of SS approaches employ a fixed threshold that is dependent on the amount of noise. These sensing approaches aren't precise since the noise is unpredictable. In literature [6, 9, 16] different techniques have been suggested in order to deal with uncertainty, such as probabilistic models. Therefore, it is important that the noise must be measured to boost the detection effectiveness of the sensing methods.

Sensitivity of SS methods is also a challenge. Where compressive sensing techniques are often incorrect, future communication systems are projected to work at lower SNR levels. Only few researchers have studied SS efficiency at lower SNR and it can be explored as a future direction [25].

The following is a simulation of channel capacity against CDF for energy detection using FBMC, as extracted from [18]. Figure 4 (a) shows channels capacity vs. CDF when there is just one PU active and four PU aren't. With 4 unfilled slots, the channel is in very bad condition. Shannon's traditional OFDM capacity in bits/sec is around 1 Shannon. In comparison to FBMC, LTE has a substantially lesser capacity. When FBMC is used, capacity begins to rise dramatically. The capacity attributable to LTE at 50% CDF for FBMC is almost 13 Shannon.

Figure 4(b) depicts the plot when a SU fills the vacant slot, keeping 3 slots open. For all CDF percentiles, OFDM capacity is nearly constant at 20 Shannon in this iteration. The LTE and FBMC capacity increased yet again. At the 50% CDF, Capacity of LTE is 5 Shannon whereas capacity of FBMC is 170 Shannon.

Figure 4(c) the plot for capacity verses during the 3rd iteration, when SU takes up again one slot and two slots are left unfilled. The capacity of the OFDM channel remains constant, but is higher than the preceding iteration i.e. at nearly 80 Shannon. For 50% LTE capacity is 25 while for FBMC it is 950.

Figure 4 (d) depicts plot when SU takes up one gain one slot, implying that not a single slot is left free. Now that all slots are filled, spectrum efficiency improves by large value. Channel capacity for FBMC, LTE, and OFDM has increased significantly. For all % of CDF, capacity of OFDM is constant at 260 Shannon. LTEs capacity at 50% CDF is 60 Shannon, whereas FBMCs capacity is 3990 Shannon.

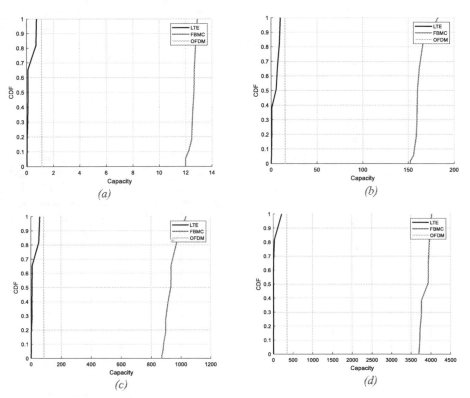

Fig. 4. The channel capacity vs. CDF plot for (a) When just one PU is present and four PU are absent, (b) When one SU takes the vacant slot, three slots remain unfilled. (c) When SU takes up one more slot, leaving two unused (d) When SU takes up one more slot, no slot is left vacant, as all slots are now filled [18].

5 Future Research Direction

1. SS performance can also be enhanced by using FBMC technology. FBMC is considered to be one of the most important technologies for 5G networks when combined with CR. To attain a high spectrum efficiency, FBMC systems make use of the spatial multiplexing gain. A transmitter and receiver are the two fundamental components of a FBMC system. Each element has a variety of antennas [20]. Signal from each antenna is sampled by an independent analog to digital converter to evaluate

the channel availability. FBMC systems are considered to improve detection while decreasing the possibilities of miss-detection and false alarm [25].

2. Energy detection method can be used for SS in filter bank [18]. The threshold in energy detection is a function of noise variance, therefore, noise variance estimation technique can be investigated in wide band spectrum sensing. Basically, fixed threshold is used for all the subbands in the filter bank. If noise variance is estimated in individual subbands, adaptive threshold scheme can be implemented. The adaptive threshold can be implemented for different stages with different spectral resolution in order to increase the probability of detection [26].

6 Conclusion

Spectrum sensing is an important function of CR through which CR is able to properly utilize the spectrum by allowing the SU to operate in the unused licensed band. Different SS methods offer a way of reusing frequency spectrum without interfering with it. Sensing many narrowband channels over a wideband spectrum is a major problem in CRs. FBMC can be used to tackle this challenge. FBMC can efficiently analyses many users with changing center frequencies and spectral dispersion between users. The filter banks provide higher bandwidth efficiency and lower side lobes desirable for spectrum sensing.

References

1. Mitola, J., Maguire, G.: Cognitive radio: making software radios more personal. IEEE Pers. Commun. 6(4), 13–18 (1999)
2. Farhang-Boroujeny, B.: Filter bank spectrum sensing for cognitive radios. IEEE Trans. Signal Process. 56(5), 1801–1811 (2008)
3. Wang, F.: Cognitive radio networks and security: a survey. J. Netw. Comput. Appl.1691–1708 (2014)
4. Masonta, M.T., Mzyece, M., Ntlatlapa, N.: Spectrum decision in cognitive radio networks: a survey. IEEE Commun. Surv. Tutor. 15(3), 1088–1107 (2012)
5. Zhang, H.: Filter Bank based Multicarrier (FBMC) for Cognitive Radio Systems. Networking and Internet Architecture. Thesis, National Conservatory of Arts and Crafts, University of Wuhan (China), (2010)
6. Mitola, J. I.: Cognitive radio. An integrated agent architecture for software defined radio (2002)
7. Anusha, M., Vemuru, S., Gunasekhar, T.: Transmission protocols in cognitive radio mesh networks. Int. J. Elect. Comput. Eng. (IJECE) 5(6), 1446 (2015). https://doi.org/10.11591/ijece.v5i6.pp1446-1451
8. Budiarjo, I., Nikookar, H., Ligthart, L.P.: Cognitive radio modulation techniques. IEEE Signal Process. Mag. 25(6), 24–34 (2008)
9. Giannakis, G.B., Tsatsanis, M.K.: Signal detection and classification using matched filtering and higher order statistics. IEEE Trans. Acoust. Speech Signal Process. 38(7), 1284–1296 (1990)
10. Sharma, I., Singh, G.: A Novel approach for spectrum access using fuzzy logic in cognitive radio. Int. J. Inf. Technol. Comput. Sci. 8, 1–9 (2012)

11. Ghozzi, M., Dohler, M., Marx, F., Palicot, J.: Cognitive radio: methods for the detection of free bands. Phys. Rep. **7**(7), 794–804 (2006)
12. Wang, B., Liu, K.J.R.: Advances in cognitive radio networks: a survey. IEEE J. Sel. Top. Signal Process. **5**(1), 5–23 (2011)
13. Amini, P., Kempter, R., Chen, R.R., Lin, L., Farhang-Boroujeny, B.: Filter bank multitone: a physical layer candidate for cognitive radios. In: Proceedings of the SDR Forum Technical Conference, pp. 14–18 (2005)
14. Farhang-Boroujeny, B.: Multicarrier modulation with blind detection capability using cosine modulated filter banks. IEEE Trans. Commun. **51**(12), 2057–2070 (2003)
15. Manesh, M.R., Kaabouch, N., Reyes, H., Hu, W.C.: A Bayesian model of the aggregate interference power in cognitive radio networks. In: 2016 IEEE 7th Annual Ubiquitous Computing, Electronics and Mobile Communication Conference (UEMCON), pp. 1–7. IEEE (2016)
16. Weiss, T.A., Jondral, F.K.: Spectrum pooling: an innovative strategy for the enhancement of spectrum efficiency. IEEE Commun. Mag. **42**(3), S8-14 (2004)
17. Salahdine, F., Kaabouch, N., El Ghazi, H.: Techniques for dealing with uncertainty in cognitive radio networks. In: 2017 IEEE 7th Annual Computing and Communication Workshop and Conference (CCWC), pp. 1–6. IEEE (2017)
18. Sheikh, J.A., Mir, Z.I., Mufti, M., Parah, S.A., Bhat, G.M.: A new Filter Bank Multicarrier (FBMC) based cognitive radio for 5g networks using optimization techniques. Wirel. Pers. Commun. **112**(2), 1265–1280 (2020). https://doi.org/10.1007/s11277-020-07101-y
19. Arjoune, Y., Kaabouch, N.: A comprehensive survey on spectrum sensing in cognitive radio networks: recent advances, new challenges, and future research directions. Sensors **19**(1), 126 (2019)
20. Amini, P., Kempter, R., Farhang-Boroujeny, B.: A comparison of alternative filter bank multi-carrier methods for cognitive radio systems. In: Proceedings of the SDR Technical Conference and Product Exposition (2006)
21. Cabric, D., Mishra, S.M., Brodersen, R.W.: Implementation issues in spectrum sensing for cognitive radios. In: Conference Record of the Thirty-Eighth Asilomar Conference on Signals, Systems and Computers, vol. 1, pp. 772–776. IEEE (2004)
22. Kumar, A., Sharma, I.: A new method for designing multiplierless two-channel filter bank using shifted-Chebyshev polynomials. Int. J. Electron. **106**(4), 537–552 (2019)
23. Sharma, I., Kumar, A., Singh, G.K.: Adjustable window based design of multiplier-less cosine modulated filter bank using swarm optimization algorithms. AEU-Int. J. Electron. Commun. **70**(1), 85–94 (2016)
24. Wang, H., Wu, B., Yao, Y., Qin, M.: Wideband spectrum sensing based on reconfigurable filter bank in cognitive radio. Future Internet **11**, 244 (2019)
25. Javed, J.N., Khalil, M., Shabbir A.,: A survey on cognitive radio spectrum sensing: classifications and performance comparison. In: 2019 International Conference on Innovative Computing (ICIC), pp. 1–8 (2019)
26. Dikmese, S., Lamichhane, K., Renfors, M.: Novel filter bank-based cooperative spectrum sensing under practical challenges for beyond 5G cognitive radios. EURASIP J. Wirel. Commun. Netw. **2021**(1), 1–27 (2021). https://doi.org/10.1186/s13638-020-01889-w

Fast Detection and Rule Based Classification of *Bharatanatyam hasta mudra*

Soumen Paul[✉] and Partha Pratim Das

Indian Institute of Technology, Kharagpur, Kharagpur, India
`soumenpaul165@gmail.com, ppd@cse.iitkgp.ac.in`

Abstract. Analysis of *Bharatanatyam* hand gestures extensively requires modern-day computer vision approaches. This paper demonstrates a real-time classification approach to these hand gestures by utilizing the MediaPipe hand model. The process commenced with hand detection and keypoint localization using MediaPipe. The keypoints were utilized to establish a rule for a particular gesture based on joint angle calculation. Real-life data were collected using our model from a well-trained dancer to set different rules. A specific gesture is classified based on the Euclidean distance measure between the joint angles of the gesture and the rule. The gesture exhibiting minimum distance would be the most matched class. The proposed work is also validated by capturing data from three dance learners with different experiences. The captured data achieved an average accuracy of 72.04%. The model took an average of 0.06 s of execution time to classify a gesture in real-time.

Keywords: Bharatanatyam · MediaPipe · Euclidean Distance · Flexion Angle

1 Introduction

Bharatanatyam is the oldest form of Indian Classical Dance that originated in the southern part of India. Initially, this dance was used in temples to express religious themes and spiritual ideas emoted by dancers with excellent footwork and impressive gestures. The theoretical base of *Bharatanatyam* was initially found in *Natya Shastra* written by Bharata Muni. But *Bharatanatyam* dance was generally taught verbally by professionals. This verbal learning method created different versions of the dance over the ages. Hence, the originality of the dance decreases over time. Also, it reduced the efficiency and knowledge of the dance professionals due to the lack of creativity available in the dance.

So it is incumbent to preserve the original steps of the intangible heritage like *Bharatanatyam* via a computerized approach. Another requirement in this context is to have an automatic dance tutoring system for a novice learner due to the unavailability of proper *gurus*. Also, efficient preservation of digital media contents through creating digital transcription or by video annotation is another

© The Author(s), under exclusive license to Springer Nature Switzerland AG 2023
D. Gupta et al. (Eds.): CVIP 2022, CCIS 1776, pp. 589–603, 2023.
https://doi.org/10.1007/978-3-031-31407-0_44

critical area of work [1]. All of these applications need real-time recognition of different elements of *Bharatanatyam* dance which include postures of a dancer, hand gestures or *hasta mudra*, facial expressions, etc. Recognizing these elements in real-time is essential for an instant feedback system.

Classification of *Bharatanatyam hasta mudra* differs from sign language gesture recognition in many ways. Use of *hasta mudra* during dance performance is free-flowing, and change of *mudra* is swift, unlike in sign language gestures. The orientation of hand gestures also changes very frequently during the dance. Also, complex light conditions, occlusion due to dancer costumes, use of different colors on the dancer's hand make the *hasta mudra* recognition problem different from the classical hand gesture recognition problem. We try to address most of these problems in our work to develop a real-time recognition application.

Hasta Mudra or hand gestures are used to convey outer events or things visually in a *Bharatanatyam* dance performance. As it is written in *Abhinaya Darpana* that the dancer should express the meaning of the song through hand gestures. Approximately 55 recognized *hasta mudras* are used in *Bharatanatyam*. Among them 32 *mudras* require only one hand and are called *Asamyukta Hasta* (see Table 1). The rest require both hands and are called *Samyukta hasta*. Each *hasta mudra* has a predefined structure and conveys different predefined semantic meanings during a dance performance. In this paper, we tried to recognize *Bharatanatyam hasta mudra* based on real-time hand detection using the MediaPipe Hand model and rule-based classification. We mainly focused on real-time classification without any involvement of sensor components or any expensive cameras or tracking devices. Currently, we use a two-dimensional webcam (e.g., Laptop camera) to identify a dancer's hand.

The rest of the paper is organized as follows:
Sect. 2 discusses previous work related to our study. In Sect. 3, existing techniques used in this paper are discussed. Section 4 discusses the proposed methodology of this paper. We present our experimental results in Sect. 5. Finally Sect. 6 concludes the paper.

2   Literature Survey

Bharatanatyam hasta mudra or human hand gesture recognition is a popular research problem in computer vision. This recognition problem is influenced by major impacts like dance analysis, sign language understanding, etc. The approach to addressing the task is two-fold - Hand Detection and Gesture Classification. Some researchers solved both tasks individually, whereas others solved the root problem as a whole. The *hasta mudra* recognition problem is somewhat more complex due to the involvement of different elements like camera position, complex background, use of different colors on hand, etc. Several other elements like different light conditions, the orientation of hands with respect to the camera position, occlusion, rotation, scaling issue, etc. are some scenarios to implement the recognition in real-time. Researchers used different handcrafted features [2] for hand detection along with different machine learning approaches for gesture

Table 1. Asamyukta Hasta Mudra

Sl No	Mudra	Sl No	Mudra
1	Alapadma	17	Mrigashirsha
2	Arala	18	Mukula
3	Ardhachandra	19	Mushthi
4	Ardhapataaka	20	Padmakosha
5	Ardhasuchi	21	Palli
6	Bhramara	22	Pataaka
7	Chandrakala	23	Sandamsha
8	Chatura	24	Sarpashirsha
9	Hamsapaksha	25	Shikara
10	Hamsasya	26	Shukatunda
11	Kangula	27	Simhamukha
12	Kapitta	28	Suchi
13	Kartarimukha	29	Tamrachuda
14	Katakaa	30	Tripataaka
15	Katakamukha	31	Trishula
16	Mayura	32	Vyagraha

recognition task [3–9]. But, handling different external elements discussed above is difficult when machine learning approaches are used.

Some researchers focused on static hand gesture recognition. For example, Kumar et al. [3] proposed an SVM based classification approach that takes feature input as Histogram of Oriented Gradient (HOG) of the hand. They also tested their classifier with different feature vectors such as SIFT, SURF, LBP, and HAAR and found the HOG feature as the best for precision and swiftness. [4] proposed a rule-based recognition system for Buddhist hand gestures using the star skeleton of the hand as a feature. It creates a contour plot to obtain the boundary of the hand then the star skeleton is calculated as the distance between two boundary pixels passing through the centroid. The dataset used in this work was taken from ancient Buddhist books and the internet. These hand-crafted features are relevant to dealing with a complex background, skin color, etc. but failed to handle occlusion, rotation and scaling problems, different light conditions, etc.

Some dynamic hand gesture recognition works are also there. A sensor-based approach published in [5] used a hand movement sensor to record different dynamic hand gestures, which consists of fingertip coordinates, palm, and wrist movements. The author used these criteria to train a KNN classifier using other distance metrics like cosine, euclidean, cubic, etc. [6] proposed an EigenTracker-based method to model dynamic hand gestures that included both hand shapes as well as trajectory information. This information was used as a feature to recognize static or dynamic hand gestures. [7] used the HOG feature and SVM technique for hand localization. Temporal features such as velocity and angle are extracted after hand detection and stored in the database. Mahalanobis distance between input gesture and database is computed for recognition. The work is addressed as real-time recognition and a solution to complex background problems. In 2021, Zhu et al. [8] published a 3D gesture recognition work based on a three-dimensional shape context. They used Kinect sensor-based depth maps to get the 3D shape context information on multiple scales. A dynamic time warping algorithm was used for gesture recognition. The author showed that the method outperforms several state-of-the-art methods on various benchmark datasets. Another work [9] based on hand-crafted features and SVM was proposed for recognition of hand gestures taken from different viewpoints. They performed trajectory extraction from an action video. Feature ensemble techniques, such as Bag of Words, LLC, were employed for the trajectory descriptors of each video. Then SVM was used for recognition. But the accuracy they got is not up to the mark.

It can be seen that researchers tried to solve different aspects of hand gesture recognition problems, such as cluttered background, rotation invariant, dynamic gestures, three-dimensional gesture recognition, and real-time recognition. But addressing all issues in one solution is somewhat complex using machine learning approaches. So, people moved into different deep learning methods to solve the recognition problem.

Several deep learning based approaches mainly convolution neural networks for gesture recognition [10–16] are attempted. In 2017, [10] proposed a two-stage deep learning-based method to detect hands in an unconstrained background. This approach trained two object detectors, RCNN and FRCNN, separately to obtain the initial estimate of the hand location. Then patch-based CNN skin detector was used to reduce the false positives. To improve the computational efficiency of the skin classifier, a regression-based image segmentation CNN was used, wherein the total variation regularization was incorporated. The method was tested using different publicly available datasets and got remarkable accuracy. However, this method does not give a good result on the ICD dataset used in the paper. The author published another work in [11], which addressed the scaling problem in hand detection work. They showed that a set of shallow parallel faster RCNN worked well than a deep faster RCNN and got accuracy as 77.1%, 86.53%, 91.43%, 74.43% for several benchmark hand gesture datasets such as Oxford Hand, VIVA, CVRR, ICD respectively. The proposed approach could detect hands as small as 15×15 pixels. But three-dimensional hand gesture recognition was not possible with this framework. In 2020, [12] worked with different singular pre-trained/non-pre-trained models and stacked ensemble CNNs for *Bharatanatyam* hand gesture recognition. The data were collected from different internet resources, consisting of diverse backgrounds compared to closed laboratory settings. All frameworks achieved an average of $> 95\%$ accuracy for both single and double hand gesture models. But due to the computational complexity of the framework and the unavailability of a sufficient ICD dataset, it was not that robust to real-time recognition. [13] proposed a two-step framework such as a deep RetinaNet-based hand detector and lightweight CNN-based hand gesture recognition. They achieved average precision of 85.5% on the ICD dataset for gesture recognition. Li et al. [14] also proposed a two-stream neural network-based approach. One stream was a self-attention-based graph CNN that models strong collaboration of hand joints. Another stream was a deep residual connection enhanced bidirectional independent RNN that extracted the temporal information for challenging gestures. The model was applied on mainly two datasets, i.e., Dynamic Hand Gesture (DHG) and First-person hand action dataset (FPHA), and achieved > 90% accuracy. Another CNN-based network was addressed in [15] where C3D architecture [17] was optimized and used for hand gesture recognition. [16] proposed a method to extract 3D hand joint features from different distance measurements. Eight layer CNN network is used for gesture recognition. The architecture achieved 94.32% accuracy on the KL_3DHG dataset.

All the networks discussed here are kind of black box recognition techniques, and the relationship of fingers cannot be visualized with these during a performed gesture. The dance tutoring system or live interpretation system requires a live user interface where a dancer can see their dance performances. The system will also be able to identify *hasta mudra* of the dancer and give feedback. This requirement needs a live recognition system and instant visualization of finger relationships used in a gesture. The design should be fast, robust, and rarely expensive. To address all these, we proposed a user interface where any performed gesture can be instantly seen, recognized, and different finger relationships can be visualized. The overall contribution of our paper is as follows:

– A live user interface is provided based on a 2D webcam by which dancer can check their live performance. A laptop camera is used in this work.
– A pre-trained hand detector architecture based on MediaPipe hand model [18] is used for hand detection. This model mainly detects 21 keypoints, i.e., bone joints of the hand, and those keypoints positions are displayed in the user interface.
– An Euclidean distance-based matching algorithm is applied based on the finger joint angles computed using keypoint coordinates.

3   Preliminaries

This section discusses all existing processes that are used in this work. First, how a hand can be detected using Blazepalm model [18] will be discussed. Next, we will discuss the hand landmark model for the keypoint localization of the hand.

3.1   Hand Detection Using BlazePalm Model

MediaPipe hand model is a hand tracking solution that predicts the skeleton of a human palm using a single RGB camera. It consists of two models: the Blazepalm detector and the hand landmark model. The Blazepalm detector operates on a fully sized input image of a hand and locates the palm on that image via an oriented bounding box. The palm detector model is used instead of the hand detector because estimating the bounding box of a rigid object like a palm is easier than the whole hand. An encoder-decoder feature extractor is used for more extensive scene-context awareness, even for small objects. Lastly, the focal loss is minimized to support a large amount of anchor achieved from high-scale variance. In a real-time tracking system, the hand detector model is run only for the first time or when the hand prediction indicates that the hand is lost. Avoiding applying a hand detector for each frame drastically reduces the computational complexity of the whole system.

3.2   Hand Landmark Model

This model takes the output bounding box as input and localizes 21 hand landmark coordinates via regression. The model is robust even to partially visible hands and self-occlusion and also very lightweight, fast, rotation, and scaling invariant. The outputs of this hand landmark model are

- 21 hand landmark three-dimensional coordinates.
- Hand flag indicating the probability of hand presence.
- Handedness marker identifies which hand is detected, i.e., left or right.

The model is trained using both real-world datasets as well as synthetic datasets. The model's architecture is shown in Fig. 1. There are three joints in each human finger except the thumb, named the Metacarpophalangeal joint (MCP), Proximal Interphalangeal Joint (PIP), and Distal Interphalangeal Joint (DIP). The thumb finger has three joints called as Interphalangeal Joint (IP), Metacarpophalangeal Joint (MCP), and Carpometacarpal Joint (CMC). These joints of five fingers, along with each finger TIP and the wrist joint, make the set of 21 hand landmarks as shown in Fig. 2.

4   Proposed Methodology

The structural position of a human palm is heavily dependent on the arrangement of fingers. So, a hand gesture can be identified based on its finger's position, orientation, and the relationship between fingers. A human finger can be bent in two main ways - Flexion and Extension. Flexion bend is done when we grab and hold an object. Extension movement is the opposite of flexion movement. A human finger can also bend sideways, but the movement is minimal. The structure of a *Bharatanatyam hasta mudra* can be defined only by the position of five fingers. A finger position can be interpreted as the amount of flexion bend of that finger. Flexion bend can be described using the angles formed in every three finger joints during bending. So, the flexion angles of all three joints are responsible for a finger position during a *mudra* formation. It is noted that, each finger flex up to certain range (given in Table 2).

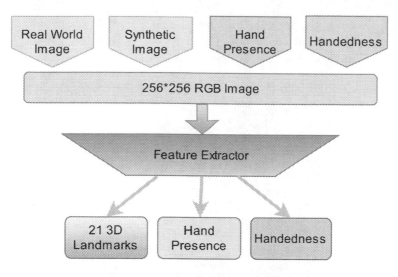

Fig. 1. Hand Landmark Model [18]

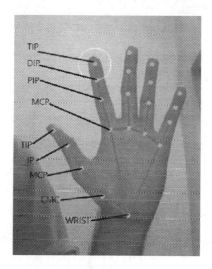

Fig. 2. Hand Keypoints

Hence, the structure of a *mudra* can be represented using a 15 flexion joint angles vector. This idea is used in this work for creating ground truths of *mudra* classification. A *mudra* is classified using the value of the joint angle vector and compared with the ground truth of all mudras. The comparison is made by calculating the Euclidean distance of the joint angle vector against all the ground truths. The whole recognition process is divided into three steps, as given below.

- Hand detection and keypoint localization using MediaPipe Hand model
- Computation of joint angles from the keypoint coordinates
- Euclidean distance computation based on the ground truth and classify mudra

Step-by-step process of the whole recognition is shown in Fig. 3.

Table 2. Range of Motion of Finger Flexion [19]

Finger Name	Joint Name	Angle Range	Standard Deviation
Thumb	CMC	49	6
	MCP	61	14
	IP	81	1
Index	MCP	80	13
	PIP	104	5
	DIP	68	11
Middle	MCP	85	15
	PIP	107	6
	DIP	70	12
Ring	MCP	87	16
	PIP	107	3
	DIP	66	9
Little	MCP	86	17
	PIP	104	6
	DIP	69	10

4.1   Hand Detection and Keypoint Localization

A dancer performs different *hasta mudra* in front of a laptop camera, which is shown in a user interface. The MediaPipe hand model is applied during capturing of the dance performance to detect and localize the keypoints of the hand. So, the hand shown in the video is enclosed by a bounding box, and the hand skeleton is highlighted (as shown in Table 3). The advantage of using the MediaPipe model is that it works well if the dancer moves their hand during the whole process. If the hand is rotated in any direction, then also the hand remains detected, and the keypoints relative position remains unchanged. This criterion makes the system more robust for real-time hand tracking. The coordinates of each keypoint in hand are tracked frame by frame for 10 s, and then the average value is calculated to get the actual coordinate of the keypoint. We track each keypoint because of constant change of coordinates due to the shakiness of the hand or any external impacts. This step gives the average coordinate value of 21 hand landmarks as output.

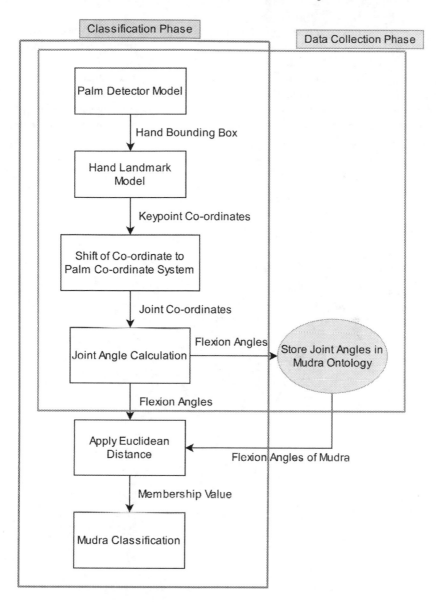

Fig. 3. Real time Mudra Classification Procedure

4.2 Calculation of Flexion Joint Angles

The keypoint coordinates extracted from the MediaPipe hand model are calculated based on the global coordinate system. Using a global coordinate system is sometimes difficult because of the constant change of hand orientation during a dance. So, we define a three-dimensional coordinate system on the palm surface as shown in Fig. 4. The X-axis is specified on the palm surface perpendicular to the finger. Y-axis is defined on the palm surface between the middle and ring finger. Z-axis is defined as perpendicular to the palm surface. The origin of the coordinate system will be the center point of the index finger MCP joint and middle finger MCP joint. All the keypoint coordinates are shifted to the palm coordinate system by subtracting the origin coordinate from all the keypoint coordinates. Then direction ratio of each finger segment between two keypoints is calculated. After that joint angle between two finger segments is calculated using those direction ratios (see Eq. 1).

$$\theta = cos^{-1}[(a1 * a2 + b1 * b2 + c1 * c2)/(|\overrightarrow{m1}| * |\overrightarrow{m2}|)] \tag{1}$$

where $(a1, b1, c1)$ = Direction ratio of first segment
$(a2, b2, c2)$ = Direction ratio of second segment
$\overrightarrow{m1}, \overrightarrow{m2}$ = Direction Cosines of both segments

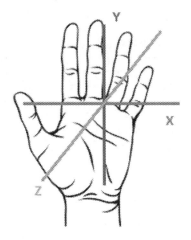

Fig. 4. Palm Co-ordinate System

Algorithm 1. Joint Angle Calculation Algorithm

1: $AngleList[1...21] \leftarrow$ Global Co-ordinates from MediaPipe Hand
2: $Origin \leftarrow (AngleList[6] + AngleList[18])/2$
3: $AngleList[1...21] \leftarrow AngleList[1...21] - Origin$
4: $dirRatio[1..4] \leftarrow$ Compute Four Direction Ratios by subtracting consecutive coordinates of a finger
5: $JointAngle[1..3] \leftarrow$ Compute joint angle using equation 1
6: Repeat step 4 and 5 for five fingers

Table 3. Skeleton of each *Asamyukta hasta mudra*

Alapadma	Arala	Ardhachandra	Ardhapataaka	Ardhasuchi	Bhramara	Chandrakala
Chatura	Hamsapaksha	Hamsasya	Kangula	Kapitta	Kartarimukha	Katakaa
Katakamukha	Mayura	Mrigashirsha	Mukula	Mushthi	Padmakosha	Palli
Pataaka	Sarpashirsha	Shikara	Shukatunda	Simhamukha	Suchi	Tamrachuda
Tripataaka	Trishula	Vyagraha				

4.3 Rule Based Classification

Each joint angle combination represents a *hasta mudra*. We have selected a trained *Bharatanatyam* dancer who performed *hasta mudra* in front of the camera. Our system simultaneously calculates joint angle combination for each *hasta mudra* and stores it in a database ontology. We used these data as ground truth for *mudra* classification. We consider that each angle combination will represent one point in a joint angle coordinate system. When a dancer is performing a *mudra*, the joint angle combination of that *mudra* must be around the ground truth of that *mudra*. When a dancer performs a hand gesture in front of a camera, all joint angles are calculated by the previously discussed methods. That joint angle combination is used to calculate euclidean distance against each ground truth. The *mudra* that gives minimum distance will be the best match, and the test sample will be classified with that *mudra* class.

5 Experimental Results

We implemented our work in an Intel i5 processor and camera system. We mainly focus on *Bharatanatyam asamyukta hasta mudra* or single hand gesture, which

Table 4. Result of Real-time Mudra Classification

Sl No	Mudra	Learner1	Learner2	Learner3	Average time (sec)	Accuracy (%)
1	Alapadma	Alapadma	Trishula	Chatura	12.86	33.33
2	Arala	Arala	Arala	Arala	12.67	100
3	Ardhachandra	Ardhachandra	Ardhachandra	Ardhachandra	12.63	100
4	Ardhapataaka	Ardhapataaka	Ardhapataaka	Ardhapataaka	12.62	100
5	Ardhasuchi	Ardhasuchi	Ardhasuchi	Ardhasuchi	12.68	100
6	Bhramara	Katakamukha	Katakamukha	Katakamukha	12.64	0
7	Chandrakala	Chandrakala	Chandrakala	Chandrakala	12.59	100
8	Chatura	Chatura	Sarpashirsha	Chatura	12.59	66.66
9	Hamsapaksha	Sarpashirsha	Sarpashirsha	Sarpashirsha	12.58	0
10	Hamsasya	Hamsasya	Hamsasya	Hamsasya	12.57	100
11	Kangula	Palli	Palli	Palli	13.21	0
12	Kapitta	Tamrachuda	Tamrachuda	Shikara	12.68	0
13	Kartarimukha	Kartarimukha	Kartarimukha	Kartarimukha	12.96	100
14	Katakaa	Katakaa	Katakaa	Katakaa	12.66	100
15	Katakamukha	Katakamukha	Bhramara	Katakamukha	12.59	66.66
16	Mayura	Mayura	Mayura	Mayura	12.58	66.66
17	Mrigashirsha	Mrigashirsha	Mrigashirsha	Mrigashirsha	12.62	100
18	Mukula	Mukula	Mukula	Mukula	12.64	100
19	Mushthi	Shikara	Shikara	Mushthi	12.58	33.33
20	Padmakosha	Padmakosha	Padmakosha	Padmakosha	12.69	100
21	Palli	Palli	Palli	Palli	12.66	100
22	Pataaka	Pataaka	Pataaka	Pataaka	12.75	100
23	Sarpashirsha	Sarpashirsha	Sarpashirsha	Sarpashirsha	12.67	100
24	Shikara	Shikara	Shikara	Mushthi	12.69	66.66
25	Shukatunda	Shukatunda	Shukatunda	Shukatunda	12.59	100
26	Simhamukha	Simhamukha	Katakaa	Simhamukha	12.59	66.66
27	Suchi	Suchi	Suchi	Ardhasuchi	12.60	66.66
28	Tamrachuda	Mukula	Tamrachuda	Mukula	12.70	33.33
29	Tripataaka	Tripataaka	Tripataaka	Tripataaka	12.68	100
30	Trishula	Trishula	Trishula	Trishula	12.61	100
31	Vyagraha	Trishula	Trishula	Trishula	12.57	0
Accuracy (%)		**77.42**	**67.74**	**70.96**	**12.67**	

has 32 variations. We have recorded data for 31 different gesture classes by a *Bharatanatyam* dance expert (it is shown in Fig. 3). We excluded *Sandamsha mudra* as it is a dynamic hand gesture, whereas we only focused on static gestures in this work. We identified three different dance learners with diverse experiences and were told to perform various *hasta mudras* in front of a laptop camera without constraint. Learner1 has the most dance experience, Learner2 is a novice, and Learner3 has moderate experience. Note that the dance learner can perform a *hasta mudra* without restriction. So, distance from the camera, orientation, and background may vary, but our system should handle all these exceptions. The result is shown in Table 4. We got an average accuracy of 72.04% for all three learners. We have also seen learner-wise accuracy and saw that accuracy depends on the experience also. We have also kept track of the execution time for the whole classification process and got an average time of 10.06 s. We kept 10 s for the accurate keypoint localization. Besides that, only an average of 0.06 s response time is needed to recognize any *mudra*.

We got the miss-classification from different learners mainly due to their limitation of accurately performing the *mudra*. Some *mudras* like *Pataaka, Ardhachandra, Palli, Arala, Mukula, etc.* are recognized accurately for all three learners because they have unique shapes. Some *mudras* are always misclassified for all learners due to their very similar shapes. For example, *Kangula* is classified as *Palli*, *Bhramara* is classified as *Katakamukha*, *Hamsapaksha* is classified as *Sarpashirsha*, *Vyagraha* is classified as *Trishula*. The model cannot distinguish them in real-time. Sometimes, the depth coordinate is not correctly identified due to the MediaPipe hand model limitation, for which a three-dimensional *mudra* structure becomes similar to a two-dimensional *mudra* structure (e.g. *Vyagraha* is classified to *Trishula*). We will check the same methodology with depth cameras like Kinect, ZED, etc., as per our future work.

6 Conclusion

This work helped us to classify *hasta mudra* during a real-time dance performance. No additional sensors other than a two-dimensional webcam are required for the real-time classification so that the system can be used with minimum cost. The system detected hand and localized 21 joints using a pre-trained MediaPipe hand model. A *mudra* was classified based on the rules created by computing joint angles. Euclidean distance was used to measure the distance between the joint angle coordinates of a mudra with the ground truths. The minimum distance gave the best match. This method achieved an average accuracy of 72.07% for different dance learners. The model worked well for various conditions like complex background, rotation and scaling invariant, and different light conditions, mainly needed in real-time classification. Though the model handled all these scenarios, keypoint detection accuracy became low for terrible light conditions. The model currently gave only class-level recognition. But for a false positive scenario, a learner may only get confused by seeing the wrong class. So, the system can be enhanced to show a list of *mudra* classes with the matching probability so that the user can understand the problem and act accordingly. The system may also suggest changes to the user during a miss-classification scenario, and the user can follow that suggestions to perform the *mudra* correctly. The model took an average execution time of 0.06 s which is fast but not instant. During a dance performance, the transition of *hasta mudra* needs to be detected, which may reduce the overall execution time because the subsequent *mudra* set of a particular *mudra* is limited and predefined. Also, we need to work on the *samyukta hasta mudra* and transition between *mudras*. These can be considered as the future work of this paper.

References

1. Mallick, T., Das, P.P., Majumdar, A.K.: *Bharatanatyam* dance transcription using multimedia ontology and machine learning. In: Mukhopadhyay, J., Sreedevi, I., Chanda, B., Chaudhury, S., Namboodiri, V.P. (eds.) Digital Techniques for Heritage Presentation and Preservation, pp. 179–222. Springer, Cham (2021). https://doi.org/10.1007/978-3-030-57907-4_10
2. Anami, B.S., Bhandage, V.A.: A comparative study of suitability of certain features in classification of bharatanatyam mudra images using artificial neural network. Neural Process. Lett. **50**(1), 741–769 (2019)
3. Kumar, K.V.V., Kishore, P.V.V.: Indian classical dance mudra classification using HOG features and SVM classifier. In: Satapathy, S.C., Bhateja, V., Das, S. (eds.) Smart Computing and Informatics. SIST, vol. 77, pp. 659–668. Springer, Singapore (2018). https://doi.org/10.1007/978-981-10-5544-7_65
4. Bhaumik, G., Govil, M.C.: Recognition of hasta mudra using star skeleton-preservation of buddhist heritage. Pattern Recognit. Image Anal. **31**(2), 251–260 (2021)
5. Sooai, A.G., Yoshimoto, K., Takahashi, H., Sumpeno, S., Purnomo, M.H.: Dynamic hand gesture recognition on 3D virtual cultural heritage ancient collection objects using k-nearest neighbor. Eng. Lett. **26**(3) (2018)
6. Patwardhan, K.S., Roy, S.D.: Hand gesture modelling and recognition involving changing shapes and trajectories, using a predictive eigentracker. Pattern Recognit. Lett. **28**(3), 329–334 (2007)
7. Lin, J., Ding, Y.: A temporal hand gesture recognition system based on hog and motion trajectory. Optik **124**(24), 6795–6798 (2013)
8. Zhu, C., Yang, J., Shao, Z., Liu, C.: Vision based hand gesture recognition using 3D shape context. IEEE/CAA J. Autom. Sinica **8**(9), 1600–1613 (2019)
9. Tran, T.-H., Nguyen, T.H., Dinh, V.S.: Significant trajectories and locality constrained linear coding for hand gesture representation. In: 2020 IEEE Eighth International Conference on Communications and Electronics (ICCE), pp. 359–364. IEEE (2021)
10. Roy, K., Mohanty, A., Sahay, R.R.: Deep learning based hand detection in cluttered environment using skin segmentation. In: Proceedings of the IEEE International Conference on Computer Vision Workshops, pp. 640–649 (2017)
11. Roy, K., Sahay, R.R.: A robust multi-scale deep learning approach for unconstrained hand detection aided by skin segmentation. Vis. Comput. **38**, 1–25 (2021)
12. Parameshwaran, A.P., Desai, H.P., Weeks, M., Sunderraman, R.: Unravelling of convolutional neural networks through bharatanatyam mudra classification with limited data. In: 2020 10th Annual Computing and Communication Workshop and Conference (CCWC), pp. 0342–0347. IEEE (2020)
13. Mohammed, A.A.Q., Lv, J., Islam, M.D.: A deep learning-based end-to-end composite system for hand detection and gesture recognition. Sensors **19**(23), 5282 (2019)
14. Li, C., Li, S., Gao, Y., Zhang, X., Li, W.: A two-stream neural network for pose-based hand gesture recognition. IEEE Trans. Cogn. Develop. Syst. **14**(4), 1594–1603 (2021)
15. Al-Hammadi, M., et al.: Deep learning-based approach for sign language gesture recognition with efficient hand gesture representation. IEEE Access **8**, 192527–192542 (2020)

16. Vasavi, P., Maloji, S., Kumar, E.K., Kumar, D.A., Sasikala, N.: 3D hand gesture representation and recognition through deep joint distance measurements. Int. J. Adv. Comput. Sci. Appl. **11**(4) (2020)
17. Tran, D., Bourdev, L., Fergus, R., Torresani, L., Paluri, M.: Learning spatiotemporal features with 3D convolutional networks. In: Proceedings of the IEEE International Conference on Computer Vision, pp. 4489–4497 (2015)
18. Zhang, F., et al.: Mediapipe hands: on-device real-time hand tracking. arXiv preprint arXiv:2006.10214 (2020)
19. Lee, K.-S., Jung, M.-C.: Ergonomic evaluation of biomechanical hand function. Saf. Health Work **6**(1), 9–17 (2015)

MFNet: A Facial Recognition Pipeline for Masked Faces Using FaceNet

Nikhil Kumar Ghanghor[iD], Chinju John[(✉)][iD], and Jayakrushna Sahoo

Indian Institute of Information Technology Kottayam, Valavoor 686635, Kerala, India
{nkghanghor18bcs,chinjuj.phd201001}@iitkottayam.ac.in

Abstract. Facial recognition is one of the most utile innovations from the Artificial Intelligence (AI) domain with extended support for secure access to protected premises and feature driven module functioning of smartphones. One of the major challenges associated with facial recognition is occlusion. There are a wide variety of occlusions that exists in images. In this work, we are trying to extract the human facial features which are being shielded by a mask. We propose a facial recognition pipeline that considers the occlusion caused by masks and retrieves the facial features which are hidden under them. The presented pipeline first focuses on enhancing the existing facial datasets by applying face masks on them, which are further fed to a facial landmark detection system. The output from the facial landmark detection system will be given to a deep neural network for learning and updating the embedded values by undergoing training in a Self - guided manner. We also train models in a supervised fashion to serve as baselines. The experimental results demonstrate that the proposed pipeline and the novel loss function introduced by us provide significantly better accuracy in recognizing masked faces compared with state-of-the-art systems for this task.

Keywords: Face recognition · Masked face recognition · Deep neural networks · Self supervised learning

1 Introduction

Current technological advancements and the admirable growth of Artificial Intelligence (AI) systems provide state-of-the-art (SOTA) solutions to cumbersome tasks with less human intervention. Organizations all over the world have started integrating and developing such systems for their in house uses. Facial recognition is one such area that could attract the interest of multinational ventures for biometric identifications of their employees.

Since the inception of the Artificial Intelligence domain, there have been diligent efforts over the decades to address the problem of facial recognition, some of such pioneering works are Eigen Faces [9], Viola Jones [10], DeepFace [8] and FaceNet [6]. In the year 2014, DeepFace [8] improved the SOTA at that time by 27% almost reaching human level accuracy in facial recognition. Almost one year

D. Gupta et al. (Eds.): CVIP 2022, CCIS 1776, pp. 604–614, 2023.
https://doi.org/10.1007/978-3-031-31407-0_45

after the introduction of DeepFace [8] FaceNet [6] was introduced which claimed to surpass the human-level accuracy in facial recognition tasks and giving SOTA results at the time of its introduction. Nowadays most of the facial recognition systems in use are built upon these SOTA models. However, the performance of these systems is questionable when it comes to *occluded* images.

Occlusion in simple words means an obstructed view of an object in three-dimensional space when the line of sight is blocked by an intervening object.

Occlusions are of three major types [14]

- Self Occlusion
- Inter Object Occlusion
- Background Occlusion

With the recent COVID-19 pandemic and the impact of its ever-growing spread on coming in contact with the infected person, it was the World Health Organization's recommendation to wear face mask and maintain social distance to reduce the spread of the virus. Now, in order to contain the spread of the virus people are supposed to wear face masks, which questions the efficiency of the existing facial recognition systems as they are configured to identify bare faces.

Through this paper, we propose a facial recognition pipeline that can be used for the facial recognition of masked faces. The paper is organized into multiple sections, in the initial paragraphs (Sections I to III), we go through some of the popular works which deal with facial recognition, and following it, the description of our dataset. In section IV, we discuss the methodology succeeding which is our proposed loss function. We have then listed and discussed the results obtained from experimental validations. The final section details the conclusion and future directions of our work.

2   Related Work

When the promising potential of AI was unveiled, there have been a considerable amount of research being done on devising efficient AI systems especially, for facial recognition. There exists a plethora of works that are still under progress on facial recognition, the discussion of which will be beyond the scope of this paper. However, we oblige to introduce some of the pioneering works being done for facial recognition as well as the discussion of a few relevant works on masked facial recognition. The Viola Jones [10] algorithm published in 2001 is unarguably one of the major milestone papers in the area. It introduced a new image representation called *Integral Image* whose construction was being done from the features rather than pixels. It then feeds this integral image representation to a learning algorithm based on Adaboost, which the authors have named as *Attentional Cascade*. The algorithm can process images extremely rapidly and achieve high detection rates.

The FaceNet [6] paper introduced in the year 2015 proposed a system that directly learns a mapping from face images to a compact Euclidean space where distances directly correspond to a measure of face similarity. It proposed an end-to-end learning system using a deep CNN architecture. It introduced a new loss known as *triplet loss* which focused on learning representations of the image in such a way that they can be represented in a compact Euclidean space. Once this space has been learned, the tasks of face recognition, face verification and face clustering can be done using any of the standard techniques such as k-nearest neighbour using the learnt facenet embeddings as feature vectors.

In the fall of the year 2017, the Face Attention Network (FAN) [11] was introduced, which focused on dealing with the problem of face recognition from occluded faces. It adopted the much popular attention mechanism [14] while implementing the network. The concept is contributed to a new anchor level of attention, which highlights the features of the face region. The FAN integrates the reproduced Oneshot RetinaNet [5] and anchor level attention and gave SOTA results on face detection benchmarks such as WiderFace [12] and MAFA [3]. The authors of the paper My Eyes Are Up Here [20] came up with an extension of the triplet loss introduced in the Facenet [6] paper. It uses Mean Squared Error as the optimization criteria between masked and unmasked representations in conjunction with the triplet loss.

A recently published work [15] explored a similar problem statement and proposed a cropping and attention-based approach for the task of facial recognition with and without masks. They have tried four different cases of facial recognition in their work which involves training on masked/unmasked data and testing with masked/unmasked data. They suggested that the shield of the mask destroys the features of the nose and mouth and to resolve this they proceeded with a cropping-based approach which is further followed by introducing attention to the convolutional neural network used for facial recognition purposes. For inducting attention they have used Convolutional Block Attention Module (CBAM) [16] and added it to each block of ResNet50 [17].

3   Dataset

We have used the Labelled Faces in the Wild (LFW) [4] dataset for our experiments. Since there are not many datasets available for masked faces, we have augmented the existing LFW dataset by using an open source tool MaskTheFace [1]. The tool supports several different mask types with different shades. We have only used the KN95 and surgical mask types for our experiments because most of the time these facial recognition systems will be deployed on premises and the people working there are supposed to be wearing one of these mask varieties. We have performed experiments on the original LFW dataset as well as the two masked versions of LFW dataset created using MaskTheFace tool (Fig. 3). The number of images and number of identities across each dataset is listed in the Table 1.

Fig. 1. Creating masked face images using Mask The Face tool

Table 1. Dataset distribution table

Dataset	No. of Identities	No. of Images
Original LFW	5749	13233
Surgical LFW	5648	12975
KN95 LFW	5622	12962

4   Methodology

The experimental pipeline which we have followed is discussed in this section, beginning with the data preprocessing section followed by the model being used for the experiments and finally the training strategy utilised is explored.

4.1   Data Preprocessing

The input image is fed to a Multi-Task Cascaded Neural Network (MTCNN) [13] which detects the facial landmarks in an input image and extracts only the regions containing facial areas present in the images as in Fig. 2. This is done because while doing any facial recognition tasks the pixels present around the face of a person are of little to no use. After the detection and extraction of these features from each image we use them for the proceeding steps. The extracted images are of size 128 * 128 which is further upsampled to 256 * 256 for our experiments.

4.2   Models

The recent success of AI systems has been attributed to the wider adoption of neural networks. The neural networks having 100s of layers and being trained on millions of data points such as ImageNet have given surprisingly good results across a variety of problems, however, training of these large neural networks on such humongous datasets requires a lot of computational resources, which is most of the times undesirable. This further led to the adoption of transfer learning in the AI community. Transfer learning involves using a pre-trained model on a different task and finetuning its weights for our own problem at hand. It gives better results compared to the approach of training from scratch that too with

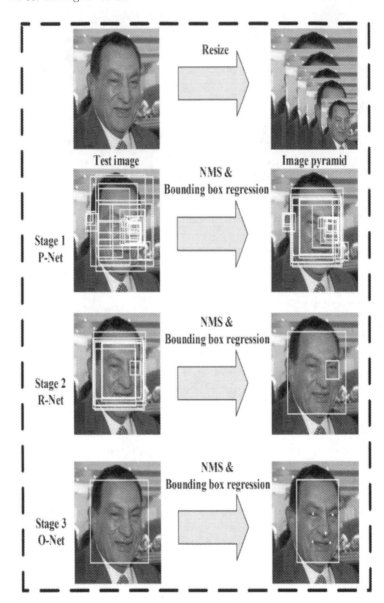

Fig. 2. MTCNN Block Diagram: Candidate windows are produced through a fast Proposal Network (P-Net), candidates are refined using a Refinement Network (R-Net). In the final stage Output Network (O-Net) produces final bounding box and facial-landmarks position.

relatively few training epochs. We have used the InceptionResNetV1 [7] model with two different checkpoints one of which was pretrained on the VggFace2 [2] dataset and the other one was pretrained on the CasiaWebFace [14] dataset.

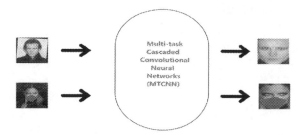

Fig. 3. Extracting faces using MTCNN

We employed two checkpoints since the ImageNet checkpoints don't give good results on facial datasets with fewer epochs. InceptionResNetV1 [7] is a hybrid network which aims to combine the ideas proposed by Inception [18] and ResNet [17] architecture together. Since Inception is a deep network and likely prone to vanishing gradient problem, InceptionResNetV1 uses residual blocks similar to the residual connections proposed by ResNet.

4.3 Training Strategy

Two different training strategies have been explored for our experiments. They are:

1. Supervised Learning (SL): The traditional way of training any Machine Learning model, when we have a labelled dataset of the form (X, y) where X is our input feature and y is its corresponding label.
2. Self-Supervised Learning (SSL): It is a relatively new idea and has gathered much attention recently where the model is being trained initially only on data without any labels. This lets the model explore the structure underlying in the data. The model trained in this fashion can be later utilized for fine tuning by providing data with their labels which is similar to a supervised learning training procedure.

We use the models with the supervised learning strategy as our baseline. In the SL setup, the InceptionResNetV1 model Fig. 4 is trained with two different checkpoints with the base network freezed and unfreezed for both the checkpoints across each of the three datasets listed in Fig. 1. Since the dataset is highly skewed given each of the identity has atleast 1 image to a maximum of 529, there are odds that the under presented classes won't be learnt by the model. In order to have a check upon this we also tried sampling strategy where only those classes which have at least 3 images are used for training by keeping the same configurations for both of them. The entire dataset was split in the ratio 80:10:10 and trained for 20 epochs using the standard CrossEntropyLoss with Adam as the optimizer. We have used ReduceLROnPlateau as our learning rate scheduler. The learning rate was set to be 0.001. The results obtained are listed in the Table 3.

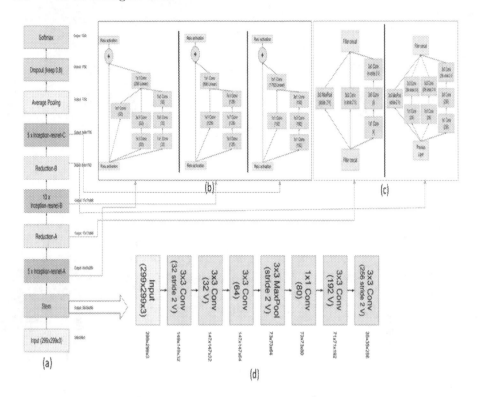

Fig. 4. InceptionResNetV1Architecture (a) Overall schematic representation of InceptionResnetV1 network (b) The three InceptionResNet modules: A, B and C (c) Reduction blocks A and B (left and right) (d) InceptionResNetV1 Stem

The training workflow which we have followed is shown in Fig. 5. In the SSL setup, we removed the classification head from the InceptionResNetV1 model and added a linear layer on top of it which outputs an embedding size of 256. We generated 12,000 triplets/sextets from the given dataset and used 8,000 for training, 2,000 for validation and 2,000 for testing purpose. The network was trained for 100 epochs with Adam as optimizer and the StepLR as the learning rate scheduler with learning rate set to be 0.001.

In addition to the triplet loss and our proposed loss function we also perform experiments using the loss function proposed by [20] named as **Triplet loss meauh**. It employs the native triplet loss to learn embeddings from anchor, positive and negative images along with minimizing the mean squared error between the representations of anchor and anchor masked image. The authors proposed that it helps the model to learn effective embeddings for both masked and unmasked faces in a joint manner.

$$L = ||f(A) - f(P)||^2 - ||f(A) - f(N)||^2 + \alpha + \sum_{i=1}^{D}(f(A) - f(A_m))^2 \quad (1)$$

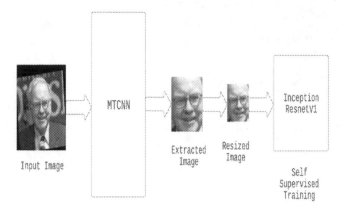

Fig. 5. Training Workflow

We have employed two different loss functions for the experiments following the SSL setup, Triplet Loss [6] and our proposed loss function which we named as *QuadTriplet Loss*. The proposed loss function is described in the subesquent section.

5   QuadTriplet Loss

To understand the notion behind QuadTriplet loss we have to introduce the triplet loss first. The triplet loss accepts triplets as its arguments which are: anchor, positive and negative, denoted as A, P and N. Here, anchor and positive indicate the samples belonging to the same class and anchor and negative are for the samples belonging to a different class. The triplet loss tries to enforce a minimum distance between A and P and at the same time maximize the distance between P and N. A self-restrained triplet loss was introduced in the work [19] for producing embeddings similar to unmasked face recognition models. Any distance metric can be used for the distance calculations and since *L2-Norm* is more promising for this purpose [6] we have used it as the metric for our distance calculations.

$$L = ||f(A) - f(P)||^2 - ||f(A) - f(N)||^2 + \alpha \qquad (2)$$

such that

$$0 < ||f(A) - f(N)||^2 - ||f(A) - f(P)||^2 < \alpha \qquad (3)$$

where α denotes the minimum margin between the positive and negative samples and $f(.)$ denotes the embedding generator function. This loss leads to an N-dimensional subspace where N denotes the embedding size of the image being fed to the loss function. Now, this loss function coupled with Siamese Network gave SOTA results on several benchmark datasets for facial recognition

We extended the idea of triplet loss to use two variants of the same dataset, the original dataset and the augmented dataset created using MaskTheFace tool.

The arguments needed by QuadTriplet are sextets of anchor, masked anchor, positive, masked positive, negative, and masked negative samples abbreviated as A, A_m, P, P_m, N, N_m.

$$L_{quadtriplet} = L_1 + L_2 + L_3 + L_4 + \alpha \tag{4}$$

$$L_1 = ||f(A) - f(P)||^2 - ||f(A) - f(N)||^2 \tag{5}$$

$$L_2 = ||f(A_m) - f(P_m)||^2 - ||f(A_m) - f(N_m)||^2 \tag{6}$$

$$L_3 = ||f(A) - f(P_m)||^2 - ||f(A) - f(N_m)||^2 \tag{7}$$

$$L_4 = ||f(A_m) - f(P)||^2 - ||f(A_m) - f(N)||^2 \tag{8}$$

$$\alpha = \alpha_1 + \alpha_2 + \alpha_3 + \alpha_4 \tag{9}$$

such that

$$0 < ||f(A) - f(N)||^2 - ||f(A) - f(P)||^2 < \alpha_1 \tag{10}$$

$$0 < ||f(A) - f(N_m)||^2 - ||f(A) - f(P_m)||^2 < \alpha_2 \tag{11}$$

$$0 < ||f(A_m) - f(N)||^2 - ||f(A_m) - f(P)||^2 < \alpha_3 \tag{12}$$

$$0 < ||f(A_m) - f(N_m)||^2 - ||f(A_m) - f(P_m)||^2 < \alpha_4 \tag{13}$$

The siamese model receives sextets as inputs and tries to minimize the loss function 4 by maintaining the constraints 10, 11, 12 and 13. These constraints enables the model to have four different hyperplanes helping to separate the masked samples of one class from masked samples of another class, unmasked samples of one class from unmasked samples of another class, masked samples of one class from unmasked samples of another class and unmasked samples of one class from masked samples of another class.

6   Results

Since the experiments were performed on the original LFW dataset as well as the two customized versions of it, the results across each dataset are grouped into a single table to have better clarity and make the results as understandable as possible. As mentioned earlier we have used two different pre-trained models, one was being trained on the VggFace2 dataset and the other one was being trained on Casia-Webface. Using these two pre-trained models four different experiments were performed on each of the three datasets. In one experimental setting, only the last layer of the InceptionResnetV1 network was fine-tuned whereas in the other setting the entire network was fine-tuned. Among all the results obtained across all three datasets which are reported in the Table 3, the experiment where the entire network was pre-trained on Casia-Webface gave the best results on both the validation as well as the test set. The motivation behind performing such an extensive set of experiments for determining our baseline was to find out the best performing model and utilise it for our SSL task. As mentioned in the Table 2 we try out triplet loss as well as our proposed loss function on original as well as surgical masked datasets. The results for the quadtriplet loss variant are reported on both masked and unmasked variants as it was designed in such a manner to emit triplets for original as well as masked images. Hence, the results reported for our proposed variant consist of both variants of the dataset. Our proposed variant gives the best accuracy of 85.41% on both masked and unmasked datasets combined.

Table 2. Results with Loss function variant across different datasets

Loss Variant x Dataset	Precision	Recall	F1-Score	Accuracy
Triplet loss (unmasked)	0.8136	0.5979	0.5924	0.8047
Triplet loss (masked)	0.7608	0.5789	0.5728	0.8138
Triplet loss meauh (unmasked + masked)	0.7283	0.7735	0.6667	0.8359
QuadTriplet loss (unmasked + masked)	0.8134	0.4359	0.4929	0.8541

7   Conclusion

This work was inspired from previous efforts to fetch facial features from mask-protected faces. Even though there are efficient models which could recognize people with high accuracy, these systems are not up to the standard when it comes to occluded images. From the observed metrics, it can be seen that our proposed variant performs at par w.r.t other model variants in terms of Accuracy as well as Precision. The dip in Recall and F1-Score could be attributed to the fact that Recall penalizes when we have more false negatives and given the random generation of triplets which was intended to incentivize negatives for learning of good embeddings. As a future scope of this work will be needing a more robust evaluation design to accurately come up with the exact recall number for this model as well as the other deep neural network models that work in the same dimension.

Table 3. Baseline results with random sampling and constrained sampling

Dataset	Model Variant	With random sampling		With constrained sampling	
		valid	test	valid	test
Original LFW Dataset	InceptionResnetV1 (the last layer) from VggFace2	22.12	39.68	35.00	34.33
	InceptionResnetV1 from VggFace2	37.7	67.95	53.74	54.07
	InceptionResnetV1 (the last layer) from Casia-webface	28.84	51.78	47.99	48.36
	InceptionResnetV1 from Casia-webface	**38.08**	**68.63**	**60.56**	**57.56**
Surgical masked LFW Dataset	InceptionResnetV1 (the last layer) from VggFace2	16.91	30.15	28.00	28.84
	InceptionResnetV1 from VggFace2	28.95	51.73	46.44	46.08
	InceptionResnetV1 (the last layer)from Casia-webface	20.21	36.39	35.71	36.82
	InceptionResnetV1 from Casia-webface	**33.70**	**60.29**	**56.33**	**56.14**
KN95 masked LFW Dataset	InceptionResnetV1 (the last layer) from VggFace2	15.73	28.40	25.94	26.93
	InceptionResnetV1 from VggFace2	24.13	44.06	43.77	41.80
	InceptionResnetV1 (the last layer) from Casia-webface	21.52	39.04	35.40	34.96
	InceptionResnetV1 from Casia-webface	**32.10**	**57.41**	**56.40**	**56.66**

References

1. Anwar, A., Raychowdhury, A.: Masked face recognition for secure authentication. arXiv preprint arXiv:2008.11104 (2020)
2. Cao, Q., Shen, L., Xie, W., Parkhi, O.M., Zisserman, A.: Vggface2: a dataset for recognising faces across pose and age. In: 2018 13th IEEE International Conference on Automatic Face Gesture Recognition (FG 2018), pp. 67–74 (2018)
3. Ge, S., Li, J., Ye, Q., Luo, Z.: Detecting masked faces in the wild with LLE-CNNs. In: 2017 IEEE Conference on Computer Vision and Pattern Recognition (CVPR), pp. 426–434 (2017)
4. Huang, G.B., Mattar, M.A., Lee, H., Learned-Miller, E.: Learning to align from scratch, vol. 1, pp. 764–772 (2012)
5. Lin, T.Y., Goyal, P., Girshick, R., He, K., Dollar, P.: Focal loss for dense object detection (2018)
6. Schroff, F., Kalenichenko, D., Philbin, J.: Facenet: a unified embedding for face recognition and clustering. In: 2015 IEEE Conference on Computer Vision and Pattern Recognition (CVPR) (2015)
7. Szegedy, C., Ioffe, S., Vanhoucke, V., Alemi, A.: Inception-v4, inception-resnet and the impact of residual connections on learning (2016)
8. Taigman, Y., Yang, M., Ranzato, M., Wolf, L.: Deepface: closing the gap to human-level performance in face verification. In: 2014 IEEE Conference on Computer Vision and Pattern Recognition, pp. 1701–1708 (2014)
9. Turk, M.A., Pentland, A.P.: Face recognition using eigenfaces. In: Proceedings of 1991 IEEE Computer Society Conference on Computer Vision and Pattern Recognition, pp. 586–591 (1991)
10. Viola, P., Jones, M.: Rapid object detection using a boosted cascade of simple features. In: Proceedings of the 2001 IEEE Computer Society Conference on Computer Vision and Pattern Recognition, CVPR 2001, vol. 1, pp. I-I (2001)
11. Wang, J., Yuan, Y., Yu, G.: Face attention network: an effective face detector for the occluded faces (2017)
12. Yang, S., Luo, P., Loy, C.C., Tang, X.: Wider face: a face detection benchmark (2015)
13. Zhang, K., Zhang, Z., Li, Z., Qiao, Y.: Joint face detection and alignment using multitask cascaded convolutional networks. IEEE Signal Process. Lett. **23**(10), 1499–1503 (2016)
14. Jalal, A., Singh, V.: The state-of-the-art in visual object tracking. Informatica **36**, 227–248 (2012)
15. Li, Y., Guo, K., Lu, Y., et al.: Cropping and attention based approach for masked face recognition. Appl. Intell. **51**, 3012–3025 (2021). https://doi.org/10.1007/s10489-020-02100-9
16. Woo, S., et al.: CBAM: convolutional block attention module. In: ECCV (2018)
17. He, K., Zhang, X., Ren, S., Sun, J.: Deep Residual Learning for Image Recognition, pp. 770–778 (2016). https://doi.org/10.1109/CVPR.2016.90
18. Szegedy, C., et al.: Going deeper with convolutions. In: 2015 IEEE Conference on Computer Vision and Pattern Recognition (CVPR), pp. 1–9 (2015)
19. Boutros, F., Damer, N., Kirchbuchner, F., Kuijper, A.: Unmasking face embeddings by self-restrained triplet loss for accurate masked face recognition. arXiv preprint arXiv:2103.01716 (2021)
20. Neto, P., et al.: My Eyes Are Up Here: Promoting Focus on Uncovered Regions in Masked Face Recognition (2021)

Deep Learning Based Novel Cascaded Approach for Skin Lesion Analysis

Shubham Innani$^{(\boxtimes)}$, Prasad Dutande, Bhakti Baheti, Ujjwal Baid, and Sanjay Talbar

Center of Excellence, Signal and Image Processing, Shri Guru Gobind Singhji Institute of Engineering and Technology, Nanded, India
{2016bec035,prasad.dutande,bahetibhakti,baidujjwal,sntalbar}@sggs.ac.in
http://www.sggs.ac.in

Abstract. Patients diagnosed with skin cancer like melanoma are prone to a high mortality rate. Automatic lesion analysis is critical in skin cancer diagnosis and ensures effective treatment. The computer-aided diagnosis of such skin cancer in dermoscopic images can significantly reduce the clinicians' workload and help improve diagnostic accuracy. Although researchers are working extensively to address this problem, early detection and accurate identification of skin lesions remain challenging. This research focuses on a two-step framework for skin lesion segmentation followed by classification for lesion analysis. We explored the effectiveness of deep convolutional neural network (CNN) based architectures by designing an encoder-decoder architecture for skin lesion segmentation and CNN based classification network. The proposed approaches are evaluated quantitatively in terms of the Accuracy, mean Intersection over Union(mIoU) and Dice Similarity Coefficient. Our cascaded end-to-end deep learning-based approach is the first of its kind, where the classification accuracy of the lesion is significantly improved because of prior segmentation. The code is available at https://www.github.com/shubhaminnani/skin/lesion.

Keywords: Skin Lesion · Deep Learning · Classification · Segmentation

1 Introduction and Related Work

Skin cancer is one of the fatal illnesses in today's world. Even though it is the least common, the disease is responsible for around 91,000 deaths every year until now [2]. Regular monitoring and early detection play a vital function in reducing the mortality rate of skin cancer and can help in precise treatment planning and improving life. Survival rates decrease significantly if skin cancer is left

Authors are greatful to Center of Excellence, Signal and Image Processing, SGGS IET, Nanded, for computing resources.

© The Author(s), under exclusive license to Springer Nature Switzerland AG 2023
D. Gupta et al. (Eds.): CVIP 2022, CCIS 1776, pp. 615–626, 2023.
https://doi.org/10.1007/978-3-031-31407-0_46

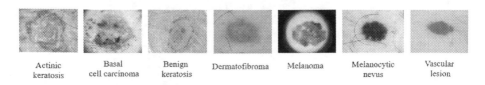

| Actinic keratosis | Basal cell carcinoma | Benign keratosis | Dermatofibroma | Melanoma | Melanocytic nevus | Vascular lesion |

Fig. 1. Classwise sample images from HAM10000 classification dataset

to be treated in an advanced stage of the disease [19]. A dermatologist examines skin images with Dermoscopy, a non-invasive diagnostic tool. This enables dermatologists to visualize delicate clinical designs of skin lesions and subsurface skin structures that are generally not visible to the unaided eye. These images of the skin are studied under a microscope to point out skin abnormalities and classify them into various types of skin cancers [1]. The enhanced dermoscopic images are free from any skin surface reflections, which helps the dermatologist to diagnose skin cancer accurately.

Skin Cancer Detection, i.e., lesion segmentation, is one of the essential and primary steps in accurate and precise treatment planning for various skin diseases. Automatic skin cancer lesion segmentation is very challenging because of the significant variations in lesion characteristics, such as size, location, shape, color, texture, and skin. The segmentation becomes more arduous due to fuzzy boundaries of lesions, poor color contrast with the surrounding skin, huge intraclass variation, and the existence of antiques such as veins and hairs. Various types of skin cancer images are shown in Fig. 1. Skin lesion segmentation has drawn researchers for over a decade because of its increased clinical applicability and demanding nature. Several image processing and supervised machine learning-based approaches are presented for accurate lesion segmentation, with pros and cons. Most studies pointed toward creating computer-aided design frameworks for skin lesions that would recognize anomalies or skin illnesses. The methods in literature usually follow a certain analysis pipeline [24]: The first step is to delineate the lesion area in the image from healthy skin, followed by automated feature extraction to compute the region of interest. The final step is to predict the type of skin lesion (classification task). Several conventional methods are available in the literature to handle the segmentation of skin lesions. The comprehensive review of different lesion segmentation algorithms is available at [5,6,16,18,23].

In recent times, deep learning techniques have outperformed all the existing state-of-the-art approaches in various computer vision studies like segmentation, detection, classification, etc. [3,4]. The availability of computing resources and huge annotated data has enabled researchers to develop supervised Deep Neural Network models to address these tasks. With the evolution of DCNN and various challenges in skin lesion latterly [8], multiple effective computational approaches have appeared to solve particular problems in this field. Regardless, the most current thriving strategies are based on CNN [10,11,27,28]. Along with lesion segmentation, deep learning approaches have improved classification

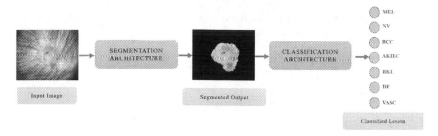

Fig. 2. Proposed two stage deep learning based framework for lesion segmentation and classification

performance, leading to better diagnosis of diseases in medical imaging. The methodologies are used to anticipate the existence of illness and recognize the classes. Recent studies demonstrated remarkable performance in classifying skin cancer using deep learning algorithms in binary classification [10] but failed to achieve comparable performance in multi-class classification.

This research aims to introduce a two-step automated system that will segment the skin lesion and then classify the disease. After a thorough literature survey, the proposed approach is an end-to-end deep learning-based approach, the first for skin lesion segmentation and classification for seven types of lesions. There is no adequate dataset available having segmentation masks and classification labels in a single dataset for seven different types of lesions. To address this, for segmentation tasks, we work with the International Skin Imaging Collaboration (ISIC) 2018 dataset [9] where images with segmentation labels are available, and for classification HAM10000 dataset [26] which consists of seven different skin lesion classes. In our two-step proposed approach, the segmentation task is initially conducted with the ISIC 2018 dataset. With a trained segmentation model, the HAM10000 dataset is segmented, where only classification labels are available. The Region of Interest(ROI) is extracted from segmented images of the HAM10000 dataset fed as input to the classification framework. The two-step framework is shown in Fig. 2.

The rest of the article is arranged as follows: Database description is given in Sect. 2. Presented methods for segmentation and classification of lesions are described in Sect. 3. Section 4 comprises evaluation metrics, experimental results, and performance analysis. This article is concluded in Sect. 5.

2   Dataset

International Skin Imaging Collaboration (ISIC) 2018 has 2594 images with corresponding ground truth labels for lesion Segmentation. The images have different sizes, from hundred to thousand, and varying width and height ratios. The image lesion has distinct appearances and is located in a different part of the skin. The HAM10000 [26] dataset is used for the classification task, consisting of seven types of lesion disease in the dermoscopy images. Figure 1 provided few images from the dataset. The standard pre-processing like scaling the values between [0,1] or [−1,1] is being implemented on entire dataset.

Table 1. Class distribution in HAM10000 dataset

Class	Number of Images	Class Percentage
AKIEC	327	3.27
BCC	514	5.13
BKL	1099	10.97
DF	115	1.15
MEL	1113	11.11
NV	6705	66.95
VASC	142	1.42

The classification dataset consists of around 10015 lesions with Actinic keratosis/Bowen's disease (intraepithelial carcinoma) (AKIEC), Basal cell carcinoma (BCC), Benign keratosis (solar lentigo/seborrheic keratosis/lichen planuslike keratosis) (BKL), Dermatofibroma (DF), Melanoma (MEL), Melanocytic nevus (NV), Vascular lesion (VASC) diseases. The data distribution is presented in Table 1, and we observe that high-class imbalance is challenging in the given datasets, where it is highly skewed towards certain classes. As a result, we observed sparse images for specific groups like DF, VASC, and AKIEC.

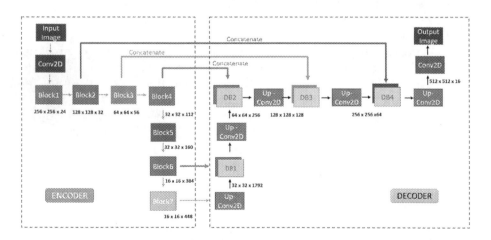

Fig. 3. Proposed encoder-decoder architecture for skin lesion segmenation

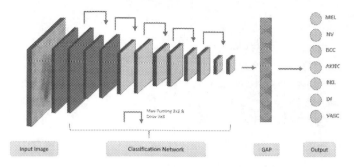

Fig. 4. General architecture for skin cancer classifier where Global Average Pooling is abbreviated as GAP.

3   Proposed Methodology

We propose a two-step framework to handle the task of segmentation and classification in skin lesions. In the first step, the images with skin lesions are segmented to generate coarse-level masks. These segmented masks are multiplied with the corresponding image to extract the coarse level lesion part in the original image, as shown in Fig. 2, which removes redundant data in the image, and these ROI images are input to the classification network that signifies the type of lesion.

3.1   Segmentation Approach

Encoder-decoder architectures are widely used in computer vision for image segmentation task [15,22]. Ronneberger et al. [20] presented U-Net, a breakthrough study for medical image segmentation comprising CNN. Generally, a feature learning block is the encoder module to capture spatial features of the input. It downsamples the input image progressively and decreases feature dimensions to catch high-level patterns of the input image. A decoder block consists of layers that upsample the feature map obtained from the encoder output with extracted spatial features. This article's encoder-decoder module is graphically presented in Fig. 3. In our approach, we designed three different encoder-decoder networks by replacing the encoder block in U-Net with popular CNN architectures such as ResNet [12], InceptionResNetV2 [29] and EfficientNets [25]. Our architecture based on an encoder-decoder module consists of contraction and expansion paths. The encoder consists of convolutional and max-pooling blocks, which downsample the image to extract high-level features. This CNN output contains denser and high-level feature maps. After every block, the number of feature maps doubles to learn the complex features accurately.

In the encoder, dense features are extracted with an output stride of 16 in each variation, where the output stride is the ratio of the input image shape to the output image shape. These extracted features work well in the classification task, but performance hampers while rebuilding the fine segmentation map. Hence, it is challenging to rebuild the segmentation map of the original input

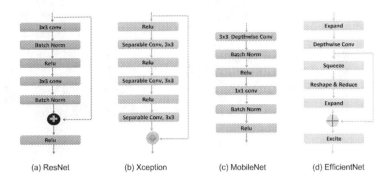

(a) ResNet   (b) Xception   (c) MobileNet   (d) EfficientNet

Fig. 5. Basic building blocks for various CNN architecture used for classification of skin lesion classes.

image dimensions from the feature map of the encoder. The decoder module builds the same U-Net decoder architecture to overcome this problem. This encoder output expands in the decoder consisting of convolutional and bilinear upsampling blocks. By concatenating low-level features from the encoder, low-level feature maps are enhanced to the corresponding block of respective size in the decoder to generate the segmented output more precisely.

3.2   Classification Approach

Convolutional Neural Network has shown tremendous progress in the task of image classification. With advancements in computational resources and fine-tuning methods, CNN fulfills the demand for performance in terms of accuracy. As shown in Fig. 4, a conventional CNN architecture consists of combination blocks of convolutional layer and downsampling layers, followed by a fully connected layer (FC) and the output class. For accurate predictions, CNN automatically pulls the patterns known as features from the input image and carries information at the output block. In the classification step of the dermoscopy, images of the HAM10000 dataset having seven classes from the are to be predicted [26]. We propose to use various classification architectures, which are also used in segmentation encoders like ResNet, Xception, MobileNets, and EfficientNets for classification tasks with an output stride of 32.

ResNets [12]: Deep neural network have shattered performance due to the problem of vanishing gradient. To overcome this problem, He et al. proposed the idea of skip connections or residual networks, as shown in Fig. 5(a). This residual network, known as ResNets, achieved improved performance. ResNet has different variants formed by increasing the residual blocks, namely ResNet18, ResNet50, and so on. ResNet consists of 3×3 convolutional layers stacked with residual or skip connection to form the residual block. For denser prediction and deeper model, maps are periodically doubled. The output of the final layer is 32 times smaller than the input shape. For an image with input shape 224×224, the output is of shape 7×7.

Xception [7]: F. Chollet et al. presented the Xception network as having superior performance. This architecture is inspired by the Inception [29]. In Xception, the Inception module in the Inception network is replaced by Depthwise separable convolution (DSC). Xcpetion architecture consisting of 36 convolutional layers grouped in 14 blocks extracts features. All the blocks except the first and last block have skip connections from the previous block. Xception has DSC with residual or skip connection as the primary building layer, as in Fig. 5(d). The output stride of the final layer is 32.

MobileNet [13]: Mobilenet architecture is a lightweight architecture having depthwise separable convolution as the core layer in building this network, as shown in Fig. 5(c). DSC is a factorized convolution consisting of pointwise 1×1 and depthwise convolution. In mobilenet to each input channel, a single filter is used depthwise followed by pointwise convolution, fed with input from depthwise convolution for stacking them together. A convolution process combines and filters the input into output in a single step. The DSC is a two-step process in which filtering is carried out in separate layers and combing in another. This division has a significant effect on model size and reduces computation.

EfficientNet [25]: CNNs are developed depending on the resource, and scaling occurs for influential performance while increasing the resources. e.g., ResNet-18 [12] can be scaled to ResNet-101 by adding some layers. The traditional procedure for scaling the network is to increase the CNN depth or depth or feed with a higher input image size. These methods have proven to improve performance but with tedious manual tuning. In [25], the author proposed a novel approach to scaling the model that uses a compound coefficient that is highly effective for structural scaling of the CNNs. Rather than arbitrarily increasing network dimensions such as resolution, depth, and width, EfficientNet scales every parameter in the compound coefficient with a fixed set of scaling factors. This network is built with mobile inverted bottleneck convolution (MBConv) [21] and squeeze and excitation optimization [14] as shown in Fig. 5(b).

4   Result and Discussion

We randomly divided the ISIC training dataset into 80% training cohort and 20% testing cohort. The dataset comprises images of varying sizes rescaled to $512 \times 512 \times 3$ for the segmentation task. The segmentation network is trained with a batch size of 8 with a loss function as the sum of cross-entropy and dice loss for 15 epochs setting the parameters for early stopping on Loss. The learning rate was maintained at 0.001 with the ADAM optimizer. In the classification task, we fed the network with an input size of 224×224 and loss function as categorical cross-entropy. The model is trained with a batch size of 8 for 30 epochs setting the parameters for early stopping on Loss. During training, we initialized the learning rate to 0.001 with the ADAM [17] optimizer. We augmented the data with various popular augmentation techniques like rotation, shearing, zooming, brightness, and flipping the original images for segmentation and classification

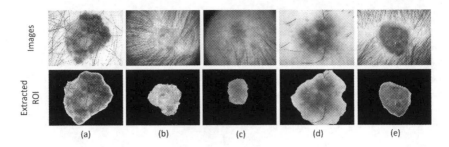

Fig. 6. Sample results ROI extracted after segmentation for classification task.

Table 2. Performance evaluation of segmentation task on test dataset in terms of Dice Score and Mean Intersection over Union

Encoder backbone	Dice Score	mIoU
Original U-Net	71.53	60.58
ResNet50	84.46	73.76
ResNet101	86.30	76.77
MobileNet	83.90	71.32
InceptionResNetV2	87.20	78.03
EfficientNetB4	89.56	81.42

tasks. The frameworks are designed with Tensorflow 2.0 and Keras open-source libraries, and the models are trained on NVIDIA P100 GPU with 16 GB memory.

For the segmentation task, U-Net is just a stack of convolutional layers, the original U-Net underperforms in this task. To experiment, we increase the depth of the network with various encoders like ResNet, MobileNet, and EffcientNet. Also, we design an asymmetric decoder, as seen in Fig. 3. Concatenation of low-level features occurs at some intervals rather than joining each block from the encoder, as proposed by Ronneberger et al. in U-Net improves performance. The modification improves performance with the proposed deep encoder with the asymmetric decoder.

After extracting the ROI by segmenting using an EfficientNet-based encoder, it is fed as input to the various state-of-the-art networks in classification like ResNet, MobileNet, EfficientNet, and Xception. As seen in Table 3, there is significant performance gain when ROI extracted skin lesion is used. For an in-depth comparison, classification is performed with different CNNs with and without ROI obtained from segmentation. The efficacy of the proposed approaches is evaluated in terms of various popular quantitative evaluation parameters. The performance of segmentation approaches is assessed in terms of the Dice Similarity Coefficient (DSC) and Mean Intersection over Union (mIoU) and the classification approach with accuracy. The performance for the segmentation task

Table 3. Performance evaluation of classification task on test dataset with and without considering ROI images

Classification Architecture	Accuracy	
	without ROI	with ROI
ResNet50	74.15	78.32
ResNet101	75.65	79.26
MobileNet	78.54	81.54
Xception	78.04	82.41
EfficientNetB0	75.05	79.14
EfficientNetB3	76.65	82.19

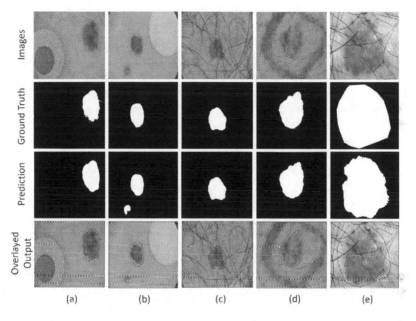

Fig. 7. Segmentation Output with EfficientNetB7 as encoder. Each column represents a lesion image, Ground Truth, segmentation predicted by the network and overlayed image of segmented output(Green) and Ground Truth(Blue). (Color figure online)

of various encoder backbones in DSC and mIoU is given in Table 2. It can be observed that EfficientNetB4 outperformed other encoders quantitatively. Segmentation outputs predicted by the model for five different images are presented in Fig. 7.

From Figs. 7(a) and 7(b), it can be observed that the proposed approach performed well even if non-skin objects are present in the image. The architecture could segment lesions, even severe occlusion, because of hairs. These segmentation results are then multiplied with the original image to extract the skin lesion, as shown in Fig. 6. It can be observed that besides skin lesions, various surrounding patterns may hamper the classifier learning. ROI from Fig. 6 (b) and (e) clearly justifies the need of lesion segmentation before classification. The performance evaluation for the classification task with and without ROI is given in Table 3. The architectures trained on images containing only lesion ROI performed better in terms of accuracy, as shown in Table 3.

5   Conclusion

Skin lesion segmentation and classification are the primary steps in designing the Computer-Aided Diagnostic (CAD) Tool and are essential for precise treatment planning. This study proposed a two-step approach with two distinct databases for skin lesion segmentation and classification. It was observed that, except for lesions, various surrounding patterns might hamper the classifier's learning. To address this, we proposed a two-step approach where in the first step, skin lesions are segmented, and in the second step, ROIs are extracted, which are given input to the classification architecture. Experimentation results showed that classification accuracy with ROI as input outperformed lesion images with surrounding patterns and was improved by 5%. We currently have the performance of the proposed approach on the publicly available dataset.

References

1. Dermoscopy and mole scans in Perth and regional WA. https://myskincentre.com.au/service/dermoscopy/ (2018). Accessed 20 Feb 2020
2. Melanoma stats, facts, and figures. https://www.aimatmelanoma.org/about-melanoma/melanoma-stats-facts-and-figures (2018). Accessed 20 Feb 2020
3. Baheti, B., Innani, S., Gajre, S., Talbar, S.: Eff-unet: A novel architecture for semantic segmentation in unstructured environment. In: 2020 IEEE/CVF Conference on Computer Vision and Pattern Recognition Workshops (CVPRW), pp. 1473–1481 (2020). https://doi.org/10.1109/CVPRW50498.2020.00187
4. Baheti, B., Innani, S., Gajre, S., Talbar, S.: Semantic scene segmentation in unstructured environment with modified deeplabv3+. Pattern Recogn. Lett. **138**, 223–229 (2020). https://doi.org/10.1016/j.patrec.2020.07.029
5. Celebi, M.E., et al.: Border detection in dermoscopy images using statistical region merging. Skin research and technology : official journal of International Society for Bioengineering and the Skin (ISBS) [and] International Society for Digital Imaging of Skin (ISDIS) [and] International Society for Skin Imaging (ISSI). **14**, 347–53 (2008). https://doi.org/10.1111/j.1600-0846.2008.00301.x
6. Celebi, M.E., Wen, Q., Hwang, S., Iyatomi, H., Schaefer, G.: Lesion border detection in dermoscopy images using ensembles of thresholding methods. CoRR abs/1312.7345 (2013). http://arxiv.org/abs/1312.7345
7. Chollet, F.: Xception: Deep learning with depthwise separable convolutions, pp. 1800–1807, July 2017. https://doi.org/10.1109/CVPR.2017.195
8. Codella, N.C.F., et al.: Skin lesion analysis toward melanoma detection: a challenge at the 2017 international symposium on biomedical imaging (ISBI), hosted by the international skin imaging collaboration (ISIC). CoRR abs/1710.05006 (2017). http://arxiv.org/abs/1710.05006

9. Codella, N.C.F., et al.: Skin lesion analysis toward melanoma detection 2018: A challenge hosted by the international skin imaging collaboration (ISIC). CoRR abs/1902.03368 (2019). http://arxiv.org/abs/1902.03368

10. Esteva, A., et al.: Dermatologist-level classification of skin cancer with deep neural networks. Nature. **542** (2017). https://doi.org/10.1038/nature21056

11. González-Díaz, I.: Dermaknet: incorporating the knowledge of dermatologists to convolutional neural networks for skin lesion diagnosis. IEEE J. Biomed. Health Inform. **23**(2), 547–559 (2019). https://doi.org/10.1109/JBHI.2018.2806962

12. He, K., Zhang, X., Ren, S., Sun, J.: Deep residual learning for image recognition. CoRR abs/1512.03385 (2015). http://arxiv.org/abs/1512.03385

13. Howard, A.G., et al.: Mobilenets: efficient convolutional neural networks for mobile vision applications (2017)

14. Hu, J., Shen, L., Sun, G.: Squeeze-and-excitation networks. CoRR abs/1709.01507 (2017). http://arxiv.org/abs/1709.01507

15. Innani, S., Dutande, P., Baheti, B., Talbar, S., Baid, U.: Fuse-PN: a novel architecture for anomaly pattern segmentation in aerial agricultural images. In: 2021 IEEE/CVF Conference on Computer Vision and Pattern Recognition Workshops (CVPRW), pp. 2954–2962 (2021). https://doi.org/10.1109/CVPRW53098.2021.00331

16. Jahanifar, M., Zamani Tajeddin, N., Mohammadzadeh Asl, B., Gooya, A.: Supervised saliency map driven segmentation of lesions in dermoscopic images. IEEE J. Biomed. Health Inform. **23**(2), 509–518 (2019). https://doi.org/10.1109/JBHI.2018.2839647

17. Kingma, D., Ba, J.: Adam: a method for stochastic optimization. In: International Conference on Learning Representations, December 2014

18. Oliveira, R.B., Filho, M.E., Ma, Z., Papa, J.P., Pereira, A.S., Tavares, J.M.R.: Computational methods for the image segmentation of pigmented skin lesions: A review. Comput. Methods Programs Biomed. **131**, 127–141 (2016). https://doi.org/10.1016/j.cmpb.2016.03.032

19. Rigel, D.S., Russak, J., Friedman, R.: The evolution of melanoma diagnosis: 25 years beyond the ABCDs. CA: Cancer J. Clin. **60**(5), 301–316. https://doi.org/10.3322/caac.20074 ,https://acsjournals.onlinelibrary.wiley.com/doi/abs/10.3322/caac.20074

20. Ronneberger, O., Fischer, P., Brox, T.: U-net: convolutional networks for biomedical image segmentation. In: Navab, N., Hornegger, J., Wells, W.M., Frangi, A.F. (eds.) MICCAI 2015. LNCS, vol. 9351, pp. 234–241. Springer, Cham (2015). https://doi.org/10.1007/978-3-319-24574-4_28

21. Sandler, M., Howard, A.G., Zhu, M., Zhmoginov, A., Chen, L.: Inverted residuals and linear bottlenecks: Mobile networks for classification, detection and segmentation. CoRR abs/1801.04381 (2018). https://arxiv.org/abs/1801.04381

22. Sultana, F., Sufian, A., Dutta, P.: Evolution of image segmentation using deep convolutional neural network: a survey. arXiv preprint arXiv:2001.04074 (2020)

23. Tajeddin, N.Z., Asl, B.M.: A general algorithm for automatic lesion segmentation in dermoscopy images. In: 2016 23rd Iranian Conference on Biomedical Engineering and 2016 1st International Iranian Conference on Biomedical Engineering (ICBME), pp. 134–139, November 2016. https://doi.org/10.1109/ICBME.2016.7890944

24. Tajeddin, N.Z., Asl, B.M.: Melanoma recognition in dermoscopy images using lesion's peripheral region information. Comput. Methods Programs Biomed. **163**, 143–153 (2018). https://doi.org/10.1016/j.cmpb.2018.05.005

25. Tan, M., Le, Q.V.: Efficientnet: Rethinking model scaling for convolutional neural networks. CoRR abs/1905.11946 (2019). https://arxiv.org/abs/1905.11946
26. Tschandl, P., Rosendahl, C., Kittler, H.: Data descriptor: the HAM10000 dataset, a large collection of multi-source dermatoscopic images of common pigmented skin lesions. Sci. Data **5**, 1–9 (2018). https://doi.org/10.1038/sdata.2018.161
27. Yu, L., Chen, H., Dou, Q., Qin, J., Heng, P.: Automated melanoma recognition in dermoscopy images via very deep residual networks. IEEE Trans. Med. Imaging **36**(4), 994–1004 (2017). https://doi.org/10.1109/TMI.2016.2642839
28. Yuan, Y., Lo, Y.: Improving dermoscopic image segmentation with enhanced convolutional-deconvolutional networks. CoRR abs/1709.09780 (2017). https://arxiv.org/abs/1709.09780
29. Zhang, X., Huang, S., Zhang, X., Wang, W., Wang, Q., Yang, D.: Residual inception: a new module combining modified residual with inception to improve network performance. In: 2018 25th IEEE International Conference on Image Processing (ICIP), pp. 3039–3043, October 2018. https://doi.org/10.1109/ICIP.2018.8451515

Attending Local and Global Features for Image Caption Generation

Virendra Kumar Meghwal$^{(\boxtimes)}$, Namita Mittal, and Girdhari Singh

Malaviya National Institute of Technology, Jaipur, Rajasthan, India
2018rcp9061@mnit.ac.in
http://www.mnit.ac.in

Abstract. Attention based deep learning architectures have been used extensively for image captioning. Early methods used attention over global features for generating captions. After the advent of local or object-level features, most researchers started using local features as they provided better performance than global features. Thus the importance of global features in caption generation has been ignored in most current methods. Though the local features provide good performance, they may not adequately capture the underlying relations between different local features. On the contrary, the global features can capture the relationship between different object/local features of the image and may provide essential cues for better caption generation. This work proposes a method that utilizes mean global features to attend to salient local features while generating caption. The global features are extracted using a CNN, and local features are extracted using a Faster RCNN. The proposed decoder utilizes these features to generate the caption. Experiments carried out on the MSCOCO dataset indicate that our approach generates better captions indicating the effectiveness of the proposed method.

Keywords: Image Captioning · Natural Language Processing · Attention · Computer Vision

1 Introduction

Each image has some meaningful content, but it is hidden in the form of pixels and is not in the form of natural language. Image Captioning helps to describe this content in the image in a natural language. However, it is a difficult task to perform as knowledge from two different domains (Computer Vision and Natural Language Processing) needs to be combined [1–3]. The majority of current methods [12–14] are based on deep learning and employ an encoder-decoder as base model. The encoder encodes the image into a vector containing features, and the decoder takes this feature vector as input to generate the corresponding caption for the image. Different encoders can generate different types of feature vectors. The feature vector in general can be classified into:

D. Gupta et al. (Eds.): CVIP 2022, CCIS 1776, pp. 627–636, 2023.
https://doi.org/10.1007/978-3-031-31407-0_47

- **Global Features:** They use a CNN to generate whole image features. The image is divided into various square grids, and features of each grid are generated using a CNN.
- **Local Features:** They are generated using an RCNN. First, bounding box regions are identified consisting of salient objects, and then features are generated for each bounding box using a CNN.

Earlier deep learning based image captioning methods utilized global features, but recent methods primarily utilize local features to provide better performance on various automatic evaluation metrics. However, the local features may not correctly capture the relationship between different local objects. In such situations, global features may be helpful as they capture whole image features which may assist in understanding the association between various objects present.

Therefore, we propose a model that utilizes both local and global image features to generate image captions. Following are the main contributions of this work:

- We present a method to combine local features with global features. As a result, the generated features have both local and global context information.
- We also propose a method to utilize local features to select salient features from the features generated above.
- We employ these networks in between the two LSTMs of the decoder for generating captions for images. We validate our approach by conducting experiments on the MSCOCO dataset. The results demonstrate our method's efficacy.

2   Related Work

With the proposal of the encoder-decoder architecture, the era of deep learning based methods for image captioning began. The early deep learning based models [1,2] used a Convolutional Neural Network (CNN) as an encoder to encode an image into a vector of visual features. This feature vector is then fed to a Recurrent Neural Network (RNN) based decoder to decode the feature vector into the caption. Many methods have been proposed for image captioning, and most of them employ an encoder-decoder framework. Recent works also utilize various types of attention, such as visual attention [3], and semantic attention [4], to improve the performance of their method. To avoid using visual attention for non-visual words, [5] proposed adaptive attention with a visual sentinel that employs global features. Another work on global features [6] proposed channel-wise multilayer spatial attention for extracting better features from CNN. Various methods [7–9] use attention over text to achieve better captions. Some [10–13] used attribute information to enhance captions. [10] proposed an attribute-based attention model to select good attributes, then the context vector for each of these attributes is attended adaptively to build the caption. In [11] a CNN fine-tuned on multi-label image dataset(MSCOCO) is used to extract features for the input image's proposed regions. Outputs of CNN for each proposal are then max pooled to get the high-level representation of the image (i.e., attributes). The LSTM then uses these attributes to generate captions. An LSTM with attributes is proposed in [12] which uses attribute information along with image features for caption generation. Five variants of LSTM-A were proposed differing in how they combine attributes with image features. An attribute refinement network is proposed in [13] which utilizes visual attention and conditional random field to get refined attributes from which few are selected through semantic attention. The final caption is generated by taking the softmax of the output of the 2-layer LSTM network and the predicted attributes.

A neural image captioner is presented in [1] which uses a CNN pretrained on image classification to extract image features, and an RNN is used to generate captions using the extracted features. Soft attention and hard attention are proposed in [19]. It utilizes attention in a CNN-LSTM framework. A network to detect semantic concepts from an image is presented in [20] which an LSTM later uses along with image features to build captions. A video event description generation model is presented in [21] which uses an image encoder and sentence encoder to extract features and then uses a concatenated feature to generate video description using a GRU based decoder. A neural network based baby talk method is proposed in [22], which first generates a sentence template [23] with empty slots and then uses a CNN-RNN framework [1] to fill the empty slots. Bottom-Up features were proposed by [14]. Their method uses a two-layer LSTM network with bottom-up and top-down attention. The first LSTM is used for attending to the mean of image features, and its output is used to attend to bottom-up features. The second LSTM generates the words using information from the first LSTM and attended bottom-up features.

Most of the existing works on image captioning use either global features or local features but not both. Some of the works that used both global and local features, include [15] in which local and global features were integrated using an attention mechanism. A two-layer stacked LSTM is used for caption generation such that the attended features are passed to the second LSTM along with the output of the first LSTM and the previous state output of the second LSTM. In [16] an adaptive global-local attention fusion method is proposed. Various combinations of global, local features, and spatial information were experimented with, and their results were compared.

3   The Proposed Work

This section first discusses the overview of the complete architecture and then discusses the proposed decoder's architecture. We also discuss the Gated Linear Unit (GLU) and multi-head attention used in the proposed architecture.

3.1   Overview of Complete Architecture

The overview of the complete architecture of the proposed model is presented in Fig. 1. We extract global features from the image using a ResNet101, and use the pre-extracted local (adaptive bottom-up) features presented in [14]. These local features are extracted using a Faster RCNN. The first LSTM takes the mean ($\bar{l}$) of local features L and attends to various features based on the input context. It outputs a hidden state vector which is concatenated with the mean ($\bar{g}$) of global features G. This concatenated vector contains two half parts: the hidden output vector and mean global features ($\bar{g}$) having same size. This is needed, as GLU requires the two parts to be of equal size. The concatenated feature vector is passed to a GLU. The GLU uses second half consisting of mean global features to refine features from the first half of the vector. A multi-head attention module then utilizes these and local features to identify salient features. These salient features are concatenated with the refined features obtained from GLU and passed to the second LSTM for the next word generation.

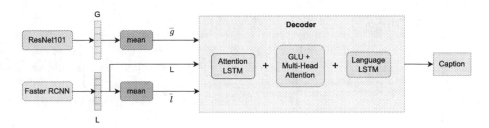

Fig. 1. The overview of complete architecture of the proposed model. (G, L, $\bar{g}$, and $\bar{l}$ denotes global features, local features, mean global features and mean local features respectively.)

3.2 Proposed Decoder Architecture

The decoder majorly consists of 2 LSTM, multi-head attention, and a GLU and is shown in Fig. 2. The first LSTM works as an attention LSTM by selecting essential features useful for the next word generation. The second LSTM works as a language LSTM by selecting the next appropriate word from the training dictionary. Between these two LSTMs, a network consisting of GLU and multi-head attention modifies the important features selected using the mean of global image features.

At the start, mean local features are concatenated with the context vector and passed to the first LSTM, which attends the local features based on the context provided. The LSTM produces a hidden state vector h_{1t} and a cell state vector c_{1t} defined as follows:

$$h_{1t}, c_{1t} = LSTM_1(x_t \oplus \bar{l}) \tag{1}$$

This hidden state output is then concatenated with global features, and the output is refined using a GLU.

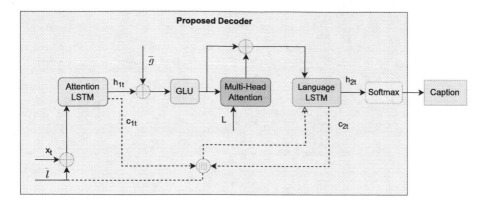

Fig. 2. A diagram representing the proposed decoder architecture. (x_t, h_{1t} and c_{1t}, and h_{2t} and c_{2t} represents context vector, hidden state vector and cell state vector of attention LSTM, and hidden state vector and cell state vector of language LSTM respectively.)

$$P = GLU(h_{1t} \oplus \overline{g}) \tag{2}$$

The multi-head attention module uses the refined features outputted by the GLU and local features to select salient features.

$$L' = MHA(L, P) \tag{3}$$

These salient features are then concatenated with refined features and passed to another LSTM, followed by a softmax unit to generate the caption words.

$$h_{2t}, c_{2t} = LSTM_2(L' \oplus P) \tag{4}$$

$$W_t = Softmax(h_{2t}) \tag{5}$$

3.3 Gated Linear Unit

A GLU divides its input vector into two equal parts (same size) and then applies sigmoid on the second part. Then, element-wise multiplication is performed between the first vector and the output of the sigmoid to get the final attended vector, as shown in Fig. 3. Its working can be represented as follows:

$$GLU(x, y) = x \otimes \sigma(y) \tag{6}$$

When x and y are equal, GLU provides an effective way of applying self-attention to a vector. In our model, the x corresponds to the hidden state vector of the first LSTM, and the y corresponds to the mean of the global image features, which are not equal. In this case, GLU helps to refine the hidden state vector based on the mean global features.

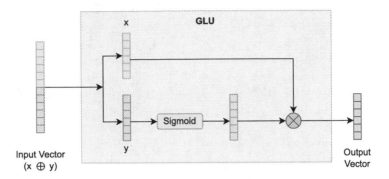

Fig. 3. A diagram representing working of the Gated Linear Unit.

3.4   Multi-head Attention

We adopt multi-head attention from [17] to identify salient features. In multi-head attention (Fig. 4), the input vector is projected into three vectors, Q, K, and V. Each of them is divided into n slices, and then using n heads, attention is applied to them. First scaled dot-product is a calculated between Q_i and K_i^T then dot product is calculated between the softmax of the output of previous dot-product and V_i vector. The final result of multi-head attention is the concatenation of the output (O_i of each head, which can be represented as follows

$$O_{mha} = O_1 \oplus O_2 \oplus ... \oplus O_n \tag{7}$$

$$O_i = Softmax(\frac{Q_i \odot K_i^T}{\sqrt{d}}) \odot V_i \tag{8}$$

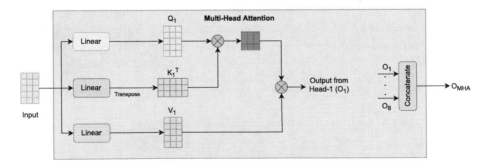

Fig. 4. A diagram depicting working of the Multi-Head Attention. (Q_1, K_1^T and V_1 represents the query vector, transpose of key vector, and value vector for 1st head respectively.)

4   Experiments

This section briefly describes various datasets, experimental settings, and evaluation metrics used for performing the experiments. Then various state-of-the-art methods are compared based on different evaluation metrics (Table 1). We also provide some captions generated by our proposed method and compare them with captions generated by the baseline method and ground truths (Fig. 5).

We trained and tested our model on MSCOCO [18] dataset. It is the most widely used image captioning dataset. It consists of 330k images, each having five captions. The experiments were performed using Karpathy split [2]. The global features are extracted using a ResNet101, and for local features, the pre-extracted adaptive bottom-up features [14] are used. Resnet101 is used to have a fair comparison with existing approaches which use the same model. During experimentation, a minibatch size of 8 and Adam optimizer are used with an initial learning rate of $2e^{-4}$. The model is trained for 60 epochs and label smoothing is used, which utilizes cross-entropy loss.

Various evaluation metrics are used to compare the proposed method with other state-of-the-art methods. BLEU [24] metric uses n-gram precision, METEOR [25] and ROUGE [26] uses sentence similarity, CIDEr [27] uses consensus based strategy and SPICE [28] uses semantic propositions to evaluate generated captions. The BLEU metric has the lowest correlation with human evaluation, METEOR has a better correlation than BLEU, and CIDEr and SPICE have the highest correlation with human judgement.

Table 1. Evaluation metric scores of various state of the art methods and our proposed method after training on MSCOCO dataset.

Method	BLEU1	BLEU4	METEOR	ROUGE	CIDEr	SPICE
Google NIC [1]	66.6	20.3	-	-	-	-
Hard Attention [19]	71.8	25.0	23.0	-	-	-
SCA-CNN [6]	71.9	31.1	25.0	-	95.2	-
GLA [15]	72.5	31.4	24.9	-	96.4	-
Adaptive Attention [5]	74.2	33.2	26.6	-	108.5	-
SCN-LSTM [20]	74.1	34.1	26.1	-	104.1	-
NBT [22]	75.5	34.7	27.1	-	107.2	20.1
BUTD [14]	77.2	36.2	27.0	56.4	113.5	20.3
ASIA [16]	**78.5**	**37.8**	27.7	-	116.7	-
Baseline	75.3	34.4	27.2	55.5	109.7	20.1
Proposed	77.7	36.6	**28.0**	**57.2**	**116.9**	**21.3**

As evident from the METEOR, CIDEr, and SPICE scores, the proposed work outperforms existing work. As METEOR, CIDEr, and SPICE have a better correlation with humans [28] thus, the proposed method generates better captions.

GT1: a man on skis showing a young child how to ski.
GT2: An adult in a red jacket is with a child in a blue snow suit on skis.
GT3: A man and a little boy on skis on a ski hill.
Baseline: a little boy standing on top of a snow covered slope.
Proposed: a man and a child are standing in the snow.

GT1: Two young women digging in to a tin pan of food in a barn.
GT2: A teenage girl holding a food dish while a little girl scoops it.
GT3: The girls are getting the feed ready for the animals.
Baseline: A man holding a plate of food with a .
Proposed: Two women holding a plate of food in their hands.

GT1: Three people walking down a sidewalk while holding umbrellas.
GT2: Three people walking down the sidewalk with umbrellas.
GT3: Three people walking with umbrellas in the rain.
Baseline: A couple of people that are walking in the rain.
Proposed: A group of people walking down a street holding umbrellas.

GT1: Two surfer with surf boards heading out to the water.
GT2: A couple of people walk on a beach with surf board.
GT3: Two surfers walk across the beach towards the ocean.
Baseline: a woman and a dog on a beach.
Proposed: Two people walking on the beach carrying surfboards.

GT1: A woman riding a bike with a basket on it.
GT2: A school girl checks her phone while riding a bike.
GT3: A woman sitting on a bike with a cellphone.
Baseline: A woman is sitting on a bench with her bicycle.
Proposed: A woman riding a bike down a sidewalk.

Fig. 5. Captions generated by the baseline and proposed model on MSCOCO dataset. GT1, GT2 and GT3 represents 3 selected ground truth sentences.

The improved performance can be attributed to our use of GLU to refine the features based on mean global features and then applying multi-head attention to attend to salient features. Also, our attention LSTM uses local features instead of global features in comparison to ASIA [16]. ASIA combines global and local features (along with spatial information) using an adaptive attention based mechanism on the other hand our model uses a combination of GLU followed multi-headed attention.

5 Conclusion and Future Work

In this paper, we propose a method that utilizes local as well as global features to generate image captions. The method concatenates the mean global features with the attended feature. It then utilizes a combination of GLU and multi-head attention to select the salient features which are used for caption generation. Our experiments demonstrate that the proposed work outperforms the existing works on various metrics, including METEOR, CIDEr, and SPICE scores, which correlate better with human evaluation, indicating that the captions generated by the proposed method are better. In future work, similar experiments can be performed using grid features instead of local features. Also, a combination of local, global, and grid features can be used for caption generation.

References

1. Vinyals, O., Toshev, A., Bengio, S., Erhan, D.: Show and tell: a neural image caption generator. In: Proceedings of the IEEE Conference on Computer Vision and Pattern Recognition, pp. 3156–3164 (2015)
2. Karpathy, A., Fei-Fei, L.: Deep visual-semantic alignments for generating image descriptions. In: Proceedings of the IEEE Conference on Computer Vision and Pattern Recognition, pp. 3128–3137 (2015)
3. Xu, K., et al.: Show, attend and tell: neural image caption generation with visual attention. In: International Conference on Machine Learning, pp. 2048–2057. PMLR (2015)
4. You, Q., Jin, H., Wang, Z., Fang, C., Luo, J.: Image captioning with semantic attention. In: Proceedings of the IEEE Conference on Computer Vision and Pattern Recognition, pp. 4651–4659 (2016)
5. Lu, J., Xiong, C., Parikh, D., Socher, R.: Knowing when to look: adaptive attention via a visual sentinel for image captioning. In: Proceedings of the IEEE Conference on Computer Vision and Pattern Recognition, pp. 375–383 (2017)
6. Chen, L., et al.: SCA-CNN: spatial and channel-wise attention in convolutional networks for image captioning. In: Proceedings of the IEEE Conference on Computer Vision and Pattern Recognition, pp. 5659–5667 (2017)
7. Mun, J., Cho, M., Han, B.: Text-guided attention model for image captioning. In: Proceedings of the AAAI Conference on Artificial Intelligence, vol. 31, no. 1, pp. 4233–4239 (2017)
8. Tavakoli, H.R., Shetty, R., Borji, A., Laaksonen, J.: Paying attention to descriptions generated by image captioning models. In: Proceedings of the IEEE International Conference on Computer Vision, pp. 2487–2496 (2017)
9. Zhou, L., Xu, C., Koch, P., Corso, J.J.: Watch what you just said: image captioning with text-conditional attention. In: Proceedings of the on Thematic Workshops of ACM Multimedia 2017, pp. 305–313 (2017)
10. Chen, H., Ding, G., Lin, Z., Zhao, S., Han, J.: Show, observe and tell: attribute-driven attention model for image captioning. In: IJCAI, pp. 606–612 (2018)
11. Wu, Q., Shen, C., Wang, P., Dick, A., Van Den Hengel, A.: Image captioning and visual question answering based on attributes and external knowledge. IEEE Trans. Pattern Anal. Mach. Intell. **40**(6), 1367–1381 (2017)

12. Yao, T., Pan, Y., Li, Y., Qiu, Z., Mei, T.: Boosting image captioning with attributes. In: Proceedings of the IEEE International Conference on Computer Vision, pp. 4894–4902 (2017)
13. Huang, Y., Li, C., Li, T., Wan, W., Chen, J.: Image captioning with attribute refinement. In: 2019 IEEE International Conference on Image Processing, pp. 1820–1824 (2019)
14. Anderson, P., et al.: Bottom-up and top-down attention for image captioning and visual question answering. In: Proceedings of the IEEE Conference on Computer Vision and Pattern Recognition, pp. 6077–6086 (2018)
15. Li, L., Tang, S., Deng, L., Zhang, Y., Tian, Q.: Image caption with global-local attention. In: Thirty-First AAAI Conference on Artificial Intelligence, pp. 4133–4139 (2017)
16. Zhong, X., Nie, G., Huang, W., Liu, W., Ma, B., Lin, C.W.: Attention-guided image captioning with adaptive global and local feature fusion. J. Vis. Commun. Image Represent. **78**, 103138 (2021)
17. Vaswani, A., et al.: Attention is all you need. In: Advances in Neural Information Processing Systems, vol. 30, pp. 5998–6008 (2017)
18. Lin, T.-Y., et al.: Microsoft COCO: common objects in context. In: Fleet, D., Pajdla, T., Schiele, B., Tuytelaars, T. (eds.) ECCV 2014. LNCS, vol. 8693, pp. 740–755. Springer, Cham (2014). https://doi.org/10.1007/978-3-319-10602-1_48
19. Xu, K., et al.: Show, attend and tell: neural image caption generation with visual attention. In: International Conference on Machine Learning, pp. 2048–2057 (2015)
20. Gan, Z., et al.: Semantic compositional networks for visual captioning. In: Proceedings of the IEEE Conference on Computer Vision and Pattern Recognition, pp. 5630–5639 (2017)
21. Kumar, K., Nishanth, P., Singh, M., Dahiya, S.: Image encoder and sentence decoder based video event description generating model: a storytelling. IETE J. Educ. **63**(2), 78–84 (2022)
22. Lu, J., Yang, J., Batra, D., Parikh, D.: Neural baby talk. In: Proceedings of the IEEE Conference on Computer Vision and Pattern Recognition, pp. 7219–7228 (2018)
23. Kulkarni, G., et al.: Babytalk: understanding and generating simple image descriptions. IEEE Trans. Pattern Anal. Mach. Intell. **35**(12), 2891–2903 (2013)
24. Papineni, K., Roukos, S., Ward, T., Zhu, W.J.: Bleu: a method for automatic evaluation of machine translation. In: Proceedings of the 40th Annual Meeting of the Association for Computational Linguistics, pp. 311–318 (2002)
25. Lavie, A., Agarwal, A.: METEOR: an automatic metric for MT evaluation with high levels of correlation with human judgments. In: Proceedings of the Second Workshop on Statistical Machine Translation, pp. 228–231 (2007)
26. Lin, C.Y.: Rouge: a package for automatic evaluation of summaries. In: Text Summarization Branches Out, pp. 74–81 (2004)
27. Vedantam, R., Lawrence Zitnick, C., Parikh, D.: Cider: consensus-based image description evaluation. In: Proceedings of the IEEE Conference on Computer Vision and Pattern Recognition, pp. 4566–4575 (2015)
28. Anderson, P., Fernando, B., Johnson, M., Gould, S.: SPICE: semantic propositional image caption evaluation. In: Leibe, B., Matas, J., Sebe, N., Welling, M. (eds.) ECCV 2016. LNCS, vol. 9909, pp. 382–398. Springer, Cham (2016). https://doi.org/10.1007/978-3-319-46454-1_24

A Study on an Ensemble Model for Automatic Classification of Melanoma from Dermoscopy Images

Anil Kumar Adepu[1] , Subin Sahayam[1]([✉]) , Rashmika Arramraju[2],
and Umarani Jayaraman[1]

[1] Indian Institute of Information Technology Design and Manufacturing,
Kancheepuram, Chennai 600127, India
{ced16i002,coe18d001,umarani}@iiitdm.ac.in
[2] Apollo Institute of Medical Sciences and Research, Hyderabad 500090, India

Abstract. Accurate melanoma classification from dermoscopy images is challenging due to low contrasts between skin lesions and normal tissue regions. The intraclass variance of melanomas in terms of color, texture, shape, size, uncertain boundary, and location of lesions in dermoscopy images adds to the complexity. Artifacts like body hair, blood vessels, nerves, ruler, and ink marks in dermoscopy images also hinder the classification performance. In this work, an inpainting technique has been studied to handle artifacts. Transfer learning models, namely EfficientNet B4, B5, DenseNet121, and Inception-ResNet V2, have been studied. A study on ensembling the results of all the mentioned models is also performed. The robustness of the models has been tested using stratified K-fold cross-validation with test time augmentation (TTA). The trained models with the mentioned inpainting technique outperformed several deep learning solutions in the literature on the SIIM-ISIC Melanoma Classification Challenge dataset. EfficientNet B5 has achieved the best AUC of 0.9287 among the stand-alone models, and the ensemble solution has achieved an AUC of 0.9297.

Keywords: Ensemble Models · Melanoma Classification · Skin Lesion Classification · Transfer Learning · SIIM-ISIC dataset

1 Introduction

Skin cancers are the most commonly diagnosed cancers worldwide with 5 million cases occurring annually [1,2]. Over the past three decades, more people diagnosed with skin cancers are more than those diagnosed with the other type of cancers [3]. Skin cancers are clinically classified into Melanoma and Non-Melanoma. Melanoma is fatal and is responsible for most of the deaths among all skin cancers, with about 9000 people dying every year [4]. It accounts for about 75% of deaths associated with skin cancers, and [5] is still increasing with an incidence of 14%. Melanoma occurs when melanocytes, the pigment-producing

D. Gupta et al. (Eds.): CVIP 2022, CCIS 1776, pp. 637–651, 2023.
https://doi.org/10.1007/978-3-031-31407-0_48

cells that give color to the skin become cancerous. Fortunately, if melanoma is recognized in the patients during the early stages and treated, the survival and prognosis of the patient improve [6,7].

The initial screening and diagnosis of melanoma include an inspection of the skin lesion using dermoscopy. Dermoscopy is a non-invasive skin imaging technique aimed at capturing an illuminated and magnified image of a skin region with increased clarity of the spots on the skin [8]. The imaging technique removes surface reflections from the skin regions, thereby enhancing the visual effects by providing more detailing of the deeper levels of skin regions. Due to such advantages, dermoscopy assessment is more widely used in the diagnosis of melanoma than a mere evaluation with naked eyes by physicians [9]. Clinical Algorithms practised by dermatologists to diagnose skin cancers include ABCD rule (Asymmetry, Border, Color and Diameter) [10], ABCDE (Asymmetry, Border, Color, Diameter, and Evolution) [11], Pattern Analysis [12], CASH algorithm (Color, Architecture, Symmetry, and Homogeneity) [13]. The diagnosis of melanoma has been improved by 5–30% [14] in comparison with the simple naked-eye examination using dermoscopy and classical clinical algorithms. However, the manual inspection made by dermatologists from dermoscopy images is usually tedious, prone to errors, and subjective too [8]. Moreover, cost-efficient population screening is only possible with automated classification techniques. So, automatic Melanoma classification models are much more necessary for early-stage recognition and diagnosis [15].

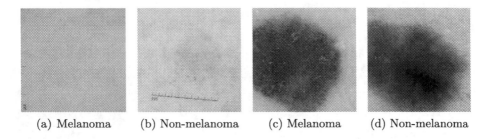

(a) Melanoma   (b) Non-melanoma   (c) Melanoma   (d) Non-melanoma

Fig. 1. Shows various challenges in the classification of melanoma and non-melanoma. (a–b) Shows a melanoma and non-melanoma with low contrast and less inter-class variation (skin vs lesion area), respectively. (c–d) Shows a melanoma and non-melanoma with high contrast but high intra-class variation (regions within the lesion area), respectively.

1.1   Clinical Challenges

The points mentioned below describes the clinical challenges and a need for automatic methods for melanoma classification,

1. Manual diagnoses are prone to human errors, time-taking, and subjective. Even experienced doctors produce varying diagnostic results [8].

2. The tumor features change with time. This makes thin melanomas more difficult to be diagnosed in the initial stages of malignancy [16].
3. Even the best dermoscopic algorithm, the Menzies method, shows a diagnostic accuracy of 81.1%, followed by the ABCD rule (79.0%), 7-point checklist (77.2%), pattern analysis (76.8%), clinical assessment being the least with (73.2%) [15].

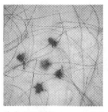   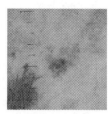

(a) Melanoma with color stains spots   (b) Non-melanoma with ruler marks   (c) Melanoma with body hair   (d) Non-melanoma with color stains and ruler marks

Fig. 2. Shows the artifacts usually present in dermoscopic image data, namely, body hair, color stains, veins, and ruler marks, which act as obstacles while solving the classification problem

1.2   Computational Challenges

1. Presence of high inter and intra-class variation of melanomas in terms of color, texture, shape, low contrast, irregular lesion boundaries, size, and location of lesions in dermoscopy images makes it difficult to classify skin lesions. Examples are shown in Fig. 1.
2. Artifacts like body hair, nerves, ruler marks, color stains, and blurring obstruct the lesion and degrade the classification performance. The mentioned scenario is depicted in Fig. 2.
3. Data non-availability and high class imbalances are a few other computational challenges.

1.3   Contributions

The contributions of the proposed work are as follows,

1. A-weighted ensemble model of Deep CNNs has been proposed for skin lesion classification task towards melanoma classification. The models considered for ensembling are, DenseNets, EfficientNets, Inception-ResNets.
2. The problem of artifact removal has been handled by employing an inpainting technique for accurate lesion classification.

3. To address the class-imbalance problem in the ISIC-2020 dataset, a Cost-Sensitive Learning technique with Focal Loss has been used.
4. Test Time Augmentation with a factor of 81 has been performed to demonstrate the robustness of the test data predictions.

2   Related Work

Automated Melanoma classification has been studied for years, dating back to works as early as 1987 [17]. Until the early 2000s, most works focused on applying low-level hand-crafted features for the melanoma classification task. These low-level features include shape [18], color [19,20], and texture [21,22]. Kusumoputro et al. [23] processed color and shape feature vectors from images, performed dimensionality reduction with principal component analysis (PCA), and employed a multi-layer perceptron for binary classification. Hameed et al. [24] extracted gray-level co-occurrence matrix features and performed the classification task with a support vector machine (SVM) classifier. Murugan et al. [25] used Gaussian filters to extract the features from lesions and classified them by employing SVM. Furthermore, to select proper low-level features, some authors also employed feature selection algorithms and used combinations of these feature sets for better classification performance [26,27].

Recently, convolutional neural networks (CNN) have been applied to solve the melanoma classification problem. The aim is to harness the discrimination capabilities, exploiting its hierarchical feature learning capabilities. Haenssle et al. [28] employed a pre-trained Inception-v4 model for classifying melanoma and melanocytic nevi. They compared their results with a large international group of 58 dermatologists. Yu et al. employed Fully Convolutional Residual models in ISIC 2016 challenge and proposed a two-stage framework performing segmentation followed by classification with the integration of multi-scale contextual information [29]. Wang et al. [30], Li and Qiao et al. [31] proposed EfficientNet-based models for solving the classification problem. R. Zhang [32] added a Fully Connected network for an EfficientNet B6 backbone and performed the classification task. J. Zhang and Yang et al. [33] used a standalone EfficientNet-B3 with Test time augmentation (TTA) for classification. Y. Zhang and Wong [34] employed a DenseNet201 for the classification task.

However, all these methods employ either hand-crafted low-level feature extraction techniques or utilize CNNs with shallow architectures or rely on the features obtained from pre-trained models on the ImageNet dataset without sufficiently considering the characteristics of melanoma. Also, despite using recent deep-CNNs, some models could not address the artifact problem that affected the classification performance. Nevertheless, there is still much more room to harness the potential of CNNs for further improving the performance of melanoma classification models aided by rigorous pre-processing techniques and robust validation strategies.

3   Methodology

3.1   Pre-processing

Skin lesions are generally present at the center part of the dermoscopy image. So, the dermoscopy images have been center-square cropped and resized to 256×256 using AREA interpolation.

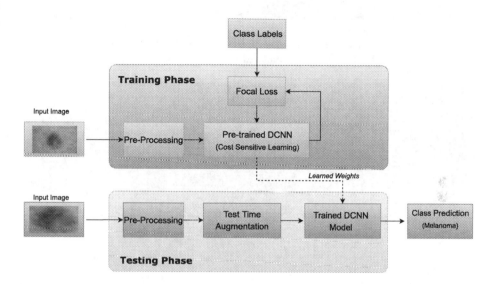

Fig. 3. Proposed Framework for Automatic Classification of Melanoma from Dermoscopy Images

Artifacts in the images obstruct the region of interest (ROI). So to remove such artifacts, an inpainting technique proposed by Telea A. [35] is applied to the dermoscopy images. To find the regions to be inpainted, the darker regions should be highlighted. It is done by performing a close operation on the grayscale version of the input image followed by a blackhat morphological operation using a cross kernel of size 17×17. It is then followed by binary thresholding. The resulting image is used for inpainting. The algorithm initially paints the boundaries followed by the inside regions of the dermoscopy image. By considering a small neighborhood around the pixel of interest, the algorithm replaces the respective pixel with the normalized weighted sum of all the neighborhood pixels. A high weightage is given to skin lesion pixels rather than the background pixels. After a pixel is inpainted, the algorithm proceeds to the next nearest pixel using the Fast Marching Method (FMM) as described in [36]. Thus, all the resized images are inpainted with the above technique to remove artifacts. The effect of the inpainting technique is shown in Fig. 4.

(a) The leftmost image is the input image, the center image is the cross kernel, and the rightmost image is the gray-scale image obtained after applying the close morphological operation.

(b) The leftmost image is the image obtained after applying black-hat morphological operation over the closed image, the center image is the binarized image, and the rightmost image is obtained after applying the in-painting technique.

Fig. 4. Artifact removal using inpainting technique

3.2   Classification Architecture

In recent years, Deep CNNs have made dramatic breakthroughs in many image classification tasks, and with the advent of the ImageNet (ILSVRC) challenge, many state-of-the-art DCNNs have been proposed over the years. In this work, four different Deep CNNs, namely, EfficientNets B4, B5, DenseNet121, and Inception-ResNet V2, have been employed to create the proposed ensemble model. The models have been chosen based on their ability to learn different features.

EfficientNets are employed to harness their scaling ability to width, resolution, and depth. The model taps the potentials of their Squeeze and Excitation blocks for channel-wise attention. It helps the classification pipeline as the tumor size is widely varying, and this scaling ability helps capture distinguishing features at multiple scales. In turn, DenseNets have to skip connections densely from one layer to all other layers, thus facilitating cumulative feature reuse at multiple scales and better feature propagation. On the flip side, Inception-ResNet V2 allows the models to learn features of the varying filter size which is an added advantage considering the widely-varying size of skin lesions in dermoscopic images. The framework to train and test with each of these models for skin lesion melanoma classification is shown in Fig. 3.

Weighted Model Ensembling. After training the four Deep CNN models, a weighted ensemble has been created. Here a pool of weights $[0.1, 0.2, 0.3 \dots, 1.0]$ is assigned for generating model ensembles. The algorithm starts by assigning the highest weight in the pool to the model that has the highest validation AUC score. For each weight 'w_i' in the pool, the weight 'w_i' is assigned to the best performing model and all other models are iterated through with an averaged weight of '$1 - w_i$' and the results are combined. The combination producing the highest AUC is noted and the weight 'w_i' is fixed for the first best model. Then, the above process is repeated for the remaining models (3 here) with the pool of weights now ranging from $[0.1, \dots, '1 - w_i']$. Thus, a fixed weight vector is obtained for all four models in the pipeline which is as follows $[0.4, 0.3, 0.2, 0.1]$.

3.3   Test Time Augmentation

Typically, augmentation of the dataset, the process of adding augmented copies of images for handling class imbalance and teaching various transformations of the original input image, is performed during a training phase. On the flip side, this data augmentation can be done at test time to obtain smoothed predictions to improve the model's performance. Test-Time Augmentation (TTA) [37] in this framework involves grouping the predictions obtained from several augmented copies of the same test image to generate a smoothed result by simply taking an arithmetic mean of the results obtained from multiple cropped patches of each test image as this can also favor removing a few unfavorable crops.

In the proposed work, a TTA factor of 81 is applied i.e., for each test and validation image, the final prediction value is taken as the average of the predictions of 81 augmented images. Detailed information about the various data augmentation operations applied is given in Table 1.

Table 1. List of Augmentations performed during Test Time Augmentation

Augmentation Type	Magnitude Range (Randomness)	Description
Random Rotation	$180° \times rand$	Rotates the image by a random value where *rand* is a random value from normal distribution ($\mu = 0, \sigma = 1$)
Random Shear	$2° \times rand$	Shears the image by a random value where *rand* is a random value from normal distribution ($\mu = 0, \sigma = 1$)
Random Zoom	$1.0 + rand/8.0$	Zooms the image along X and Y axes by a random value where *rand* is a random value from normal distribution
Random Shift	$2.0 + rand$	Shifts the image along X and Y axes by a random value where *rand* is a random value from normal distribution ($\mu = 0, \sigma = 1$)
Random flip	0.5	Randomly (50% chance) flips an image along horizontal or vertical axis
Random Saturation	$[0.7, 1.3]$	Saturates an image with a random value from the given range
Random Contrast	$[0.8, 1.2]$	Adjusts the contrast of an image with a random value from the given range
Random Brightness	$[-0.1, 0.1)$	Adjusts brightness by adding a random value chosen from the given range to each pixel

4   Experimental Results

4.1   Dataset

The proposed framework has been evaluated on the SIIM-ISIC Melanoma Classification Challenge public dataset hosted on Kaggle. It is a subset of data collected from the International Skin Imaging Collaboration (ISIC) Archive [38], which is the largest open-sourced database of high-quality dermoscopic images of skin lesions. The dataset is collected from about 2,056 patients from three continents with about 33,126 representative images in the train set and 10982 images in the test set. In the training data, 425 images turned out to be duplicated (as reported by challenge organizers) and so have been removed. In the remaining 32701 images, 32120 belong to non-melanoma (class 0), and 581 belong to melanoma (class 1). The dataset is highly imbalanced with around 1.8% melanoma images. The test data does not contain ground truth information.

4.2   Hyper Parameters

The class imbalance issue has been addressed using cost-sensitive learning along with Focal Loss [39]. This is a Cross-Entropy Loss variant that assigns a higher weight to the minority class. The strategy helps mitigate the class imbalance problem. It generally gives better performance when compared to data-augmentation techniques. In this setting, the Focal Loss is formulated as,

$$J_{FL} = -\alpha_t(1 - p_t)^\gamma \log(p_t)$$

where,

$$p_t = \begin{cases} p & \text{if } y = 1 \\ 1 - p & otherwise \end{cases}, \text{and} \alpha_t = \begin{cases} \alpha & \text{if } y = 1 \\ 1 - \alpha & otherwise \end{cases}$$

and, α_t is the weighting factor and $\gamma >= 0$ is a tunable focusing parameter, and 'y' is the ground-truth. When $\gamma = 0$, Focal Loss is equivalent to Weighted Binary Cross Entropy Loss.

The models have been trained using Rectified Adam optimizer [40] with an initial Learning rate of 0.00032. This has been preferred as the Adaptive learning methods (conventional Adam) have a large variance in the early stages of training. To reduce the variance, rectified Adam optimizer uses smaller learning rates for the first few epochs while training.

The best model weights have been saved using the Model Checkpoints callback available in the Keras API. EarlyStopping callback with patience of 5 has been used to avoid overfitting. ReduceLROnPlateau callback has been used to dynamically alter the learning rate by a factor once a patience value is reached. The learning rate is increased by 0.3 after a patience value of 2 in the proposed work.

4.3   Stratified K-fold Cross Validation

To preserve the class distribution in the K subsets, a stratified K-fold has been used in this work ($K = 5$). Each K subset resembles the original training data distribution. The training data has been divided into five subsets, with around 6000 images per subset preserving the class distribution *i.e.*, in each subset of 6K images, 1.8% corresponds to melanoma, and the remaining corresponds to non-melanoma.

4.4   Evaluation Metrics

The metric employed for the evaluation of the ISIC competition is Area Under ROC Curve (AUC). Other metrics used in this framework are Accuracy (ACC), Specificity (SPE), and Sensitivity (SEN).

$$ACC = \frac{TP + TN}{TP + TN + FP + FN},$$

$$SEN = \frac{TP}{TP + FN}, \quad SPE = \frac{TN}{TN + FP}$$

ROC (Receiver Operating Characteristic) Curve is a graph of two parameters, i. True Positive Rate, and ii. False Positive Rate. The more the area under this curve, the more the AUC score and the better the model classification performance.

$$TPR(SEN) = \frac{TP}{TP + FN}, \quad FPR(1 - SPE) = \frac{FP}{FP + TN}$$

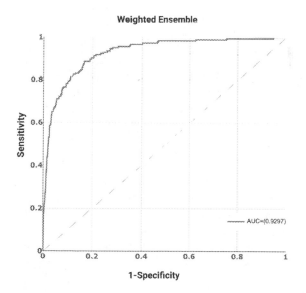

Fig. 5. AUC Score of the proposed Weighted Ensemble Model

4.5   System Implementation

The proposed method is implemented in Python3 based on Keras with TensorFlow backend v2.4.0. All the models have been trained on TPU-v3 8-core pods over the Kaggle platform. For all the images in the dataset, a center crop of 256×256 size to focus on the region of interest (ROI). All the images are processed into the inpainting block for artifact removal. Then, all images are converted into and stored in the format of TensorFlow record files with the ".tfrec" extension. It drastically reduces the training times with faster input pipelines while building TensorFlow models. During train time, these '.tfrec' files are decoded, and each individual encoded image is decoded back into a 3-channel color image with values ranging from 0-255. The images are scaled down to the 0-1 range using Feature Scaling. For a given image I,

$$\text{Scaled Image, } I_{scaled} = \frac{I}{255.0}$$

To enhance the training efficiency, the model weights are initialized with noisy_student weights [41] in EfficientNets and imagenet weights in the rest of the other models.

All the models have been trained for an average of 40 epochs per fold. They stopped around that range due to EarlyStopping callback to avoid overfitting. Average time per epoch = 47 s.

Table 2. Comparison with other state of the art solutions on ISIC-2020 Test Data

Authors	AUC
J. Zhang and Yang et al. [33]	0.9010
Li and Qiao et al. [31]	0.9090
R. Zhang [32]	0.9170
Wang et al. [30]	0.9190
Y. Zhang and Wong [34]	0.9250
Ours (stand-alone model)	**0.9287**
Ours (weighted-ensemble)	**0.9297**

The efficiency of the model increases with depth and training with fewer data results in overfitting. Lequan Yu et al. [29] during their participation in the ISIC-2016 (winners) challenge faced the same issue. Their ResNet101 was overfitting with the limited training data and under-performed. Similarly, all eight models of EfficientNets have been trained on the ISIC 2020 dataset and it is found that EfficientNet B5, followed by EfficientNet B4, gave the best performance on the ISIC-2020 dataset outperforming other deeper networks like B6 and B7. B5 is initialized with noisy-student weights and trained from scratch on the skin lesion images. The B5 model produces 2048 feature maps of 8×8 size from the last convolution layer. Similarly, the EfficientNet B4 produces 1792 feature maps of 8×8 size. Also, in all of the DenseNets available of varying depths, DenseNet121 gave better performance compared to others. It produces 1024 feature maps of 8×8 size. An Inception-ResNet V2 which produces 1532 feature maps of 6×6 size has also been trained.

Finally, four models have been used namely, EfficientNet B5, B4, Dense-Net121, and Inception-ResNet V2 to create a weighted ensemble framework. In all four models, the last Fully Connected Layer has been discarded from the network trained on the ImageNet dataset and replaced with a Global Average Pooling (GAP) layer. A GAP layer is better than a series of Dense layers because it has a lesser number of parameters and is computationally cost-efficient. After the GAP layer, a 1-class Output layer with Sigmoid activation has been added, the output of which is the probability of the input being malignant. The total number of parameters for each of the models in the proposed framework is listed below in Table 3.

Table 3. Classification results of our ensemble and stand-alone models on ISIC-2020 Test data and the parameters in each of the models of the proposed work

Model	AUC	ACC	SEN	SPE	Parameters
EfficientNet B5	0.9287	0.9665	**0.5410**	0.9769	28,515,569
EfficientNet B4	0.9280	0.9644	0.5300	0.9750	17,675,609
Dense Net 121	0.9185	0.9650	0.4860	0.9766	7,038,529
Inception-ResNet V2	0.9109	0.9612	0.4918	0.9726	54,338,273
Ensemble	**0.9297**	**0.9681**	0.5245	**0.9789**	

5   Discussions

The proposed work has been tested and evaluated on the ISIC-2020 dataset. The results are as shown in Table 3. All our results shown in this work are from the Live Leaderboard of the ISIC-archive website under the "SIIM-ISIC Melanoma Classification Challenge Live Leaderboard" tab with the Team name "IIITDM"[1]. The final results of each standalone model are taken as the arithmetic mean of the results from all five folds. Of all the stand-alone models, the EfficientNet B5 model gave the best results. The optimal weight vector obtained for our weighted ensemble model for EfficientNet B5, B4, DenseNet121, Inception-ResNet V2 is, Weight-Vector: [0.4, 0.3, 0.2, 0.1], respectively. The weighted ensemble gave an

---

[1] SIIM-ISIC Melanoma Classification Challenge Live Leaderboard.

improvement of about 0.1, 0.16, and 0.2 in terms of AUC, ACC, and SPE, respectively, when compared to that of the best stand-alone model. In terms of sensitivity, the ensemble model underperformed when compared to that of the stand-alone EfficientNet B5. It could be due to the averaged results of stand-alone models which become more smooth, thus resulting in a lesser sensitivity score. As shown in Fig. 5, with a testing AUC score of 0.9297, the solution is the current state-of-the-art on the ISIC-2020 dataset compared to that of the previous one of 0.9250 by Y. Zhang, and Wong [34]. The proposed work is compared with other state-of-the-art solutions as shown in Table 2.

6 Conclusions and Future Work

In this work, the potentials of Deep CNNs for solving the problem of skin lesion classification toward Melanoma recognition has been explored. The concept of residual learning with dense connectivity in DenseNets facilitates feature propagation and feature reuse. Squeeze and excitation blocks to capture inter-channel dependencies in EfficientNets addressed the problem of high inter-class similarities and proved to be an immediate solution to handle the complex challenges in melanoma classification. These models gave promising results in solving the classification task. The inpainting technique proved to be an efficient tool to address the artifact removal problem. It significantly improved the performance of the model on the classification task. Techniques like Test Time Augmentation and Stratified K-fold showed the robustness of the models. Focal Loss proved to be an efficient tool compared to the vanilla version of Binary Cross-Entropy (BCE) loss for handling highly imbalanced datasets. The ensemble model gave better results compared to the stand-alone models although at a trade-off of higher computational costs.

Nevertheless, there is still a potential room for improving the performance by employing other pre-processing techniques and robust training strategies. As part of future work, the authors plan to make an ablation study with different components viz., inpainting block, TTA block, etc. used in the classification pipeline. The potential of Knowledge Distillation techniques will be harnessed to address the drawbacks of ensemble learning by reducing the computational costs without compromising on the performance. Furthermore, methods and models to improve the sensitivity of detecting melanoma in the imbalanced dataset will be explored.

References

1. Rogers, H.W., Weinstock, M.A., Feldman, S.R., Coldiron, B.M.: Incidence estimate of nonmelanoma skin cancer (keratinocyte carcinomas) in the us population, 2012. JAMA Dermatol. **151**(10), 1081–1086 (2015)
2. Siegel, R.L., Miller, K.D., Jemal, A.: Cancer statistics, 2016. CA: Cancer J. Clin. **66**(1), 7–30 (2016)
3. Stern, R.S.: Prevalence of a history of skin cancer in 2007: results of an incidence-based model. Arch. Dermatol. **146**(3), 279–282 (2010)

4. US Cancer Statistics Working Group: United states cancer statistics: 1999–2010 incidence and mortality web-based report. Atlanta: US Department of Health and Human Services, Centers for Disease Control and Prevention and National Cancer Institute, vol. 201 (2013)

5. Jerant, A.F., Johnson, J.T., Sheridan, C.D., Caffrey, T.J.: Early detection and treatment of skin cancer. Am. Fam. Phys. **62**(2), 357–368 (2000)

6. Balch, C.M., et al.: Final version of the American joint committee on cancer staging system for cutaneous melanoma. J. Clin. Oncol. **19**(16), 3635–3648 (2001)

7. Freedberg, K.A., Geller, A.C., Miller, D.R., Lew, R.A., Koh, H.K.: Screening for malignant melanoma: a cost-effectiveness analysis. J. Am. Acad. Dermatol. **41**(5), 738–745 (1999)

8. Binder, M., et al.: Epiluminescence microscopy: a useful tool for the diagnosis of pigmented skin lesions for formally trained dermatologists. Arch. Dermatol. **131**(3), 286–291 (1995)

9. Silveira, M., et al.: Comparison of segmentation methods for melanoma diagnosis in dermoscopy images. IEEE J. Sel. Top. Signal Process. **3**(1), 35–45 (2009)

10. Stolz, W.: Abcd rule of dermatoscopy: a new practical method for early recognition of malignant melanoma. Eur. J. Dermatol. **4**, 521–527 (1994)

11. Blum, A., Rassner, G., Garbe, C.: Modified ABC-point list of dermoscopy: a simplified and highly accurate dermoscopic algorithm for the diagnosis of cutaneous melanocytic lesions. J. Am. Acad. Dermatol. **48**(5), 672–678 (2003)

12. Pehamberger, H., Steiner, A., Wolff, K.: In vivo epiluminescence microscopy of pigmented skin lesions. I. pattern analysis of pigmented skin lesions. J. Am. Acad. Dermatol. **17**(4), 571–583 (1987)

13. Henning, J.S., Dusza, S.W., Wang, S.Q., Marghoob, A.A., Rabinovitz, H.S., Polsky, D., Kopf, A.W.: The cash (color, architecture, symmetry, and homogeneity) algorithm for dermoscopy. J. Am. Acad. Dermatol. **56**(1), 45–52 (2007)

14. Garnavi, R., Aldeen, M., Bailey, J.: Computer-aided diagnosis of melanoma using border-and wavelet-based texture analysis. IEEE Trans. Inf. Technol. Biomed. **16**(6), 1239 1252 (2012)

15. Dolianitis, C., Kelly, J., Wolfe, R., Simpson, P.: Comparative performance of 4 dermoscopic algorithms by nonexperts for the diagnosis of melanocytic lesions. Arch. Dermatol. **141**(8), 1008–1014 (2005)

16. Bono, A., et al.: Melanoma detection. Dermatology **205**(4), 362–366 (2002)

17. Cascinelli, N., Ferrario, M., Tonelli, T., Leo, E.: A possible new tool for clinical diagnosis of melanoma: the computer. J. Am. Acad. Dermatol. **16**(2), 361–367 (1987)

18. Mishra, N.K., Celebi, M.E.: An overview of melanoma detection in dermoscopy images using image processing and machine learning. arXiv preprint arXiv:1601.07843 (2016)

19. Stanley, R.J., Stoecker, W.V., Moss, R.H.: A relative color approach to color discrimination for malignant melanoma detection in dermoscopy images. Skin Res. Technol. **13**(1), 62–72 (2007)

20. Cheng, Y., et al.: Skin lesion classification using relative color features. Skin Res. Technol. **14**(1), 53–64 (2008)

21. Ballerini, L., Fisher, R.B., Aldridge, B., Rees, J.: A color and texture based hierarchical K-NN approach to the classification of non-melanoma skin lesions. In: Celebi, M., Schaefer, G. (eds.) Color Med. Image Anal., pp. 63–86. Springer, Dordrecht (2013). https://doi.org/10.1007/978-94-007-5389-1_4

22. Tommasi, T., La Torre, E., Caputo, B.: Melanoma recognition using representative and discriminative kernel classifiers. In: Beichel, R.R., Sonka, M. (eds.) CVAMIA 2006. LNCS, vol. 4241, pp. 1–12. Springer, Heidelberg (2006). https://doi.org/10.1007/11889762_1

23. Kusumoputro, B., Ariyanto, A.: Neural network diagnosis of malignant skin cancers using principal component analysis as a preprocessor. In: 1998 IEEE International Joint Conference on Neural Networks Proceedings. IEEE World Congress on Computational Intelligence (Cat. No. 98CH36227), vol. 1, pp. 310–315. IEEE (1998)

24. Hameed, N., Hameed, F., Shabut, A., Khan, S., Cirstea, S., Hossain, A.: An intelligent computer-aided scheme for classifying multiple skin lesions. Computers 8(3), 62 (2019)

25. Murugan, A., Nair, S.A.H., Kumar, K.S.: Detection of skin cancer using SVM, random forest and KNN classifiers. J. Med. Syst. 43(8), 1–9 (2019)

26. Ganster, H., Pinz, P., Rohrer, R., Wildling, E., Binder, M., Kittler, H.: Automated melanoma recognition. IEEE Trans. Med. Imaging 20(3), 233–239 (2001)

27. Celebi, M.E., et al.: A methodological approach to the classification of dermoscopy images. Comput. Med. Imaging Graph. 31(6), 362–373 (2007)

28. Haenssle, H.A., et al.: Man against machine: diagnostic performance of a deep learning convolutional neural network for dermoscopic melanoma recognition in comparison to 58 dermatologists. Ann. Oncol. 29(8), 1836–1842 (2018)

29. Yu, L., Chen, H., Dou, Q., Qin, J., Heng, P.A.: Automated melanoma recognition in dermoscopy images via very deep residual networks. IEEE Trans. Med. Imaging 36(4), 994–1004 (2016)

30. Xingguang, J., Yuan, W., Luo, Z., Yu, Z., et al.: Deep neural network for melanoma classification in dermoscopic images. In: 2021 IEEE International Conference on Consumer Electronics and Computer Engineering (ICCECE), pp. 666–669. IEEE (2021)

31. Li, C., Qiao, Z., Wang, K., Hongxing, J.: Improved efficientnet-B4 for melanoma detection. In: 2021 IEEE 2nd International Conference on Big Data, Artificial Intelligence and Internet of Things Engineering (ICBAIE), pp. 127–130. IEEE (2021)

32. Zhang, R.: Melanoma detection using convolutional neural network. In: 2021 IEEE International Conference on Consumer Electronics and Computer Engineering (ICCECE), pp. 75–78. IEEE (2021)

33. Jiang, Y., Huang, R., Shi, J., et al.: Efficientnet-based model with test time augmentation for cancer detection. In: 2021 IEEE 2nd International Conference on Big Data, Artificial Intelligence and Internet of Things Engineering (ICBAIE), pp. 548–551. IEEE (2021)

34. Zhang, Y., Wang, C.: SIIM-ISIC melanoma classification with densenet. In: 2021 IEEE 2nd International Conference on Big Data, Artificial Intelligence and Internet of Things Engineering (ICBAIE), pp. 14–17. IEEE (2021)

35. Telea, A.: An image inpainting technique based on the fast marching method. J. Graph. Tools 9(1), 23–34 (2004)

36. Sethian, J.A.: A fast marching level set method for monotonically advancing fronts. Proc. Natl. Acad. Sci. 93(4), 1591–1595 (1996)

37. Shanmugam, D., Blalock, D., Balakrishnan, G., Guttag, J.: When and why test-time augmentation works. arXiv preprint arXiv:2011.11156 (2020)

38. Rotemberg, V., et al.: A patient-centric dataset of images and metadata for identifying melanomas using clinical context. Sci. Data 8(1), 1–8 (2021)

39. Lin, T.Y., Goyal, P., Girshick, R., He, K., Dollár, P.: Focal loss for dense object detection. In: Proceedings of the IEEE International Conference on Computer Vision, pp. 2980–2988 (2017)
40. Liu, L., Jiang, H., He, P., Chen, W., Liu, X., Gao, J., Han, J.: On the variance of the adaptive learning rate and beyond. arXiv preprint arXiv:1908.03265 (2019)
41. Xie, Q., Luong, M.T., Hovy, E., Le, Q.V.: Self-training with noisy student improves imagenet classification. In: Proceedings of the IEEE/CVF Conference on Computer Vision and Pattern Recognition, pp. 10687–10698 (2020)

Challenges in Data Extraction from Graphical Labels in the Commercial Products

K. C. Shahira$^{(\boxtimes)}$ ⓘ and A. Lijiya ⓘ

National Institute of Technology Calicut, Kozhikode, India
{shahira_p170096cs,lijiya}@nitc.ac.in

Abstract. Text detection from images is an important and challenging computer vision task. It has a wide variety of applications in reading signboards in autonomous navigation, document image analysis, as well as in assisting visually disabled population. This article presents the need for text extraction of various sizes and fancy typefaces to recognize the text in graphical labels of daily consumables. A dataset of graphical labels of daily consumables and medicines is collected and annotated for further detection using Yolo-v5. We compare the performance of the existing optical character recognition (OCR) system on synthetic datasets and real-world datasets, emphasizing the significance of small text detection from images. It summarizes the limitations in text recognition in the real-world scenario with examples and plausible solutions. We focus on enhancing the OCR for small text extraction on these pictorial labels so that the visually impaired shopper never misses out on critical information.

Keywords: Data Extraction · OCR · Text Recognition · Scene Text Recognition · YoloV5

1 Introduction

Text extraction from images is a well-studied problem in computer vision in recent years. The reading challenges by ICDAR [1] are conducted to reduce the difference in text recognition rate between machines and humans. Extraction of textual content enhances the information in the image of which it is a part. Whether a document or a natural image, it can be extracted using different methods.

The captions or product descriptions given in the daily consumables or medicine bottles are difficult to be read by people aged 40 and above. This is because, aging causes presbyopia, to adult vision, it is difficult to focus on reading. Moreover, the small font sizes make it difficult for people who use spectacles to gather the information. Most commercial products emphasize improving the graphics' aesthetic value, and this further reduces the readability of important information. Identifying a product in the market with its trademark textual element can be done by any text recognition API like cloud vision API by Google or smartphone applications like Taptapsee, which assist visually impaired people

© The Author(s), under exclusive license to Springer Nature Switzerland AG 2023
D. Gupta et al. (Eds.): CVIP 2022, CCIS 1776, pp. 652–663, 2023.
https://doi.org/10.1007/978-3-031-31407-0_49

in choosing the products. The issue is in determining the relevant information from the printed text. When compared to sensitive information such as allergen information, expiry date, or batch number, a large portion of the product information in the graphics is irrelevant. The small font of the content makes it strenuous to read by normal eyesight.

Fig. 1. A framework for extracting significant textual information from a product image. Prior to text recognition, the region of interest goes through pre-processing, and the final result can be read by a TTS.

As a solution to this, the relevant information or the region of interest (RoI) can be located using object recognition integrated into a mobile application. Extracting the RoI and the text recognition is done using OCR. The text recognised can be delivered to TTS, which will read out the captions to help the visually impaired. The architecture for the same is presented in Fig. 1; here the input sample is an image of medicine, from which the region of interest is recognised and pre-processed for further text extraction, such as the batch number and expiry date.

In this article, we also present the various methods to recognise the small text in a product image and identify the various limitations of the existing OCR in identifying the multi-oriented, diverse and small fonts.

The remainder of this article is organised as follows: Sect. 2 examines recent techniques towards text recognition from scenes and documents. The proposed methodology and results are discussed in Sect. 3. Section 4 is devoted to challenges in reading the text, while Sect. 5 concludes the article by discussing future developments.

2   Related Works

This section discusses the background and the state-of-the-art methods in both object detection and text recognition.

Scene Text Recognition. Text recognition involves text detection or identifying the textual region in an image followed by the recognition of the text. Scene text recognition (STR) [8–10, 14] identifies the text in any complex scene, which has applications in document image analysis to street text view detection in autonomous navigation. Modern OCRs include Google Tesseract, AbbyFinder, and Amazon Rekognition, trained on neural networks to recognize words instead of focusing on single characters. Document text extraction is a subfield of STR where text recognition is done with OCR with 99% accuracy. However, when applied to natural scenes, the same OCR methods detect text with a lower accuracy due to varying font sizes and various illumination conditions.

Object Detection. Object detection deals with detecting instances of objects in an image into their respective categories (like cars, buildings). This involves localization of the object and classifying into respective classes. A successful object detection was carried out in 2001 by Viola et al. [2], where they introduced a framework for face detection using handcrafted feature extraction followed by feature selection based on AdaBoost. Despite the tremendous complexity in terms of both time and space, this was an effective object detection framework.

The success of the object detection method is attributed to the pioneers in deep learning, Convolutional Neural Networks (CNN) [14] and its ability to learn high-level feature representations of an image. The achievement of deep learning methods is due to the high computing capacity provided by GPU and the benchmark datasets accessible.

In 2014, the region-based object detection (RCNN) used CNN to find the region of object proposals. Object recognition can be divided into two classes: single-stage detectors and multi-stage detectors. In multi stage, it starts with first extracting some region of interest (or bounding boxes) and then applying classification on these boxes. RCNN and its modified versions-Fast RCNN and Faster-RCNN fall in this category. In single-stage detectors, the box prediction and classification are carried out simultaneously, contrary to multi-stage detectors. Single-shot detectors (SSD) [12] and all the versions of Yolo-v5 [5] belong to this category. We use Yolo-v5 [7] for region-of-interest identification as it is a single-shot detector and is faster than its counterparts.

3   Methodology

The framework is implemented in python 3.6 using Tensorflow. Yolo-v5 is used for object detection, followed by text recognition in the extracted region of interest, using Python wrapper for Tesseract. Figure 1 describes the proposed pipeline.

3.1   Dataset Collection and Pre-processing

The data comprises of images of daily use products which are collected by using a smart phone camera with a focus on product details such as price and expiry date, a sample image is given in Fig. 2. The captured 700 images is then augmented by using a data library called Augmentor. Data augmentation uses affine transformations like rotation and translation, to increase the data size to 3000 images. The data is then manually annotated to determine the region of interest.

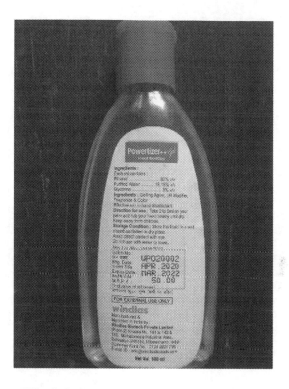

Fig. 2. A sample image with the RoI marked

The pre-processing involves the conversion of the RGB image to binary, followed by canny edge detection and opening operation. The opening involves erosion followed by dilation. Erosion shrinks the image objects and removes the small anomalies, while dilation expands them and fills the holes and broken areas. Skew correction to correct the RoI orientation is done as well. The pre-processing on RoI is given in Fig. 3.

3.2   Region of Interest Identification

We assume that the region of interest contains critical information such as price and expiration date. This RoI is identified using a Yolo-v5 based object detection algorithm. The structural details of the model used is given in Fig. 4. The backbone, neck and output make up the network's three basic structural components. The backbone section concentrates on obtaining feature information from input images, the neck part combines the gathered feature information and produces feature maps at three different scales, and the output part uses these feature maps to identify objects.

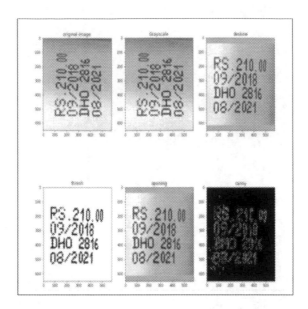

Fig. 3. Pre-processing on the RoI extracted.

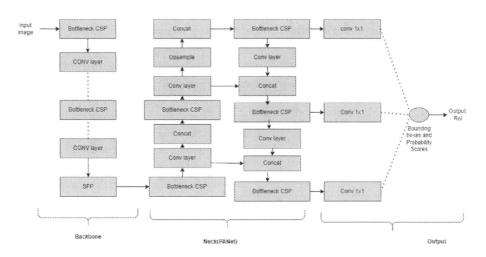

Fig. 4. Architecture of YOLOv5 [7]. The model Backbone extracts essential features from an input image and the model head output the objectness scores and bounding boxes by applying anchor boxes to features

Manual annotation of the RoI is using the LabelImg tool, which generates the corresponding '*.json*' files. Annotations can also be saved as '*.xml*' files in Pascal-VOC [4] format or text files in Yolo-v5 format. The image and the '*.json*' file is the input to the object detector. Yolo-v5 object detector is trained on 80% of dataset images and the 20% is used for validation. We acquire the bounding box coordinates after using the Yolo-v5 algorithm and crop out the region of interest, followed by pre-processing like grayscaling, opening, thresholding, and deskewing. The accuracy of object detection by Yolo-v5 is 84%, indicating the need for more training data. The region of interest extracted by Yolo-v5 undergoes pre-processing before text extraction.

3.3 Text Detection

The text detection from the RoI is done with two OCR networks. Firstly, Pytesseract, a python wrapper for Google's tesseract-OCR engine. It works in a step-wise manner where the first step is Adaptive Thresholding by which the original images are converted into binary images. In the next step, it extracts character outlines followed by finding the text and lines and then text recognition. Secondly, we use a simple-OCR based on a standard CRNN architecture. It is trained on a synthetic generated text dataset with the help of the Text Recognition Data Generator (*trdg*). The *trdg* library generates text image samples which can be used to train an OCR system. Testing is done on a few synthetic images from the MjSynth [11] dataset. Figure 5 illustrates the comparison of the output of the OCR on the real data and synthetic data [11]. The recognition rate in real input images varies from image to image, depending on the quality and size of fonts.

4 Results and Discussions

4.1 Evaluation Metrics

The performance of object detection module can be evaluated using the metrics: *(a)* IoU *(b)* Accuracy *(c)* Precision, *(d)* Recall, *(e)* F-score. We evaluate the RoI extraction using b,c,d and e given by Eq. 1 to Eq. 4. The evaluation metrics are given by the following equations:

$$Precision = \frac{TP}{TP + FP} \tag{1}$$

$$Recall = \frac{TP}{TP + FN} \tag{2}$$

$$Accuracy = \frac{TP + TN}{TP + FP + TN + FN} \tag{3}$$

$$F1 = 2 \cdot \frac{Precision \cdot Recall}{Precision + Recall} \tag{4}$$

The performance text recognition is evaluated by character level accuracy (accuracy$_{CL}$) which is the ratio of the number of characters correctly recognised η_c to the total number of characters N_c.

$$Accuracy_{CL} = \frac{\eta_c}{N_c} \qquad (5)$$

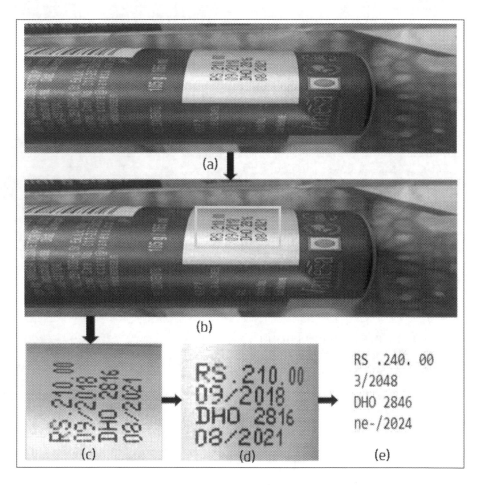

Fig. 5. Steps involved in finding the region of interest followed by text extraction. *(a)* Input image, *(b)* Region Identification, *(c)* RoI extracted, *(d)* Skew corrected RoI, and *(e)* Text detected

4.2   Region Identification:

The RoI extraction is done by Yolo-V5 and the accuracy is 84% on custom dataset. Figure 5 represents the overall results on a product image qualitatively. The learning curve is given by Fig. 6, it depicts the precision, recall and mean average precision mAP. mAP is a metric used for object detection models, which is the average of AP. It compares the ground-truth bounding box to the detected box and returns a score. The higher the score, the more reliable the model's detections are. The quantitative results of RoI identification is given in Table 1.

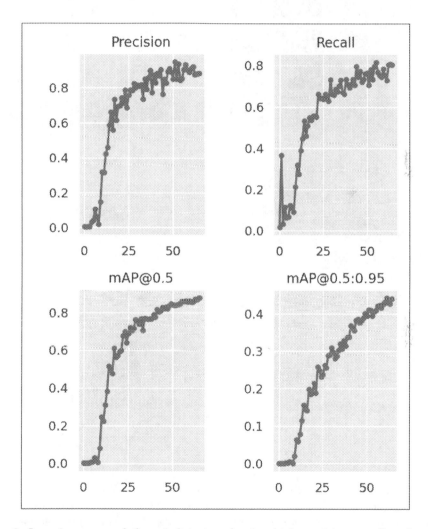

Fig. 6. Learning curve of the roi detector showing high precision, recall and mean average precision (mAP) at different thresholds - 0.5 and 0.95

Table 1. Precision, Recall and F1-score for the RoI detector

Metrics	Value
Precision	0.883
Recall	0.803
F1-score	0.841

Fig. 7. *(a)* A few synthetic images from MJSynth [11] dataset and predicted text on top of each word image, *(b)* A random image from the real world data and the predicted output.

4.3   Text Recognition

Figure 7 gives the qualitative comparison of text recognition on the actual data and synthetic data. The qualitative and the quantitative results depicts that text extraction results need more accuracy in real data. This is because the baseline OCR used is trained for digitally born images. The recognition rate varies for synthetic and real data. Because of the various font sizes and several of the difficulties listed in the following section, the recognition fluctuates among the real-world data.

5   Challenges in Reading Text

This paper focuses on the difficulties in comprehending the text, as seen in Fig. 8. The textual elements of the figure are highlighted, and some of them are hard to understand with the human eye. A few of the issues includes the following:

1. **Materials Used for Packing:** The materials used in packaging differ from one product to the next. Text printed on paper-like materials is easier to read than those written on aluminium surfaces. These surfaces cause reflection problems, therefore we'll require image processing techniques that can enhance such photos without compromising information.
2. **Illumination:** The illumination conditions at the time of image acquisition introduces distortions to the image leading to false detections.
3. **Impaired products:** Sometimes the packets can be wrinkled, making it difficult to read.

Fig. 8. Text at the bottom of an aluminium container blurred by mist, date of expiry specified on the crimp of tubes, artistic fonts, transparent prints that camouflage with the juice bottles are just few examples of challenges in comprehending the text.

4. **Graphics:** The combination of colors used for printing, used to improve the aesthetics, causes difficulty in identifying the text from the clutter.
5. **Artistic Fonts:** Making the words legible and understandable for machines should not mean accepting archaic designs. However, the product names are printed in beautiful typefaces which are difficult to be read by an OCR.
6. **Lack of Standard:** The majority of items place a greater emphasis on visuals than on important information such as allergen information. The product name and other product offerings are printed in large font, while the essential content is dispersed around the product, with some at the top and others at the bottom *etc.* There should be common norms regarding where the product's sensitive information should be placed.

We have sophisticated technology and algorithms, but interpreting critical data like expiry date is not feasible with either technology or the naked eye. So, what is the significance of printing? This can be solved only by making changes to the policy, which should set a standard like minimum font size, font color. The textual information should be readable by the color blind people as they cannot perceive the printing in numerous colors. If possible, the products should include braille/tactile print to assist the blind.

6   Conclusion and Future Work

In this work, we discuss the challenges in text localization in the case of small fonts in the consumables using a text detection framework. This work aims to improve the end-user experience by solving for the information availability for them. To that end, a dataset of commonly used consumables and medicines is compiled and annotated for the most sensitive information of interest, like expiry date. We notice that the text extraction from these products is accurate for large fonts, but reading the crucial contents of the products designated in small font sizes is less accurate. The RoI is extracted with 84% accuracy, and text recognition achieved 80% word-level accuracy using the synthetic dataset and 36% accuracy on real world data. But the work shows promise in improving this accuracy. We are working on enhancing text recognition accuracy and providing audio descriptions of the output images to visually challenged persons.

Acknowledgement. We thank all the reviewers for their comments on this paper. We would also like to thank Gaurav Kumar and Rishav, BTech students of NITC, for all their contributions in completing this work.

References

1. Karatzas, D., et al.: ICDAR 2015 competition on robust reading. In: 2015 13th International Conference on Document Analysis and Recognition (ICDAR), pp. 1156–1160. IEEE (2015)
2. Viola, P., Jones, M.J.: Robust real-time face detection. Int. J. Comput. Vision **57**(2), 137–154 (2004)

3. Wu, S., Wieland, J., Farivar, O., Schiller, J.: Automatic alt-text: computer-generated image descriptions for blind users on a social network service. In: Proceedings of the 2017 ACM Computer Supported Cooperative Work and Social Computing, pp. 1180–1192 (2017)
4. The Pascal Visual Object Classes Home. http://host.robots.ox.ac.uk/pascal/VOC/
5. Ge, Z., Liu, S., Wang, F., Li, Z., Sun, J.: Yolo-v5x: exceeding Yolo-v5 series in 2021, arXiv preprint arXiv:2107.08430 (2021)
6. Yakovlev, A., Lisovychenko, O.: An approach for image annotation automatization for artificial intelligence models learning. Adapt. Autom. Control Syst. 1(36), 32–40 (2020)
7. Ge, Z., Liu, S., Wang, F., Li, Z., Sun, J.: Yolo-v5x: exceeding Yolo-v5 series in 2021. https://arxiv.org/abs/2107.08430
8. Mishra, A., Alahari, K., Jawahar, C.V.: Top-down and bottom-up cues for scene text recognition. In: 2012 IEEE Conference on Computer Vision and Pattern Recognition, pp. 2687–2694. IEEE (2012)
9. Shi, B., Bai, X., Yao, C.: An end-to-end trainable neural network for image-based sequence recognition and its application to scene text recognition. IEEE Trans. Pattern Anal. Mach. Intell. 39(11), 2298–2304 (2016)
10. Zhu, Y., Yao, C., Bai, X.: Scene text detection and recognition: recent advances and future trends. Front. Comput. Sci. 10(1), 19–36 (2016)
11. Simonyan, K., Vedaldi, A., Zisserman, A.: Deep inside convolutional networks: visualising image classification models and saliency maps. In: Workshop at International Conference on Learning Representations (2014)
12. Liu, W., et al.: SSD: single shot MultiBox detector. In: Leibe, B., Matas, J., Sebe, N., Welling, M. (eds.) ECCV 2016. LNCS, vol. 9905, pp. 21–37. Springer, Cham (2016). https://doi.org/10.1007/978-3-319-46448-0_2
13. Reddy, S., Mathew, M., Gomez, L., Rusinol, M., Karatzas, D., Jawahar, C.V.: Roadtext-1k: text detection and recognition dataset for driving videos. In: 2020 IEEE International Conference on Robotics and Automation (ICRA), pp. 11074–11080. IEEE (2020)
14. Goodfellow, I., Bengio, Y., Courville, A.: Deep Learning. MIT Press, Cambridge (2016)

A Novel Deep Learning Method for Thermal to Annotated Thermal-Optical Fused Images

Suranjan Goswami[1]([mail]) [ID], Satish Kumar Singh[1] [ID], and Bidyut Baran Chaudhuri[2] [ID]

[1] Computer Visions and Biometrics Lab, Indian Institute of Information Technology, Allahabad, India
suranjan_arcade@yahoo.co.in
[2] Techno India University, Salt Lake, Kolkata, India

Abstract. Thermal Images profile the passive radiation of objects and capture them in grayscale images. Such images have a very different distribution of data compared to optical colored images. We present here a work that produces a grayscale thermo-optical fused mask given a thermal input. This is a deep learning based pioneering work since to the best of our knowledge, there exists no other work which produces a mask from a single thermal infrared input image. Our method is also unique in the sense that the deep learning method we are proposing here employ the Discrete Wavelet Transform (DWT) domain instead of the gray level domain. As a part of this work, we also prepared a new and unique database for obtaining the region of interest in thermal images, which have been manually annotated to denote the Region of Interest on 5 different classes of real world images. Finally, we are proposing a simple low cost overhead statistical measure for identifying the region of interest in fused images, which we call as the Region of Fusion (RoF). Experiments on 2 different databases show encouraging results in identifying the region of interest in the fused images. We also show that these images can be processed better in the mixed form rather than with only thermal images.

Keywords: Thermal Imaging · Fusion · Thermo-Optical Mask · Deep Learning

1 Introduction

Compared to optical images, thermal Images are difficult to work with because the objects are not well segregated like optical images and the different signatures are visible in black and white. Thermal Infrared (TIR) images work on the principle of passive thermal radiation, as opposed to reflected light in optical images or Near Infrared (NIR) images. Moreover, thermal images are produced by radiation, which are of higher wavelength than visible light, leading to a lower resolution. As such, while there exist works like [2–4] which focus on thermal images, we did not come across any work which tries to fuse thermal and optical images represented in the grayscale domain directly using a single thermal input to create a fusion image, which we call a mask. While we have presented a work [5] which tries to prepare color images in a fused domain, that is different from our present work, because we try to create a fused image which can be used in the optical domain. For example, we can do Deep Learning (DL) based colorization trained only on optical images, which would not be possible with the work described in [5]. We demonstrate this in Fig. 3. We also support our hypothesis via quantitative scores shown in Table 2 and Table 3.

Our work is specifically focused on data synthesis in a single grayscale level instead of a mask in the RGB or the 3 channel luminance-chrominance (LAB) domain and thus we have different data distributions for our deep network. We anticipate that our work will be useful in domains that need the input from thermal images to process the data for further information like medical imaging, drone imaging at night, forensic images etc. Also, our method is unique in the sense that we are proposing a network that works on a transformed space (DWT). Our network creates different levels of parallel pathways for DWT transform and captures the data distribution at different levels of abstraction [21]. Finally, we return to the normalized gray-level image domain, the reason for which is described in Sect. 2.1. Non DL methods on fusion of thermal images include works like [17] which works on contour formation, [16] for long range observation and [15], which handles multiple thermal image fusion for focus improvement. The DL based methods usually need more data, but in many cases such methods outperform even humans. Some examples are generation [22], image coloring [18] or medical image diagnosis [23]. Thus, in specialized areas, DL based methods are used to handle jobs that are difficult in classical methods. This is the motivation for our current work. We hypothesize that these images should be better processed by a machine learning method, which is trained to work on either optical or thermal images with nominal retraining in comparison to images of the opposing domains. In Sec.3, we show this in our blind testing method. We also provide objective measures in support of our claim in Table 2, where we compare our results with comparisons on further variations of our network, like changing the levels of sub-bands or adding skip connections. We also provide results from an unbiased database, called VT5000 [14], to show that our method works on images from a wide range of sources in Fig. 3 and Table 3.

Our proposed dataset [19] is based on an existing database [6], which contains complex real-world thermal images and their corresponding optical images belonging to 5 classes, namely nature, modern infrastructure, animal, human and crowd which we collected over a period of 1.5 years. These images were selected from our work on cross domain colorized images [5], which were not annotated. We manually annotated all collected images and marked the Regions of Interest (ROI). Since these were real (non-synthetic) images, the total process needed about 300 working hours to complete. We also present a simple new statistical measure for obtaining the region which has modified most in the output image in comparison with the input image. We call such region as the Region of Fusion (RoF).

Thus, the main contributions we are proposing in this work are:

- We demonstrate that it is possible to produce grayscale fused images containing information from both the thermal and optical images.
- We introduce a novel DL architecture that works on a separate logical space (DWT) than the input or output space (normalized images).
- We demonstrate the results on a separate dataset to show that our method can work irrespective of the subject of the data.

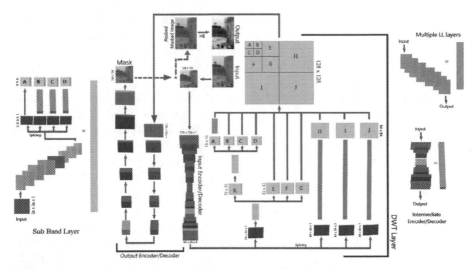

Fig. 1. Deep Learning Model proposed for our work. The pink block represents an LL layer comprised of a combination of the individual encode_same blocks, the yellow ones are encode_same, blue represents encode_half and the red ones are encode_double. The intermediate encoder/decoder has been simplfied into a single orange block. The grey blocks are spliced single depth layers obtained by separating the 4 layers of an output block. The last red layer is a single depth Conv2D layer with sigmoid activation. The averaging is represented by the * operator, the dotted lines represent the post DL steps and HE stands for Histogram Equalization. Detailed information on the model layers is available in Table 1.

- We introduce a unique dataset [19], containing annotated thermal images across multiple classes based on our existing database [6].
- We define a simple statistical score for focusing on a region of interest in fused images.

2 Proposed Method

We are using a deep network to produce a mask. This mask is then statistically fused using Eq. (4), followed by Histogram Equalization to create the final output. The output mask is created by training the model to optimize the loss from an input thermal image to an output image which is the thermal image embedded with the optical-thermal average in the annotated region. This ensures that only a particular region in the thermal image is different in the output image. The deep model we are using is described in Fig. 1 and Table 1.

2.1 Deep Network

Our network can roughly be divided into 3 different blocks: Input Encoder/Decoder, DWT Layer and Output Encoder/Decoder. We use 2 sets of encoder/decoders to process the data before and after the nth (3rd in our case) level decomposition, as shown in Fig. 1.

In Table 1, all output layers have a depth equal to the number of filters used as the function arguments for convolution. Thus, for example, the second layer has a shape of 64 x 64 x 16 when using an input shape of 128 x 128 in the first layer. For slicing layers, outputs have a depth of 1 (i.e., it is a 2D matrix only). The Input Encoder/Decoder is a basic encoder coupled with a decoder with Convolutional 2D Transpose layers (instead of Upsampling2D layers) to preserve the gradient in between the layers. Also, we do not form a complete encoder-decoder, but put 1 less layer of the input dimension for feeding into the first level of our DWT layer. The Output Encoder/Decoder is also a general encoder decoder which creates the final mask.

Table 1. Deep Network Layer details.

Base Layer Name	Details (dwf = 4)	Description
encode_same (input, filter, kernel, dropout = True, normalization = True)	Conv2D {W (3,3), S: (1,1)} leakyReLU () if (normalization = True): Batch Normalization() if (dropout = True): DropOut(0.5)	Creates an output layer of the same size as the input layer, with the specified depth (filter)
encode_half (input, filter, kernel, dropout = True, normalization = True)	Conv2D {W (3,3), S: (2,2)} leakyReLU () if (normalization = True): Batch Normalization() if (dropout = True): DropOut(0.5)	Creates an output layer of half the size (length/width) as the input layer, with the specified depth (filter)
encode_double (input, filter, kernel, dropout = True, normalization = True)	Conv2D Transpose{W (3,3), S: (2,2)} leakyReLU () if (normalization = True): Batch Normalization() if (dropout = True): DropOut(0.5)	Creates an output layer of double the size (length/width) as the input layer, with the specified depth (filter)
LL (input, filter, kernel, dropout = True, normalization = True)	Conv2D {W (3,3), S: (1,1)} ReLU () if (normalization = True): Batch Normalization() if (dropout = True): DropOut(0.5)	Creates an output layer of the same size as the input layer, with the specified depth (filter), using ReLU activation function

(*continued*)

Table 1. (*continued*)

Base Layer Name	Details (dwf = 4)	Description
intermediate_enc_dec (input, kernel, dropout = True, normalization = True)	p = encode_same (input, dwf) p = encode_half (input, dwf*4) p = encode_ half (input, dwf*16) p = encode_same (input, dwf*64) p = encode_double (input, dwf*16) p = encode_double (input, dwf*4, False) p = encode_same (input, 1, False, False)	Combination of encode_same, encode_half and encode_double blocks to create an encoder-decoder like structure used in the network
sub-band	ca1, ch1, cv1, cd1 = slice along last axis (input) ll = LL (ca, dwf) ll = LL (ll, dwf*4) ll = LL (ll, dwf*16) ll = LL (ll, dwf*32) ll = encode_half (ll, dwf*64) ll = encode_same (ll, dwf*16) ll = encode_same (ll, dwf*4) ll = encode_same (ll, dwf) ca2, ch2, cv2, cd2 = slice along last axis (input) hl = intermediate_enc_dec (ch1) lh = intermediate_enc_dec (cv1) hh = intermediate_enc_dec (cd1)	Creates 4 layers of sub bands for processing at the next level, at half the dimension size as the input and processes the inputs at the current level

Our method does not convert an input thermal image completely into a full optical mask, but instead minimizes the loss against a partial output image which has an averaged area embedded into the input thermal image. The output mask is obtained by using a 2D Convolutional layer with the sigmoid activation which normalizes the output to (0, 1) values.

We wanted to check if we could work in the Discrete Wavelet transform (DWT) domain instead of the usual normalized image domain for our fusion. The reasoning for this is that 2 Dimensional DWT (2DDWT) works on iteratively smaller scales of an image by halving the 2 axes of an input image, processing it and then reconstructing it back. In fact, this is similar to the logic of an encoder-decoder, except that an encoder-decoder based CNN works on the spatial domain and 2DDWT works on the frequency domain. Since conversion from the spatial to the frequency domain is a standard signal processing algorithm, our assumption was that a logically sound sufficiently complex deep network should be able to intuitively model this. We refer to the standard notation representing the DWT frequency bands as LL (low-low), LH (low-high), HL (high-low) and HH (high-high). In fact, this is precisely the reason we alternate between 2 different blocks of deep network for modelling the LL blocks as opposed to the other (LH, HL, HH) blocks in our model. As can be noticed, for the LL blocks, we specifically use ReLU as the activation function, while we use LReLU for other blocks. In 2DDWT, LL blocks are confined to lie between 0 and a positive integer, which doubles in value with every successive iteration, which is the reason we use ReLU, which is not the case for the other bands.

It needs to be noted here that we design our model to represent only till the 3rd level decomposition. However, theoretically, one could go even deeper. We did not opt for this because of two reasons. Firstly, the size of our data was 128x128. We could not have data at the 256x256 size since the database we used had several images which had a maximum size of 240 in one dimension. Secondly, another level of decomposition would bring the output size of the patches down to 2x2, which would render our method unusable as at such lower patch sizes, logical relations in between patches of images become pixel like. Since we are considering images with local relations, this would be counter intuitive to our method. Also, at some point, the increase in complexity would overrule the optimization of the loss.

We decide to generate a method that is able to create patches of localized data by making an encoder-decoder structure for each scale of resolution we work on. This is because we find that a localized encoder-decoder structure is able to lower the absolute loss by about 20%, as opposed to using patches with more depth (at the same resolution). We provide a quantitative study of these networks by comparing their results in Table 2 and Table 3 and the qualitative results are presented in Fig. 3. We use Adaptive Moment Optimization (ADAM) [25] as the optimizer because our model tries to optimize the loss function similar to what ADAM is doing as explained below.

The optimizer tries to lower the loss by changing values of nth moment, which is defined in Eq. (1):

$$m_n = E[X^n], \tag{1}$$

where X represents the data and E is the expectation. Since ADAM works by minimizing loss through moving average optimization, with the help of 2 constants ($\beta_1 = 0.9$ and $\beta_2 = 0.999$), the kth mini-batch moving averages at the ith level reduces to:

$$\hat{m}_k = \frac{mk}{1 - \beta_1^i}, \hat{v}k = \frac{\hat{v}k}{1 - \beta_2^i}, \tag{2}$$

where m and v represent the moving averages.

Thus, we see that as the level goes deeper, the loss becomes lower and more local. The local convergence of ADAM optimizer has been relied on heavily for its choice of optimizer and has been already proven in [23]. This is what we are trying to achieve with our method as well, wherein the levels are logically represented by the parallel paths of the DWT layer described in Table 1.

However, there is another hyper parameter, the loss function, which forms an integral part of a deep network. We use *logcosh* as the loss for our current model. As stated in [1], if we consider wavelet based data, geodesic distance based on the Riemannian manifold is a good estimator as a distance measure. Since the Riemannian manifold is a part of the hyperbolic plane and according to [13], we can consider barycentric coordinates to be geocentric in nature. Thus, we decide to use the *logcosh* loss measure representing the logarithm value of the hyperbolic cosine of the error predicted, given by

$$logcosh(x) = \begin{cases} \frac{x^2}{2} & for x \ll 1 \\ abs(x) - log(2) & otherwise \end{cases} \tag{3}$$

where x stands for the input in Eq. (3). Once we have the mask from our deep network, we fuse it with the thermal prior according the simple averaging rule:

$$O_i = (T_i + M_i)/2, \tag{4}$$

where O_i represents the averaged output image pixel, T_i is the corresponding thermal prior pixel and M_i is the equivalent mask pixel for each ith pixel. We are trying to obtain an image that already has the thermal image as a part of the output. Both T and M have the same shape so that they can be averaged.

Finally, we go on to histogram equalize the fused image in order to obtain a final output image which has a better distribution of illumination for higher visibility. Here we would like to point out that there is no meaning to equalizing a thermal image. This is because thermal images are already histogram equalized by the capturing device since thermal images use all 256 levels of illumination. This is evident from the thermal bar present on the right side of thermal images. We present a comparison of the thermal input, the fused image and the final output for different networks in Fig. 3 and Fig. 4.

2.2 Region of Fusion (RoF)

When looking at research works focused on fusion, we have noted that there is no objective measure which could provide a bounding box for the localized regions of fusion. This is relevant in works such as this one, where we are focusing on regions which should have localized content for fusion.

Hence, we propose a relative measure called Region of Fusion (RoF), based on localized Region of Interest (ROI). This method is fully customizable in regards to the distance metric that is used to calculate the region similarity and can be used on fusion methods which are either DL or statistically based. It has a low computational complexity depending on the size of the image and the similarity measure being used. The idea behind the method is to take a score for the variation of a full image between the thermal and the fused output and then calculate the area of both. We iteratively reduce the height and width of the region by 1 and check the percentage reduction of variation with the percentage reduction in area. If variation is less than the change in area, we stop and define the region as the final region. The algorithm is discussed in details as Algorithm 1.

As can be understood from the Algorithm 1, the measure for similarity (or dissimilarity) can be changed as needed. We have used the sum of the square of difference of pixel values as a measure of dissimilarity in our case, but one can use other scores, like Structural Similarity Index Measure (SSIM).

Also, since this is an unbiased score, one can opt to combine existing DL based fusion methods like [11, 12] with our score to provide a better measure of the fused region to focus on the output. It may be noted that while RoF can model any fusion based distribution for a region of interest, the data distribution needs to be on the same scale. For example, if we work with data distributions modelled on Wavelet transformed data (without converting it back into an image), which are multi resolution data distributions containing several scales of an image, it would not work. This is because RoF is designed to work on data in a single scale only, by determining a local maximum for the bounding box.

ALGORITHM 1: Region of Fusion

Input: Thermal-Fused grayscale image pair

Output: Fused Image with a RoF: (x1, y1) to (x2, y2)

1.   for each image pair in list:

2.   obtain image size as x = (0 to m), y = (0 to n)

          This section increments the value of x from 0 to m iteratively to calculate where
          the ratio of similarity scores between 2 consecutive regions becomes lower than
                    the ratio of their areas and defines x1 as the point where it stops

3.   check ← 0

4.   while x < m, with x1 ← 0, y ← n:

5.   if check == 1:

6.   x ← x - 1

7.   continue

8.   calculate the measure of similarity between the thermal and the fused image patch
          for region (x = (x1 to m),   y = (0 to n)) as M1

9.   calculate the measure of similarity between the thermal and the fused image patch
          for region (x = (x1 to m-   1), y = (0 to n)) as M2

10.   calculate the area A1 ← ((m-x) * n) and A2 ← ((m- (x+1)) * n)

11.   if M1 / M2 < A1 / A2:

12.   x ← x+1

13.   x1 ← x

14.   else:

15.   check ← 1

          This section decrements the value of x from m to 0 iteratively to calculate where
          the ratio of similarity scores between 2 consecutive regions becomes lower than
                    the ratio of their areas and defines x2 as the point where it stops

16.   check ← 0

17.   while x > x1, with x2 ← m, y ← n:

18.   if check == 1:

19.   x ← x-1

20.   continue

21.   calculate the measure of similarity between the thermal and the fused image patch
          for region (x = (m to   x2), y = (0 to n)) as M1

22.   calculate the measure of similarity between the thermal and the fused image patch
          for region (x = (m-1   to x2), y = (0 to n)) as M2

23.   calculate the area A1 ← ((m- x) * n) and A2 ← (((m-1) - x)) * n)

24.   if M1 / M2 < A1 / A2:

25.   x ← x-1

26.   x2 ← x

27.   else:

---

28.   check ← 1

29.   repeat steps 3 – 15 keeping x as constant area (x1 : x2) and varying y from (0 to n) to get y1

30.   repeat steps 16 – 28 keeping x as constant area (x1 : x2) and varying y from (n to y1) to get y2

31.   draw a box on the fused image from (x1, y1) to (x2, y2) to get the RoF

32. end for loop

2.3 Database

We use the thermal-visual paired image dataset [19] for our work. It was presented as a part of our work in [5]. We use 10 random cuts of the input images, while keeping the annotated region inside the cut. This is because we are trying to create a model which is able to create a localized region for the final output instead of a uniform fused image.

The database we propose has 1873 thermal images hand annotated by us. The annotation in rectangular bounding boxes is done using the tool VGG Image Annotator (VIA) [7]. We annotate the images into 5 different classes, Nature (nat), Animal (ani), Human (hum), Crowd (cro) and Modern Infrastructure (inf). Each image may have multiple annotated objects inside it, which is how we are able to obtain more than one training image for each individual annotated image.

However, the database [6] also contained the paired visual equivalent for each of these thermal images, which has lent a way to augment our dataset further. We applied an optical ROI bounding box algorithm on the optical images to create additional data. The logic behind this is that since we are proposing a localized fusion method, the fusion should occur from both directions. There might be objects present in the optical domain which are not clearly visible in the thermal domain (objects at the same thermal profile range), and vice versa. We came across different object identification algorithms like [8, 9], but most of them were either image classifiers only or did not provide multiple bounding boxes over a single image. Moreover, since the database we were using as our background base was focused on multiple classes of different sizes and was not of a very high resolution, we wanted to find a low overhead high accuracy algorithm which would be able to fit our case. Thus, we decided to opt for DEtection TRansformer (DETR) [10] for our problem. DETR is a state of the art localized low cost object annotator which has multiple object classes, trained on optical images.

We use the public code that they provide, and obtain object annotations on the optical images in the database and transpose these boxes on their thermal counterparts to finally obtain the localized database we are using for our use. Of course, since we have only 5 classes in our annotation, we simplify the annotation provided by DETR into our annotation labels by changing classes like bus, car, laptop, truck etc. into Modern Infrastructure, sheep, horse etc. into animal class and so on. The final database we propose [6] has 5 different classes labeled as a number from 1 to 5.

Once this is done, we take 10 random cuts around the annotated region, for each of the images with individual annotations constraining the minimum size for each image to be 128 x 128. Finally, we combine the thermal and optical information in the annotated region following Eq. (4). We finally obtain 123570 image pairs, which we use in our work. It should be noted that since there is no extra restriction on the annotated region size, our final database for the model comprises of images of widely differing sizes, which we normalize to 128 x 128 for keeping parity in the input and output image sizes in the deep network. The reason we did not impose a restriction on the dimensions of the image used for training other than a minimum size is because this action ensured that our data was widely varied, even with a 10 cross augmentation. While this did result in most of our data being irregularly stretched, it ensured a sufficiently distinct dataset for the DL method. This was demonstrated by our validation data as well.

However, while this did ensure a good fit for our DL method, it could still be argued that our method might be over-fitting the dataset to provide a highly optimized result. Hence, we also tested our method on the dataset VT5000 [14]. This dataset contains 5000 pairs of unique data. However, the problem with this dataset is that every pair of image has a single region of annotation, and in most cases, the annotation was not very relevant. For example, in multiple images with a human and a football, the football has been annotated, while the human was not. This not only meant that the dataset was inadequately annotated, it also meant that the general size of the annotated region in the dataset is extremely low. The size of the relevant region goes down even further when we resize the images to 128 x 128 to fit into our network. Nonetheless, we use our network to train against this dataset, and provide both qualitative and quantitative results showing that our method works with an external dataset, which has no repeated data. These results are presented in Fig. 3 and Table 3.

In short, we demonstrate that our method works with images captured via different kinds of thermal imagers, FLIR E40 and Sonel KT400, the 2 thermal imagers we use to capture our annotated data, and FLIR SC620, T640 and T610, all of which are used to capture images for the VT5000 dataset [14].

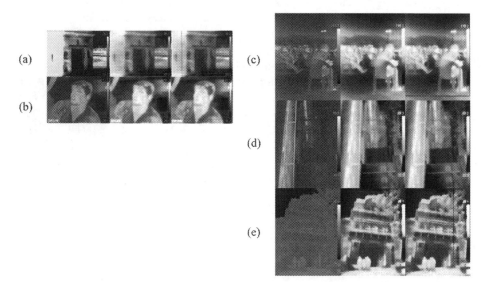

Fig. 2. A comparison of different images showing their RoF. (a) and (b) are images obtained via the FLIR E60 and (c), (d) and (e) are obtained via Sonel KT400 and have different image resolutions. The leftmost images are thermal inputs, the middle ones are Histogram Equalized masked outputs and the right most images are the outputs obtained after running the RoF algorithm on the images in the middle. The black boxes represent the RoF.

3   Experimental Results

We use 3 different objective scores to evaluate our method. Since we did not find any image fusion evaluation score, we choose Structural Similarity Index Measure (SSIM) [20], Cosine-similarity (cossim) and Mean Square Error (MSE) for our quantitative evaluation. SSIM represents the similarity between 2 images at the same scale with the consideration that pixels which lie closer to each other spatially are strongly related to each other. On the other hand, MSE tries to quantify absolute difference between 2 images by simply comparing them at the pixel level and cossim compares the absolute error, but with the full images considered as vectors. These scores are denoted in Table 2 and Table 3.

There are 3 columns in Table 2. These are the scores for the proposed method, the proposed method with 1 less sub band, and the proposed method with the skip connections. The DL method with the skip connections has everything else same, along with concatenation layers between the input encoder-decoder and the output encoder-decoder. On the other hand, the DL network with one less sub band only has lowest sub

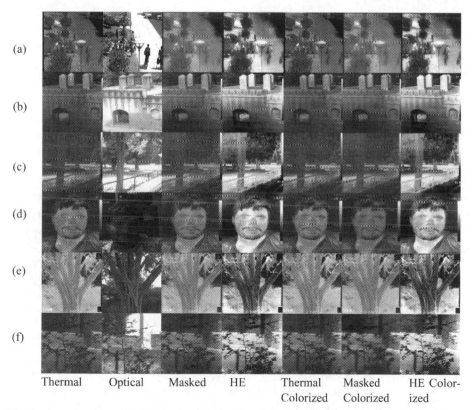

(a)						
(b)						
(c)						
(d)						
(e)						
(f)						

Thermal   Optical   Masked   HE   Thermal   Masked   HE Color-
                                      Colorized Colorized ized

Fig. 3. A comparison of different images used for input versus the different outputs we obtain along with a blind testing done by colorizing the images with a network trained exclusively on optical images. HE represents Histogram Equalized masked images. All of the colorization is via the method in [18].

band levels at 16 x 16, instead of 8 x 8. It retains the skip connections. All of them use the same data for training, validation and testing.

We provide qualitative results to demonstrate this in Fig. 4, where we show the comparison of the images obtained as output from the different DL networks.

We use 3 different measures of similarity. The first column shows how similar our averaged output is to the thermal images. Similarly, the third column shows their similarity with the visual counterparts. The middle one is the similarity of the thermal images to their optical counterparts and provides the baseline against which we compare our values. Of course, the scores between the thermal and the averaged output is much better than the ones between the optical and the average output, because we fuse the mask with the thermal image before comparison.

As a part of the objective study, we also present scores for the 3 similarity measures on the VT5000 [14] dataset. Similar to the trend seen in Table 2, all scores for the visual vs output masked images and thermal vs output images are better than the thermal vs visual scores except for MSE. We include a discussion on the scores for both Table 2 and Table 3 in Sect. 4. Each row has 2 bold scores to denote the best comparisons in 2 different domains.

4   Discussion

Since there is no direct method of comparison for showing that our method produces a significantly different output (as all of it is in grayscale domain and optical features incorporated in the mask are not immediately identifiable), we opt for an indirect method to show this. We use a neutral testing method of coloring of the thermal image and the final output that we are producing. The coloring is done via the method explained in [18] for optical image colorization. We use the online demo method they provide for the same, without training it on our database for the blind testing, to remove any bias.

As can be seen in Fig. 3, the Histogram Equalized (HE) images contain more texture as compared to the thermal images. This is especially noticeable in image (a), (c) and (e). We include (d) since it has a noticeably bad optical image since the setting for the photograph, possessing a bad illumination. We include images captured both at a short distance (face image (d)), as well as images far away. It needs to be noted that when we are considering images for subjects very close by, due to the physical difference of location of the thermal and the optical sensor, the perspective of the thermal and the optical images change. We demonstrate this in [5] as well. The image (d) is an example of this. We still include a data point from this category to show that our method is robust enough to process such images as well.

We use a purely optical trained colorization technique [18] to show that our method produces a significantly different output because it is an unbiased method. The texture difference can be clearly seen in (a), (c) and (f) in Fig. 3, where the masked and HE colorized image has better real-world colors compared to the thermal input, thus demonstrating our point. The colors in (b), on the other hand, show that the top of the structure, which had a greenish hue in the thermal colorized output, changes to a more natural yellowish sun-lit range. While the colors for (d) and (e) do not mirror real world natural colors, we would again like to stress that colorization was not an aim of our current work.

In fact, our method is unlikely to produce accurate colorized images using an optical colorization method since it has thermal image information embedded as a part of the output. We include these images to show that our method produces texture in the fused images.

We can also note that in the HE colorized images for (d) and (e), the facial features and the features on the tree are both more easily identifiable visually as compared to the thermal (or masked) colorized images as well. Out of the 6 images presented, (a) is from the VT5000 dataset, and (b-f) are from the dataset we are proposing. However, if there exist thermal images which have very well-defined levels of separation in between objects, our method would not perform as well since the texture might be interpreted as noise by a machine learning method.

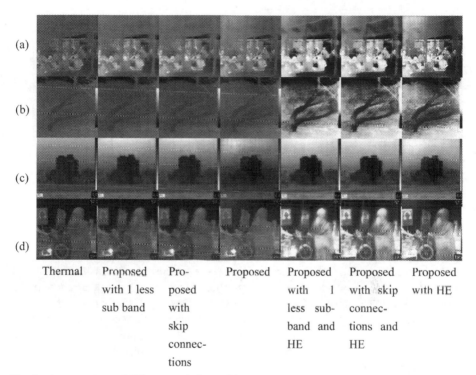

Fig. 4. A comparison of different variations of the proposed network with their outputs. HE stands for Histogram Equalized

For both our quantitative and our qualitative results, in Table 2, and Fig. 4, we present 3 variations of our network. The first is the proposed method with 1 less sub band and skip connections added between the input encoder-decoder and the output encoder-decoder via concatenation, the second is the proposed network with skip connections and the third is the proposed network (without skip connections). As we have shown in [5], skip connections do not always produce better results, especially when the input and the output images are in different domains, as is the case here. This can be verified both by the scores presented in Table 2, as well as the images presented in Fig. 4. While the scores in Table 2 do show better results in the SSIM and the MSE scores when comparing the output domain images with their thermal input counterparts, it can be noticed that the proposed network provides better scores in every other area. In fact, if we average the scores for the thermal and the optical image comparisons, we see that except for SSIM, where the scores are slightly better for the proposed network with skip connections, every other score provides better quantitative results for the proposed network. This is logically consistent as well, since the input encoder decoder is likely to have noticeable characteristics of the input thermal image.

Table 2. Objective score comparison between thermal images, optical images and the masked average outputs on the proposed dataset. Larger is better for SSIM and cos-sim and smaller is better for MSE.

Scores	Thermal vs output			Thermal vs visual	Visual vs output		
	Proposed with skip	Proposed with 1 less sub band	Proposed		Proposed with skip	Proposed with 1 less sub band	Proposed
SSIM	**0.72**	0.69	0.54	0.20	0.254	0.252	**0.29**
cos-sim	0.961	0.95	**0.964**	0.90	**0.93**	0.92	**0.93**
MSE	**352.6**	353.3	781.55	7473.6	6988.6	6976	**5963.67**

We also train our proposed method using the dataset presented in VT5000 [14] and present the scores for the same in Table 3 for a quantitative evaluation of a large external dataset. Except for MSE, every other score is better with the proposed network. We can see that the network actually improves the output distribution to be closer to the optimal output we are hypothesizing in Fig. 3 (a) as well, where the color scheme for the HE output image is much better than the thermal input.

We can see the effects of the various DL networks shown in the qualitative results presented in Fig. 4, where the output images for the proposed network have better optical characteristics as compared to the other 2 networks. This is especially noticeable in the HE images presented in Fig. 4, since the illumination becomes more pronounced because of histogram equalization. If we look at the apparel of the people present in (a) in Fig. (4), we can see that there is a clear presence of texture. This is missing in HE images for the other 2 variations of the proposed network.

In (d), if we focus on the area of the person where their head is covered, we can see that except for the proposed network, the other 2 variations of the DL method creates an indistinct luminated patch around the head of the person in the picture. This is a direct result of mistaken illumination levels in that region. This can also be noticed in the trunk region of the tree at the base in (b) and the upper left corner of the building in (c). Both of these regions have better illumination separation similar to optical images, as is reflected via the scores presented in Table 2 and Table 3 as well.

We show the results from our measure of fusion, RoF in Fig. 2. The images we use here are those which are published in [6] as being unregistered. Thus, we did not have the optical counterparts of these images, and they were not used in training our DL algorithm. We obtain the HE masked images for each of the thermal inputs and then run our RoF identifying algorithm on them. The texture difference is relevant in case of images (a), (b) and (c), where we see a clear region of interest. In case of (d), the region is around almost the full image. However, in (e), the region is quite outside the expected region of interest. This is because, in (e), we see that the thermal image has well defined levels of separation for regions. However, our method does detect a region where the score varies enough to make a RoF. In images such as this, since the thermal image itself is well segmented and possess well defined visual features, we would not opt for a fusion method. However, we include this result to show that this case may also occur.

The results from both datasets are shown in Fig. 3 and the quantitative scores are presented in Table 2 and Table 3. We also used 438 images for testing on a blind dataset comprising of images that were unregistered in the dataset we proposed, some

Table 3. Objective score comparison between thermal images, optical images and the masked average outputs on VT5000. Larger is better for SSIM and cos-sim and smaller is better for MSE.

Scores	Thermal vs output	Thermal vs visual	Visual vs output
SSIM	**0.546**	0.21	0.229
cos-sim	**0.97**	0.90	0.931
MSE	9624.7	8640.18	**8301.16**

of which we present in Fig. 2 as a part of our qualitative results for demonstrating RoF. We use a 95% to 5% split for training/test-validation. We further break the test-validation data into 50% each for validation and testing sets. This is maintained in both experiments involving our dataset as well as the one conducted on VT5000.

5 Conclusion

We present a novel method demonstrating weighted partial thermal-optical fusion. The model is both unique in its scope of work and the theoretical basis, wherein we show that the calculations are based on a separate logical space, constructed on the principles of 2 Dimensional Discrete Wavelet Transform. We also introduce a simple statistical score for identifying regions with significantly different distribution in output fused images. Lastly, we introduce a unique database [19] containing annotated thermal images on varying classes as a part of this work for public use.

All experiments were carried out on a machine with i5 7600 processor with 16 GB RAM and a RTX 2080 Super with 8 Gbps GDDR6 memory. All coding was done on Python with Keras 2.2.4, using Tensorflow 1.13.1 as the backend. On an average, one epoch of the proposed DL network took about 21 min to complete with a batch size of 64 using generators for data loading. The total number of parameters were 45810743, out of which 23936 were non trainable with an input image size of 128 x 128. The proposed algorithm reached loss saturation by the 24th epoch. The thermal imagers used for creating the dataset were FLIR E40 and Sonel KT400. All facilities and equipment were provided by Computer Vision and Biometrics Lab (CVBL), IIITA, India.

References

1. Garcin, L., Younes, L.: Geodesic image matching: a wavelet based energy minimization scheme. In: Rangarajan, A., Vemuri, B., Yuille, A.L. (eds.) EMMCVPR 2005. LNCS, vol. 3757, pp. 349–364. Springer, Heidelberg (2005). https://doi.org/10.1007/11585978_23

2. Berg, A., Ahlberg, J., Felsberg, M.: Generating visible spectrum images from thermal infrared. In: Proceedings of the IEEE Conference on Computer Vision and Pattern Recognition Workshops, pp. 1143–1152 (2018)

3. Tao, D., Shi, J., Cheng, F.: Intelligent colorization for thermal infrared image based on CNN. In: 2020 IEEE International Conference on Information Technology, Big Data and Artificial Intelligence (ICIBA), vol. 1, pp. 1184–1190. IEEE (2020)

4. Liu, S., Gao, M., John, V., Liu, Z., Blasch, E.: Deep learning thermal image translation for night vision perception. ACM Trans. Intell. Syst. Technol. (TIST) 12(1), 1–18 (2020)

5. Goswami, S., Singh, S.K.: A simple mutual information based registration method for thermal-optical image pairs applied on a novel dataset. In: 2022 3rd International Conference for Emerging Technology (INCET), pp. 1–5. IEEE (2022). Thermal Visual Paired Dataset. https://doi.org/10.21227/jjba-6220

6. Dutta, A., Gupta, A., Zissermann, A.: VGG image annotator (VIA) (2016)

7. Wu, B., Jia, F., Liu, W., Ghanem, B.: Diverse image annotation. In: Proceedings of the IEEE Conference on Computer Vision and Pattern Recognition, pp. 2559–2567 (2017)

8. Chen, M., Zheng, A., Weinberger, K.: Fast image tagging. In: International Conference on Machine Learning, pp. 1274–1282. PMLR (2013)

9. Carion, N., Massa, F., Synnaeve, G., Usunier, N., Kirillov, A., Zagoruyko, S.: End-to-end object detection with transformers. In: Vedaldi, A., Bischof, H., Brox, T., Frahm, J.M. (eds.) ECCV 2020. LNCS, vol. 12346, pp. 213–229. Springer, Cham (2020). https://doi.org/10.1007/978-3-030-58452-8_13

10. Kulkarni, S.C., Rege, P.P.: Pixel level fusion techniques for SAR and optical images: a review. Inf. Fusion 59, 13–29 (2020)

11. Yadav, S.P., Yadav, S.: Image fusion using hybrid methods in multimodality medical images. Med. Biol. Eng. Comput. 58(4), 669–687 (2020). https://doi.org/10.1007/s11517-020-02136-6

12. Rustamov, R.M.: Barycentric coordinates on surfaces. In: Computer Graphics Forum, vol. 29, no. 5, pp. 1507–1516. Blackwell Publishing Ltd, Oxford (2010)

13. Tu, Z., Ma, Y., Li, Z., Li, C., Xu, J., Liu, Y.: RGBT salient object detection: A large-scale dataset and benchmark. arXiv preprint arXiv:2007.03262 (2020)

14. Zhong, X., Lu, T., Huang, W., Ye, M., Jia, X., Lin, C.W.: Grayscale enhancement colorization network for visible-infrared person re-identification. IEEE Trans. Circ. Syst. Video Technol. 32, 1418–1430 (2021)

15. Yaroslavsky, L.P., Fishbain, B., Shteinman, A., Gepshtein, S.: Processing and fusion of thermal and video sequences for terrestrial long range observation systems (2004)

16. Liu, B., Zhu, W., Huo, G.: An image fusion algorithm of infrared thermal and optical images for pig contour. Trans. Chin. Soc. Agric. Eng. 29(17), 113–120 (2013)

17. Iizuka, S., Simo-Serra, E., Ishikawa, H.: Let there be color! Joint end-to-end learning of global and local image priors for automatic image colorization with simultaneous classification. ACM Trans. Graph. (ToG) 35(4), 1–11 (2016)

18. Goswami, S., Singh, S.K., Chaudhuri, B.B.: Thermal Optical Annotated Multi Class Image Dataset. https://doi.org/10.21227/80yz-h738

19. Wang, Z., Bovik, A.C., Sheikh, H.R., Simoncelli, E.P.: Image quality assessment: from error visibility to structural similarity. IEEE Trans. Image Process. 13(4), 600–612 (2004)

20. Li, J., Yuan, G., Fan, H.: Multifocus image fusion using wavelet-domain-based deep CNN. Comput. Intell. Neurosci. 2019 (2019)
21. Wang, Z., Chen, Z., Feng, W.: Thermal to visible facial image translation using generative adversarial networks. IEEE Signal Process. Lett. **25**(8), 1161–1165 (2018)
22. Zhou, W., et al.: Ensembled deep learning model outperforms human experts in diagnosing biliary atresia from sonographic gallbladder images. Nat. Commun. **12**(1), 1–14 (2021)
23. González, A., et al.: Pedestrian detection at day/night time with visible and FIR cameras: a comparison. Sensors **16**(6), 820 (2016)
24. Bock, S., Weiß, M.: A proof of local convergence for the Adam optimizer. In: 2019 International Joint Conference on Neural Networks (IJCNN), pp. 1–8. IEEE (2019)
25. Buetti-Dinh, A., et al.: Deep neural networks outperform human expert's capacity in characterizing bioleaching bacterial biofilm composition. Biotechnol. Rep. **22**, e00321 (2019)

A Compact-Structured Convolutional Neural Network for Single Image Denoising and Super-Resolution

S. Deivalakshmi[✉] and J. Sudaroli Sandana

Department of Electronics and Communication Engineering, National Institute of Technology,, Tiruchirappalli, India
deiva@nitt.edu

Abstract. In this work, a simple and compact-structured convolutional neural network (CNN) entitled as Denoising and Super-Resolution (DnSR) network for single image denoising and super resolution (SISR) is presented. Using sparsity property (a smaller number of large intensity values and a larger number of small intensity values), the training of DnSR is made to converge early. We obtain the sparsity by learning residuals of image pixels instead of learning raw image pixels particularly for SR. We use a smaller receptive field of the image patch for faster training. We use gradient clipping to train DnSR net with an extremely large learning rate to overcome gradient inconsistency during training. An end-to-end mapping is done by learning the complex mapping between low-resolution (LR) image patches and the corresponding residual of high resolution (ΔHR) image patches using DnSR net. The proposed DnSR net uses a smaller number of parameters (approximately 3 times lesser) than the existing state-of-the-art (SOTA) SRCNN method. The proposed DnSR provides superior reconstruction accuracy with less artifacts when compared to other SOTA methods. The performance of the DnSR is assessed qualitatively and quantitatively using different image quality metrics.

Keywords: Denoising · Super-resolution · low-resolution · receptive field · residual learning · sparsity

1 Introduction

Obtaining a high-resolution (HR) image from corresponding low-resolution (LR) image(s) without artifacts is the main aim of image super-resolution (SR). Denoising aims at restoring visually pleasing images from a noisy image (LR). For simplicity, we consider low-resolution and noisy images as LR images. Many LR images or a single LR image can be used to obtain an HR image. The HR image can be obtained from multiple samples of the same LR image like frames of a video. If the HR image is obtained from the corresponding single LR image, then it is called Single Image Super-Resolution (SISR). To super resolve an image by a factor of n across width and breadth, each LR pixel must predict new pixel values which makes the task severely

D. Gupta et al. (Eds.): CVIP 2022, CCIS 1776, pp. 682–695, 2023.
https://doi.org/10.1007/978-3-031-31407-0_51

ill-posed. SISR is a very popular low-level vision task which has applications in medical field, security and surveillance imaging. Early upscaling methods like 'Bicubic' interpolation and Lanczos resampling [1], up-samples the images but introduces blurs by employing smoothing priors. A strong and sharp edge reconstruction must be done to produce visually plausible images. Interpolation based [1] method failed to reconstruct sharp edges. These techniques used smooth priors to super resolve an image which made images to contain artifacts like blurring and ghost edges at irregular regions of the image. Reconstruction based [2, 3] SISR methods struggle with the strong and sharp reconstruction of non-smooth details like edges and irregular patterns. These methods produce waterlike colors and ringing artifacts. Learning based methods [4–10] overcame these artifacts with accurate reconstruction and good perceptual quality. The learning-based methods utilizes patch recurrence and self-similarity properties of natural images to achieve better reconstruction accuracy. Example-based techniques [4–10] employed the correspondence between LR and HR patches. Internal example-based methods and external example-based methods are two categories of example-based methods. Internal example-based SISR method samples HRLR patches from an image, it's down sampled version, thereby estimates the SR image using the patch replacement technique. External example based SISR methods extract example HRLR patches from separate collection of images (and from their down scaled versions).

The proposed DnSR method is based on external example based SISR. Dong et al. [9] proposed SRCNN for SISR using simple three-layered structure, which had drawn a good attention in research groups to develop different deep CNN models for achieving SR. SRCNN has simple, compact structure and offers better performance than the existing state of-the-art (SOTA) conventional approaches for SISR. The SRCNN method has many limitations as the training procedure took three days to converge because of a small and a constant learning rate used for training. SRCNN also considered different patch sizes of input and output for different upscaling factors. The denoising methods [11–15] proposed based on filtering, effective priors and dictionary learning is used for comparison. Filter based denoising was used in [11]. Discrete Cosine transform (DCT) was used in [12] for denoising and deblurring. Effective priors were used in [13] for denoising.

In this work, a simple and compact-structured convolutional neural network (CNN) named as Denoising and Super-Resolution (DnSR) network for single image denoising and super resolution (SISR) is proposed. Using sparsity property, the training of DnSR is made to converge early and learn the residuals of image pixels instead of learning raw image pixels particularly for SR. In addition, gradient clipping is used to train DnSR net with an extremely large learning rate to overcome gradient inconsistency during training.

The major contributions of the proposed work are as follows:

- A new CNN model for single image denoising and super resolution is proposed entitled as the DnSR net. To the best of our knowledge, there has not been any simple (with only 3-layers) deep learning based denoising and super resolution network proposed yet.
- For the faster training convergence of the proposed DnSR net, the property of sparsity is employed. The sparsity nature is attained through learning residuals of image pixels instead of learning raw image pixels for SISR.

In the rest of the paper, we discuss the following: Section II comprises the related work. The proposed DnSR network architecture is included in section III. Section IV describes the experimental results and discussions on single image denoising and SR. Conclusions are given in section V.

2 Related Work

Most of the example-based methods learned a mapping between LR-HR patches. Yang et al. [4] proposed a sparse representation based on LR-HR mapping. This method searches for an LR patch sparse representation, and then use the obtained coefficients to produce the HR output. Yang et al. [4] also exploited the similarity of sparse representations on patches by conjointly training two dictionaries of LR-HR image patch pairs. Bevilacqua et al. [5] proposed a non-negative neighbor embedding based SISR in which each LR feature vector is expressed as a weighted-linear combination of k nearest neighbors in the dictionary. The methods proposed in [4, 5] required more time for forming dictionaries and training the formed dictionaries. The memory requirement is also one of the limitations of dictionary based SISR [4, 5] methods. Timofte et al. [6] used the anchored regression of dictionary atoms to compute the nearest neighbors rather than using Euclidean distance. The method proposed by Timofte et al. [6] overcame the time complexity of the dictionary based [4, 5] methods up to some extent without sacrificing the quality of the SR output image. Zeyde et al. [7] proposed a regularization as a local sparse-land model based on image patches. Huang et al. [8] used transformed self-exemplars for SISR. All the above methods are based on 3 consecutive operations i) patch extraction as pre-processing ii) patch optimization and iii) patch aggregation as post-processing operations.

C.Dong et al. [9] proposed SRCNN (Super-Resolution Convolution Neural Network), which is a deep learning based SISR motivated by Sparse Coding (SC) [4] method. The three layered deep SRCNN has a light weight and simple structure. Each layer operations are as follows: i) the first layer extracts different features from the image patches ii) the second layer helps to learn non-linear mapping of features and iii) the third layer helps in the reconstruction of the image. The SRCNN training procedure took 3 days on a GTX 770 GPU, which is the major drawback of the SRCNN. Even though the SRCNN has compact structure, its convergence speed is very slow because of a very small and constant learning rate for training. Further, C. Dong et al. [10] accelerated the SISR using deconvolution layer as the output layer.

A blend of Non-Local Means (NLM) filter and its method noise adaptive thresholding using wavelets was presented in [11]. NLM require self-similarity of the image for restoration, otherwise it over-smoothens the sharp edges. Foi et al. [12] proposed an approach for image filtering using shape adaptive discrete cosine transform (SA-DCT). Elad et al. [13] proposed the sparse representation based denoising technique using Singular Value Decomposition (K-SVD) algorithm. The KSVD method learns dictionaries from the image for denoising and suffers by high computational burden. Zoran et al. [15], used effective priors to restore the whole denoised image from the Expected Patch Log Likelihoods (EPLL). The deep learning-based methods gain popularity because of availability of modern powerful GPUs and abundant data to train. The proposed DnSR net is accelerated by decreasing the kernel size in the middle layer. The key advantage of kernel size reduction in middle layer is the decrease in the number of parameters to be optimized.

3 Proposed Algorithm

In this section, we present a deep architecture based Denoising and Super-Resolution network. The proposed DnSR contains 3 convolutional layers as shown in Fig. 1. The first layer helps to extract different features, the second layer aids for non-linear mapping and the final layer helps for reconstruction. The first layer contains 128 kernels with each of size 9×9, which extracts 128 features. The second layer contains 64 kernels of size $1 \times 1 \times 128$, here 128 features are non-linearly mapped to 64 features. The learned 64 features corresponds to HR image residuals.

3.1 Color Transformation

The color (RGB) image which is to be super resolved is transformed into the YCbCr image (Contrast /Brightness of the image only matters for SR so, color components are not altered). Y channel alone is considered as input to the network for super-resolution as it is the only component perceived by the human eye. We convert color images into gray images for denoising. The network output is basically the residual of the denoised or super-resolved image. To obtain the SR image, the residual image must be added to the 'Bicubic' interpolated image for SISR and the image corrupted by the Gaussian noise for denoising respectively. This process produces the Y channel of the SR image. The Cb and Cr channels are super-resolved by just interpolating them with 'Bicubic' interpolation. Then the three channels are concatenated to form the YCbCr color space SR image. To get the color image, the YCbCr image must be transformed back to the RGB domain. For fair comparison with other denoising methods [11–15], we use only gray images.

3.2 DnSR Architecture

The DnSR algorithm targets at learning complex mapping among LR (noisy or Low resolution) and HR residual patch pairs. A function f is learned between the LR image and residual of the HR image patches. The first layer is represented as a kernel operated on an LR image. The equivalent operation of the first layer (Conv1) is:

$$X = \Theta_1 * LR + B_1 \qquad (1)$$

where Θ_1 and B_1 are the vectors of weights and biases of n_1 kernels used in the first layer. Symbol '*' denotes the convolution operator. Here each convolution kernel has the size of $1 \times k_1 \times k_1$. Where k_1 is the individual kernel size. The Rectified Linear Unit (ReLU1) activation will operate on the first layer output X and produce an equivalent intermediate output as follows:

$$f_1(X) = \max(0, X) \qquad (2)$$

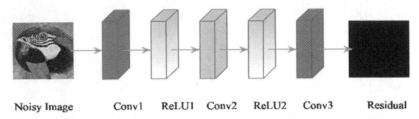

Fig. 1. Architecture of the proposed DnSR network

The second convolution layer (Conv2) will operate on the output of ReLU1 and produces an intermediate output along with ReLU2 as follows:

$$f_2(X) = \max(0, \Theta_2 * f_1(X) + B_2) \tag{3}$$

The second layer maps n_1 dimensional features to the n_2 dimensional feature space by non-linear mapping. Where Θ_2 denotes the parameter vector of the n_2 kernels each of size $n_1 \times k_2 \times k_2$. Each n_2 dimensional vector corresponds to features of a residual HR patch. The final convolutional layer (Conv3) produces an output which is the required final SR residual image.

$$\Delta SR = f_3(X) = \Theta_3 * f_2(X) + B_3 \tag{4}$$

The final learned function $f_3(X)$ is used to get the residual counter part of the SR image. The final SR image is the summation of the LR image and the residual of the SR image is.

$$SR = LR + \Delta SR \tag{5}$$

The training algorithm used in the proposed work is provided as Algorithm 1 to understand the patch extraction and training procedure. We extract a patch of size P × P from the LR image at an arbitrary location. The output patch of size O × O is extracted from the HR image at the same location which is used for the LR patch extraction by moving (O − P)/2 pixels horizontally and vertically. At the same selected location, a patch of size O × O is extracted from the LR image. The extracted patches from HR images and LR images are subtracted to form residual of the HR image.

Algorithm 1: Training Procedure of DnSR for Denoising and SISR.

Input: Training set of images, input size P, output size O, Number of training samples S, number of kernels and kernel size in each layer (n_1, k_1), (n_2, k_2) and (n_3, k_3).

Output: Trained model (optimized parameters) for estimating the residual image of SR.

1. Load the training set of images
2. for $i = 1$ to S do
3. Extract patches from the images (LR and HR) having input size P and output size O, at the location $(1 \leq m \leq N_1 - P + 1, 1 \leq n \leq N_2 - P + 1)$, where (N_1, N_2) is the size of the LR images.

4. The extracted patches at the location (m, n) from the LR image form the input LR patch tensors $(LR_i \in R^{(1 \times 1 \times P \times P)})$. From the location $(m-(P-O)/2, n - (P-O)/2)$ extract patches of size O × O from the LR and the corresponding HR images. Subtracting the extracted LR patches from the respective HR patches forms the target residual patch tensors $(\Delta HR_i \in R^{(1 \times 1 \times O \times O)})$. 5

5. End

6. A function $f: LR \to \Delta HR$ is learned using the DnSR by optimizing the mean squared loss.

$$L(\Theta) = \frac{1}{s} \sum\nolimits_{i=1}^{s} \left\| f\left(LR^i, \Theta, B\right) - \Delta HR^i \right\|^2 + \lambda \|\Theta\|^2 \qquad (6)$$

where Θ represents the parameters of DnSR network and λ is the weight decay factor.

3.3 Computational Complexity

The computational complexity of the proposed DnSR is computed based on the following formula.

$$O\{(\sum\nolimits_{l=1}^{3} n_{l-1} \times k_l^2 \times n_l) \times S_{HR}^2 \qquad (7)$$

where l is the layer index and $\{k_l^2\}_{l=1}^{3}$ is the size of the kernels used in each layer. $\{n_l\}_{l=1}^{3}$ is the number of kernels used in each layer and $n_0 = 1$. S_{HR} is the size of the HR image. The deeper the network with larger kernel size, the more the number of parameters to be estimated which in turn increases the computational complexity. The deeper models give better performance at the cost of learning more parameters.

3.4 Kernel Size and Parameters

Table 1 gives the detailed analysis of the kernels in each layer and parameters used. The total number of parameters that the SRCNN [9] used was 57184. Our implementation used only 20160 which is 2.84 ($\approx$ 3) times smaller. Training with a smaller number of parameters is faster, obviously our implementation is faster when compared to the most popular deep learning based SRCNN technique. The SRCNN used a smaller number of kernels as compared to our implementation but in the middle layer, it used a kernel of spatial size 5 × 5. The middle layer kernel size drastically increases the number of parameters to be estimated. So, the major contribution of parameters is from the middle layers. To overcome the middle layer parameter issue, we reduce the spatial size of the middle layer kernels to 1 × 1. Even though the number of parameters used was less than approximately 3 times, we achieved better restoration quality. The faster and better restoration quality is because of learning in sparser way by using residuals instead of raw image pixels.

Table 1. Proposed network specifications

Layer Index (l)	Kernel Size	Number of kernels	Parameters
1	9×9	128	10368
2	1×1	64	8192
3	5×5	1	1600
Total parameters		20160	

4 Experimental Analysis

The datasets used for training the DnSR and experimental results on different benchmark test datasets are provided in this section.

4.1 Dataset

The '91-images' dataset provided by Yang *et al.* [4] is the widely used dataset for training in all the SR methods which we also used for comparison. We use the same dataset for denoising. The original SRCNN was trained with a very large number of images (395909 images) from ILSVRC 2013 ImageNet dataset [16]. The comparison is done with the learning-based methods [8, 10] trained on the '91images' dataset and SRCNN [9] that used ImageNet dataset. For denoising performance, we compared it with conventional methods [11–15]. To utilize the dataset fully, we adopt the data augmentation used in [10]. We augment the data through scaling by 0.6, 0.7, 0.8 and 0.9 and rotate each image by 90, 180, and 270 degrees respectively. So, total images become 1820. For validation, 20 separate images from the validation set of the 'BSD500' [17] are used. For test results comparison, we used three datasets 'Set5' [5], 'Set14' [7] and 'B100' [17] for SISR. 12 widely used images shown in Fig. 3 and 'BSD68' [17] datasets are used for denoising.

4.2 Training Parameters

The trained model hyper-parameters are provided in this section. The network has three layers along with the feature extraction layer and reconstruction regression layer. Training uses mini batches of size 64. The Stochastic Gradient Descent (SGD) with Momentum set to 0.9 (this works well for most all the applications) is used as optimizer. For weight and bias initialization, we use the best method provided for Rectified Linear Units (ReLU) in He et al. [20]. The regularization (weight decay) factor is set to 0.0001. For faster convergence, gradient threshold method is used to clip the gradients that exceed the gradient threshold of 0.01. All experiments are trained for 100 epochs (27450 iterations with 64 samples in each mini batch). Learning rate schedular is followed for training. The initial learning rate is set to 0.1 and for every 20 epochs, the learning rate is reduced by 10 percent. In total, the learning rate is reduced four times. The learning procedure is stopped when 100 epochs are completed. Training takes roughly 12 h on NVIDIA GeForce 710 GPU. Testing is done on CPU with I5 processor, 32 GB RAM and clock frequency of 3.20 GHz. MATLAB 9.5 is used for both training and testing.

Table 2. The average results of the various performance metrics on 'SET5' [5] dataset for SISR.

Method	Scale	PSNR	SSIM	IFC
Bicubic [1]	2	33.66	0.9299	6.09
	3	30.39	0.8681	3.52
	4	28.42	0.8104	2.35
SelfEx [8]	2	36.49	0.9535	7.82
	3	32.61	0.9091	4.74
	4	30.32	0.8621	3.18
FSRCNN [10]	2	36.57	0.9532	7.75
	3	32.60	0.9067	4.52
	4	30.11	0.8499	2.76
SRCNN [9]	2	36.66	0.9542	8.05
	3	32.75	0.9090	4.54
	4	30.48	0.8628	3.01
DnSR	**2**	**36.87**	**0.9554**	**8.11**
	3	**32.81**	**0.9105**	**4.88**
	4	**30.51**	**0.8631**	**3.25**

Table 3. The average results of the various performance metrics on 'SET14' [7] dataset for SISR.

Method	Scale	PSNR	SSIM	IFC
Bicubic [1]	2	30.23	0.8687	6.09
	3	27.54	0.7736	3.41
	4	26.15	0.7019	2.24
SelfEx [8]	2	32.21	0.9034	7.59
	3	29.15	0.8196	4.17
	4	27.39	0.7518	2.89
FSRCNN [10]	2	32.28	0.9052	7.47
	3	29.12	0.8178	4.10
	4	27.19	0.7422	2.55
SRCNN [9]	2	32.45	0.9067	7.69
	3	29.29	0.8216	4.20
	4	27.50	0.7513	2.74
DnSR	**2**	**32.52**	**0.9080**	**7.76**
	3	**29.31**	**0.8216**	**4.26**
	4	**27.54**	**0.7513**	**2.76**

Table 4. The average results of the various performance metrics on 'B100' [13] dataset for SISR.

Method	Scale	PSNR	SSIM	IFC
Bicubic [1]	2	29.56	0.8431	5.64
	3	27.21	0.7384	3.12
	4	25.96	0.6674	1.97
SelfEx [8]	2	31.17	0.8853	6.84
	3	28.29	0.7841	3.70
	4	26.84	0.7106	2.46
FSRCNN [10]	2	31.23	0.8863	6.91
	3	28.29	0.7832	3.60
	4	26.73	0.7045	2.26
SRCNN [9]	2	31.36	0.8879	7.16
	3	28.41	0.7863	3.83
	4	26.90	0.7103	2.39
DnSR	2	31.44	0.8896	7.19
	3	28.42	0.7865	3.78
	4	26.93	0.7105	2.50

Table 5. The average results of the various performance metrics on 'SET12' dataset for denoising.

Method	Noise level	PSNR	SSIM
NLM [11]	10	33.68	0.9077
	20	30.81	0.8606
	30	28.87	0.8041
SA-DCT [12]	10	35.17	0.933
	20	31.5	0.8728
	30	29.44	0.819
K-SVD [13]	10	35.48	0.9331
	20	31.86	0.8779
	30	29.7	0.8301
GHP [14]	10	35.44	0.9274
	20	32.01	0.8858
	30	29.9	0.8366
EPLL [15]	10	35.48	0.9342
	20	31.92	0.8811

(*continued*)

Table 5. (*continued*)

Method	Noise level	PSNR	SSIM
	30	29.88	0.8318
DnSR	**10**	**35.65**	**0.9351**
	20	**32.02**	**0.8827**
	30	**29.91**	**0.837**

Table 6. The average results of the various performance metrics on 'BSD68' [13] dataset for denoising.

Method	Noise level	PSNR	SSIM
NLM [11]	10	31.5	0.8619
	20	28.32	0.7917
	30	26.53	0.726
SA-DCT [12]	10	32.97	0.9104
	20	29.24	0.8203
	30	27.34	0.7495
K-SVD [13]	10	33.12	0.913
	20	29.38	0.8248
	30	27.45	0.7549
GHP [14]	10	33.16	0.9086
	20	29.61	0.8379
	30	27.57	0.7622
EPLL [15]	10	33.31	0.9149
	20	29.62	0.8338
	30	27.76	0.7631
DnSR	**10**	**33.37**	**0.9156**
	20	**29.73**	**0.835**
	30	**27.8**	**0.7708**

4.3 Comparison with the State-Of-The-Art (SOTA) Methods

The quantitative and the qualitative results of the proposed DnSR for both SISR and Denoising are presented along with the other SOTA techniques.

1) Quantitative comparison. We compare the proposed DnSR method with existing SOTA methods, which used '91images' dataset for training. For better comparison, we also trained our network on the same dataset. We compare our implementation with the methods SelfEx [8], FSRCNN-s [10] and SRCNN [9]. For denoising performance of the

DnSR, we compared with the methods proposed in NLM [11], SADCT [12], K-SVD [13], GHP [14] and EPLL [15]. All the methods are compared based on the published source codes. Quantitative comparisons are done with the generally used performance measures like Peak Signal to Noise Ratio (PSNR), Structural Similarity Index Measure (SSIM) [18], Information Fidelity Criterion (IFC) [19]. Tables 2, 3 and 4 present all the metrics mentioned above for the 'Set5' [5], 'Set14' [7] and 'B100' [17] datasets for SISR respectively. The denoising performance of DnSR is assessed by measuring quantitative metrics like PSNR and SSIM for different noise standard deviations on 12 widely used images shown in Fig. 3 and on 'BSD68' [17] dataset. Tables 5 and 6 represents the denoising results in terms of PSNR and SSIM for the 12 widely used images shown in Fig. 8 and 'BSD68' [17] dataset corrupted by 'Gaussian' noise with standard deviations of 10, 20 and 30.

The DnSR is the top consistent performer for denoising. The EPLL [15] performance is better than all the remaining techniques. The features learned in each layer using convolutional kernels are different for each of the noise standard deviations ($\sigma = 10, 20, 30$), as the DnSR is trained separately for different noise densities.

4.4 Qualitative Results

Sharp edge portions from the 'bird' image in the Fig. 2 is extracted and zoomed to observe the edge details. The reconstruction capability of all the methods is assessed by zooming the extracted patches. If the zoomed portions are artifact free, then the restoration accuracy of that method is high. The sharp details are recovered accurately with no artifacts using the DnSR method. The PSNR value of the SR image produced by the DnSR method is 0.64 dB higher than the next best method SRCNN. All images are better viewed on color displays.

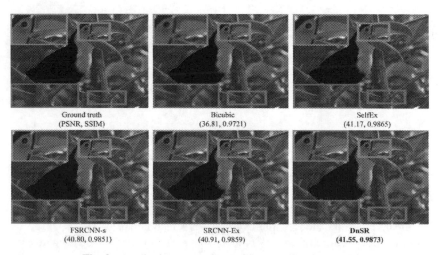

Ground truth
(PSNR, SSIM)

Bicubic
(36.81, 0.9721)

SelfEx
(41.17, 0.9865)

FSRCNN-s
(40.80, 0.9851)

SRCNN-Ex
(40.91, 0.9859)

DnSR
(41.55, 0.9873)

Fig. 2. Qualitative comparison with up scaling factor of 2

Fig. 3. Set12 images

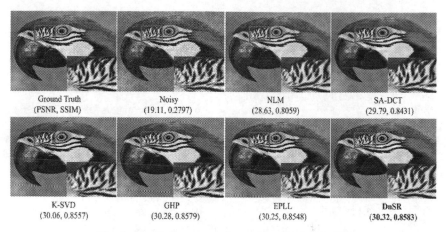

Fig. 4. Qualitative comparison with noise level of 30

From Fig. 4, it is clear that the denoising performance of the DnSR method is better in terms of the quantitative measures and the perceptual quality when compared to other methods.

4.5 Run Time

From the testing time given in Table 7 for SISR, the proposed DnSR is the fastest method. The DnSR is 10.68 times faster when compared to the next best method FSRCNN.

Table 7. Testing time (in seconds) comparison on 'SET5' dataset for up scaling of 2

Method	SelfEx	FSRCNN	SRCNN	DnSR
Time (Sec)	35.93	2.35	3.26	0.22

5 Conclusion

The proposed DnSR is simple, compact and lightweight with very few parameters that are to be learned. The simple and light weight structured DnSR provides faster image restoration and better perceptual quality when compared to SRCNN. Residual learning is also one of the reasons for the fastness of the DnSR. The DnSR is eleven times faster than the FSRCNN, which is faster than all the other methods used for comparison. The DnSR surpassed all the model-based denoising methods for different noise standard deviations. In future, this work can be extended for SISR and denoising in transformed domain (Wavelet or DCT) with deep convolutional layers.

References

1. Sun, J., Xu, Z., Shum, H.Y.: Image super-resolution using gradient profile prior. In: 2008 IEEE Conference on Computer Vision and Pattern Recognition, Anchorage, AK, pp. 1–8 (2008). https://doi.org/10.1109/CVPR.2008.4587659
2. Baker, S., Kanade, T.: Limits on super-resolution and how to break them. In: IEEE Transactions on Pattern Analysis and Machine Intelligence, vol. 24, no. 9, pp. 1167–1183 (2002). https://doi.org/10.1109/TPAMI.2002.1033210
3. Mallat, S., Yu, G.: Super-resolution with sparse mixing estimators. IEEE Trans. Image Process. **19**(11), 2889–2900 (2010). https://doi.org/10.1109/TIP.2010.2049927
4. Yang, J., Wright, J., Huang, T.S., Ma, Y.: Image super-resolution via sparse representation. IEEE Trans. Image Process. **19**(11), 2861–2873 (2010). https://doi.org/10.1109/TIP.2010.205 0625
5. Bevilacqua, M., Roumy, A., Guillemot, C., Alberi-Morel, M.L.: Low-complexity single-image super-resolution based on nonnegative neighbor embedding. In: Proceedings British Machine Vision Conference pp. 135.1–135.10 (2012). https://doi.org/10.5244/C.26.135
6. Timofte, R., De Smet, V., Van Gool, L.: A+: adjusted anchored neighborhood regression for fast super-resolution. In: Cremers, D., Reid, I., Saito, H., Yang, M.-H. (eds.) ACCV 2014. LNCS, vol. 9006, pp. 111–126. Springer, Cham (2015). https://doi.org/10.1007/978-3-319-16817-3_8
7. Zeyde, R., Elad, M., Protter, M.: On single image scale-up using sparse-representations. In: Boissonnat, J.D., et al. (eds) Curves and Surfaces. Curves and Surfaces 2010. Lecture Notes in Computer Science, vol. 6920, pp. 711–730. Springer, Berlin (2012).https://doi.org/10.1007/978-3-642-27413-8_47
8. Huang, J., Singh, A., Ahuja, N.: Single image super-resolution from transformed self-exemplars. In: 2015 IEEE Conference on Computer Vision and Pattern Recognition (CVPR), Boston, MA, pp. 5197–5206 (2015). https://doi.org/10.1109/CVPR.2015.7299156
9. Dong, C., Loy, C.C., He, K., Tang, X.: Image super-resolution using deep convolutional networks. IEEE Trans. Pattern Anal. Mach. Intell. **38**(2), 295–307 (2015). https://doi.org/10.1109/TPAMI.2015.2439281
10. Dong, C., Loy, C.C., Tang, X.: Accelerating the Super-Resolution Convolutional Neural Network. CoRR, abs/1608.00367 (2016).http://arxiv.org/abs/1608.00367
11. Shreyamsha Kumar, B.K.: Image denoising based on non-local means filter and its method noise thresholding. SIViP **7**(6), 1211–1227 (2012). https://doi.org/10.1007/s11760-012-0389-y
12. Foi, A., Katkovnik, V., Egiazarian, K.: Pointwise shape-adaptive DCT for high-quality denoising and deblocking of grayscale and color images. IEEE Trans. Image Process. **16**(5), 1395–1411 (2007). https://doi.org/10.1109/TIP.2007.891788
13. Elad, M., Aharon, M.: Image denoising via sparse and redundant representations over learned dictionaries. IEEE Trans. Image Process. **15**(12), 3736–3745 (2006). https://doi.org/10.1109/TIP.2006.881969
14. Zuo, W., Zhang, L., Song, C., Zhang, D.: Texture enhanced image denoising via gradient histogram preservation. In: 2013 IEEE Conference on Computer Vision and Pattern Recognition, Portland, OR, pp. 1203–1210 (2013). https://doi.org/10.1109/CVPR.2013.159

15. Zoran, D., Weiss, Y.: From learning models of natural image patches to whole image restoration. In: 2011 International Conference on Computer Vision, Barcelona, pp. 479–486 (2011). https://doi.org/10.1109/ICCV.2011.6126278

16. Deng, J., Dong, W., Socher, R., Li, L.J., Li, K., Fei-Fei, L.: ImageNet: a large-scale hierarchical image database. In: 2009 IEEE Conference on Computer Vision and Pattern Recognition, Miami, FL, pp. 248–255 (2009). https://doi.org/10.1109/CVPR.2009.5206848

17. Martin, D., Fowlkes, C., Tal, D., Malik, J.: A database of human segmented natural images and its application to evaluating segmentation algorithms and measuring ecological statistics. In: Proceedings Eighth IEEE International Conference on Computer Vision. ICCV 2001, Vancouver, BC, Canada, vol. 2, pp. 416–423 (2001). https://doi.org/10.1109/ICCV.2001.937655

18. Wang, Z., Bovik, A.C., Sheikh, H.R., Simoncelli, E.P.: Image quality assessment: from error visibility to structural similarity. IEEE Trans. Image Process. 13(4), 600–612 (2004). https://doi.org/10.1109/TIP.2003.819861

19. Sheikh, H.R., Bovik, A.C., de Veciana, G.: An information fidelity criterion for image quality assessment using natural scene statistics. IEEE Trans. Image Process. 14(12), 2117–2128 (2005). https://doi.org/10.1109/TIP.2005.859389

20. He, K., Zhang, X., Ren, S., Sun, J.: Delving deep into rectifiers: surpassing human-level performance on ImageNet classification. In: 2015 IEEE International Conference on Computer Vision (ICCV), Santiago, pp. 1026–1034 (2015). https://doi.org/10.1109/ICCV.2015.123

A Case Study of Rice Paddy Field Detection Using Sentinel-1 Time Series in Northern Italy

Fabio Dell'Acqua$^{(\boxtimes)}$ (ID) and David Marzi

Department of Electrical, Computer, Biomedical Engineering, University of Pavia,
Pavia, Italy
`fabio.dellacqua@unipv.it`

Abstract. Whereas a vast literature exists reporting on mapping of rice paddy fields in Asia based on spaceborne data, especially from radar sensors, comparatively little has been done so far on the European context, where production is much smaller in absolute terms. From a scientific standpoint, it would be interesting to characterize rice paddy fields in terms of typical annual trend of radar response in a context where seasons follow different patterns with respect to the Asian one. In this manuscript we report a case study on a designated set of rice paddy fields in northern Italy, where the largest fraction of European rice paddy fields are located. Building on previous work, more in-depth analysis of the time trends of radar response is carried out, and some preliminary conclusions on features usable in mapping are presented.

Keywords: Satellite-based mapping · rice paddy fields · Copernicus

1 Introduction

Spaceborne remote sensing has been widely used for rice paddy mapping in Southern Asian contexts, where most of global rice production takes place. Rice is however grown also in Europe, although to a much smaller extent, and cultivation practices in Asia and Europe are different for cultural, environmental and climatic reasons. Methods for rice mapping developed for Asian production [1–3] may not be so effective in Europe. Here, rice mapping needs specific investigation, starting from identification of the features observed in satellite data that may be leveraged to discriminate rice paddy fields from other types of land cover.

Once these features are defined, the information extracted for mapping rice may possibly be used also to enhance food traceability; satellite-based information on development stages, for example, can be leveraged to provide independent verification to claims issued by producers, or to cross-check compliance with production specifications with special regards to organic labeling requirements.

Indeed, satellite data can assist with monitoring crops on a broad geographical scale, gathering precise and timely information on the phenological status

Partly supported by the Italian Space Agency through Contract n. 2021-7-U.0 CUP n. F15F21000250005.

and development of vegetation [3–6], detecting signals of emerging problems, while also building independent records of the crop status. This can ultimately lead to facilitate third-party cross-checking of organic claims [7].

In this paper we provide some preliminary research results that may help filling the current research gap in rice paddy field mapping in the specific context of European rice. The paper is organized as follows: Sect. 2 introduces the data used, Sect. 3 presents the operations done on the data to test the classifier and discusses the peculiarities discovered, Sect. 4 draws some conclusions from the work done.

2   Data Sources

2.1   Land Cover: The DUSAF Repository

Land cover information, and specifically location and extent of rice paddy fields, was sourced from the open geoportal of the Lombardy region. Here, the land cover repository DUSAF ("*Destinazione d'Uso dei Suoli Agricoli e Forestali*"), a database that contains information on the use or characteristics of soils or vegetation cover, can be freely downloaded in .shp *shapefile* format. Many versions exist, each referring to a specific year. The most complete at the time of experiments was DUSAF 6.0, reporting the situation of 348.378 fields in 2018. The land cover layer was created through photointerpretation of aerial photos and SPOT 6/7 multispectral satellite images captured in year 2018 on the entire regional territory [8]. Each item in the file contains information related to an individual field about its location, extension, type of crop, etc. Items were filtered to keep only fields whose attributed crop type was *rice*.

The site of Parasacco, in south-western Lombardy, was selected as a specific spotlight area, due to the availability of ground truth information from local farmers for year 2018.

2.2   Spaceborne Radar Data

Sentinel-1 data was selected as the spaceborne data source for these experiments, thanks to the open data policy granted by the Copernicus initiative. Plans included data from two additional systems, namely COSMO/SkyMed Second Generation (CSG) and SAOCON; however, the availability of ground truth only for year 2018 prevented the use of the latter satellites, which were deployed later. The selection of the analyzed areas were still made considering CSG and SAOCON footprints, as reported below, to enable future comparison among different years. This conveys to the additional advantage of reducing the number of polygons (farmland fields) to be considered; the entire set of over 350 k instances would in fact require too long processing times even in GEE.

Figure 2 shows the intersection of CSG and SAOCOM footprints leading to identify the area where all satellites provide homogeneous time series.

On the identified area, Sentinel-1 data was selected by location and time frame with a specific function in the Google Earth Engine (GEE) repository.

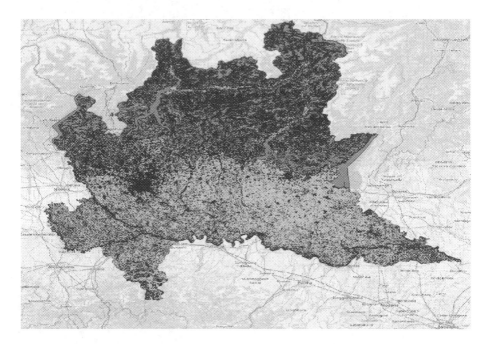

Fig. 1. Farmland polygons (in green) from DUSAF 6.0 visualized in QGIS environment. The black background represents the geographical extent of the Italian Region of Lombardia. DUSAF polygons are available only withing the boundaries of this Region. (Color figure online)

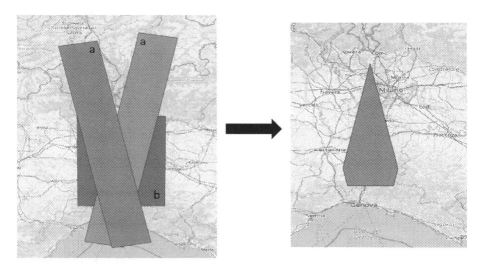

Fig. 2. Satellite data footprints. Left: (a) - CSG asc/desc footprints, (b) - SAOCON footprint. Right: intersection of the considered footprints

The entire chain of pre-processing [9] is already implemented on the selected data. The selected polarization was HV, as this is believed to be more sensitive to the emergence of plants from water in rice paddy fields.

3   Data Processing

After identifying the Region of Interest (RoI) as explained in the previous section, rice fields were singled out within the RoI. Figure 3 visually represents the process, which narrowed down the polygon set to 27 k units (all farmland in RoI) and then to 550 units (rice paddy fields in RoI).

Inputs to the classifiers were then created for each of the 550 polygons by considering time sequences of reflectivity averaged across all pixels in the considered polygon. Time sequences were composed of 61 samples, consistently with a revisit time of Sentinel-1 around 6 d. Each sequence was then filtered with the Savitzky-Golay filter [10], a method used to smooth data based on local least-squares polynomial approximation, to reduce the impact of noise while still sufficiently preserving the temporal trends of the curve. The Butterworth low-pass filter [11] was also tested, but turned out to remove too aggressively high-frequency features that were useful for classification.

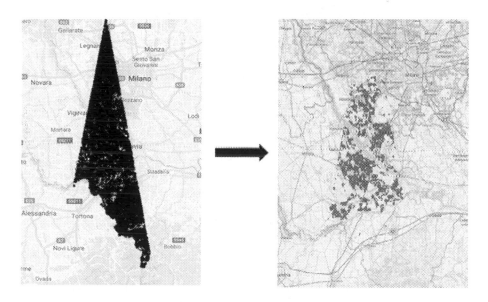

Fig. 3. Left: in black, intersection between RoI and farmland polygons in DUSAF. Right: in red, rice paddy fields in the intersection. Underlying maps from Google Maps and OpenStreetmap respectively. (Color figure online)

The 550 series were then analysed along the time axis. It was found that 12 series were composed of 90 samples instead of 60, due to an error in catalog entry details, which causes some among the eligible images to be picked more than once. Duplicate samples were then suppressed, thus reducing the number of series to 538.

In line with [12], the average across all series for any given acquisition was first computed to determine the average time trend of rice paddy fields; the result, shown in Fig. 4, reports the well-known plunge in spring. The absolute minimum falls as expected between satellite pass number 20 and number 30, corresponding to the April-May period. The minimum is surrounded by two local maxima usually associated with tillage and emergence respectively.

Next, the classifier presented in [12] was tested on the 538 identified rice fields. The expected result was to see all classified as rice, but -interestingly- 106 fields were classified as non-rice, corresponding to an unsatisfying omission rate of 23% approximately.

The reason for such a high error rate was investigated by separately analyising time trends for fields classified as rice (*rice* set) and those classified as non-rice (*non-rice* set). The result, presented in Fig. 5 made some features to emerge, which were hidden in the general average. The erroneously classified fields share large tracts of the time response with the general average presented in 4, but differ significantly in the spring plunge.

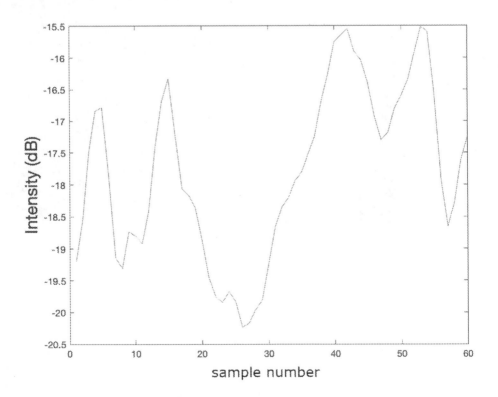

Fig. 4. Reflectivity time series averaged across all fields

Further analysis was conducted on the homogeneity of behaviour in the two sets (*rice* and *non-rice*), by computing variance across the entire set for every sample along the time series. The results are presented in Fig. 6.

The unexpected result of comparison is that - especially in the distinctive interval of spring - the *non-rice* set features more similar values than the *rice* set, meaning that somehow the *non-rice* set is more consistent in its temporal trend than the other. This suggests that the *non-rice* set may be a class of its own.

Further investigation was needed to obtain an explanation. The temporal series of radar backscatter for both *rice* and *non-rice* sets were visually represented in a pseudocolor palette in Fig. 7, where the horizontal axes represent the progress of time in the form of satellite pass number, and the vertical axes represent the order number of the considered field. The level of radar backscatter is represented by the blue-to-yellow palette, with blue representing the weakest intensity of backscattered power. The association of colors with backscatter levels expressed in dB is visible on the scale to the right.

The graphs reveal some interesting facts that tend to remain hidden when considering only the mean across all fields. A first note is that, for correctly classified rice fields, the spring minimum tends to take place in two different

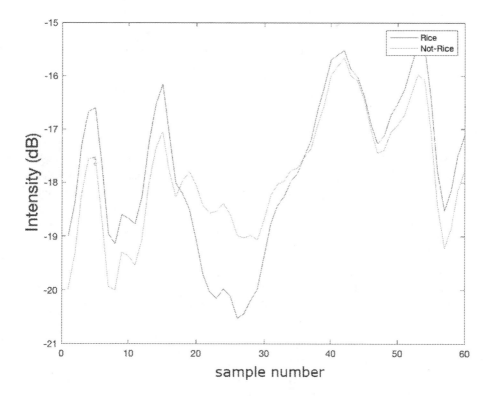

Fig. 5. Comparison of reflectivity time series for *rice* and *non-rice* polygons

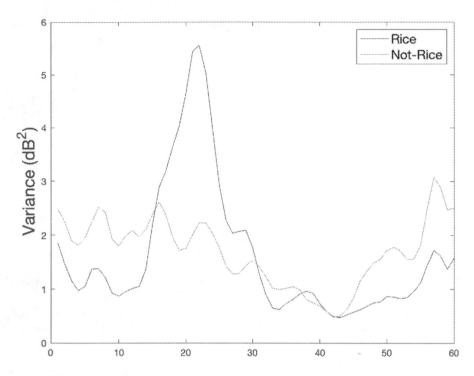

Fig. 6. Comparison of variance at each date for *rice* and *non-rice* sets

dates, which may partly justify the higher variance observed in this period of year. This is higlighted in Fig. 8, and is attributed to two different cultivation practices, with different submersion periods.

The other interesting fact is that periods of low and high backscatter tend to be homogeneous across the *rice* and *non-rice* classes, as visible by comparing the two graphs in Fig. 7. Some of this shared behaviour can be explained by weather conditions, that are in common: for example, the low backscatter observed across all fields around the 10th and 55th pass of satellites could be linked to very rainy weather, which probably led to persistent puddles in the fields, causing mirror reflection and thus reducing backscatter. Other shared features like backscatter peaks just after the 40th pass of the satellite could be attributed to harvesting, which leaves residuals on the terrain causing diffuse reflection. These latter features support that the DUSAF attribution to the class rice is correct, and it is the radar-based classification criterion that needs to be refined in order to accommodate a variability of behaviour that was not initially foreseen.

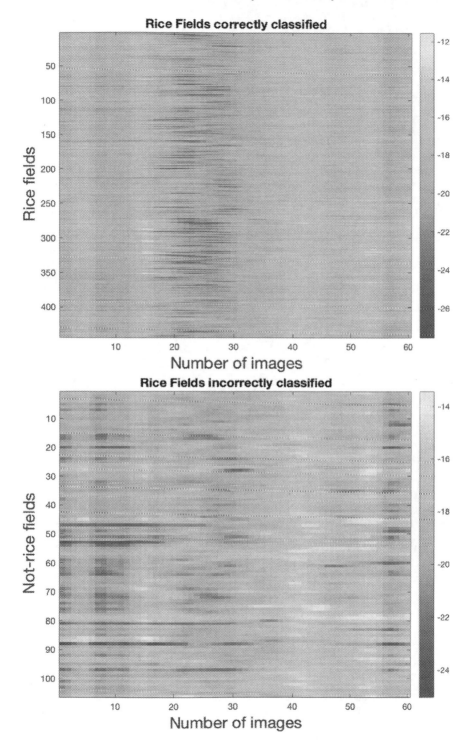

Fig. 7. Pseudocolor representation of radar reflectivity for sample sets classified as *rice* (above) and *non-rice* (below). The horizontal axes report the satellite pass number, and the vertical axes represent the order number of the considered field.

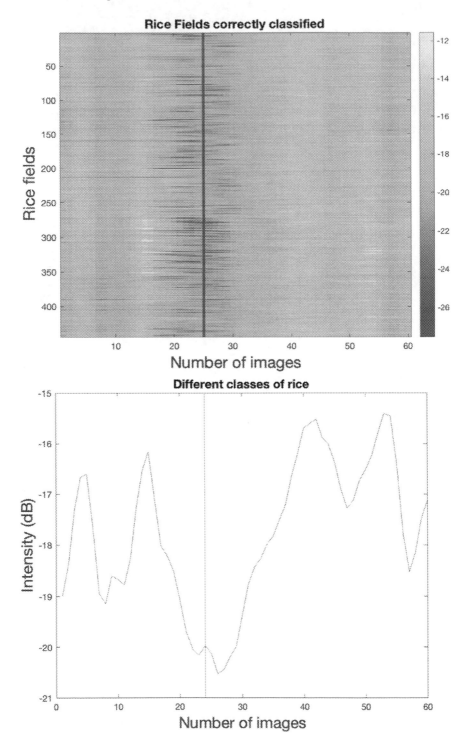

Fig. 8. Pseudocolor representation of radar reflectivity for sample sets classified as *rice*. The vertical black line marks a watershed, likely between two different cultivation practices which involve different flooding periods.

4   Conclusions

In this paper, we have analysed time series of Sentinel-1 images over rice paddy fields in Italy, and discovered some facts that may be leveraged in large-scale classification of European rice paddy fields.

A large, apparent error rate in applying a previously developed classifier to S-1 data led to discover that the classifier was somehow oversimplifying the rice class, and different types of rice need slightly different approaches for mapping. The classified needs modifications to accommodate different prototype behaviours. Radar data can help distinguishing the various stages of the cultivation process, discriminating the cultivation techniques, and differentiating the types of rice.

Future developments will involve data from the other two considered platforms, namely COSMO Second Generation (CSG) and SIASGE. Such data will be used to assess how spatial resolution and wavelength may affect the results.

Another important implication is that it is possible to replace the first version of this classifier with a more advanced classifier, based on neural networks that will be able not only to recognize rice fields but also to recognize their types.

Acknowledgements. The authors wish to thank Vincenzo Curcio for carrying out the experiments described in this paper in the framework of his final graduate thesis work. This research was partly funded by the Italian Space Agency (ASI) in the framework of project "MultiBigSARData" n.2021-7-U.0 - CUP F15F21000250005.

References

1. Lopez-Sanchez, J., Cloude, S., Ballester-Berman, J.: Rice phenology monitoring by means of SAR polarimetry at X-band. IEEE Trans. Geosci. Remote Sens. **50**, 2695–2709 (2011)
2. Xu, L., Zhang, H., Wang, C., Zhang, B., Liu, M.: Crop classification based on temporal information using sentinel-1 SAR time-series data. Remote Sens. **11**, 53 (2019)
3. Zhou, D., Zhao, S., Zhang, L., Liu, S.: Remotely sensed assessment of urbanization effects on vegetation phenology in China's 32 major cities. Remote Sens. Environ. **176**, 272–281 (2016)
4. Pastor-Guzman, J., Dash, J., Atkinson, P.: Remote sensing of mangrove forest phenology and its environmental drivers. Remote Sens. Environ. **205**, 71–84 (2018)
5. Siachalou, S., Mallinis, G., Tsakiri-Strati, M.: A hidden Markov models approach for crop classification: linking crop phenology to time series of multi-sensor remote sensing data. Remote Sens. **7**, 3633–3650 (2015)
6. Albanesi, E., Bernoldi, S., Dell'Acqua, F., Entekhabi, D.: Covariation of passive-active microwave measurements over vegetated surfaces: case studies at L-band passive and L-. C-and X-Band Active. Remote Sens. **13**, 1786 (2021)
7. Marzi, D., De Vecchi, D., Iannelli, G.: The ESA KSA Vialone project: new business from space in organic farming. ESA Earth Observation Phi-Week, Frascati (Rome), Italy, 9th-13th September 2019 (2019)

8. Lombardia, R.: Uso e copertura del suolo in regione Lombardia. https://www.regione.lombardia.it/wps/portal/istituzionale/HP/DettaglioServizio/servizi-e-informazioni/Enti-e-Operatori/Territorio/sistema-informativo-territoriale-sit/uso-suolo-dusaf/uso-suolo-dusaf

9. Filipponi, F.: Sentinel-1 GRD preprocessing workflow. In: MDPI Proceedings, vol. 18 (2019). https://www.mdpi.com/2504-3900/18/1/11

10. Savitzky, A., Golay, M.: Smoothing and differentiation of data by simplified least squares procedures. Anal. Chem. **36**, 1627–1639 (1964). https://doi.org/10.1021/ac60214a047

11. Selesnick, I., Burrus, C.: Generalized digital Butterworth filter design. IEEE Trans. Sig. Process. **46**, 1688–1694 (1998)

12. Marzi, D., Garau, C., Dell'Acqua, F.: Identification of rice fields in the Lombardy region of Italy Based on time series of sentinel-1 data. In: 2021 IEEE International Geoscience And Remote Sensing Symposium IGARSS, pp. 1073–1076 (2021)

The UNICT-TEAM Vision Modules for the Mohamed Bin Zayed International Robotics Challenge 2020

Sebastiano Battiato[1], Luciano Cantelli[2], Fabio D'Urso[1],
Giovanni Maria Farinella[1], Luca Guarnera[1(✉)],
Dario Calogero Guastella[2], Rosario Leonardi[1], Alessia Li Noce[2],
Giovanni Muscato[2], Alessio Piazza[1], Francesco Ragusa[1],
Corrado Santoro[1], Giuseppe Sutera[2], and Antonio Zappalà[2]

[1] Department of Math and Computer Science, University of Catania, Catania, Italy
luca.guarnera@unict.it
[2] Department of Electrical Electronic and Computer Engineering,
University of Catania, Catania, Italy

Abstract. Real-world advanced robotics applications cannot be conceived without the employment of onboard visual perception. By perception we refer not only to image acquisition, but more importantly to the information extraction required to carry out the robotic task. In this paper the computer vision system developed by the team of the University of Catania for the Mohamed Bin Zayed International Robotics Challenge 2020 is presented. The two challenges required to: 1) develop a team of drones for grasping a ball attached to another flying vehicle and to pierce a set of randomly placed balloons, 2) to build a wall by adopting a mobile manipulator and a flying vehicle. Several aspects have been taken into account in order to obtain a real-time and robust system, which are crucial features in demanding situations such as the ones posed by the challenges. The experimental results achieved in the real-world setting are reported.

Keywords: MBZIRC · UAV detection · Object detection · Object recognition · Pose estimation · Vision tracking

1 Introduction

The Mohamed Bin Zayed International Robotics Challenge (MBZIRC) is an international robotics competition involving universities and research centers from all over the world. MBZIRC poses challenging tasks for robotics systems in real-world applications. Our team participated in challenges 1 and 2 of the 2020 edition of the MBZIRC. A brief description of the two challenges is given below, whereas a detailed video showing all the challenges of the competition can be found at the link below[1].

---

[1] https://www.youtube.com/watch?v=u106Vy-XJ7c.

D. Gupta et al. (Eds.): CVIP 2022, CCIS 1776, pp. 707–719, 2023.
https://doi.org/10.1007/978-3-031-31407-0_53

1.1 Challenge 1

Challenge 1 arena (approximate size $100 \times 60\,\mathrm{m}$) includes a set of randomly placed balloons, attached to fixed-height poles from the ground. Inside the arena there is also an *enemy* Unmanned Aerial Vehicle (*UAV*) with a detachable soft ball, tethered to the drone via a semi-rigid cable. The enemy drone follows a 3D trajectory, with random location and orientation.

A team of up to 3 UAVs has to autonomously detect both the attached ball and the balloons. The ball has to be detached from the *enemy* UAV (thus resembling the 'neutralization' of a malicious transport), whereas the balloons have to be pierced. The mission has to be accomplished within 15 min.

1.2 Challenge 2

Challenge 2 arena (approximate size $50 \times 60\,\mathrm{m}$) will have four piles of bricks, each pile consisting of similar bricks (in size and color). The bricks' cross-section size is $0.2 \times 0.2\,\mathrm{m}$, whereas the length can be $0.3\,\mathrm{m}$, $0.6\,\mathrm{m}$, $1.2\,\mathrm{m}$, and $1.80\,\mathrm{m}$ (with different related colors). This challenge requires a team of up to 3 UAVs and an Unmanned Ground Vehicle (*UGV*) to autonomously locate, pick, and assemble the bricks, in order to construct a wall. The bricks can be picked and placed collaboratively by team members. The robots must assemble the bricks in a pre-specified color sequence. The Challenge 2 duration is 25 min.

This paper will mainly focus on the computer vision solutions adopted to carry out the tasks required by the two Challenges. The remainder of the paper is organized as follows: Sect. 2 reports a state-of-the-art related to the problems of object detection, recognition and pose estimation; our proposed solutions are described in Sect. 3 and the related experimental results are shown in Sect. 4. Section 5 presents the robotic platforms developed and the final hardware adopted for the vision system. Conclusions are reported in Sect. 6.

2 Related Work

In this section we discuss the studies related to the different modules composing the overall computer vision system.

2.1 Object Detection and Recognition

Object Detection and Recognition is a well established topic in Computer Vision. A large body of research has investigated how to detect and recognize objects to describe an image [20], localize them in the scene to enable a robot to perform autonomous navigation and landing [1,3].

For recognition purposes, some approaches extract image patches from region proposals and perform classification of them [7,8,10], whereas others classify a fixed set of evenly spaced square windows [26]. The authors of [24] proposed FasterRCNN, an evolution of the approach described in [7], in which the heuristic of finding region proposals has been replaced with a dedicated Region Proposal Network (*RPN*). Authors of [9] added an extra branch to the FasterRCNN object detector for predicting class-specific object masks, in parallel with the existing object classifier and bounding box regressor. Among the others, YOLO [23] is considered state-of-the-art for real-time object detection. In particular, YOLOv3 is an evolution of its previous versions [21,22] which uses a novel multi-scale training paradigm and proposes a technique to jointly train on object detection and classification. The authors of [33] proposed an optimization methods to train deep networks for object detection and segmentation. In [13] IoU-Net has been introduced to improve bounding box localization. Authors of [15] proposed an approach to detect an object bounding box as a pair of keypoints (top-left corner and bottom-right corner) using a single CNN. A recent work proposed SiamMask [31], a method able to perform both visual object tracking and semi-supervised video object segmentation in real-time using a Siamese Network paradigm. ScratchDet [35] is another recent method to perform object detection by training an object detector from scratch focusing on the Batch-Norm optimization. The authors of [32] performed single-stage object detection, combining the advantages of both fine-tuning pre-trained models and training from scratch to reduce the task gap between classification and localization. To avoid the problem of scale variation of objects a Trident Network to generate scale-specific feature maps is proposed in [16]. The authors of [28] presented an evolution of Non-Maximum Suppression (*NMS*) to filter by ranking the candidates using a novel Learning-to-Rank (*LTR*) model via a learning procedure.

Taking into account the aim of the MBZIRC challenge and the timely onboard computation required for the autonomous system, we have used an object detection method based on YOLOv3 [23] to perform real-time drone detection.

2.2   Object Pose Estimation

The methods of object detection described above are able to localize the objects of interest with a bounding box in an image. However, for many real-world tasks the location of an object in a image is not sufficient and the estimation of the 3D pose of the detected objects with respect to the camera is needed. For instance, the estimation of the 3D object pose is crucial for tasks such as grasping, manipulation or inspection in robotics [5], augmented reality [18,19] or autonomous navigation [3,4,25].

Classic approaches exploit one modality (e.g., RGB images) or multiple modalities as input (e.g., RGB and depth). The authors of [11] presented LINEMOD, a method based on multi-modal data to detect 3D objects in the scene. In particular, they used a combination between RGB images and a dense depth map. In [12] a framework based on LINEMOD for automatic modeling, detection and tracking of 3D objects with Kinect has been proposed. The authors built the templates of the objects from 3D models to estimate the 6-degree-of-freedom pose (6-DOF)in real-time. A popular method to estimate the 6-DOF camera pose is PoseNet [14]. It is based on a deep network architecture which performs camera relocalization in an end-to-end manner from RGB images only.

A recent work on 3D object detection and 6D pose estimation exploiting only RGB images has been presented in [34]. This method (named DPOD) uses an additional RGB pose refinement network to optimize the 6-DOF pose computed using PnP and RANSAC. One more approach in the context of pose estimation is DenseFusion [30]. It focuses on estimation of the object pose using both RGB and depth and exploit a novel dense fusion network to extract pixel-wise dense features. In [29] an approach to perform 6-DOF object pose estimation based on training a deep neural network using synthetic and photorealistic data has been proposed.

Since our autonomous system has to detect the pose of objects with rather limited on-board capabilities, in our development we have used an approach based on LINEMOD [11], with the aim of detecting the ball attached to the enemy drone in the first challenge, as well as to estimate the pose of the bricks for the second challenge.

3   Method

3.1   Ball Detection

The aim of our approach is to provide the autonomous system with the ability to detect the soft ball attached to the enemy UAV. We decided to use an approach based on the detection of texture-less objects [11] considering the specification of the ball to be detected and tracked. An efficient template matching method was developed which considers only the input image and its gradient in order to detect the objects of interest (i.e., the ball). The input signals are discretized into bins and, using a linearized response maps [12], we minimize cache misses and allow for heavy parallelization. After detecting the ball in the input image, the 3D coordinates of the center of the ball are estimated. The developed algorithm outputs the best match with respect to the templates of the training set and, hence, the returned 3D coordinates of the center of the ball (x, y, z) are the ones associated to the best match. In particular, the z coordinate represents the distance between the ball and the camera. To improve the accuracy of the ball detection algorithm, we have performed color analysis, considered the temporal relationships between consecutive frames as well as performed the resize of the input frame. Since the color of the ball is known in advance, the implemented method performs color segmentation in order to filter ahead only those pixels which can be related to the ball. To further strengthen the detection phase, a temporal analysis was carried out, implementing the following pipeline:

1. The candidate with the highest score is analyzed, saving the position (x, y) of the ball in its frame;
2. Considering the output of the previous step, for each next frame if the candidate with the highest score is within a neighborhood of a number of pixels with respect to the position of the previous one, a "*success*" counter is incremented and the position information is updated with the current ones, otherwise a "fail" counter is incremented;

3. If the "*success*" counter reaches a predefined value, the candidate is considered a true positive, while if the fail counter reaches a high value the information is discarded and the pipeline re-started;

The final position of the ball is computed by applying a smoothing over time by weighting with a proportion of 60% for the current position and 40% for the previous one. Figure 1 shows some results obtained for the detection of the ball. If the identified object is a potential candidate, it is represented inside a red bounding box (right in the figure), whereas, when the candidate is confirmed, it is depicted inside a green bounding box (left in the figure).

Fig. 1. Example of detection and center estimation of the ball. The bounding box is colored in red if the detection condition is not already satisfied (left), otherwise the bounding box is green (right). (Color figure online)

3.2 Drone Recognition

The aim of our method is to detect and localize the target UAV regardless of the type of drones that appears in the scene. Our approach is composed by three main stages: 1) object detection and localization on the images acquired by the on-board camera for both target drone and fellow drones, 2) temporal bounding box recognition to discriminate each drone in the scene, 3) exclusion of bounding boxed which are not related to the target drone taking into account fellow drones positions.

Our approach is based on YOLOv3 [23] that allows real-time computation. The input is only the RGB image and the model outputs the location of the drones in the images as 4D coordinates related to the bounding box (x, y, w, h), as well as the class of each detected drone (i.e., target vs non-target). A generalized version of the algorithm with temporal analysis, which considers the steps described in the pipeline used for the ball detection task, has been implemented. In particular, candidates are analyzed and vectors are used to memorize the various positions and counters. An *ID* is associated to each identified drone by comparing the positions among all the elements detected in the scene.

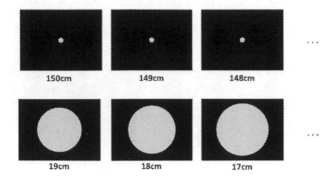

Fig. 2. Training templates generated in Blender considering a distance from the camera between 17 and 150 cm.

3.3   Brick Recognition

We have developed an algorithm able to perform a multiple detection and pose estimation of bricks of different size and colors. In particular, gradient based template matching and color-based filters have been used to distinguish them. We have adapted the algorithm used for the ball detection (see Sect. 3.1) to detect and recognize multiple bricks. Also in this case, to improve the accuracy of the detection algorithm for the brick, further considerations have been made related to the color-based filter and temporal smoothing. The filtering operation on the color is the same implemented for the ball detection algorithm and the temporal analysis is similar to the one used for the drone recognition to assign an *ID* to each bounding box.

4   Experimental Settings and Results

4.1   Ball Detection

For the training phase of our template-based matching approach we have generated the templates using Blender [2]. The considered ball has a diameter in the 0.10–0.15 m range. Samples related to a ball placed at a distance ranging from 17 to 150 cm have been considered. Examples of the generated templates are shown in Fig. 2.

We tested the method with gradient extracted from both color and gray-scale images. When color images are used in the detection phase, 3D pose estimation of the ball is more accurate and robust to the background changes. To improve the performance of the method, the resolution of the input image has been reduced from 640×480 pixels to 320×240 pixels. This was also useful to obtain an improvement on the computational time of about 3 times.

Table 1. The training accuracy described by: 1) average of the Intersection of Union (Avg IOU) of the bounding box, 2) classification accuracy, 3) accuracy in finding an object in the scene, 4) error in finding wrong objects in the scene.

AVG IoU	Accuracy Class	Accuracy Object	Accuracy No Object
0.94	0.99	0.99	0.0006

4.2 Drone Recognition

To train our network we have acquired 13 videos using an Odroid OCam camera with a focal length of 2.65 mm and an angle of view of 74° × 110° × 150°, using a resolution of 1280 × 960 at 30 fps. Different models of drones have been placed at a fixed position and videos have been acquired walking around the drone at various distances (from 1 to 60 m). Afterwards, we have annotated the frames with bounding boxes around the drones to be detected using the VGG Annotator tool [6]. In Fig. 3 some labeled frames are shown.

Fig. 3. Some frames acquired with the OCam camera with bounding box annotation.

We used 10 videos to finetune our model pre-trained on COCO dataset [17] and the remaining 3 videos to test the model. During training phase, we used a learning rate of *0.001*, momentum of *0.9* and decay of *0.0005*. The training accuracy is shown in Table 1.

At test time we fixed the hyperparameter *thresh* equal to 0.25. We report some test frames processed using our trained object detector in Fig. 4.

To further test the generalization capability of the detection algorithm when using a different camera, we performed experiments on videos depicting drones taken from the web. The videos include drones appearing with different perspectives and lighting conditions. Qualitative experiments pointed out that the

Fig. 4. Some test frames processed with our trained object detector.

Fig. 5. Qualitative results on videos acquired with different cameras, points of view and lighting conditions.

detector is robust also considering different settings. Some results of the detection are depicted in Fig. 5.

The proposed algorithm works in real-time. We tested its performance using two embedded boards with Nvidia GPU: a Jetson TX1 and a Jetson TX2. The algorithm has been tested in a real scenario with data acquired by a standard webcam with a resolution of 640 × 480 pixels at 25 fps. As expected, the performance shown in Table 2 highlights that the object detector has the best performance on Jetson TX2. We compared the fast version of Yolo (tiny Yolo) with our standard version obtaining similar performances in terms of speed and accuracy. The computational speed limit was caused mainly by the limits of the acquisition frame rate of the camera.

Table 2. Evaluation of the performances using two embedded boards with Nvidia GPU: Jetson TX1 and Jetson TX2.

Model	Board	Speed (Fps)
Yolo	TX1	3
Tiny Yolo	TX1	13
Yolo	TX2	22
Tiny Yolo	TX2	22

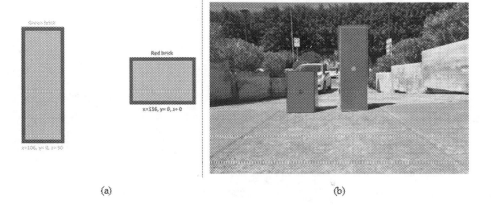

(a)   (b)

Fig. 6. (a) Example of training templates used by our algorithm. (b) Multiple detection of bricks.

4.3   Brick Recognition

To train our template-based method we have generated training templates for each brick using again Blender. To build our training set of templates we have changed the distance between the camera and the bricks, as well as the pose of the bricks which we wanted to estimate in an efficient and effective way. Each training template is associated to a specific pose of the brick and its distance from the camera. Figure 6(a) shows an example of two different training templates considering the specification of the challenge. The left-hand one is related to a green brick class, whereas the right-hand template is related to a red brick class.

We have tested the proposed algorithm to detect and localize multiple bricks with two different colors (red and green) in real scenario. Figure 6(b) qualitatively shows the results achieved in such a scenario.

5   The Robotic Platforms

For Challenge 1 the tracker drone (i.e., the one employed for the ball capture) has been built from a DJI Spreading Wings S900 with a specifically designed gripper, as shown in Fig. 7. The arms of the gripper are controlled by 3 servos,

Fig. 7. The tracker drone with the custom gripper developed for Challenge 1.

Fig. 8. The custom mobile manipulator developed for Challenge 2.

one for each arm, whereas 3 passive arms, follow the active ones. A custom developed net has been also designed and built to help the capture of the ball.

For Challenge 2 a custom rover (Fig. 8) has been built and tested using direct drive hub motors. Wheel encoders have been installed for odometric estimation. A manipulator (AUBO i-5) has been adopted to pick and place the bricks. The UAVs are based on DJI F550 frames and equipped with a custom magnetic gripper to capture and release the bricks [27]. A similar gripper has been mounted as end-effector tool of the manipulator as well.

The onboard cameras are the OCam 1CGN-Uplus by Odroid, whereas computer vision algorithms are executed by the Jetson TX2. The desired accuracy in the localization is ensured by on-board RTK-DGPS systems, receiving the corrections from a base station.

6   Conclusions

In this paper the computer vision modules developed by the team of the University of Catania for the MBZIRC 2020 have been presented and discussed. The outcome of such vision modules is crucial for the remainder of the control system and the strategy developed for the challenges.

The achieved results proved the effectiveness of the proposed method, both in terms of robustness against potential sources of error (i.e. varying background, light conditions and perspective) and time constraints in data processing with onboard computationally limited hardware.

References

1. Battiato, S., et al.: A system for autonomous landing of a UAV on a moving vehicle. In: Battiato, S., Gallo, G., Schettini, R., Stanco, F. (eds.) ICIAP 2017. LNCS, vol. 10484, pp. 129–139. Springer, Cham (2017). https://doi.org/10.1007/978-3-319-68560-1_12
2. blender online community: blender - a 3d modelling and rendering package. Blender foundation, blender institute, Amsterdam. https://www.blender.org
3. Cantelli, L., et al.: Autonomous landing of a UAV on a moving vehicle for the mbzirc. In: Human-Centric Robotics- Proceedings of the 20th International Conference on Climbing and Walking Robots and the Support Technologies for Mobile Machines, CLAWAR 2017, pp. 197–204 (2018)
4. Choi, J., Chun, D., Kim, H., Lee, H.J.: Gaussian yolov3: an accurate and fast object detector using localization uncertainty for autonomous driving. In: The IEEE International Conference on Computer Vision (ICCV) (2019)
5. Collet, A., Martinez, M., Srinivasa, S.: The moped framework: object recognition and pose estimation for manipulation. I. J. Robot. Res. **30**, 1284–1306 (2011)
6. Dutta, A., Zisserman, A.: The VIA annotation software for images, audio and video. In: Proceedings of the 27th ACM International Conference on Multimedia. MM 2019, ACM, New York, NY, USA (2019)
7. Girshick, R.: Fast R-CNN. In: Proceedings of the IEEE International Conference on Computer Vision, pp. 1440–1448 (2015)
8. Girshick, R., Donahue, J., Darrell, T., Malik, J.: Rich feature hierarchies for accurate object detection and semantic segmentation. In: Proceedings of the IEEE Conference on Computer Vision and Pattern Recognition, pp. 580–587 (2014)
9. He, K., Gkioxari, G., Dollár, P., Girshick, R.: Mask R-CNN. arXiv preprint arXiv:1703.06870 (2017)
10. He, K., Zhang, X., Ren, S., Sun, J.: Spatial pyramid pooling in deep convolutional networks for visual recognition. CoRR abs/1406.4729 (2014)
11. Hinterstoisser, S., et al.: Multimodal templates for real-time detection of texture-less objects in heavily cluttered scenes. In: 2011 International Conference on Computer Vision, pp. 858–865, November 2011
12. Hinterstoisser, S., et al.: Model based training, detection and pose estimation of texture-less 3d objects in heavily cluttered scenes. In: Lee, K.M., Matsushita, Y., Rehg, J.M., Hu, Z. (eds.) ACCV 2012. LNCS, vol. 7724, pp. 548–562. Springer, Heidelberg (2013). https://doi.org/10.1007/978-3-642-37331-2_42

13. Jiang, B., Luo, R., Mao, J., Xiao, T., Jiang, Y.: Acquisition of localization confidence for accurate object detection. In: The European Conference on Computer Vision (ECCV) (2018)
14. Kendall, A., Grimes, M., Cipolla, R.: Convolutional networks for real-time 6-dof camera relocalization. CoRR abs/1505.07427 (2015)
15. Law, H., Deng, J.: Cornernet: Detecting objects as paired keypoints. In: The European Conference on Computer Vision (ECCV), September 2018
16. Li, Y., Chen, Y., Wang, N., Zhang, Z.: Scale-aware trident networks for object detection. In: ICCV 2019 (2019)
17. Lin, T.-Y., et al.: Microsoft COCO: common objects in context. In: Fleet, D., Pajdla, T., Schiele, B., Tuytelaars, T. (eds.) ECCV 2014. LNCS, vol. 8693, pp. 740–755. Springer, Cham (2014). https://doi.org/10.1007/978-3-319-10602-1_48
18. Marchand, E., Uchiyama, H., Spindler, F.: Pose estimation for augmented reality: a hands-on survey. IEEE Trans. Vis. Comput. Graph. $22(12)$, 2633–2651 (2016)
19. Marder-Eppstein, E.: Project tango. In: Special Interest Group on Computer Graphics and Interactive Techniques Conference, SIGGRAPH 2016, Anaheim, CA, USA, 24–28 July 2016, Real-Time Live! p. 25 (2016)
20. Ortis, A., Farinella, G., Torrisi, G., Battiato, S.: Exploiting objective text description of images for visual sentiment analysis. Multimedia Tools Appl. **80**, 22323–22346 (2020)
21. Redmon, J., Divvala, S., Girshick, R., Farhadi, A.: You only look once: unified, real-time object detection. In: Proceedings of the IEEE Conference on Computer Vision and Pattern Recognition, pp. 779–788 (2016)
22. Redmon, J., Farhadi, A.: Yolo9000: better, faster, stronger. arXiv preprint arXiv:1612.08242 (2016)
23. Redmon, J., Farhadi, A.: Yolov3: an incremental improvement. CoRR abs/1804.02767 (2018)
24. Ren, S., He, K., Girshick, R., Sun, J.: Faster R-CNN: towards real-time object detection with region proposal networks. In: Advances in Neural Information Processing Systems, pp. 91–99 (2015)
25. Rosano, M., Furnari, A., Farinella, G.M.: A comparison of visual navigation approaches based on localization and reinforcement learning in virtual and real environments. In: International Conference on Computer Vision Theory and Applications (VISAPP) (2020)
26. Sermanet, P., Eigen, D., Zhang, X., Mathieu, M., Fergus, R., Lecun, Y.: Overfeat: integrated recognition, localization and detection using convolutional networks. In: International Conference on Learning Representations (ICLR2014) (2014)
27. Sutera, G., Guastella, D.C., Muscato, G.: A lightweight magnetic gripper for an aerial delivery vehicle: design and applications. ACTA IMEKO **10**(3), 61–65 (2021)
28. Tan, Z., Nie, X., Qian, Q., Li, N., Li, H.: Learning to rank proposals for object detection. In: The IEEE International Conference on Computer Vision (ICCV) (2019)
29. Tremblay, J., To, T., Sundaralingam, B., Xiang, Y., Fox, D., Birchfield, S.: Deep object pose estimation for semantic robotic grasping of household objects. In: Conference on Robot Learning (CoRL) (2018)
30. Wang, C., et al.: Densefusion: 6d object pose estimation by iterative dense fusion (2019)
31. Wang, Q., Zhang, L., Bertinetto, L., Hu, W., Torr, P.H.: Fast online object tracking and segmentation: a unifying approach. In: Proceedings of the IEEE Conference on Computer Vision and Pattern Recognition (2019)

32. Wang, T., Anwer, R.M., Cholakkal, H., Khan, F.S., Pang, Y., Shao, L.: Learning rich features at high-speed for single-shot object detection. In: The IEEE International Conference on Computer Vision (ICCV) (2019)
33. Wu, Y., He, K.: Group normalization. In: The European Conference on Computer Vision (ECCV) (2018)
34. Zakharov, S., Shugurov, I., Ilic, S.: Dpod: 6d pose object detector and refiner. In: The IEEE International Conference on Computer Vision (ICCV), October 2019
35. Zhu, R., et al.: Scratchdet: training single-shot object detectors from scratch. In: Proceedings of the IEEE/CVF Conference on Computer Vision and Pattern Recognition, pp. 2268–2277 (2019)

ResUNet: An Automated Deep Learning Model for Image Splicing Localization

Nitish Kumar[✉][iD] and Toshanlal Meenpal[iD]

Department of Electronics and Communication Engineering,
National Institute of Technology Raipur, Raipur, India
{nkumar.phd2018.etc,tmeenpal.etc}@nitrr.ac.in

Abstract. With the advances in digital media, images have been used as one of the most significant sources of information and communication in the modern society. However, images can be manipulated easily with the widespread availability of advanced image editing tools. Image splicing is one of the most popular image forgery methods in which a portion of one image is copied and stitched into another image for misleading the information. Hence, detection of image splicing forgery has become a significant research problem in multimedia forensic. Many splicing detection algorithms have been developed using traditional hand-crafted features, but these algorithms could not perform well on many post-processed or geometrically transformed spliced images. Hence in this paper, a new encoder-decoder architecture using convolutional neural network (CNN) is designed to locate the spliced region in an image. A hybrid CNN model called ResUNet is proposed in which encoder part of standard UNet architecture is replaced by ResNet 50 to analyze the discriminating feature between tampered and untampered regions. The proposed model is evaluated on CASIA v2.0 a benchmark dataset and experimental results demonstrate the proposed model turned out to be more efficient and accurate in splicing localization than other existing techniques.

Keywords: Image forgery detection · Image splicing detection · Splicing localization · ResNet 50 · UNet

1 Introduction

The advent of the multimedia age coupled with the tremendous usability of the internet and social media has made the digital image a preeminent source of information. In many cases, digital images have been produced as a source of primary evidence, published in newspaper or used in medical imaging for diagnostic purpose as well. But with the development of contemporary image editing applications and tools, image manipulation has become extremely easy with freely available advanced software. Image manipulation is practiced for unethical intention by creating forged images, raises the major concern of authenticity and

Fig. 1. An illustration of the formation of image splicing forgery where part of image 2 is copied and stitched into image 1 to form a spliced image.

reliability of digital images. On social media, in magazines, and on news channels, forged images can be found anywhere. Hence, there is a need of effective and robust forgery detection technique in image forensics.

Image forgery is executed by changing the graphic content to provide misleading information through an image [28]. Image forgery is mostly categorizes into three parts: Copy-move forgery, image splicing and image inpainting forgery [40]. Copy-move forgery involves the copying and pasting of an object or region within the same image [19]. Several copy-move forgery detection and localization techniques have been developed [1]. Some of the recent work done for the detection of copy-move forgery is discussed in [12,23,26]. Image inpainting forgery is used for removing any object and empty region is filled using elementary patches from the untampered region of the image [18,36]. In splicing forgery, some content of an image is copied and inserted into another image for adding or hiding any information. An example of formation of spliced image is illustrated in Fig. 1. Image splicing is most widely adopted and simple approach for creating forgeries in images. With the advanced, handy and widely available image processing softwares, spliced images are created in a way that makes splicing traces imperceptible to human eye.

Based on the abnormalities at the boundary of the spliced region, several methods have been developed for the detection of image splicing. [40]. Traditional methods using hand-crafted features are mostly based on essential image property [9,35], image compression property [20,22] and device property [17]. These algorithms have been designed to counter specific conditions but they fail to detect the forgery in other condition. For example, a JPEG-based method designed to detect double compression but it fails in detecting forgery in multiple compression situation. In recent years with the advent of deep learning, convolutional neural networks (CNN) have been widely used in the field of computer vision and also investigated successfully in image forensic. CNN based approaches performed better as compared to conventional approaches [3, 21].

In this paper, a CNN-based image authentication framework is proposed for the localization of splicing forgery. Here, encoder-decoder based CNN architecture is proposed to segment out the spliced region from a given image. In this method, state-of-the-art U-net architecture [30] is used which consists of 8 encoder and 8 decoder layers with skip connections. The encoder layer of U-net is replaced by state-of-the-art ResNet-50 network [13] which performed better for image classification. In this way ResUNet, a fusion network is proposed which is a combination of ResNet-50 and U-net architecture. Spliced mask generation is a binary classification task for detection of tampered and untampered pixels. The output layer of the proposed architecture uses the sigmoid activation function to generate a binary mask. On the CASIA v2.0 dataset, the proposed network is trained and its performance is evaluated. In addition, the results are compared with some prominent algorithms.

The rest of this article is organised as follows. In Sect. 2, significant existing works related to image splicing detection are discussed. A CNN-based proposed ResUnet architecture is presented for splicing forgery localization in Sect. 3. Extensive experiments and performance evaluation of proposed model have been performed in Sect. 4. Conclusion and future scope is present in Sect. 5.

2   Related Work

In recent years, several approaches have been suggested for image splicing detection and localization. These approaches can be broadly classified into two categories: Traditional feature-based techniques and CNN-based techniques. An overview of some of the significant work related to these two categories is discussed in this section.

In the first category, researchers have used image features like texture, edge and color features and frequency domain features with machine learning based classifiers. A natural image model using statistical features for image splicing detection was introduced in [33]. These statistical features which include moment of wavelet sub bands are acquired from the test image. Multi-size block discrete cosine transform (MBDCT) coefficients generate two dimensional arrays. Performance of the natural image model was evaluated on the columbia uncompressed image splicing detection evaluation dataset (CUISDE) and achieved an accuracy of 91.87%. This natural image model was improved in [14] by considering intra-block and inter-block correlation between DCT coefficients. Alongwith DCT domain, Markov features are also extracted in discrete wavelet transform (DWT) domain. Support vector machine recursive feature elimination was used as feature selection (SVM-RFE) and classification of authentic and spliced images was done by support vector machine (SVM) classifier. Zhang et al. [39]

also extracted features from MBDCT in their proposed methodology with image quality metrics (IQM). In [24], the steerable pyramid transform (SPT) was combined with local binary pattern (LBP) as feature descriptors and used SVM as classifier for splicing detection. Agrawal et al. [2] transformed the input image in undecimated wavelet transform (UWT) domain and then extracted the Markov features. Park et al. [27] proposed the co-occurrence matrix in wavelet domain using pair of wavelet differences. Jaiswal et al. [15] proposed hybrid features set consist of histogram of oriented gradients (HoG), DWT, LBP and laws texture energy (LTE) and logistic regression was used as classifier. Kanwal et al. [16] introduced a new texture feature otsu based enhanced local ternary pattern (OELTP) in their proposed work. The methods discussed till now have focused only on detection of forged images but not on the localization of forged region. Zhu et al. [41] explored the noise level function in their proposed methodology and localize the spliced region.

In the second category, deep learning-based splicing detection and localization methods are discussed. A CNN based deep learning model was introduced in [29] for extracting dense features. An SVM classifier was trained for the detection of spliced images. Chen et al. [8] analyzed camera response function (CRF) for detection and localization of splicing forgery. In this work, first edges were analyzed by intensity-gradient bivariate histogram and then deep-learning architecture is designed for localization of forged edges. In [21], three different varients of fully convolutional networks (FCNs) was trained along with a conditional random field (CRF) for the prediction of pixel level splicing forgery. In [11], CNN features along with DWT features were extracted from the input image and trained with SVM classifier for the detection of spliced image. Wang et al. [34] selected three features which are edge features, YCbCr features and photo response non-uniformity (PRNU) from the input image in their proposed method. Selected features were combined by automatically assigning the weight during CNN training to get the best ratio of weight. In [4], ResNet-conv was utilized as initial feature map which was trained further with Mask-RCNN to generate the spliced mask. ResNet was also included as a backbone for feature extraction in [25] with fully connected network for the classification of authentic and spliced images.

Traditional feature extraction based forgery detection methods always need the prior information about the visual content of the image for the selection of features and exhibit limitations in many cases like smoothing, blurring, compression and so on. Further, deep learning-based approaches came up with impressive results as discussed above in the field of image forensics and overcome the above mentioned limitations as well. With this motivation, proposed work introduced the deep learning based ResUNet architecture for the localization of spliced region in an image.

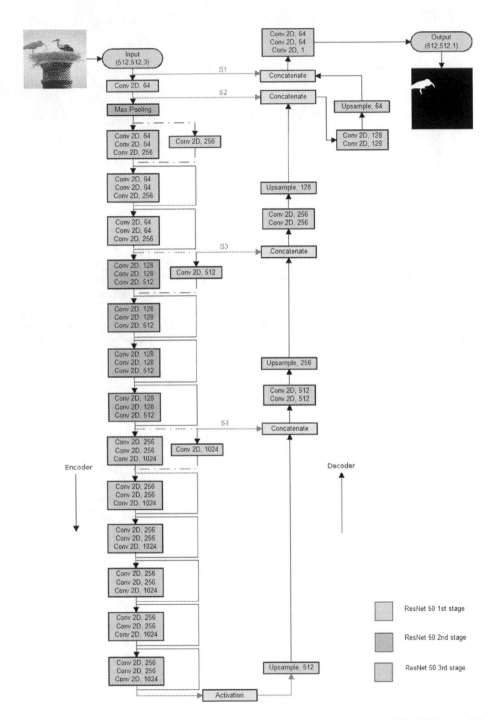

Fig. 2. Overview of the detailed architecture of encoder-decoder based ResUNet model

3   Proposed CNN-based Spliced Region Localization Model

Finding and locating the spliced region in an image is the primary goal of this work. An automated deep CNN-based encoder-decoder architecture named ResUNet is proposed to achieve this goal. The proposed ResUNet model consists of two main parts: encoder and decoder as shown in Fig. 2. The encoder part of the model extracts the high level features to get the contextual information. Major operations involved in the encoder are convolution, batch normalization and activation. However, the decoder part of the model collect the information about spatial location. Upsampling and concatenation of two inputs, one from the decoder's previous layer and the other from the same layer of the encoder, are two of the key actions of the decoder. Here, spliced region detection is considered as a binary classification problem depending on whether each pixel of an image is spliced or not. To solve this problem, sigmoid activation function is used for generation of binary mask as spliced region of the image, at the output of the model. In this section, encoder and decoder part of the proposed ResUNet is discussed in detail.

3.1   ResUNet-encoder

In the proposed ResUNet model, encoder is the part of standard ResNet-50 architecture [13]. ResNet-50 achieved a benchmark performance for the image classification problem. Some of the major advantages of this network are optimal formation of various layers, easy optimization of residual block and improving accuracy by increasing the network depth. Transfer learning approach is introduced for faster convergence at the model initialization. Hence, the weights of ResNet-50 which are already trained on ImageNet dataset [31], are used at the time of training.

Input of the ResUNet model is the image of size $(512 \times 512 \times 3)$. Initially, the encoder performs the convolution of the input image having kernel size of 64, followed by batch normalization. Following this, Max-pooling with a stride of (2×2) is used to reduce the input size. Thereafter, out of four residual stages of ResNet-50, three stages are included here in cascade. In each residual stage, convolution block is followed by identity blocks. In the first residual stage, there are three blocks with the kernel size (64, 64, 256). In each block, convolution is followed by batch normalization and activation function. ReLU is used here as an activation function. There are four blocks in the second residual stage with the kernel size (128, 128, 512) and six residual blocks in the third stage with kernel size (256, 256, 1024). Blocks of three different stages are shown with different color in the given Fig. 2. Output of the encoder is connected with the decoder through an activation function which is called as bridge connection.

3.2   ResUNet-Decoder

Decoder part of the ResUNet model comprise of three major blocks: upsample, concatenation and convolution. There are four stages in the decoder and in each stage upsample is followed by concatenation and then convolution block. The upsample blocks perform the deconvolution by applying transpose convolution. The kernel size of four upsample blocks are (64, 64, 512), (128, 128, 256), (256, 256, 128) and (512, 512,64). The concatenation blocks take two inputs, one from the previous upsample block and other from the encoder block which is identical in shape with upsample block. There are four connection from encoder part at each concatenation block. These connections are called as skip connection and marked as S1, S2, S3 and S4. The conactenated output is followed with two successive convolution, where batch normalisation and the activation function are applied after each convolution. At the last layer of the decoder, convolution is applied with kernel size of 1 by considering the problem as two class classification as spliced pixel and original pixel. Sigmoid activation function is used at the end of decoder for pixel-wise classification of spliced region. If $P(S_n)$ is defined as the probability distribution of two classes where 0 represent spliced and 1 represent original. Here, the S function is used to estimate the probability, and the prediction label is obtained by maximising $P(S_n)$ and $\hat{S} = argmax P(S_n)$. Hence, the model will generate the binary mask of size (512, 512, 1) as per the detected spliced region in an image.

4   Implementation and Results

This section deals with the experimental setup, dataset decription, training and validation details and performance evaluation of the proposed ResUNet model. Implementation of the ResUNet is carried out in Python 3.6.8 using Keras 2.2.4 running on Windows 10 with NVIDIA Quadro P2000 GPU.

4.1   Dataset Description

Training of the ResUNet model and its performance evaluation is carried out on the CASIA v2.0 [10] benchmark spliced image dataset. There are a total of 12,614 color images in this dataset out of which 7491 are authentic images and 5123 are spliced images. Since, The dataset consists on unequal number of authentic and spliced images. Hence, to avoid the data imbalance and classifier bias issue, same number of authentic and spliced images are picked randomly for the experiment. 4000 images are selected for training and 1000 images for validation. For testing the proposed model, 270 images are selected randomly which are not part of training and validation.

4.2   Model Training and Initialization

Various parameters need to be initialized before starting the model training. In context of convergence speed, model initialization plays a significant role. In this experiment, model is initialized with weights of ResNet 50 which is pre-trained on ImageNet database [31]. The learning rate is set to 0.01 and the momentum is set to 0.9 when using the stochastic gradient descent optimizer.

Predicted mask loss is calculated using a binary cross-entropy loss function. The number of epochs set for model training is 100.

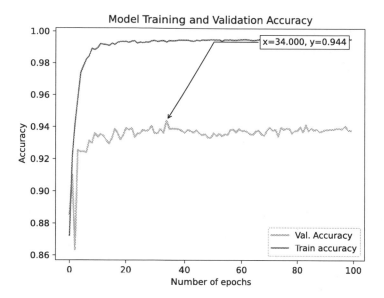

Fig. 3. Training and validation accuracy of the proposed ResUnet model with respect to number of epochs.

4.3   Evaluation Metrics

Mostly there are two kinds of metric used for evaluation of forgery detection: image level metrics and pixel level metrics. Accuracy is used here as image level metric and Intrsection over Union (IoU) [18] is used as pixel level metric. IoU metric is more stringent metric for performance evaluation of predicted mask. It is defined as the ratio of intersection to the union of number of pixels of ground truth mask and predicted mask. The range of IoU lies between 0 to 100% and higher the value of IoU, higher will be the similarity of predicted mask with ground truth. IoU can be computed using Eq. 1 for a given image where G is its ground truth mask and P is the predicted mask.

$$IoU(P,G) = (\frac{P \cap G}{P \cup G}) \tag{1}$$

4.4   Performance Evaluation

Various parameters are used to assess the presented model's performance. Training accuracy of the proposed model achieves 99.5% whereas validation accuracy

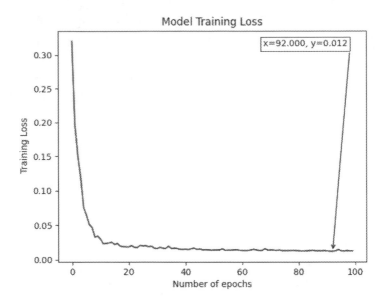

Fig. 4. Evaluation of loss of the proposed model with respect to number of epochs.

achieves 94.4% with respect to number of epochs as shown in Fig. 3. Training loss of the proposed model is also evaluated and achieves 1.2% loss as shown in Fig. 4. From Fig. 3 and 4, convergence of the model training with initialization of pre-trained weights can be observed. Training of the model converges after 70 epochs which is very less for training a large image database.

Results of the proposed model is represented in Fig. 5 on various images of CASIA v2.0 dataset [10], where for each spliced image, their ground truth, predicted mask and IoU score are reported. It is evident from the result that the proposed model has outperformed in localization of the spliced region. The proposed model has achieved an overall splicing detection accuracy of 92%. The IoU score of 270 images are plotted in Fig. 6 and the model has achieved the mean IoU value as 82.1% which is marked by horizontal line in this figure.

4.5 Comparative Analysis with Existing Methods

The effectiveness of the proposed architecture is pursued with the state-of-the-art. Splicing localization results of different methods based on their IoU score on CASIA v2.0 dataset is shown in Fig. 7. Comparison of the proposed model is presented with CNN_LSTM [5], Mantra-Net [37], MFCN [32], RRU-Net [7], SE-Network [38] and R-CNN [6] models. Figure 7 shows that the proposed model outperformed existing methods.

Spliced Image   Ground Truth Mask   Predicted Mask   IoU Score

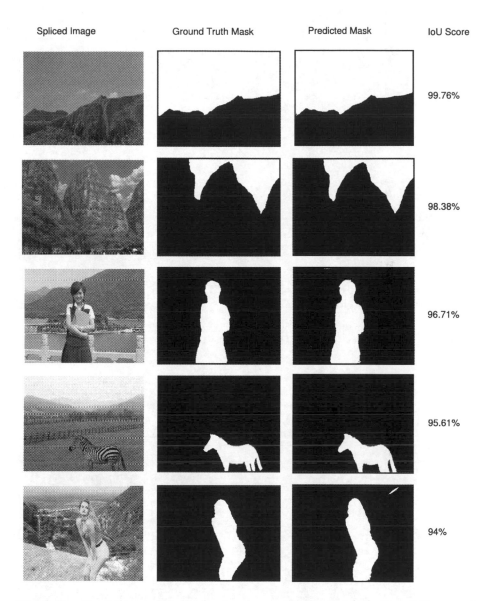

Fig. 5. Results of the predicted spliced region on CASIA v2.0 [10] where IoU score of individual predicted mask is shown.

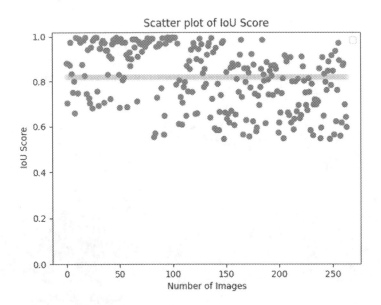

Fig. 6. Plot of IoU score on test images from CASIA v2.0 [10] dataset where horizontal line represent the mean IoU value.

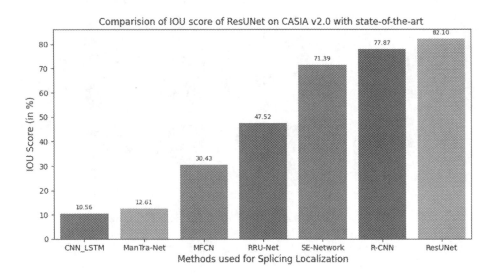

Fig. 7. Comparison of IoU score of the proposed model with existing methods on CASIA v2.0 dataset

5   Conclusion and Future Scope

One of the most popular and simplest approaches to image forgery is image splicing. In this article, a novel encoder-decoder based ResUNet model using CNN is proposed for the detection and localization of image splicing forgery. Encoder of the proposed model is part of ResNet 50 architecture which has proven its performance for image classification. Decoder of the proposed model is identical to the decoder of UNet architecture which is introduced for the generation of mask image. On the CASIA v2.0 dataset, performance of the proposed model is evaluated and accessed by computing Accuracy and IoU metrics. Encoder of the proposed model is initialized with weights pretrained on ImageNet database prior to the model training. Extensive experiments have demonstrated the superiority of the proposed model. The proposed model has achieved 92% accuracy and 82.1% mean IoU score which shows the effectiveness of the splicing detection.

The proposed model has some limitations. This model is designed only for image splicing forgery and performance is evaluated only on CASIA V2.0 dataset. This work can be extended for the design of robust forgery detection for any kind of image forgery and can be evaluated on various existing benchmark datasets. Further, there is a need for design of detection algorithm for computer generated fake images also.

References

1. Abd Warif, N.B., et al.: Copy-move forgery detection: survey, challenges and future directions. J. Netw. Comput. Appl. **75**, 259–278 (2016)
2. Agarwal, S., Chand, S.: Image forgery detection using markov features in undecimated wavelet transform. In: 2016 Ninth International Conference on Contemporary Computing (IC3), pp. 1–6. IEEE (2016)
3. Ahmed, B., Gulliver, T.A., alZahir, S.: Image splicing detection using mask-rcnn. Sig. Image Video Process. **14**(5), 1035–1042 (2020)
4. Ahmed, B., Gulliver, T.A., alZahir, S.: Image splicing detection using mask-rcnn. Sig. Image Video Process **14**(5), 1035–1042 (2020)
5. Bappy, J.H., Roy-Chowdhury, A.K., Bunk, J., Nataraj, L., Manjunath, B.: Exploiting spatial structure for localizing manipulated image regions. In: 2017 IEEE International Conference on Computer Vision (ICCV), pp. 4980–4989 (2017). https://doi.org/10.1109/ICCV.2017.532
6. Beijing, C., Xingwang, J., Ye, G., Jinwei, W.: A quaternion two-stream r-cnn network for pixel-level color image splicing localization. Chin. J. Electron. **30**(6), 1069–1079 (2021)
7. Bi, X., Wei, Y., Xiao, B., Li, W.: Rru-net: the ringed residual u-net for image splicing forgery detection. In: 2019 IEEE/CVF Conference on Computer Vision and Pattern Recognition Workshops (CVPRW), pp. 30–39 (2019). https://doi.org/10.1109/CVPRW.2019.00010
8. Chen, C., McCloskey, S., Yu, J.: Image splicing detection via camera response function analysis. In: Proceedings of the IEEE Conference on Computer Vision and Pattern Recognition, pp. 5087–5096 (2017)

9. Chen, C., Ni, J., Huang, J.: Blind detection of median filtering in digital images: a difference domain based approach. IEEE Trans. Image Process. **22**(12), 4699–4710 (2013). https://doi.org/10.1109/TIP.2013.2277814

10. Dong, J., Wang, W., Tan, T.: Casia image tampering detection evaluation database. In: 2013 IEEE China Summit and International Conference on Signal and Information Processing, pp. 422–426. IEEE (2013)

11. El-Latif, A., Eman, I., Taha, A., Zayed, H.H.: A passive approach for detecting image splicing based on deep learning and wavelet transform. Arabian J. Sci. Eng. **45**(4), 3379–3386 (2020)

12. Goel, N., Kaur, S., Bala, R.: Dual branch convolutional neural network for copy move forgery detection. IET Image Process. **15**(3), 656–665 (2021)

13. He, K., Zhang, X., Ren, S., Sun, J.: Deep residual learning for image recognition. In: Proceedings of the IEEE Conference on Computer Vision and Pattern Recognition, pp. 770–778 (2016)

14. He, Z., Lu, W., Sun, W., Huang, J.: Digital image splicing detection based on markov features in DCT and dwt domain. Pattern Recogn. **45**(12), 4292–4299 (2012)

15. Jaiswal, A.K., Srivastava, R.: A technique for image splicing detection using hybrid feature set. Multimedia Tools Appl. **79**(17), 11837–11860 (2020)

16. Kanwal, N., Girdhar, A., Kaur, L., Bhullar, J.S.: Digital image splicing detection technique using optimal threshold based local ternary pattern. Multimedia Tools Appl. **79**(19), 12829–12846 (2020)

17. Korus, P., Huang, J.: Multi-scale analysis strategies in prnu-based tampering localization. IEEE Trans. Inf. Forensics Secur. **12**(4), 809–824 (2016)

18. Kumar, N., Meenpal, T.: Semantic segmentation-based image inpainting detection. In: Favorskaya, M.N., Mekhilef, S., Pandey, R.K., Singh, N. (eds.) Innovations in Electrical and Electronic Engineering. LNEE, vol. 661, pp. 665–677. Springer, Singapore (2021). https://doi.org/10.1007/978-981-15-4692-1_51

19. Kumar, N., Meenpal, T.: Salient keypoint-based copy-move image forgery detection. Australian J. Forensic Sci. 1–24 (2022)

20. Lin, Z., He, J., Tang, X., Tang, C.K.: Fast, automatic and fine-grained tampered jpeg image detection via DCT coefficient analysis. Pattern Recogn. **42**(11), 2492–2501 (2009)

21. Liu, B., Pun, C.M.: Locating splicing forgery by fully convolutional networks and conditional random field. Sig. Process. Image Commun. **66**, 103–112 (2018)

22. Luo, W., Huang, J., Qiu, G.: Jpeg error analysis and its applications to digital image forensics. IEEE Trans. Inf. Forensics Secur. **5**(3), 480–491 (2010)

23. Meena, K.B., Tyagi, V.: A copy-move image forgery detection technique based on tetrolet transform. J. Inf. Secur. Appl. **52**, 102481 (2020)

24. Muhammad, G., Al-Hammadi, M.H., Hussain, M., Bebis, G.: Image forgery detection using steerable pyramid transform and local binary pattern. Mach. Vis. Appl. **25**(4), 985–995 (2014)

25. Nath, S., Naskar, R.: Automated image splicing detection using deep CNN-learned features and ANN-based classifier. Sig. Image Video Process. **15**(7), 1601–1608 (2021)

26. Niyishaka, P., Bhagvati, C.: Copy-move forgery detection using image blobs and brisk feature. Multimedia Tools Appl. **79**(35), 26045–26059 (2020)

27. Park, T.H., Han, J.G., Moon, Y.H., Eom, I.K.: Image splicing detection based on inter-scale 2d joint characteristic function moments in wavelet domain. EURASIP J. Image Video Process. **2016**(1), 1–10 (2016)

28. Qazi, T., et al.: Survey on blind image forgery detection. IET Image Process. **7**(7), 660–670 (2013)
29. Rao, Y., Ni, J.: A deep learning approach to detection of splicing and copy-move forgeries in images. In: 2016 IEEE International Workshop on Information Forensics and Security (WIFS), pp. 1–6. IEEE (2016)
30. Ronneberger, O., Fischer, P., Brox, T.: U-net: convolutional networks for biomedical image segmentation. In: Navab, N., Hornegger, J., Wells, W.M., Frangi, A.F. (eds.) MICCAI 2015. LNCS, vol. 9351, pp. 234–241. Springer, Cham (2015). https://doi.org/10.1007/978-3-319-24574-4_28
31. Russakovsky, O., et al.: Imagenet large scale visual recognition challenge. Int. J. Comput. Vis. **115**(3), 211–252 (2015)
32. Salloum, R., Ren, Y., Kuo, C.C.J.: Image splicing localization using a multi-task fully convolutional network (MFCN). J. Vis. Commun. Image Representation **51**, 201–209 (2018)
33. Shi, Y.Q., Chen, C., Chen, W.: A natural image model approach to splicing detection. In: Proceedings of the 9th Workshop on Multimedia & Security, pp. 51–62 (2007)
34. Wang, J., Ni, Q., Liu, G., Luo, X., Jha, S.K.: Image splicing detection based on convolutional neural network with weight combination strategy. J. Inf. Secur. Appl. **54**, 102523 (2020)
35. Wang, W., Dong, J., Tan, T.: Effective image splicing detection based on image chroma. In: 2009 16th IEEE International Conference on Image Processing (ICIP), pp. 1257–1260 (2009). https://doi.org/10.1109/ICIP.2009.5413549
36. Wang, X., Niu, S., Wang, H.: Image inpainting detection based on multi-task deep learning network. IETE Techn. Rev. **38**(1), 149–157 (2021)
37. Wu, Y., AbdAlmageed, W., Natarajan, P.: Mantra-net: manipulation tracing network for detection and localization of image forgeries with anomalous features. In: 2019 IEEE/CVF Conference on Computer Vision and Pattern Recognition (CVPR), pp. 9535–9544 (2019). https://doi.org/10.1109/CVPR.2019.00977
38. Zhang, Y., Zhu, G., Wu, L., Kwong, S., Zhang, H., Zhou, Y.: Multi-task se-network for image splicing localization. IEEE Trans. Circ. Syst. Video Technol. **32**(7), 4828–4840 (2022). https://doi.org/10.1109/TCSVT.2021.3123829
39. Zhang, Z., Kang, J., Ren, Y.: An effective algorithm of image splicing detection. In: 2008 International Conference on Computer Science and Software Engineering, vol. 1, pp. 1035–1039. IEEE (2008)
40. Zheng, L., Zhang, Y., Thing, V.L.: A survey on image tampering and its detection in real-world photos. J. Vis. Commun. Image Representation **58**, 380–399 (2019)
41. Zhu, N., Li, Z.: Blind image splicing detection via noise level function. Sig. Process. Image Commun. **68**, 181–192 (2018)

Author Index

Printed in the United States
by Baker & Taylor Publisher Services